Expert On

Visual Bas

Design and Development

Expert One-on-One™
Visual Basic® 2005
Design and Development

Rod Stephens

Wiley Publishing, Inc.

Expert One-on-One™ Visual Basic® 2005 Design and Development

Published by
Wiley Publishing, Inc.
10475 Crosspoint Boulevard
Indianapolis, IN 46256
www.wiley.com

Published by Wiley Publishing, Inc., Indianapolis, Indiana

Published simultaneously in Canada

ISBN: 978-0-470-05341-6

Manufactured in the United States of America

10 9 8 7 6 5 4 3 2 1

Library of Congress Cataloging-in-Publication Data:

Stephens, Rod, 1961-
Expert one-on-one Visual Basic 2005 design and development / Rod Stephens.
p. cm.
Includes index.
ISBN-13: 978-0-470-05341-6 (paper/website)
ISBN-10: 0-470-05341-0 (paper/website)
1. Microsoft Visual BASIC. 2. BASIC (Computer program language) I. Title.
QA76.73.B3S8335 2007
005.2'768--dc22
2006036646

For general information on our other products and services please contact our Customer Care Department within the United States at (800) 762-2974, outside the United States at (317) 572-3993 or fax (317) 572-4002.

Wiley also publishes its books in a variety of electronic formats. Some content that appears in print may not be available in electronic books.

Credits

Executive Editor
Robert Elliott

Development Editor
Kevin Shafer

Technical Editor
John Mueller

Production Editor
Eric Charbonneau

Copy Editor
Kim Cofer

Editorial Manager
Mary Beth Wakefield

Production Manager
Tim Tate

Vice President and Executive Group Publisher
Richard Swadley

Vice President and Executive Publisher
Joseph B. Wikert

Graphics and Production Specialists
Carrie A. Foster
Denny Hager
Stephanie D. Jumper

Quality Control Technician
Laura Albert

Proofreading and Indexing
ConText
Techbooks

About the Author

Rod Stephens started out as a mathematician but, while studying at MIT, discovered the joys of programming, and has been programming professionally ever since. During his career, he has worked on an eclectic assortment of applications in such fields as telephone switching, billing, repair dispatching, tax processing, wastewater treatment, and training for professional football players.

Stephens has written 15 books that have been translated into half a dozen different languages, and more than 200 magazine articles covering Visual Basic, Visual Basic for Applications, Delphi, and Java. He writes three weekly newsletters (`www.vb-helper.com/newsletter.html`) that contain quick tips, tricks, and examples for Visual Basic developers.

His popular *VB Helper* Web site (`www.vb-helper.com`) receives several million hits per month, and contains thousands of pages of tips, tricks, and example code for Visual Basic programmers, as well as example code for this book.

Currently, Stephens is an author, consultant, and instructor at ITT Technical Institute.

Other Books by Rod Stephens

Visual Basic 2005 Programmer's Reference	ISBN: 0-7645-7198-2
Visual Basic .NET and XML	ISBN: 0-471-12060-X
Visual Basic Graphics Programming, Second Edition	ISBN: 0-471-35599-2
Bug Proofing Visual Basic Graphics	ISBN: 0-471-32351-9
Custom Controls Library	ISBN: 0-471-24267-5
Ready-to-Run Visual Basic Algorithms, Second Edition	ISBN: 0-471-24268-3
Ready-to-Run Visual Basic Code Library	ISBN: 0-471-33345-X

Acknowledgments

Thanks to Bob Elliott, Kevin Shafer, and all of the others who make producing any book possible.

Thanks also to technical editor John Mueller for making sure I wasn't putting my foot too deeply in my mouth and for helping to add extra depth to the book. Visit `http://www.mwt.net/~jmueller` to learn about John's books and to sign up for his free newsletter *.NET Tips, Trends & Technology eXTRA*.

Contents

Introduction

Visual Basic 2005, together with the .NET Framework, provides a wonderfully powerful development environment. With these tools, developers can build amazingly powerful applications relatively quickly and easily.

With this power, however, comes great complexity. Many books are available that discuss the Visual Basic language, and if you need to build a relatively simple application, those are generally sufficient. No books, however, address the complex issues that surround the development of more complicated Visual Basic applications. None discuss design, modeling, user-interface design, or testing for Visual Basic applications.

These books also don't cover some of the important advanced topics that don't fit well into introductory books. They generally don't have the time to cover threading, reflection, advanced memory management, and printing in the depth necessary to make them useful for building really advanced applications.

Expert One-on-One Visual Basic 2005 Design and Development fills the gaps that these books leave surrounding Visual Basic development. It explains the design activities that are necessary before Visual Basic development can begin. It covers processes that occur after development (such as deployment, update management, and testing) that are essential to a successful Visual Basic project, but that are not part of the language itself. Finally, it covers advanced topics that are useful in real-world applications, but that are given little attention in other books.

Why Visual Basic?

A Visual Basic programmer's joke asks, "What's the difference between Visual Basic .NET and C#? About three months!" The implication is that Visual Basic .NET syntax is easier to understand, and building applications with it is faster. Similarly, C# programmers have their jokes about Visual Basic, implying that C# is more powerful.

In fact, Visual Basic is *not* a whole lot easier to use than C#, and C# is *not* significantly more powerful. The basic form of the two languages is very similar, aside from a few stylistic differences. A good C# programmer can crank out a small application as quickly as a Visual Basic developer can, and a good Visual Basic programmer can churn out object hierarchies and graphics code as effectively as a C# developer.

What many developers forget, however, is that building a successful application goes far beyond spitting out mountains of code. The code must work today, tomorrow, and for the entire life of the application.

Far more important than the programming language is the way developers use the language. I have seen code written in C, FORTRAN, and even assembly language that was so well structured and documented that practically anyone could modify the code with a minimal chance of adding obscure bugs. I've also seen a 56,000-line Visual Basic project that was so poorly designed and documented that even developers who had worked with the project for years could spend a week or more making a simple change, and have about a 50 percent chance of adding new bugs that would take another week or two to fix.

So, does that mean your choice of language is irrelevant? Almost, but not quite. First, the development environment plays a very important role in modern application development. Visual Studio provides unmatched tools for programming, debugging, and refactoring code. IntelliSense makes it easier to remember what parameters a routine needs. Auto-completion makes it easy to use longer, more descriptive variables. Design-time syntax-checking highlights suspicious code as you type it. XML comments and attributes let you make classes, methods, and events even more self-documenting than ever before. All of these tools make writing effective, reliable, maintainable code in the Visual Studio languages much easier than in many other languages that have less support from their development environments.

Though Visual Studio provides all of these tools, it cannot force you to use them properly, and here Visual Basic gives you a slight edge. Visual Basic has always been a very descriptive language. Its keywords are reasonably self-documenting and provide extra context to help you figure out what's going on. A piece of C# or C++ code containing several nested loops inside a subroutine may end with a series of many closing brackets. There's no extra information to help you remember what the brackets are ending. You can (and should) add comments to make this obvious, but the language doesn't force you to, so many programmers don't bother.

In contrast, Visual Basic ends a block of code with appropriate `End Do`, `End If`, `End Sub`, and other statements that make it obvious what type of block is ending. Although you should still add comments to indicate the purpose of the block of code that is ending, Visual Basic provides some basic annotation by itself.

Because Visual Basic is more descriptive than the other Visual Studio languages, it encourages developers to adopt a more descriptive style, too. Every time you write a `For` loop, you see keywords that help confirm the purpose and extent of the loop. Visual Basic is transparent, so developers are more inclined to make their own code transparent.

(The .NET Framework also sets a good example by providing long, descriptive variable, class, method, and event names. Class names such as `SortedList` and method names such as `DrawRectangle` are so easy to understand that it's easy to adopt similar habits of writing descriptive names.)

No programming language can force you to write good code. But Visual Studio provides powerful tools that reduce barriers to writing good code. They make it so easy to construct self-descriptive code that there's no excuse to write dense, opaque code full of obscure, inconsistent abbreviations. By performing its own chores in a self-descriptive way, Visual Basic gives you a little extra help in keeping your own code lucid. Use C# if you like, but I prefer to grab every advantage available.

Who Should Read This Book

This book is intended for advanced Visual Basic programmers. It assumes that you already have experience with Visual Basic 2005 and are comfortable with the language. The book does not cover any language fundamentals, and does not include any refresher material. If you feel that you need more experience with Visual Basic, see my book *Visual Basic 2005 Programmer's Reference* (Indianapolis: Wiley, 2005).

The topics I present in this book are as advanced as possible. In some cases, however, I have included simpler code to give background for a more advanced topic. But the goal of every part of the book is to explain advanced material that is either complex, hard to find in other places, or both.

Note that not all advanced material is complicated or difficult to understand. For example, the following statement summarizes one of the most important concepts in this entire book:

Programs are written for people, not computers.

In fact, this statement is so important that if you learn nothing else from this book, you will have received your money's worth. However, once you truly understand this idea (which I'll discuss further later in the book, notably in Chapter 14, "Development Philosophy"), it's completely obvious. Still, this is an advanced concept. I have never seen it written down explicitly in another book, and many developers only figure it out after years of debugging other people's code.

How This Book Is Organized

This book's chapters are grouped into four parts.

Part I: Design

The chapters in this part of the book cover activities that occur before programming begins. They describe development and design approaches, and some useful design techniques. Many programmers skimp on these phases, and later pay a huge price when their initial assumptions prove inappropriate for the application.

Chapter 1, "Language Selection," describes some of the issues that you should consider when picking a development language. The book assumes you will use Visual Basic, but this chapter describes some of the language's shortcomings. While you may stick with Visual Basic, it's worth understanding some of the language's weak spots, and what you can do about them. If you know where trouble may arise, you can more easily cope with it. In extreme cases, you may be able to move some of the more troublesome modules into a library written in another language and call the library from your Visual Basic code.

Chapter 2, "Lifecycle Methodologies," discusses different lifecycle methodologies such as the waterfall, iterative prototyping, and staged delivery models. It explains why Visual Basic is a particularly good tool for building applications iteratively. Most developers become accustomed to a particular methodology and never change. Even if you know you will be using iterative prototyping to build your application, it's worth taking the time to understand the best features of alternative approaches so that you can try to steal the best ideas from them all.

Chapter 3, "Agile Methodologies," explains different development strategies, such as agile development methods like extreme programming (XP), test-first development, and design by contract (DBC). It includes references to information on Microsoft's Web sites about using Visual Studio for agile development.

Chapter 4, "Object-Oriented Design," discusses issues in object-oriented design. It introduces the Universal Modeling Language (UML) and gives some tips for designing an object-oriented system. It explains how Visual Studio Team Suite and Visual Studio Team Architect support UML, and mentions a few other UML tools that developers can use. It tells how to gain a complete understanding of an application by viewing design from different perspectives, such as user interface, document, and data perspectives. It explains how to get the greatest benefit from object-oriented ideas, such as encapsulation, polymorphism, loose coupling, and component-oriented design.

Chapter 5, "User-Interface Design," explains important user-interface concepts. It explains the rule of 7 +/– 2 and tells how to use containers such as tab strips and scrolling controls to display large amounts of data. It discusses the merits and drawbacks of SDI and MDI applications, and examines menus, toolbars, and keyboard shortcuts. It also explains techniques for customizing the user interface for particular users and locales.

Chapter 6, "Data Storage Design," discusses different data storage and retrieval strategies. It explores options such as relational databases, XML, flat text files, the System Registry, compiled in data, resource files, and INI files. It explains how a program can serialize and deserialize its data. Note that this chapter does not cover relational database design in depth. For example, it does not explain normalization and indexing in great detail, instead referring to other books for more information.

Chapter 7, "Design Patterns," provides an introduction to design patterns and anti-patterns in Visual Basic. It explains what design patterns and anti-patterns are, describes some of the most useful, and refers the reader to other books such as *Visual Basic Design Patterns* by Mark Grand and Brad Merrill (Indianapolis: Wiley, 2005) for additional details.

Part II: Meta-Development

The chapters in this part of the book discuss writing tools that are used by application developers. These include add-ins that give design-time support to developers, custom controls and components that can be placed on forms, and techniques that let the user execute scripts at run-time. A good library of meta-development tools makes later development easier and less error-prone.

Chapter 8, "Snippets, Macros, and Add-ins," explains how to write add-ins for the Visual Basic 2005 development environment. It briefly describes code snippets and explains when it is appropriate to use them rather than add-ins.

Chapter 9, "Scripting," explains how a program can allow the end user to write and execute scripts. It tells how to let the user execute SQL statements, VBA code, and VB .NET scripts. It explains how a program can expose its object model so that the user can control it with VB .NET scripting. This chapter also tells how a developer can use the same scripting techniques to give an application new functionality after it has been compiled.

Chapter 10, "Custom Controls and Components," explains how to build custom controls. It describes the three main approaches for building custom controls: `UserControl`, subclassing, and from scratch. It also explains how to build a special particularly useful type of custom control called extender providers, and includes examples of some extremely useful data validation *extender providers*.

Chapter 11, "Property Support," explains how to build custom property editors for use by custom controls. It also tells how to use type converters to allow editors such as the Properties window at design time and the `PropertyGrid` control at run-time to edit complex properties of an object.

Chapter 12, "Attributes and XML Comments," explains useful attributes that you can use to "decorate" code. These attributes make extra information available to other developers (or yourself) who use the code later so that it is easier to use the code correctly.

Part III: Development

The chapters in this part of the book explain topics relating to the main body of the application's development work. These chapters focus on the process of writing code, and some approaches that make writing code more effective. They do not dwell on language features and syntactic issues.

Chapter 13, "Documentation," explains how a more complex project should be documented. It describes the special XML documentation comments supported by Visual Basic 2005, and provides advanced examples that show how to use them to automatically generate documentation and help files.

Chapter 14, "Development Philosophy," explains advanced coding concepts that make development and maintenance of complex applications easier. It discusses ideas such as advanced design for testing, defensive and offensive programming, and writing code for people, not computers. These ideas are particularly useful in large projects with possibly changing staff because they provide context for new developers moving onto a project.

Chapter 15, "Coding Standards," explains my particular set of coding standards that make reading code easier. It explains the differences between my standards and those used by Microsoft and others. These standards offer a starting point for developing the rules that you decide to adopt. No set of standards is perfect, but using any standard is better than not following any standard.

Chapter 16, "Bug Proofing," explains steps that developers can take to make bugs easier to find and repair. These methods are essential in large, complex applications. This chapter explains shortcomings of the `Try Catch Finally` blocks and shows how to work around them. It explains how to use application-level events to catch all of an application's errors, and discusses advanced methods that allow the program to record and recover from errors.

Chapter 17, "Testing," explains advanced debugging and testing techniques. It explains black box, white box, and unusual condition testing. It explains regression, routine, module, and integration testing, and tells how to estimate the quality of a project. It describes the free NUnit testing tool and how it fits into a test-driven approach. It also describes the unit-test support built into Visual Studio 2005 Team System.

Chapter 18, "Deployment," explains the deployment strategies available to Visual Basic 2005 applications. It shows how to provide extensibility by loading new modules and scripts into previously compiled applications. It also explains how to use serialization to allow backward and forward compatibility.

Part IV: Specific Techniques

The chapters in this section explain specific advanced techniques that are useful in many applications. Whereas the earlier chapters deal with general design and development issues, these chapters explain approaches to handling particular tasks that arise on many development projects.

Chapter 19, "Splash Screens," explains how to quickly build impressive splash screens and About dialogs. It covers such techniques as shaped forms, rotated text, and links to Web pages. While this is probably the least advanced (but most fun) chapter in the book, you should give the topic its due. Splash screens and About dialogs are some of the first ways in which users and clients interact with an application, so they set the mood. A good splash screen shows your enthusiasm for the application, and tells your user that you take care of the little details that make a program useful.

Chapter 20, "Printing," explains how to print in Visual Basic .NET. It shows how to use the standard .NET printing techniques to wrap text across pages and flow text around objects. It also describes a more natural procedural approach to printing that is more intuitive for most developers, and lets you display items such as page-by-page counts that are difficult when using the standard .NET printing model.

Chapter 21, "Threading," explains how to use the new threading tools provided by Visual Basic 2005. With computer hardware speeds leveling off, multi-threading is one of the best ways to improve performance of intensive applications, but it comes with its own set of risks and assumptions. This chapter explains some of the issues involved in multi-threaded applications, such as access to the user interface thread and concurrency issues.

Chapter 22, "Reflection," explains one of the most powerful features in Visual Basic .NET: reflection. It shows how a program can use reflection to learn about modules, objects, properties, and methods in its own code, and in other assemblies. It also explains how a program can use reflection to load modules that were written after the application was compiled.

Chapter 23, "Memory Management," explains memory-management issues. It describes the garbage collector, shows how to implement and invoke `Dispose` methods, and how to use weak memory references to improve memory management.

How to Use This Book

There are two obvious approaches to using this book. First, you can read it cover-to-cover. That presents the book's parts in their most natural order: design, meta-development, development, and specific techniques.

Second, you can jump into the book to read about topics that currently interest you. If you want to build some custom controls to perform data validation in text boxes, you can read Chapter 10, "Custom Controls and Components."

Many of the techniques described in this book are much more useful if you keep them in mind during development. It is more difficult to go back and retrofit good programming practices onto code that you have already written. For that reason, you should read relevant chapters *before* you need them. You may want to at least skim the entire book so that you have a good idea of what topics are covered. That way, when you prepare to start a new development phase, you will know if a chapter contains information that you should look at more closely.

What You Need to Use This Book

To read this book and understand the examples, you will need no special equipment. You don't really even need Visual Basic, and many of these techniques apply to other languages as well.

To use Visual Basic .NET and to run the examples found on the book's Web page, you need any computer that can reasonably run Visual Basic .NET. That means a reasonably modern, fast computer with a lot of memory. See the Visual Basic .NET documentation for Microsoft's exact requirements and recommendations.

To build Visual Basic .NET programs, you will also need a copy of Visual Basic .NET. The examples shown here were written and tested in Visual Basic 2005 under Windows XP, but most will run with few or no modification in earlier versions of Visual Basic .NET and older operating systems. Some of the programs may not run in the Vista operating system. Visit the book's Web site at `www.vb-helper.com/one_on_one.htm` for updated Vista-compatible examples.

Much of the Visual Basic 2005 release is compatible with Visual Basic .NET 2003 and earlier versions of Visual Basic .NET, so you can make many of the examples work with earlier versions of Visual Basic .NET. You will not be able to load the example programs downloaded from the book's Web site, however. You will need to copy and paste the significant portions of the code into your version of Visual Basic .NET, and you may need to make a few changes. If you get stuck, email me at `RodStephens@vb-helper.com` and I'll try to point you in the right direction.

Don't bother trying to run the examples with a pre-.NET version of Visual Basic such as Visual Basic 6. The changes between Visual Basic 6 and Visual Basic .NET are huge, and many Visual Basic .NET concepts don't translate well into Visual Basic 6. With some experience in C#, it would be much easier to translate programs into that language.

p2p.wrox.com

For author and peer discussion, join the P2P forums at `p2p.wrox.com`. The forums are a Web-based system for you to post messages relating to Wrox books and related technologies and interact with other readers and technology users. The forums offer a subscription feature to email you topics of interest of your choosing when new posts are made to the forums. Wrox authors, editors, other industry experts, and your fellow readers are present on these forums.

At `http://p2p.wrox.com`, you will find a number of different forums that will help you not only as you read this book, but also as you develop your own applications. To join the forums, just follow these steps:

1. Go to `p2p.wrox.com` and click the Register link.
2. Read the terms of use and click Agree.
3. Complete the required information to join, as well as any optional information you wish to provide, and click Submit.
4. You will receive an email with information describing how to verify your account and complete the joining process.

You can read messages in the forums without joining P2P, but in order to post your own messages, you must join.

Once you join, you can post new messages and respond to messages other users post. You can read messages at any time on the Web. If you would like to have new messages from a particular forum emailed to you, click the "Subscribe to this Forum" icon by the forum name in the forum listing.

For more information about how to use the Wrox P2P, be sure to read the P2P FAQs for answers to questions about how the forum software works, as well as many common questions specific to P2P and Wrox books. To read the FAQs, click the FAQ link on any P2P page.

The Book's Web Site

On the book's Web site, `www.vb-helper.com/one_on_one.htm`, you can do the following:

- Download the examples in this book
- Download other Visual Basic programming examples
- View updates and corrections
- Connect to the Wrox discussion group for this book
- Read other readers' comments and suggestions

This book was written using Visual Basic 2005 under Windows XP. The book's Web page will include any modifications that the examples need to run in the Vista operating system.

If you have corrections or comments of your own, please send them to me at `RodStephens@vb-helper.com`. I will do my best to keep the Web site as up-to-date as possible.

Subscribe to one of my three newsletters at `www.vb-helper.com/newsletter.html` to receive weekly tips, tricks, and examples for Visual Basic programming. I also announce any updates to my books in the newsletters, so if you sign up, you'll learn when there are updates.

Part I
Design

In this Part:

1

Language Selection

The chapters in this part of the book cover activities that occur before programming begins. They describe development and design approaches, and some useful design techniques. Many programmers skimp on these phases, and later pay a huge price when their initial assumptions prove inappropriate for the application.

This chapter describes some of the issues that you should consider when picking a development language. The book assumes you will use Visual Basic, but this chapter describes some of the language's shortcomings. While you may stick with Visual Basic, it's worth understanding some of the language's weak spots and what you can do about them. If you know where trouble may arise, you can more easily cope with it. In extreme cases, you may be able to move some of the more troublesome modules into a library written in another language such as C# or C++, and call the library from your Visual Basic code. For example, C++ and C# handle pointers more transparently than Visual Basic does. If you need to use a library to control special-purpose hardware, it may be easier to call that library's routines from C++ or C#, particularly if the library was written in one of those languages.

One of the other times I've found this sort of thing useful is with "unsafe" array manipulation for graphics processing. A program can obtain a pointer to the memory containing an image's pixel data. A C# program can treat the pointer as a reference to an array, whereas a Visual Basic program must use API functions to copy the pointer's memory into a new array and, after the program has finished manipulating the array, it must copy the result back to the pointer's location. If you place the graphics-processing code in a C# module and call it from Visual Basic, you can avoid these two memory copies and save some time.

Language Addiction

If you surf the Web looking for reviews of languages, you'll find a very strong correlation between the programming language a person uses and the language he or she thinks is best. You can find lots of C# and C++ programmers who can tell you all about the bad points of Visual Basic, and plenty of Visual Basic developers who will tell you at length what's wrong with C# and C++. When you use a language extensively, that's the one you find most natural, and anything else seems strange.

If you speak to developers who have used several languages extensively, you'll generally get a very different response. These developers tend to say that most languages do pretty much the same thing, just in different ways, and the choice isn't that big a deal. In particular, I know a lot of programmers who have used both Visual Basic and C# for several years and they agree that the languages are practically identical. Many have a personal preference, but very few people with a lot of experience claim that one language is clearly superior to all others in all situations.

During my career, I've used quite a few languages, including Pascal, assembly, FORTRAN, C, C++, Delphi, PostScript (many developers don't even know it's a programming language), some graphics programming languages, various flavors of BASIC, and an assortment of Visual Basic versions such as VBA, VBScript, and Visual Basic versions 3 through 2005. Each of these languages has its strengths and weaknesses.

Disadvantages

The following section describes some of the most common objections raised against Visual Basic and explains whether these are real, significant objections; a problem that is easy to work around; or merely a matter of perception.

Interpreted, Not Compiled

Visual Basic does not produce a compiled executable. Instead it produces Intermediate Language (IL) code that is interpreted at run-time by the Command Language Runtime (CLR). This has a couple of important consequences.

First, interpreting code reduces execution speed. Visual Basic uses a just-in-time (JIT) compiler so after a program has executed a piece of code, it should be compiled and run at faster speeds later. However, running the code the first time will still be a bit slower than it will be in a truly compiled language.

Second, a computer must have the CLR and the .NET Framework installed to interpret the Visual Basic program's IL code. These not only increase the installation complexity, but they are also quite large and getting larger with each new release. Whereas the Visual Basic 6 run-time libraries took about 1MB compressed, the .NET Framework 2.0 needed to run Visual Basic 2005 programs weighs in at 22.4MB compressed, and expands to 280MB of disk space when installed (610MB if you're running 64-bit Windows).

Third, IL code is relatively easy to read, so even distributed as an "executable," a Visual Basic or C# application is relatively easy to reverse-engineer. Code obfuscators that rearrange code, rename variables so they are harder to understand, and so forth are available, but the result is still easier to read than a compiled executable.

Lutz Roeder's excellent "Reflector for .NET" program allows you to easily view IL code for .NET assemblies written in Visual Basic, C#, C++, IL, Delphi, and Chrome. It will even display code in those languages that could have generated the IL code. For example, you can load a compile application and Reflector will show you C# code that is roughly equivalent. This tool for comparing the IL generated by similar pieces of Visual Basic and C# code — the res always the same. You can download Reflector and some other useful tools at `www.ais` `roeder/dotnet`.

How important are these objections? Programmers often focus on speed but, as I'll a later in this book, usability and correctness are more important than speed for most applications. If an application spends most of its time waiting for user input and calling a database engine, pure CPU speed isn't an issue. With today's fast computers and JIT compilation, speed is usually not a problem.

C# uses IL just as Visual Basic does, so there's no reason to think using C# will improve performance. Some languages such as Delphi may give better performance because they use better compiler optimization techniques. Assembly can also give better performance, but only if you write good assembly code, and the difficultly is rarely worth it.

Installing huge run-time libraries can be a serious issue. If you're developing software for use within your company, you may be able to require users to download a 22.4MB file that uses 280MB of disk space when installed. However, if you want to allow customers to download your program from the Internet, this may be a problem. For example, a 56K modem would take almost an hour to download the file. Once customers have the run-time libraries installed, they will not need to download them for future Visual Basic applications, but downloading them the first time could be problematic. Even with Visual Basic's new Click-Once Deployment, it's much easier for the user to run a self-installing Java application on whatever browser he or she prefers.

Finally, IL security can be a big issue for some applications. Many companies are protective of their software, and the chance of reverse-engineering has made many of them reluctant to adopt Visual Basic .NET. For many applications, you can easily deduce the code from the user interface. Any programmer can figure out how to make menus, dialogs, and reports. Often, there is only a small part of the application that is proprietary. If security is a real concern, you may be able to move that small piece of code into a library written in a truly compiled language such as C++.

When considering whether the reduced security provided by IL is a show-stopping issue, ask yourself these questions:

- ❑ How likely is it that someone will try to reverse-engineer the code?
- ❑ Does the program contain real proprietary information that you need to protect? Or, is most of the code obvious from the user interface?
- ❑ Can you pull the sensitive pieces out and compile them into a compiled library?

You can also use obfusticators to deter casual hackers. Some of the latest obfusticators do a pretty good job of making the code so confusing that it will be easier for a hacker to rewrite the application from scratch, rather than to sift through the scrambled code. If you do use an obfusticator, you should also use Lutz Roeder's Reflector program to see what the resulting IL looks like. If you're not confused by the result, a hacker won't be either.

uage Features

Visual Basic has an intuitive, self-documenting syntax but it also has a few annoying quirks. In an attempt to make every customer happy, Microsoft has left in some features and options that it probably should have removed. These are generally syntactic annoyances and don't cause much trouble if you are aware of them:

- *Strict Type Checking*—Type checking in Visual Basic .NET is stricter than it was in Visual Basic 6, but it's still looser than in some other languages. For example, by default, Visual Basic 2005 doesn't let you assign an Integer to a String (`s = 12`), but it will allow you to assign an Integer to a Long (`long_var = integer_var`). Sometimes that's what you want to do, but sometimes it's an indication that there's something wrong with your design. It also costs some execution time as the value is converted from one data type to another.
- *Option Explicit*—This option shouldn't be optional, it should always be on. I've never seen an example where turning this option off was necessary.
- *Option Strict*—This option should also always be on. Unfortunately, there are very rare cases when it's convenient to bypass type checking and turn Option Strict off (for example, when coercing parameters in and out of library function calls). If you must turn Option Strict off, do so in the smallest module you can build to get the job done. Use partial classes, if necessary, so that Option Strict is on in the rest of the application.
- *IIF*—Generally, an IIF statement is harder to read than a corresponding multi-line `If Then Else` statement, although I have seen cases where IIF can make a series of very simple statements easier to compare. IIF is also less efficient than `If Then Else` because it always evaluates both results even though only one is used. Usually you can avoid IIF.
- *Pointers*—Visual Basic uses references to refer to objects rather than actual pointers. That makes working with true pointers somewhat awkward. For example, if an API routine returns a pointer to a chunk of memory that contains one of several different data structures, it's more difficult to bully the result into the right kind of Structure type in Visual Basic than it is in languages such as C++ that use pointers explicitly. However, explicit use of pointers and manual memory allocation leads to some of the most difficult kinds of bugs to find in C++. The times when I've missed pointers have been pretty rare, so on the whole, Visual Basic is better off with references. The Marshal class provides methods that coerce pointers from one data type to another, so usually a Visual Basic program can produce the correct results with a little extra work.
- *Strings*—In Visual Basic, a String is more than a pointer to a series of characters in memory as it is in C and C++. If your application performs extremely complex string manipulation, those languages may give better performance. On the other hand, you can convert Strings in Visual Basic into an array of characters, and then manipulate the entries in the array. You couldn't use C-style character pointer arithmetic, but you can use array indices.
- *Garbage Collection*—The garbage collection techniques used by .NET take control of memory management away from the developer. The garbage collector can run at any time, and you have almost no control over when or how it does its job. You also cannot tell when an object will finally be destroyed and its resources freed (this is called *non-deterministic finalization*). That forces you to implement other methods such as the IDispose interface to allow the program to free resources before an object is garbage-collected. The garbage collector makes some of these issues more complicated than necessary, but they should only be a real showstopper in real-time applications.

A famous story from the MIT artificial intelligence laboratory illustrates how garbage collection can hurt real-time systems. A robotics application was supposed to track a thrown ball and catch it with a robot arm. In one trial, the machine vision system found the ball, tracked its trajectory, calculated its future trajectory, and then stopped for garbage collection. By the time garbage collection had finished and the computer moved the robot arm, the ball had hit the floor and bounced away.

- `AndAlso` *and* `OrElse` — The `AndAlso` and `OrElse` operators perform logical evaluation with short-circuiting. For example, consider the statement `A AndAlso B`. If `A` is `False`, then there's no reason to evaluate `B`, so Visual Basic doesn't bother. In the statement `A And B`, Visual Basic evaluates both `A` and `B`, even if `A` is `False`. If `A` and `B` are simple Boolean values or variables, this doesn't matter much. If they represent time-consuming function calls, `AndAlso` and `OrElse` can be much faster than `And` and `Or`. It would probably be better if `And` and `Or` used short-circuit evaluation, because that is generally more efficient, but Microsoft left the definitions of `And` and `Or` the way they were in Visual Basic 6 for backward compatibility.

The only time when you would want to always evaluate `A` *and* `B` *is if* `A` *and* `B` *were routines that have side effects such as updating global variables or opening files. Writing functions with side effects such as these is a bad programming practice, so this shouldn't be an issue anyway.*

- *Routine Libraries* — Visual Basic doesn't allow you to build a library that contains nothing but functions and subroutines. Instead, you must create a class library. The user of the library must make an instance of the class, and then use the object's methods to take action. Though this can sometimes be an annoyance, it's not too hard to live with.
- *Inline Code* — Visual Basic does not allow you to include inline code written in other languages. For example, you cannot include a small section of assembly or C# code to handle a particularly tricky or CPU-intensive task. You can, however, place that code in a separate library written in another language and call it from Visual Basic, although there will be a slight overhead in making the library call.
- *Macro Expansion* — Visual Basic does not allow inline macro expansion as provided by C++. This kind of macro expansion replaces a macro reference with a chunk of code at compile time. You can get much the same effect by placing the code in a subroutine instead of a macro definition. This may make the code slightly less efficient, but it makes issues such as setting breakpoints in the code much simpler.

Multiple Inheritance

Some languages support *multiple inheritance* (where a class can inherit from more than one parent class). For example, if you have a `Vehicle` class and a `Domicile` class, you could make the `MotorHome` class inherit from both to gain the properties and methods of both `Vehicle` and `Domicile`.

Though it's not too hard to come up with believable examples where multiple inheritance might make sense (`MotorHome`, `HouseBoat`, `EmtFirefighter`), I have yet to see a real application where that sort of inheritance was absolutely crucial. You can always implement classes such as these by using the facade design pattern. For example, the `EmtFirefighter` class would contain objects from the `Emt` (for "emergency medical technician") and `Firefighter` classes. It would then delegate calls to its properties and methods to those objects. Although this would be less automatic, it would be easier to understand and would also encourage a simpler, flatter object hierarchy.

Platform Dependencies

After you compile a Visual Basic application into IL, you use the CLR to execute the IL code. Microsoft provides support to use those libraries on Windows platforms, but, in theory, you could run on any platform that provides run-time support for IL.

The Mono project (`www.mono-project.com`) is an Open Source effort to support .NET applications in various operating systems. Currently, Mono lets you build and run .NET applications on Windows, Unix, Linux, Solaris, and Mac OS X. It also supports Java, Python, and other languages, in addition to C# and Visual Basic. See the Mono Web site `www.mono-project.com` for more information.

Between .NET's native support on Windows and Mono, .NET applications should run on the vast majority of PCs in use. An application written in Java or another Web-based language can run on those operating systems, and also on any other system that supports modern Web browsers, so such an application would have slightly greater portability.

Often, desktop applications built with Visual Basic provide a better user experience than those built with Java. Desktop applications have fewer restrictions than Java applications, and some things that are trivial in Visual Basic are much more difficult in Java, particularly if the Java application needs to run in a browser that doesn't support the same features available on the desktop.

However, there seems to be a growing feeling that "good enough is good enough" — that the restrictions imposed by Java are worth the ability to run by simply pointing a browser at the appropriate URL.

I prefer the performance and flexibility you usually get from desktop applications rather than Java, but there's much to recommend the "good enough is good enough" philosophy. When Visual Basic 3 was released, I had spent just over a month working on a C++ application. When I gave Visual Basic 3 a try, I was able to reproduce everything I had built within that month in only four days. There were some things that Visual Basic 3 could not do that were possible in C++, but they meant extra work and were things I was willing to live without for the sake of a 75 percent reduction in development time. I moved to Visual Basic because it was good enough, so I can understand the idea that Java is good enough for some applications.

Upgrading from Visual Basic 6

Visual Basic .NET includes an upgrade wizard that converts Visual Basic 6 code into Visual Basic .NET. Unfortunately, the wizard isn't very good. Microsoft claims the wizard can handle as much as 85 percent of Visual Basic 6 code without intervention, but in practice, the results aren't very good and a typical application requires a lot of manual rewriting.

However, this is still better than nothing. Even if the wizard converts only a small fraction of the code correctly, it's a head start that you wouldn't get if you wanted to port a Visual Basic 6 application to C++ or Java.

GUI Building

Believe it or not, the fact is that building graphical user interfaces (GUIs) in Visual Basic is so easy that it can actually cause problems. It's extremely easy for an inexperienced developer to slap together an awkward interface that's difficult for users to understand.

This is a problem with the developer rather than Visual Basic. The development environment gives you the tools you need to build a good or bad interface. It's up to the developer to learn how to use the tools wisely. The fact that it's more difficult to build GUIs in some other languages may force developers to spend more time on design, but that's time you should spend no matter what language you are using.

Verbosity

Many C++ and C# developers think Visual Basic is too verbose and that code is easier to read and write if it doesn't include as many characters. Though Visual Basic does require more typing, it is also more self-documenting. If the goal were to write programs as tersely as possible, all developers would use assembly code. Only a tiny part of application development is spent actually typing code. Far more time is spent reading code and looking for bugs.

In any case, Visual Studio's excellent IntelliSense makes it unnecessary for programmers to type out most class, variable, property, and method names in their entirety. Usually, you only need to type a few characters. If Visual Studio can figure out what choices might match (as when you're accessing an object's properties), it provides a list. If you're starting a new line, you can press Ctrl+spacebar to get a list of possible matches. Then you can quickly select one without additional typing.

I teach introductory Visual Basic courses where I always stress IntelliSense and, after a few weeks with the students, Ctrl+spacebar. It's particularly effective if you name controls and variables consistently. For a text box, type **txt** *and press Ctrl+spacebar to get a short list of the available choices. After a few weeks, the students become experts at using Ctrl+spacebar.*

Power and Flexibility

Probably the silliest disadvantage to Visual Basic (but perhaps the one that has the most impact on developers) is the perception that Visual Basic is less powerful than Java, C++, and C#. Although those languages are more difficult to learn, they are not significantly more powerful. They all run on the same hardware and can all do more or less whatever the hardware supports. In fact, C# and Visual Basic are practically identical, aside from their syntactic differences.

The fact that many pre-.NET Visual Basic developers were self-taught and that many came to Visual Basic via Visual Basic for Applications (VBA) makes Visual Basic seem more ordinary to many managers, and lends an extra mystique to Java, C++, and C#.

Salaries for Java, C++, and C# programmers also tend to be higher than those of Visual Basic developers. This is probably partly because of the perception that those languages are more powerful, the fact that they are more difficult, and the fact that there are far more Visual Basic developers available in the job marketplace.

All of these facts sometimes lead management to prefer those languages to Visual Basic, although there really isn't much justification on the basis of power or flexibility.

Advantages

Visual Basic does have some legitimate disadvantages, but it has many advantages as well. The following sections describe some of the most important advantages Visual Basic has over other common programming languages.

Self-Documenting

Visual Basic's syntax makes it much more self-documenting than other languages. Its keywords are spelled out and easy to read. Statements that close blocks such as `End Do` and `Next employee` explicitly tell you what block is ending—in this case a `Do` loop and a loop involving a variable named `employee`. This makes the code much easier to read than code that ends blocks with braces.

The `Next` statement that ends a `For` loop allows you to explicitly give the variable controlling the loop, specifying exactly which loop is ending. Although you are not required to include this variable, you should because it makes the code more self-documenting. The following code shows a small example:

```
For i As Integer = 0 To 100
    ...
Next i
```

Unfortunately, you cannot similarly attach the name of the variable controlling an `If Then` block, `Do` loop, or other structure. That makes some sense, because these statements are often controlled by Boolean expressions rather than simple variables. You can, however, include the controlling expressions in a comment after the closing statement. The following code shows how you might add comments to a `Do` loop and an `If Then Else` block:

```
Do Until all_done
    ...
Loop ' Until all_done

If num_employees <= 100 Then
    ...
ElseIf num_employees <= 500 Then ' If num_employees <= 100 Then...
    ...
Else ' If num_employees <= 100 Then ... ElseIf <= 500 ...
    ...
End If ' If num_employees <= 100 Then ... ElseIf <= 500 ... Else ...
```

As is shown in the last two comments, you don't need to include every detail of the block; you just need to include enough so that someone remembers the block to which the statement belongs.

The .NET Framework also uses nice, long, descriptive class, property, and method names, making it self-documenting as well. That makes using the Framework easier, and provides a good example to encourage Visual Basic developers to use similarly descriptive names.

Prototyping and Simple Applications

It is extremely easy to build user interface prototypes with Visual Basic. For many applications, you can put together a simple application in a few hours and get feedback from the customer before starting any really difficult development. Providing a prototype quickly is far more effective than making users visualize what an application will look like through drawings or textual descriptions.

Visual Basic is also extremely effective for building very simple applications. In a matter of minutes, you can build a basic database application that lets you add, query, update, and delete records in a database. Though you would need to spend some extra effort to make such an application bulletproof, adding validations, and so forth, you can quickly build prototypes or throwaway programs for your own use.

IDE

Visual Studio is an excellent integrated development environment (IDE) for programming and debugging code. IntelliSense makes it easier to correctly enter complex parameter lists. Breakpoints and watches make stepping through code easy. The call stack browser lets you jump through the code to see how pieces call each other.

Other languages provide their own IDEs and, though some such as Delphi's are quite good, Visual Studio is an outstanding IDE.

Language Relatives

Visual Basic is a close relative to several other languages, including the following:

- *VBA* (*Visual Basic for Applications*) — Used as a macro language by the Microsoft Office products and can be used for scripting in other applications.
- *VBScript* — Used in ASP applications to build interactive Web applications. VBScript is very similar to the Visual Basic language. In contrast, JavaScript is more like VBScript than Java.
- *Visual Basic "Classic"* — Although Visual Basic .NET is different in many ways from Visual Basic 6 and earlier versions, the languages have much in common. As the "Y2K problem" showed, software often lives far beyond its expected lifetime. While Visual Basic .NET is Microsoft's path of the future, legacy Visual Basic "Classic" applications will continue to need support and even development for many years to come.

This makes translating code between these languages relatively easy, so applications that you write in one may be useful in others. By using Visual Basic, you acquire skills and a code base that can be helpful in building desktop, Web, and scripted applications.

While the syntax details of Visual Basic and C# differ, the languages have a common enough structure that it's not too hard for a Visual Basic developer to read C# code. Though translating C# code line-by-line into Visual Basic is not as straightforward as translating VBA code, it is relatively easy to get the general idea of C# code and then rewrite it. That gives Visual Basic developers another source for ideas and solutions to common problems.

Garbage Collection

Although the garbage-collection scheme used by Visual Basic .NET has its drawbacks, it also has some advantages. Memory allocation is often the most difficult part of C and C++ applications to debug and maintain. If you forget to free allocated memory, the application has "memory leaks" and uses more and more of the system's memory over time. If you free the same memory twice, the memory system can crash. If you forget that you have freed a piece of memory and then later try to use it, the program may crash.

The nature of these bugs often means problems are obvious only long after the program executes the incorrect code. For example, suppose a program frees the memory holding an object. It may be much later that the program tries to access that object, causing a crash. Because the effects of these errors may occur long after their causes, these bugs can be extremely difficult to locate.

Visual Basic's garbage collection scheme avoids all of these problems by removing your memory management responsibility. When the garbage collector runs, it frees memory that cannot be accessed by the application. If a piece of memory such as an object reference is still usable by the program, the garbage collector leaves it alone. This prevents all of these memory-related bugs.

Large Talent Pool

It's hard to find reliable data about the number of developers currently using Visual Basic. At one time, Microsoft claimed there were more than 3.2 million Visual Basic 6 users (`msdn.microsoft.com/isv/technology/vba/overview/default.aspx`). They have also claimed more than 3.5 million Visual Studio users (`msdn.microsoft.com/vstudio/extend/vsta/default.aspx`), although they don't specifically mention which version of Visual Studio, and 1 million Visual Basic .NET users (`msdn.microsoft.com/netframework/technologyinfo/Overview/default.aspx`).

Whatever the numbers, it's clear that there are a *lot* of developers who use Visual Basic of one form or another. This in itself doesn't mean Visual Basic is the best language, but it does mean that there is a large pool of Visual Basic talent available. It means there are active newsgroups and forums where you can ask questions if you need help, and that there are plenty of developers that you can hire if you need extra hands on a project.

Summary

Although Visual Basic is an excellent programming language, the choice of language is not always trivial. Whether Visual Basic is right for you depends on your application.

Arguments that Visual Basic is less powerful or slower than languages such as C# are just plain wrong. All high-level languages have about the same capabilities and any missing features are usually easy to supply with a few well-chosen libraries. Still, Visual Basic does have a few legitimate drawbacks.

If you only need your application to run on Windows operating systems, then Visual Basic is fine. If you need to run on other systems, you will need support for running IL code. Mono may be an acceptable solution for Unix, Linux, Solaris, and Mac OS X, and there have been rumors that Microsoft is bringing support for C# to the Mac OS, but support will probably be better on Windows platforms.

Visual Basic does not provide multiple inheritance, so if your application architecture requires multiple inheritance, you may want to use another language. I have never seen a real-world application that truly *required* multiple inheritance, so if you only use it in a few places, you may be able to redesign the application slightly to avoid it. If all else fails, you can mimic multiple inheritance in limited cases by using a facade design pattern.

Though Visual Basic .NET is as fast as C# and is much faster than earlier versions of Visual Basic, it is still an interpreted language, and a truly compiled language may give better performance for extremely CPU-intensive applications. Most applications are limited by factors other than CPU use, however. Many applications spend most of their time waiting for user input, database requests, network access, or file access, and making the code itself faster may not help much. If you are writing a high-performance real-time application where every clock cycle counts, you may need to move to a truly compiled language. However, for most applications, you can move selected CPU-intensive pieces of code into compiled libraries and call them from Visual Basic when necessary.

Another consequence of the IL is that a Visual Basic .NET application requires a 280MB run-time library. Even in today's environment of cheap hard drives, that's a lot of disk space. More important, however, is that downloading such a large library takes a long time. That will prevent many users with only casual interest from downloading your application from the Internet, particularly users with slower network connections. Once customers have installed one .NET application, the run-time library will already be installed so they won't need to download it again. However, the first installation can be painful.

Visual Basic's interpreted nature also lets developers read IL code relatively easily. That makes it much simpler to reverse-engineer Visual Basic or C# applications to either steal useful code or exploit weaknesses in the code. Obfusticators can make code much more difficult to read, but not as hard as truly compiled code.

Finally, many C, C++, and C# developers complain about Visual Basic's verbosity. You can reasonably argue that this is a matter of personal preference, but I claim it's something more. Extra verbosity makes the language more readable, and that's absolutely crucial for debugging and maintaining any complex application. You can add extra comments to C++ or C# code to make it more maintainable, but Visual Basic has extra help built in. That leads to the most important concept in this book:

> *Programs are written for people, not computers.*

If you were writing only for the computer, you would use 0s and 1s, or at least some form of assembly language rather than a high-level language. The computer doesn't care what language you use. It's all 0s and 1s when the CPU executes it. The reason you use a high-level language is to make programming, understanding, debugging, and maintaining the code easier *for people*. Any feature that makes the code easier for a human to read and understand gives you an advantage that you should not lightly throw away in the name of conciseness.

Taking all of these factors into account, you need to decide whether Visual Basic is the right language for your application. Performance and capability are critical issues far less often than the ability of programmers to write, debug, and maintain the code, so Visual Basic makes an excellent choice.

Once you've picked a programming language, whether it is Visual Basic or something else, you're still not ready to start writing code. There are plenty of other tasks that you should perform before starting to build any non-trivial application. Chapter 2, "Lifecycle Methodologies," discusses different patterns for bringing a project through to produce a finished application. The chapters after that one describe other pre-coding design and development activities that you should study before you get down to the serious business of programming. If you stint on these phases, you may start coding sooner, but you may later pay a huge price when you need to debug and maintain the application.

2

Lifecycle Methodologies

An application's lifecycle covers its entire existence, starting with a vaguely formed idea and lasting through design, development, deployment, and use by customers. The lifecycle may include any number of revisions and new releases, and ends when the last copy of the application is no longer used and the whole thing is relegated to history. An application's lifecycle may last 30 years and span dozens of releases and enhancements, or it may be cut short during design when developers decide the application is impractical or doesn't adequately meet customer needs.

Whether an application is intended to last a month, a year, or indefinitely, you need to manage its lifecycle. For a simple, one-use throwaway application, you may spend very little time in lifecycle management. For longer-lived applications, you may need to spend considerable effort to ensure that the application moves as smoothly as possible from the idea stage to a usable product, and that it remains usable as long as possible, or at least as long as it is needed.

This chapter describes several different lifecycle methodologies that you can use to manage different kinds of applications. It discusses the strengths and weaknesses of each method, and explains which work best when developing in Visual Basic.

Lifecycle Stages

All lifecycle strategies use the same fundamental stages arranged in various ways. In one approach, some stages may be made longer or shorter. In another approach, some stages may be reduced practically to the point of non-existence, whereas others are repeated several times. Often, different stages blur together with one overlapping another. However, every approach uses the same basic stages to one extent or another. The following sections describe these basic stages.

Idea Formulation and Refinement

Every application begins as an idea. Someone gets a notion about some program that might be useful.

Sometimes the idea is only a vague notion, such as, "Wouldn't it be great if we had a program that could generate reports for us?" Other times, the idea may be fully formed from the start with the idea maker knowing exactly what the program must do.

Once the basic idea is discovered, it should be discussed with others who might have different insights into the desired result. As many people as possible should have a chance to provide input, making suggestions, additions, and improvements until you know pretty much what the application should do.

Many different people might provide useful feedback in this stage of the lifecycle. People who will eventually use the application (the customers) know what they need to accomplish. If the application will help with an existing process, the customers know how the process is currently performed. Though the application doesn't need to follow the same approach that the customers use now, it's worthwhile examining the current methods to see if they contain any useful ideas.

The supervisors and managers of the final users also often have useful insights. Even if these people won't use the application daily, they sometimes have a higher-level view of the environment in which the application will run. They may be able to suggest ways to expand the scope of the application to handle other related tasks. They may also be able to restrict the scope of the idea to avoid duplicating other efforts that may not be obvious to the end users.

It is frequently useful to ask people to daydream during this phase. Ask questions such as, "In an ideal world where anything is possible, what would you like the application to do?" The idea-makers may decide they want a telepathic interface that can guess what items are in inventory at any given moment. Ideas like this one may sound outlandish to the customers, but recent innovations in radio frequency identification (RFID) do basically that. Now is not the time to stifle creativity.

Application architects, user interface designers, programmers, and developer types are often involved at the idea formulation and refinement phase, but their participation is not necessary, and it is sometimes even detrimental. These people know which application features are easy to build and which are not. In an effort to keep the ideas realistic, they may inhibit the other idea-refiners and close down useful avenues of exploration before their final payback is discovered. Though one feature may be unrealizable, discussing it may spawn other more useful ideas. It's better to have lots of unrealistic ideas that are later discarded than to miss a golden opportunity.

Happy accidents are not uncommon. Ice cream cones, chocolate chip cookies, the implantable pacemaker, penicillin, Post-it Notes, and Scotchgard were all invented by people trying to do something else (an ice cream seller ran out of bowls, Ruth Wakefield thought the chips would dissolve, Wilson Greatbatch was trying to make a device to record heartbeats, Alexander Fleming was studying nasal mucus but his samples were contaminated by mold, the glue used by Post-its was an attempt to make a better adhesive tape, and Scotchgard came from efforts to improve airplane fuels).

Although you are unlikely to accidentally invent the next blockbuster three-dimensional action adventure game while trying to build a better billing system, you may stumble across a better way to identify at-risk customers. In a dispatch system I worked on, we added a mapping feature that let dispatchers see the routes that repair people were scheduled to follow. We thought this was a minor feature, but it turned out to be the easiest way for the dispatcher to see where everyone was at the same time, so the dispatchers used it all the time. A fortunate accident.

Just as experienced developers can stifle creativity, too much executive participation can restrict the scope of the project. Eventually, the application's lifecycle must consider real-world factors such as schedule and cost, but that can be left for later. It's better to have too many good ideas and then pick out the best for implementation, rather than to stop at the first set of usable ideas you stumble across.

In many projects, particularly those with a large existing group of users, some of the users will be generally against the whole idea of the project. Sometimes this resistance is caused by inertia ("We've done fine without it so far"). Sometimes it's caused by a general fear of a loss of power, respect, or control. Sometimes it's caused by a general fear or dislike of change.

If you ignore this person, he or she can become a real difficulty, spreading fear and dissent among the users. However, if you recruit this person into the development effort at the beginning, he or she can become a tremendous asset. This person is likely to see things from a different perspective than the management and programming team members, and can provide valuable input. Often, this person will also become one of the project's greatest proponents. Once the other users see that this person has been won over, they often follow.

One person who should definitely be consulted during idea development is the idea's originator. Even if the idea changes greatly during refinement, it's worth keeping this person involved, if for no other reason than to make the idea seem appreciated. People with usable ideas are important, and if you yank the project away, you may never get another idea from this person again.

Eventually, you may run across someone who is so committed to an original idea that he or she won't allow the idea to change and grow. This person keeps pulling the idea back to its earliest form no matter how much others try to stretch and improve the idea. I've seen this on several projects. Often the perpetrator has recently learned about a new concept or technique, and is determined to use it no matter what.

In some cases, you can civilly explain to the person that the idea has outgrown the original concept and that it is time to move on. Occasionally, you may need to appeal to a higher level of management to make a decision stick.

At the end of the idea formulation and refinement stage, you do not need a schedule, cost estimates, an architectural design, a user interface design, or anything else that is directly related to writing code. Those all come later.

Another danger at this stage is the person who wants to rush headlong into development. Managers often want to move quickly to produce something they can hold up to show progress. Developers often want to hurry along to their favorite part of the lifecycle: development. Although you eventually need to actually build something, it's a mistake to end the idea stage too early. If you dash off into development with the first workable idea, you may be missing out on all sorts of wonderful opportunities.

At this point, you should have a pretty good idea of the application's goals. The list of goals may be very short, as in, "Pull data from a specific database and enter it into an Excel workbook." The list may be extremely large, containing hundreds of "must haves," "nice to haves," and "wild wishes." The next stage, requirements gathering, refines these possibly vague ideas and makes them more concrete and measurable.

Team Building

This isn't really a stage in an application's lifecycle. Rather, it's an ongoing activity that should start early and last throughout the project. Ideally, you should start building a solid team of supporters during idea formulation and refinement, and build on that core as the lifecycle progresses.

This core team should include people who will be involved in all phases of the lifecycle. It can include customers, designers, developers, management, and customer support people, although you may need to rein in some of these people during different stages. For example, during the idea formulation and refinement phase, developers should not dwell on what is easy to program, and managers should not focus exclusively on time and expense.

Two people who are particularly useful starting with the very earliest phases of the project lifecycle are a customer champion and a management patron.

The *customer champion* represents the final users of the application. Often, this person is (or was) one of those users, or is their direct supervisor. This person understands the needs of the users inside and out, and can make informed decisions about which features will be most useful in the finished application. This person must have the respect of the other users, so any decisions he or she makes will be accepted. This person should be able to sign off on the project and say that it has officially achieved its goals.

It is also extremely helpful to have a customer champion with an easygoing attitude of give and take. During later stages of the lifecycle, you may discover that some features are much harder to implement than you had originally planned. At that point, it's tremendously valuable to have a customer champion who understands the realities of software development, and who knows that insisting on sticking to the original design may mean cost and schedule slips. The best attitude here is one of, "The details don't matter, as long as the finished application lets the users do their jobs."

People who have played the role of customer champion before often understand this give-and-take approach. If your champion doesn't have experience with development, you can start laying the groundwork for this type of interaction during the idea formulation and refinement phase. Use phrases such as, "We'll see how hard that would be when we get into the design phase" and "If we start running out of time, perhaps we can defer that feature until release two."

Customers familiar with the traditional Waterfall lifecycle model described later in this chapter may have more trouble with this concept. In that model, requirements are laid out early and exactly in the cycle, and they must be followed strictly with little or no room for negotiation. A devoted Waterfall enthusiast can make development difficult.

Fortunately, most people who are really dedicated to their jobs don't care about the details too much as long as they can do their jobs well. Most customers don't insist on sticking to a plan long after the plan has proven flawed (although I've met several managers with that attitude).

The *management patron* is someone with enough influence in the company to ensure that the project moves forward. This person doesn't necessarily need to be involved in the project's day-to-day decisions, but should be aware of the project's progress and any high-level issues that may need to be resolved (such as the need for staff, budget, and other resources).

Practically anyone with decision-making power can play this role, depending on the scope of the application. For small projects that will be used by only one or two users, I've worked with patrons who were first-tier managers with only one or two direct reports. For applications that would affect hundreds of users and thousands of customers, I've worked with corporate vice presidents who oversaw tens of thousands of employees. On a particularly interesting football-training project, Hall of Famer Mike Ditka was one of our management patrons.

Two types of people that you may want to avoid for the role of patron are the soon-to-be-ex-managers and people with lots of enemies.

If management changes, the new management may not have the same commitment to your project as your previous patron. Sometimes, new management may cancel or weaken support for a project to discredit the previous management, to provide resources for new pet projects, or just to make a change. Unless you have a strong customer champion, keeping the project on track may be difficult. Of course, you probably won't know if your company is about to be sold and a new management team installed, but if you know that a particular supervisor is up for retirement in six months, you might want to identify possible replacements and decide whether the transition is likely to be smooth.

If your management patron has lots of enemies, you may be in for an arduous project lifecycle. Political infighting can make it difficult to attract and keep good team members, obtain needed resources, or gain and keep customer confidence.

I worked on one project with particularly nasty politics. Corporate vice presidents were slugging it out for control of this application and control of software development in general. At times, developers faced threats and blatant attempts to sabotage the code. Fortunately, we had a strong customer advocate and good customer buy-in, so the project was eventually a success, but it was a long, hard battle to keep the project on track.

To avoid this sort of situation, you must take a look at the environment in which the potential patron works. If it's a hostile environment full of political infighting, you may want to look for another management sponsor. Battling heroically against all odds to bring the customers the best possible application despite adversity brings a certain satisfaction after the fact, but it can make for a pretty grim couple of years during development.

Requirements Gathering

After the idea has had some time to ferment, you need to take a closer look at it and specify its features more precisely. You need to decide exactly what the features you have identified mean. You need to describe them with enough detail so that developers can understand what is necessary.

You also need to define the application's requirements with enough precision to determine whether the finished application has met its goals. The requirements must include specific measurable goals and milestones that you can use to unambiguously decide whether the application has achieved its objectives.

For example, the following statement is a measurable goal: "When a user modifies a customer record, the program will make an 'audit trail' record storing the date and time, the user's name, the customer ID, and the type of data changed. Supervisors (and only supervisors) will be able to view these records by date, user, and type of change." This is a nice concrete statement that you can easily verify by trying it out in the program.

Many projects bog down at the finish while developers and customers bicker over whether the application meets its goals. This is particularly a problem in projects that follow the Waterfall lifecycle model described later in this chapter because that model makes changing the goals difficult. During the project, if you discover that the goals are outdated, or that they do not solve a useful problem, it may be difficult to adapt and revise the application's design. That can lead to fighting between the developers who did what they thought they were supposed to do (implement the original requirements) and customers whose needs are not satisfied by the original requirements.

Other common requirements statements specify desired performance. For example, "When the user requests a customer order for processing, the program will display the next order within five seconds." This statement is reasonable and measurable, but requires a bit more clarification. What may be possible with a few users on a fast network may be impossible if the network is congested and hundreds of users try to access the database at the same time.

A more precise requirement should specify the system's load and allow for some fluctuation. For example, "When the user requests a customer order for processing, the program will display the next order within five seconds 95 percent of the time with up to 100 users performing typical duties." This may still be difficult to test, but at least it's fairly clear.

I worked on one project where performance testing was performed by a group of 20 users in the same room. The test leader had every user type in exactly the same data at the same time and press the Enter key simultaneously. They quickly learned that this was not a realistic test because it is very unlikely that every user would want to access the same customer record at exactly the same time. More realistic tests used fake jobs to simulate real work with users working jobs and requesting new ones at their own paces.

One useful method for characterizing requirements is to build *use cases*. These are scripted scenarios that portray a user trying to work through a common task. For example, an emergency dispatch system might include a use case where the user takes a phone call from someone reporting a house fire, records necessary information, reviews and possibly overrides recommendations for the units to dispatch, and dispatches the units.

You can find some example use cases at `www.objectmentor.com/publications/usecases.pdf`.

At this stage, the requirements should not specify a solution to the use cases. In fact, a use case should specify as little about the solution as possible. It should not indicate how the user answers the phone, records necessary information, views recommended units, and approves the dispatching selection. It should just indicate the things that must happen, and leave the details open for later design.

During the requirements gathering stage, you should also categorize ideas by their degree of importance. At a minimum, you should make a list of "must haves," "nice to haves," and "wild wishes." You may even have a category of "don't need" for items that you've decided are really not such great ideas after all.

Depending on the lifecycle model you follow, items may move between these categories during later stages of development. You may find an idea that you put in the "wild wishes" category is more important than you thought. Or, changes in the users' rules and regulations might make a "nice to have" feature mandatory.

This phase is one point where various lifecycle approaches can differ. The best strategy is to avoid any actual design at this stage and focus on results. Rather than specifying exactly *how* the application should perform its actions, describe the *results* of those actions and what the actions will accomplish. Instead of designing a customer entry form, just say there will be a customer entry form where the user can enter customer data with links to order and payment information. Leave the details for the following design phases.

This approach works particularly well with iterative approaches where everyone expects changes to the design. It doesn't usually work as well with stricter Waterfall models where people expect every last detail of the application to be chiseled in stone before any of the work begins. With that approach, requirements gathering sometimes turns into a search for an exact specification. Avoid this as long as possible. That kind of specification makes explicit and implicit assumptions about the design, and you haven't started the design yet.

If your development environment requires that you begin a specification at this point, begin the design, too, either formally or informally. Try to do enough design work to support your decisions in the specification. If you don't have time to design the features properly, you may be able to reuse ideas from existing applications. If you've written an order-taking form before, reuse the ideas that worked well in that application. While you may not have time to perform a detailed design analysis, you can piggyback on the analysis you used for the previous application.

Feasibility Analysis

Feasibility analysis occurs at two levels. At a higher level, you must decide whether the project as a whole can succeed. At a lower level, you must decide which features should be implemented.

High-Level Feasibility Analysis

At a high level, it is the process of deciding whether the project as a whole is possible given your time, staffing, cost, and other constraints. At this scale, the goal is to determine whether the project will be possible and worthwhile as quickly as possible. If the project is not viable, you want to know that as soon as possible so you can bail out without spending more time and money on it than necessary.

It's much cheaper to cancel a project after a 1-month feasibility study involving 3 people than it is to cancel a project that has been running with 20 staff members for 2 years. If people cost about $100,000 per year, then the difference is spending $25,000 on a feasibility study versus wasting $4 million.

In this sense, feasibility analysis is a bit like poker. Many people think the goal in poker is to get the best hand possible. The true goal is to decide whether you have the winning hand as quickly as possible. If you are going to lose, you need to get out quickly before you bet a lot of money in the pot. If you think you are going to win, you want to drag the betting out as long as possible to get as much money in the pot as you can.

Because the goal of high-level feasibility analysis is to determine the overall fitness of the project as soon as possible, you must start working on it as soon as you can. If the ideas you come up with during a month of idea formulation and refinement are not worth expending some effort, cancel the project, write off the $25,000 you invested studying the ideas, and use the $3.975 million you saved on another project. If the refined ideas you develop during a month of requirements gathering no longer seem useful, again abandon the project, forget the $50,000 you've spent so far, and invest the $3.95 million you saved on something else. (You can see from this example that the sooner you cancel the project the more time and money you save.)

As time and the project move on, you should gain an increasingly accurate idea of whether the project as a whole is viable. After doing some preliminary design work, you should have an idea of how complicated the application is. It's usually around this time that most organizations make a final decision about whether to commit to the project. Beyond this point, the amount of money invested in the application becomes large enough that people get in trouble and careers can be ruined if they admit they made a mistake and suggest that the project be canceled.

After making a detailed high-level design, you should have at least some guesses about how many people you will need and how long the project will take.

One project that I worked on should have been canceled long before it actually was. Part of its design turned out to be significantly more complicated than expected. After wasting a bit under a year working on the application, several quick changes in management lead to the project being mothballed. It was a small project and didn't last too long, so it probably wasted less than $500,000. If we had realized that the project was unfeasible sooner, we might have been able to change the design and finish six months late and $250,000 over budget, or we could have canceled the project and saved six months and $250,000.

For an even more dramatic example, a friend of mine once worked on a huge multi-billion dollar spacecraft project involving hardware and software. At some point, most of the participating engineers realized that it was unfeasible. Unfortunately, the company had already invested a lot of money in it and was thoroughly committed at a high level. The project manager suggested that the project was impossible and was promptly fired. After a few months, the new project manager reached the same conclusion, made the same suggestion, and suffered the same fate. This loop repeated a couple more times before the project's failings were too large even for upper management to ignore and it finally went under. Had the company listened to the first project manager, who knows how much time and money they could have saved.

With better information about how hard the project is as time goes on, you can make a more informed decision about whether to continue. Until the point of full commitment, the result of your analysis should either be "cancel the project" or "continue until we have more information." Try to delay full commitment until you are absolutely certain that the project can succeed.

A project was a rewrite of an enormous application that had been written and modified over many years in several different versions of Visual Basic. The rewritten version was poorly designed, and the new features that were added provided only a small benefit. I don't know how much money was spent on this rewrite, but I wouldn't be surprised to learn it was $6 million or more.

Furthermore, I predict another rewrite will be necessary, hopefully with a greatly improved design, within the next few years as the company transitions to a new development platform.

Even a year into this project, the project team could have seen the clues that the new development platform was coming, canceled the first rewrite, and invested $3 million in savings on moving to the new platform a bit sooner. The users would have lost only relatively small enhancements and gotten the final, improved version of the system a year sooner.

Low-Level Feasibility Analysis

At a lower level, you must determine which features can and should be implemented given your time, cost, and other constraints.

After the requirements-gathering phase, you should have a good idea of what the project's features are and how much benefit they will provide. You should know which features fall into the "must have," "nice to have," and "wild wish" categories.

Now is the time for quick negotiation with your customer champion to decide which features make it into the official requirements specification, which are deferred until a later release, and which are dropped completely.

To help your customer champion understand the tradeoffs, you should phrase levels of difficulty in terms of costs and exchanges. For example, "We can give you this feature, but it will delay release by six months." Or, "If we implement this feature and keep our original schedule, then we will have to defer this other feature." Or, "We can separate the development of this piece from the rest of the project and hire four additional developers for six months (at a cost of $200,000)." Then it's up to the customer champion to decide which options are acceptable to the users.

Initially, you may have only a vague idea about how difficult the various features are to implement. As is the case with high-level feasibility analysis, you will have a better understanding of how difficult different features are to build as time marches on.

Also as is the case with the high-level analysis, it is best to keep your options open as long as possible, rather than committing to specific features, until you have a decent idea about how difficult they will be to build. If you discover that a feature is harder (or easier) to provide than you originally estimated, that's the time when having a customer champion with an easygoing give-and-take nature is invaluable. It's also when iterative lifecycle methodologies described later in this chapter are most useful, and the Waterfall model brings the most pain.

High-Level Design

During high-level design, architects lay out the application's main systems and begin to outline how they interact with each other. They describe main groups of functions, such as order entry, billing, customer management, reporting, database processing, Web Services, inter-process communication, and so forth.

The high-level design should not specify how the systems work, just what they do. To the extent that you understand them, you can also sketch out the interactions among the systems and some of the features that they will implement. For example, experience with previous applications may suggest a particular set of tables that you will want to use in storing customer data in a database. Or, if you know that the application will need to pull files from FTP servers on the Internet, you may want to tentatively specify the FTP routines that you used on a previous project.

The high-level design generally should not specify particular classes. For example, it can say, "We'll have a tax form where the user can fill in customer data describing their fuel tax payments and usage," but it wouldn't define a `Customer` class and dictate how that class should store fuel tax information. It also would not lay out the exact user interface for this form. Both of those tasks come later.

At this stage, it is extremely important that you make the application's different systems as decoupled as you can. There should be as little interaction among these major systems as possible, while still getting the job done. Every interface between two systems is a point where the teams building the systems must communicate, negotiate, and debug differences in code.

If the systems have only a few well-defined interactions, the teams can work through them relatively quickly. If many of the systems interact in lots of different ways, the teams will spend a considerable amount of time trying to understand each other's code, negotiating (sometimes arguing) over interfaces, and debugging those interfaces, leaving less time to actually write code. A good decoupled design lets a developer focus on the code within the system he or she is developing, while spending a minimum of time studying the details of the other systems.

Lower-Level Design

During successively lower levels of design, developers add additional detail to the higher-level designs. They start sketching out exactly what is needed to implement the high-level systems that make up the application.

While building the lower-level designs, you should be able to flesh out the interfaces between the application's systems. This is the real test of whether the higher-level designs defined cleanly separated major systems. If the systems must interact in many poorly defined ways, you may need to step back and reconsider the high-level design. If two systems require a large number of interactions, then perhaps they should be combined into a single system.

At the same time, you should try to make each system small enough so that a team of four or five developers can implement it. If a system will require more than five developers, you should consider breaking it into two or more subsystems that separate teams can implement independently.

Some of the design patterns described in Chapter 7, "Design Patterns," can help you separate closely coupled systems. For example, the *mediator* pattern helps separate two closely related systems so developers can work on them separately. Instead of having code in the one system directly call code in the other, the code calls methods provided by a mediator class. The mediator class then forwards requests to the other system.

Figure 2-1 shows the situation graphically. The top of the figure shows two systems that are tied closely together. On the bottom, a mediator sits between the systems to loosen the coupling between them.

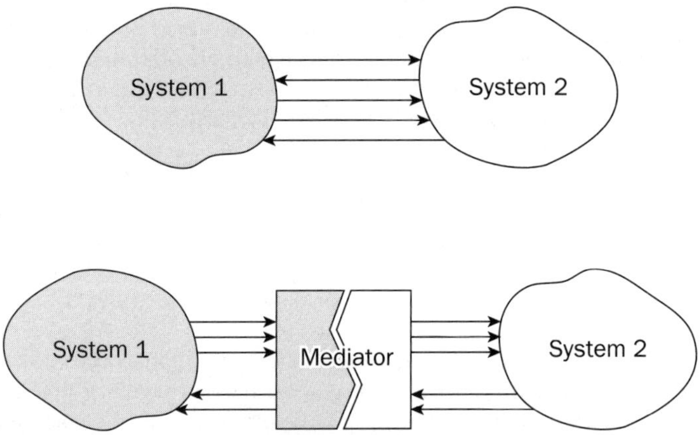

Figure 2-1: The mediator design pattern can help decouple two closely related systems.

Note that the mediator in Figure 2-1 complicates the design somewhat. In this example, the mediator doubles the number of arrows required, so the amount of communication in the application has increased. The reason this design can help is that the mediator isolates the two systems from each other so that the code in one doesn't need to know the details of the code in the other. This lets the two systems evolve independently and lets developers work on them separately.

System 1 can make calls to the mediator in more or less whatever way it wants, and those calls need not change, even if the code in System 2 that eventually handles the calls changes. Similarly, System 1 can handle calls by the mediator in a consistent way, and hopefully remain unchanged even if the code in System 2 that starts those calls must change.

At some point, however, the mediator must be able to translate calls by System 1 into services provided by System 2, and vice versa, so the application does require more code. The point isn't to reduce the amount of code, but to decouple the two systems so that developers can focus on their own systems and not worry about the other system's details. The new design is more complicated, and, generally, extra complication decreases the application's reliability. By separating the two systems, however, the mediator makes building the two systems easier, and that should increase their reliability. You should still consider the added complexity before you start throwing mediators between every pair of classes in the application; otherwise, the cure may be worse than the disease.

There are several other design patterns that you can use to help make designs easier to implement. For example, the *adapter* and *facade* design patterns provide an extra interface layer for a system to help insulate the rest of the application from changes in the system. For more information on design patterns, see Chapter 7.

Implementation

The implementation phase is when programmers write code to build the application. It is what most programmers think of when they think about software development.

This is clearly an important part of application building because the application cannot exist unless someone eventually writes some code. However, implementation is only one part of a much larger process, and you cannot ignore the other phases of development.

The application is not useful if it doesn't solve the users' problems, so it is essential that the application's initial ideas, purpose, and requirements make sense to the users. If the users need a toaster, it does no good to build a microwave oven.

If the high- and lower-level designs don't further the requirements, developers again end up building the wrong application. The users ask for a toaster, but the design is for a grill.

If the high- and lower-level designs don't specify a system that can actually be built, the application fails. The users ask for a toaster, the design specifies a nuclear-powered toaster with a multilingual voice interface that uses artificial intelligence to optimize toast-doneness while minimizing time and power consumption. The users end up with a pile of metal and circuitry that can burn bread, but can't make toast in any language (and is probably radioactive).

Even after the application is properly built, it must be tested. Every non-trivial application contains bugs. Eventually, the users will discover that the toaster cannot handle whole-wheat bread or bagels. It is less expensive and gives the application an impression of higher quality if you can discover and fix these problems before the application ships.

Finally, the users' needs change over time. The users will discover that they need to toast scones and other breads that were not considered in the original specification and design. Eventually, bugs will also pop up in even the most thoroughly tested application. If you do not provide maintenance down the road, you limit the application's lifespan.

Implementation is an important part of application development, and for programmers, at least it's usually the most fun, but it's far from the beginning or end of the story.

Testing

In most projects, testing begins only after programmers have written a lot of code. In extreme cases, testing only starts after the application has been fully assembled.

It is a well-known fact that bugs are easiest to find and remove when they are detected as soon as possible after they are inserted into the project. If a bug is introduced to the code early in the implementation phase, it can be very difficult to find if you wait until the entire application is built to look for it.

Unfortunately, programmers have a natural tendency to assume that their code is more or less correct and needs little or no testing. This makes some sense because, if you knew that your code contained a bug, you would fix it. When you spend a lot of time writing a routine and handling all of the possible errors you can think of, it's easy to underestimate the possibility of errors that you didn't think of.

Because of this tendency to think that code is correct, programmers often don't spend as much time testing as they should, particularly early on when bugs are easiest to detect and fix. To counter the programmers' naturally optimistic approach to testing, you may need to coax, cajole, or coerce developers into testing thoroughly enough.

Programmers often have blind spots when testing their own code. It's easy to look over a piece of code and see what you *think* is there rather than what is *really* there. It's also easy for a programmer to think the code handles all possible cases when it really hasn't. If you knew about a situation that wasn't handled in your subroutine, you would modify the code to handle it.

> *The human brain is amazingly good at seeing what it thinks is there instead of what is really there. For an example, see how hard it is to decipher the following sentence: It's dwnrght embrrssngly esy t rd txt evn if yu rmv mst of th vowls! If it's that easy for your brain to fill in missing vowels in a sentence, how hard can it be to fill in one or two missing details in program code?*

To ensure that code is tested reasonably objectively, you may want to have programmers review each other's code rather than (or in addition to) their own. The tester can review the code without preconceptions acquired while writing the code. The tester is more likely to see what is *really* there and to think of unusual cases that the code's original author may not have.

Probably the most common types of testing used by larger projects are unit testing, system testing, regression testing, and user acceptance testing.

Unit Testing

Unit testing examines "code units." These are regarded as the smallest usable collections of code that can be meaningfully executed. The goal is to exercise every path through the code in a variety of different ways to flush out any bugs in the code.

Unfortunately, many subroutines are difficult to test until lots of other routines are written, too. Before you can test the code that prints customer orders, you need the code that creates a customer order. That code may depend on other routines that load customer and inventory data from the database, and forms that let the user build the order.

Testing these routines as a unit is fine as far as it goes, and may very well uncover bugs. However, when you test multiple routines as a single unit, it's often difficult to ensure that you cover all of the paths through the code in each of the routines. Though you may be able to create a customer order and print it, it may be difficult to test all of the possible combinations of ways to create a customer order with various data available and printed in every possible way. While testing these routines as a unit, you may test the paths among the routines, but you may leave paths within the routines untested.

Suppose each of the routines contains about 10 possible paths of execution. To exercise each routine's paths of execution separately, you would need to run about 10 tests for each of the five code routines (print, make order, load customer data, load inventory data, and load the form that builds the order), making a total of about 50 tests.

Now, suppose you want to test the paths through the routines as a single unit. If the paths of execution within the routines are independent, then there are 10^5 = 100,000 possible paths of execution to test. Ideally, you would test all of those paths, but in practice, even the most pessimistic developer will have trouble writing that many test cases.

In addition to incomplete coverage, another drawback to testing groups of routines as a unit is that it can be difficult to locate and fix a bug when you do encounter one. If a piece of data isn't printing correctly, the error may have been caused by the printing routine, the code that generates a customer order, the customer or inventory data in the database, or the forms that let you build the order.

You can minimize all of these problems if you test each routine separately as soon as it is written. This sort of routine-level test lets you more easily follow each of the routine's paths of execution. It lets you localize bugs more precisely to the routine that contains them. It also lets you test the code while it is still fresh in your mind, so it will be easier to fix any bugs that you do find.

> *Two well-known facts about bugs are that they come in swarms and that fixing a bug is likely to create a new bug. When you find one bug, you are likely to find others in related code. If you catch a bug right after writing a routine, chances are good that any related bugs are also inside the routine and you can catch them all relatively easily. If you test a group of routines as a unit and find a bug, it is more likely that additional bugs will be in the unit's other routines, so they will be harder to find and fix.*
>
> *Part of the reason that fixing bugs is likely to create new bugs is that you usually fix bugs long after you (or someone else) originally wrote the code that contains the bug. The code is no longer fresh in your mind, so you need to re-learn the code before making changes. If you don't understand the code completely, your changes are likely to create new bugs. Routine-level testing helps with this problem by letting you test the code right after you write it, so it's still fresh in your mind.*

Routine-level testing is not always easy. Sometimes the code to test a routine can be twice as long as the routine itself, but routine-level testing is *always* worth the extra effort. Even if you don't find any bugs in the code, you will have some evidence to believe that the code works, rather than an unsubstantiated feeling of general correctness.

Of course, there's always the possibility that the test code will contain errors. Sometimes the testing code will incorrectly report that a routine contains a bug when it doesn't. While trying to fix the imaginary bug, you will probably discover the bug in the testing code, but that can be easier if you keep in mind that it's a possibility. (Of course, you can't assume every bug is in the testing code either! Assume the bug is real, but keep your eyes open.)

System Testing

System testing examines how the application's systems interact. It includes overall tests of the entire application to see how all the major components work together and how they interact with each other. It incorporates tests that exercise all of the use cases and other provisions defined in the requirements phase. System testing should also cover as many typical and unusual cases as possible to try to discover unexpected interactions among the application's code units.

You can think of the system tests as unit tests on a larger scale. During a unit test, you try to test all of the routines within an application system. During system tests, you try to test all of the units (and their routines) within the entire application.

System testing has the same drawbacks as unit testing. It is difficult to cover all possible paths through the application's code at this level. When you do detect a bug, it is often difficult to determine which routines caused the problem. After you find a bug's incorrect code, it can be difficult to remember how the code is supposed to work, making it harder to fix the bug and increasing the chances that you will introduce new bugs.

To avoid these problems, you should try to catch bugs at a lower level if possible. Ideally, you catch most bugs during routine-level testing when it's easiest and safest to fix them. A few bugs will slip through to the unit testing level where it's harder to diagnose and treat bugs. Hopefully, very few bugs will remain at the system testing level where debugging is most difficult and most error-prone.

Figure 2-2 shows the different levels of testing graphically. Routine testing exercises execution paths within a routine (represented by thin arrows). Unit testing exercises paths of execution between routines in a unit (represented by thicker dashed arrows). System testing exercises the application as a whole, testing paths of execution between units or subsystems (represented by very thick arrows).

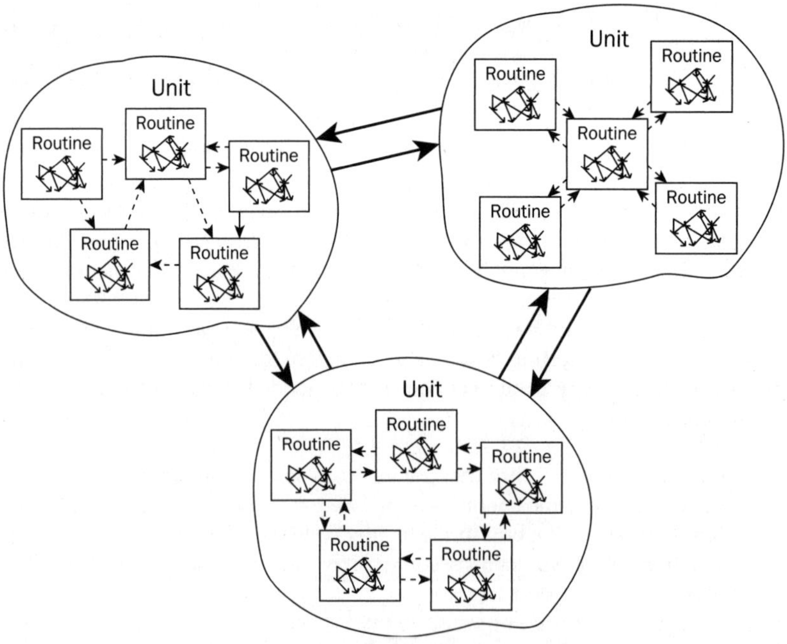

Figure 2-2: Routine, unit, and system testing exercise paths of execution at different levels.

Even if you perform extensive lower-level testing, however, system-level testing is still necessary. While most bugs have small scope and are contained within a single routine, some only occur when many different routines interact. You will not find those bugs until you perform higher-level unit and system testing.

Regression Testing

Regression testing is the process of retesting the system to try to detect changes in behavior caused by changes to the code. When you modify a piece of code to fix a bug, improve performance, or otherwise change the way in which the code works, you should test the application thoroughly to see if the change had any unintended consequences.

Changing code (whether to fix bugs or to add new features) is likely to add new bugs to the code. This is partly because you are unlikely to remember exactly how the original code was written when you are modifying the code.

To reduce the chances of introducing new bugs, you should carefully examine the code surrounding the change you are going to make to ensure that you understand the code in context. Ideally, you should also understand any routines that the nearby code calls, and any other routines that call this code. Only if you understand the code's position within the rest of the application do you have a reasonable chance of making a change without introducing errors.

After making the change, you should run as many regression tests as possible to look for changes that you may have made to the application's behavior. You can buy software-testing tools that can automatically perform these tests for you. Typically, these products perform a series of actions, either scripted or captured by watching you perform the same steps in the user interface, and then they look for specific results. For example, a test result might require that a certain text box contains a specific piece of text. Some of these programs can capture images and verify that the image matches one saved in an earlier "training run."

These sorts of regression testing tools provide some evidence that the application hasn't been broken by your change, at least at a high level. Unfortunately, they don't offer any help in locating and fixing a bug if you detect one. Your only real defense is to perform regression testing *every* time you make a change. Then, if a test identifies a bug, you have reason to believe that the problem is with the change you made most recently.

Sadly, most developers don't work this way. Often, a programmer will be given a long list of bugs to fix and enhancements to make. The programmer makes a bunch of changes to the code and then performs some tests to see if anything is broken. If the tests are cumbersome, and particularly if they are not automated by a regression testing tool, the programmer may make *a lot* of changes before testing them. If a test discovers a bug, it can be hard to figure out which change caused the bug.

Some development teams run automatic regression testing nightly. That's a good practice to ensure that a change doesn't cause a bug that slips past developers, but it's not enough. If you modify the code, you should not wait until the nightly tests. Instead, run the regression tests after you make each change.

Although regression testing is a reasonable way to look for changes at a high level, an even better way to test code changes is to re-run the module- and unit-level tests that you used when you originally wrote the code. Then, if you detect a bug, the tests are more likely to localize it, so it will be easier to find and fix.

Unfortunately, most developers do not save any test code that they may have written for a routine. The weakest developers don't write code to test their new routines in the first place. Better developers write tests for their code, but then throw the test code away after the routine is working properly. The best developers write test code and then save it forever. Admittedly, it can be inconvenient to save the huge number of test routines that may be necessary to test every routine in a large application. In some projects, the test code can be twice as large as the application itself. However, disk space is cheap and your time is valuable. It's much better to save old test routines and never need them than it is to skip testing a code modification and then spend hours tracking down a new bug later in the project's development.

To make finding test routines easier, store them in files with names similar to the code they test. For example, you might store test routines for the code in module `SortRoutines.bas` in the file `Test_SortRoutines.bas`. Keep the test code in the same sort of source code control system you use to store the application's code, back it up on a regular schedule, and treat it as a valuable asset, not an afterthought.

User Acceptance Testing

During user acceptance testing, key users examine the application to see if it satisfies the requirements. Usually, your customer champion and other key users perform these tests. The testers should work through all of the use cases defined during the requirements gathering phase. They should also try out all of the typical and unusual cases they can think of in every possible combination, trying to find circumstances that were not anticipated by the developers and that are not handled correctly by the program.

In some projects, you may be able to make the final version of the application available for every user to experiment with during their free time before the final installation. If you do this, however, ensure that the version of the application that you make available is either finished, or nearly finished, and contains no known bugs. You can disable certain features if they are not yet available, but don't give the users a fragile application. A buggy version will only give the users a bad impression of the quality of the project, so they will not accept the final version as wholeheartedly. It's okay to give the customer champion, management patron, and other project team members a preliminary version that may have some problems, but keep that version away from the general user population.

In fact, it's generally a good idea to give the customer champion and other team members access to preliminary versions as soon as they are available so you can get feedback early enough that it is still useful. This idea is discussed further in the later parts of this chapter that explain prototyping strategies such as Iterative Prototyping.

Deployment

During the deployment phase, you make the application available to the users. Sometimes, this is a massive rollout to every user at the same time. Often, particularly for applications headed to a large user audience, the application is installed in staged rollouts where several groups of users get the application at different times.

Visual Studio's ClickOnce Deployment system makes installing Visual Basic .NET applications a lot easier than installation has been in the past, but it's still not trivial. In a large installation, there will probably be some users who will have difficulty installing the application themselves. At a minimum, some users will be bothered by the long time needed to download the .NET Framework necessary to run Visual Basic .NET applications, particularly if they access the network using a slower modem.

You should at least provide explicit instructions telling the users what to expect during download and installation. It's even better if the project team or the company's IT department can install the application for the users.

A particularly troublesome issue with large installations these days is the number of operating system versions that the users may be running. If your application is built in-house for a particular company, you may be able to require that all of the users have the same operating system and software environment. If the project is for distribution to external customers, or if the company cannot require that all users have the same operating system, you may discover that the application works differently for different users.

Sometimes it's not even the operating system or the software installed that causes a problem, but the combination of operating system, software installed, and software previously installed. I recently did some maintenance work on a project that was running incorrectly on only a few installations out of hundreds of customers. It turned out that those computers had at one time run a previous version of Microsoft Excel and then upgraded to a newer version. The application was confused by Registry entries left behind by the earlier version, and I had to add code to take this unusual situation into account.

It can be difficult to test a new application on every possible operating system. Some of the possibilities include Windows 95, Windows 98, Windows 98 SE, Windows ME, Windows 2000, Windows NT (various versions), Windows XP, and the soon-to-be-released version code-named Vista. You could also consider the Home and Professional editions of some of these, plus non-Microsoft operating systems such as Linux, Solaris, Max OS X, and Unix, which can use Mono (`www.mono-project.com`) to run .NET applications.

It's unlikely that you'll have a dozen or so computers sitting around with all of these operating systems on them. It's even unlikely that you can run more than a couple of them on virtual computers such as Microsoft's Virtual PC. It's still less likely that you'll have the time to install each of these from scratch, so that you know the application doesn't depend on anything else that may happen to be installed on the developers' machines.

Usually, development teams test the application on one or two operating systems, and then require that users have those operating systems. They may say that the application *might* work on others, but that they make no guarantees. They may then handle users on other operating systems on a case-by-case basis, possibly adding new operating systems to the list of those supported over time.

No matter which operating systems you decide to support, it's generally worth trying to install and run the application on a "clean" system that has just been built with nothing installed on it. During the clean installation, it's not unusual to discover that some of the code depends on another application such as the Microsoft Office products Excel, Word, Access, or Outlook.

Support

Many programmers consider application development to be over after the code is written and tested, but there is still plenty of work to do later in support of the application. Support includes recording, tracking, and fixing bugs. It includes helping users solve problems and explaining how to use the application. It may include providing training materials and classes. Depending on the lifespan of the application, support can also include major future releases to fix bugs and implement new features.

You can reduce the amount of work needed for some of these support tasks by providing good online help and documentation. If the users can use the help and documentation to easily figure out how to do something, they won't need to call you and ask.

Many developers think that you should write documentation at the end of the project after all of the code has been written. One advantage to this approach is that the application doesn't change much after this point, so you can write documentation and help files without worrying about making extensive changes later.

Unfortunately, the end of application development is often rushed so projects are frequently released to the users with inadequate documentation and help. It's better if documentation begins as soon as possible, even though some of it must be rewritten as the application changes.

Documentation can start with the requirements and can describe the purpose of the application on a high level. As the user interface is prototyped and revised, the documentation can be revised to match.

In some organizations, the programmer who implements a feature writes the first version of its user documentation. Other writers (dedicated documentation specialists if they are available) should modify the documentation as necessary to ensure that the user can understand it. The customer champion and possibly other users should also review the documentation to verify that it makes sense to them.

ClickOnce Deployment makes installing new applications easier than it has been in the past. It makes installing new versions of an existing program even easier. If the new version of the program was written using the same version of the .NET Framework, then you only need to install the application itself and you don't need to copy the Framework onto the user's computer again. Instead of downloading and installing several hundred megabytes, you may only need to download a few hundred kilobytes.

Just because installing new releases is relatively easy, that doesn't mean you should take advantage of ClickOnce to inundate the user with a flood of updates and fixes. Releasing new versions too often gives the users the (probably correct) impression that the application is unstable and insufficiently planned, even if the releases add newly requested functionality rather than fixing bugs.

New releases also make the users learn about whatever new features are in the release, taking time away from their normal jobs. Users who are forced to read about new features every week may come to dread the new releases. They may decide that the application is adding to their workload even if it only takes 20 minutes per week to read about new features and the application saves the users hours every day. After a while, users may stop reading about the new enhancements, so they can't take advantage of them anyway. What's the point of having frequent releases if the users don't know about the new features?

I once worked at a company where everyone had Windows XP installed and automatic updates enabled. We probably averaged about one mandatory update per week, and sometimes a flurry of updates would appear on the same day. Even though many of these updates were in response to new Internet viruses and other threats, the frequent updates did nothing to enhance our perception of the quality and stability of Windows XP.

To protect your application's appearance of reliability, avoid unnecessary releases. Save up minor bug fixes and enhancements and release them all at once in a bigger release. For example, you might have a major release once per year, and a minor release six months after the major release.

You can further improve the perception of stability if you schedule the releases far in advance. You may occasionally need to release a new version quickly to implement urgently needed features or to protect against a new Internet threat, but it does nothing for your image to push out mysterious security updates with no warning on a regular basis.

Lifecycle Models

The previous sections described the basic tasks of application development:

- Idea formulation and refinement
- Team building
- Requirements gathering
- Feasibility analysis
- Design
- Implementation
- Testing
- Deployment
- Support

Any application development effort must address each of these basic tasks in some manner. Some of these clearly take a particular position in the life of the project. For example, deployment and support must happen after the code is written and tested. Other tasks, such as team building and documentation, can occur throughout the project's lifetime.

Different lifecycle models arrange the remaining tasks in different orders to provide various levels of predictability and flexibility. These models focus on the smaller subset of tasks shown in the following list:

- Idea formulation
- Requirements gathering
- Design
- Implementation
- Testing
- Deployment and support

The following sections describe some of the most common lifecycle models. They explain how the models arrange the basic tasks and discuss how these models apply to Visual Basic .NET development.

Throwaway

A *throwaway application* is one that you plan to use for only a short time. Usually, this kind of application is a developer tool intended to make some specific task easier, and then it is discarded.

This type of application generally doesn't require a very formal development process. You don't need to spend days on idea formulation, requirements gathering, and different levels of design. You just sit down and pound out some code. If it doesn't work, you adjust it slightly until it gets the job done, and then you throw it away.

There's nothing wrong with this development model, as long as it really is a small project that you won't need later. One of the few dangers to this model is that the tool may turn out to be more useful than you originally planned. If you let other developers use it and it becomes popular, then other users may not let you throw it away. You may be stuck maintaining a program that you spent very little time designing. The program may be difficult to debug, and it may be difficult to add new features that the impromptu user population demands. If the project lives long enough and is in enough demand, you may need to rebuild it using a more elaborate development model.

If you have a small project that you only need for a specific task, go ahead and use the throwaway model. Just be certain that you really can throw it away when you are finished.

Waterfall

In the *Waterfall* model, the major phases of development follow each other in the following strict order:

- Idea formulation
- Requirements gathering
- Design
- Implementation
- Testing
- Deployment and support

Control flows from one stage of development to the next in a simple predictable fashion, similar to the way water falls down a series of ledges in a cascade. Figure 2-3 shows the process graphically.

Because the control in Figure 2-3 actually falls down a series of steps, this model is also sometimes referred to as the *cascade* model or the *staircase* model. Some developers also call this the *lifecycle* model, although that term rather misleadingly implies that other development models don't last throughout a project's life.

The team works on idea formulation until it can think of no other useful ideas, and then moves on to requirements gathering. The team then writes requirements documents that completely specify the system and moves on to the design phase only after the system is completely described. Based on the specification, the project architects make the application's high- and lower-level designs. When the design is complete, programmers implement the design. After the code is written, the team members perform system-level testing and user acceptance testing. Finally, the project is released to the users and long-term support begins.

One advantage of the Waterfall model is that it is predictable. The requirements specification indicates exactly what the application will do. Later, designers and programmers can refer to the requirements to see exactly what they should be doing.

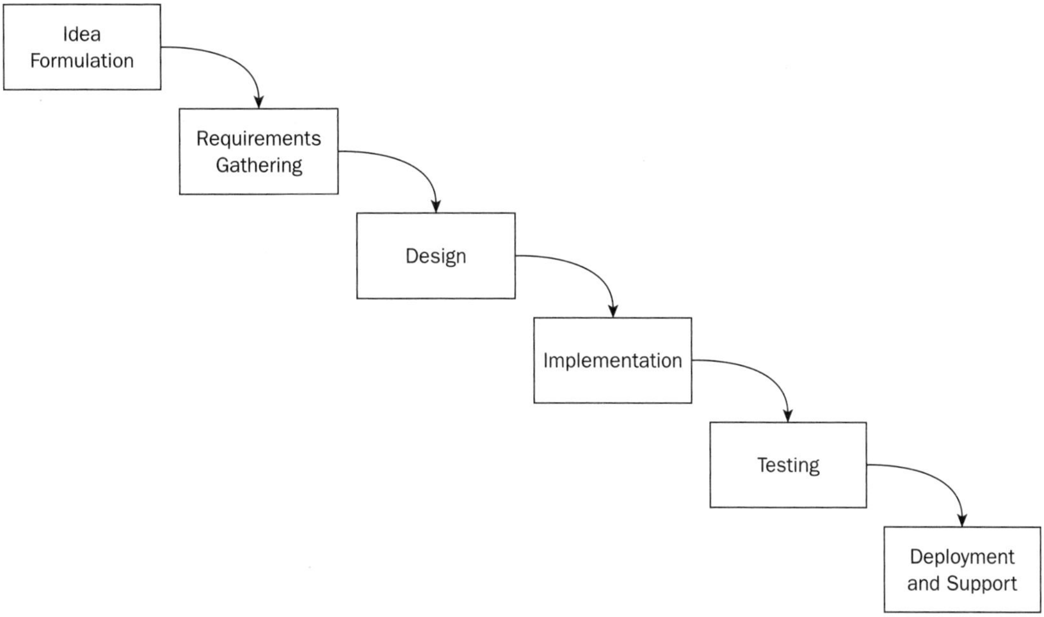

Figure 2-3: In the Waterfall lifecycle model, control falls from one step to the next like water in a cascade.

The high- and low-level designs explain exactly how the application will do its job. Later, programmers can refer to the design documents to understand how to write the code they are supposed to be implementing.

Testing is simpler because all of the code is available. You don't need to worry about one routine depending on another before it can be tested, because all of the code is ready.

Another advantage to the Waterfall model is that it makes it easier to write online help, documentation, and training materials. After the specification and design phases, the application's user interface is fully defined. At that point, technical writers can begin converting the specification and design into materials that the users and training department can work with. Because this can begin relatively early in the project, there's plenty of time to write high-quality documentation and training materials.

Although the Waterfall model has a few advantages, it is not as flexible as the other models described shortly. If the project is small and extremely well-defined, the Waterfall model can help you get the job done fairly quickly with little time wasted iterating through different feature, design, and implementation approaches.

However, if the initial requirements or designs are incorrect, it may be difficult to fix the application and produce a usable result. When you move on from one stage of development, team members assume that it is correct, and moving back to make changes can be difficult.

For example, suppose you have designed a system that downloads product data from a Web site, uses it to update a local database, and then generates reports using the data. After the design is complete, different teams of developers can start working on the code that downloads the data, inserts it into the local database, and generates the reports. Because the specification describes exactly what the program needs to do, and the design explains exactly how the code will do it, the groups can work independently.

Now, suppose you discover a problem in the way the data is stored in the local database. Perhaps the local database cannot easily store the image data that you were planning to download from the Web. You could remove the image data from the application's requirements, but that will affect all three of the groups working on this part of the application. The download group may already have written code that downloads all of the data, including the images. The report-generating group may have already written code to produce reports complete with images. These groups can modify their code to meet the altered requirements, but it may require updating a lot of code, and that can introduce a bumper crop of bugs.

The Waterfall model doesn't *cause* this sort of change. It was a mistake in the design (selecting that database technology) that gave rise to false assumptions (that you could store images in the database) and caused the real problem. By assuming that each stage of development is complete before moving on to the next, the Waterfall model just makes it more difficult to fix this sort of problem.

Serial Waterfalls

You can represent multiple application releases with the Waterfall by connecting Waterfalls one after another, as shown in Figure 2-4.

To build multiple releases with the Waterfall model, simply feed the results of one Waterfall into the beginning of another. Take the results of the previous iteration into account when you start the idea formulation phase of the next.

In addition to any bug fixes and feature enhancements that you have identified with the current version of the application, you can also consider how the previous development efforts worked out. If you found that lots of bugs were introduced during the design phase, spend extra time on this round's design phase. If you found that system testing found a lot of bugs that were difficult to track down, encourage the programmers to spend more time on routine and unit testing.

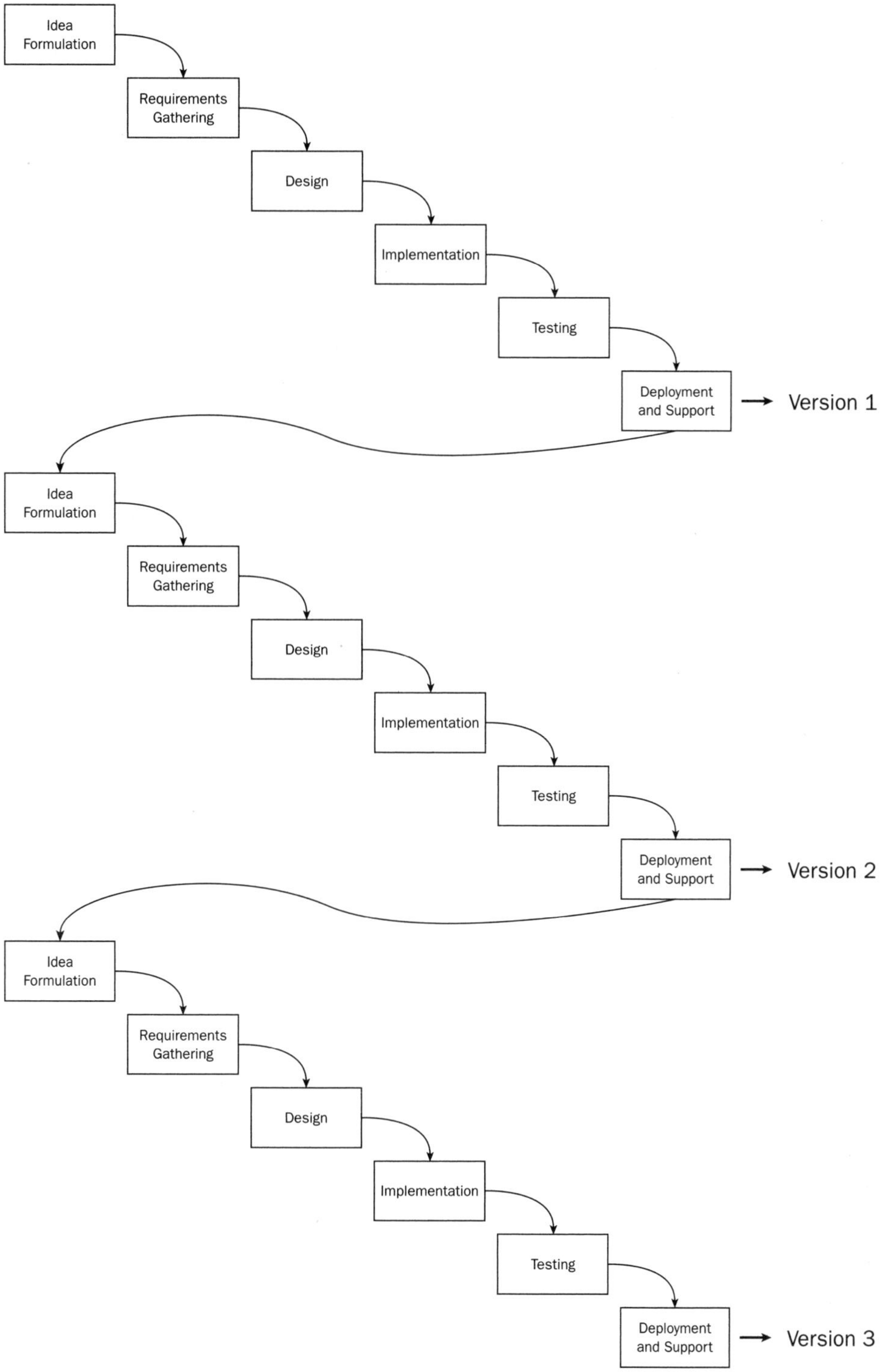

Figure 2-4: You can use multiple serial Waterfalls to model multiple releases.

Overlapping Waterfall

In practice, the different phases of development in the Waterfall model often overlap, as shown in Figure 2-5.

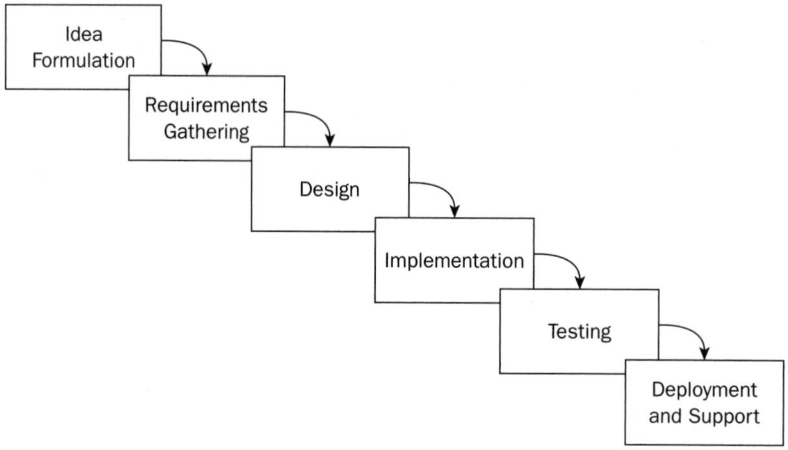

Figure 2-5: The phases in a Waterfall model may overlap.

After you have defined the application's basic theme, some team members can start working on the main requirements, while others continue with idea formulation and refinement. When pieces of the requirements are finished, application architects can begin high-level design for those pieces. Once the designs for a system are finished, programmers can start writing the code.

Waterfall with Feedback

The biggest disadvantage to the Waterfall model is the assumption that each phase is complete and correct before the next phase begins. If you really can finish each phase correctly, the Waterfall model lets you move steadily and confidently forward with no looking back. When problems do arise, however, they can be very difficult to fix.

The Waterfall model with feedback gives you a formal path for letting one phase feed back into the previous one. The project generally flows down the cascade, but sometimes you can paddle against the current to fix a mistake in the previous step.

Figure 2-6 shows this model graphically. The basic flow is downward and to the right, but, if necessary, you can work back upstream (dashed arrows).

As is the case in a kayak, however, moving back against the current is difficult. All of the project's team members usually work on the same phase of development at the same time. If you discover a flaw introduced in the previous phase, other developers may already be working under the flawed assumption.

To fix the previous phase, many team members may need to redo their work to satisfy the new assumptions. That gives them a chance to introduce a whole new set of bugs and, if you don't catch them right away, you will need to fix them during the next phase of development.

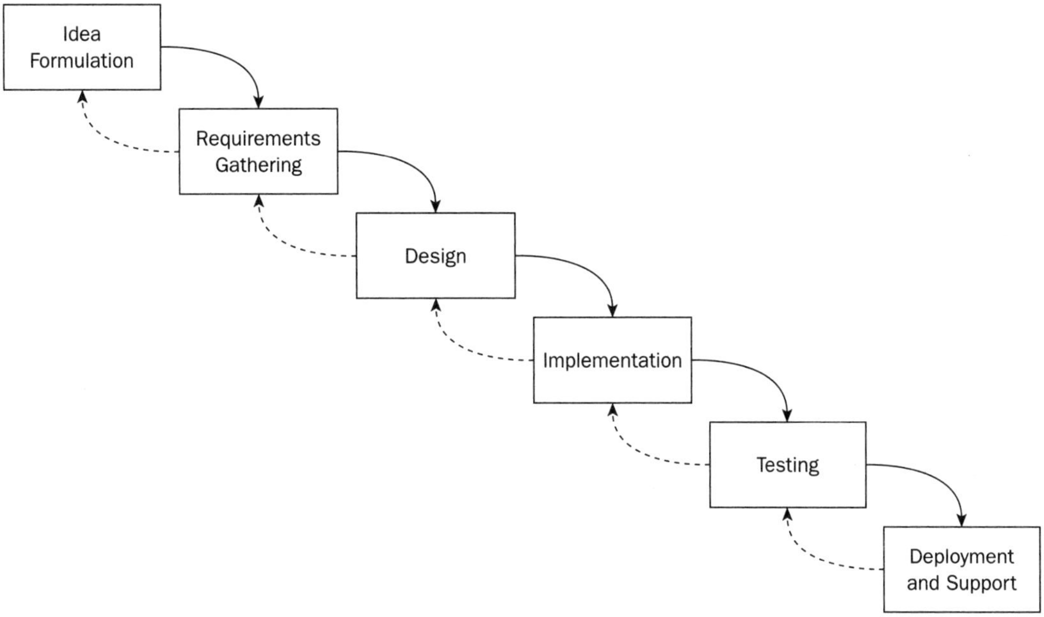

Figure 2-6: The Waterfall model with feedback lets one phase correct a previous phase.

Repairing mistakes in phases earlier than the previous one can be even more difficult. For example, you may discover a mistake in the requirements while you are writing code. You're merrily whittling away at a hand-crafted hash table when you realize that a hash table won't solve the user's problems after all. Instead, you need a priority queue.

Fixing the problem at this point is much harder. Everyone thought that the application needed a hash table and was working under that assumption. Now you need to move all the way back to the requirements gathering phase and modify the application's requirements to require a priority queue.

Changes to the requirements will cause additional changes to the design. You need to discard the design for the hash table and design a priority queue. You'll need to change both the high- and low-level designs. You'll also probably need to update the user interface design to let the user interact with the new queue.

The new design will also impact other subsystems that were supposed to add and remove items from the hash table. The design for those subsystems must now be modified to work with a priority queue instead.

Finally, the changes to the designs will have a large impact on the implementation. The code that implements the hash table must be removed and replaced by new priority queue code. Any other routines that interacted with the hash table must now be updated to follow the new design that uses the priority queue. As usual, those modifications provide additional opportunities for developers to add new bugs to the code.

The Waterfall model with feedback is better than the pure Waterfall model because it acknowledges that you may not get every phase of development absolutely perfect the first time through. Unfortunately, making changes retroactively can still be difficult.

Even with feedback, the Waterfall model is rather inflexible. It can work well if you have experience with the type of application you are developing, and you can get through the requirements gathering and design phases without too many errors, but it leaves little room for mistakes.

Prototyping

A *prototype* is a simplified version of the application that you can use to help build the real application. There are several ways you can use prototypes. You can use them to give the users an idea of how the finished application will work. You can use them to test user interface ideas or code designs.

A prototype does not necessarily need to perform tasks in the same way as the final application. It can be used purely for a proof of concept, and may not implement any actual features at all. For example, instead of actually processing input data and producing an output, the prototype might read the input and return values from a predefined output file. Though the program wouldn't be doing any real calculation, it would still let the users see how the final application will work.

You can build a prototype for almost every phase of application development. You can build mockups and user interface prototypes to let users visualize the finished application and help determine requirements. You can use prototypes during the design phase to try out different user interface approaches, and to test architectures that are less familiar to you so you can make the best design decisions. You can make prototypes to study different coding approaches during implementation. You can even build prototype documentation tools to show the users how the system will display its online help and documentation.

Once a prototype has served its purpose, different prototyping models have different approaches to what you do with it. Some throw the prototype away, whereas others try to get useful code out of it. The following sections describe some of the most important prototyping models.

Visual Basic is particularly well-suited for prototyping approaches. Its powerful user-interface design tools make building user-interface prototypes fast and easy. In a matter of minutes, you can make a mock-up of a user interface complete with multiple forms, menus, buttons, lists, labels, text boxes, and any other user-interface element you might need. You can quickly give the menus and buttons stub routines that display message boxes so that users can better understand where different actions will take place without actually building them. Later, as the project develops, you can add code to implement these features.

IntelliSense helps you remember how to correctly use routines and properties, so it's fairly easy to put code together even if you have not spent a great deal of time studying the interfaces between different modules and classes. Attributes placed on properties and methods make it easy for other developers to find and understand calls to your routines, again making it easier to plug different systems together. Optional parameters and overloading make it easy to create new versions of a routine while allowing developers to keep older versions in existing code.

You can even use the `ObsoleteAttribute` class to mark a method as no longer supported. You can make Visual Basic raise a warning at compile time while still allowing existing code to use the method. Later, when you have modified the code to call a different routine, you can make Visual Basic generate an error if the obsolete method is called, making it easy to find any remaining occurrences.

Eventually, you will need to modify the prototype code to bring it up to release quality. For example, you will need to remove obsolete routines, standardize code attributes and comments, remove unused overloads, and test for dead code no longer used by the prototype.

Between its GUI capabilities, usage hints provided by tools such as IntelliSense, and usage-defining tools such as code attributes, Visual Basic provides a very powerful environment for putting together prototypes quickly and easily.

Throwaway Prototyping

A *throwaway prototype* is just what it sounds like. You build a prototype to demonstrate ideas to users, test user-interface designs, and try out pieces of code. After you receive feedback from the users, pick the best user interface, or decide which coding approach will work best, you discard the prototype and start over.

In this model, the prototype is basically a design tool. It helps you decide what approach to take when building the final application, but you do not expect to use the code inside the prototype. The code in the finished application may implement the same features as the prototype, but it may be in a very different way. By specifying the result rather than the method, the prototype acts much as the development process's requirements phase does. It tells developers what to build, but leaves the choice of how to do it for later.

Because the prototype's code will not be part of the finished system, programmers can take shortcuts to save time. They can skimp on documentation, use mocked-up data rather than performing calculations, display pre-built images instead of creating images on-the-fly, skip proper error handling, and so forth.

One danger of the throwaway prototype approach is that, after the prototype has served its purpose, programmers will be tempted to reuse its code. Because the programmers took shortcuts, the prototype does not contain the type of high-quality code that you want in the finished application, so reusing it is a mistake. If you initially plan to throw the prototype away, then you should do so and start building the real application from scratch.

Iterative Prototyping

Iterative Prototyping is also called *successive refinement* or *evolutionary prototyping*.

In an Iterative Prototype, you start with idea formulation and requirements gathering more or less as usual. In some applications where the final result isn't completely known or the work environment is uncertain, you may need to leave some of the details for later. The prototyping will help solidify requirements as development continues.

After you have some idea of the application's requirements, you design a minimal prototype that demonstrates some features of the final application. Often, this is a simple user interface prototype that displays an assortment of menus and forms. You build and test the prototype, study it, show it to the users, and decide what changes you need to make to move the prototype closer to the final result that the users need. Using feedback from the users and your own experiences in building and using the initial prototype, you design enhancements to make a second version of the prototype. You implement the enhancements, test them, and again show them to the users.

You continue this process, analyzing the current prototype, designing enhancements, implementing the changes, and testing them until the prototype becomes the final application.

Figure 2-7 shows the process graphically. Idea formulation and requirements gathering work as usual. You then enter a loop, repeatedly designing, implementing, and testing better and better versions of the prototype until the final prototype is good enough for the users to install.

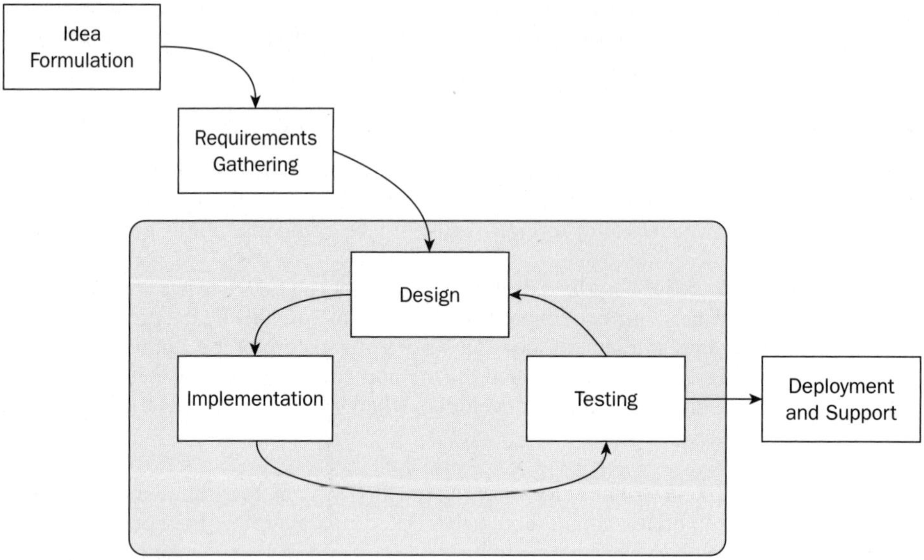

Figure 2-7: In Iterative Prototyping, you repeat the cycle of design, implementation, and testing until you build a prototype that is good enough to be the final application.

Iterative Prototyping gives you the same phases as the Waterfall model, but the repeated trips through the design/implement/test cycle give you extra flexibility. If the requirements are not fully defined during the requirements phase, you can use successive trips through the cycle to clarify and define them. If the users' needs change during development, another trip or two through the cycle can make adjustments.

> *On several occasions, I've worked on projects in conjunction with much larger development organizations that followed a strict Waterfall model. Their typical implementation cycle from idea formulation to deployment could last two, three, or even more years. By the time the application was ready to go into operation, the business environment had often changed, so the final application did not solve at least some aspects and sometimes any of the users' problems. Iterative Prototyping avoids that problem by adjusting the successive prototypes to track changing business needs.*

Iterative Prototyping is also sometimes represented by a spiral, as shown in Figure 2-8, so it is sometimes called the *spiral model*. This representation implies that the prototypes zoom in until they satisfy the requirements at the middle, and, at that point, the most recent prototype becomes the finished application. Unfortunately, that downplays Iterative Prototyping's most powerful features: the ability to handle uncertain or changing requirements.

I've also seen the spiral drawn from the inside out. Idea formulation and requirements gathering feed into the middle of the spiral, and successive development cycles move farther and farther out, implying that each prototype is bigger and more complete than the previous one.

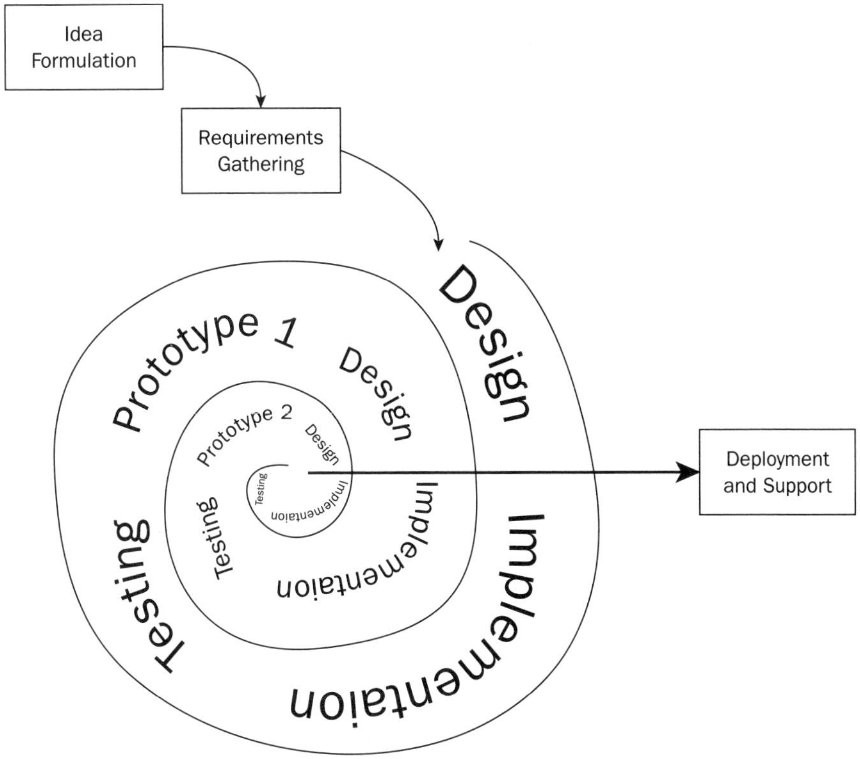

Figure 2-8: Iterative Prototyping spirals in on the finished system.

Finally, I've heard projects based on variations of the Iterative Prototyping model called *hardened prototypes*. The idea is to start with a prototype that demonstrates most of the application's desired features, but that doesn't have much error checking and other safety features. The prototype is then "hardened" to make it stronger and more resistant to failure. When the prototype is sufficiently bulletproof, it is released as the final application.

Staged Delivery

When you use Iterative Prototyping, a key question is, "When is the prototype good enough to use as the final application?" Do you need to go through three iterations? Four? More? The correct answer depends on the answers to several questions such as, "How many of the requirements are satisfied by the latest prototype?" and "How hard will it be to satisfy the remaining requirements?"

If the current prototype only satisfies some of the requirements, and it will be fairly easy to handle most of the requirements in the next prototype, then you may want to wait. If the current prototype handles most of the users' needs and you know it will be difficult to get funding to build the next prototype, then you may want to release the latest version to the users.

Staged Delivery is a variation of Iterative Prototyping that partly avoids this question by releasing several versions of the prototype to the users when the prototypes are ready. You should release a prototype to the users when it provides enough benefit to offset the inconvenience of releasing a new version of the prototype.

If the latest version provides big benefits and installing it isn't too difficult, you should give it to the users. If the latest version only adds a few small features to the previous prototype and would require the users to convert all of their data files to a new format, you should delay release until a later prototype that provides greater benefit.

Figure 2-9 shows this model graphically. Each trip through the Design-Implementation-Testing cycle may or may not produce a new version of the application.

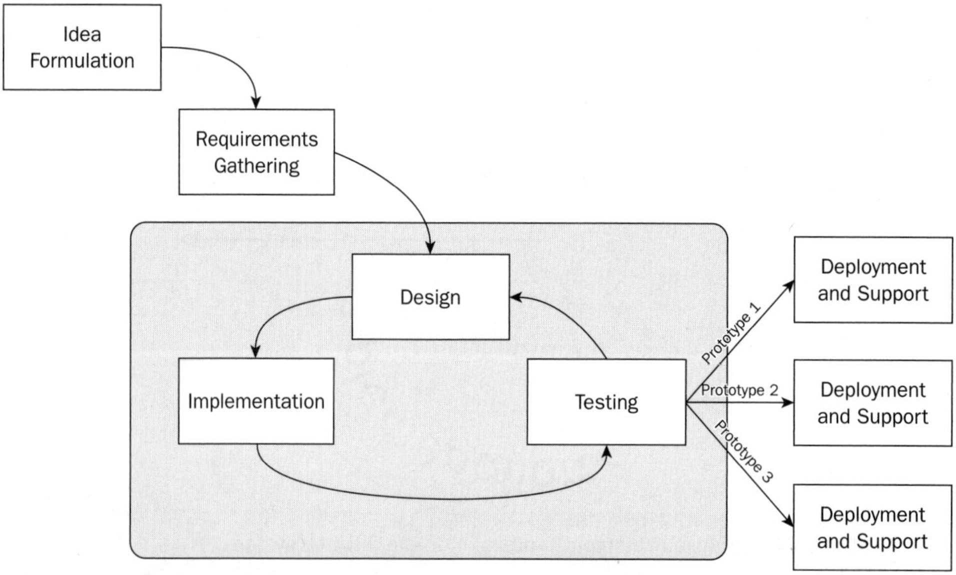

Figure 2-9: In Staged Delivery, each trip through the Design-Implementation-Testing cycle may produce a new version of the application.

Sometimes Staged Delivery is called the *spiral staircase* model. Each trip through the Design-Implementation-Testing cycle is a trip around the staircase. When you finish the Testing part of each trip around the staircase, you decide whether you should let a copy of the prototype "get off the stairs" and head for the users. Figure 2-10 shows this representation.

Staged Delivery has a couple of advantages. It lets you release something useful to the users as quickly as possible. As soon as a prototype's value outweighs the pain of release, you can give it to the users.

Staged Delivery gives the users many opportunities to test the application and provide feedback. That makes it very good at tracking uncertain requirements. If the users don't initially know what they need, they will probably have a much better idea after using the first few versions.

Similarly, Staged Delivery can track changing requirements relatively easily. If changes in the business environment require changes to the application, the next design cycle can take the new requirements into account. Handling fuzzy and changing requirements is usually extremely painful with the Waterfall model.

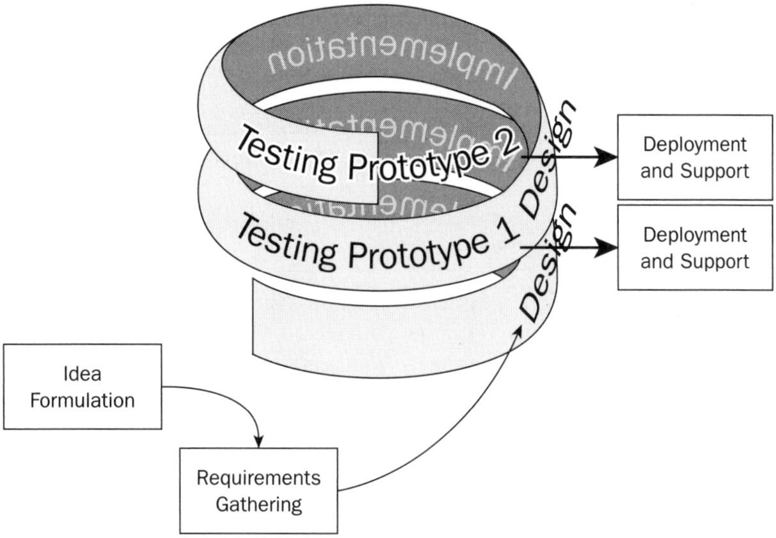

Figure 2-10: You can think of Staged Delivery as a spiral staircase.

Although Staged Delivery has several advantages over other models, it has a couple of drawbacks. First, because each prototype version is a potential candidate for release to the users, you must spend extra time writing its code. In an Iterative Prototyping approach, you can defer some error-handling code, documentation, testing, and other tasks until you approach the application's final version. In the Staged Delivery model, you must handle these tasks before every prototype release.

A second drawback to Staged Delivery is that it requires extra training for the users. Each time a new version of the application is released, the users must learn how to use its new features. Even if the differences are fairly simple, users must make a mental switch to the new version.

If the new features in each version are important to the users, the new releases may give the impression that you are responsive to the customer's needs. However, if the new releases contain only minor improvements, the users may feel that frequent releases are a waste of their time.

Deadline and Cost Cutoffs

Deadline cutoff and *cost cutoff* are variations on prototyping approaches. You can base them on either the Iterative Prototyping or Staged Delivery models.

You start both variations with idea formulation and requirements gathering as usual. You then enter a series of Design-Implementation-Testing cycles. If you are following a Staged Delivery model, you release interim versions of the application after the test phases as usual. If you are following an Iterative Prototyping model, you can defer some of the error handling, documentation, and other late-stage tasks for the final iterations. No matter which model you use, it is important that each prototype contains high-quality code so that you can quickly finish it off and release it as a finished application.

In the deadline cutoff variation, a pre-defined project deadline eventually approaches. At that point, you polish up the latest prototype, adding extra error handling, documentation, and anything else you've deferred in the earlier development cycles, and release the result to the users.

The cost cutoff variation is similar to the deadline version except that you wrap up development and release the program when you run out of money, instead of when a deadline approaches.

You can also combine these two variations and release the application's final version when either a deadline approaches or when the money runs out.

These approaches have the same strengths and weaknesses as the basic Iterative Prototyping and Staged Delivery methods. The only difference is in how you decide when to end development. Instead of repeating the Design-Implementation-Testing cycle until you satisfy enough of the requirements, you work until you reach the time or cost limit.

This can be an effective way to manage a project with limited time or money, although the users must be prepared to live with a less-than-perfect result. To give the users the best result possible, it is important that you prioritize the requirements so the most critical features are implemented in the earliest prototypes.

Mix and Match

None of these models is set in stone, and you can modify them to best suit your needs. For example, you might use Iterative Prototyping where each trip through the Design-Implementation-Testing cycle includes a full Waterfall model complete with formal requirements gathering.

You could start with a basic Waterfall model through idea formulation, requirements gathering, and design. Then you could implement the application's different systems by following an Iterative Prototyping approach. When the separate systems were finished, you would integrate them and finish the Waterfall model's testing and deployment stages.

You could begin by following an Iterative Prototyping strategy. In the middle of the project, the business environment might change so that the users have an urgent need for a working application. You could then switch to Staged Delivery and add extra error handling, documentation, and testing to create an interim application. After releasing this version, you could return to the Iterative Prototyping model and make the final release only after satisfying all of the remaining requirements.

My favorite approach is Iterative Prototyping with one main prototype and a few smaller ones. Depending on the application, the project might begin with a small user interface prototype to help the users understand how they will use the finished application. After listening to feedback and making any necessary corrections, the developers build the major prototype, implementing as many of the required features as possible.

The users evaluate this version to ensure that it adequately satisfies the requirements. If changes are necessary, developers may show the users one or two new versions containing small changes. After this point, the developers harden the code adding error handling, documentation, and so forth to produce the final release.

This method works well with small to medium-sized applications where development is relatively fast. The initial user-interface prototype helps define and clarify the requirements. Later prototypes can handle small changes to the requirements, although having the second prototype implement most of the application's features rather than building several smaller prototypes makes it somewhat harder to handle large changes.

Summary

All lifecycle models use the same basic phases:

- Idea formulation
- Requirements gathering
- Design
- Implementation
- Testing
- Deployment and support

The various models differ in how they arrange these stages. The Waterfall model puts each stage after the previous one, requiring that you finish each phase completely before beginning the next one. Variations on the Waterfall model allow overlapping phases and limited feedback to previous stages.

Prototyping models use application prototypes to gather information about the project's requirements. Throwaway prototype models use prototypes only to learn about what the application should do, and then discard the prototypes. Iterative Prototyping and Staged Delivery build on the prototypes, making the code more robust and adding more features until the prototype has satisfied the users' requirements and it becomes the final application.

Developers have been using the lifecycle methodologies described in this chapter for decades. They have been tested over generations of developers and have been found reliable when used properly. They are particularly effective when requirements are well-known before development starts, but they don't respond well to uncertain or changing requirements. The Waterfall model in particular handles changes to requirements quite poorly.

Fairly recently, new approaches have emerged that handle uncertain and changing requirements more effectively than these traditional approaches. Driven partly by the frenetic pace of development during the period of explosive Web growth in the late 1990s, these methods rapidly adjust to changes in requirements or to fix glitches in the development process itself.

Chapter 3, "Agile Methodologies," describes some of these newer agile models and explains how you can adopt them in whole or part for Visual Basic development.

3

Agile Methodologies

Chapter 2, "Lifecycle Methodologies," discussed several models for managing a project throughout its lifespan. This chapter explains newer "agile" approaches to controlling development. While the more traditional approaches focus on predictive planning to guide the project, these methods react quickly and change the project's direction as needed to move toward the eventual goal of producing a finished application.

This chapter describes agile development methods in general, and spends a little extra time on the Crystal Clear and Extreme Programming models. It describes some of the techniques that make agile methods successful, including pair programming, test-driven development, and design by contract. Even if you don't adopt agile methods in their entirety, some of these techniques may be useful to you in more traditional lifecycle models.

The first sections in this chapter focus on the goals of agile development. They describe some of the approaches developers have taken, their advantages, and their rationale. Later sections compare these methods to the more traditional methodologies described in Chapter 2 and cover some of the dangers and disadvantages in agile programming.

Agile Programming

Agile programming is as much an attitude or philosophical approach as a strictly defined methodology. The basic principle behind agile development is that the development lifecycle should be quick and responsive. It should be able to adjust rapidly to changing requirements, and should be able to take advantage of new innovations as they occur.

Different variations of agile development have such names as Crystal Clear, Scrum, Adaptive Software Development, Feature Driven Development, and Lean Software Development. Another form of agile development, Extreme Programming, is described in more detail later in this chapter. You can learn more about other agile methods on the Web or in books that focus on agile development such as *Crystal Clear: A Human-Powered Methodology for Small Teams* by Alistair Cockburn

(Boston: Addison-Wesley Professional, 2004), *Agile and Iterative Development* by Craig Larman (Boston: Addison-Wesley Professional, 2003), and *Managing Agile Projects* by Kevin Aguanno (Lakefield, Ontario, Canada: Multi-Media Publications Inc., 2005).

Though different agile methods have different details, they share some common themes. In 2001, a group of prominent agile developers got together and assembled what is now called the Agile Manifesto. The short summary of the manifesto at `agilemanifesto.org` is as follows:

Individuals and interactions over processes and tools

Working software over comprehensive documentation

Customer collaboration over contract negotiation

Responding to change over following a plan

These rather vague statements try to convey the agile philosophy, rather than specific rules to follow. The idea is that developers should place greater importance on building a flexible, usable, effective application than on following rigidly defined methods to build a complete specification and then follow it to the letter.

The following text shows the manifesto's principles in slightly greater detail. Some of these points are more concrete rules that you can actually follow:

Our highest priority is to satisfy the customer through early and continuous delivery of valuable software.

Welcome changing requirements, even late in development. Agile processes harness change for the customer's competitive advantage.

Deliver working software frequently, from a couple of weeks to a couple of months, with a preference to the shorter timescale.

Business people and developers must work together daily throughout the project.

Build projects around motivated individuals. Give them the environment and support they need, and trust them to get the job done.

The most efficient and effective method of conveying information to and within a development team is face-to-face conversation.

Working software is the primary measure of progress.

Agile processes promote sustainable development. The sponsors, developers, and users should be able to maintain a constant pace indefinitely.

Continuous attention to technical excellence and good design enhances agility.

Simplicity — the art of maximizing the amount of work not done — is essential.

The best architectures, requirements, and designs emerge from self-organizing teams.

At regular intervals, the team reflects on how to become more effective, then tunes and adjusts its behavior accordingly.

The emphasis is on producing small software releases very quickly with constant feedback from users to ensure that development continues toward a useful goal.

Crystal Clear

The Crystal Clear methodology reduces the Agile Manifesto to seven principles. You can find a detailed description of these principles in the chapter, "Crystal Clear Applied: The Seven Properties of Running an Agile Project," of the book *Crystal Clear: A Human-Powered Methodology for Small Teams* (you can find this chapter at `www.awprofessional.com/articles/article.asp?p=345009&seqNum=1`). The following list summarizes those principles:

- *Frequent Delivery* — Each iteration should take only a few weeks, not the months or years sometimes required by other lifecycle models. Each cycle should produce a high-quality release-ready application, although post-release activities such as documentation are often neglected.
- *Reflective Improvement* — After each iteration, the team makes a list of the things that are working and those that are not. It then continues using the methods that work and improves the things that are not working. Even if things go badly wrong, the team should be able to get back on track in the next iteration or two.
- *Osmotic Communication* — Communication occurs frequently, so all of the team members can listen in, preferably with all of the team members in the same room. For example, if all of the developers work in a large "bullpen" style office, they can listen in on each other's conversations. Naturally, this kind of "eavesdropping" style of communication is more difficult with large teams. (However, some developers may be uncomfortable in the "bullpen" style office and get the feeling that someone is constantly looking over their shoulders. Some managers may think this encourages developers to work hard and only on business-related projects, but it may also lead to a stressful environment that chases away good developers.)
- *Personal Safety* — The work environment encourages developers to speak up when they see problems without fear of retaliation. Developers respect each others' opinions and discuss issues openly. (As is the case with osmotic communication, the real world sometimes makes this sort of assumption difficult. We've all met "prima donna" developers who have extremely high opinions of their own abilities, and it is difficult to build an atmosphere of trust with them around. In some cases, it may be best in the long run to keep some of these developers apart so they don't sour the rest of the team.)
- *Focus* — Developers stay focused on clearly defined tasks and high-priority items to control their workload. (Occasionally, however, developers may need a break from crucial program elements. Building a quick, unrelated programming tool or attending a conference can help keep developers fresh. Google employees are expressly told to spend a certain percentage of their time experimenting to see what they can accomplish.)
- *Easy Access to Expert Users* — Developers have quick, easy access to expert users so that they can get prompt authoritative feedback and guidance on changing requirements. (Developers should keep themselves under control, however, and not become total pests. Frequent interruptions can reduce the experts' productivity at their normal jobs and can be frustrating for them. In some projects, I have worked with experts assigned full-time to our project, but at other times the users had to handle their normal workloads in addition to answering our questions. In that kind of situation, you must be sensitive to the experts' situations and not overwhelm them.)

- *A Strong Development Environment*—This includes the tools that you would want for any development effort such as a source code control system and automated testing tools. Alistair Cockburn, the author of the *Crystal Clear: A Human-Powered Methodology for Small Teams* book (Boston: Addison-Wesley Professional, 2004), also argues that developers should perform frequent integration—as often as several times per day, but no less than once every other day. He calls this "continuous integration-with-test." Frequent integration combined with good testing tools lets developers move forward confidently.

Again, the emphasis is on producing small software releases very quickly with constant feedback from users to ensure that development continues toward a useful goal. Specific principles (such as reflective improvement, osmotic communication, and personal safety) help keep the team working smoothly at a rapid pace.

Extreme Programming (XP)

The Agile Manifesto and *Crystal Clear* focus on a set of relatively high-level goals and procedures. For example, frequent releases, reflective improvement, and quick user feedback are tools that help keep development on track. They do not address the day-to-day process of writing code.

Extreme Programming (`www.extremeprogramming.org`) uses similar concepts, but also adds a few more concrete rules for guiding everyday development.

The book *Extreme Programming Explained: Embrace Change* by Kent Beck and Cynthia Andres (Boston: Addison-Wesley, 2004) lists five key values that are central to Extreme Programming:

- *Communication*—Communication occurs frequently and informally within the development team.
- *Simplicity*—Code starts simply and is later modified, if necessary, to build a better solution.
- *Feedback*—Expert users provide frequent feedback. The team provides feedback to itself to improve the development process.
- *Courage*—This is the idea that developers should bravely push forward writing code for their immediate needs, and not focus on code they will need to write later. Developers focus on the current simpler needs, rather than on the more complicated modified code they may need to write later.
- *Respect*—Developers respect each other. They work together to improve each others' code and take each others' suggestions seriously.

Advocates of Extreme Programming also recommend embracing changes and making incremental change, rather than making large-scale changes all at once. Extreme Programming also assumes that the code is frequently tested so that the releases have high quality.

If you compare these values to the list of principles for Crystal Clear given in the previous section, you will see some parallels. Both emphasize communication, user feedback, and improving the development process (reflective improvement in Crystal Clear, feedback in Extreme Programming). Both stress frequent, incremental, high-quality releases, rather than fewer large releases.

You can also see some of the same potential drawbacks. Frequent communication and trust can be difficult with some developers. Some of the team's stronger personalities may have trouble giving total respect to less-experienced members. Occasionally, it's better to place a bit of distance between troublesome developers and the others so the team as a whole functions smoothly.

In addition to these higher-level values and principles, Extreme Programming requires developers to follow the 12 specific practices described in the following sections.

Whole Team

The development group works as a unified team, ideally in a single location sharing a large workspace. Proximity and a relaxed team atmosphere make it easy for team members to ask and answer questions whenever necessary.

The team will certainly include programmers. Often, it will include customers, or at least someone who represents the customers' interests. Depending on the scope of the project, it may also include project managers, testers, documentation writers, trainers, and others. Extreme programming works best with small teams, so that often a single person fills several of these roles.

The Planning Game

In the "planning game," users and developers sit down and discuss the next round of development. Users describe features that they need implemented. Developers estimate the times and costs needed to implement the features. The users then pick the most important features for inclusion in the next release. The result is a short list of changes and additions to the current solution that developers can implement in a few weeks.

One of the key points of the planning game is to select the features that will be added to the next release. This focus encourages users to think in terms of releases with some features deferred for one, two, or more release cycles. Keeping track of deferred features can help lay the groundwork for long-term planning and future planning games.

One problem with this sort of planning is that it can be hard for the participants to commit to difficult tasks. Suppose a particular feature will take four weeks to implement, but the goal is to select features that can be implemented in no more than three weeks. Unless you can find a way to break the large task into smaller pieces, it is easy to defer this large task indefinitely. At some point, you need to admit that the task is necessary and "lose" the planning game to get the job done.

Simple Design

The application uses the simplest design possible to achieve its goals at every step. Programmers focus on the immediate needs, and don't worry about building general solutions to later problems. Test-driven development (described later) promotes this idea of keeping the design as simple as possible while getting the job done.

Developers are often prone to "featuritis," adding unnecessary bells and whistles to code because they are interesting or improve flexibility. It is better to get the immediate job done as simply and quickly as possible and only make more complicated changes later when they prove necessary.

Design Improvement

An Extreme Programming project starts with a simple design and grows more complicated as necessary over time. Because Extreme Programming favors frequent small builds, the overall design grows incrementally. Sometimes decisions that made sense when a particular piece of code was written don't make sense later as the project expands.

As development progresses, the code is *refactored* as necessary to improve the overall design. Redesign activities focus on consolidating redundant code, improving consistency, and decoupling subsystems.

Small Releases

Like other agile methods, Extreme Programming uses many small releases to work rapidly toward the final solution. Small releases give the users frequent chances to provide feedback and give the developers frequent opportunities to improve the design, the requirements, and the development process itself.

Continuous Integration

After a piece of code successfully passes its tests, it is integrated into the system. All of the system's tests must run after the new code is added. In Extreme Programming, this system integration should be performed several times each day if possible.

Continuous integration ensures that the code always has high quality. Before a piece of code is permanently added to the system, its authors have tested it, added it to the code base, and tested the whole system to ensure that the new code didn't break anything. The system may have some missing features, but the features that are present have been tested.

Coding Standard

The project should have a set of coding standards that all users follow. The standards should cover such things as the following:

- Class, variable, and routine naming conventions
- Calling conventions, such as how parameters are named and whether they are declared `ByVal` or `ByRef`
- Commenting conventions for routines, modules, and code
- Standards for using the `With` or `Using` keywords, defining loop variables, and so forth
- Error-handling conventions

Using a common code style makes it easier for developers to understand each other's code, and can prevent petty disputes over style that might otherwise arise during pair programming.

Collective Code Ownership

The Extreme Programming team as a whole owns the code, not particular developers or pairs. That means if you find a problem in a piece of code that has been checked into the system, you check it out, modify it, retest it, check the code back in, and retest the system to ensure that you didn't break anything else.

You may need to ask other developers for information about code they wrote, but you should not regard that code as their property. It belongs to the project and the project team as a whole.

System Metaphor

The system's metaphor is an all-encompassing story that describes the system. This should be an intuitive parallel to some process that all of the developers can easily understand. The developers can use the metaphor to think about the relationships among the system's pieces, and to pick names that go together reasonably well.

For example, Windows uses a desktop metaphor, where folders contain files and you put files you no longer need in a wastebasket. Until you empty the wastebasket, you can retrieve files from it if you decide you really need them.

With this metaphor, it is easy to think of consistent names for most of the operations a program might need to perform: `CreateFile`, `PutFileInFolder`, `MoveFileToWastebasket`, `MoveFolderToWastebasket`, `ListWastebasketContents`, `RemoveFromWastebasket`, `EmptyWastebasket`, `ArrangeDesktop`, and so forth. Names such as `DeleteFile`, `PermanentlyDelete`, and `ReorderIcons` don't fit the metaphor, so they are not as good.

If you can't think of a reasonably intuitive metaphor, you can at least give names to all of the major systems and classes so that developers can use them to generate other consistent names. For example, if a dispatching application uses network classes named `StreetNode` and `StreetLink`, developers can easily generate related names such as `ConnectStreetNodes`, `TraverseStreetLinks`, and so forth.

Pair Programming

In pair programming, two programmers work together to write a single piece of code. They design, write, test, and debug the code together as a two-person team. One person, the *driver*, types at the computer while the other, the *observer* or *navigator*, reads the results and thinks about the direction of the steps to come. The two programmers switch roles periodically (some recommend at least every half hour) to keep both fresh, and to allow both to develop their pair programming skills.

People are naturally very good at filling in pieces that are missing from a puzzle. When you write code and later when you read the code you wrote, you sometimes see what you think is there instead of what is *really* there. That's why programmers sometimes stare right at a bug for hours without actually seeing it.

One way traditional development efforts try to improve code quality is by holding code reviews, where a programmer steps through his code and explains it to the other programmers. Often, the process of holding the review enables the programmer who wrote the code to spot bugs. The act of slowing down and describing the code verbally often forces the programmer to see the code that is actually there and that makes the bugs obvious.

Pair programming lets programmers take advantage of the same phenomenon while writing every line of code. If one person verbally describes the code while typing it into the computer, and the other person listens and reads along, the code is reviewed by two people in four different ways (speaking, typing, listening, and reading) and the programmers are more likely to catch any mistakes.

One way to proofread a novel takes advantage of this same principle of reviewing text in two different ways at the same time. Two reviewers read the book together, taking turns where one reads aloud (in a whisper to conserve their voices) and the other follows along silently. If a word is missing or extraneous, one reviewer may mentally correct the mistake, but if the other does not, then the error is immediately apparent.

Pair programming can also help less-experienced developers improve their skills by working with a more experienced developer. It can act as a form of apprenticeship to help the junior programmers learn new techniques more quickly than they could on their own. It is important that the pair switch roles periodically, however, even if one programmer is more experienced than the other. Both developers must participate, or the experienced programmer may end up doing all of the work while the apprentice sits quietly, removing the multiple-point-of-view benefit provided by pair programming.

Pair programming can help overcome some of the difficulties that less-experienced developers may face when using other agile methods. When requirements change frequently, junior programmers who require more guidance may have trouble quickly adapting to the new circumstances, and may need extra help to get settled in the new direction. When paired with a more senior developer, the junior programmer can still make progress relatively quickly. Two novice programmers paired together might make adequate progress on simple, well-defined tasks, but you wouldn't want that team to tackle the trickier parts of the system without guidance.

Pair programming also has some less-tangible benefits, such as faster team building and fewer interruptions (people are more reluctant to interrupt a pair).

Pair programming does have a few drawbacks. Some programmers prefer to work alone and may find working too closely with a partner to be irritating. Very advanced developers may find it particularly difficult to work with junior developers. Pairing a coding wizard with a novice may reduce the wizard's productivity. Sometimes it may be better to let the wizard work alone, particularly when deadlines are approaching. Often, though, it's worth at least some loss of productivity to put more "eyes on the code" and to give the novice some extra experience and insight.

Differences in coding styles can cause friction between paired developers. You can avoid some of this problem by creating a project code standard and requiring all of the developers to follow it. Then, instead of arguing over who has the better system for naming variables, the pairs can just blame the style standard for any deviations from their preferred styles and move forward. (They may even bond a bit during a joint complaining session.)

Test-Driven Development

One of the main goals of Extreme Programming is to produce code that is of high quality at all times. One approach to achieving that goal is test-driven development.

In *test-driven development* (also called *test-first development*), you write the tests first, and then you write code to pass the tests. You then run the code against the tests. If there are any problems, you revise the code and run the tests again. You repeat this process until the code passes all of the tests.

Of course, when you design code to pass a test, you must assume that the test is correct. If the test is wrong, it will drive you to write perfectly working code that does the wrong thing. Take some time with the tests and ensure that they test the right thing. If the code doesn't satisfy a test, ensure that you understand why, and be certain that it's because the code is wrong, not because the test is flawed.

Sometimes during initial development or while you are fixing the code to pass a test, you may think of another test case that you didn't consider before. At that point, you can add the new test to the suite you have already written. Before you do, however, you should consider whether the test is really necessary or whether it would be possible to restrict the requirements to prohibit that particular test case. Restricting the requirements usually leads to simpler code that can be easier to debug and maintain.

For example, suppose you need to write a routine to sort a list of customer names. You write some tests that generate random lists of names, pass them into the sorting routine, and then verify that the returned results are sorted. The test software performs any number of trials with lists of customer containing from 1 to 100,000 customers.

You write the sorting code, run the tests on it, and fix some bugs. While fixing the code, you realize that the routine won't work if two customers have exactly the same name, or if the list of customers contains zero entries.

In this case, you probably need the code to handle the case where two customers have exactly the same name. How many Jane Smiths and Manuel Garcias are in your local phone book? You should write a new test that runs the software on customer lists that contain duplicates.

However, your application may have other requirements that make a zero-item customer list impossible. Perhaps the user cannot get to the form that displays the sorted list unless there are entries in it. In that case, you may want to note in the requirements that this situation is impossible, so you don't need to write code to handle it or test against it.

> *You might also include a* `Debug.Assert` *statement in the code to verify that the list has at least one item. Then, if the program somehow manages to pass an empty customer list to the routine, the program will stop so that you can figure out why this is happening and fix it.*

Figure 3-1 shows the process graphically.

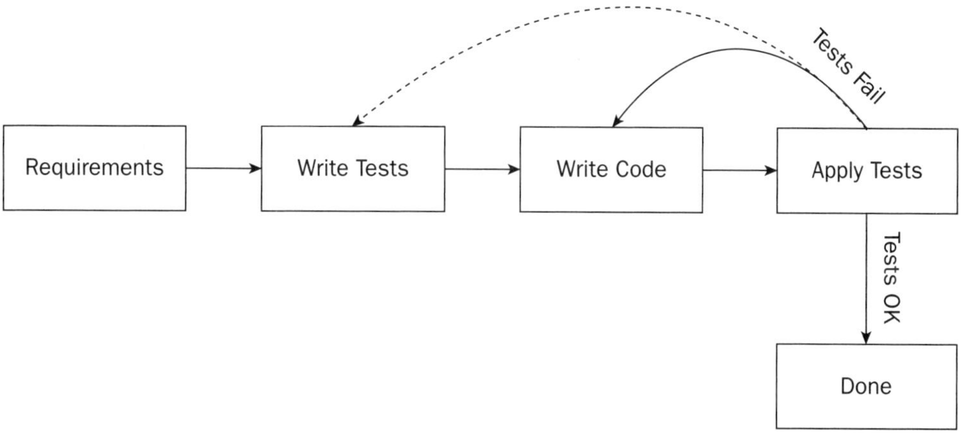

Figure 3-1: In test-driven programming, you write tests first and then code. As long as the tests fail, you fix the code and possibly write more tests.

Test-driven development has many advantages. To write the tests, you must understand the requirements, but you don't need to know yet how to write the code. This keeps you focused on the code's usage and results, rather than its implementation. This focus on usage is similar to the design by contract approach described later in this chapter.

That, in turn, helps you write tests that determine whether the code meets the requirements, rather than determining whether the code does what you *think* it does. Just as your brain can fill in missing pieces in a puzzle or subroutine, it can also predispose you to write tests that evaluate the code you wrote, rather than the code that you *should have written*. If you're not on guard, it's very easy to write code that only tests the cases you thought of when you wrote the code, and not all of the cases that the requirements demand.

It's also easy to write just one or two tests, and then assume that if the code passes those, it must pass any others that you might write. Some developers don't write any tests for their code, at least at the routine level, and they just assume that it will work. After all, if they knew there was a problem in the code, they would have fixed it. Since they don't know of any problems, the code must be correct. Because test-driven development places test writing first, programmers have no excuse to skip writing tests. Even the most delusional developers cannot claim that their code works correctly if it doesn't exist yet.

Sometimes test-driven development leads to simpler code. Because the programmer is writing code that only satisfies a specific set of tests, there's less temptation to add extra bells and whistles that don't lead to passing the tests.

Finally, test-driven development ensures that every piece of code is covered by some automated test. That makes automated module and unit testing easier, so the code is more likely to be tested thoroughly.

Test-driven development is not completely without drawbacks. If you write a routine to perform a minimal set of tests, and later discover that the routine needs to do more, you must spend additional time revising the tests in addition to modifying the code.

Though testing gives you some confidence that your code works, it is far from a guarantee. Ideally, your tests would try out every possible combination of inputs and verify the results. In practice, it's rare that you can test with *every* possible set of input values. In that case, testing doesn't guarantee correctness and, if you design the tests poorly, it may add a false level of confidence to code that doesn't work.

Designing tests is itself a bit of an art form. Generally, it's a good idea to test inputs near the boundaries of allowed values; very big and very small values. Depending on the code, you should test with values in the middle of the allowed values, empty and missing inputs, lots of duplicate inputs, and inputs sorted forward and backward. Try a large assortment of values that seem typical for the application, in addition to a variety of values that seems weird or unusual. Try illegal values and verify that the code catches them.

Even with all of these tests, you can't be sure to catch every possible bug. What if the test code is written incorrectly so that it doesn't actually catch any bugs at all? One approach that many test-driven developers use to prevent that particular error is to start writing the actual code with a version that doesn't work, and then verify that the testing code realizes it. For example, you might have a sorting subroutine return the same values it receives as input, so any tests that did not start with already sorted data should detect an error.

Another drawback to test-driven development is that it can be difficult to write good tests for certain kinds of development before the code is written. For example, it's hard to write programmatic tests for graphical and GUI code beforehand. Suppose a program should display the locations of sales representatives on a map. You can buy regression-testing tools that will take a snapshot of the map so that you can later tell if a test achieved the same result. However, it would be difficult for you to manually generate the map ahead of time so that you could compare the code's output to it.

Testing for these sorts of projects may require extensive manual review of use cases, at least until you have generated some verified output that you can use for future comparisons during regression testing.

Sustainable Pace

Agile methods produce a lot of small releases on very short time scales. When short time spans are involved, it's easy to feel pressure to meet tight deadlines. If developers work frantically, racking up overtime to meet the short deadlines imposed by Extreme Programming, they will burn out after one or two development cycles.

To allow the developers to continue to produce these small, quick releases, you must set a reasonable pace. It's reasonable for developers to work overtime once in a while. It's not reasonable to expect them to work overtime for months at a time.

If developers aren't meeting the schedule most of the time in 40 hours per week, then something's wrong. If that happens, you need to adjust the planning game, so you estimate longer delivery times for the features requested by the users.

Other Extreme Practices

Kent Beck, author of *Extreme Programming Explained*, adds a few more practices to provide additional detail. The following gives my interpretations of his new terms:

- *Customer Team Member* — The team should include at least one member who represents the application's eventual customers. This can be an expert user, a manager of the customers, or someone else who has an intimate understanding of the customers' needs. This person provides constant feedback, and takes the lead in deciding what features are the most important during the planning game.
- *User Story* — The user story is a description of how a particular system feature will work. These stories are typically brief, providing just enough information to estimate the difficulty of implementing the feature during the planning game. The features described by a story should be small enough for one person (or pair) to complete within one development cycle. Larger stories should be broken up, if possible.
- *Acceptance Testing* — The customer team member writes acceptance tests that determine when the features described by a story have been built. The programmers help the customer code the acceptance tests so they can be run automatically every time a new piece of code is added to the application just like any other set of tests.
- *Open Workspace* — This emphasizes that the whole team works together in an easily accessible environment so that they can raise questions, give answers, and collaborate quickly and easily.

Extreme Programming Weaknesses

Extreme Programming has many benefits, but, like every other method, it has some drawbacks.

In more formal lifecycle models such as the Waterfall model, change requests must be formally approved before developers can begin design and development work. In Extreme Programming, customers who are part of the development team can request new features with little or no approval, possibly leading to a proliferation of unnecessary bells and whistles.

In theory, those sorts of requests will not arise because they violate the rule of using the simplest possible design. To keep these items in check, customers and developers should ask during the planning game whether a feature is really necessary and helpful to the users, or whether it is a gratuitous complication.

An Extreme Programming project doesn't have formal documentation of requirements before the project starts and the requirement grow incrementally over time. Some companies may have trouble justifying a $1 million or $2 million budget to let a group of rogue programmers run loose for a year or two with no milestones or verifiable requirements.

This attitude reflects a cultural incompatibility between the organization and the Extreme Programming method (or any agile method, for that matter). The company should consider the project more as a series of smaller projects that makes up a journey of discovery leading toward an eventual solution. Or, to put it more concretely, you don't need to commit $2 million and two years. You only need to commit resources for the next couple of development cycles. If things are headed the wrong way, you can make corrections during the next cycle.

A final drawback to Extreme Programming is that it seems to be an all-or-nothing decision. I've seen some articles arguing that you don't get the benefits of Extreme Programming unless you follow all 12 of the official practices. Rapid development cycles don't work if you don't allow for design improvement over time through refactoring. Pair programming doesn't work smoothly unless you have a good metaphor and coding standards. Frequent integration doesn't work well unless you produce high-quality code using test-driven development.

I don't think you can say that these techniques have no value unless you do them all together. A good coding standard, pair programming, test-driven development, and working at a sustainable pace will each provide a benefit when added to any lifecycle methodology, whether it's agile, iterative or throw-away prototyping, or the Waterfall model.

You might not get as big a benefit as you would if you take a deep breath and take the plunge into Extreme Programming in a giant leap. Jumping in with both feet will at least help you make a clean break from your current development pattern. But there's no reason why you can't enter the shallow end of the Agile Development pool if your organization isn't ready for the whole package.

Agile Versus Traditional Lifecycles

If you compare agile methods to the lifecycle methodologies described in Chapter 2, you'll see that agile development is a variation of Iterative Prototyping. Because of the emphasis on frequent releases, it's basically Iterative Prototyping on a caffeine buzz.

Each iteration may include a complete series of lifecycle phases and may contain idea formulation, requirements gathering, feasibility analysis, high- and low-level design, implementation, and testing. Agile methods encourage frequent releases, but you don't necessarily need to give the new software to the end users. Instead, you can give minor releases to expert users so that they can give you feedback and guide the next round of development. Later, you can give only major releases to the end users when the application has accumulated enough benefits to justify the turmoil caused by installing new software.

To keep development nimble, agile methods favor lots of relatively small, quick iterations with lots of feedback from the users between each. The users may even provide feedback while iterations are under construction, not waiting for each prototype to be finished. The idea is to move toward the final application in lots of tiny steps that are continuously guided toward the goal. Each development cycle should only take a few weeks, and should produce a result that is close to release quality.

You can compare this to the Waterfall model, which makes one enormous step that you hope lands squarely on the desired result. If the requirements in the Waterfall model are incorrect, or the users' needs change during development, then the Waterfall model marches on like an unstoppable juggernaut to produce the inappropriate result specified by the requirements. Agile methods adjust as needed during the next development cycle to move back toward a usable result.

Agile development requires constant communication between users and developers. Communication is necessary at all levels of development, so customers, project managers, architects, user interface designers, programmers, testers, and document writers must all be involved.

To make communication easier, all of these people usually meet "face-to-face" in person, by phone, or in conference calls. Because of the fast pace, the decisions made during these conferences are sometimes not recorded as diligently as they would be if they were made during the planning stages of a more formal lifecycle process such as the Waterfall model. You can combat this possible failing by writing up any decisions made at these meetings. Send those notes to everyone involved so they can respond if they think there was a misunderstanding or if they think of new related issues.

Decisions are made quickly, so sometimes all of the consequences may not be completely clear until after the next round of development starts. If you keep each iteration's timeframe small enough, then you cannot go too far astray with an incorrect decision before you (hopefully) catch the problem during the next development cycle.

Agile Strengths and Weaknesses

Agile methods work particularly well for small teams of developers who work at the same location. You may also get good results if the team members are geographically separated, but in frequent contact via conference calls, although you will lose the Crystal Clear benefit of osmotic communication.

> *I've worked on several projects where we had customers move to our site for several months to provide constant testing and feedback. That type of instant feedback would have been impossible over a long distance, even with daily conference calls.*

One drawback to the agile methods is the sheer amount of communication necessary. For small projects involving four or five developers, having a meeting or conference call that involves the entire team is practical. Having even eight or ten developers work in the same large room is also possible. However, if the development group involves 40 or 50 team leaders, architects, designers, developers, and user experts, that type of conference isn't productive.

If every member of the group must communicate with every other member, the number of possible communication paths increases with the square of the number of participants. A project with 4 members has 16 possible communication pairs. A project with 50 members has 2,500 possible communication pairs, and even shaking everyone's hands would be an all-day affair.

Large projects also make building quick, incremental builds difficult. The goal of agile methods is to make every iteration at least close to release quality. If you need to integrate and test hundreds or thousands of subroutines during each cycle, you are unlikely to be able to make a new release-quality build every week or two.

To apply agile methods to larger projects, you need to break the project down and compartmentalize the pieces so that developers can work on each piece independently. Smaller project teams can apply agile methods to their pieces, and the pieces can later be assembled into the finished application. With this approach, you might use a Waterfall model to provide the basic structure, and then use agile methods to fine-tune the application's pieces.

However, any large changes discovered by one team's agile methods may have a ripple effect and impact the other teams, breaking their separation. If that occurs, you quickly lose the benefits of agile development and you are left with a rather leaky waterfall. To prevent a potential disaster, you should not skimp on the Waterfall's planning and design phases. You better make sure that the pieces of the application really are completely separate before you turn the smaller teams loose with agile methods.

Agile methods work well when you have the following:

- Experienced developers who can easily adapt to change
- A small team at a single location
- A non-critical application where uncertainty in timeline and functionality are okay
- Incorrect or imprecise specifications
- Changing requirements
- Users who don't mind frequent small releases in exchange for new features

Agile methods generally don't work well when you have the following:

- Inexperienced developers who need frequent guidance
- A large team, or team members at several locations
- Critical deadlines or requirements
- A corporate culture that requires a more formal process
- A large user population where frequent installations will be bothersome

Design by Contract

Informally, *design by contract* (DBC) is a process for describing what classes and routines expect as inputs and do as a result. A class should specify the conditions that it always maintains to be valid (*invariants*). Routines should specify the conditions they expect to see when they are called (*preconditions*) and the results they will produce (*postconditions*).

For example, a `Customer` class's contract might say that it should always have non-blank `FirstName` and `LastName` values. The class's `PrintInvoice` method might require that the object have unbilled orders associated with it as a precondition, and it might promise that those orders will be flagged as billed as a postcondition after it has generated an invoice.

If a contract is violated, you want the program's execution to stop immediately so that you can examine the code, see how the contract was violated, and fix it.

In his book *Object-Oriented Software Construction*, Bertrand Meyer (Upper Saddle River, NJ: Prentice Hall, 2000) identifies the following contract-defining items:

- *Assertion* — This is a simple logical statement that an object or routine can assert is true. For example, suppose a work assignment application matches employees with work they can perform. After performing a series of tests to find an employee who can perform a particular job, the program could assert that the employee actually *can* do the job. If the code picks an employee who cannot handle the job, the contract is violated and program execution stops.
- *Class Invariant* — This is a condition that remains true throughout an object's lifetime. The contract is violated if the invariant is ever false. For example, the `Customer` class might require that the `FirstName` and `LastName` fields always have non-blank values.
- *Method Precondition* — This is a condition that a method requires to be true when it is called. The code calling the routine must guarantee that the precondition is satisfied. For example, a `Customer` class's `PrintInvoice` method might require that its `Customer` object have associated `Order` objects that have not yet been billed when the method is called.
- *Method Postcondition* — This is a condition that a method guarantees to be true after it is called. For example, a `Customer` class's `PrintInvoice` method might guarantee that any associated `Order` objects are flagged as billed after the method returns.

You could also add to the list *method invariants* — conditions that should remain true throughout a method's execution. For example, the `Customer` class's `PrintInvoice` method should not modify the `Customer` object's data except in certain specific ways such as setting the `LastInvoicedDate` value. It should not modify the customer's name, address, or frequent buyer status.

Ideally, invariants, preconditions, and postconditions would be handled by the programming language so that they would not clutter up the main body of code. They would also be inherited by derived classes and those classes should be able to restrict, enhance, or override the inherited conditions.

Unfortunately, Visual Basic doesn't have these features. It does, however, have a fairly useful `Debug.Assert` statement. In an application compiled as a release build, `Debug.Assert` does nothing.

In an application compiled as a debug build, `Debug.Assert` evaluates a Boolean expression. If the expression is false, execution stops with an error message so that you can examine the code and figure out what caused the assertion to fail. This is where you would fix the problem with your violated contract.

You can also use the `#If` compiler directive to execute code only when the program is running as a debug release. The following code shows how your code can check conditions only if it is running in a debug build. If the program is running in a release build, the `DEBUG` compiler constant is not true so the `#If` block skips the tests.

```
#If DEBUG Then
    ' Perform tests here...
#End If
```

The following code shows how you can use `Debug.Assert` and `#If` to implement assertions, class invariants, method preconditions, and method postconditions in Visual Basic:

```
Public Class Customer
    ' Class Invariant: FirstName and LastName must be non-blank.
    ' Ensure this in constructors and property procedures.
    Public Sub New(ByVal first_name As String, ByVal last_name As String)
        FirstName = first_name
        LastName = last_name
    End Sub

    Private m_FirstName As String = ""
    Public Property FirstName() As String
        Get
            Return m_FirstName
        End Get
        Set(ByVal value As String)
            ' Invariant: FirstName must be non-blank.
            value = value.Trim()
            Debug.Assert(value.Length > 0, "FirstName value must be non-blank")

            m_FirstName = value
        End Set
    End Property

    Private m_LastName As String = ""
    Public Property LastName() As String
        Get
            Return m_LastName
        End Get
        Set(ByVal value As String)
            ' Invariant: LastName must be non-blank.
            value = value.Trim()
            Debug.Assert(value.Length > 0, "LastName value must be non-blank")

            m_LastName = value
        End Set
    End Property

    ' A collection of Order objects.
    Public Orders As New Collection

    ' Print an invoice for unbilled Orders.
    Public Sub PrintInvoices()
        ' Precondition: There must be unbilled Orders.
#If DEBUG Then
        Dim has_unbilled_order As Boolean = False
        For Each test_order As Order In Orders
            If (test_order.BilledOnDate = Nothing) Then
                has_unbilled_order = True
                Exit For
            End If
        Next test_order
        Debug.Assert(has_unbilled_order, _
```

```
                "Customer " & FirstName & " " & LastName & _
                " has no unbilled Orders before PrintInvoices")
#End If

            ' Assertion: The printer must be ready.
            Debug.Assert(g_PrinterIsReady, _
                "The printer is not ready in subroutine PrintInvoices")

            ' Generate and print the invoices.
            ' ...

            ' Postcondition: All Orders have been billed.
#If DEBUG Then
            For Each test_order As Order In Orders
                Debug.Assert(test_order.BilledOnDate <> Nothing, _
                    "Customer " & FirstName & " " & LastName & _
                    " has unbilled Orders after PrintInvoices")
            Next test_order
#End If
    End Sub
End Class
```

The `Customer` class should provide the invariant that `FirstName` and `LastName` are always non-blank. To do this, the class's constructor takes `first_name` and `last_name` parameters and assigns them to the class's `FirstName` and `LastName` properties. Visual Basic passes the values to the `FirstName` and `LastName` property procedures.

The `FirstName` and `LastName` property `Set` procedures trim their input values and use `Debug.Assert` to verify that the properties' new values are non-blank.

This code ensures that `Customer` objects always meet their contracted obligations to ensure that `FirstName` and `LastName` are non-blank, as long as those values are modified *only* through the class's constructor and property procedures. Other parts of the class must not modify the private variables `m_FirstName` and `m_LastName`. Instead, they should use the property procedures so that those procedures can enforce the invariant.

The `PrintInvoices` subroutine demonstrates method preconditions, method postconditions, and a simple assertion. When it starts, the routine uses an `#If DEBUG Then` statement to execute test code only while in a debug build. The test code loops through the object's `Order` collection looking for an `Order` object with an uninitialized `BilledOnDate` value. If it finds an `Order` with `BilledOnDate` equal to `Nothing`, the code sets the Boolean variable `has_unbilled_order` to true and stops looking. After it has finished examining the `Orders`, the test code uses `Debug.Assert` to require that `has_unbilled_order` is true.

If the program gets past this test, it enforces an assertion. It uses `Debug.Assert` to verify that the `g_PrinterIsReady` global variable has a true value.

After the routine generates and prints invoices, it uses an `#If DEBUG Then` statement to perform a test that enforces a postcondition. This test loops through the `Customer's Orders` collection and uses `Debug.Assert` to ensure that every `Order` object's `BilledOnDate` is not `Nothing`.

Note that the `PrintInvoices` subroutine checks its postcondition at the end. If the subroutine exits before reaching this test, the postcondition is not verified. If you want to ensure that postconditions are verified, you may want to adopt a coding standard that requires all routines to exit from a single point immediately after verifying any postconditions.

An alternative approach would be to wrap the main computation in a new routine that performs the precondition checks, calls the main computation routine, and then verifies the postconditions, as shown in the following code:

```
Public Sub PrintInvoices()
    ' Precondition: There must be unbilled Orders.
    ...

    ' Perform the actual computation.
    DoPrintInvoices()

    ' Postcondition: All Orders have been billed.
    ...
End Sub
```

This approach makes the main computation routine simpler and easier to read by removing all of the messy precondition and postcondition code. Now that routine only needs to contain code that deals directly with its main task (plus any assertions you need to make).

Another potential problem to watch for in this code is exception handling. If the code throws an exception, control may pass out of the wrapper routine without passing through the postcondition tests. That may or may not be appropriate for your application. The routine's contract may stipulate that the postcondition only holds if the routine completes normally. If that's the case, then you're done.

If you want to enforce the postcondition even if the routine throws an exception, move the call to the main computation routine and the postcondition testing into a `Try Catch Finally` block, as shown in the following code. Visual Basic executes the postcondition check in the `Finally` section, even if subroutine `DoPrintInvoices` throws an exception and this code re-throws it the `Catch` section.

```
Public Sub PrintInvoices()
    ' Precondition: There must be unbilled Orders.
    ...

    Try
        ' Perform the actual computation.
        DoPrintInvoices()
    Catch ex As Exception
        ' Rethrow the exception.
        Throw ex
    Finally
        ' Postcondition: All Orders have been billed.
        ...
    End Try
End Sub
```

Using design by contract in this way is in some ways very similar to test-driven development where the tests are incorporated into the routine as postconditions. While test-driven development requires you to run the tests when you have finished writing or modifying the code, this technique makes the code automatically re-test itself every time it executes.

To get the full benefits of test-driven development, you should write the postcondition testing code before you write the main body of the computation. See the earlier section, "Test-Driven Development," to see why it is important to write the tests before you write the code.

Preconditions and general assertions are new additions to your testing toolkit that go beyond test-driven development. They add an extra dimension to testing that can catch false assumptions that might make your routine return incorrect results. By pinning the blame on the inputs and intermediate results, preconditions and assertions help narrow down the area in which a bug might lie. They help you focus more quickly on the actual problem, while letting you avoid searching through your code for problems that lie elsewhere.

I want to make one final point about design by contract. To get the greatest possible benefit from it, you need to make contracts as precise and demanding as possible. The preconditions should check for every possible situation that could cause the routine to go wrong. They should verify that every incoming parameter is present and in a valid format. It may help to imagine yourself as a lawyer and that the contract is the only thing protecting your client (the subroutine) from being sued. If someone else's code calls your routine, your tests must either flag the data as invalid, or return a valid, usable result.

Microsoft Tools for Agile Development

Visual Studio Team System includes a tool called Microsoft Solutions Framework (MSF) for Agile Software Development. Microsoft partners are working on integrating tools to support specific agile methodologies, such as Scrum and Feature Driven Development.

Here's how Microsoft describes this tool:

> **MSF for Agile Software Development is a scenario-driven, context-based, agile software development process that utilizes many of the ideas embodied in Visual Studio Team System. This process incorporates proven practices developed at Microsoft around requirements, design, security, performance, and testing. MSF for Agile for Software Development is the first agile process for the end to end software development lifecycle.**

MSF for Agile Development is based in part on the processes Microsoft has been using for several years to develop its own products. (Given how late some of those products have been over the last few releases, this may not seem like much of an endorsement.)

Visual Studio Team System is a tool designed to integrate all participants in application development. It includes roles for the entire development team, including customers (which it calls "business stakeholders"), project managers, architects, developers, and testers. It contains tools for collaboration, so all of the team members can work closely together. It integrates such development aspects as source code control, and metric reporting to help the development team track its progress.

MSF is a customizable set of processes that help lead the development effort. It provides guidance for different tasks and stages of development.

You can learn a lot more about MSF for Agile Development at `msdn.microsoft.com/vstudio/teamsystem/msf/msfagile/default.aspx`. This page includes links to articles describing Microsoft's vision of agile development, overviews of the agile development process in general, blogs related to the tool, and other useful information.

Summary

This chapter described agile methods for controlling application development. Whereas traditional life-cycle models rely on predictive planning, agile methods are reactive. They produce a quick, small result; compare it to the desired outcome; and then adjust accordingly. Instead of a large, planned progression toward a goal that is well-planned-out in advance, they make lots of little steps to constantly improve the application until it is usable.

Agile development is not for every project. It works best with relatively small projects where the whole development team works in the same location so communication can be fast and easy. It handles uncertain or changing requirements more easily than less-reactive methodologies such as the Waterfall model.

Some have argued that you're not really doing Extreme Programming unless you follow all 12 of the "official" Extreme Programming practices, but you can still get some benefit by applying a subset of the agile techniques to other development models. Any model will benefit from coding standards, test-driven development, and design by contract. It may not be Extreme Programming but Iterative Prototyping with design by contract is better than Iterative Prototyping without.

Both this chapter and Chapter 2 focused on control of the development process at a high level. Chapter 4, "Object-Oriented Design," turns to the lower-level task of object-oriented design. This is the first step on the path from requirements representing the users' needs and desires to the code that will satisfy them.

4

Object-Oriented Design

This chapter discusses how to design the classes that make up the application. It explains the major goals of object-oriented programming, and how they relate to the application's classes.

This chapter also explains how you can use different views of the system to get a better understanding of the application as a whole. It introduces the Universal Modeling Language (UML), which you can use to help specify and understand the application before you start building it, and describes some UML design tools that you can use to model the application.

The Bug Hunter Example

The sections in this chapter explain different ways to characterize an application. They discuss the program from the point of view of the users, architects, developers, and others.

To make the discussion easier, each section works with the same example: a hypothetical bug tracking application named Bug Hunter. This application allows users to enter bug reports. A bug manager reviews each report and assigns it to an appropriate developer. The developer reviews the bug, tries to reproduce it, fixes the bug (hopefully), and clears the bug. A release coordinator then performs regression testing, revises the application and user documentation, and then releases a new version of the code.

In some cases, the bug can follow a different path, looping back to a previous state. For example, if the assigned developer cannot reproduce the bug, it is sent back to the user for clarification. If regression testing shows that the bug fix broke something, the bug is sent back to the developer for reevaluation.

Throughout this process, users can view the status of a particular bug to see if it is new, under review, assigned, under study, fixed, or released. The user can generate reports showing information about bugs, selected and ordered in various ways, such as a particular bug, all bugs, bugs with certain severity levels, bugs submitted during a particular time range, or bugs in various states (new, assigned, fixed, and so forth).

The bug manager and release coordinator can also select reports that are not available to the users (such as the code modules containing the bugs, the developers who wrote code containing bugs, and so forth).

Building an Object Model

Before you can start building an application, you must identify the classes that you will use. Once these classes are defined, they will quickly become intertwined with the developers' code. Changing, removing, or replacing them later becomes very difficult. You may be able to add new properties and methods to a class. However, making large changes is time-consuming and likely to affect the existing code.

To avoid needless drudgery and frustration, you should spend extra time at the beginning of the project identifying the major classes that you will use, spelling out their roles and responsibilities, and defining (at least in general terms) their properties, methods, and events.

The following sections describe some methods you can use to pick classes for developers to use.

Picking Candidate Classes

One way of picking candidate classes is to take a close look at the project's written specification or description, and highlight all of the nouns in the text. For now, focus on nouns that are objects, such as document, user, and report. Skip concepts and activities, such as testing and evaluation. The nouns you have highlighted are the candidate classes.

The following text is the description of the Bug Hunter application with the candidate nouns in bold:

> *This **application** allows users to enter **bug reports**. A **bug manager** reviews each **report** and assigns it to an appropriate **developer**. The **developer** reviews the **bug**, tries to reproduce it, fixes the **bug** (hopefully), and clears the **bug**. A **release coordinator** then performs regression testing, revises the **application** and **user documentation**, and then releases a **new version of the code**.*
>
> *In some cases, the **bug** can follow a different **path**, looping back to a previous **state**. For example, if the assigned **developer** cannot reproduce the **bug**, it is sent back to the **user** for clarification. If regression testing shows that the **bug** fix broke **something**, the **bug** is sent back to the **developer** for reevaluation.*
>
> *Throughout this process, **users** can view the **status** of a particular **bug** to see if it is new, under review, assigned, under study, fixed, or released. The **user** can generate **reports** showing information about **bugs**, selected and ordered in various ways, such as a **particular bug**, **all bugs**, **bugs with certain severity levels**, **bugs submitted during a particular time range**, or **bugs in various states** (new, assigned, fixed, and so forth).*
>
> *The **bug manager** and **release coordinator** can also select **reports** that are not available to the **users** (such as the **code modules** containing the **bugs**, the **developers** who wrote **code** containing **bugs**, and so forth).*

Next, combine any duplicates and make a list. Add comments, if necessary, to clarify a word's meaning. For example, the word "something" is too vague to be useful by itself. The following list shows the bold nouns from the previous text:

- all bugs (report)
- application
- bug
- bug manager
- bug report
- bugs in various states (report)
- bugs submitted during a particular time range (report)
- bugs with selected severity levels (report)
- code modules containing the bugs (report)
- developer
- new version of the code
- particular bug (report)
- path (a bug report's path through the states/statuses)
- release coordinator
- something (a piece of code broken by a bug fix)
- state (of a bug report)
- status (of a bug report)
- the developers who wrote code containing bugs (report)
- user
- user documentation

Note that picking candidate classes in this way requires that you have a good specification. If the specification is vague, it won't include all of the nouns that you will need for the classes. The specification is the starting point for building a list of candidate classes, not the final story. If something seems to be missing, take another look at the specification and see if it completely describes what the program needs to do.

Converting Candidates into Classes

After you compile the initial candidate list, you must look over the items and decide which will make good classes, and what interactions there are among them.

This list contains some items that represent the same concepts. The items "state" and "status" are really the same concept, so you can remove one of them. Let's remove "state." Similarly, "bug" and "bug report" represent the same idea, the data about a bug, so let's remove "bug."

Looking at the list, you can see a couple of general categories. There are several different kinds of reports. There are also four kinds of people: user, bug manager, developer, and release coordinator. You should pull these related objects out into groups. Such groups of objects often indicate a close relationship, and may be a sign of inheritance, composition, or other close coupling.

Think about the groups and decide whether these objects are the same type of thing at some level, or whether they are just closely related. In this example, user, bug manager, developer, and release coordinator are all the same sort of thing: people. It's even easier to see that all of the reports are types of reports.

Because the objects are the same sort of thing, it probably makes sense to combine them by making them inherit from parent classes. Study these items further and see how much they have in common because they are the same type of thing. The people items all have characteristics of people: name, address, phone number, and so forth.

Different people will also have different permissions for using application features. For example, the bug manager and release coordinator can make reports showing bugs by module or developer, whereas the users cannot.

The report items are less well-defined at this point, so it's a bit more difficult to know what they have in common. Drawing on previous experience with other applications, however, you can guess that they will all need methods for building the report, setting report parameters, saving the report into a file, printing, exporting the report for analysis in a spreadsheet and possibly other file formats, and so forth.

Armed with this information, you can *generalize* the groups by pulling their common features into a parent class, and making the items in the previous list child classes.

Now, consider the remaining items and think about the types of roles they will play in the application. Decide whether the item represents a single piece of data, a more complex data structure with multiple fields, something that performs an action (or on which important actions are performed), or a combination of these.

You can model a single piece of data by using normal variables such as strings, integers, or arrays of similar simple data types.

You can implement a complex data structure in Visual Basic by using either a structure or a class. Both structures and classes can provide methods, so you can use either to represent something that performs actions.

> *The difference between a structure and a class in Visual Basic is mainly one of how the item is allocated. A structure is allocated when it is declared, whereas a class is allocated when you use the* `New` *keyword. For example, if you declare an array of 1,000 structures, Visual Basic allocates memory for them when it reaches the declaration. If you allocate 1,000 class objects, Visual Basic only allocates memory for references to the objects, and doesn't create the objects themselves until you initialize them individually by using the* `New` *statement. There are also a few additional differences (such as the fact that structures don't have constructors). I usually use classes, at least partly because they can have constructors.*

The "bug report" item contains information about a bug, so it represents a piece of data. It is also a very central concept to the system: a user creates it, the bug manager assigns it, a developer works it, and the release coordinator releases it. It takes part in reports and requires user documentation. The fact that this item plays a role in so many activities indicates that it is something special. Let's make it a class.

In the earlier description of Bug Hunter, "application" refers to Bug Hunter in a fairly general way, and it doesn't really do anything specific. At most, you could use it to represent application properties such as the version number, release date, and so forth. Because this information changes rarely (only when new versions are created) and because the "application" item doesn't need to perform any action, let's tentatively remove it from the list. The program will store application information such as version number in the program's properties and in the data describing a bug report.

> *I've seen many systems where object enthusiasts insist on creating objects for even small items such as this. They would create an* `ApplicationInformation` *class whose sole purpose is to load and save these few data values. I prefer to initially keep these items simple and make them more elaborate later only if it proves absolutely necessary.*

Similarly "new version of the code" refers to a new program build to fix a bug. The new code itself is stored outside of the program in some sort of source code control system. Though this is an important part of the Bug Hunter system as a whole, it's not properly part of the code.

The "user documentation" item also refers to something external to the program. Updating the documentation is an important activity, but it's not part of Bug Hunter. Even if the program displays the documentation online, it is the release coordinator, not the program, that updates the documentation. You could add a property to the "bug report" object to record the version number of the documentation produced in response to the bug, but even that may not be necessary. It's more common for the documentation to include a revision history that will indicate that it was revised because of the bug.

The "path" item represents the path a bug report takes through the system as it is created, assigned, worked, and released. Whether you need to keep this item depends on whether you really care about the job's path through the system or whether you just need to know that the job follows *some* path. In some applications it is important to know an object's complete history.

For example, if you are processing financial information, you may need to establish a chain of custody so you know exactly who did what to the data and when. In that case, you might want to implement an audit trail system where the application saves a record every time the data is modified (and possibly viewed).

For Bug Hunter, let's assume that you just want to know that a bug report flows through the system and you don't need to remember all of the steps, so let's remove "path" from the list.

The "status" item represents a bug report's current state in the system. This item takes specific values such as `New`, `Assigned`, and `Released`. The "status" item is a single enumerated value that applies to a bug report, so let's make it a property of the "bug report" object. In the Visual Basic code, let's make the list of possible values an enumerated type.

Finally, the "something (a piece of code broken by a bug fix)" item represents the code that was fixed. This is another item that lies outside of Bug Hunter's code. However, the program's description says that the bug manager should be able to generate reports showing bugs by module and bugs by developer. To provide those reports, the program must know where the bugs occurred and who created the bugs. These are fairly simple data items, and the program won't do anything with them other than report them, so let's make these properties of the "bug report" item. After fixing a bug, the developer should enter this information in the "bug report" data.

Figure 4-1 shows the initial object model.

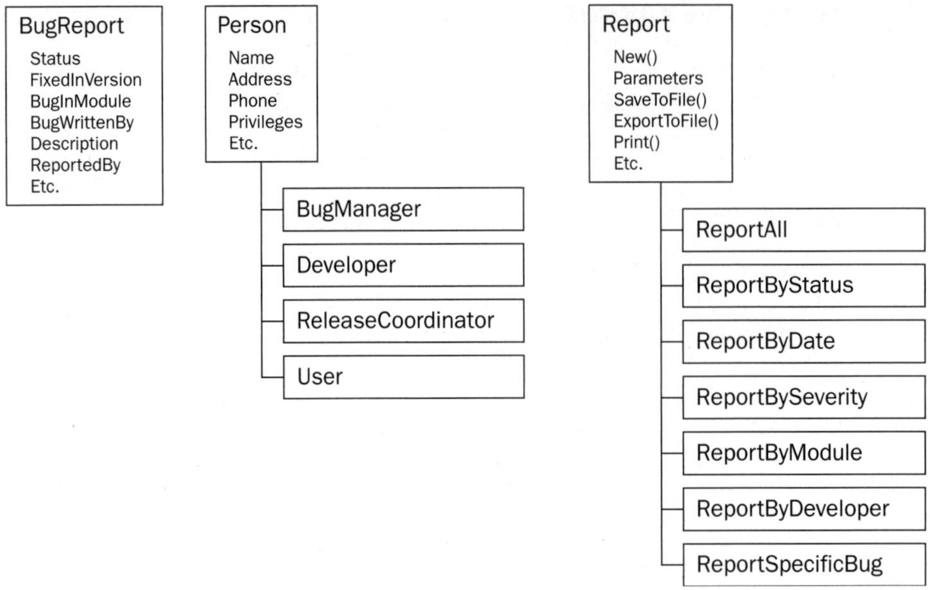

Figure 4-1: The initial object model contains objects extracted from the program's description.

Adding Internal Classes

Sometimes an application's object model needs additional classes that don't correspond to the physical objects mentioned in the project description. These classes provide features that the developers need to build as parts of the system, but they are often hidden from the users.

Sometimes you may know that these classes are necessary from previous experience. In a similar application, you may have used a `PriorityQueue` class that you think will be useful for keeping bug reports ordered by priority.

Other times you will discover that you need new classes as you develop the classes that you have already defined. You may discover that the `Report` object's `ExportToFile` method would best be implemented by a group of classes that can handle different export formats (such as tabbed text, comma-separated value, Excel workbook, and others).

You may find additional classes when you apply design patterns to the application's design. Model-view-controller, facade, adapter, and other design patterns add new classes to the design.

It's often useful to look at the places where the application interacts with the outside world to identify new classes. That includes places that read or write files, such as the `ExportToFile` method mentioned earlier. It also includes places where the application must read or send email, upload or download files from the Internet, print reports, send faxes, interact with Windows or other applications, and interact with different components of your application.

Adding Database Classes

A particularly common interaction is with a database. Many programs read and write data in a database, and they can use classes to make that easier. Higher-level classes can act as factories for reading and writing certain other kinds of objects. For example, a `DbPersonFactory` class might have methods that can build and save `Person` objects in the database. A database-level class might provide methods for inserting, updating, querying, and deleting data. Higher-level classes could use its methods instead of accessing the database directly.

Separation between the day-to-day development classes and the database is important so that developers don't need to remember the details of the database's structure and the particular database engine's access methods. For example, Access and Oracle databases delimit dates differently. The database classes should hide this from higher-level classes.

However, I've worked on several applications where developers got carried away and added too many extra layers of classes trying to increase the separation between the developers and the database. That made tracing a piece of data through the system almost impossible. I've seen code that climbed through 30 or 35 layers of call stack involving dozens of objects to retrieve a relatively simple piece of data. This is not only inefficient, but it's also incredibly hard to debug.

Use classes for separation, but strive for broad, shallow object hierarchies, instead of very long inheritance chains or deep stacks of method calls.

Often, the tables in a database map naturally to classes within the program. Perform a quick study of the program's data needs and design a preliminary database. Now see if any of the tables should correspond to classes.

Tables that are related in the database often correspond to classes that are related in a similar way. Bug Hunter will probably need a `BugReports` table to store information about bugs and a `People` table to store information about people.

There are two one-to-many relationships between the `BugReports` table and the `People` table because each `BugReports` record will contain references to the `User` who created the report and the `Developer` who is assigned to it. These are one-to-many relationships because each `BugReports` record refers to a single creating user and assigned developer, while each user or developer can be associated with any number of `BugReports` records.

You will probably want to model this relationship by giving the `BugReport` class references to the corresponding `User` and `Developer` objects.

Studying Different Design Views

It has been repeatedly shown that the longer it takes to find a bug in an application, the more difficult it is to fix. Design decisions are particularly important, because you make them near the beginning of the project and because they have such wide-ranging consequences. A big mistake in the initial design can make the entire project fail.

One of the easiest ways to make big design mistakes is to not understand the application thoroughly. If you don't understand the customers' needs, you can't design classes to satisfy them. If you don't understand the application's internal needs, you can't design the classes that it needs to get the job done.

To gain the best possible understanding of the system, you should look at the application from as many points of view as possible. Some of the different views you should consider include the following:

- *Object View*—Perform an object-oriented analysis to define likely classes to represent the physical objects in the system. Group and combine objects, build an inheritance hierarchy, refine the objects, and so forth.
- *GUI View*—Sketch out a rough user-interface design. Then think about the types of data the program will need to support that interface. Often, the items displayed on the screen match underlying classes. Chapter 5, "User-Interface Design," has more to say about designing the application's user interface.
- *Data View*—Identify the data that the system needs. Decide where the data should reside: in classes, global variables, or someplace else. Design the database if you need one and see if the tables in the database naturally map to classes.
- *Document View*—In many applications, the users work on some sort of document. In Bug Hunter, the central document is a bug report. Often these documents correspond to classes. Mentally follow the documents through the system and identify the entities that interact with them. In Bug Hunter, these are the different kinds of people and reports. Often, these entities should also be implemented as classes.
- *Case View*—Step through the use cases that you and the users have defined for the application. See if the classes you have defined contain all of the necessary ingredients to handle the use cases. Look for new nouns in the use cases that might make good classes.

The Universal Modeling Language (UML), described later in this chapter, can help you characterize the details of different aspects of the application's design and behavior. It gives you a representation that you and the other application designers can use to study the design meaningfully. Later, it can give developers guidance so they share a common vision of how the system should work.

UML also gives you several new views from which to examine the system, so even if you are the sole designer and developer on the project, you may get some benefit from using UML.

Improving the Classes

For years, object-oriented developers have focused on three important characteristics of object-oriented languages: encapsulation, polymorphism, and inheritance. These three principles make classes more powerful and easier to use with fewer chances for errors.

Unfortunately, many focus so tightly on those three principles that they forget the purpose behind the dogma. By keeping in mind the reasons why those three concepts are useful, you can generalize them and apply similar principles to higher-level design tasks. Most experienced developers understand that a well-designed class should provide encapsulation, polymorphism, and inheritance. It's less clear how you can apply the underlying concepts to improve the design of higher-level entities such as application systems and subsystems.

The following sections describe encapsulation, polymorphism, and inheritance. They also extract the underlying ideas and explain how you can apply them to the application's higher-level organization.

Encapsulation

Encapsulation is the idea that a class should wrap up its implementation details in a tight little package. The class provides an interface (properties, methods, and events) that lets other parts of the program interact with the class's objects, but it keeps the details about how it does its job a closely held secret.

Many programmers justify encapsulation by saying that it makes the rest of the program less dependent on the class's code. If you later need to change the way the class works, you will not need to modify the rest of the program to work with the new code.

For example, suppose an `Invoice` class looks up a customer's data and the list of items that customer has purchased, adds up the items' prices, and prints an invoice. The main program can create an `Invoice` object and call its `MakeInvoice` method to make and print an invoice.

Now, suppose the company decides to create a new Preferred Customer program that gives any customer a 10 percent across-the-board discount on every order after the customer has purchased $10,000 worth of goods. You need to modify the `Invoice` class so it checks the value of the customer's previous orders. If the customer has placed $10,000 worth of orders, the `Invoice` class applies the 10 percent discount and prints the invoice.

Because the `Invoice` class encapsulates the invoice generation and printing process, you don't need to change the rest of the application. The main program still creates an `Invoice` object and calls its `MakeInvoice` method exactly as before. The details of how the `MakeInvoice` method works is safely hidden from the main program.

You can also think of the ability to change one part of the application without messing up another part as *loose coupling*. The different systems are related, but loosely enough that changes to one don't necessarily require changes to the others. Although developers think of encapsulation as a class-level concept, loose coupling applies equally to all levels of the project. Keeping the user interface, report generation, invoicing, inventory, and other major systems as loosely coupled as possible means changes to one are less likely to require changes to the others.

A second part to encapsulation that is sometimes overlooked is the simple fact that it hides information about the class's internals. This is such an integral part of encapsulation that encapsulation is sometimes called *information hiding*.

Even if hiding the class's internals didn't promote loose coupling, it would still have a large benefit for developers because it allows them to use the class without worrying about what's going on beneath the surface, thus reducing the developer's cognitive load. The developer can use the class and assume that it works.

This may seem like the smaller of encapsulation's two effects, but it can have a big impact, particularly if you apply the idea to the higher levels of the application design. If the report generation system hides its internal details from developers, those developers can work on their own pieces of code, calling the report generation system as needed, without worrying about how it works.

On a large project where different teams implement the application's various systems, keeping the systems as independent as possible is absolutely crucial. You must allow the teams to work separately to get their pieces of the application done as quickly as possible. Information hiding allows members of one system's team do their jobs without needing to consult with the members of the other teams.

One really strong way to promote loose coupling is to build parts of the application as dynamic link libraries (DLLs), components, and controls. Most developers have the sense that classes in these kinds of modules are separate entities. That makes them less likely to try to break the class's encapsulation than they might be if the class was simply another class in the same code base. Putting the class in a separate code library adds a "barrier to messing around" with the code.

Of course, if it's harder to modify the library's code, then you'd better spend some extra time up front to ensure that the library can handle all of the requests that the developers will need to make of it. The extra work at the beginning will be more than repaid by the additional isolation you get between the application's systems.

To summarize, encapsulation really includes two concepts: loose coupling and information hiding. Both of these are beneficial when you build a class, but they are also useful at the higher levels of application design.

Hide as many of the details as possible within a class. Provide public access to the bare essentials that other code needs to get the job done. If it later turns out that a piece of vital information that is hidden within the class must be exposed, you can add it later. It's better to start out too restrictive and loosen access than it is to start too loose and create dependencies that will be hard to implement, debug, and maintain.

Polymorphism and Inheritance

Encapsulation, polymorphism, and inheritance are the three main characteristics of object-oriented programming. As the previous section explains, you can maximize encapsulation in your classes and system-level design to make the application easier to build, debug, and maintain.

Polymorphism and inheritance, however, are more descriptions of objects, rather than advice on how to use them.

Polymorphism means the ability to use one object as if it were another type of object. In particular, it means that the code should be able to treat an object as if it had the type of its ancestor classes. You should be able to treat a `User` object as if it were a `Person` because `User` is a child class of `Person`. `User` is a type of `Person`, so a `User` is actually also a `Person`. Note that the reverse is not true: a `Person` is not necessarily a type of `User`.

In practice, this means that you can pass a `User` object into a routine that expects a `Person`. You can also store a `User` object in a variable that is a reference to a `Person`.

Inheritance means that derived classes inherit the properties, methods, and events of their parent classes. A `User` object has all of the features of a `Person` object, possibly with some additional features. The `User` class may also modify some of the `Person` features (for example, overriding or shadowing them).

It's hard to see how you would change a class's definition to gain the most benefit from polymorphism and inheritance, much less how to apply those principles at a higher design level. It helps to ask why these capabilities are useful.

Both polymorphism and inheritance provide forms of code reuse. If a routine manipulates derived classes as if they belonged to the parent class, you don't need to write separate routines to handle each derived class. If you write a routine to send email to a `Person` object, you don't need to write separate routines to deal with `User`, `BugManager`, `Developer`, and `ReleaseCoordinator` objects.

Similarly, inheritance allows derived classes to reuse the code in their parent classes. If the `Person` class defines `Name`, `Address`, and `Phone` properties, you don't need to define those properties in the `User`, `BugManager`, `Developer`, and `ReleaseCoordinator` classes.

To take the greatest advantage of polymorphism, design and later program with the highest-level, most abstract object types that you can. Suppose the application needs a piece of code that generates a report listing bugs by date created and then prints the report. Rather than making the code work with a `ReportByDate` object, write it to work with a variable from the parent class `Report`. Then you can reuse the code to work with other kinds of reports. You may need to add some additional code to create the different kinds of reports (or use a factory object to create the report without knowing what type it is), but the rest of the routine should be the same for each report type.

To get the most out of inheritance, move functionality as high up the inheritance hierarchy as possible. If the derived classes all have similar functionality, move the functionality into the parent class. Then the benefits of inheritance follow automatically.

> *These ideas of looking for ways to make code more general sometimes contradict the agile philosophy of implementing the simplest possible solution for the given situation without regard for code you will need to write later.*
>
> *For example, if you need to sort a list that could contain up to three integers, a simple series of* `If Then` *statements will suffice. There's no need to waste extra time writing a powerful routine that uses the bucketsort algorithm to sort huge numbers of values of arbitrary data types. That version will be harder to write, debug, and maintain, and would provide no additional advantage over the simpler solution.*
>
> *Though the keep-it-simple philosophy is important for agile development (and actually applies to non-agile development, too), there's no need to be intentionally stupid. If you see an opportunity to make the code more flexible without a lot of extra effort, take it. This is particularly important during the early stages of design where decisions will have far-reaching consequences.*

When you write a subroutine or design a class, ask yourself if small changes would make it more general. Can you make the routine work with more generic ancestor objects? Can you move common features into a parent class? Both of these will promote code reuse.

UML

Universal Modeling Language (UML) is a design tool that developers can use to model a system's behavior. The idea is that a set of UML diagrams, use cases, and other depictions are to software engineers what blueprints are to structural engineers and architects. Once you have a UML representation of an application, you should be able to send that representation to all of the developers so that everyone has the same view of how the system should behave. With this common vision, the developers can then start implementing their separate pieces of the systems, confident that they are all working toward the same goal.

In addition to providing a consistent model of the application's behavior for the developers, some projects use UML to allow the users to help specify and understand the application. Unfortunately, UML is not intuitively obvious. It takes some training and practice to use UML effectively. Few users have experience with UML, and training them in its use can be difficult and time-consuming. Even after they understand the ideas of UML, they may not have a good understanding of what the diagrams really mean. If you have sophisticated users that either already understand UML or who pick it up quickly, you can use UML to help ensure that the design implemented by the developers matches the expectations of the users as specified by the diagrams. If your users don't have previous experience with UML, you might want to focus only on the most intuitive diagrams: use case diagrams and activity diagrams.

In the projects I've worked on, we always tried to interact with the users in their own language. We used simple tools that they use regularly and that are comfortable for them, such as word processing applications, spreadsheets, email, telephones, and face-to-face conversations. We wanted them to focus on their knowledge of the problem space and not get bogged down trying to learn UML or other development tools. We wanted the users to concentrate on what they wanted to happen, and let the developers make software architecture decisions.

The following sections describe the most common types of diagrams defined by UML. The intent of these sections is to give you an idea of what UML can do, not to be an exhaustive tutorial. They describe only relatively simple versions of the diagrams. UML is a fairly complicated tool and includes many detailed variations. To really learn UML, see a book about the subject such as *Professional UML with Visual Studio .NET* by Andrew Filev et al. (Indianapolis: Wrox, 2002) or *UML in Practice: The Art of Modeling Software Systems Demonstrated thorough Worked Examples and Solutions* by Pascal Roques (Indianapolis: John Wiley & Sons, 2004).

Use Case Diagrams

A use case is a script for an action that the users will perform with the system. It describes the steps that a user will follow to perform some specific task. When the application is finished, the users can run through the use cases to verify that the application can handle them all.

The use cases for the bug reporting system describe how the users perform various actions. For example, these would include the following:

- User enters a bug report.
- Bug manager reviews a bug and assigns it to a developer.
- Developer reproduces the bug, studies it, fixes it, and moves it into the "fixed" state.
- Developer fails to reproduce the bug and returns it to the user for more information.
- Developer reproduces the bug, studies it, discovers it should be better handled by another developer, and returns it to the bug manager for reassignment.
- Release coordinator tests the fix and releases a new executable and user documentation.
- User generates a report giving a specific bug's status.
- User generates a report listing all bugs with a specific state (for example, "open").
- User generates a report listing all bugs with a specific priority (for example, "high").
- Bug manager generates a report showing all bugs by code module.
- Bug manager generates a report showing total time spent clearing bugs in code by code module.

An application such as this one could easily have several dozen use cases. Depending on the number and types of reports needed, it could have more than 100 use cases.

> *I've worked on projects with a wide variety of use case needs. Some projects have only a couple of fairly straightforward use cases. One of my most recent projects had only one use case, but it was extremely complex, involving about two dozen steps and close to 1,000 data entry fields. Other projects I've worked on had more than 100 use cases.*
>
> *A project's complexity and flexibility determines the number of use cases. In fact, the number of use cases you and the users can come up with is a reasonable first measure of how complex an application will be, although sometimes a fairly simple but powerful application can provide enough flexibility to handle a large number of use cases.*

Typically, a use case is a script that explains what each of the *actors* in the scenario need to do. It should specify *what* needs to be done, but not *how* it should be done. The application's design will determine how the actors accomplish their tasks.

For example, the use case for entering a new bug report might look like the following:

> **The user enters data describing the bug including:**
>
> - **Bug priority**
> - **Date and time of bug**
> - **Description of what the user was trying to do**
> - **Description of actions the user took**
> - **Description of what actually happened**
> - **Error messages received**
> - **Operating system and computer hardware**
> - **Application version**
>
> **The program should automatically display the user's ID and include it in the bug report.**
>
> **After the user has entered the data, the application should save the bug report and flag it so the bug manager can review and assign it.**

The purpose of the UML *use case diagrams* is to help you visualize how the system's actors interact with the use cases. They also show how the use cases relate to each other by showing which actors perform the use cases. For example, the "User enters a bug report" use case is related to the "User creates bug reports" use cases because the same actor performs them: the user.

Use cases are drawn as ellipses. Actors are drawn as stick figures. Lines connect the actors to the use cases that they perform.

To keep the use case diagrams simple, use cases are grouped into categories. Instead of listing every possible user report use case, the diagram contains a single object representing the "generate basic reports" group of use cases.

Figure 4-2 shows a use case diagram for the Bug Hunter application.

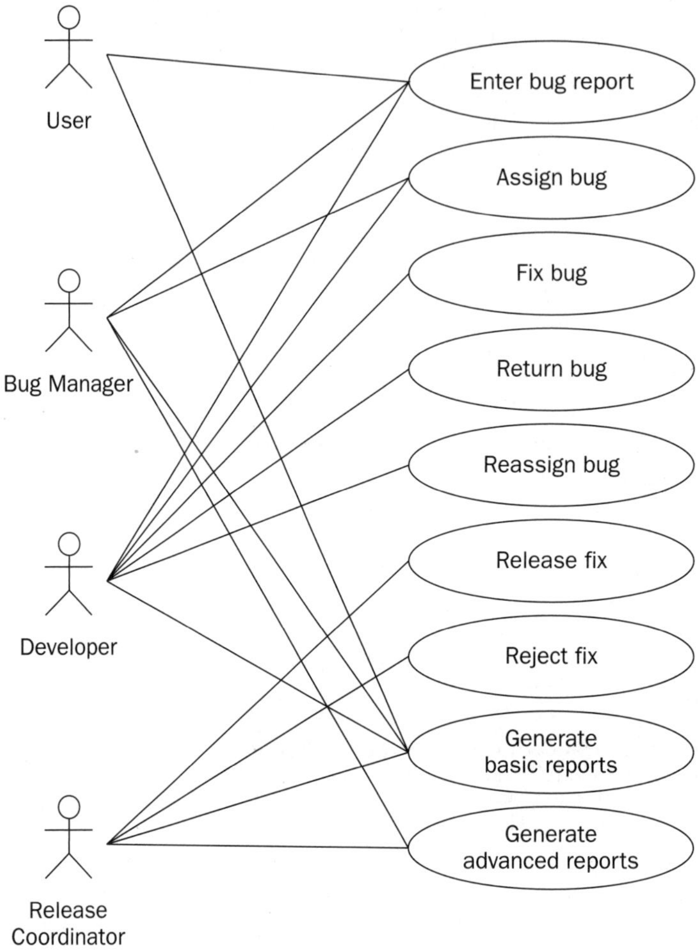

Figure 4-2: Use case diagrams show the relationships between actors and use cases.

The diagram also helps clarify who performs which actions for use cases that may not have been initially spelled out in the requirements. In this example, the diagram shows that every actor can generate basic reports (bugs by severity, bugs by status), but only the bug manager and release coordinator can generate advanced reports (bugs by module, bugs by developer).

From Figure 4-2, you can also see that some use cases are naturally grouped in a one-to-one mapping with certain actors. For example, only the developer performs the "Fix bug," "Return bug," and "Reassign bug" use cases, so you could group them into a larger category of "Developer cases." Similarly you could group the "Release fix" and "Reject fix" use cases into "Release coordinator cases."

Use case diagrams can help the users understand the different roles the systems will define. This example defines four roles: user, bug manager, developer, and release coordinator. The use case diagram shows which activities these actors will perform. Often, you can use this as a basis for the application's permission model.

Class Diagrams

Class diagrams show how the major entities in the system are related to each other. These form a static view of the system showing relationships among objects in the system, and do not consider the system's dynamics (such as the flow of information or method call sequences).

Figure 4-3 shows the simplest diagram to represent a class. It is labeled at the top with the class's name. The next section lists the class's properties. Below that are the class's methods.

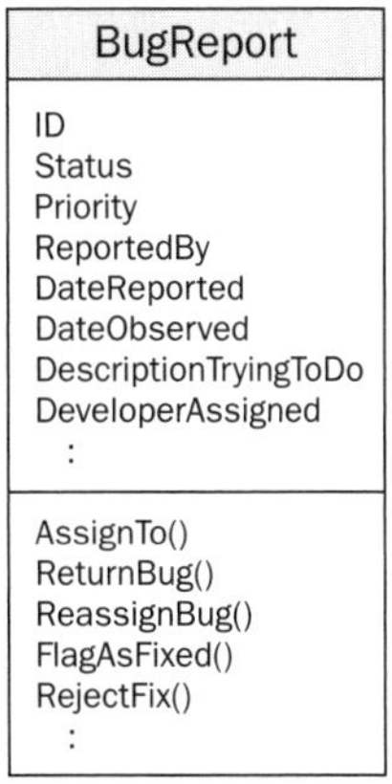

Figure 4-3: A simple class diagram shows a class's name, properties, and methods.

You can define much more complicated versions of the class diagram if you like to show details such as property data types, method parameters and return types (for functions), and events. Some UML drawing tools add icons to the left of the entries to indicate property or method. If you add every possible piece of information, however, the class diagrams can become so cluttered that they are hard to use. Start with simple diagrams and add details only if you need them. Often, a very simple diagram such as the one shown in Figure 4-3 is good enough to let you work on high-level design and study communications among classes.

A class diagram can show relationships among application domain objects. Those are the objects that the users are familiar with, and include data objects such as the bug report, reports the user may generate, and so forth.

You can use other class diagrams to study the classes that the program's code will use. The objects in that diagram might include queues, objects representing database tables, and so forth. Generally, these diagrams are meaningful only to the developers, and not the users.

To indicate relationships among classes, you draw lines between them. Arrowheads and labels further define the types of relationships.

To indicate that one class is inherited from another, use a hollow triangular arrowhead pointing to the parent class. Figure 4-4 shows an *inheritance diagram* that indicates the `User`, `BugManager`, `Developer`, and `ReleaseCoordinator` classes inherit from the `Person` class.

To indicate a non-inheritance relationship between two classes, use a solid line. If only one of the classes is aware of the other, use an arrowhead to point to the class that is unaware of the other. You can add labels to indicate the number of objects from each class in the relationship.

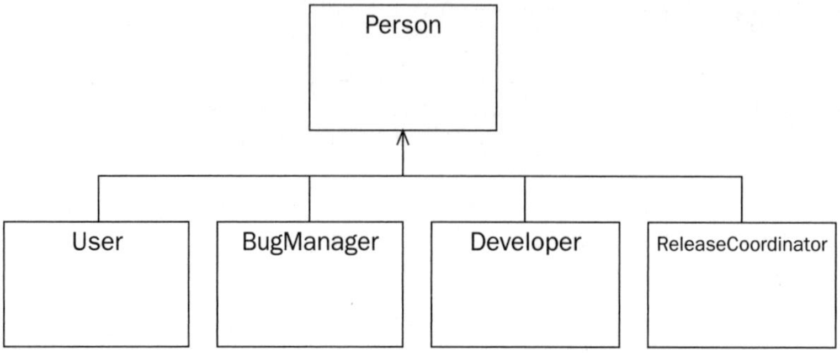

Figure 4-4: A class diagram can show an inheritance hierarchy.

In the *relationship diagram* shown in Figure 4-5, the `ReportSingleBug` object represents a report about a single bug. It is associated in a one-to-one relationship with the `BugReport` object representing the selected bug report. The `ReportSingleBug` object knows about the `BugReport`, but the `BugReport` object does not need to know about the `ReportSingleBug`, so the line connecting them has an arrowhead pointing toward `BugReport`. Each `ReportSingleBug` is associated with a single `BugReport` object, so the right end of the relationship is labeled with a 1.

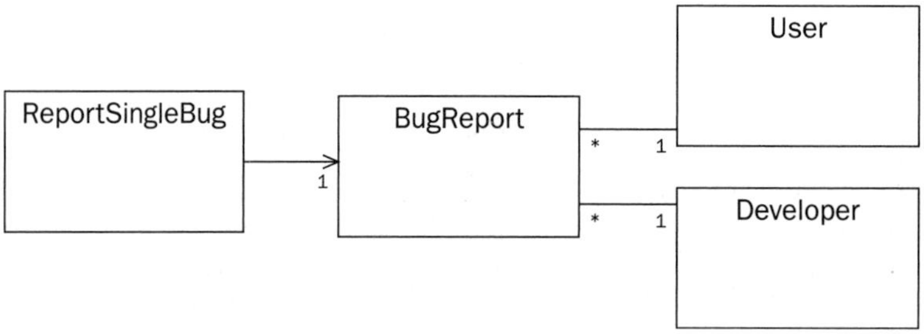

Figure 4-5: A class diagram can show relationships.

Each `BugReport` object is related to the `User` who reported the bug and the `Developer` assigned to the bug. Each `BugReport` is associated with one `User` and `Developer`, but the `Users` and `Developers` can be associated with any number of `BugReports`, so the lines are labeled with a 1 by the `User` and `Developer` and a * (meaning "any number") by the `BugReport`.

Sometimes relationships are labeled to describe the relationship. The relationship diagram shown in Figure 4-6 shows three relationships with the `BugReport` class. Here `User` creates `BugReports`, `BugManager` assigns `BugReports`, and `Developer` works `BugReports`.

Each of the diagrams shown in this section focuses on only a small part of the application. The goal is to clarify part of the application's behavior or design, not to model the entire application in a single massive diagram. It is frequently useful to make several diagrams that display different aspects of the system such as an inheritance hierarchy, relationships, dependencies, and so forth. Often, it's useful to focus on the objects involved in a specific use case or transaction chain of events. For example, Figure 4-5 shows the objects that would be involved in printing a report about a specific bug.

These sorts of class diagrams don't capture the step-by-step flow during a sequence of events, however. For those, you can use sequence diagrams.

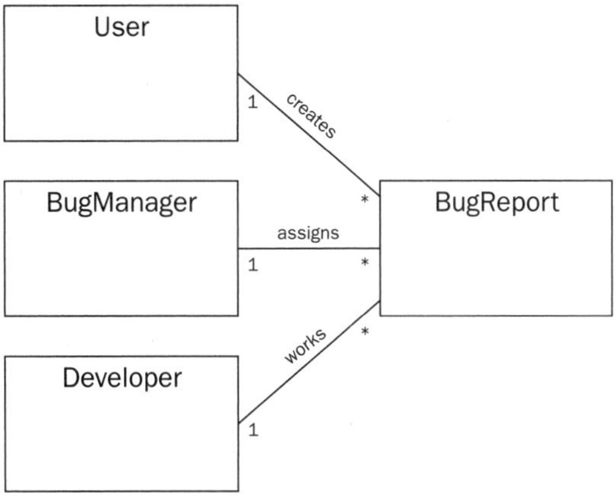

Figure 4-6: Labels can describe relationships.

Sequence Diagrams

Sequence diagrams use a timeline of events to describe a dynamic feature of the application. Across the top of the diagram is a series of objects that will participate in the exchange. Below each object is a dashed line called the object's *lifeline* that indicates time progressing downward. A narrow rectangle along the lifeline (called an *activation*) represents times when the object is performing some action.

As time moves on, objects send messages to each other to communicate and request actions. Usually, a message in this context is simply a Visual Basic subroutine or function call. A sequence diagram represents messages as arrows from one object's lifeline to another's. Arrows for synchronous calls get solid arrowheads and those for asynchronous calls get open arrowheads. Returns from messages (returns from subroutine and function calls or raised events) are represented as backward-pointing dashed arrows.

Figure 4-7 shows a sequence diagram for a user generating a report of bugs with a particular status. The names of the objects at the top are underlined to indicate that they are specific instances of classes, rather than the classes themselves.

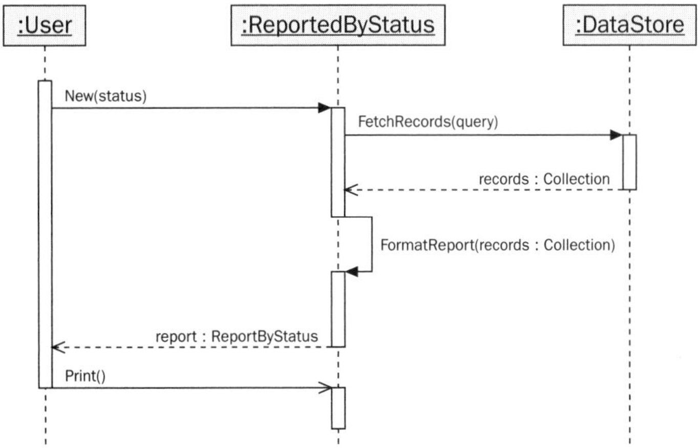

Figure 4-7: A sequence diagram shows a sequence of messages that implement some action.

The syntax for specific objects is the object's name, followed by a colon, followed by the object's class. For example, the name `submitter:User` means a `User` object named `submitter`. If you don't need to give a name to an object, you can omit the name as shown in Figure 4-7 to use *unnamed objects*.

The `User` object creates a new `ReportByStatus` object. The diagram represents this by sending a `New` message to the `ReportByStatus` object. The `User` passes a parameter named "status" in the `New` message so the `ReportByStatus` object knows what status to use when selecting bugs for the report.

Next the `ReportByStatus` object sends a `FetchRecords` message to a `DataStore` object, passing it a parameter named "query." In this example, query might be a SQL statement that selects the desired bug reports.

The `FetchRecord` call to the `DataStore` object returns a value called "records" that has type `Collection`.

The `ReportByStatus` object now sends itself a `FormatReport` message with a records collection as a parameter.

After it has finished formatting the report, the original call to `New` returns the new `ReportByStatus` object. The `User` then calls the `ReportByStatus` object's `Print` method asynchronously. At that point, the `User` object's involvement ends and its activation stops. The `ReportByStatus` object handles the `Print` request and then its activation stops as well.

Activity Diagrams

An *activity diagram* is a simplified representation of the steps that occur during an event sequence that is less time-oriented than a sequence diagram. Figure 4-8 shows an activity diagram describing the tasks shown in Figure 4-7.

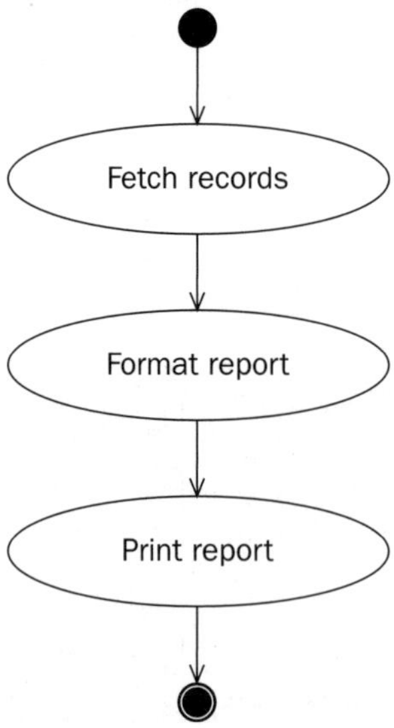

Figure 4-8: An activity diagram shows a sequence of events in an intuitive way.

A dark circle represents the start of the activity that the diagram represents, and a dark circle with an extra ring around it represents the end. This type of diagram is usually more intuitive than a sequence diagram like the one in Figure 4-7, so it is more meaningful to users.

More-complicated activity diagrams can include `If-Then` style branches, loops, and other more elaborate structures. When you add all of the bells and whistles, an activity diagram looks a lot like an old-fashioned flow chart.

Figure 4-9 shows an expanded and reformatted version of the activity diagram in Figure 4-8. This version is called the *swimlane* version, because it shows the objects performing the actions in columns much as lap swimmers move down the lanes in a swimming pool.

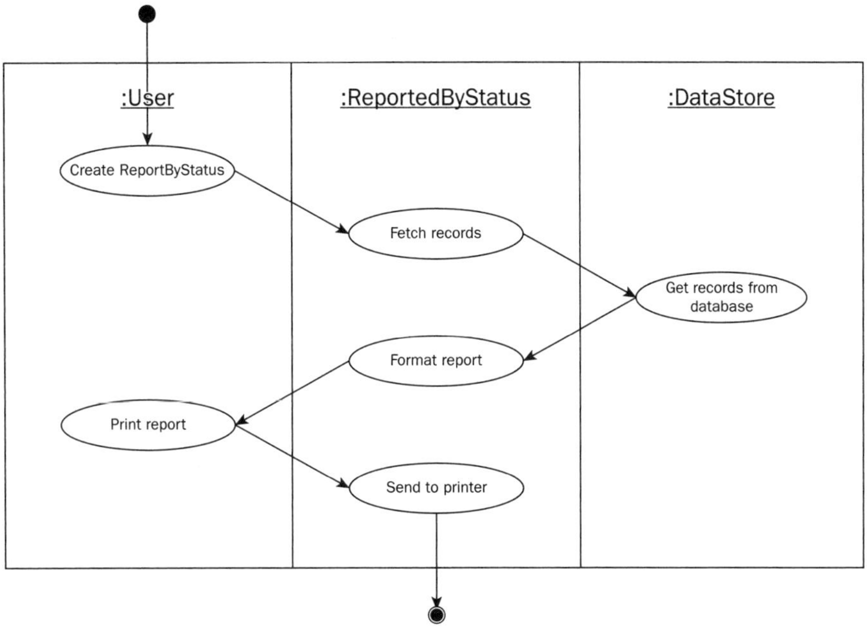

Figure 4-9: A swimlane activity diagram provides more detail about what object performs each action.

In a sense, the swimlane diagram in Figure 4-9 is a combination of the activity diagram shown in Figure 4-8 and the sequence diagram shown in Figure 4-7. It provides more detail than the activity diagram, but is still intuitive enough that most users should be able to understand it. The sequence diagram shows even more detail including method calls, return values, and asynchronous calls, but it's intended to help developers, and is usually too confusing for users.

State Chart Diagrams

A *state chart diagram* shows the states that an object is in over time. Figure 4-10 shows the state of a `BugReport` object as it passes through the system.

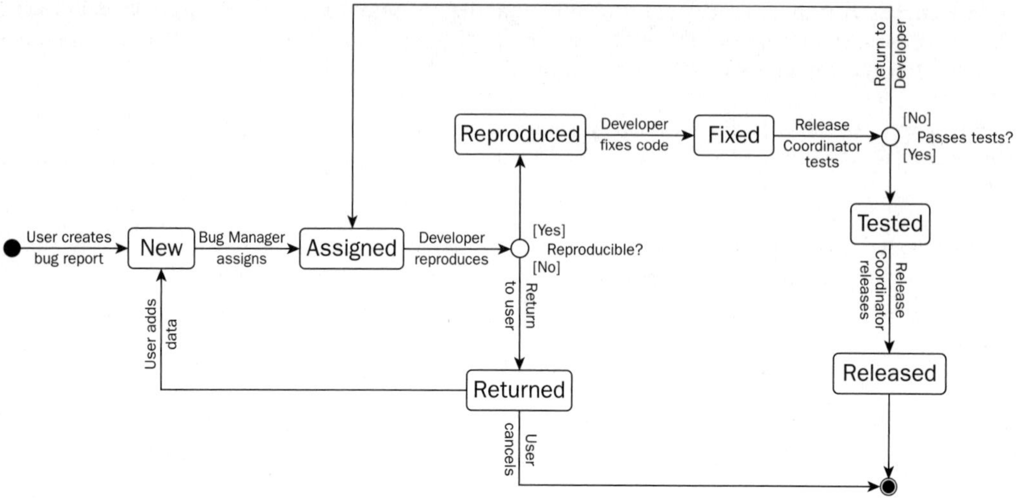

Figure 4-10: A state diagram shows an object's states over time.

You can further break down some transitions to show sub-states. For example, you could break the "developer fixes code" step into the sub-steps "study code," "modify code," "unit test," "document code," "update manual," and "flag as fixed." You could then draw a state diagram for this sequence of events, as shown in Figure 4-11.

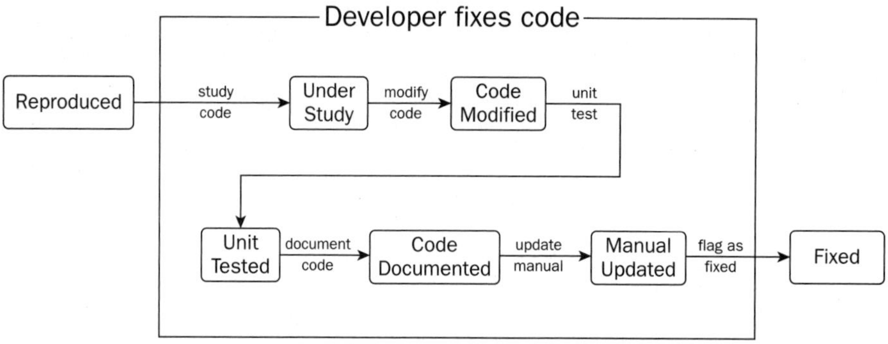

Figure 4-11: You can break a state transition into sub-transitions and sub-states.

To aid tracking `BugReport` objects through the system, the bug report data may actually include a `State` or `Status` field to indicate its state in the system. This field would take the values `New`, `Assigned`, `Reproduced`, `Returned`, `Fixed`, `Tested`, and `Released`. It might not need to include the sub-states `Under Study`, `Code Modified`, `Unit Tested`, `Code Documented`, and `Manual Updated`. Those are logical states that the bug report passes through as the developer works on it. The developer might need to use different tools while the report moves through these different states, so it may be important to include them in the model of the system, but you probably don't need to store them in the database.

Other objects might have states that are not ever explicitly recorded in the object's fields. For example, a `Developer` object has states corresponding to the `BugReport` states shown in Figure 4-11. Those states would be `Studying Code`, `Modifying Code`, `Unit Testing`, `Documenting Code`, and `Updating Manual`. A state diagram for the `Developer` object would include those states, although you may not need to store the state in the `Developer` class.

Component Diagrams

A *component diagram* shows interactions among the application's self-contained, modular parts of the system. These pieces of the application are often called *systems, subsystems*, or *components*. You can also think of them as libraries or tools that support other parts of the application.

Components are drawn either as boxes with the text "<<component>>" at the top, or as boxes containing a box attached to two smaller boxes. UML 1.0 specifies a different notation with the box attached to two smaller boxes containing the component. Figure 4-12 shows these three notations.

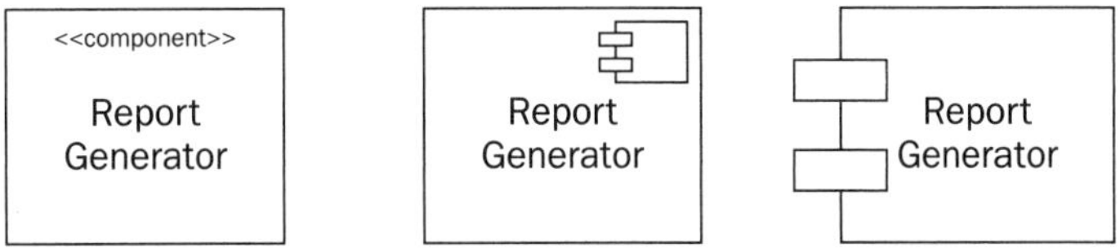

Figure 4-12: UML 2.0 allows the left and middle representations for a component, whereas UML 1.0 specifies the representation on the right.

You can model dependencies between components with dashed arrows. If a component provides an interface, you attach a small circle to the component with a line. If a component requires an interface, you attach a semicircle to the component with a line. Together, an interface provided and required makes a "ball and socket."

Figure 4-13 shows a component diagram describing part of the Bug Hunter application's report generation code. The main Reporting Module is dependent on the Printer Services component, so a dashed arrow points from Reporting Module to Printer Services. Reporting Module needs an interface to the Report Generator and Report Generator provides the needed interface, so those components are connected with a ball and socket link. Finally, the Report Generator needs an interface to the Data Store, and the Data Store component provides the interface, so those components are also connected by a ball and socket link.

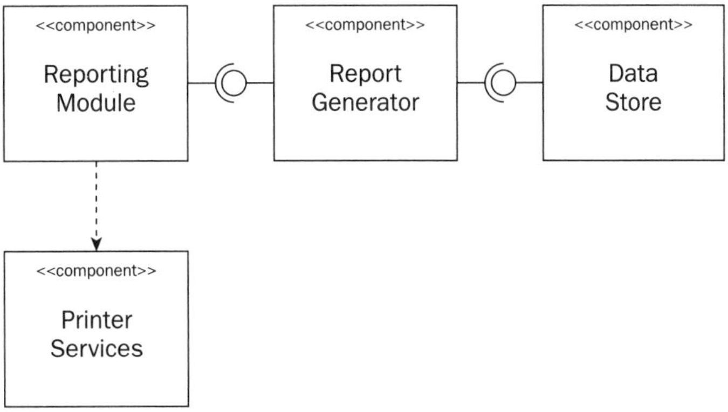

Figure 4-13: A component diagram represents dependencies and interfaces among components.

Component diagrams represent interactions among high-level application design objects, so they are purely for the benefit of the developers. They are usually meaningless to users, so there's little point in inflicting them on the users.

Deployment Diagrams

A *deployment diagram* shows the configuration of the physical hardware that will run the application. Objects in the diagram are called *nodes*. UML 2.0 says that a *device* is a node that executes artifacts, where an *artifact* is a piece of data that the system produces or uses, including executable files. Other types of nodes include objects such as routers, modems, and printers that form part of the system but that don't hold artifacts. Lines between the nodes show their connections.

Figure 4-14 shows a deployment diagram for the Bug Hunter application. All of the application's nodes are connected to a router. The router also connects to the corporate LAN, so users of the application's computers can access the rest of the company's online resources.

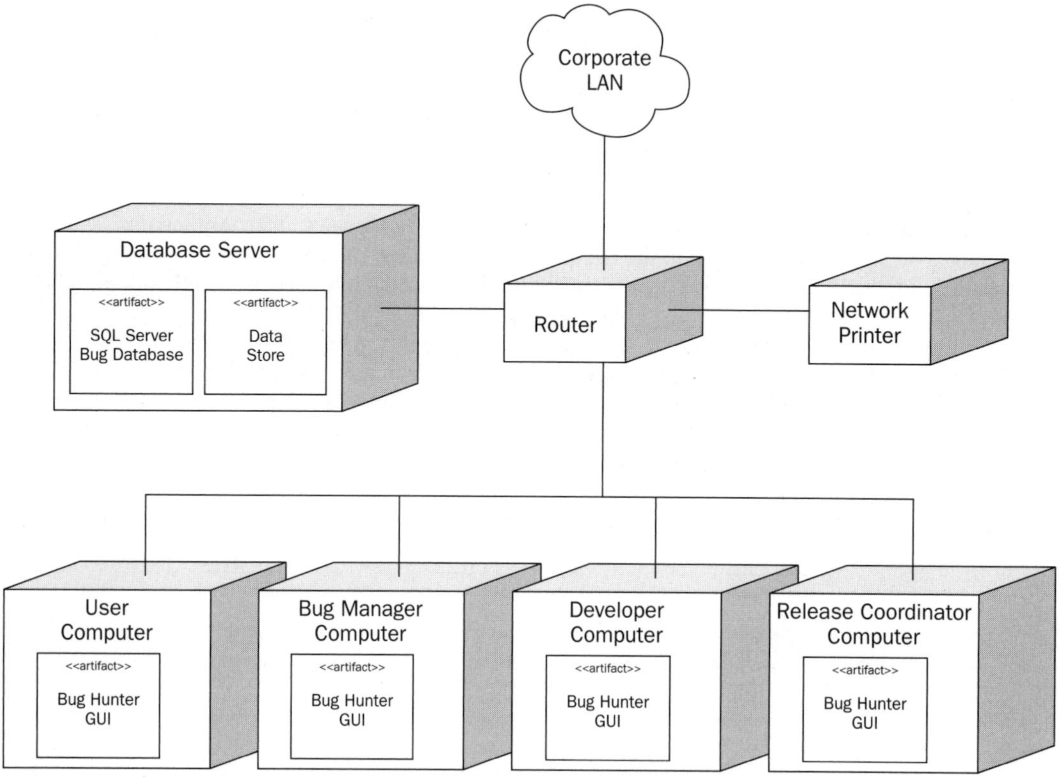

Figure 4-14: In this deployment diagram, nodes are connected by a simple network.

A Database Server computer stores the bug data in a SQL Server database. It also contains the Data Store component responsible for managing the data.

The computers used by the users, bug manager, developers, and the release coordinator are all connected to the router. Each of these computers runs the Bug Hunter's graphical user interface.

Finally, the router is connected to a network printer, so all of the computers can print reports.

Because the deployment diagram deals with the system's implementation, you might think it is for developers only. Actually, users typically are very interested in the deployment configuration. They either already own or must purchase the hardware that will run the application.

The users may need to restructure their environment to fit the deployment diagram. They may need to move computers around, add routers, buy printers, re-cable buildings, and so forth. These sorts of changes are usually very time-consuming, and the users might need to start planning months in advance.

The users may also want to change the deployment diagram to represent a preferred scenario. For example, they may want to move "heavier" artifacts onto new server machines so that the users can continue using their existing computers with lighter loads. When you show the users the deployment diagram, you may learn that they have remote users, so a local network won't work. In that case, you may need to adjust the diagram to allow for remote access over the Web.

Show the deployment diagram to the users early in the development cycle so that they can provide feedback before you make major architectural decisions.

UML Summary

UML defines diagramming functions that you can use to study an application's behavior and design. You can use it to make a large number of diagrams for modeling different aspects of the system. Not all applications are the same, however, so some of the diagrams make little sense for some applications.

Use case diagrams help you understand which groups of users perform what actions. If you are building a single-user application, this doesn't make much sense. It would be a waste of time and energy to draw a diagram with a single actor on the left connected to all of the use cases on the right.

Similarly, a sequence diagram is useful for studying calls between various objects as time passes. They can be particularly helpful when several classes are involved, and when some of the calls are asynchronous. They are not useful when one object synchronously calls a single method in another class.

I've seen several projects where developers believed (or were told) that it was necessary to provide every possible UML diagram for reasons of completeness. Figure 4-15 shows a typical result. Sometimes a picture is worth 1000 words. In this case, it's only worth nine: "The User object calls the `BugReport` object's Initialize method." The diagram is correct, but hardly worth the effort.

If a UML diagram doesn't make sense for your application, don't bother to draw it. The goal is to specify the system's behavior and design precisely so that you can study it and develop a common understanding with users, other designers, and developers. It's not to create a bunch of diagrams with little to say.

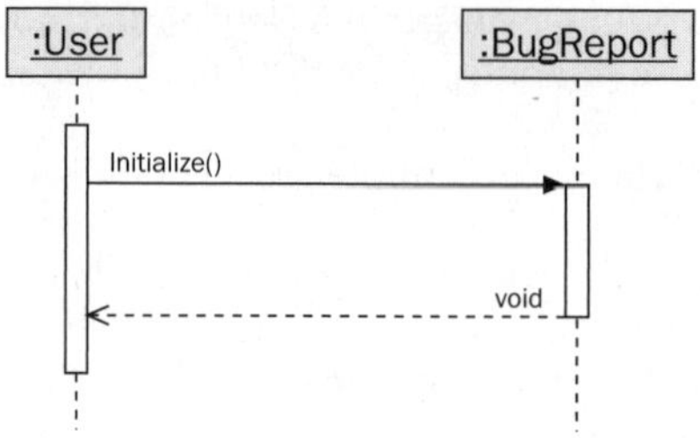

Figure 4-15: This UML diagram doesn't say anything that you can't say in a few words.

UML Tools

You can draw UML diagrams on paper by hand, or with any drawing application. If you want extra support for UML-specific operations, you have plenty of tools to choose from.

The Objects by Design Web site has a table listing more than 100 UML tools at `http://www.objectsbydesign.com/tools/umltools_byCompany.html`. The tools range in price from free to more than $11,000, work on a wide variety of platforms (including Windows, Linux, Unix, Java VM, and MacOS), and are intended for use with an assortment of languages and development environments (such as Java, Delphi, Smalltalk, Visual Studio, and Visual Basic).

Microsoft's Visio Enterprise Architect product, which is available as part of Visual Studio 2005 Team System or Visual Studio Professional with MSDN Premium, includes support for activity, collaboration, component, deployment, sequence, statechart, static structure, and use case diagrams. It is also integrated to an extent with Visual Studio.

To use Visio to "reverse-engineer" an application, load the application in Visual Studio. Open the Project menu, open the Visio UML submenu, and select Reverse Engineer. Visio will open and gather information about the application's classes.

You can then use Visio to draw UML diagrams representing different aspects of the system. Figure 4-16 shows Visio editing a sequence diagram similar to the one shown in Figure 4-7.

To make a sequence diagram similar to the one shown in Figure 4-16, right-click the project in Model Explorer in the lower-left part of the form. In the context menu, open the New submenu, and select Sequence Diagram to create the new diagram.

From the UML Sequence tab in the toolbar (above the Model Explorer), drag three Object Lifeline tools onto the diagram. Double-click an object to display the dialog shown in Figure 4-17. Enter the name you want for the object, and use the Classifier drop-down list to select the object's class. In this example, the class is `SequenceDiagramTest` (the project's name) followed by `User` (the class).

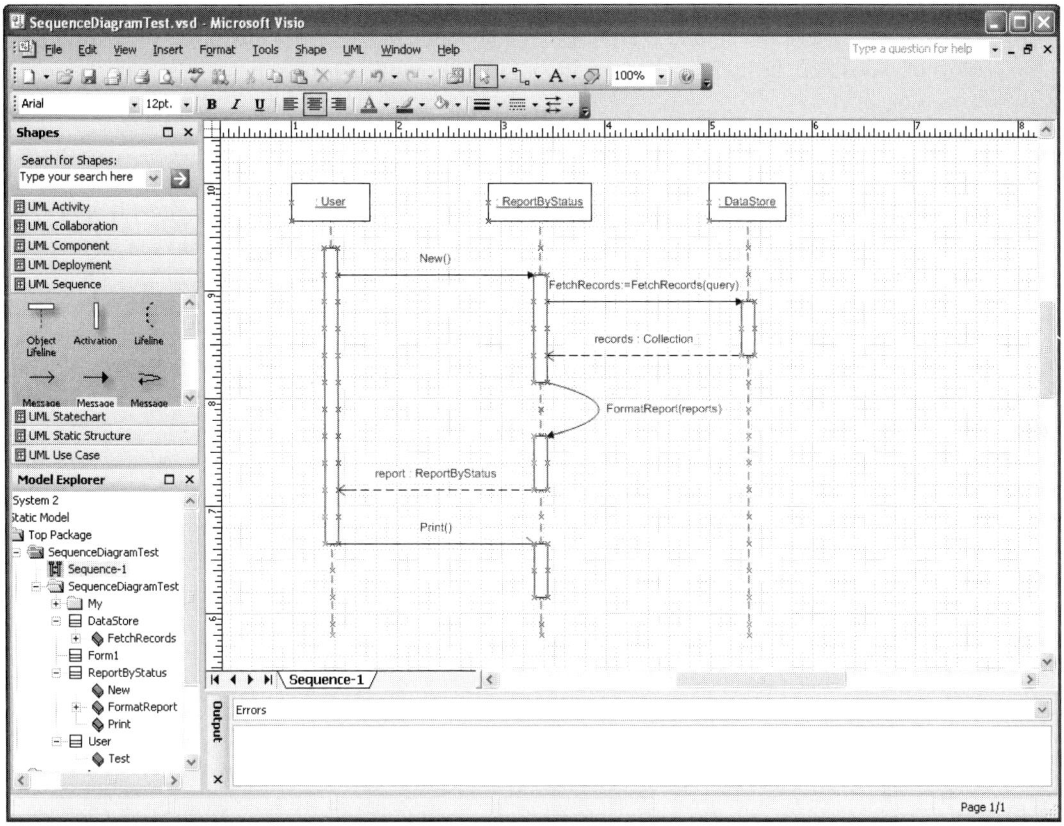

Figure 4-16: You can use Visio to build UML diagrams such as this sequence diagram.

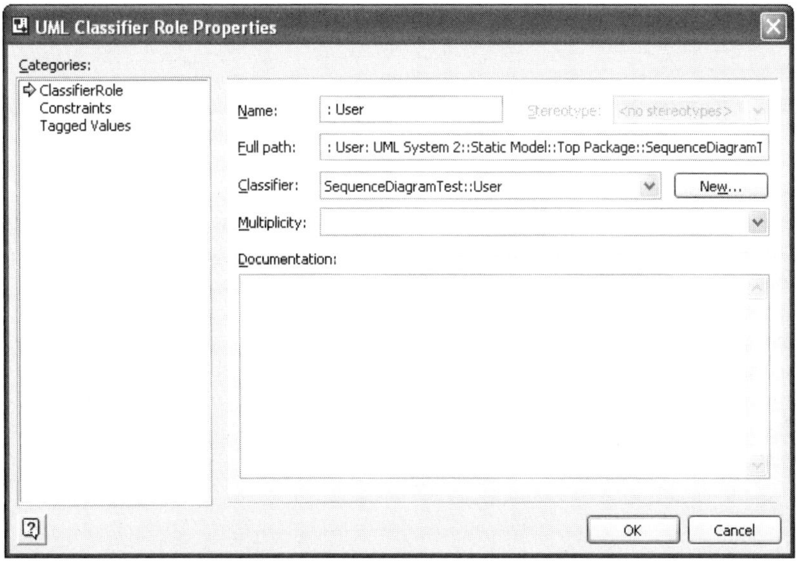

Figure 4-17: Use this dialog to set an object's name and class.

Next, drag activations, messages, and other diagram tools from the UML Sequence toolbox tab onto the diagram. You can anchor the tools to each other so they move together. For example, if you drag an object to a new position, its lifeline and activations, and the endpoints of any messages attached to the object move with it.

Double-click these items to set their properties. For example, if you double-click a message leading from the `User` object to the `ReportByStatus` object, you'll see the dialog shown in Figure 4-18. Use the Operation drop-down list to select the `ReportByStatus` method that you want to call. The dialog automatically displays the method and any parameters that it takes. I selected the `FetchRecords` function in Figure 4-18. Visio knew that `FetchRecords` takes a parameter named `query`, so it included it in the message shown in Figure 4-16.

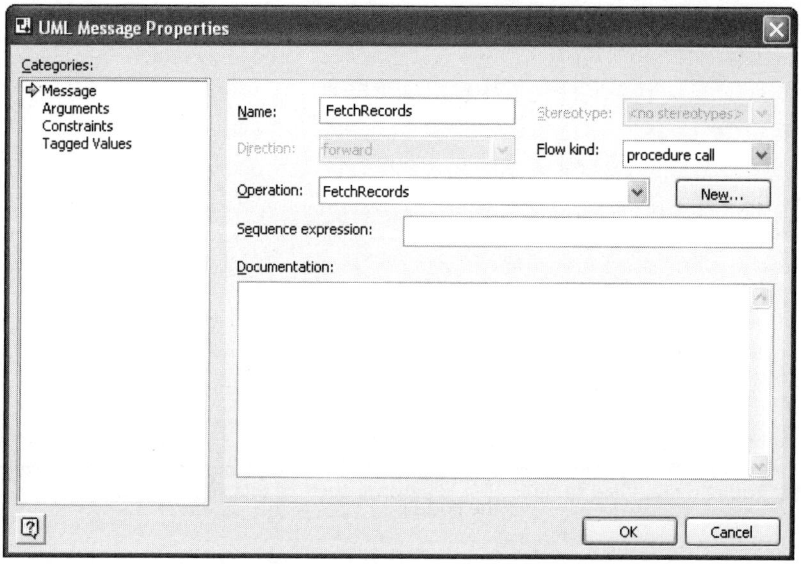

Figure 4-18: This dialog lets you describe a message call.

Unfortunately, when Visio "reverse-engineers" an application, it takes a snapshot of the project's classes. If you later change the classes, Visio will not reload the project to learn about the changes. In that case, you must reverse-engineer the project again, rebuilding any diagrams that you built before in Visio.

In addition to using Visio to diagram the structure of an existing project, you can also use Visio to design the structure for a new project. Start Visio, open the File menu's New submenu, cascade to the Software sub-submenu, and select UML Model Diagram.

Drag tools onto the diagram to create a static class model of the application. You can build classes, data types (such as enumerated types), inheritance relationships, and other design features.

When you have a design you like, open the UML menu's Code submenu and select Generate. In the dialog that appears, select the design items that you want to generate, and pick the directory where Visio should put the new code.

Visio is a very complicated application that provides a huge number of options for building UML diagrams and generating a basic code implementation. See the Microsoft Visio Web site for more information about the product's features. See the Visio documentation and online help for details about how to take full advantage of Visio's capabilities.

Summary

This chapter discussed ways you can design the classes that make up an application. Start by reading the requirements documents, system description, and use cases, looking for physical objects that would make good classes. Merge duplicates and look for closely related objects that might indicate inheritance, containment, or other class relationships.

Add any internal objects that you know you will need, possibly from previous experience with similar applications. You may also add classes as you develop the design, particularly when you apply design patterns.

To ensure that you have a good understanding of the system, look at it from a variety of viewpoints. Consider the application's data needs. Often, the tables in the database map naturally to objects. Think about the places where the application interacts with outside systems (such as other applications, the file system, or the network). Finally, consider the application's user interface. Sometimes classes sit behind the user interface elements to provide support for them.

You can use UML to model various aspects of the application's structure and behavior, both to study the application and to provide users, architects, and developers with the same view of the system.

Chapter 5 discusses user-interface design. While a good object-oriented design makes the system buildable, a good user-interface design makes it usable. Without a good user interface, the application may fail, no matter how flexible and robust the code is.

5

User-Interface Design

Chapter 4, "Object-Oriented Design," explored issues in high-level object-oriented design. However, the best application architecture and design in the world won't save a program unless it helps the users do their jobs. The application must be easy enough to use that the users can do their jobs better with the program than without.

This chapter explains some important user interface (UI) design concepts. It describes some of the rules you should follow and the techniques you should use to build a system that is useful, powerful, engaging, and natural to the users.

Many developers believe that UI design is a simple matter of following common sense. Some of the rules of interface design are intuitively obvious, but others are fairly subtle. Individually, the rules for producing a good UI design seem obvious, but to build the best application possible, you must fully exploit every possible advantage, not just those that seem like common sense.

This chapter begins by discussing a user-centered design philosophy that keeps UI design in perspective. It helps you remain focused on the user.

The chapter then discusses the characteristics of types of users. Different groups of users have different skills and different deficiencies. If you take the users' strengths, weaknesses, and environments into account, you will arrive at a better design.

The remainder of the chapter describes different kinds of forms and design principles that you should follow to make a clean, smoothly running UI. By minimizing distractions and following design guidelines that lead the user toward performing the job correctly, the UI can make the users as productive as possible.

UI Design Philosophy

It may sound a bit wishy-washy, but good UI design begins with the proper attitude. Developers must remember that the goal is not to show off the latest cool controls and UI techniques. It's not to build unique, attention-getting designs, or to show off all of the colors of the rainbow. It's not even to display the application's data. Instead, the goal of UI design is to devise an interface that lets the users perform their jobs as efficiently as possible.

To build the most efficient design, you must keep the users in mind while you are designing the application's UI. You should try not to think about the software behind the screen, the object-oriented design, or the application's database structure. You should focus on the users and their needs.

Some of the consequences of this attitude are obvious, while others are fairly subtle. The following sections explain some of the results of this user-centric philosophy. It explains some of the goals of UI design at a very high intuitive level. Later parts of the chapter explain techniques you can use to achieve these goals.

Give the User Control

The customer should always be in the driver's seat. The application is merely a tool to help the customer get a job done. The customer is neither a slave servicing the application's demands, nor a supplicant begging for the application's attention.

The user should be active, not responsive. The user has a task and performs it. The program doesn't perform the task with the user's help; the user performs the task with the application's help.

The program should phrase interactions with the user to emphasize the user's control. It should be reasonably concise to save time, but it should also be humble. It should say things such as "ready for input," rather than "enter values." The emphasis is that the program is ready to do the user's bidding, not that the program is commanding the user to enter data.

I've seen many systems that tried to perform complex tasks automatically and then let the user handle the small percentage of cases where the program isn't up to the task. In most of those applications, the "small percentage" turned out to be fairly significant, so the users ended up doing a lot of work. Because the program hid the easy cases, the users got less practice, and their skills actually atrophied over time, so they were less able to handle the exceptional cases. There's nothing wrong with making the users' jobs easier. After all, that's what the application is supposed to do. If you think the program can do all of the work, however, you'd better be sure it really does all of the work.

Focus on Tasks

Users perform tasks, so the goal of the application should be to help them perform those tasks. Rather than thinking about the data available to the user, you should think about the jobs they perform and what they need to perform them.

For example, suppose a billing representative needs to examine a delinquent customer's data and decide whether to send a gentle reminder letter, send a stern warning letter, or discontinue service. A data-centric approach might be to display the customer's data and then let the user decide what to do.

The problem with this approach is that it includes all of the customer's data. It might include the customer's name, address, phone number, account number, previous orders, product configuration, payment history, outstanding balance, and so forth. What the user really needs for this task, however, is the customer's payment history and records of any previous correspondence. All that extra data can distract the user, and make it more difficult to focus on the essential information needed to finish the task. Even if the critical data is nicely separated and easy to find, the presence of the other data adds to the complexity of the screen and slows the user down.

A task-centric approach to this problem would display the customer's billing history and list of previous correspondence. It might also display the customer's name, just to give the user a sense of working with a person, but it doesn't need to include the customer's address, phone number, account number, order history, and other data. All of that information should be easily available in case the user needs it, but it should be hidden if the user won't typically need it.

Advise, Don't Act

The application can provide default values, give hints, suggest actions, and make actions available to the user, but it should not perform actions on its own unless those actions are an integral part of its job.

A popular management aphorism is that it is easier to ask forgiveness than it is to ask permission. The idea is that it is sometimes better to take action (even if it later turns out to be wrong) than it is to do nothing. This idea makes sense when it's difficult to make a decision or get approval to take a particular action, but it doesn't make sense when the decision is quick and easy to make.

Even if the program can save the user some time and trouble by taking action automatically, it should not do so unless it has a good chance of taking the proper action. It's better to do nothing than it is to take action and apologize 85 percent of the time. Abraham Lincoln never saw a computer but his words apply equally to people and programs: "Better to remain silent and be thought a fool than to speak out and remove all doubt."

The Visual Studio development environment is an example of an application that doesn't automatically take action. If you accidentally misspell a keyword or variable name, Visual Studio doesn't automatically correct it for you. Instead it provides support to make it easier for you to fix the problem, as shown in Figure 5-1.

Rather than correcting the error, Visual Studio flags it with a wiggly underline and a little red rectangle. If you hover the mouse over the error, a tooltip appears describing the error and a small information icon pops up. If you click the icon, a drop-down list appears, describes the problem, and lists possible solutions.

In contrast, Microsoft Word automatically corrects spelling, replaces certain characters with others (for example, replacing straight quotation marks with "smart" quotation marks), and makes other improvements as you type. These are an integral feature of Word, just as applying styles is, so it makes some sense for Word to take action by itself. Note, however, that Word allows you to deactivate these features. If your program can automatically provide this sort of convenience feature, you should let the user turn it off as well.

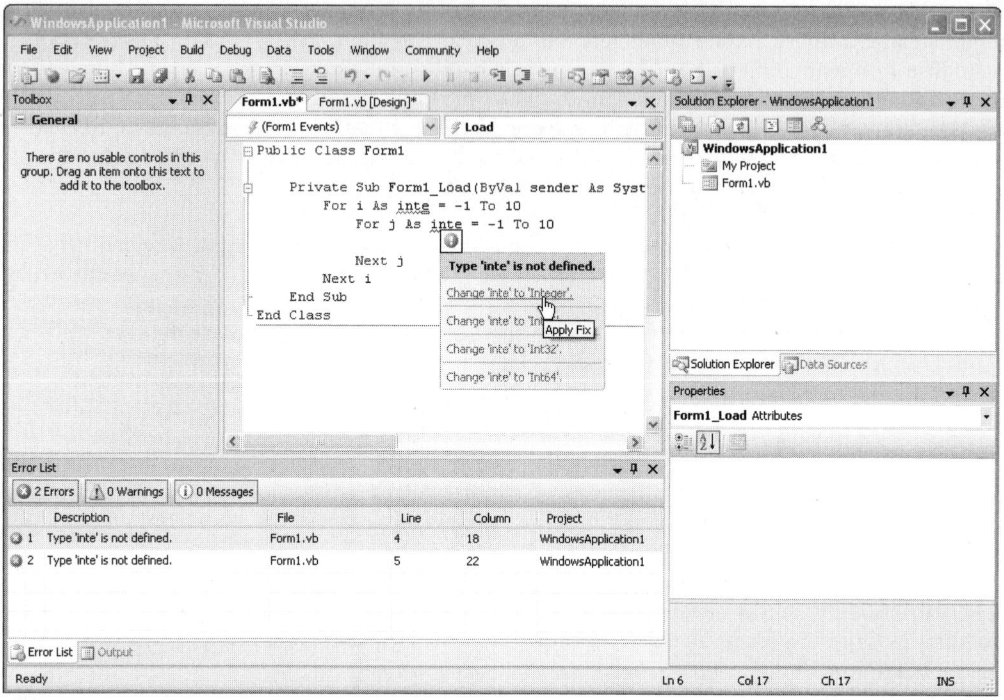

Figure 5-1: Visual Studio does not automatically correct spelling errors.

Help Users Do the Right Thing

Though the program shouldn't do the users' jobs for them, it can constrain the specific actions that the users can take. By using restrictive controls, it can help the users avoid mistakes. For example, by using combo boxes and lists, you can ensure that the user selects only valid items.

Suppose an address form provides text boxes for city, state, and ZIP code. The user can enter any old garbage in those fields, so you will need to write additional code to validate the fields. More importantly, if the user does make a mistake, he or she will have to waste time correcting it later.

Now, suppose your form includes a combo box listing all of the cities in your distribution area. The user picks a city from the list, and the program fills in the state and ZIP code. Now the user cannot enter an incorrect city, state, or ZIP code, nor can the user enter invalid combinations of those values. For example, the user cannot enter a city with the wrong state and ZIP code.

You can also restrict text boxes so that they allow only numeric input, input that matches patterns such as ###-###-#### for telephone numbers, and so forth.

A program can use regular expressions to verify that strings match certain patterns. Although they are not covered fully in this book, the section "Making a Better Add-in" in Chapter 8, "Snippets, Macros, and Add-ins," explains how to build add-ins that create properties that are validated by regular expressions. The section "Building Extender Providers" in Chapter 10, "Custom Controls and Components," describes how to build extender providers that use regular expressions to validate controls.

Make your forms as restrictive as possible to prevent the user from making mistakes that must be fixed later.

Users

Before you can write the best application for a user, you need to understand who the user is. You need to understand the user's point of view, job, work environment, and abilities. It's remarkable how many developers write applications without really knowing who will use them.

Understand the User's Job

The first thing you should do when starting a new project is learn about the user's job. If you don't know what the user does, you won't be able to write an application to help do it.

Read any documentation or training materials that the users have that describes the job. Then talk to the users. Warn them that you're going to ask a lot of stupid questions and then do so. Almost everyone likes to answer questions about their jobs and you'll probably have no trouble getting answers.

Sit with the users and watch them do their jobs. Ask what's hard, what's easy, what's normal, and what's unusual. Ask what they like and don't like about the job. Ask what they would change, what they would keep the same, and why.

When I worked for GTE Laboratories, developers were regularly sent to a training center where telephone personnel were trained. We spent several days crawling in cable vaults, visiting switching offices, learning how to splice telephone cables, trying out the techniques for diagnosing line faults, and learning as much as we could about phone company operation in general. It provided some very important perspective (and some funny stories) for many of the projects that I worked on later.

Then do the same with another user. And another. Get perspectives from users who play different roles. Sit with the person who knows the whole process inside and out (there's at least one in every office) and get a supervisor's perspective.

If you can, try performing the job yourself.

The more you understand about the user's job, the better you'll be able to write an application to help.

Respect the User

Just because your users don't understand how to write software doesn't mean they are stupid or in any way less important than you. Often, the users have spent years in training and performing their jobs, and there's no way you can expect to acquire their level of expertise in just a few hours or days. Fortunately, your goal isn't to become as good as the users at their jobs; it's to understand their jobs well enough to build an application that can help.

At one company I worked for, an employee's badge had a big star on it for every five years of service. Typically, the expert users we worked with had four or five stars. Even many of the hourly "craft" workers had 10 or 20 years of experience and performed relatively complicated technical jobs.

Never think that the users' jobs are trivial or inconsequential. Your job is to translate the needs of the users into an application that can help them do their jobs. Without your users, you wouldn't have a job.

If you alienate your users, development can become a nightmare. At best, you'll face a lack of cooperation and little or no feedback leading to an ineffective application. At worst, you'll be replaced by someone who understands the importance of the users in the grand scheme of things.

Understand the User's Environment

While you are working on an application, it's important to focus on what the application does and how it works, but it's also important to keep the user's large environment in the back of your mind.

Do the users work with other important applications? If so, your program will probably need to share screen real estate with other programs. Will your application need to interact directly with those systems? If it won't now, might it later?

Do the users work in a noisy environment? If so, sounds won't be very useful in your application.

Do the users all work in the same space? In that case, lots of sound may interrupt other users trying to get their jobs done.

I once built a few applications for a billing center where the users wore very sensitive telephone headsets to talk to the customers. Even the sounds of their typing were sometimes picked up on the phone. The applications they used needed to stay quiet.

Do the users work mostly with the keyboard, the mouse, or some other input device? If the users' hands are always full, or they wear heavy gloves, the application may need a voice interface.

What kind of computers will the users have? It's very common for software developers to work on very powerful up-to-date computers while the eventual users have older, sluggish systems with little memory, full hard drives, and lethargic network connections. Developing on a powerful computer will save you time, but be sure to think about the target platform, particularly when you consider the response time issues described later in this chapter.

While you develop in one environment, the users perform their jobs in another. To build the most useful application possible, you need to see your system in the context of the users' complete environment.

Understand User Types

Users come in all shapes and sizes with different sets of skills and expectations. Although you cannot take into account every difference between users, you should think about large classes of users that you are likely to encounter. Two particularly important dimensions to consider are the users' ages and their physical differences.

Younger users have better vision and hearing, faster reaction times, and better memory than senior users. They also have higher level of reading comprehension and have finer motor control.

Older users may have weaker vision and hearing, slower reaction times, and trouble positioning the mouse precisely.

Interestingly, children share some characteristics of both groups. They have good hearing and vision but are still developing their reactions and fine motor skills.

Unless you know that your group of users includes only people of a certain age, you should plan to support as wide an audience as possible. Overall, the world's population is aging, so over time, a larger percentage of your potential users will be older. It makes sense to spend additional effort making the application easier to use for this growing segment of your user population.

That means using larger fonts and icons to support weakening vision, and larger buttons to support declining fine motor skills. It also means reducing the importance of sounds in the UI.

In addition to age-related differences, users may have physical differences that affect how they use an application. About 10 percent of men and 1 percent of women have some form of color blindness. Unless you have a very small user population, odds are you will have some users that have trouble distinguishing certain colors. To help those users, you should not rely solely on color (particularly red and green) to convey important information.

One check you can perform is to put the computer in high-contrast mode using the Accessibility applet settings and see if the application is still readable. If you can't understand the application in this mode, chances are some of your users won't be able to understand it either.

Some users may have different skills than others. Touch typists can work much more quickly if you don't force them to use the mouse. Users experienced with the numeric keypad can enter numbers extremely quickly if you let them use the keypad. All users slow down greatly if you force them to switch frequently between the keyboard and mouse.

Cultural difference may also play a role in how users interpret your system. Culture obviously affects such issues as language, but it also has many subtler differences. For example, different images and colors can have different interpretations in different parts of the world. In some parts of the world, a dog represents a faithful friend, whereas in others it symbolizes a sneaky, cunning, and degraded person.

Finally, your user population may include those with physical handicaps such as impaired vision, hearing, memory, and motor control. You can help some of these users with the same techniques that help older users: larger fonts and icons, bigger buttons, and not relying on sound alone. You can also look at the checklist at `www.webaim.org/standards/508/checklist` to help make applications more accessible.

Good UI design helps further by providing textual representations, non-mouse alternatives for performing actions, and hints and guides to reduce the user's memory load.

Forms

There are several kinds of forms an application may need. You can group these into the following categories:

- *Main forms* provide a base from which a user begins a work sequence. Some applications have a single main form that controls all other forms. Other applications have several main forms that control different aspects of the system. For example, a control panel application might provide an assortment of tools that let you manage different processes. Usually main forms are resizable.
- *Secondary forms* provide additional detail for main forms.
- *Dialogs* give the user feedback or let the user enter data immediately. Dialogs are modal so the user must dismiss them before interacting with the rest of the application. Main and secondary forms are modeless.

Having lots of forms connected in unusual ways is confusing. As users open and close forms, they can become disoriented. Later, they may have trouble figuring out how they got into the position they're in, how to get to a particular form, or how to backtrack to a previous position. You can make this a lot less confusing by minimizing the ways in which users can navigate between forms. You can also make navigation simpler by minimizing the number of levels in the hierarchy.

For example, Visual Studio provides a main form that includes everything else. It can launch secondary forms that are code editors, form editors, resource pages, and so forth. Those secondary forms display dialogs such as warnings, property editors, and wizards, but they generally don't display new forms. The dialogs are modal, so you need to finish using them and close them before you can go back to the rest of the project. This hierarchy has only two levels containing a single main form and secondary forms contained inside the main form. It is usually better to have a shallow hierarchy of forms so the user cannot get too lost.

Another possible design uses a set of accessor forms that provide access to main forms. For example, you might have a series of search forms that let the user look for orders, customers, and inventory items. Once you have found a set of items, you could open a new form to view that item. This item view form might include secondary forms to provide additional detail, or it might include all of the item's detail, possibly by using tabs.

Instead of using accessor forms to search for items, you could use search dialogs launched by a main application form. That would make the most sense if the user spends relatively little time searching and lots of time working with the item view forms. If the user spends a lot of time searching and monitoring lists of items, it is reasonable to make the accessor forms instead of dialogs.

One way you can decide whether a form should be a main form is to ask whether it should appear in the taskbar. Main forms belong in the taskbar, while secondary forms and dialogs do not. In the previous design, you would want the main application form and the item view forms to be in the taskbar. You would probably not want to show the accessor forms in the taskbar.

MDI versus SDI

You can sometimes use a *multiple-document interface* (MDI) to make managing the program's forms easier. An MDI application uses a single large form to hold child forms. The user can move, resize, and even iconify the child forms, but they always sit within the MDI parent form. Visual Studio is an MDI application with a main form containing any number of form editors, code editors, and other child forms.

In contrast, a *single-document interface* (SDI) does not contain a main form that holds the others. Each form sits separately on the user's desktop and the user manages them separately. Microsoft's Paint, Notepad, and WordPad programs are all SDI applications. When you open a bitmap in Paint, or a text file in Notepad or WordPad, Windows creates a new independent instance of the application with its own taskbar icon.

If your application deals with very complicated data, you can even create a hybrid with characteristics of both SDI and MDI applications. For example, you can make an application that launches MDI parent windows as needed. The main form could be an MDI parent form containing a series of MDI accessor forms as children. When the user selects an item from an accessor, you could launch a new MDI parent form to display its data. That form could contain its own MDI child forms to provide details about the selected item.

SDI has the advantage that it is simple, easy to build, and easy to understand. It has the disadvantage that it can only reasonably hold information about a single entity.

MDI has the advantages that it can hold any number of windows and that it keeps them grouped together. In addition to providing a container for the child windows, the parent window can provide tools for arranging the children by tiling, cascading, minimizing, and maximizing them. A disadvantage of MDI windows is that it's more confusing to manage a collection of windows. Secondary windows that are not MDI children aren't integrated into the whole, but if you make them MDI children, it's easy to lose the connection between a secondary window and the main window to which it is related. It's also more difficult to tell how the menu bar works, because the commands on it depend on the child window that currently has the focus.

Which option is best depends on your application. In the end, you need to balance simplicity with flexibility, and pick the simplest solution that can satisfy the users' needs.

Resizing Forms

Main forms should generally be resizable. Secondary forms may be resizable or not, depending on how much information they need to display. If a secondary form can show all of its information in a limited space, give it a fixed size. If all of the information won't fit on the form at once, you can let the user resize it to see more data.

Dialogs should generally not be resizable. One common exception to this rule is the unfolding or expanding dialog. In an *unfolding dialog*, a button allows the user to show or hide additional advanced information. For example, look at the `ColorDialog` shown in Figure 5-2. If you click the button labeled "Define Custom Colors >>", the dialog expands, as shown in Figure 5-3.

Note that the expansion button includes the characters ">>" at the end to tell the user that the dialog can expand. Ideally, the dialog expands to the right. If the dialog is too wide, some applications expand the dialog downward, although they usually still use the characters ">>" to indicate the expansion, which is somewhat misleading because the expansion isn't to the right.

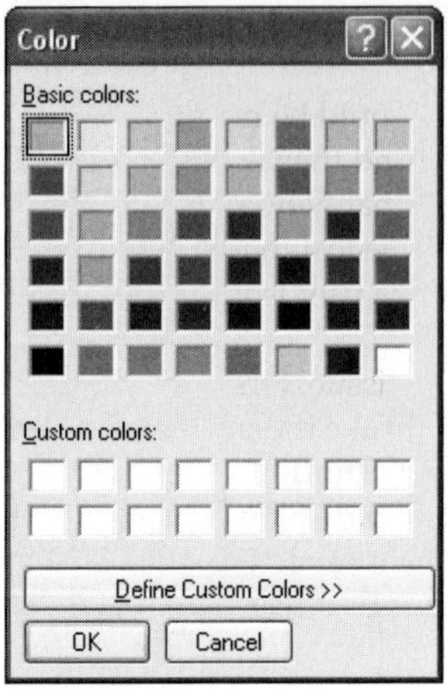

Figure 5-2: The `ColorDialog` starts in this small state.

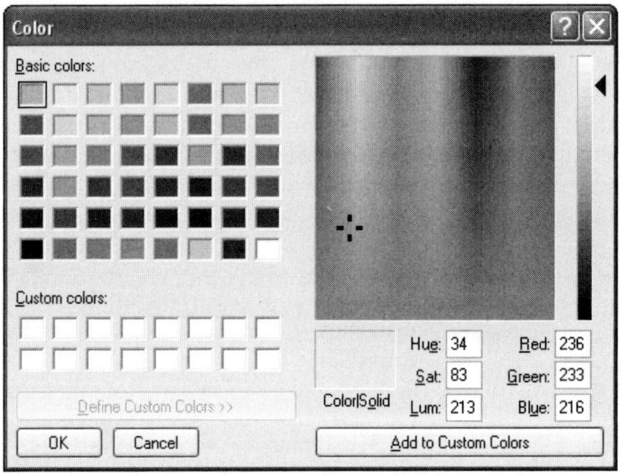

Figure 5-3: Click the "Define Custom Colors >>" button to expand the `ColorDialog` to this state.

In some designs, the expansion button's caption changes after it is pressed, and it then allows the user to collapse the expansion. In this example, the button's caption might change to "<< Hide Custom Colors."

You can also make an argument for allowing the user to resize dialogs that contain a large amount of information. For example, a selection dialog might let the user pick from a list of thousands of customer accounts. In that case, the user might want to make the dialog very tall to see more of the list at one time. If you know the list will hold between few dozen items and perhaps 100 items, make it large enough to show a substantial portion of the list (10 or 12 items) and make it a fixed size. If the list will contain several hundred items, make the dialog resizable. Better still, restrict the information in the list to make it smaller, or consider moving the functionality into a secondary screen with search capabilities.

Message boxes should never allow resizing.

One special trick for message boxes should be mentioned, however. Sometimes an application presents a long, complex message to the user, and then asks that the user report the message to the developers. That's completely unfair. The user probably doesn't understand the technical parts of the message and there's a good chance something will be lost in translation. Besides, the users shouldn't need to transcribe long messages into an email. The user is your customer, not your secretary.

There are several ways to address this issue. First, have the program record the error in a log or automatically email it to developers. Second, make the message short and meaningful enough that the user can understand it and pass it along to you. Third, if you really need a long diagnostic message sent to developers, write your own message box and display the information in a read-only text box so the user can copy and paste the information into the email. Finally, provide a "Report Error" button on the message box to let the program email the message directly. You've probably seen similar buttons on error dialogs in recent versions of Windows.

Editors

An *editor* allows a user to modify a piece of data that is presented in a read-only format. For example, a student information form might show a student's name, address, classes, and so forth. If you wanted to update the student's address, you would click a button or use a menu to display a student editor. You would modify the student's data and then close the editor.

In this scenario, the editor could be either a secondary form associated with the student information form, or it could be a dialog. The advantage of making the editor a form is that you can move it around, resize it, and pull up other forms for comparison or to find other information. You can also take as long as you want to finish updating the record before saving it or canceling your changes.

One disadvantage to this approach is that different forms might display different versions of the data. In this example, the student information form shows the old data, while the editor shows the data you are now typing. After you save or discard your changes in the editor, the program can update the information form, but until then, the two will disagree.

Putting editors in secondary forms also requires you to keep track of the form. If you open an editor and then get sidetracked working with another student's records, you may have trouble coming back later and figuring out what you were doing with the editor.

If the editor is in a modal dialog, you are forced to deal with it completely before you can interact with any other part of the application. You cannot lose the editor among the other forms you have open, and you cannot forget what you were doing with the editor. The disadvantage is that you cannot consult other forms while you are working with the editor.

If the item you are editing is fairly simple and won't require data lookup or comparison with other forms, make it a dialog. If the item is complex, will require lookups and comparisons, or may take a long time to finish, put the editor in a secondary form.

The Properties Window in Visual Studio uses simple modal editors for many properties. If you click the drop-down arrow to the right of the Anchor or Dock properties, Visual Studio displays a little drop-down image where you can click on areas to specify the property's value. If you click the drop-down arrow to the right of the Text property, a small text box appears where you can enter multi-line text. You can also think of the drop-down lists associated with enumerated properties as tiny editors. All of these property editors are modal.

Property Sheets

A *property sheet* is fundamentally the same as an editor with a special format. Usually, a property sheet contains several controls that let the user set values for several properties of a single object. If the object has many properties, they can be grouped into tabbed property pages within the property sheet. Figure 5-4 shows a property sheet that contains two property pages and is used by CorelDRAW! to let you set a font's properties.

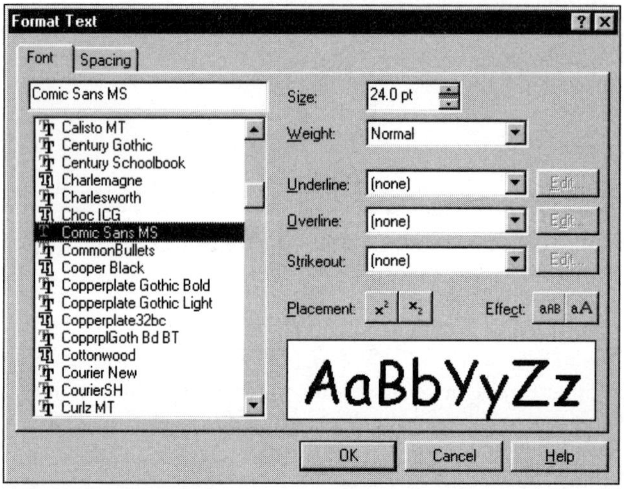

Figure 5-4: CorelDRAW! uses this property to let you set a font's properties.

One common style for property sheets is to provide OK, Cancel, and Apply buttons. When the user clicks the Apply button, the program tentatively applies the property sheet's current settings to the object so the user can see what the effect would be. The user can then click OK to make the choices permanent, or Cancel to undo the choices.

Property sheets used in this way are usually modal dialogs, so the user must finish setting the property values before working with other parts of the application.

Visual Studio comes with a `PropertyGrid` control that you can use as an alternative to traditional property pages. This control automatically displays an object's properties and lets the user edit them. Figure 5-5 shows a `UserPropertyGrid` displaying the properties for an `Employee` object defined in the program's code.

The `PropertyGrid` control is less friendly than a traditional property sheet, so users will need some additional training and practice if you use one in your application. Visual Studio has proven that this can be a powerful and effective method for editing object properties, however. This control is not a standard used in many applications, but that may soon change.

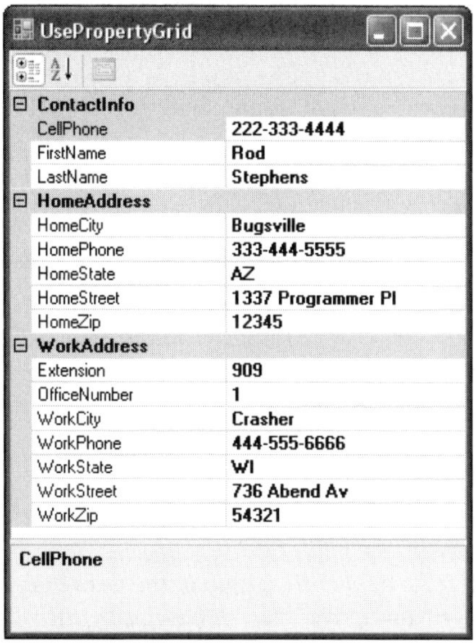

Figure 5-5: The `PropertyGrid` control displays an object's properties automatically.

Design Principles

Visual Studio's forms and controls do a huge amount of work for you, and they generally follow good design principles. For example, by default, the text in a `GroupBox` caption uses a different color than the text used in `Labels` and `TextBoxes`. That makes it easier for experienced users to tune out the `GroupBox` captions and focus on the essential data. If you don't change the default appearance of a `GroupBox`, it will automatically improve the form's design.

Visual Studio also properly formats menus, displays cascade indicators, draws keyboard accelerators and menu shortcuts, activates objects in response to keyboard accelerators and menu shortcuts, displays objects appropriately when enabled or disabled, positions menus so they remain on the screen, and performs a myriad of other tasks that you normally take for granted.

While Visual Studio's controls give you a lot of help, it's still useful to know some of the design principles that they bring into play. For example, you should know why the `GroupBox` uses a different color and not change it unnecessarily.

The following sections explain a series of design principles and techniques that you should be aware of when you build your application's forms. In some cases, Visual Studio will apply them for you if you let it. In others, you will need to do the work yourself.

All of these ideas have a single goal: to provide the user with the most helpful and efficient application possible. In broad terms, that means making the users' jobs easier. The program should minimize the users' visual, mental, memory, and motor workloads to make working with the application as smooth as possible.

Prototype in Stages

Don't jump into Visual Studio and start slapping controls on forms right away. Start slowly. Working with your users, sketch out some form designs on paper or a whiteboard. Kick around ideas and try to come up with some basic designs for various forms, and an idea of how those forms will fit together to let the users perform their tasks.

Focus on the users' tasks, not the data or overall goals. Work through the tasks one at a time, and verify that you have designed screens to handle them all.

Only after you have decent sketches of your forms should you build prototypes of the forms in Visual Studio. Then, before you rush out and start putting code behind the controls, show them to your users and get their feedback. Seeing the actual forms may give the users new insights that you should consider before committing to a bunch of code.

Promote Form Flow

When a user works with a form, he or she must look at the data that it contains. The user's eye travels across the form taking in data, scanning for instructions, and generally analyzing the form to figure out what it contains and what he or she needs to do with it.

To make scanning the form as easy as possible, the user's eye should travel in an orderly way over the data, not jump back and forth all over the place. While the user has something to say about where his or her eye roams, a lot of eye movement is controlled by the form's arrangement. You need to arrange the form's controls to promote a smooth flow over the data.

Use a roomy, symmetric, balanced layout. An aesthetic layout makes the user's eye flow naturally across the form.

The human brain is a powerful pattern-matching tool. Finding patterns and order is one of the things that humans do well, and it's why humans are so good at tasks such as face and voice recognition, which are difficult for computers. If the data shows pleasing, symmetric, and balanced patterns, the user's brain can correctly guess where the next piece of data should be, and the user's eye will naturally follow the pattern. If the form's layout is cramped, uneven, and misaligned, the user will have greater trouble finding the pattern and may get lost.

Figure 5-6 shows an unbalanced form. Figure 5-7 shows the same controls arranged in a more balanced way. In this version, the group boxes are all the same size, even though their contents don't take up the same amount of room.

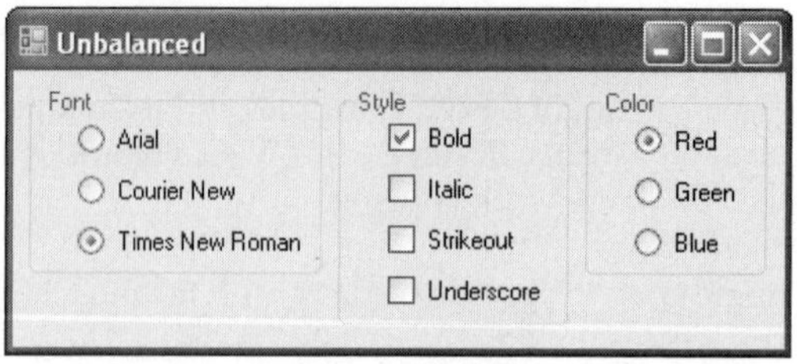

Figure 5-6: An unbalanced form is uncomfortable and makes form flow awkward.

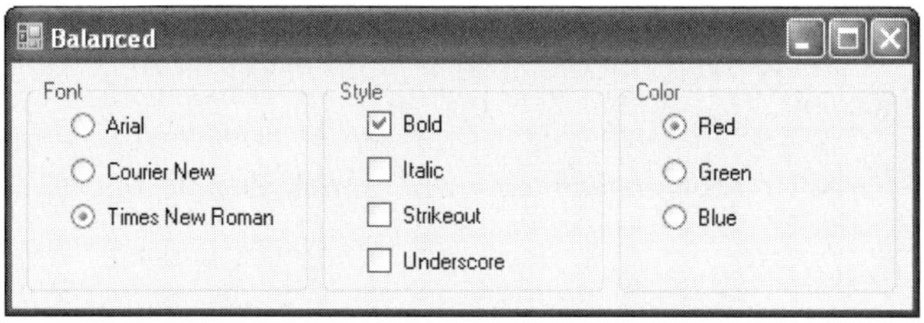

Figure 5-7: A balanced form feels natural and smooth.

To minimize eye movement, keep related items close together. This also helps minimize mouse movement when the user is manipulating the data.

Use big targets to make pointing and selection with the mouse easier. That means using larger fonts and buttons. Of course, larger targets mean the user's eyes and mouse must move farther between the controls. To strike a balance between large targets and small eye and mouse movements, start with normal system default sizes for buttons and fonts, and make the application adjust according to the user's system settings. If the user selects large fonts, the application can display larger fonts. The section "Support Resizing" later in this chapter has more to say about accommodating larger fonts.

Avoid making the user switch between the keyboard and mouse. Moving your hand from the keyboard to the mouse and then positioning the mouse can take one or two seconds. If the user is performing "head down" typing, the break can be very distracting. Try to group keyboard and mouse tasks so that the user isn't forced to switch frequently.

> *One place where this switch is required by many applications is in entering address information. The user types a name, street, and city, then uses the mouse to pick a state from a combo box, and then switches back to the keyboard to enter the ZIP code. You can make this kind of entry easier if you use a* `ComboBox` *with* `DropDownStyle` *set to* `DropDown` *instead of* `DropDownList`*. Then the user can type the* `State` *value in addition to using the drop-down list. Note that this means the program must later validate the user's entry to make sure the value is valid.*

Use restraint. Don't go overboard with bright colors. You might consider allowing the users to set their own color preferences. That would allow users who have trouble distinguishing colors to adjust the colors to suit their needs. However, this can greatly complicate the application and, if you pick a good selection of system colors, shouldn't really be necessary. Consider using design applications that check for color problems. These programs can show you what the application would look like to older or color-blind users.

> *If you let the users pick their own colors, someone will eventually pick black text on a black background, and you'll be called in to figure out how to get them up and running again. You can make it easier to solve this and other customization problems by providing a Restore Defaults button. Provide shortcuts and accelerators so you can trigger this button even if the interface is so messed up that you can't find the button.*

Don't use every fancy control just because it's available. Complicated controls take longer to use. Use the simplest control that can reasonably do the job. For example, pop-up calendars look nice, but are cumbersome. If the user knows the date he or she needs to enter, it's much faster to just type it with the keyboard. Pop-up calendars are useful if the user needs to browse for a date, as when he needs to see what dates in a future month fall on what days of the week.

Emphasize the unusual. Normal ordinary data should be calm and peaceful. Data that is unusual, risky, or containing an error should stand out. Flag these types of data with an `ErrorProvider` control or a different background color.

Don't use computer jargon or abbreviations. Use plain, simple English and the user's terminology.

> *I worked for the telephone company GTE. Like most companies, they have their own rather large collection of technical abbreviations and jargon. Terms such as POTS (plain old telephone service) and TelCo (a telephone company) were common in the workplace, so they were allowed in the UI.*

Start with the most important information in the upper left and move down and across to the right. Minimize the movement of eyes and mouse. Use screen elements to draw the user's eyes in this direction. Some screen characteristics that determine eye movements include the following:

- Graphics draws the eye more than text.
- Color draws the eye more than black and white.
- Bright, saturated colors (red, green) draw the eye more than "washed out" colors.
- Dark areas draw the eye more than light areas.
- Unusual shapes draw the eye more than simple shapes.
- Big objects draw the eye more than small objects.

Put keyboard accelerators on labels to help the user navigate without using the mouse. If the user presses the accelerator, focus jumps to the control following the label in the tab order. For example, if the label First Name comes before the first name text box in the tab order, then, when the user presses Alt+F the focus jumps to the first name text box.

Set an appropriate tab order to move the user through the form. Put buttons at the bottom or right of the form, and make them last in the tab order. Be sure to place labels in the tab order immediately before the controls they identify so that their keyboard accelerators work properly.

Use completion aids where appropriate. For example, after a date field, you could put a label saying "(mm/dd/yy)" to give the user a hint about the format you expect.

Identify required and optional fields. Lately, putting an asterisk (*) after a field's label has become quite popular, particularly on Web sites. Sometimes the asterisk is in a different color than the label. You could also flag required fields with a different background color or border style. Be sure not to pick bright colors that will draw the user's eye and become distracting.

Do not use auto-tab unless the user will fill out a long series of fields to their maximum widths. For example, if the user must enter ten numbers with exactly five digits each in a row, auto-tab can save time. Often, the user will not necessarily fill a field completely and, in that case, auto-tab is confusing.

Visually differentiate text boxes, labels, instructions, headers, and groups. Text boxes are naturally different because they are inside boxes. Visual Studio's group boxes display their captions in a different color. If you include labels used as instructions or headers, change their color, font, or size to make the difference noticeable. This allows more advanced users to more easily ignore these prompts and focus on the key data in text boxes.

Use the TrueType fonts that are available on most Windows systems: Courier New, Times New Roman, and Arial. By default, Visual Studio uses the MS Sans Serif font. That font should be available on Windows systems, so it should also be a safe choice. Unless you know your users have a particular font, don't use it.

Left-justify text; right-justify numbers.

Display brief results to the user in message boxes or labels. If the message is so long that the user will need to scroll, provide scroll bars. Either put a label inside a panel with scroll bars, or put the message inside a read-only text box.

If the user might want to copy and paste a result, put the result in a read-only text box. The user cannot modify the text box's value, but can highlight it and copy it to the clipboard.

Group Related Items

Group related items visibly. Surround closely related items in a group box. Use the group box's caption to indicate how they are related.

Separate less closely related groups of items with white space or a line. You can also group objects by giving them a differently colored background, although don't go overboard with bright colors. The background should draw attention to the group, not to itself.

Figure 5-8 shows a form with three kinds of grouping. The Contact Information and Newsletters group boxes contain information that is closely related. Inside the Contact Information group box, vertical white space separates address, phone, and Internet information. Inside the Newsletters group box, horizontal space divides the items into two columns.

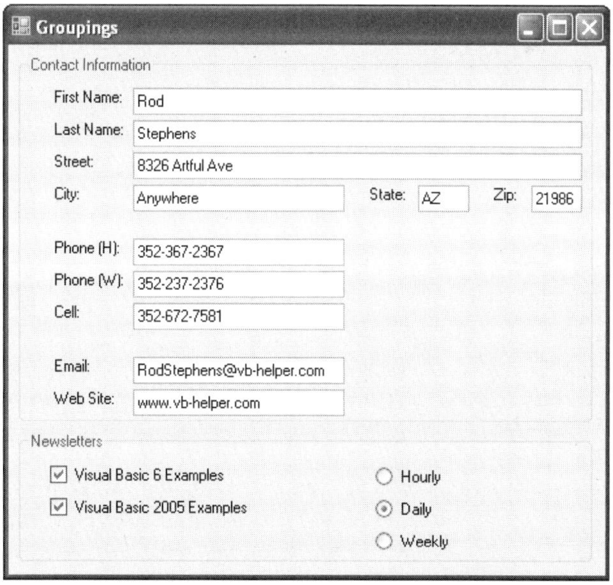

Figure 5-8: This form uses group boxes, vertical white space, and horizontal columns to group items.

Align elements within and across groups. Also, align group box borders, even if adjacent group boxes don't need the same amount of space.

Support Resizing

Ideally, a form should be useful at any size. If the user needs to compare the form's data to data on other forms, he or she may need to shrink the form until it is quite small. To make this kind of comparison possible, the form should make its most important data visible, even when it is fairly small. Usually that means putting the most important data in the upper left. If the user might need to view other data while the form is small, provide scroll bars.

If the user is focusing solely on this form, he or she may want to maximize it so that it covers the whole screen. This not only allows the form to display more information, but it also hides the rest of the desktop so the user faces fewer distractions.

The form should adjust its controls to take full advantage of its current size. The `Dock` and `Anchor` properties let controls resize with the form. This is particularly useful for list boxes, grids, and other controls that contain scrolling areas because they resize with the form, and hide or display their scroll bars as necessary.

Figure 5-9 shows a form that resizes its controls to take advantage of its current size. The First Name, Last Name, Street, and City fields are anchored on the top, left, and right, so they expand horizontally as the form does. The State and ZIP code fields and their labels are anchored on the top and right, but not the left, so they move with the form's right edge. The list at the bottom is anchored to the top, bottom, left, and right, so it expands vertically and horizontally as the form does.

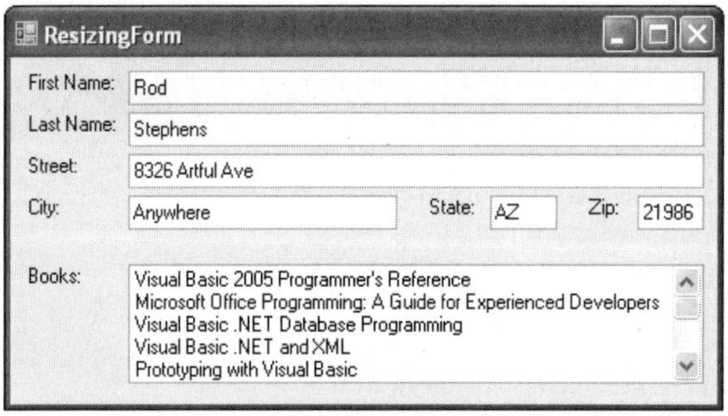

Figure 5-9: This form's fields expand to take advantage of the form's size.

List boxes and other scrolling areas can be quite difficult to use if they are too small. If you shrink this form so that the list box displays fewer than four items, the thumb inside the scroll bar disappears, and you can only scroll through the list using the up and down arrow buttons or by using the keyboard (clicking an item and using the arrow keys, Page Up, Page Dn, Home, and other keys). This is particularly annoying if the list contains a lot of items. Imagine using the up and down arrows to scroll through a list of 50 states.

The problem is much worse if the user must select multiple items from the list. In that case, some selections won't be visible when the list is too small, so the user won't be able to see the current selections.

The form's First Name, Last Name, Street, and City text boxes are also difficult to use if the form is too narrow. To prevent the user from making the form too small to be useful, its `MinimumSize` property is set to `435,221`, so the user cannot make it smaller than 435x221 pixels.

Taking advantage of the form's full size can be tricky. It can mess up the nice layout you devise, ruining the form's symmetry and balance. If you don't pick the resizable controls carefully, it can spoil control alignment and, in some cases, even make controls overlap.

Support Different Font Sizes

Windows supports different base system font sizes. To change the font sizes in Windows XP, right-click the desktop and select Properties. On the Appearance tab, click on the "Font size" drop-down list and select Normal, Large Fonts, or Extra Large Fonts. Then click OK.

Using large fonts can help those with vision problems, a group of users that is growing as the general population ages. Large fonts can also help those with very high-resolution monitors. Sometimes it's useful to use a very large number of pixels per inch on the screen for graphics work but it makes normal fonts measured in pixels very small. The solution is to use large fonts with the small pixels.

When you change the system's font size, Windows automatically increases the size of menus, menu items, dialogs, and other screen elements, but it does not change the size of the fonts used within your application. However, Visual Studio does provide a few features that make it easier for you to support different font sizes.

First, by default, Visual Studio automatically resizes forms if you change their font sizes. If you enlarge a form's font to match the system's selected size, the form resizes to fit the font.

Second, controls on a form inherit the font used by their container. For example, if you change a group box's font, all of the buttons, labels, text boxes, and other controls inside the group box inherit the new font. Because all controls are contained inside the form, changing the form's font changes every control's font.

Note that this doesn't work if you modify a control's font. If you change a label's font at design time, then the label keeps that font, even if its container's font changes.

Figure 5-10 shows a form containing two group boxes. I changed the font used by the right group box to detach it from the form's font. When this program starts, its code enlarges the form's font. You can see that the left group box and its contained controls grew to match while the group box on the right and its controls did not. Visual Studio also enlarged the form and the group boxes.

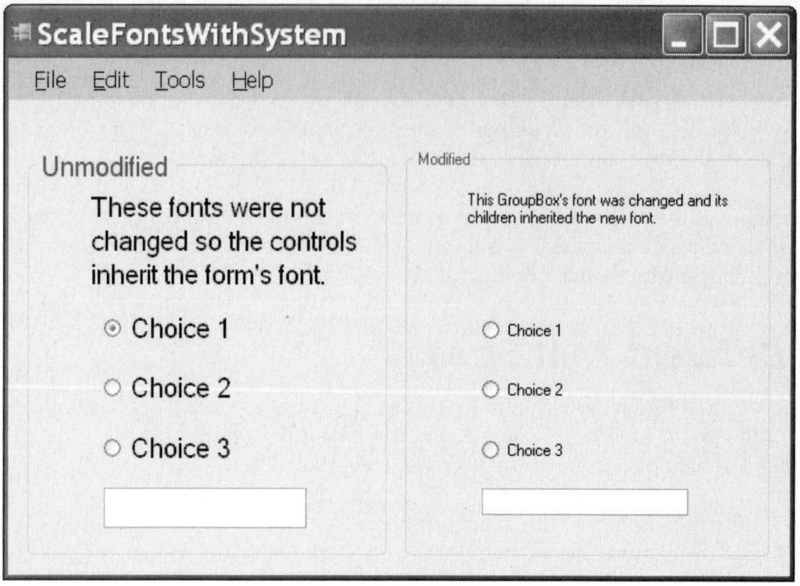

Figure 5-10: By default, a control inherits its container's font.

Before taking the image of the form in Figure 5-10, I set the system to use extra large fonts, and you can see those fonts in the title bar and menus. The following code shows how this program adjusts the form's font to match:

```
Public Class Form1
    Private Const SMALL_CAPTION_FONT_SIZE As Single = 9.75
    Private Const SMALL_DEFAULT_FONT_SIZE As Single = 8.25
    Private Const FONT_SCALE As Single = _
        SMALL_DEFAULT_FONT_SIZE / SMALL_CAPTION_FONT_SIZE

    Private Sub Form1_Load(ByVal sender As System.Object, _
     ByVal e As System.EventArgs) Handles MyBase.Load
        Me.Font = New Font( _
            Me.Font.FontFamily, _
            SystemFonts.CaptionFont.Size * FONT_SCALE)
    End Sub
End Class
```

The program defines constants holding the font sizes used by the form when the system is using normal sized fonts. When the form loads, it creates a new `Font` object using its current font family, and the system's caption font size is scaled to produce a corresponding form font size. (You can download this example at `www.vb-helper.com/one_on_one.htm`.)

If you don't modify the fonts used by the controls on a form, this code will set the font size for every control on the form automatically.

This technique provides a pretty good result with very little work on your part, but it's not completely perfect. It resizes most, but not all, kinds of controls. In particular, it doesn't resize picture boxes. The resizing also doesn't always produce the best appearance, and some items look better if they are rearranged after resizing.

One trick for handling different system font sizes explicitly is to use Visual Basic's localization features to build "fake locales" for the different sizes. First, build the basic form design, giving it whatever controls you want to display when the system is using the normal font size.

Then set the form's `Localizable` property to `True` and set its `Language` property to a language that you know you will never need to use for internationalization. For my example program, I used "Uzbek (Latin, Uzbekistan)" and "Uzbek (Cyrillic, Uzbekistan)." Next, modify the controls on the form for the new size. Make fonts larger, resize controls, add bigger pictures to pictures boxes, and so forth.

Pick another fake locale for extra large fonts and repeat the process. You can make even more fake locales if you want to support other configurations.

Now, add the following code to the form:

```
Imports System.Threading
Imports System.Globalization

Public Class Form1
    Public Sub New()
        SetFormLocale()

        ' This call is required by the Windows Form Designer.
        InitializeComponent()

        ' Add any initialization after the InitializeComponent() call.

    End Sub

    ' Pick the correct size "locale."
    Private Sub SetFormLocale()
        ' See how big the system fonts are.
        Dim culture_info As CultureInfo
        If SystemFonts.CaptionFont.Size < 10 Then
            ' Use the default locale.
            culture_info = New CultureInfo("")
        ElseIf SystemFonts.CaptionFont.Size < 15 Then
            ' Use the large fake locale.
            culture_info = New CultureInfo("uz-UZ-Cyrl")
        Else
            ' Use the extra large fake locale.
            culture_info = New CultureInfo("uz-UZ-Latn")
        End If

        ' Set the locale.
        Thread.CurrentThread.CurrentCulture = culture_info
        Thread.CurrentThread.CurrentUICulture = culture_info
    End Sub
End Class
```

Subroutine `SetFormLocale` looks at the system's caption font size and uses a series of `If Then` statements to pick the appropriate fake locale. It creates a `CultureInfo` object for the locale and sets the thread's `CurrentCulture` and `CurrentUICulture` to that object. This makes the program load resources from the appropriate locale-specific resource file when it builds the form.

The form's constructor `Sub New` calls subroutine `SetFormLocale`. Note that it must do this before the form creates its controls in the call to `InitializeComponent`. (You can download this example at `www.vb-helper.com/one_on_one.htm`.)

This technique lets you select a locale when a form loads, but it can't change a form's locale after it is loaded. Sometimes you might want to let the user select the form's scale at run-time instead of relying on the system's font settings. The following code changes a form's locale after it has been loaded:

```
Imports System.Globalization
Imports System.ComponentModel

Public Class Form1
    Private Sub ApplyLocale(ByVal locale_name As String)
        Dim culture_info As New CultureInfo(locale_name)
        Dim component_resource_manager As New ComponentResourceManager(Me.GetType)
        component_resource_manager.ApplyResources(Me, "$this", culture_info)

        For Each ctl As Control In Me.Controls
            ApplyLocaleToControl(ctl, component_resource_manager, culture_info)
        Next ctl
    End Sub

    Private Sub ApplyLocaleToControl(ByVal ctl As Control, _
     ByVal component_resource_manager As ComponentResourceManager, _
     ByVal culture_info As CultureInfo)
        component_resource_manager.ApplyResources(ctl, ctl.Name, culture_info)

        For Each child As Control In ctl.Controls
            component_resource_manager.ApplyResources( _
                child, child.Name, culture_info)
        Next child
    End Sub

    Private Sub radEnglish_CheckedChanged(ByVal sender As System.Object, _
     ByVal e As System.EventArgs) Handles radEnglish.CheckedChanged
        ApplyLocale("en-US")
    End Sub

    Private Sub radGerman_CheckedChanged(ByVal sender As System.Object, _
     ByVal e As System.EventArgs) Handles radGerman.CheckedChanged
        ApplyLocale("de-DE")
    End Sub
End Class
```

Subroutine `ApplyLocale` loads the resources for a locale into a form that is already loaded. It creates a `CultureInfo` object for the locale, makes a `ComponentResourceManager` for the form, and calls its

ApplyResources method to make the manager load the resources for the form (in the resource file, the form's name is "$this"). Next, the code calls ApplyLocaleToControl for each of the controls contained in the form.

Subroutine ApplyLocaleToControl calls the resource manager's ApplyResources method to load a control's resources from the locale-specific resource file, and then recursively calls itself for each control contained in the initial control.

When the user clicks the radEnglish or radGerman radio buttons in the example program, the event handlers call subroutine ApplyLocale, passing in the appropriate locale name. (You can download this example at www.vb-helper.com/one_on_one.htm.)

> *If you are writing an application for international use, you shouldn't use these techniques to load fake locales when the form loads or when the user picks one. Instead, design the form for the locales you will really support and let Visual Studio automatically select the appropriate resources for the user's system.*

If you really need to support multiple sizes for multiple languages, you could probably define a matrix of fake locales for each combination: English normal, English large, German normal, German large, and so forth. It will probably be easier to let Visual Studio pick the locale, update the font sizes, and then write code to rearrange any picture boxes or other controls that don't resize properly.

Optimize Menus

Use standard menus and menu items in their normal arrangement with their typical keyboard accelerators and shortcuts whenever possible. Users expect the File menu to be on the left, and for it to contain a Save command with Ctrl+S as a shortcut. Changing this traditional arrangement will slow the user down, and may lead to errors when the user switches from one application to another.

Visual Studio makes building a standard menu easy. First, add a MenuStrip control to the form. Right-click the MenuStrip and select Insert Standard Items. Figure 5-11 shows the result.

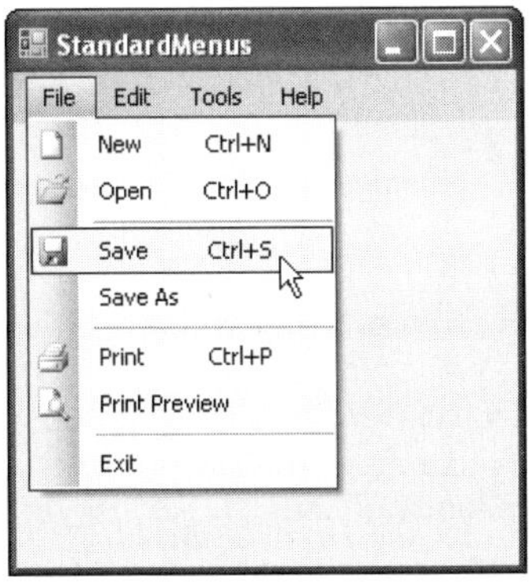

Figure 5-11: To build standard menus, place a MenuStrip on the form, right-click it, and select Insert Standard Items.

The following list shows the menus and keyboard shortcuts created by the Insert Standard Menus command.

- File
    - New (Ctrl+N)
    - Open (Ctrl+O)
    - Save (Ctrl+S)
    - Save As
    - Print (Ctrl+P)
    - Print Preview
    - Exit
- Edit
    - Undo (Ctrl+Z)
    - Redo (Ctrl+Y)
    - Cut (Ctrl+X)
    - Copy (Ctrl+C)
    - Paste (Ctrl+V)
    - Select All
- Tools
    - Customize
    - Options
- Help
    - Contents
    - Index
    - Search
    - About

Add code for the menu items that you want to use and delete the others.

Strangely, only the About dialog displays an ellipsis (...) on the right to indicate that it opens a dialog. You should modify the captions of the menus to add ellipses to the Save As, Print Preview, Customize, Options, Contents, Index, and Search menu items.

When menu items are unavailable, disable them instead of deleting them. That lets the user see the items so that he or she knows where they are. It can be frustrating to remember that the system has a particular menu command, but be unable to find it. If the item is disabled, the user can at least see it and try to figure out how to enable the command.

Context menus handle unavailable items a little differently than standard menus. Context menus are tied to specific controls and data, so their contents should reflect the item to which they are tied. That means a menu attached to a text box holding a name might contain different items than one attached to a text box displaying a student's quiz score. Those menus should not contain the same items with the unavailable entries disabled. Instead, they should contain only the items that are relevant for their purposes.

Of course, some of a context menu's items may still be disabled if they are currently unavailable. For example, if the program is in a state that does not allow you to change a student's quiz score, the Reset Score command might be present, but disabled on the quiz score text box's context menu.

Favor breadth over depth in menu design. Deep menu systems contain many hidden items and make it hard for the user to find things. Ideally, the menu should have around four to eight choices per level, and a maximum of two or three levels.

If the application works with some sort of document, provide a most recently used (MRU) file list in the File menu to let the user quickly reload a document. Note that the documents need not be files on the system. For example, they could be customer records in a database.

If you are building an MDI application, provide a Windows menu that contains commands that help the user manage the child windows. When you create an MDI parent form, Visual Studio automatically gives it a Windows menu with appropriate items. It even provides code to implement the basic menu commands.

Use Space Wisely

In many applications, squeezing all of the data the users needs onto a form can be a challenge. In non-graphical legacy systems, screen navigation can be difficult, and the user cannot display multiple windows to compare data on different forms. To give users all of the data they need, those systems often crammed hundreds of fields onto a single screen. If you are rewriting such a system, users will be used to having all of that data available, and you need to find a way to present it efficiently. Ideally the user should be able to view all information at once without resizing or scrolling, but that's not always possible.

Visual Studio gives you several tools for putting large amounts of data on a form. Controls such as `ListBox`, `ListView`, and grids can scroll their contents. The `TreeView` control lets the user expand and collapse parts of the tree to show only parts of a potentially enormous amount of data.

The `TabControl`, `SplitContainer`, and `Panel` controls allow the user to adjust the information visible in a group of other controls that do not provide scrolling themselves. For example, if you put a large group of labels and text boxes inside a `Panel` with `AutoScroll` set to `True`, the user can scroll through the controls if necessary. If you place two scrollable `Panels` inside a `SplitContainer`, the user can adjust the relative sizes of the two `Panels` and scroll their contents.

The `TabControl` control (yes, "Control" is part of its name) is particularly useful for handling very large amounts of related data. Break the data into manageable pieces and place each on a separate tab. For a customer database, you might have tabs for contact information, order history, payment history, and correspondence.

I've used tabbed forms successfully in many applications. They put enormous amounts of data at the users' fingertips while conserving screen space.

When you put items inside a scrollable panel, split container, or a series of tabs, try to ensure that any items that the user will need to compare are visible at the same time. Putting a customer's order history and payment history on separate tabs will make it difficult for the user to compare them. Of course, in theory, the user may want to look at just about any two pieces of data at the same time, so you need to prioritize. Plan for the user's most common tasks and make them as easy as possible. It's okay if less-common tasks take a little more effort.

Design Good Headers

Use header labels to identify groups of controls and areas on the form. Visually distinguish headers so more-advanced users can quickly identify them and ignore them. The `GroupBox` control provides its own header that is distinguished by a different color. You can also make headers use ALL CAPS.

While changing header font size and style is nice way to distinguish headers, it makes resizing the form's fonts more difficult, so you may want to stick with color and ALL CAPS instead.

Use consistent header structure. If some headers are nouns, make them all nouns. Don't say "Addresses" for one header and "User Contacts" in another. Either say "User Addresses" and "User Contacts," or just "Addresses" and "Contacts." Don't say "Enter Data" in one area and "Data" in another.

Spell out headers rather than using abbreviations. Even if the users have no trouble realizing that TelNo is short for "Telephone Number," their recognition will be slightly faster if you spell it out. If you are pressed for space, use "Phone Number" or just "Phone" instead of an abbreviation.

Though you should avoid abbreviations, it's okay to use abbreviations from the users' domain if the users are very familiar with them, particularly if they represent complex ideas that would be hard to spell out. In the telephone industry, POTS stands for "plain old telephone service" and TelCo stands for "telephone company." The users are so accustomed to those terms that spelling these out would probably slow recognition.

Be sure headers are consistent across all forms. Use the same header captions when two forms display the same kind of data. Consistency will help new users learn to use the application, and makes it faster and easier for all users to locate specific pieces of data.

Preserve State

If the user typically performs tasks over long periods of time that may span days, resuming an interrupted task after restarting the application can take a long time. To make this easier, the application should save its state when closing and return to that state when it restarts. It should reopen any windows that were open before and position them where they were last time. It should also configure the forms as they were last time. For example, it should select the tab that the form had selected when the program was closed.

If the users typically don't perform long tasks, the idea of restoring their working state is not as critical. You might redisplay search forms and other forms that control the application so the user can get started with new tasks quickly, but the program might not need to restore specific customer forms.

Undo and Redo

Undo and redo features are very helpful for users trying to explore an application. They let users know that they can experiment without fear of damaging the system and its data. They also help users undo potentially disastrous mistakes made accidentally.

Unfortunately, building an undo and redo system is fairly difficult, and Visual Studio doesn't provide much help.

One approach is to store a snapshot of the system's state in a collection every time the user makes a modification. To undo a change, the program restores the previous snapshot from the collection. To redo a removed action, the program restores the next snapshot from the collection.

The following code demonstrates this approach. This simple program lets you draw dots of random sizes on the form. Click to draw a dot. Use the Data menu's Undo and Redo commands to undo and redo dots.

```
Imports System.Xml.Serialization
Imports System.IO

Public Class Form1
    ' A dot object.
    <Serializable()> _
    Public Class Dot
        Public X As Integer
        Public Y As Integer
        Public Radius As Integer

        Public Sub New()
        End Sub
        Public Sub New(ByVal new_x As Integer, ByVal new_y As Integer, _
         ByVal new_radius As Integer)
            X = new_x
            Y = new_y
            Radius = new_radius
        End Sub

        Public Sub Draw(ByVal gr As Graphics)
            gr.DrawEllipse(Pens.Black, X - Radius, Y - Radius, _
                2 * Radius, 2 * Radius)
        End Sub
    End Class

    ' Snapshots for undo/redo.
    Private m_Snapshots As New Collection
    Private m_CurrentSnapshot As Integer = 0
    Private Const MAX_SNAPSHOTS As Integer = 5

    ' The current dots.
    Private m_NumDots As Integer = 0
    Private m_Dots() As Dot

    Private Sub Form1_Load(ByVal sender As Object, _
```

```
    ByVal e As System.EventArgs) Handles Me.Load
        ' Save an empty snapshot.
        SaveSnapshot()
    End Sub

    ' Make a new dot.
    Private Sub Form1_MouseDown(ByVal sender As Object, _
     ByVal e As System.Windows.Forms.MouseEventArgs) Handles Me.MouseDown
        MakeDot(e.X, e.Y)

        Me.Invalidate()
    End Sub

    ' Make a dot.
    Private Sub MakeDot(ByVal X As Integer, ByVal Y As Integer)
        Dim rand As New Random
        Dim new_dot As New Dot(X, Y, rand.Next(10, 30))

        m_NumDots += 1
        ReDim Preserve m_Dots(0 To m_NumDots - 1)
        m_Dots(m_NumDots - 1) = new_dot

        ' Save a snapshot.
        SaveSnapshot()
    End Sub

    ' Save a snapshot.
    Private Sub SaveSnapshot()
        ' Remove any snapshots after the current one.
        Do While m_Snapshots.Count > m_CurrentSnapshot
            m_Snapshots.Remove(m_Snapshots.Count)
        Loop

        Dim xml_serializer As New XmlSerializer(GetType(Dot()))
        Dim string_writer As New StringWriter()
        xml_serializer.Serialize(string_writer, m_Dots)
        m_Snapshots.Add(string_writer.ToString())

        string_writer.Close()
        string_writer.Dispose()

        ' Make sure we don't have too many.
        Do While m_Snapshots.Count > MAX_SNAPSHOTS + 1
            m_Snapshots.Remove(1)
        Loop

        m_CurrentSnapshot = m_Snapshots.Count
    End Sub

    ' Restore a snapshot.
    Private Sub RestoreSnapshot()
        Dim xml_serializer As New XmlSerializer(GetType(Dot()))
        Dim string_reader As New StringReader( _
            CStr(m_Snapshots.Item(m_CurrentSnapshot)))
```

```
        m_Dots = DirectCast(xml_serializer.Deserialize(string_reader), Dot())
        If m_Dots Is Nothing Then
            m_NumDots = 0
        Else
            m_NumDots = m_Dots.Length
        End If
        string_reader.Close()
        string_reader.Dispose()

        Me.Invalidate()
    End Sub

    ' Draw the dots.
    Private Sub Form1_Paint(ByVal sender As Object, _
     ByVal e As System.Windows.Forms.PaintEventArgs) Handles Me.Paint
        e.Graphics.Clear(Me.BackColor)
        For i As Integer = 0 To m_NumDots - 1
            m_Dots(i).Draw(e.Graphics)
        Next i
    End Sub

    Private Sub mnuDataUndo_Click(ByVal sender As System.Object, _
     ByVal e As System.EventArgs) Handles mnuDataUndo.Click
        If m_CurrentSnapshot > 1 Then
            m_CurrentSnapshot -= 1
            RestoreSnapshot()
        End If
    End Sub

    Private Sub mnuDataRedo_Click(ByVal sender As System.Object, _
     ByVal e As System.EventArgs) Handles mnuDataRedo.Click
        If m_CurrentSnapshot < m_Snapshots.Count Then
            m_CurrentSnapshot += 1
            RestoreSnapshot()
        End If
    End Sub
End Class
```

This program takes advantage of the powerful serialization capabilities provided by the `XmlSerializer` class. The code begins with a simple `Dot` class that stores a dot's size and position. The class is marked as `Serializable` and has a `Draw` method that draws the dot on the form.

The `m_Snapshots` collection holds the system's saved state information. The value `MAX_SNAPSHOTS` determines how many snapshots the program will save at a time.

The `m_Dots` array stores the dots that the program is currently displaying.

When the form loads, its `Load` event handler calls subroutine `SaveSnapshot` to save a snapshot of the program with no dots.

If you click the form, the form's `MouseDown` event handler calls subroutine `MakeDot` to make a new dot. It then invalidates the form, so it redraws.

Subroutine `MakeDot` creates a `Dot` object with a random radius and adds it to the `m_Dots` collection. It then calls `SaveSnapshot` to save the system's new state. Routines such as this one that change the program's state that should save snapshots.

Subroutine `SaveSnapshot` removes any snapshots after the one that is currently visible. This happens if you undo a few actions and then make a new action. It then creates an `XmlSerializer`, passing the constructor the type of object that it will serialize (an array of `Dot` objects). It makes a `StringWriter` to hold the result and serializes the `m_Dots` array. The result is an XML string representing the array. The following text shows a serialization holding three `Dots`:

```
<?xml version="1.0" encoding="utf-16"?>
<ArrayOfDot xmlns:xsi="http://www.w3.org/2001/XMLSchema-instance"
xmlns:xsd="http://www.w3.org/2001/XMLSchema">
  <Dot>
    <X>102</X>
    <Y>183</Y>
    <Radius>27</Radius>
  </Dot>
  <Dot>
    <X>68</X>
    <Y>83</Y>
    <Radius>25</Radius>
  </Dot>
  <Dot>
    <X>138</X>
    <Y>124</Y>
    <Radius>17</Radius>
  </Dot>
</ArrayOfDot>
```

Subroutine `SaveSnapshot` stores the serialization string in the `m_Snapshots` collection. Then, if the collection contains too many snapshots, the subroutine deletes the oldest ones. Finally, it sets the current snapshot index to indicate the last one in the collection.

Subroutine `RestoreSnapshot` recovers a snapshot. Like subroutine `SaveSnapshot`, it makes an `XmlSerializer` to work with arrays of `Dot` objects. It gets the snapshot pointed to by `m_CurrentSnapshot` and deserializes it to re-create the `m_Dots` array. It then invalidates the form so that the form's `Paint` event handler can draw the objects in the new `m_Dots` array.

The form's `Paint` event handler simply loops through the objects in the `m_Dots` array and invokes their `Draw` methods.

When the user clicks the Undo button, the program subtracts one from `m_CurrentSnapshot` and calls `RestoreSnapshot` to recover that snapshot. When the user clicks the Redo button, the program adds one from `m_CurrentSnapshot` and calls `RestoreSnapshot` to recover that snapshot. (You can download this example at `www.vb-helper.com/one_on_one.htm`.)

This example uses an array of very simple `Dot` objects to store its state. You can use any arbitrary set of classes instead, as long as a single object represents the root of the application's state. In this example, the root is the `m_Dots` array. It could just as well have been some sort of `DrawnPicture` object containing various objects representing ellipses, rectangles, lines, text, and other drawing elements. XML serialization is a powerful technique that lets you easily save and restore representations of the objects that hold the application's state.

The serialization also gives you an easy way to save and restore the application's state in a file. If you write the serialization into an XML file, you can later deserialize the file to restore the application to its former state.

Instead of storing a serialization string, you could store objects in the snapshot collection. In this example, you would make a copy of the `m_Dots` array for each snapshot and store it in the collection.

Accommodate Different Skills Levels

Users with different levels of experience with the application need different types of assistance to use the application efficiently. Beginners need lots of prompts, headers, and instruction. They need memory prompts to help them remember what commands they can use under different circumstances. They explore menus to find appropriate commands and may need online help.

Expert users need fewer hints and guidance. They can remember the tasks they need to perform so they are able to take advantage of keyboard shortcuts and accelerators. They don't need to navigate menus to find what they need, and they rarely need online help.

To satisfy both kinds of users, you should display information that gives help as unobtrusively as possible. Beginners can look for the tips and hints, while experts easily ignore them. Making the guiding information easy to ignore lets expert users work more quickly.

> *In a way this is similar to the idea of information hiding described in Chapter 4. There, the goal was for a class to hide all of its internal information that is not absolutely necessary from outside code. Here, the idea is to make information accessible, but in a way that lets users view or ignore it as they see fit. The user, not the program, decides what information is necessary.*

The application should also provide multiple ways to perform the same tasks. It should allow beginners to find commands in menus, while experts use shortcuts.

Some developers think providing multiple ways to perform the same task is a goal in itself. Adding several commands to do the same task in different menus only makes the menus confusing. Instead, you should provide different methods that will help users of different abilities.

The following list describes hints and guides you can make available to novices without unduly distracting expert users:

- Provide a "Tip Of The Day" feature when the application starts. Put a "Do not show this again" checkbox on the tip's form so that users can turn it off when they no longer need it. Allow them to turn it back on through the Tools menu's Options command.
- Provide context-sensitive instructions in a status bar at the bottom of the form.
- Provide all of the currently available commands in the menus so that beginners can find them.
- Provide tools and commands in a toolbar. Intermediate-level users who can recognize tools by their icons can use these instead of navigating the menus.

- Provide tooltips for every control with a purpose that isn't completely obvious.
- Provide textual instructions in the form. Make the text visually distinctive (for example, with a lighter font) so that expert users can ignore it.
- Provide context-sensitive help.
- Provide online help. Include lots of examples showing how to perform typical tasks. Take advantage of the fact that people are very good at learning from examples.
- Provide online tutorials.

The following list describes shortcuts that you can make available to advanced users without confusing beginners:

- Provide keyboard accelerators for menu commands and buttons.
- Provide accelerators on the labels that come before important text boxes in the tab order so that expert users can quickly jump to the field.
- Provide shortcut key combinations such as Ctrl+S to save so expert users don't need to open the program's menus.
- Provide context menus attached to specific controls and areas on the form. Beginners may use the main menus instead, but advanced users will be more productive using context menus.
- Provide methods for the user to customize the application. Let the user build customized toolbars that contain the commands the user needs most frequently. Let the user customize the fields shown in query results. Beginners will use the initial default values, but experts will know what tools they need most and what values they need to see.

Use subtle error indicators when a field contains invalid data, rather than stopping the user's workflow. For example, highlight invalid fields with a different background color or use an `ErrorProvider` control to flag the field. Beginners will notice the indicator right away and try to fix the problem.

If you use an `ErrorProvider` control, give the control a meaningful message that tells the user what is wrong and how to correct it. The user can see this message by hovering the mouse over the `ErrorProvider`. Figure 5-12 shows the `ErrorProvider` control displaying an error message.

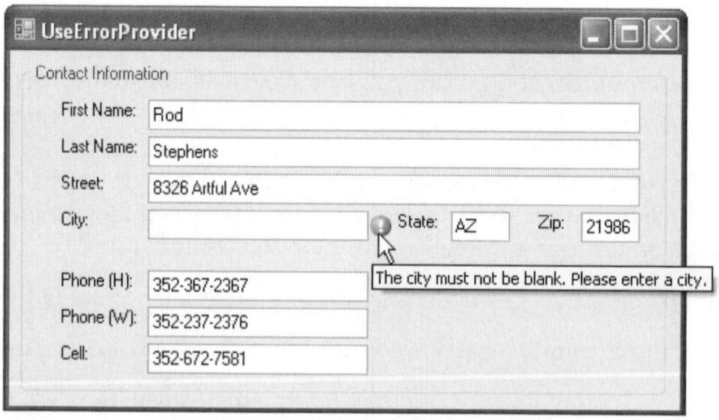

Figure 5-12: The `ErrorProvider` control displays a message if you hover the mouse over it.

More-advanced users who are performing "head down" data entry will not notice the flag until later, so they can continue entering other data uninterrupted.

Many of the tools you give to beginners can also help expert users on occasion. A user who has years of experience with the application as a whole is basically a beginner when it comes to performing rare and unusual tasks.

Provide Appropriate Feedback

The application must give the user prompt and appropriate feedback so that the user knows what has happened. When the user performs a task, the application should let the user know whether task was completed successfully. If there is a problem, it should tell the user how to resolve it.

The strength and intrusiveness of the response should be in proportion to the importance and frequency of the task. If the user performs a task continuously and mistakes are easy to correct, the application can provide subtle feedback.

For example, suppose the application uses an `ErrorProvider` to flag data format errors in text boxes. When the user enters a value and tabs to the next field, the fact that the `ErrorProvider` does not appear is sufficient feedback that the field's value is correct. This is a very frequent interaction, so the feedback is very subtle.

However, the feedback when an error occurs is less subtle. In that case, the `ErrorProvider` blinks several times and displays an error icon. It still doesn't interrupt the user's workflow, but the error is quite obvious.

When the user performs more powerful and unusual tasks, the program should provide stronger feedback. When the user launches a time-consuming process, for example, the program should provide feedback while the operation continues to let the user know what it is doing. When the task finishes, it can display a message box telling the user it is finished and display its results.

The program should provide continuous feedback to tell the user what state it is in. If the program can enter different modes of operation, it should give an indication of its current mode. For example, Microsoft Word can operate in insert mode where the text you type is inserted before the following text, or in overwrite mode where new text replaces old text. The status bar at the bottom displays the text "OVR" when Word is in overwrite mode. When Word is in insert mode, the "OVR" is grayed out.

This actually isn't a great design because "OVR" is a fairly cryptic abbreviation instead of being spelled out, and the grayed-out "OVR" doesn't tell you that you are in insert mode. The item in the status bar is also an active button that toggles Word between overwrite and insert modes, even when it's grayed out and looks disabled. A checkbox labeled "Overwrite" might be better. But at least Word provides a continual mode indicator!

The program should also indicate if data is outdated. For example, suppose the user queries a database to get a list of the highest priority jobs. As new jobs come into the database, the display will be out of date.

Visual Studio's database model is basically batch-oriented, so it's rare that the program knows its data is up to date. The program fetches data from the database, works with it for awhile, and then updates the database. In many applications, it's safer for the user to assume that the data is out of date, unless the program does something to lock a record for its own use. In that case, the program should flag the locked data so that the user knows that it is up to date and that other users cannot modify the data until they release it.

Users expect prompt results. If the program appears to do nothing for too long, the user may wonder if something has gone wrong or if the program has crashed. If a task will take a long time to complete (more than about one second), the program should give appropriate feedback to the user.

Users can keep their attention on the application while waiting for about five seconds. If a delay is longer than that, the user becomes impatient. To prevent the user from growing annoyed, you need to display a larger, more obvious indication to the user that the task may take awhile.

The following table shows appropriate feedback for tasks of various durations.

Duration	Feedback
Under 1 second	None.
1–5 seconds	Wait cursor on all forms.
5–10 seconds	A modal "Working" dialog that goes away automatically when the task finishes.
10 seconds–1 minute	A modal dialog with a progress bar indicating progress. When the program finishes the task, it automatically replaces the dialog with a "Done" message box.
More than 1 minute	A modal dialog with a progress bar indicating progress, a label continuously showing the estimated time remaining, and a label indicating the subtask that the program is currently performing. Only report subtasks that take long enough for the user to read about them so that there isn't a stream of rapidly blinking text. The dialog can include an "Automatically close when finished" checkbox. If this box is not checked, the program should replace the dialog with a "Done" message box when it finishes.

Sounds are generally quite annoying to the users, particularly if they work in a common area so everyone hears whatever sounds are playing on each others' computers.

Don't use sound to notify the user about anything important. The user may have turned down the computer's volume, may have hearing problems, or may have broken speakers.

If you do use sound to help get the user's attention, use one of the standard system sounds, not an interesting or cute music file. Cute sounds don't seem so cute when your coworkers must listen to them hundreds of times a day. Combine the sound with a visible indicator in case the user does have the sound turned off or is away from the computer when the event occurs and misses the sound.

Avoid moving or blinking objects. They are extremely attention-getting, so they draw the user away from anything else he or she might prefer to do before responding to your message. If you do display a blinking object to tell the user about an urgent situation, make it blink a few times and then stop (like the `ErrorProvider` does).

Consistency

At every level of UI design, be consistent. Design main forms, secondary forms, and dialogs consistently. Place buttons in the same position on all dialogs, either at the bottom or on the right. Use similar font styles for headings, labels, instructions, and data.

Give forms with similar purposes similar sizes, colors, and layouts. Use similar menus, toolbars, status bars, accelerators, and keyboard shortcuts. Capitalize field labels, headings, and form captions in the same ways. Use similar navigational methods to let the user move between forms.

The more the forms have in common, the easier it is for the users to figure out how to use them. Consistency promotes learning. Even after the users have experience with the application, consistency lets them perform their jobs faster and with fewer mistakes.

A good consistent design makes your application stand together as a whole, rather than appearing to be a collection of randomly generated forms that were thrown together with little design and planning.

Summary

User-interface design is a huge field. To build a usable, clean, elegant UI, you must consider a myriad of factors, including the characteristics of the users, their work environment, their jobs, and the tasks that are common and those that are unusual. You must also follow good design principles to encourage users with different roles and skill levels to get the most out of the application.

Even then your work is not done. You should observe the users interacting with the application and determine what parts work smoothly and efficiently, and what parts need to be redesigned.

This chapter should be enough to get you started, but there's a lot more to good design. For more information about UI design, see a more specialized book such as *The Essential Guide to User Interface Design* by Wilbert Galitz (Indianapolis: John Wiley & Sons, 2002).

For lighter reading, I also recommend the book The Design of Everyday Things by Donald Norman (New York: Basic Books, 2002). It discusses more general design issues for physical objects, rather than software (doors, doorknobs, teapots, and so forth). Many of the ideas also apply to UI design, and can give you a general feel for what makes a good design and what doesn't.

This chapter and Chapter 4 show two different aspects of an application's design. Chapter 6, "Data Storage Design," shows a third aspect of design: how the data behind the application is arranged, stored, retrieved, and presented to the user.

6

Data Storage Design

The first step in building an application is to design it. The better your design is, the fewer problems you will encounter later when you write the code. To make the best design possible, you need to look at the design from several points of view.

Chapter 4, "Object-Oriented Design," looks at design from an object-oriented perspective. It explains how to select and refine the classes that will implement the application's behavior. Chapter 5, "User-Interface Design," looks at design from the user's perspective. It explains how to lay out the application's forms to make them as intuitive and useful as possible to the user.

This chapter considers another aspect of design: how the data is stored. In the real world, the large majority of applications store data in relational databases, but that's not the only option, and it's not always the best option. This chapter discusses different methods you can use to store different kinds of data. It talks briefly about relational databases, focusing on their strengths and weaknesses so that you know when they are appropriate.

It then discusses alternatives for storing data such as compiled-in data (data stored in constants and other code elements), the System Registry, and various text file formats. Even if you do need a relational database (and most applications do), there may be other pieces of information that are better stored by one of these other methods.

Relational Databases

Most large applications and many smaller ones use relational databases to store their data. There's no room in this book to do justice to the topic, so I'm not going to try. For more in-depth information about relational databases, see a book specifically about them, such as one of the following:

- *Beginning Visual Basic 2005 Databases* by Thearon Willis (Indianapolis: Wrox, 2005)
- *Visual Basic Database Programming* by Rod Stephens (Indianapolis: Que, 2002)
- *Expert One-on-One Visual Basic 2005 Database Programming* by Roger Jennings (Indianapolis: Wrox, 2005)

There isn't room to cover relational databases in much depth here, but I do want to cover a few aspects of relational databases so that you can compare them to the alternatives, and select the best data storage method for your application.

A relational database stores data in tables. You can think of a table as a grid where each column represents a specific piece of data (such as a name, address, phone number, or image). Each row in the table represents a set of column values that are related. For example, a row in the `Customers` table would contain data for a specific customer. Figure 6-1 shows a simple `Customers` table represented as a grid.

Customers						
CustomerId	FirstName	LastName	Street	City	State	Zip
2178	Ann	Ace	2451 Elm St	Bugsville	AZ	88382
172	Bill	Blaugh	254 2nd Ave	Bugsville	AZ	88381
97	Cindy	Cheerful	One Oak Ter	Programmeria	AZ	88390
3287	Dan	Dwelph	196 Draklin	Programmeria	AZ	88389
2176	Eva	Eversnor	13 Prime Pl	Abend	AZ	88376
1927	Fred	Catabalpas	8472 32nd St	Bugsville	AZ	88382
2981	Gina	Parnathus	91 Horus Ln	Abend	AZ	88376
274	Harry	Pan	3131 Duke Ct	Bugsville	AZ	88381

Figure 6-1: A row in a table contains values that are related.

Rows are also called *records,* and columns are also called *fields,* so a record contains a collection of related fields.

A relational database may contain many tables, as shown in Figure 6-2.

Storing data in this grid-like arrangement may sometimes be useful, but the real power of a relational database comes when you define relationships among the tables. For example, suppose the `Customers` table represents customers and identifies each customer with a `CustomerId`.

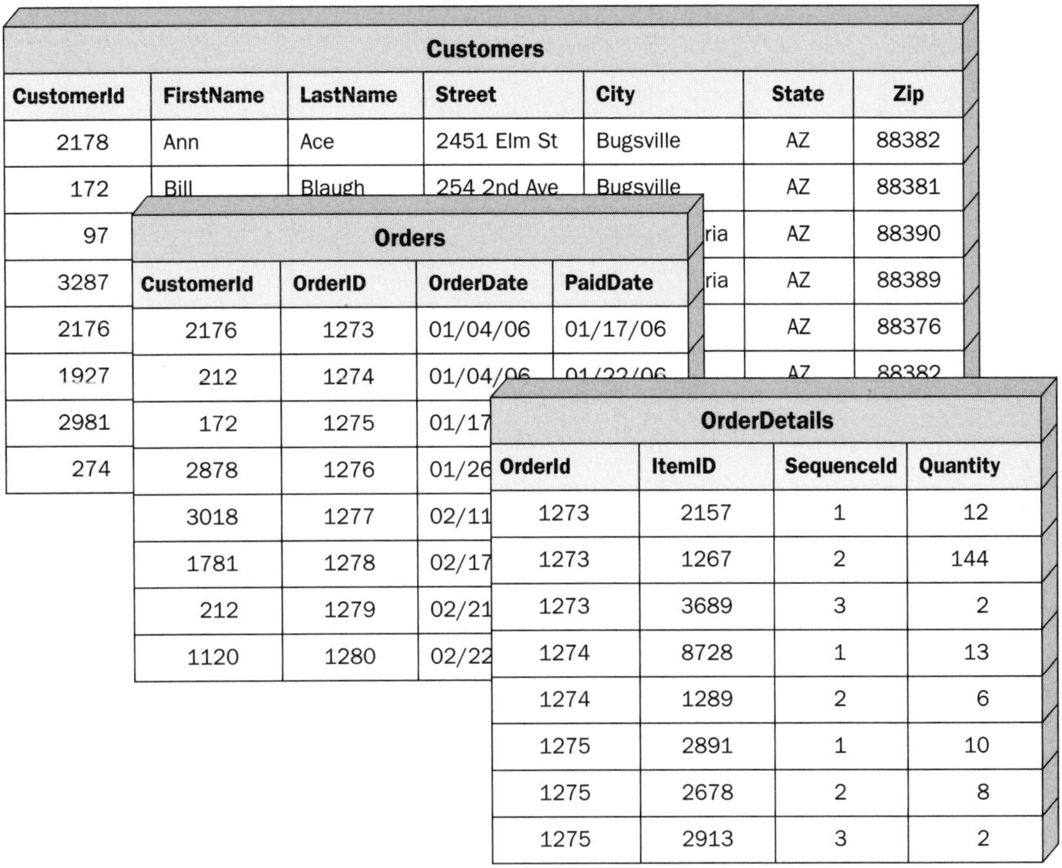
Customers
CustomerId FirstName LastName Street City State Zip
2178 Ann Ace 2451 Elm St Bugsville AZ 88382
172 Bill Blaugh 254 2nd Ave Bugsville AZ 88381
97 ria AZ 88390
3287 ria AZ 88389
2176 AZ 88376
1927
2981
274
Orders
CustomerId OrderID OrderDate PaidDate
2176 1273 01/04/06 01/17/06
212 1274 01/04/
172 1275 01/17
2878 1276 01/26
3018 1277 02/11
1781 1278 02/17
212 1279 02/21
1120 1280 02/22
OrderDetails
OrderId ItemID SequenceId Quantity
1273 2157 1 12
1273 1267 2 144
1273 3689 3 2
1274 8728 1 13
1274 1289 2 6
1275 2891 1 10
1275 2678 2 8
1275 2913 3 2

Figure 6-2: A relational database contains multiple tables, each containing multiple rows of fields.

The `Orders` table represents orders placed by the customers. It identifies the customer who placed an order with a `CustomerId` field. It identifies each order with an `OrderId` field.

The `OrderDetails` table contains information about the items that make up an order. It identifies the order that contains an item with an `OrderId` field.

Figure 6-3 shows how `Customers`, `Orders`, and `OrderDetails` tables are related graphically. In this figure, customer 2176 placed an order represented in the `Orders` table by a record with `CustomerId 2176`. That order has `OrderId 1273`. The order item details for that order are the records in the `OrderDetails` table with `OrderId 1273`.

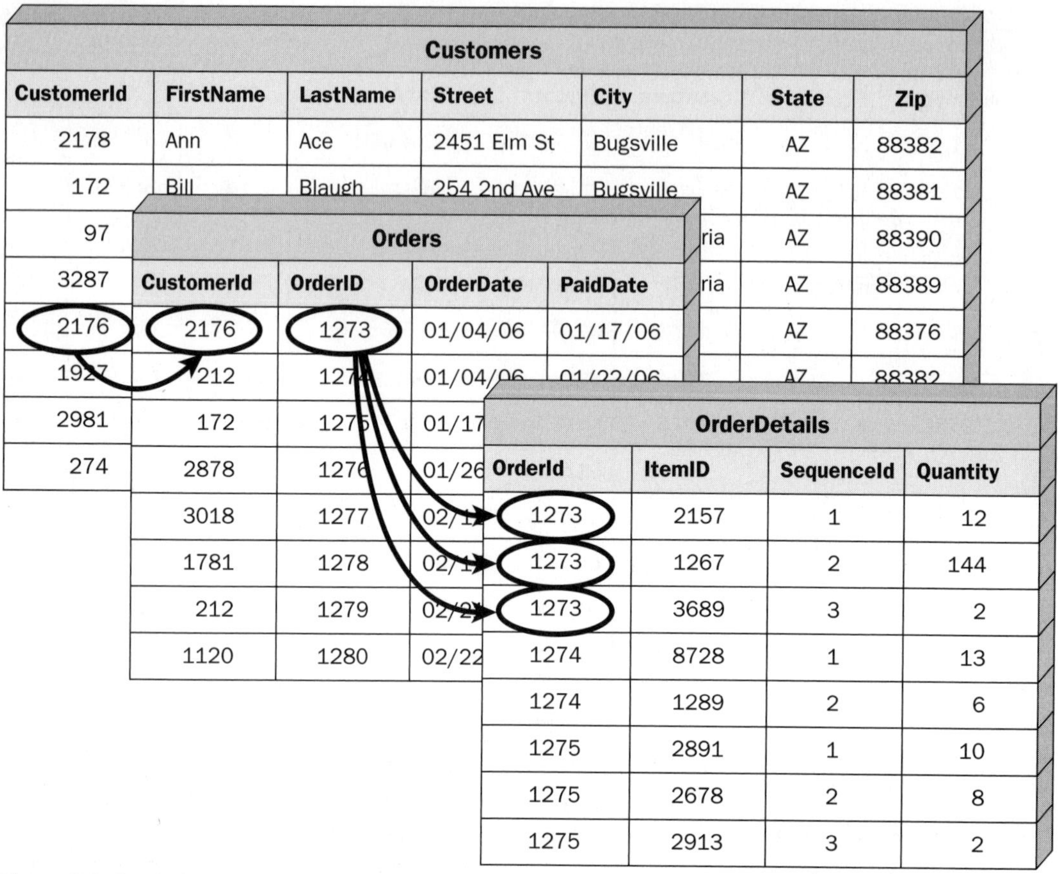

Figure 6-3: A relational database uses field values to form relationships among records in tables.

Relational databases support the Structured Query Language (SQL), an English-like language that tells a database engine what records to retrieve from the database. You can use SQL statements to join together tables and select related records. For example, the following query selects information about orders placed by customer 2176. It returns them ordered by `OrderId` and then `SequenceId`:

```
SELECT FirstName, LastName, Orders.OrderId, OrderDate, PaidDate, _
       ItemId, Quantity
FROM Customers, Orders, OrderDetails
WHERE Customers.CustomerId = 2176
  AND Customers.CustomerId = Orders.CustomerId
  AND Orders.OrderId = OrderDetails.OrderId
ORDER BY Orders.OrderId, SequenceId
```

This example searches for `Customers` records with the desired `CustomerId`, joins the resulting records with records in other tables, and sorts the result.

Relational databases can define indexes on tables to make searching them for specific values faster. For example, you could build an index for the `Orders` table's `CustomerId` field to make searching for records with a particular `CustomerId` faster.

Relational databases also provide for aggregating values: taking sums, averages, and so forth. Taken together, all of these features make relational databases very useful for searching, combining, sorting, and reporting on data. Those are the strengths of relational databases.

Those features can be very useful in an application, particularly for typical business data describing such entities as customers, employees, orders, inventory, and invoices. They can even be useful for storing information about the classes that the program uses. For example, the program might define a `Customer` class and store information about it in the `Customers` table. The database itself won't save and restore `Customer` objects, but it wouldn't be hard to write code to move values from a `Customer` object and a `Customers` record in the database and vice versa.

Though relational databases are good at representing table-like data, they are not as good at representing complex data structures.

For example, consider the small hierarchical data structure shown in Figure 6-4. Each node in the tree contains some information and has a collection of references to child nodes.

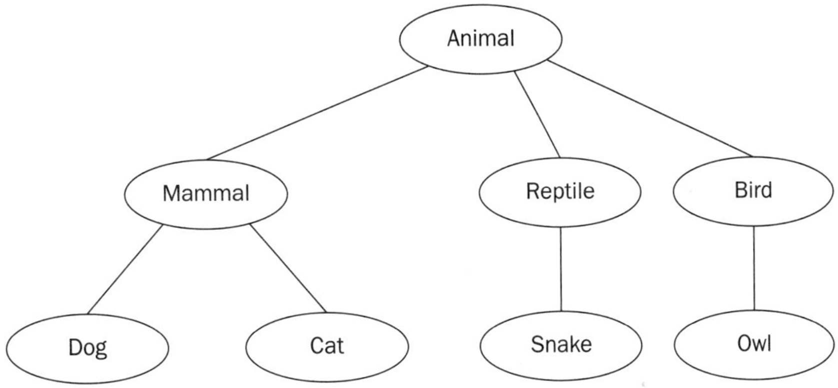

Figure 6-4: Each node in this hierarchical data structure has a collection of references to child nodes.

One way to represent this data in a relational database is to build a `Nodes` table and a `Children` table. The `Nodes` table contains each node's information and a `NodeId`. The `Children` table connects `NodeId` values to `ChildId` values.

Figure 6-5 shows the previous tree stored in a database with this structure. Arrows show how to trace out the top two levels of the tree. Start at the root node with `NodeId 1`. Next, find the records in the `ChildNodes` table with `NodeId 1` and their `ChildId` values give you the IDs of the children of node 1.

To build the entire tree, you need to examine the `ChildNodes` records for each of the child nodes you found in the previous step. You continue in this manner, searching the `ChildNodes` table for the children of the nodes you have found so far, until you find all of the nodes.

To use a similar database design to store a network-like data structure, change the name of the `ChildNodes` table to `Neighbors` and change the name of the `ChildId` field to `NeighborId`. Now the `Neighbors` table lists the nodes that are adjacent to a node in the network. Restoring the network from the database is a little more complicated than it is with a tree because you need to beware of loops. For example, if the network is undirected, if node A has node B as a neighbor then node B also has node A as a neighbor.

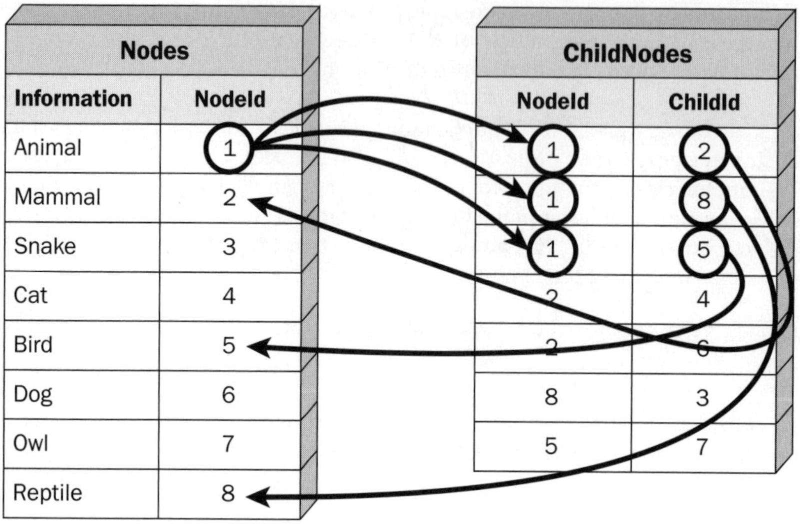

Figure 6-5: These tables store a hierarchical data structure.

Figure 6-6 shows a more compact database design. In addition to information and a `NodeId`, each node's record now contains the index of its parent in the tree. To find a node's children, now you search for `Nodes` records where the `ParentId` refers to the node whose children you are trying to find.

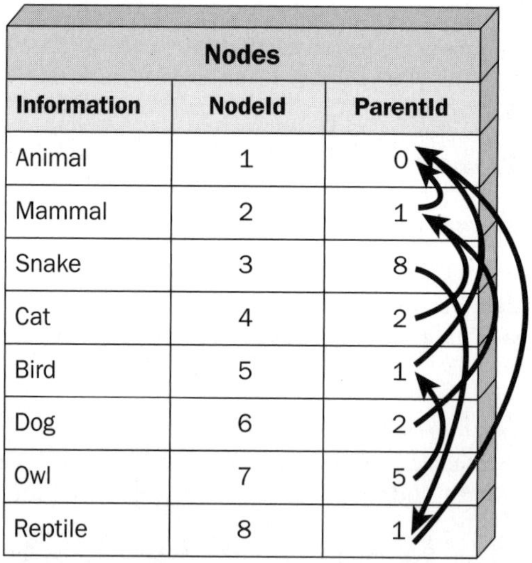
Nodes
Information | NodeId | ParentId
Animal | 1 | 0
Mammal | 2 | 1
Snake | 3 | 8
Cat | 4 | 2
Bird | 5 | 1
Dog | 6 | 2
Owl | 7 | 5
Reptile | 8 | 1

Figure 6-6: This design stores a hierarchical data structure more efficiently.

Although these database designs work, they are not very efficient because you need to perform a separate database search to find each node's children. If you have 1,000 nodes in the tree, you'll need to perform 1,000 separate searches.

I worked on one application that built and manipulated huge trees representing products stored in a relational database. A typical tree could easily have 20,000 nodes, so loading a tree could take 20,000 or more database queries. Even with the tables indexed, it took quite a while. I left that project before they addressed this issue, although I did some tests that indicated that a serialized tree stored in XML would have reduced the load time from around five minutes to less than five seconds. The section "XML," later in this chapter says a bit more about XML.

Relational databases are great if you stick to their strengths: searching, joining tables, and ordering and aggregating results. It's also relatively straightforward to save and restore simple objects in a relational database.

However, though you can coerce a relational database into storing more complicated data structures, it's often quite inefficient. You can make them store a tree or network, but you're often better off considering a different data structure.

Note that you can also combine relational databases with other approaches. For example, you can store Extensible Markup Language (XML) text in a relational database and then use the XML data to represent a hierarchical data structure. Unless the application needed a lot of relatively small trees, however, the relational database wouldn't add much to the solution.

Relational Database Products

All of the major relational database products (such as SQL Server, Access, Oracle, Informix, and MySql) provide about the same level of functionality. Some provide more features than others, but they all provide basic searching, joining, and sorting. Look at the product documentation to compare them and pick the one best suited for your development team.

The most obvious choices for many Visual Basic developers are the two Microsoft database products: Access and SQL Server. Each has its benefits and drawbacks.

Microsoft Access is extremely simple to use. It's also very easy to distribute an Access database with an application. You simply copy the database onto the target computer and install the appropriate database engine. Then the application can open the database and use it. You don't need to install (or pay for) the Access product on the target computer. In fact, you can use other tools to build the database initially, so you don't really even need the Access product installed on the developers' machines.

Although Access is the product used by many Visual Basic developers, it does have a few drawbacks. First, it does not provide the same level of support for multiple users that the more powerful database products do. Second, the amount of data an Access database can hold is limited. In particular, any single table can hold no more than 1GB or 2GB of data, depending on the version of Access.

In SQL Server, a table can contain as much data as will fit on the computer's disks. SQL Server also supports some additional features that Access does not (such as database triggers, views, and transaction logging).

SQL Server is more complicated to manage, however. It's also a lot more expensive and it must be installed on the end users' computers, so you need to buy additional licenses for them.

Ideally, you would develop your program using Access, and then switch to SQL Server if you discover that the application has outgrown Access's more limited capabilities. Unfortunately the code is substantially different for working with Access or SQL Server.

Fortunately, Microsoft has recently provided an alternative growth path. The Microsoft SQL Server 2005 Express edition is a slightly restricted version of SQL Server that is available for free. The main restriction is that a SQL Server Express database cannot have a total size greater than 4GB, while the size of a full SQL Server database is limited by the available disk space.

This means you can build your application with the free SQL Server Express product. Later, if you discover that your database has grown too big, you can buy a more complete version of SQL Server. When you use SQL Server Express, you still need to install SQL Server Express on the end users' computers, which is more difficult than installing the database drivers for use with Access, but at least it won't cost you a lot of money.

Learn more about SQL Server Express at `http://www.microsoft.com/sql/editions/express/default.mspx`. Compare the features of SQL Server Express with other versions of SQL Server at `http://www.microsoft.com/sql/prodinfo/features/compare-features.mspx`.

Compiled-In Data

The least-flexible way to include data in an application is to compile it into the code. You simply type values into strings literals, assign values to constants, and so forth. Because the data is embedded in the code, you cannot make changes to it without recompiling.

Though this isn't a very flexible technique, it has a few advantages. Loading data in compiled code is relatively fast, and it's fairly difficult for the user to mess with the data. In contrast, it's fairly easy for a user to read and modify data stored in an Access database.

You can get slightly more flexibility by putting data in a dynamic link library (DLL) and linking the DLL into the application. You still cannot make changes to the data without recompiling, but at least you only need to recompile the DLL and not the whole application. If you don't do anything to break compatibility (changing function names, removing classes, and so forth), the main program can use the new version of the DLL without recompiling.

Normally, a Visual Basic executable does not require a specific version of an assembly containing a class library. You can change that behavior to require a specific version, but only if you strongly name the assembly. Unfortunately, this requires a long sequence of arcane steps, so read the following paragraphs closely.

Start by creating a new class library project. In Visual Studio, select the File menu's New Project command, select the Class Library template, enter the library's name (for example, **CompiledInDataLibrary**), and click OK.

Add code to the class library. For example, the following code defines a `CompiledInData` class with one public function named `GetInstructions`:

```
Public Class CompiledInData
    Public Function GetInstructions() As String
        Return "Here are instructions for version 1.1"
    End Function
End Class
```

Set the project's version number. In Project Explorer, double-click My Project. On the Application tab, click the Assembly Information button. Enter the assembly's major, minor, build, and revision numbers, as shown in Figure 6-7, and click OK.

Figure 6-7: Enter the assembly's major, minor, build, and revision numbers.

Save the project so that you have a project directory to use if you haven't already done so.

Before you can sign the assembly, you need to generate a strong name key file. To do that, you need to use the Strong Name tool, `sn.exe`. To make using this tool easier, you can add its location to your path. In Windows XP, open the Control Panel and start the System applet. On the Advanced tab, click the Environment Variables button, edit the Path system variable, and add the following path to the end (assuming `sn.exe` is in the default location):

```
C:\Program Files\Microsoft Visual Studio 8\SDK\v2.0\Bin
```

Alternatively you can add the following statement to the end of your system's `AUTOEXEC.BAT` file and reboot:

```
PATH "C:\Program Files\Microsoft Visual Studio 8\SDK\v2.0\Bin";%PATH%
```

Now, create the strong name key file. Open a command window (select the Start menu's Run command, type **cmd**, and press Enter) and go to the assembly's directory. At the command prompt, enter a command similar to the following one. You can give the strong name key file a different name if you like:

```
sn -k CompiledInDataLibrary.snk
```

Back in Visual Studio, you need to enable assembly signing. Double-click My Project again if you closed it, go to the Signing tab, and check the "Sign the assembly" box. Click the "Choose a strong name key file" drop-down, select <Browse...>, select the key file you just created, and click Open. The result should look like Figure 6-8.

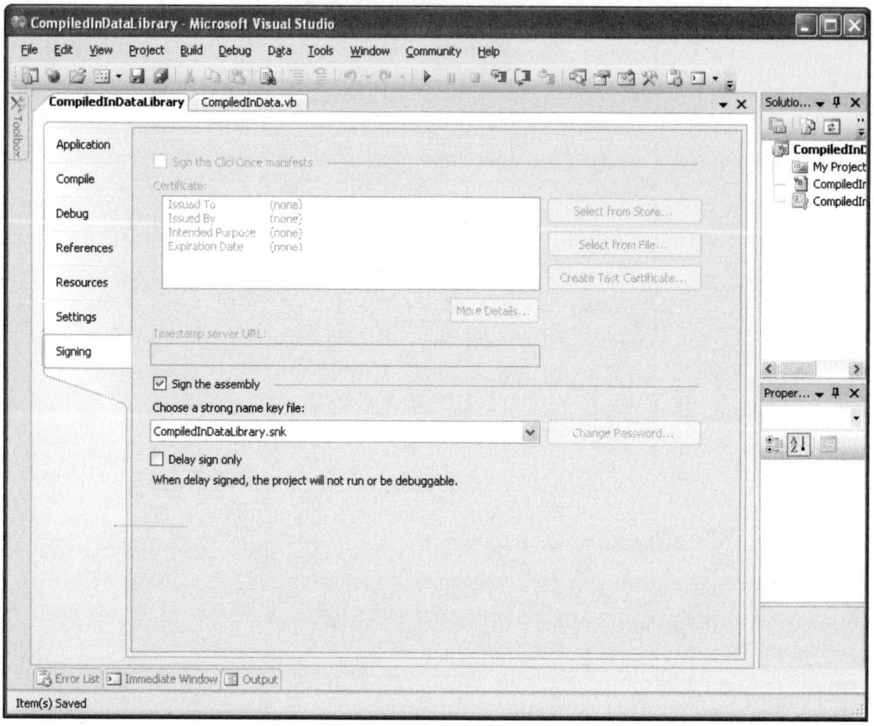

Figure 6-8: Select the strong name key file.

Save the project and build the library.

You have now built the strongly named DLL assembly and are ready to make an application to test it.

Select the File menu's New Project command, select the Windows Application template, enter the application's name (for example, **UseCompiledInData**), and click OK.

In Project Explorer, double-click My Project, click the References tab, click the Add drop-down, and select Reference. On the Add Reference dialog, click the Browse tab, select the DLL you just created, and click OK.

Select the new reference. Then, in the Properties Window, set the Specific Version property to True, as shown in Figure 6-9. This tells the executable to require the exact version that is referenced. The Version column in Figure 6-9 shows that the library had version 1.0.0.1 in this example.

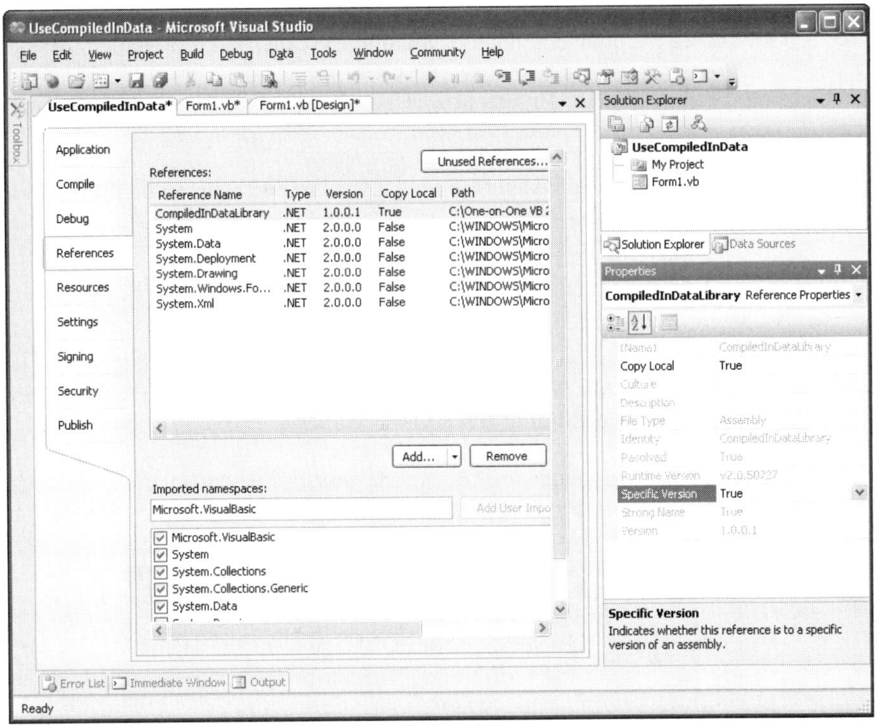

Figure 6-9: Set the class library reference's Specific Version property to True.

Now you can finally use the compiled assembly. Add a Label named `lblMessage` to the program's form and add the following code to the form:

```
Public Class Form1
    Private Sub Form1_Load(ByVal sender As System.Object, _
     ByVal e As System.EventArgs) Handles MyBase.Load
        Dim compiled_in_data As New _
            CompiledInDataLibrary.CompiledInData
        lblMessage.Text = compiled_in_data.GetInstructions()
    End Sub
End Class
```

When the program starts, it creates a new `CompiledInData` object from the class library, and displays the result of its `GetInformation` function in the label.

If you compile and run the program, you should see the text "Here are instructions for version 1.1."

Here's where the useful part begins. Open the library project and change the `Return` statement in function `GetInstructions` to the following:

```
Return "Here are instructions for version 1.2"
```

Rebuild the library and copy the DLL into the directory where the `UseCompiledInData` project built its executable. You should see the older copy of the DLL there already. Just replace it.

Without rebuilding the `UseCompiledInData` project, run the executable in that directory. You should see the new message "Here are instructions for version 1.2."

So far so good. This is what you would expect if you hadn't jumped through all the hoops to strongly name the library. You can update the data by replacing the old version of the DLL with a new version.

Now, open the library project and change the `Return` statement to the following:

```
Return "Here are instructions for version 2.0"
```

In Project Explorer, double-click My Project; click the Application tab; click the Assembly Information button; and change the major, minor, build, and revision values to 1.0.0.2.

Again, rebuild the library and copy the new DLL into the directory where the `UseCompiledInData` project's executable is. Now, when you try to run the executable, you'll see the message shown in Figure 6-10.

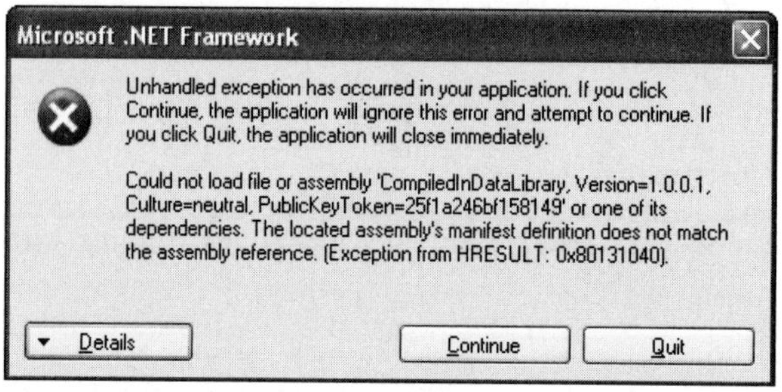

Figure 6-10: A Visual Basic executable won't run with a new version of a strongly named DLL.

To make the application work with the new version of the library, open the executable project. In Project Explorer, double-click My Project. Select the References tab, click the library's reference, and click the Remove button. Then use the Add drop-down as before to add a reference to the new DLL. Rebuild the executable project, and the compiled executable will be ready to go.

Be sure you make the proper kind of build. If you copy the DLL into the executable project's `bin/Debug` *directory, be sure you are making a Debug build.*

By default, Visual Basic determines the kind of build automatically. If you use the Build menu to compile the project, it assumes you are making a Release build. If you compiled the project by running it from the Debug menu, Visual Basic assumes you are making a Debug build.

If you don't want Visual Basic to make this choice for you, use the Configuration Manager to select the configuration that you want to make. When you install Visual Basic, the Configuration Manager is hidden. To make it available, select the Tools menu's Options menu. In the Projects and Solutions section, select the General page, check the "Show advanced build configurations" box, and click OK.

Now you can use the Configuration Manager command in the Build menu to display the dialog shown in Figure 6-11. Use the drop-down in the upper left to select the Debug or Release configuration.

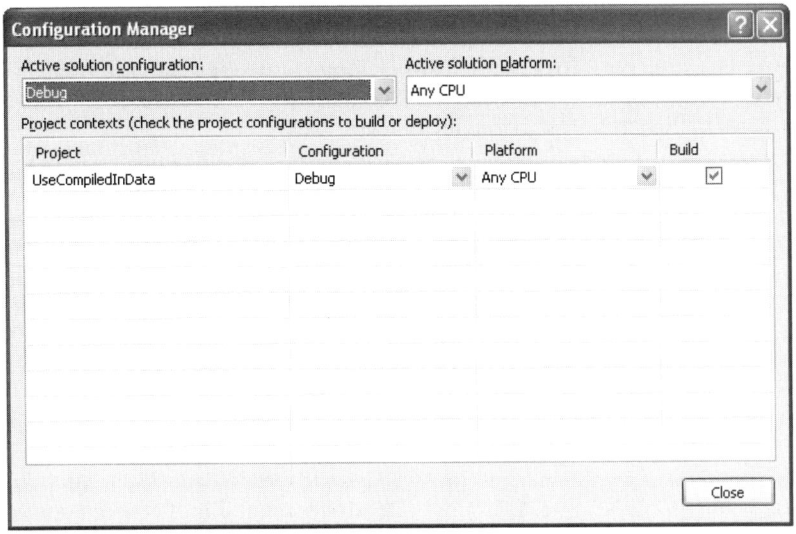

Figure 6-11: The Configuration Manager lets you select Debug or Release builds.

Using these techniques, you can make changes to the compiled-in data and allow the executable to view the changes simply by copying the new DLL into the executable's directory.

Note that you can change the file version information (see Figure 6-7) without breaking compatibility. You can use the file version to keep track of different versions of the DLL without changing the assembly version information, which would force you to recompile the executable.

If the changes you make will require an update to the executable, you can change the library's version information so the old executable won't work with it.

All of this is a lot of work to ensure that an old executable cannot run with a new library under some circumstances. A different approach would be to give the library a subroutine called `VerifyCompatibility`. The executable program would call that routine, passing in some identifying value such as its version number. `VerifyCompatibility` would examine the value, decide whether the library can work for that version of the executable, and throw an error if there will be problems. This wouldn't be quite as foolproof as using a strong named library, and it requires a little extra work to write and use `VerifyCompatibility`, but it would be a lot less confusing.

Resource Files

Resource files contain values that the program can read at run-time. One of the more interesting uses for resource files is to allow forms to automatically display in more than one language. To localize a form in this way, open the form in the form designer. Place controls on the form and set their properties as usual.

Next, set the form's `Localizable` property to `True`. In the Properties Window, click the form's `Language` property, click the drop-down arrow on the right, and pick one of the languages on the list.

When you do this, Visual Studio creates a new resource file representing the language you selected. If you modify the form, the changes are stored in the language-specific resource file. You will probably need to change the text in the form's caption, labels, group boxes, and other controls on the form for the new language. You may also need to display different icons or pictures, or use different colors for the new language. All of these changes go into the resource file.

The resource files are normally hidden, but you can see them if you click the Show All Files button in Solution Explorer. The resource files lie below the form's branch. The default file used when no better localized file is available for the user's system is named after the form and has an `.resx` extension. Other resource files add a locale identifier before the extension.

For example, suppose you build a form named `Form1` and then localize it for German. Visual Studio builds a hidden default resource file named `Form1.resx` and a resource containing the German modifications named `Form1.de.resx`.

When the application starts, it automatically picks the best resource file based on the computer's settings. If the computer is using German, it picks the German resource file. If the computer is not using German, it picks the default resource file. When it loads a form, the application automatically uses the values from the selected resource file.

In addition to using the resource files automatically, your code can pull values from the files. If you want to use the same value for every language, you can add them to the project's main resource file. In Solution Explorer, double-click My Project and select the Resources tab. Use the drop-downs to add resources to the file. Now your code can retrieve values from the project resources.

For example, suppose you add two string resources named `FileNotFoundMessage` and `FileNotFoundCaption` to the program's resource file. Then you could use the following code to display the message with the desired caption:

```
MessageBox.Show(My.Resources.FileNotFoundMessage, My.Resources.FileNotFoundCaption)
```

To create a new resource file, open the Project menu and select Add New Item. Pick the Resources File template, give the file a name, and click OK.

To create different resource files for different locales, create another resource file with the same name, but with a locale identifier before the `.resx` extension. Then the application will automatically pick the appropriate file when it runs.

Example program `UseResources` includes resource files named `StringResources.resx` and `StringResources.de.resx`. Each defines string resources named `HelloMessage` and `HelloCaption`. Double-click a resource file to open it in the resource editor. Figure 6-12 shows Visual Studio editing the `StringResources.de.resx` file. Notice the `StringResources.resx` and `StringResources.de.resx` files at the bottom of Solution Explorer.

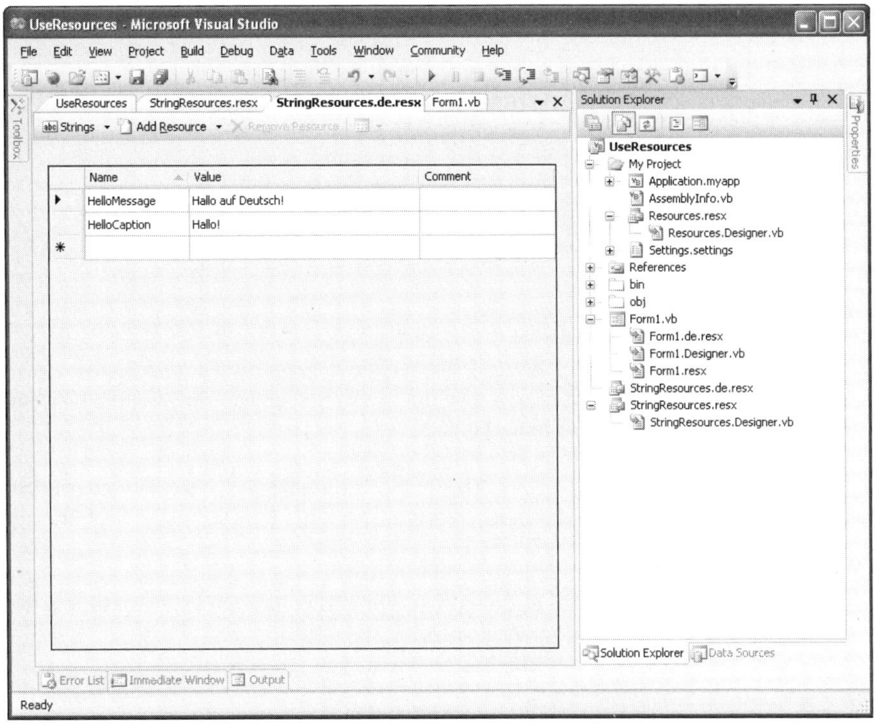

Figure 6-12: A resource file can contain strings, icons, and images.

The `UseResources` program uses the following code to display a message when you click the Click Me button. (You can download this example at `www.vb-helper.com/one_on_one.htm`.)

```
' Display the value "Hello" stored in the resource files.
Private Sub btnClickMe_Click(ByVal sender As System.Object, _
 ByVal e As System.EventArgs) Handles btnClickMe.Click
    MessageBox.Show( _
        My.Resources.StringResources.HelloMessage, _
        My.Resources.StringResources.HelloCaption)
End Sub
```

Setting your system to use other languages would make testing localized applications cumbersome. Fortunately, you can make the program switch locales at run-time. Add the following code to a form to make it pick a new locale:

```
Imports System.Threading
Imports System.Globalization

Public Class Form1
    Public Sub New()
        MyBase.New()

        ' Set the culture.
```

```
        Dim culture_info As New CultureInfo("de-DE")
        Thread.CurrentThread.CurrentUICulture = culture_info
        Thread.CurrentThread.CurrentCulture = culture_info

        ' This call is required by the Windows Form Designer.
        InitializeComponent()

        ' Add any initialization after the InitializeComponent() call.

    End Sub
    ...
End Class
```

When the form is created, the constructor executes. It calls `MyBase.New` to ensure that its parent class's constructor is called. Next, the code makes a new `CultureInfo` object representing German, and sets the current thread's culture properties to that object.

The code then calls `InitializeComponent`. This is the automatically generated subroutine that loads the form's controls. Because the code has specified the German `CultureInfo` object, the application uses the resources in the German resource file.

Now, when the user clicks the Click Me button, the program displays the values stored in the appropriate resource file. Figure 6-13 shows the program displaying the message when the locale is set to German. (You can download this example at `www.vb-helper.com/one_on_one.htm`.)

Figure 6-13: Program `UseResources` displays messages in English or German.

Resource files are useful places to store strings and images for the program to use. You can use different resource files to support different languages, and the application will automatically pick the best file that it can for the computer's configuration.

Satellite Assemblies

The earlier section, "Compiled-In Data," explained how you can use class libraries to provide easily updatable data. You can combine this idea with the resource files described in the previous section to implement *satellite assemblies.*

A satellite assembly is an assembly that contains only resource files. To create a satellite assembly, start a class library, delete the initial class, and add resource files as usual.

Now, you can make a program access the resources in these assemblies much as you can have it attach to any other class library. The following code shows how a program can load string resources from a satellite assembly at run-time:

```
Imports System.Resources
Imports System.Reflection

Public Class Form1
    Private Sub btnClickMe_Click(ByVal sender As System.Object, _
     ByVal e As System.EventArgs) Handles btnClickMe.Click
        ' Make an Assembly representing the resource assembly.
        Dim satellite_assembly As Assembly = _
            Assembly.LoadFrom("SatelliteAssembly.dll")

        ' Make a resource manager.
        Dim resource_manager As New ResourceManager( _
            "SatelliteAssembly.StringResources", _
            satellite_assembly)

        ' Display the message.
        MessageBox.Show( _
            resource_manager.GetString("HelloMessage"), _
            resource_manager.GetString("HelloCaption"))
    End Sub
End Class
```

When you click the `UseSatelliteAssembly` example program's Click Me button, the code creates an `Assembly` object to represent the satellite assembly DLL.

Next, it makes a `ResourceManager` object to get resources from the assembly. The constructor parameter `SatelliteAssembly.StringResources` gives the assembly's root namespace (`SatelliteAssembly`) and the name of the resource file within the DLL (`StringResources`).

Now the program can use the `ResourceManager`'s methods to get resources from the assembly. In this example, it uses the `GetString` method to get the values of the `HelloMessage` and `HelloCaption` resources. (You can download this example at `www.vb-helper.com/one_on_one.htm`.)

Just as you can replace a class library with a new version and run without recompiling the main program, you can also replace a satellite assembly without recompiling the main program. Simply copy the new DLL into the executable's directory and you're ready to run.

Satellite assemblies have the same advantages as resource files with the additional benefit that you can update them over time relatively easily.

System Registry

The System Registry is a good place to store small amounts of data. Generally, it is intended to hold configuration data for an application, although you can also use it to store a modest amount of other data. Typically, it is used to store application options and state information such as the positions of the windows that were open the last time the user closed the application.

Probably the most common use of the Registry is to store most recently used (MRU) file lists. The following code shows an `MruList` class that attaches an MRU list to a form:

```
Public Class MruList
    Private m_ApplicationName As String
    Private m_FileMenu As ToolStripMenuItem
    Private m_NumEntries As Integer
    Private m_FileNames As Collection
    Private m_MenuItems As Collection

    Public Event OpenFile(ByVal file_name As String)

    Public Sub New(ByVal application_name As String, _
     ByVal file_menu As ToolStripMenuItem, ByVal num_entries As Integer)
        m_ApplicationName = application_name
        m_FileMenu = file_menu
        m_NumEntries = num_entries
        m_FileNames = New Collection
        m_MenuItems = New Collection

        ' Load saved file names from the Registry.
        LoadMruList()

        ' Display the MRU list.
        DisplayMruList()
    End Sub

    ' Load previously saved file names from the Registry.
    Private Sub LoadMruList()
        Dim file_name As String
        For i As Integer = 1 To m_NumEntries
            ' Get the next file name and title.
            file_name = GetSetting(m_ApplicationName, _
                "MruList", "FileName" & i, "")

            ' See if we got anything.
            If file_name.Length > 0 Then
                ' Save this file name.
                m_FileNames.Add(file_name, file_name)
            End If
        Next i
    End Sub

    ' Save the MRU list into the Registry.
    Private Sub SaveMruList()
        ' Remove previous entries.
        If GetSetting(m_ApplicationName, "MruList", "FileName1", "").Length > 0 _
         Then
            DeleteSetting(m_ApplicationName, "MruList")
        End If

        ' Make the new entries.
        For i As Integer = 1 To m_FileNames.Count
            SaveSetting(m_ApplicationName, "MruList", "FileName" & i, _
```

```
                m_FileNames(i).ToString)
        Next i
    End Sub

    ' MRU menu item event handler.
    Private Sub MruItem_Click(ByVal sender As System.Object, _
     ByVal e As System.EventArgs)
        Dim mnu As ToolStripMenuItem = DirectCast(sender, ToolStripMenuItem)

        ' Raise the OpenFile event for the menu's file name.
        RaiseEvent OpenFile(DirectCast(mnu.Tag, String))
    End Sub

    ' Display the MRU list.
    Private Sub DisplayMruList()
        ' Remove old menu items from the File menu.
        For Each mnu As ToolStripItem In m_MenuItems
            m_FileMenu.DropDownItems.Remove(mnu)
        Next mnu
        m_MenuItems = New Collection

        ' See if we have any file names.
        If m_FileNames.Count > 0 Then
            ' Make the separator.
            Dim sep As New ToolStripSeparator
            m_MenuItems.Add(sep)
            m_FileMenu.DropDownItems.Add(sep)

            ' Make the file items.
            For i As Integer = 1 To m_FileNames.Count
                Dim mnu As New ToolStripMenuItem( _
                    "&" & i & " " & FileTitle(m_FileNames(i).ToString))
                AddHandler mnu.Click, _
                    New System.EventHandler(AddressOf MruItem_Click)
                mnu.Tag = m_FileNames(i).ToString
                m_MenuItems.Add(mnu)
                m_FileMenu.DropDownItems.Add(mnu)
            Next i
        End If
    End Sub

    ' Add a file to the MRU list.
    Public Sub Add(ByVal file_name As String)
        ' Remove this file from the MRU list
        ' if it is present.
        Dim i As Integer = FileNameIndex(file_name)
        If i > 0 Then m_FileNames.Remove(i)

        ' Add the item to the beginning of the list.
        If m_FileNames.Count > 0 Then
            m_FileNames.Add(file_name, file_name, m_FileNames.Item(1))
        Else
            m_FileNames.Add(file_name, file_name)
        End If
```

```
            ' If the list is too long, remove the last item.
            If m_FileNames.Count > m_NumEntries Then
                m_FileNames.Remove(m_NumEntries + 1)
            End If

            ' Display the list.
            DisplayMruList()

            ' Save the updated list.
            SaveMruList()
        End Sub

        ' Return the index of this file in the list.
        Private Function FileNameIndex(ByVal file_name As String) As Integer
            For i As Integer = 1 To m_FileNames.Count
                If m_FileNames(i).ToString = file_name Then Return i
            Next i
            Return 0
        End Function

        ' Remove a file from the MRU list.
        Public Sub Remove(ByVal file_name As String)
            ' See if the file is present.
            Dim i As Integer = FileNameIndex(file_name)
            If i > 0 Then
                ' Remove the file.
                m_FileNames.Remove(i)

                ' Display the list.
                DisplayMruList()

                ' Save the updated list.
                SaveMruList()
            End If
        End Sub
    End Class
```

The `MruList` class declares a public event `OpenFile` that it raises when the user selects a file from the MRU list.

The class's constructor saves the application's name so that it will know the part of the Registry where it should store values. It also saves a reference to the form's File menu and the maximum number of entries the MRU list should hold. (This is four in most applications, but some let the user set it.) The constructor creates new collections to hold the files' names and menu items. It then calls `LoadMruList` to load the file names from the Registry, and `DisplayMruList` to create appropriate File menu items.

The `SaveSetting` and `GetSetting` routines used by the program store and retrieve values from the following Registry area:

```
HKEY_CURRENT_USER\Software\VB and VBA Program Settings
```

Within that area, the routines work in a sub-key named after the application, inside a sub-sub-key with a given section name. In the `MakeMruList` example program available for download on the book's Web site, the program name is MakeMruList and the section where the program stores values is called MruList. The file names are FileName1, FileName2, and so forth.

Subroutine LoadMruList uses the GetSetting function to fetch file names from the Registry. It uses an integer variable to loop from one to the maximum number of files that the MRU list can hold. For each, it uses GetSetting to get a file name from the Registry. When it gets a non-blank value, it adds the file name to the m_FileNames collection.

Subroutine SaveMruList saves the file names in the m_FileNames collection into the Registry. First, it uses GetSetting to see if the FileName1 entry is in the Registry. If that value is present, the subroutine uses DeleteSetting to remove the entire MruList section containing all of the file names.

Next, the routine loops through the file names in the m_FileNames, saving each into the Registry.

The MruItem_Click event handler executes when the user clicks an MRU menu item. It converts the event's sender into the ToolStripMenuItem object that raised the event. It then raises the MruList class's OpenFile event, passing it the name of the file stored in the ToolStripMenuItem object's Tag property.

Subroutine DisplayMruList makes menu items in the File menu. First, it removes any items that it had previously added to the menu. If the m_FileNames collection contains any file names, the subroutine adds a separator to the end of the File menu. It then loops through the names, adding new ToolStripMenuItems to the File menu. It uses the AddHandler statement to make the MruItem_Click subroutine handle each item's Click event. It also stores the file's name in the ToolStripMenuItem's Tag property.

Subroutine Add adds a new file to the MRU list. The main program calls this routine when it opens a file or saves a file with a new name. The subroutine removes the file name from the m_FileNames collection if it is there, and then adds the file name to the beginning of the collection. If the collection now has more than the allowed number of items m_NumEntries, the routine removes the last one. Subroutine Add finishes by calling DisplayMruList to update the File menu and by calling SaveMruList to save the new list into the Registry.

Many applications don't bother to save configuration information such as the MRU list until the application ends. That means the information is not saved if the program crashes. This is doubly annoying to the user—first because the application crashed, and second because it didn't save the configuration information that the user may have spent quite some time modifying.

To avoid this problem, I make my applications save changes to the configuration information as soon as the change occurs. It happens quickly enough that the user doesn't notice it, and it prevents data loss if the program crashes.

Helper function FileNameIndex simply looks through the m_FileNames collection and returns a file name's index in it.

Finally, subroutine Remove removes a file name from the m_FileNames collection. The main program should call this method if it tries to open a file and fails, so the file is removed from the File menu. The subroutine uses function FileNameIndex to look for the file name in the m_FileNames collection. If it finds the name, the routine removes it from the collection, calls DisplayMruList to update the File menu, and then calls SaveMruList to save the change.

The MakeMruList example program (which you can download at www.vb-helper.com/one_on_one.htm) demonstrates the MruList class. It also includes some code that keeps its data safe. For example, if you modify a file and try to exit, it asks if you want to save your changes. Download the program and take a look to see the details.

The Registry is a pretty good place to store short pieces of configuration information. Each user's information is stored in a separate `HKEY_CURRENT_USER` hive in the Registry so they can each have their own configurations.

The Registry is not a great place to store large amounts of information, however. Saving and retrieving information is a bit awkward, and the Registry is bloated enough, even on a small system.

INI Files

In earlier versions of Windows, applications stored their configuration information in *initialization files*. These are text files with an `.ini` extension that contain values in a simple format. The file is divided into sections indicated by a section name inside square brackets. Each section contains value names followed by corresponding values. The following code shows an INI file containing two sections named `MruList` and `QueryResultFields`:

```
 [MruList]
FileName1=C:\Program Files\SalesTracker\FY2006.xls
FileName2=C:\Program Files\SalesTracker\FY2005.xls
FileName3=A:\books.xml
FileName4=C:\Program Files\SalesTracker\Notes.txt

[QueryResultFields]
Field1=FirstName
Field2=LastName
Field3=Assignment
Field4=TotalSales
Field5=ClosingPercentage
```

When it invented the System Registry, Microsoft told developers to store configuration information there instead of in INI files. Although support for INI files has declined, you can still use them to store information.

In fact, Microsoft seems to be moving back toward using INI files because it's easier to copy an application's settings in an INI file to a new computer than it is to add entries to the Registry.

The `GetPrivateProfileString` and `WritePrivateProfileString` API functions read and write entries in an INI file. The following code shows how example program `UseIniFile` (available for download at `www.vb-helper.com/one_on_one.htm`) saves and restores its size and position when it starts and stops:

```
Imports System.Text
Imports System.IO

Public Class Form1
    Private Declare Auto Function GetPrivateProfileString Lib "Kernel32" ( _
        ByVal lpAppName As String, _
        ByVal lpKeyName As String, _
```

```
        ByVal lpDefault As String, _
        ByVal lpReturnedString As StringBuilder, _
        ByVal nSize As Integer, _
        ByVal lpFileName As String) As Integer
    Private Declare Auto Function WritePrivateProfileString Lib "Kernel32" ( _
        ByVal lpAppName As String, _
        ByVal lpKeyName As String, _
        ByVal lpString As String, _
        ByVal lpFileName As String) As Integer

    ' Load the previously saved position.
    Private Sub Form1_Load(ByVal sender As System.Object, _
     ByVal e As System.EventArgs) Handles MyBase.Load
        Dim ini_file_name As String = IniFileName
        Dim l As Integer = Integer.Parse( _
            GetIniString(ini_file_name, "Position", "Left", "100"))
        Dim t As Integer = Integer.Parse( _
            GetIniString(ini_file_name, "Position", "Top", "100"))
        Dim w As Integer = Integer.Parse( _
            GetIniString(ini_file_name, "Position", "Width", "400"))
        Dim h As Integer = Integer.Parse( _
            GetIniString(ini_file_name, "Position", "Height", "300"))
        Me.SetBounds(l, t, w, h)
    End Sub

    ' Make using GetPrivateProfileString a little easier.
    Private Function GetIniString(ByVal file_name As String, _
     ByVal section_name As String, ByVal key_name As String, _
     ByVal default_value As String) As String
        Const MAX_LENGTH As Integer = 500
        Dim string_builder As New StringBuilder(MAX_LENGTH)
        GetPrivateProfileString(section_name, key_name, default_value, _
            string_builder, MAX_LENGTH, file_name)
        Return string_builder.ToString()
    End Function

    ' Save the current position.
    Private Sub Form1_FormClosing(ByVal sender As Object, _
     ByVal e As System.Windows.Forms.FormClosingEventArgs) Handles Me.FormClosing
        Dim ini_file_name As String = IniFileName()
        WritePrivateProfileString("Position", "Left", Me.Left.ToString(), _
            ini_file_name)
        WritePrivateProfileString("Position", "Top", Me.Top.ToString(), _
            ini_file_name)
        WritePrivateProfileString("Position", "Width", Me.Width.ToString(), _
            ini_file_name)
        WritePrivateProfileString("Position", "Height", Me.Height.ToString(), _
            ini_file_name)
    End Sub

    ' Return the INI file's name.
    Private Function IniFileName() As String
        Dim ini_file_name As String = Application.StartupPath
        ini_file_name = ini_file_name.Substring(0, ini_file_name.LastIndexOf("\"))
```

```
            ini_file_name = ini_file_name.Substring(0, ini_file_name.LastIndexOf("\"))
            Return ini_file_name & "\UseIniFile.ini"
        End Function
    End Class
```

The code begins by declaring the `GetPrivateProfileString` and `WritePrivateProfileString` API functions.

When the form loads, its `Load` event handler calls function `IniFileName` to get the name of the INI file the program uses. It then uses function `GetIniString` to get the values of the `Left`, `Top`, `Width`, and `Height` values in the file's `Position` section. If the INI file doesn't exist, or if a value is missing from the file, the function returns the default value it is passed. The code then uses the form's `SetBounds` method to size and position the form.

Function `GetIniString` creates a `StringBuilder` object. It then calls the `GetPrivateProfileString` API function to get a value from the INI file. It returns the value that the API function places in the `StringBuilder`.

When the form unloads, its `FormClosing` event handler saves the form's size and position. It uses `IniFileName` to get the name of the API file. It then calls the `WritePrivateProfileString` API function to save its size and position values into the file.

Function `IniFileName` simply returns the name of the INI file to use. I put it in a separate function so the `Load` and `FormClosing` event handlers wouldn't have to duplicate the same code.

The following code shows an INI file created by the `UseIniFile` program:

```
[Position]
Left=34
Top=33
Width=323
Height=100
```

INI files are somewhat old-fashioned, but they have a few advantages over the System Registry. They are plain-text files, so they are easy to view and edit. To edit the Registry, you need to use a tool such as `RegEdit`, which is cumbersome. It's also a bit risky. If you mess up the Registry, you can do a lot of damage, possibly even making your system unbootable. If you mess up an INI file, the worst you can do is confuse the application and INI values are usually easy to fix.

It's easy to share INI files across multiple computers simply by putting them in a shared directory. Then the program can read the configuration values no matter which computer you are using. Generally, different computers should not share Registries, so data in the System Registry is not shared across computers.

If you want each user to have separate configuration values, you can name the INI files after the users. For example, you might put the user's name in the file name as in `UseIniFile_rod.ini`.

Like the Registry, INI files are good for storing relatively small amounts of information. Because they are easy to share, they make storing configuration information easy in environments where users work on multiple computers.

XML

Extensible Markup Language (XML) is a language for storing data in a hierarchical format. Without going into too much detail, you define tags to contain the data. Each opening tag has a corresponding ending tag. Tags must be properly nested, and a single root tag must hold all other data tags. For more information on XML files, see a book about them such as my book *Visual Basic .NET and XML* (Indianapolis: Wiley, 2002).

The following code shows a small XML file:

```
<Configuration>
    <Position>
        <Left>100</Left>
        <Top>100</Top>
        <Width>400</Width>
        <Height>300</Height>
    </Position>
    <Colors>
        <BackColor>White</BackColor>
        <ForeColor>Dark Blue</ForeColor>
    </Colors>
</Configuration>
```

Visual Basic provides tools that make saving and loading XML data easy. Just as you can save settings in the System Registry or an INI file, you can save them in an XML file. The following code shows how example program `UseXmlFile` (which you can download at `www.vb-helper.com/one_on_one.htm`) saves and restores its position when it starts and stops:

```
Imports System.Xml
Imports System.IO

Public Class Form1
    ' Load the previously saved position.
    Private Sub Form1_Load(ByVal sender As System.Object, _
     ByVal e As System.EventArgs) Handles MyBase.Load
        ' See if the XML file exists.
        Dim xml_file_name As String = XmlFileName()
        If File.Exists(xml_file_name) Then
            ' Load the XML file.
            Dim dom_document As New XmlDocument
            dom_document.Load(XmlFileName())

            ' Set the form's size and position.
            For Each child_node As XmlNode In _
             dom_document.DocumentElement.ChildNodes
                Select Case child_node.Name
                    Case "Left"
                        Me.Left = Integer.Parse(child_node.InnerText)
                    Case "Top"
                        Me.Top = Integer.Parse(child_node.InnerText)
                    Case "Width"
                        Me.Width = Integer.Parse(child_node.InnerText)
                    Case "Height"
```

```
                        Me.Height = Integer.Parse(child_node.InnerText)
                End Select
            Next
        End If
    End Sub

    ' Save the current position.
    Private Sub Form1_FormClosing(ByVal sender As Object, _
     ByVal e As System.Windows.Forms.FormClosingEventArgs) Handles Me.FormClosing
        Dim dom_document As New XmlDocument

        ' Make the <Position> tag.
        Dim position_node As XmlNode = dom_document.CreateElement("Position")
        dom_document.AppendChild(position_node)

        ' Make the child tags.
        Dim child_node As XmlNode
        child_node = dom_document.CreateElement("Left")
        child_node.InnerText = Me.Left.ToString()
        position_node.AppendChild(child_node)

        child_node = dom_document.CreateElement("Top")
        child_node.InnerText = Me.Top.ToString()
        position_node.AppendChild(child_node)

        child_node = dom_document.CreateElement("Width")
        child_node.InnerText = Me.Width.ToString()
        position_node.AppendChild(child_node)

        child_node = dom_document.CreateElement("Height")
        child_node.InnerText = Me.Height.ToString()
        position_node.AppendChild(child_node)

        ' Save the file.
        dom_document.Save(XmlFileName())
    End Sub

    ' Return the XML file's name.
    Private Function XmlFileName() As String
        Dim xml_file_name As String = Application.StartupPath
        xml_file_name = xml_file_name.Substring(0, xml_file_name.LastIndexOf("\"))
        xml_file_name = xml_file_name.Substring(0, xml_file_name.LastIndexOf("\"))
        Return xml_file_name & "\UseXmlFile.xml"
    End Function
End Class
```

The form's `Load` event handler checks to see if the XML file exists. If the file exists, the program creates an `XmlDocument` object and uses it to load the file. It uses the `XmlDocument`'s `DocumentElement` to find the data root element (named `Position`) in the file and loops through that element's children. It uses the text that the children contain to set the form's `Left`, `Top`, `Width`, and `Height` properties.

The program's `FormClosing` event handler creates a new `XmlDocument` object. It creates an element named `Position` and adds it to the document's child collection. It then creates an element named `Left`, sets its contained text to the value of the form's `Left` property, and adds the element to the `Position` element's children. The code repeats this process to make elements for the `Top`, `Width`, and `Height` values. Finally, the event handler calls the `XmlDocument`'s `Save` method to save the file.

One of the quirkier features of Visual Basic's XML classes is that you need to use the `XmlDocument` *object to create an element, and then you must append it to another element's collection of children. You might think you could use* `New` *to create a new element, or that the* `XmlNode` *class might provide a method to create a child element and add it to the child collection in a single step, but that's not the case.*

The following code shows an XML file created by the `UseXmlFile` program:

```
<Position>
  <Left>994</Left>
  <Top>33</Top>
  <Width>257</Width>
  <Height>141</Height>
</Position>
```

XML files have many of the same advantages as INI files. You can share them simply by putting them in a shared directory, so you can read their values from multiple computers. XML files are plain-text, so they are easy to read and modify if necessary. By using XML files instead of the Registry, you also avoid the risk of damaging the Registry. As is the case with INI files, you can let multiple users have their own versions of the files by adding the users' names to the file names.

Unlike INI files, XML files are hierarchical. The example shown here uses a hierarchy only two levels deep, but an XML file can store a hierarchy of any depth. That makes them ideal for storing large amounts of tree-like data.

One application I worked on saved and restored trees containing tens of thousands of nodes in just a few seconds.

You can also use serialization to save and restore many items in an XML file in a single step. Simply build an object that contains the configuration data and serialize into a file. The section "Undo and Redo" in Chapter 5 shows an example of serialization. For more information about serialization, see a book about XML such as my book *Visual Basic .NET and XML* (Indianapolis: Wiley, 2002).

Other Text File Formats

INI and XML files are just text files with a specific format. You can use any text file in a similar manner to save and restore data. For example, you could use the following comma-separated value (CSV) file to store a form's position. The two columns in this file hold a property and value:

```
Left,994
Top,33
Width,257
Height,141
```

This kind of file is not naturally hierarchical like an XML file is, but you can add some extra dimension to it either by adding more columns, or by embedding hierarchical data in the values. The following file contains an additional column, giving the name of the form to which the values apply:

```
Main,Left,994
Main,Top,33
Main,Width,257
Main,Height,141
NewCustomer,Left,360
NewCustomer,Top,241
NewCustomer,Width,500
NewCustomer,Height,330
```

The following version includes the form's name and the property name in the first column:

```
Main.Left,994
Main.Top,33
Main.Width,257
Main.Height,141
NewCustomer.Left,360
NewCustomer.Top,241
NewCustomer.Width,500
NewCustomer.Height,330
```

You can use other delimiters such as tabs, semicolons, vertical bars, and so forth to build similar files. Unfortunately, parsing these files is a bit more difficult than reading INI or XML files.

Visual Basic's `Input` and `Write` functions make reading and writing values in a file reasonably straightforward, although you must read the data in the same order in which it was written, so it is harder to handle new or obsolete values in different versions of the file. The files are also not as self-documenting as INI and XML files.

Object Databases

An *object database* or *object store* is a database that saves and restores objects. It may also provide query capabilities. If you search the Internet, you can find commercially available object databases, but it's also not too hard to build your own.

For example, you can store an object's properties as fields in a relational database. Write methods to make loading and saving objects easier. For example, the `SaveNewObject` method would create a new record holding an object's properties; `UpdateObject` would update an object's record; `FetchObject` would use the values in a record to initialize the object; and so forth.

You can even take advantage of the relational database's searching features to let you find objects in different ways. For example, overloaded versions of the `FetchCustomer` function might take a customer ID number (integer), a phone number (string), or first and last names as parameters. They would use the parameters to query the database and then return an initialized `Customer` object. The following code shows stubs for these functions:

```
' Fetch a Customer by ID number.
Public Function FetchCustomer(ByVal customer_id As Integer) As Customer

End Sub
```

```
' Fetch a Customer by phone number.
Public Function FetchCustomer(ByVal phone_number As String) As Customer

End Sub

' Fetch a Customer by first and last name.
Public Function FetchCustomer( _
 ByVal first_name As String, _
 ByVal last_name As String) As Customer

End Sub
```

In an alternative approach, you could store only identifying information and serializations in the database. The `XmlSerializer` class allows an application to serialize an object into an XML string, and later deserialize the string to re-create the original object. You can store an object's serialization in the database together with identifying information (such as customer ID, phone number, and first and last names). To fetch an object, you would search on the identifying information, and then use the serialization to re-create the object.

This method helps isolate the database structure from the class definitions somewhat. If you add or remove properties from a class, you don't need to change the database's structure unless you change some of the identifying information fields. One disadvantage to this method is that you can only search on the identification fields that are explicitly included in the database's tables, not on the other fields as you usually can in a relational database.

These techniques can be reasonably effective for simple objects where there is a one-to-one correspondence between objects and records in the database. In this example, the database would use fields in the `Customers` table to initialize a new `Customer` object. These methods don't work as well if the objects are complex structures containing references to other objects.

For example, a `Customer` object might contain a collection of references to `Order` objects representing past orders. Each `Order` object might hold a collection of `OrderItem` objects that give information about the items in the order. In that case, when you fetch a `Customer`, you might want its `Orders` and `OrderItems` to be fetched also. You can handle this in a similar way by providing methods to save and restore `Order` and `OrderItem` objects, but it does complicate matters.

Another tricky issue is object uniqueness. If you fetch by using the same customer ID twice, you might want the `FetchCustomer` method to return a reference to the same object. To do that, the program would need to keep track of the objects that it has created so that it can return new references to them. It will also need some method for tracking items so that it knows when it is safe to remove them from its list of items.

If you need this kind of functionality, you might consider buying a true object database. Alternatively if the application doesn't need a huge number of objects, you could save and restore all of the objects as a single data structure in a serialization. See the section "Undo and Redo" in Chapter 5 for information on serializing and deserializing data structures.

Summary

Most large Visual Basic applications store data in a relational database, but that is not your only option.

If the program needs some read-only data, you can compile it right into the code. If you put the data in a class library DLL, you can update the data without recompiling the main program.

Resource files let you store read-only information such as strings and images that the program might need to display. You can use localized resource files to let the program automatically use the values that are most appropriate on the user's system.

Just as you can store compiled-in data in a DLL, you can also store resources in a DLL called a satellite assembly. These allow you to change resources without recompiling the application.

In the past, Microsoft has recommended that you store configuration information in the System Registry, and that's a reasonable place to put some values. Each user has his or her set of values in the Registry on each computer. Recently, Microsoft has started telling developers to store configuration information in INI files so that you can install them on other computers just by copying them.

If you want to let users access their configuration values on more than one computer, you can place the values in shared text files in INI, XML, CSV, or other formats. XML files are particularly useful for storing large amounts of hierarchical data.

Finally, if you need to perform querying, sorting, and aggregation, you can use a relational database. Relational databases don't store hierarchical and network data as effectively as XML files, but their searching capabilities are generally a lot easier to use.

The chapters so far in this book have covered various activities that occur before programming begins. They have focused on different kinds of application design, including lifecycle methodologies, object-oriented design, user-interface design, and data storage issues.

Chapter 7, "Design Patterns," discusses another aspect to design: design patterns. A design pattern is a set of classes working together to provide a solution to a common application-engineering problem. Once you understand design patterns, you can apply them to your project to handle design issues in a reasonably standardized and well-understood manner.

7

Design Patterns

A *design pattern* consists of one or more objects that together perform some useful task. In a sense, a design pattern is an algorithm for using classes to do something useful. It's a recipe for building part of an application. A design pattern may include objects from a single class, or an ensemble of classes working together.

As you refine your application's design, you should start looking for common design patterns. You may discover a group of classes that implement a pattern. You may also find a group of classes that you could rewrite to follow a pattern. In either case, if you can rewrite your design to follow a design pattern, then you can take advantage of the solutions that other developers have developed to solve the same problem. That can save you time and gives you some confidence that the solution will work correctly so you can move on to design other parts of the application.

Some patterns also make an application easier to implement, debug, and maintain. For example, the Adapter and Facade patterns described later in this chapter help decouple classes so they are less tightly related. That lets you build, debug, and modify the classes with less impact on the rest of the application.

Since the seminal book *Design Patterns* by Gamma et. al (Boston: Addison-Wesley, 1995) was published, all sorts of patterns have been devised for data access, integration, interoperability, services, security, Web Services, configuration, exceptions, testing, threat modeling, legacy applications, project management, and many more. This chapter, or even this whole book, doesn't have room to cover them all. Rather than just listing the names of a bunch of design patterns with no explanation, this chapter describes in more detail some of the patterns that I have found most useful in the applications that I've built.

A lot of the design pattern books treat their patterns in a very formal way with introductory sections for each pattern giving a synopsis, context, "forces," and other sections eventually leading up to a solution, which is often so simple it's anticlimactic. In some cases, the prelude sections are so stilted and full of technical diagrams that they're practically unintelligible. This chapter takes a much more intuitive approach.

For a more complete treatment of design patterns, see a book entirely about them such as the original *Design Patterns*. This book was written by four authors (Gamma, Helm, Johnson, and Vlissides), who are sometimes called "the gang of four," so the book is also sometimes called "the gang of four," or GOF.

You can also see the book *Visual Basic Design Patterns* by Mark Grand and Brad Merrill (Indianapolis: Wiley, 2005).

The patterns that I find most useful can be grouped into three categories: creation patterns, relation patterns, and behavior patterns.

Creation Patterns

Creation patterns are patterns that deal with how objects are created. The Clone pattern provides a way to make new objects by copying existing ones. The Factory pattern uses one class to create instances of other classes.

Clone

Sometimes it's useful to make an exact copy of an existing object. That's what a clone is: a copy of an object that is initialized with the same property values as the object from which it was cloned.

The *Clone pattern* is usually called the *Prototype pattern* in the design pattern literature. The idea is that the application can make a new object based on a prototype object by cloning the prototype.

It's relatively easy to allow cloning in Visual Basic. Simply add a `Clone` function to a class that returns a new instance of the class with the same parameters as the existing object.

In fact, Visual Basic's `Object` class provides a `MemberwiseClone` method that returns a new object with the same property values as the original object. Because all classes are descendants of the `Object` class, they can all have the `MemberwiseClone` method.

The following code shows how a program might make a clone of a `Customer` object named `old_customer`:

```
Dim new_customer As Customer = DirectCast(old_customer.MemberwiseClone, Customer)
```

The `MemberwiseClone` method returns a generic `Object` so this code uses `DirectCast` to convert the result into a `Customer` object.

To make cloning objects a little easier, you can make a `Clone` method that wraps up the call to `MemberwiseClone`. The following code shows how a simple `Customer` class can use `MemberwiseClone` to implement a `Clone` method:

```
Public Class Customer
    ' Code omitted...

    ' Return a shallow clone.
    Public Function Clone() As Customer
```

```
        Return DirectCast(Me.MemberwiseClone(), Customer)
    End Function
End Class
```

Now the main program can use this method, as in the following code:

```
Dim new_customer As Customer = old_customer.Clone()
```

The `MemberwiseClone` method makes a new copy of an object and initializes its fields to the same values used by the original object. That works well for simple data types such as `Integer` or `String` but it doesn't work as well with references to other objects.

For example, suppose an `Order` item contains a reference to a `Customer` object. When you clone an `Order`, should the clone contain a reference to the same `Customer` object as the original, or should it contain a reference to a new `Customer` object that has been cloned from the original? If the new `Order` has a reference to the existing object, then changes to the joint `Customer` object are shared by both `Orders`. If the new `Order` object has a reference to a new copy of the `Customer`, then changes to the two `Customer` objects happen independently.

A clone that uses the same references as the original object is called a *shallow copy*. The `MemberwiseClone` method makes shallow copies. A clone that uses references to new objects is called a *deep copy*.

> *You could also define partially deep copies if you want to. For example, suppose an* `Order` *item has references to a* `Customer` *object, and a collection of references to* `OrderItem` *objects that describe the items that are included in the order. You might want an* `Order` *clone to share the same* `Customer` *object as the original, but get its own new* `OrderItems` *collection. This would let you easily make a new order for an existing customer. This kind of partially deep clone would be defined for a particular application, so there aren't really any standards for defining them.*

The following code shows an `Order` class that can make shallow or deep copies:

```
Public Class Order
    Public OrderCustomer As Customer
    Public OrderItems As New List(Of OrderItem)

    ' Code omitted...

    ' Return a deep or shallow clone.
    Public Function Clone(ByVal deep As Boolean) As Order
        ' Start with a shallow clone.
        Dim new_order As Order = DirectCast(Me.MemberwiseClone(), Order)

        ' If appropriate, copy deeper data.
        If deep Then
            With new_order
                ' Clone the OrderCustomer.
                .OrderCustomer = Me.OrderCustomer.Clone()

                ' Clone the OrderItems list.
                .OrderItems = New List(Of OrderItem)
                For Each order_item As OrderItem In Me.OrderItems
                    .OrderItems.Add(order_item.Clone())
```

```
                Next order_item
            End With
        End If

        Return new_order
    End Function
End Class
```

The `Order` class contains a reference to a `Customer` object and a generic list of `OrderItem` objects.

The `Clone` method takes a parameter indicating whether it should return a shallow or deep copy. The function starts by using `MemberwiseClone` to make a shallow copy. If it should make a deep copy, it then sets the new object's `Customer` and `OrderItem` references to clones of the original objects.

In this example, the `Customer` and `OrderItem` classes don't contain any references, so they only provide shallow copies, and the `Order` class's `Clone` method doesn't need to pass a parameter into the `Customer` and `OrderItem` class's `Clone` methods. If those classes did support shallow and deep cloning, you would probably want to pass the same deep parameter into those methods.

The following code shows how the `Clones` example program demonstrates cloning in the `Customer` and `OrderItems` classes:

```
Private Sub Form1_Load(ByVal sender As System.Object, _
 ByVal e As System.EventArgs) Handles MyBase.Load
    Dim txt_originals As String = ""
    Dim txt_clones As String = ""

    ' Make and clone a Customer.
    Dim cust1 As New Customer("Rod", "Stephens", "1337 Leet St", "Bugsville", _
        "AZ", "87654")
    Dim cust2 As Customer = cust1.Clone()
    txt_originals &= "*** cust1:" & vbCrLf & cust1.ToString() & "----------" & _
        vbCrLf
    txt_clones &= "*** cust2:" & vbCrLf & cust2.ToString() & "----------" & vbCrLf

    ' Make and clone an Order.
    Dim order1 As New Order
    With order1
        .OrderCustomer = New Customer("Bob", "Hacker", "123 Decompile Ct", _
            "Attatash", "ME", "01234")
        .OrderItems.Add(New OrderItem("Cookies", 12))
        .OrderItems.Add(New OrderItem("Pencil", 2))
        .OrderItems.Add(New OrderItem("Notebook", 6))
    End With

    ' Make a shallow clone.
    Dim order2 As Order = order1.Clone(False)

    ' Make a deep clone.
    Dim order3 As Order = order1.Clone(True)

    ' Modify the original Order object.
    With order1.OrderCustomer
```

```
            .FirstName = "Mindy"
            .LastName = "Modified"
            .Street = "12 Altered Ave"
            .City = "Changed City"
            .State = "AL"
            .Zip = "98765"
        End With
        With order1.OrderItems(0)
            .Item = "Rice (grain)"
            .Quantity = 10000
        End With

        ' Display the three Orders.
        txt_originals &= "*** order1: " & vbCrLf & order1.ToString() & _
            "----------" & vbCrLf
        txt_clones &= "*** order2: " & vbCrLf & order2.ToString() & _
            "----------" & vbCrLf

        txt_originals &= "*** order1: " & vbCrLf & order1.ToString() & _
            "----------" & vbCrLf
        txt_clones &= "*** order3: " & vbCrLf & order3.ToString() & _
            "----------" & vbCrLf

        ' Display the results.
        txtOriginals.Text = txt_originals
        txtClones.Text = txt_clones
        txtOriginals.Select(0, 0)
        txtClones.Select(0, 0)
    End Sub
```

The code first creates `Customer` object. Its constructor initializes its properties. The code uses the `Customer` class's `Clone` method to make a copy of the object. It then uses the objects' `ToString` methods to add textual representations of the objects to a pair of output strings.

Next, the program makes an `Order` item, attaches a `Customer` object, and fills its `OrderItems` list with `OrderItem` objects. It then makes shallow and deep clones of the `Order` object. It modifies some of the values in the original object, and then adds textual representations of all three objects to the output strings. The code finishes by displaying the result strings.

Figure 7-1 shows the result. Notice that the `Customer` object on the top left is the same as its clone on the right. The original `Order` item named `order1` on the left matches the shallow copy `order2` on the right. The deep copy `order3` does not match, because it got its own new `Customer` and `OrderItem` objects when it was copied, so those items were not modified when the program altered the original `Order`'s data.

Visual Basic defines an `ICloneable` interface to make cloning more consistent. Unfortunately, the interface defines a `Clone` method, but it doesn't take a parameter indicating whether it should be a deep or shallow copy, and it returns a generic `Object` instead of a more specific object type.

The intent is that the program will use `MemberwiseClone` to make a shallow copy, and `Clone` to make a deep copy. In either case, the main program must use `DirectCast` to convert the returned `Object` into an appropriate type.

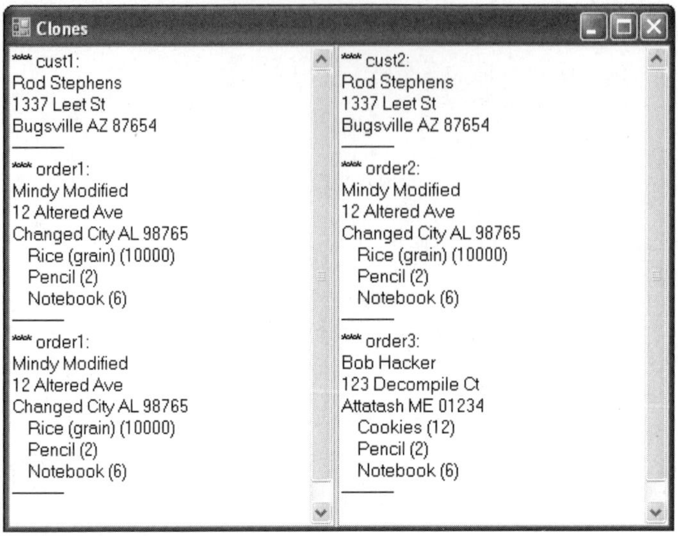

Figure 7-1: Program `Clones` demonstrates shallow and deep clones.

The `ICloneable` interface doesn't provide much advantage over simply writing your own `Clone` method that takes a parameter indicating the kind of copy to make and returning a specific object type. Unless you need to work with another class that requires the `ICloneable` interface, you are just as well off writing your own `Clone` method.

Factory

A *factory* is a class that provides a means for creating instances of other classes. The main program creates the `Factory` object and calls a method to create an instance of another class. Usually the factory could return more than one type of object depending on the circumstances. Pulling the decision-making process into the class helps isolate the main program from information about those created classes.

Suppose it's hard to decide what type of object to create. Perhaps the type of object depends on the user's selections, the value of a calculation, or the data in a file. In that case, the program must perform some sort of complicated test, and then create the appropriate object.

For example, suppose the user opens a file that might be a bitmap, text file, or database. The program must create a different kind of object to handle each choice. If `file_info` is a `FileInfo` object representing the selected file, then you could use code similar to the following to create the right object. Here, `FileProcessor` is a parent class from which `BitmapProcessor`, `TextFileProcessor`, `MdbProcessor`, and `OtherProcessor` are derived:

```
' Make an appropriate FileProcessor.
Dim file_processor As FileProcessor = Nothing
Select Case file_info.Extension.ToLower
    Case ".bmp"
        file_processor = New BitmapProcessor(file_info)
    Case ".txt"
        file_processor = New TextFileProcessor(file_info)
    Case ".mdb"
```

```
        file_processor = New MdbProcessor(file_info)
    Case Else
        file_processor = New OtherProcessor(file_info)
End Select

' Tell the FileProcessor to do its thing.
fp.ProcessFile()
```

The `Select Case` statement examines the file's extension and creates an object of the appropriate `FileProcessor` subclass. The program then calls the processor's `ProcessFile` method to take action.

This code works, but it locks information about the file types into the main program's code. If you later needed to change the types of files supported, or the method by which the program decides which type of processor to build, you must update the main program.

You can pull the intelligence out of the main program into its own class by making a `Factory` class. The `FileProcessorFactory` class shown in the following code holds the logic to create different kinds of `FileProcessor` subclasses:

```
' Make various kinds of FileProcessor objects.
Public Class FileProcessorFactory
    Public Function MakeFileProcessor(ByVal file_name As String) As FileProcessor
        Dim file_info As New FileInfo(file_name)

        ' See what kind of file this is.
        Dim file_processor As FileProcessor = Nothing
        Select Case file_info.Extension.ToLower
            Case ".bmp"
                file_processor = New BitmapProcessor(file_info)
            Case ".txt"
                file_processor = New TextFileProcessor(file_info)
            Case ".mdb"
                file_processor = New MdbProcessor(file_info)
            Case Else
                file_processor = New OtherProcessor(file_info)
        End Select

        Return file_processor
    End Function
End Class
```

This class contains a `Select Case` statement similar to the one shown previously, but now it's not tied into the main program.

The main program could use the following code to process files:

```
' Make a FileProcessorFactory.
Dim fp_factory As New FileProcessorFactory()

' Make a FileProcessor.
Dim fp As FileProcessor = fp_factory.MakeFileProcessor(dlgOpen.FileName)

' Tell the FileProcessor to do its thing.
fp.ProcessFile()
```

The code makes a new `FileProcessorFactory` object and calls its `MakeFileProcessor` function to make an object from one of the `FileProcessor` subclasses. It then calls that object's `ProcessFile` method.

> *Notice that the factory creates instances of classes that all inherit from the* `FileProcessor` *base class. In general, the objects that the factory creates should either come from the same ancestor class, or implement the same interface so the main program can do something meaningful with them. Otherwise, the program will need to use some sort of test such as* `If TypeOf returned_object Is Class1 Then...` *and so forth. That pulls logic about the subclasses back into the main program and defeats much of the purpose of the factory.*

For another example, suppose you build a base class named `ErrorProcessor`. The subclass `EmailErrorProcessor` sends error messages to a developer and the subclass `LogFileErrorProcessor` logs error messages into a file. When an error occurs, the program checks environment variables to see whether it should log errors into a file or send email. If it should send email, it checks other variables to decide to whom it should send the mail. You could put all of these tests in the main program and repeat them every time there is an error message, but it would be better to make an `ErrorProcessorFactory` to create an object from the appropriate `ErrorProcessor` subclass.

I have also seen programs where developers made a factory class for each concrete class that they will want to create. For example, a `CustomerFactory` object creates a `Customer` object. Sometimes there may be a `FactoryBase` class from which the specific factory classes inherit. The `FactoryBase` class would define a `CreateInstance` function or some other method for creating an instance of the concrete class.

In this scenario, you can use the factory objects to defer creating the concrete objects. For example, you can pass a `CustomerFactory` object into a subroutine that may need to make a `Customer` object. If the routine decides it doesn't need a `Customer` object, it doesn't need to create one. If the `Customer` class is complicated and hard to initialize, not creating a `Customer` can save the program some time and memory.

Similarly, you can pass a factory object into a subroutine that can later use it to create an object from the concrete class, all without knowing what type of object it is creating. In this approach, the decision about the type of object was made earlier when you picked the appropriate factory class, but actually creating the object has been deferred.

One misuse of factory classes that I've seen is when the program uses a set of factory classes to immediately create instances of their classes. For example, the program creates an `InvoiceFactory` object and then immediately uses it to create an `Invoice` object. In that case, you could just as well have moved any initialization code from the `InvoiceFactory` into the `Invoice` class's constructors. Another variation would be to give the `Invoice` class a public shared function that returns an `Invoice` object. Either of these solutions avoids having to have the `InvoiceFactory` class, avoids the need to create instances of that class, and moves logic dealing with the `Invoice` class inside that class where it belongs.

Relation Patterns

Relation patterns deal with the ways in which objects are related to each other. They affect the object-oriented structure of the application. The Adapter, Facade, and Interface patterns all provide front-ends to classes. They allow one class to interact with one or more other classes in as simpler, more isolated way. That can help decouple the classes so they are easier to write, debug, and maintain separately.

Adapter

An *Adapter class* provides an interface between two classes. It lets two classes cooperate when they otherwise couldn't because they have mismatched interfaces.

For example, suppose you have written an event logging system that can log messages into a file or email messages to a developer. Now, suppose you decide you also want to be able to send messages to a pager. The method your code uses to log messages into a file or send them in an email doesn't work the same way as the Web Service that you would call to send the message to a pager.

To make the existing classes work with the new pager class, you could write an Adapter between them. The Adapter would let the main program call methods in the same way it does now when using a log file or email. It would then pass requests along to the Web Service in whatever format it requires. Figure 7-2 shows the situation graphically.

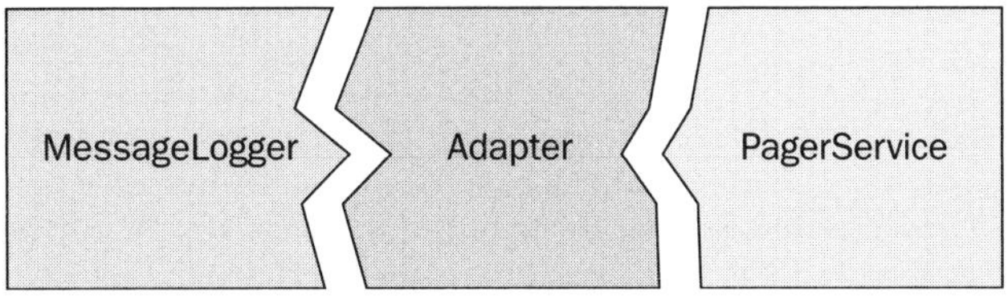

Figure 7-2: An Adapter allows a program to work with an incompatible class.

Because the Adapter wraps up another object, in this case a Web Service, it is also sometimes called a Wrapper.

The Adapter pattern is closely related to the Interface and Facade patterns.

Facade

A *Facade* is basically an interface to a large and potentially complicated collection of objects that perform a single role. For example, a program might use `DataGatherer`, `ReportFormatter`, and `ReportPrinter` classes to build and print reports. You can make printing reports simpler by hiding the process behind a Facade. Figure 7-3 shows the idea graphically.

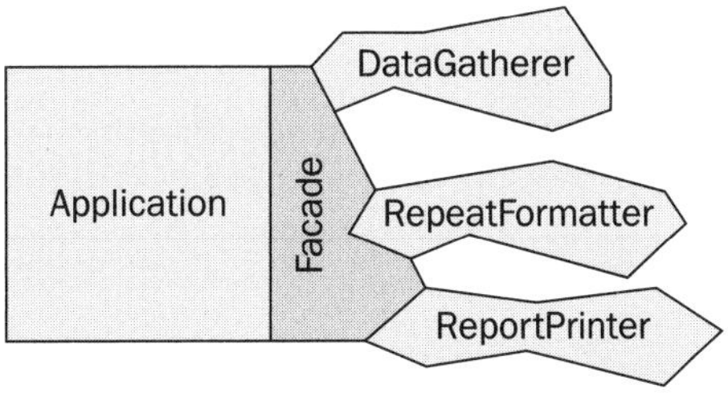

Figure 7-3: A Facade presents a simple interface for a complex collection of objects.

Note that the classes do not need to be strictly contained in the Facade. For example, the `DataGatherer` *class could be used in other operations, perhaps to build a report for display rather than printing. In that case, you might want another Facade to hide the details of report display.*

Interface

An *Interface* is basically the same as an Adapter, but it is used for a different purpose. You use an Adapter to allow existing incompatible classes to work together. You use an Interface to isolate two classes so they can evolve independently. It helps keep two classes loosely coupled.

For example, suppose your application generates a series of reports with a standard format. Early in the project, you may not have completely finalized the report format or the data that will be displayed in the reports. If you make the `CustomerOrder` class call the `ReportGenerator` class directly, then you will need to change the `CustomerOrder` code whenever the `ReportGenerator` code changes. When the data stored in the `CustomerOrder` class changes, you may also need to make changes to the `ReportGenerator` class.

To decouple the classes and make development easier, you can insert an Interface between the two classes. The `CustomerOrder` class calls Interface methods and the Interface passes them along to the `ReportGenerator`. Now if you make changes to one of the classes, you only need to make corresponding changes to the Interface and the other class can remain unchanged.

In practice, changes to one class often require changes to the other despite the Interface. For example, if you add new data to the `CustomerOrder` class, you'll eventually need to change the `ReportGenerator` to display the new data.

However, the Interface lets you change `CustomerOrder` without changing `ReportGenerator` right away. The developers working on that class can continue their work independently, and process the new data when they are ready to do so.

I've worked on a couple of projects where tight coupling between classes made it very difficult for developers working on the classes to get anything done. The first class would change and the second class would break until it was updated. The next day the second class would change and first would break until it was fixed. Adding an Interface between the two allowed them both to move forward more quickly.

Behavior Patterns

Behavior patterns deal with the behavior of parts of the application. The Abstract Base Class pattern uses a base class to determine the properties and behavior of derived classes.

Chain of Responsibility and Chain of Events allow a program to apply a series of methods to an object or event until one of them handles it.

The Command pattern lets you treat a method as an object that you can pass around to different pieces of code. Commands can be useful for implementing the Chain of Responsibility, Chain of Events, and Strategy patterns.

Delegation is a technique where one object uses other objects to provide some of its behavior. The Model, View, Controller pattern allows a group of relatively simple classes to let the user view and modify data in complex ways. Both the Delegation and the Model, View, Controller patterns deal with ways classes can work together to simplify complex behavior.

The Property Procedure pattern describes a standard method for implementing properties that makes them easier to debug.

The Snapshot pattern describes a technique for allowing code to save an object's state and later restore it to that state without knowing the object's internal details.

Finally, the Strategy pattern encapsulates a strategy or algorithm. While the Chain of Responsibility and Chain of Events apply several methods until one works, the Strategy pattern allows a program to apply a single one of a number of different approaches.

Abstract Base Class

The idea behind an *Abstract Base Class* is so simple that it's almost not worth describing as a design pattern. However, it is an important idea, so it's probably better to give it too much attention rather than not enough.

When you derive a set of child classes from a parent class, the program can treat objects from the child classes as if they were members of the parent class. That's the object-oriented principle of *polymorphism*.

For example, suppose you are making a drawing application and you want to make classes representing drawn objects such as rectangles, ellipses, polygons, stars, text, and so forth. Each of these has some shared characteristics such as an (X, Y) position, width, height, fill color, outline color, and line style. If the objects are to draw themselves, they must also provide some sort of `Draw` method.

To allow the main program to treat all of these objects in the same way, you can pull out these common characteristics and place them in a parent class named `Shape`. Now the program can store objects in a collection of `Shapes`. It can loop through the collection calling each method's `Draw` method and it can examine each object's size and position.

While the program must be able to create objects from the ellipse, rectangle, and other child classes, it wouldn't make much sense to create a `Shape` object. The `Shape` class represents an abstraction of the child classes, not a particular shape itself. It can store a position, size, and colors, but if you called its `Draw` method, what would it draw?

To ensure that the program doesn't try to create a `Shape` object, you can make the class *abstract*. An *abstract class* is one that cannot be instantiated. In contrast, a *concrete class* is one that is not abstract, so you can create instances of it. In Visual Basic, you can make a class abstract by adding the `MustInherit` keyword to its declaration.

The following code shows an abstract `Shape` class:

```
' The abstract Shape parent class.
Public MustInherit Class Shape
    Public Location As Rectangle
    Public FillColor As Color
```

```
    Public ForeColor As Color

    ' The constructor is protected so the child classes must
    ' provide constructors for the program to use.

    ' Save the location and colors.
    Public Sub New(ByVal shape_location As Rectangle, ByVal fill_color As Color, _
     ByVal fore_color As Color)
        Location = shape_location
        FillColor = fill_color
        ForeColor = fore_color
    End Sub

    ' Methods.
    Public MustOverride Sub Draw(ByVal gr As Graphics)
End Class
```

The `Shape` class's declaration includes the keyword `MustInherit`, so the program cannot make an instance of this class directly.

The `Shape` class defines public `Location`, `FillColor`, and `ForeColor` variables that are shared by all of its child classes. It then defines a constructor that uses parameters to initialize these variables.

> *If you declare a constructor as* `Protected`*, only that class and any derived classes can use it, so the main program will not be able to use the constructor. If this is the only constructor, then the program cannot make an instance of the class. This essentially makes the class abstract.*

Next, the `Shape` class declares a `Draw` method. The `MustOverride` keyword makes this is an *abstract method declaration* that provides no implementation (notice that there is no `End Sub` statement). Any concrete ancestor classes must override this method and provide a concrete implementation. The declaration in the `Shape` class defines the signature of the method. In this case, the method must be a subroutine, not a function, and must take a single `Graphics` object as a parameter.

> *Note that a class with an abstract method must be an abstract class. In Visual Basic, that means if the class has a* `MustOverride` *method, then it must be declared* `MustInherit`.
>
> *Note also that only concrete child classes* must *provide an implementation of the abstract method. If you declare a child class* `MustInherit`*, then it doesn't need to override the method. Its descendants can do it instead.*

The following code shows the concrete `RectangleShape` class derived from the `Shape` class:

```
' Rectangle.
Public Class RectangleShape
    Inherits Shape

    ' Constructor. Delegated to the Shape class.
    Public Sub New(ByVal shape_location As Rectangle, ByVal fill_color As Color, _
     ByVal fore_color As Color)
        MyBase.New(shape_location, fill_color, fore_color)
    End Sub
```

```
        ' Draw the rectangle.
        Public Overrides Sub Draw(ByVal gr As System.Drawing.Graphics)
            Using the_brush As New SolidBrush(FillColor)
                gr.FillRectangle(the_brush, Location)
            End Using
            Using the_pen As New Pen(ForeColor)
                gr.DrawRectangle(the_pen, Location)
            End Using
        End Sub
    End Class
```

The `RectangleShape` class defines a constructor that uses the `Shape` class's constructor to save location and color information.

The class provides a concrete `Draw` method. It makes a brush and fills the rectangle; then makes a pen and outlines the rectangle.

You can easily make other classes to draw ellipses and other shapes. The `EllipseShape` class would be identical to the `RectangleShape` class, except the `Draw` method would draw an ellipse instead of a rectangle. Other classes might need additional information. For example, a `PolygonShape` class would need to store the points it will connect. A `TextShape` class would need to know what font to use and what text to draw.

The following code shows how the `AbstractBaseClass` example program works:

```
Imports System.Collections.Generic

Public Class Form1
    ' The collection of Shapes to draw.
    Private m_Shapes As New List(Of Shape)

    Private Sub Form1_Load(ByVal sender As System.Object, _
     ByVal e As System.EventArgs) Handles MyBase.Load
        ' Make some Shapes.
        m_Shapes.Add(New RectangleShape(New Rectangle(50, 20, 50, 120), _
            Color.Orange, Color.Red))
        m_Shapes.Add(New EllipseShape(New Rectangle(80, 60, 90, 180), _
            Color.Blue, Color.DarkBlue))
        m_Shapes.Add(New RectangleShape(New Rectangle(20, 80, 210, 40), _
            Color.Lime, Color.DarkGreen))
        m_Shapes.Add(New EllipseShape(New Rectangle(10, 150, 250, 50), _
            Color.Pink, Color.Teal))

        ' Redraw.
        Me.Invalidate()
    End Sub

    ' Draw the shapes.
    Private Sub Form1_Paint(ByVal sender As Object, _
     ByVal e As System.Windows.Forms.PaintEventArgs) Handles Me.Paint
        e.Graphics.Clear(Me.BackColor)
        For Each a_shape As Shape In m_Shapes
            a_shape.Draw(e.Graphics)
```

```
        Next a_shape
    End Sub
End Class
```

The program declares a generic `List Of Shape` objects to store drawing objects. When the form loads, the program creates some `RectangleShape` and `EllipseShape` objects and adds them to the collection.

When the form's `Paint` event handler fires, the program clears the form and loops through the `Shape` collection, calling each object's `Draw` method.

Figure 7-4 shows the program in action.

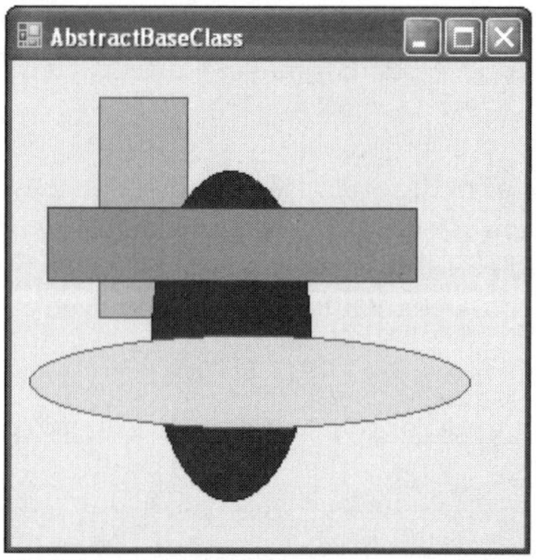

Figure 7-4: Program `AbstractBaseClass` uses concrete child classes to draw rectangles and ellipses.

An abstract base class is useful for specifying features that must be implemented by child classes, and when it doesn't make sense for the program to create instances of the base class.

Chain of Responsibility

In the *Chain of Responsibility pattern*, some sort of message, task, or other item that must be handled is sent to a series of objects until one of them processes it. This frees the code that must handle the item from needing to know how the item must be handled.

Normally, the classes that process the item provide a function that examines the item and returns `True` if the object completely handled the item.

The following code shows an abstract `NumberHandler` class. The abstract `WasHandled` function returns `True` or `False` to indicate whether the object processed an integer parameter.

```
Public MustInherit Class NumberHandler
    Public MustOverride Function WasHandled(ByVal value As Integer) As Boolean
End Class
```

Child classes must override the `WasHandled` function. The following code shows a `PowerHandler` class that displays a message if the input value is a power (greater than 1) of some other integer (for example, 16 = 2 ^ 4):

```
Public Class PowerHandler
    Inherits NumberHandler

    ' Return True if we handle this item.
    Public Overrides Function WasHandled(ByVal value As Integer) As Boolean
        If value < 0 Then value = -value
        If value < 4 Then Return False

        For base As Integer = 2 To CInt(Sqrt(value))
            Dim power As Double = Log(value, base)
            If CInt(power) = power Then
                ' value = base ^ power.
                MessageBox.Show(value.ToString() & " = " & _
                    base.ToString() & "^" & power.ToString(), _
                    "Power", MessageBoxButtons.OK, MessageBoxIcon.Information)
                Return True
            End If
        Next base

        ' Not a power.
        Return False
    End Function
End Class
```

The `WasHandled` function first ensures that the input value is non-negative. If the value is less than 4, the function returns `False`, because the values 0 through 3 are not powers of other integers.

Next, the program loops through base values between 2 and the square root of the input value. It takes the logarithm of the value using the base. If the result is an integer, then the value is a power of the base, so the function displays a message and returns `True`.

If the input value is not a power of any of the bases, it is not a power, so the function returns `False`.

Example program `ChainOfCommand` uses the following code to evaluate numbers:

```
Public Class Form1
    Private m_Handlers As New List(Of NumberHandler)

    ' Make the chain of command.
    Private Sub Form1_Load(ByVal sender As System.Object, _
     ByVal e As System.EventArgs) Handles MyBase.Load
        m_Handlers.Add(New PrimeHandler())
        m_Handlers.Add(New PowerHandler())
        m_Handlers.Add(New EvenHandler())
        m_Handlers.Add(New UnhandledHandler())
    End Sub

    ' Process a number.
    Private Sub btnProcess_Click(ByVal sender As System.Object, _
```

```
        ByVal e As System.EventArgs) Handles btnProcess.Click
            Dim value As Integer = Integer.Parse(txtValue.Text)

            For Each handler As NumberHandler In m_Handlers
                If handler.WasHandled(value) Then Exit For
            Next handler

        End Sub
    End Class
```

When the program's form loads, the code makes a List of `NumberHandler` objects and adds subclasses of the `NumberHandler` class to the list. `PrimeHandler` processes prime numbers, `PowerHandler` processes numbers that are powers of other numbers, and `EvenHandler` processes even numbers.

The `UnhandledHandler` class processes every number by displaying a message box saying the number was unhandled. It's usually a good idea to place a similar catch-all object at the end of the chain of command to deal with any items that are not processed earlier. At a minimum, this object can display an error message to the user or log the event.

If you enter a value in the `ChainOfCommand` example program and click the Process button, the code loops through the list of handlers. It calls each handler's `WasProcessed` function and exits the loop if the function returns `True`.

This example tries each of its handlers in the order in which they were added to the handler list, but you could apply the handlers in any order that makes sense. For example, you might sort the handlers by priority and apply the higher priority items first.

For a concrete example, suppose you have created classes that process error messages in various ways. Perhaps you would first like to try sending an email to developers, then try writing the error into a log file, and, finally, display a message to the user. You can give each of the objects a priority and sort the list of handlers so that the program tries them in priority order.

Note that an object's `WasHandled` function should return `True` only if the item is *completely* handled so that other handlers don't need to look at it. An object's `WasHandled` function might take some action to partially handle the item, and then return `False` to give other objects a chance to perform additional processing.

For example, suppose when there's an error you want to notify the user and log the file in some way. Then the `NotifyUserErrorHandler`'s `WasHandled` method could display a message and return `False`. Next the program would let the `EmailErrorHandler` and `LogErrorHandler` objects also process the message.

Chain of Events

A *Chain of Events* is similar to a Chain of Command, but it is somewhat more specific. A Chain of Command sends an item to a series of handler objects to see if any of them can process the item. A Chain of Events sends an event to a series of event handlers to allow them to handle it.

The `ChainOfEventsSimple` example program uses the `NumberProcessor` class shown in the following code to monitor an integer value. When its value is changed, the `NumberProcessor` raises a `NumberChanged` event.

```
Public Class NumberProcessor
    Private m_Value As Integer
    Public Property Value() As Integer
        Get
            Return m_Value
        End Get
        Set(ByVal value As Integer)
            m_Value = value
            RaiseEvent NumberChanged(m_Value)
        End Set
    End Property

    Public Delegate Sub NumberChangedDelegate(ByVal value As Integer)
    Public Event NumberChanged As NumberChangedDelegate
End Class
```

When the program starts, it uses the following code to register three event handlers for the `NumberChanged` event:

```
Private m_NumberProcessor As New NumberProcessor

' Add events to the NumberProcessor.
Private Sub Form1_Load(ByVal sender As System.Object, _
 ByVal e As System.EventArgs) Handles MyBase.Load
    AddHandler m_NumberProcessor.NumberChanged, AddressOf CheckPrime
    AddHandler m_NumberProcessor.NumberChanged, AddressOf CheckPower
    AddHandler m_NumberProcessor.NumberChanged, AddressOf CheckEven

    m_NumberProcessor.Value = Integer.Parse(txtValue.Text)
End Sub
```

If you change the value in the program's text box, the following code updates the `NumberProcessor`, it raises its `NumberChanged` event, and the three event handlers execute:

```
' Set the new integer value.
Private Sub txtValue_TextChanged(ByVal sender As System.Object, _
 ByVal e As System.EventArgs) Handles txtValue.TextChanged
    If IsNumeric(txtValue.Text) Then
        m_NumberProcessor.Value = Integer.Parse(txtValue.Text)
    End If
End Sub
```

The event handlers defined by example program `ChainOfEventsSimple` indicate whether the current number is prime, a power, or even in three text boxes.

This method is relatively straightforward. It allows more than one event handler to process the same event. It doesn't give the same flexibility as the Chain of Command pattern described in the previous section, however, because it doesn't give you control over how the events are applied. You cannot determine the order in which they are executed, although in practice, they are executed in the order in which they were registered, so you have some control. They also don't give you the option of stopping after an event handler has successfully processed the event.

You can provide these extra features if you use a custom event. The following code shows a new version of the `NumberProcessor` class that provides a custom `NumberChanged` event:

```
Public Class NumberProcessor
    Private m_Value As Integer
    Public Property Value() As Integer
        Get
            Return m_Value
        End Get
        Set(ByVal value As Integer)
            m_Value = value
            RaiseEvent NumberChanged(m_Value, False)
        End Set
    End Property

    Public Delegate Sub NumberChangedDelegate(ByVal value As Integer, _
        ByRef was_handled As Boolean)
    Private m_EventDelegates As New List(Of NumberChangedDelegate)

    Public Custom Event NumberChanged As NumberChangedDelegate
        AddHandler(ByVal value As NumberChangedDelegate)
            m_EventDelegates.Add(value)
        End AddHandler

        RemoveHandler(ByVal value As NumberChangedDelegate)
            m_EventDelegates.Remove(value)
        End RemoveHandler

        RaiseEvent(ByVal value As Integer, ByRef was_handled As Boolean)
            was_handled = False
            For Each a_delegate As NumberChangedDelegate In m_EventDelegates
                a_delegate(value, was_handled)
                If was_handled Then Exit For
            Next a_delegate
        End RaiseEvent
    End Event
End Class
```

A custom event handler has three sections: `AddHandler`, `RemoveHandler`, and `RaiseEvent`.

The `AddHandler` section stores information about a delegate that is being registered. This example adds the delegate to a list.

The `RemoveHandler` section removes a delegate from the list.

The `RaiseEvent` section invokes the delegates when the `NumberProcessor` object raises its `Number Changed` event. In this example, the `NumberChangedDelegate` is declared with two parameters: a value passed by `value` and a Boolean variable named `was_handled` passed by reference. The invoked event handler should set this to `True` if it has completely processed the event.

In this example, the `RaiseEvent` code loops through the stored delegates, invoking each until one of the sets `was_handled` to `True`. That lets the program skip any remaining event handlers.

Example program `ChainOfEvents` uses event handlers that check a number to see whether it is prime, a power, or even. If any of the event handlers takes action, it displays an appropriate message and sets `was_handled` to `True` so that the program skips the remaining event handlers.

Custom events don't give you an easy way to prioritize event handlers (other than the fact that they are executed in the registration order). If you need to order the handlers more dynamically, use the Chain of Command pattern described in the previous section.

Command

In the *Command design pattern*, an object represents an action. The program can perform the action by calling the object's `Execute` method.

Command objects are useful when you want to pass the action around for use later, and you don't want the code that is carrying and using the object to know the details of what the command does. This decreases the coupling between the code and the action, and makes working with both easier.

For example, suppose a report generator class gathers data and formats a report. You could pass the generator a command object that provides a `ProcessReport` method. After it has built the report, the generator can call the command object's `ProcessReport` method without knowing whether the report will be printed, saved into a file, or emailed to a user.

You can pass a variety of command objects to allow for contingencies. For example, you could pass an order processing routine an object to invoke if the customer has an unpaid balance, another object to invoke if the requested items are out of stock, a third object to invoke if the order is processed successfully, and so forth.

Visual Basic provides a couple of ways you can implement the Command design pattern. The more common approach is to build a class that provides an `Execute` method, instantiate the class, and pass the resulting object to the code that needs it.

The following code shows a simple command class. Its constructor takes a parameter, giving the message that the object will later display, and saves the message in a private variable. The `Execute` method displays the following message:

```
Public Class ExecuteClass
    Private m_Message As String
    Public Sub New(ByVal message As String)
        m_Message = message
    End Sub

    Public Sub Execute()
        MessageBox.Show(m_Message, "ExecuteClass", _
            MessageBoxButtons.OK, MessageBoxIcon.Asterisk)
    End Sub
End Class
```

A second approach is to pass a delegate to a routine that can invoke it later. With this method you don't need to build an extra class just to perform a simple action. This is more confusing to many programmers, however.

The `Commands` example program uses the following code to demonstrate each of these methods:

```
Public Class Form1
    Private Delegate Sub ExecuteDelegate()

    Private Sub Form1_Load(ByVal sender As System.Object, _
     ByVal e As System.EventArgs) Handles MyBase.Load
        btnGoodDay.Tag = New ExecuteDelegate(AddressOf SayGoodDay)
        btnGutenTag.Tag = New ExecuteClass("Guten Tag")
    End Sub

    Private Sub SayGoodDay()
        MessageBox.Show("Good Day", "SayGoodDay", _
            MessageBoxButtons.OK, MessageBoxIcon.Asterisk)
    End Sub

    Private Sub btnGoodDay_Click(ByVal sender As System.Object, _
     ByVal e As System.EventArgs) Handles btnGoodDay.Click
        Dim btn As Button = DirectCast(sender, Button)
        Dim execute_delegate As ExecuteDelegate = _
            DirectCast(btn.Tag, ExecuteDelegate)
        execute_delegate()
    End Sub

    Private Sub btnGutenTag_Click(ByVal sender As System.Object, _
     ByVal e As System.EventArgs) Handles btnGutenTag.Click
        Dim btn As Button = DirectCast(sender, Button)
        Dim execute_object As ExecuteClass = DirectCast(btn.Tag, ExecuteClass)
        execute_object.Execute()
    End Sub
End Class
```

The program defines the `ExecuteDelegate` type as a reference to a simple subroutine that takes no parameters. When the program starts, its `Load` event handler sets the Good Day button's `Tag` property to a delegate representing the form's `SayGoodDay` subroutine.

Next, the program sets the Guten Tag button's `Tag` property to a new instance of the `ExecuteClass`.

When you click the Good Day button, the button's event handler converts the event's sender into the button that caused the event. It casts the button's `Tag` property into an `ExecuteDelegate` and executes it. This delegate refers to the `SayGoodDay` subroutine so that routine runs and displays the message "Good Day."

When you click the Guten Tag button, the button's event handler converts the event's sender into the button that caused the event. It casts the button's `Tag` property into an `ExecuteClass` object and calls its `Execute` method. That method displays the message "Guten Tag" stored by the object's constructor when it was created in the form's `Load` event handler.

Delegates are useful when you need to pass a single routine in a fairly local context and you don't want to create a new class. Most developers find delegates more confusing than objects, however, so you may prefer to use objects.

Delegation

Like abstract base classes, delegation is a simple but important technique. *Delegation* is the process of one object using another to provide features. It gives a result similar to those of inheritance, but without actually using inheritance.

To provide Delegation in Visual Basic, give one class a reference to another class. To provide the features of the second class, the object calls the methods provided by its referenced object.

For example, suppose you've built a `House` class that has the properties `NumberOfBedrooms`, `NumberOfBathrooms`, `SquareFeet`, and `PricePerSquareFoot`. It also has a `CalculateValue` function that returns the house's estimated value based on its square feet and price per square foot.

Suppose you also have a `Vehicle` class that has the properties `MilesPerGallon`, `FuelCapacity`, and `FuelRemaining`. `Vehicle` also has a `CalculateRange` function that uses `MilesPerGallon` and `FuelRemaining` to estimate the distance the `Vehicle` can travel before running out of fuel.

Now, suppose you want to make a `MotorHome` class that has the characteristics of both a `House` and a `Vehicle`. Visual Basic does not allow multiple inheritance, so `MotorHome` cannot inherit from both classes.

One solution to this problem is to make `MotorHome` inherit from the `House` class. Then give it a private variable of type `Vehicle`. To provide the features of a `Vehicle`, make the `MotorHome` call the properties and methods provided by this private object.

Figure 7-5 shows the idea graphically.

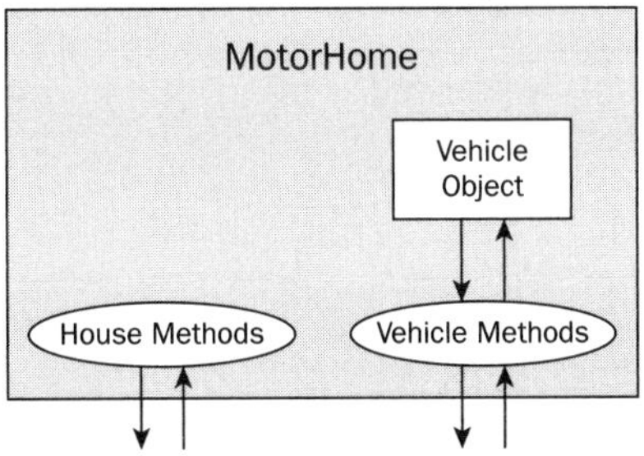

Figure 7-5: In Delegation, an object uses other objects to provide its behavior.

The following code shows simple `House` and `Vehicle` classes:

```
Public Class House
    Public NumberOfBedrooms As Integer
    Public NumberOfBathrooms As Single
    Public SquareFeet As Integer
    Public PricePerSquareFoot As Single

    ' Return estimated value.
    Public Function CalculateValue() As Single
        Return SquareFeet * PricePerSquareFoot
    End Function
End Class

Public Class Vehicle
    Public MilesPerGallon As Single
    Public FuelCapacity As Single
    Public FuelRemaining As Single

    ' Return estimated range.
    Public Function CalculateRange() As Single
        Return MilesPerGallon * FuelRemaining
    End Function
End Class
```

The following code shows the `MotorHome` class:

```
Public Class MotorHome
    Inherits House

    ' The Vehicle we delegate to.
    Private m_Vehicle As New Vehicle

    Public Property MilesPerGallon() As Single
        Get
            Return m_Vehicle.MilesPerGallon
        End Get
        Set(ByVal value As Single)
            m_Vehicle.MilesPerGallon = value
        End Set
    End Property

    Public Property FuelCapacity() As Single
        Get
            Return m_Vehicle.FuelCapacity
        End Get
        Set(ByVal value As Single)
            m_Vehicle.FuelCapacity = value
        End Set
    End Property

    Public Property FuelRemaining() As Single
        Get
            Return m_Vehicle.FuelRemaining
```

```
            End Get
            Set(ByVal value As Single)
                m_Vehicle.FuelRemaining = value
            End Set
        End Property

        ' Return estimated range.
        Public Function CalculateRange() As Single
            Return m_Vehicle.CalculateRange
        End Function
    End Class
```

`MotorHome` inherits from the `House` class, so it doesn't need any extra code to provide the `NumberOfBedrooms`, `NumberOfBathrooms`, `SquareFeet`, and `PricePerSquareFoot` properties or the `CalculateValue` function.

The `MotorHome` class declares a reference to a private `Vehicle` object named `m_Vehicle`. It uses that object's properties and methods to implement its own `MilesPerGallon`, `FuelCapacity`, and `FuelRemaining` properties, and its `CalculateRange` function.

In this example, `MotorHome` inherits from `House` and delegates to `Vehicle`. You could just as easily have made `MotorHome` inherit from `Vehicle` and delegate to `House`. The `House` class is a little more complicated than the `Vehicle` class, however, so that solution would require `MotorHome` to implement more delegation code.

You could also make `MotorHome` delegate to both the `House` and `Vehicle` classes. Then `MotorHome` could inherit from some other class.

Note that you don't need to implement all of the features defined by an object that you are using for delegation. For example, suppose you make `MotorHome` inherit from `Vehicle` and delegate to a `House` object. You may decide that `NumberOfBedrooms` is irrelevant for a `MotorHome`, so you would simply not provide property procedures to delegate that value to the `House` object.

Another situation where delegation is useful is when one object is made up of others. For example, an `Order` might contain `Customer` and `Address` objects. Rather than giving the `Order` class its own properties and methods for managing customer and address data, you can give it references to private `Customer` and `Address` objects. Then, for example, the `Order` object's `City` property would delegate to the private `Address` object's `City` property.

Delegation is useful when you want an object to provide features implemented by another class, but you cannot use inheritance.

Model, View, Controller

The *Model, View, Controller (MVC) pattern* is the most complicated pattern described in this chapter. It's complicated in part because it involves more than two classes working together. It's also complicated because in real-world applications a single object often plays more than one role in the pattern. It's very common for an object to act as a view and a controller. For example, a text box allows a user to enter a new value for a data item, and it also displays the item's value.

Other combinations are less useful. One of the key benefits of the MVC pattern is that it separates the roles of model, view, and controller so that they are easier to understand separately. Ideally, you would keep views and controllers separate, too. In practice, however, many controls that act as controllers (such as text boxes and sliders) also display a representation of the data, so they are also views. An example of separate views and controllers would be a numeric up/down button acting as a controller with an associated label acting as a view. The more separate you can keep the objects, the easier it is to understand their roles.

This pattern involves three basic kinds of objects:

- A *model* is an object that represents some sort of data. It provides methods that allow other pieces of code to examine and modify the data.
- A *view* needs to know about the data provided by a model. Often a view displays the data in some form so that the user can see it.
- A *controller* modifies the data provided by a model. Often, controllers are tied to user interface elements such as text boxes, list boxes, or sliders, and those controls' event handlers use the controller to modify the data.

If a view needs to receive notification about changes to the data, it registers itself with the view. Then, when the data changes, the view notifies all of the registered views so that they can read the new data, display information to the user, or whatever else is appropriate.

The basic flow of data is fairly straightforward: a controller uses the model's methods to modify the data, the model notifies its registered views, and the views take action to handle the new data. The flow gets more confusing when the same object must play more than one of these roles.

For example, the `ModelViewController` example program shown in Figure 7-6 models ten integer test scores. The label at the bottom displays a view. The text boxes on the right act both as views and controllers because you can type new values into them. The graph is also both a view and controller because it lets you click and drag to change a value.

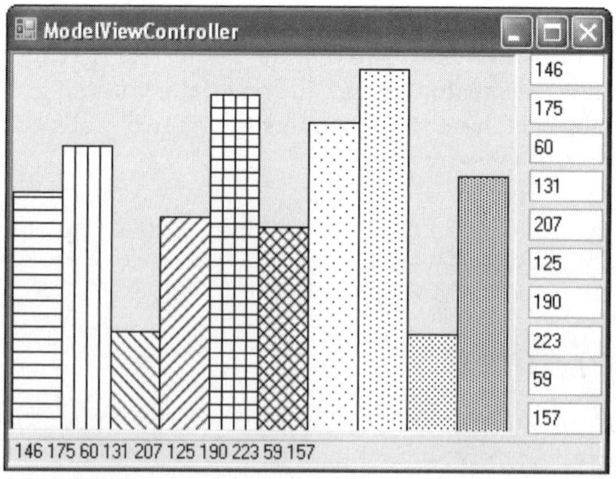

Figure 7-6: Program `ModelViewController` displays data in text boxes, a label, and a graph.

The following code shows the program's `ScoreModel` class:

```
' Stores score data.
Public Class ScoreModel
    Private m_MaxValue As Integer

    ' We raise this event when data is modified.
    Public Event DataModified(ByVal index As Integer)

    Public Sub New(ByVal max_value As Integer)
        m_MaxValue = max_value
    End Sub

    ' Get or set a value.
    Public Const MaxValue As Integer = 9
    Private m_Values(0 To MaxValue) As Integer
    Public Property Value(ByVal index As Integer) As Integer
        Get
            Return m_Values(index)
        End Get
        Set(ByVal value As Integer)
            If value < 0 Then value = 0
            If value > m_MaxValue Then value = m_MaxValue
            m_Values(index) = value

            ' Notify views.
            RaiseEvent DataModified(index)
        End Set
    End Property
End Class
```

The class's `m_MaxValue` variable stores the largest value allowed. The program uses this to fit the data to the `PictureBox` that will hold the graph. The class's constructor saves this value.

The ten scores are saved in the `m_Values` array. Property procedures let other pieces of code get and set the values.

The property set procedure ensures that the new value is between `0` and `m_MaxValue`, updates the saved value, and then raises its `DataModified` event. This event lets views know that the data has been modified.

The following code shows the `ScoreController` class. Its constructor stores a reference to the `ScoreModel` that the object controls. The write-only property `Value` allows the controller to set a value in the model.

```
' Modifies score data.
Public Class ScoreController
    Private m_ScoreModel As ScoreModel

    Public Sub New(ByVal score_model As ScoreModel)
        m_ScoreModel = score_model
    End Sub

    ' Set a score value.
```

```
        Public WriteOnly Property Value(ByVal index As Integer) As Integer
            Set(ByVal value As Integer)
                m_ScoreModel.Value(index) = value
            End Set
        End Property
    End Class
```

The following code shows an abstract `ScoreView` base class:

```
    ' Displays score data.
    Public MustInherit Class ScoreView
        Protected WithEvents m_ScoreModel As ScoreModel
        Public Sub New(ByVal score_model As ScoreModel)
            m_ScoreModel = score_model
        End Sub

        ' Redisplay the data.
        Protected MustOverride Sub m_ScoreModel_DataModified(_
         ByVal index As Integer) Handles m_ScoreModel.DataModified
    End Class
```

The `ScoreView` class declares a `ScoreModel` variable named `m_ScoreModel`. It uses the `WithEvents` keyword, so it can easily catch the model's `DataModified` event. The class also declares the event handler, using the `MustOverride` keyword, so any derived classes must provide a concrete implementation for the event handler.

The `ScoreLabelView` class shown in the following code is a concrete child class of the `ScoreView` class:

```
    ' Displays score data in a label.
    Public Class ScoreLabelView
        Inherits ScoreView

        Private m_Label As Label

        ' Save the ScoreModel and Label.
        Public Sub New(ByVal score_model As ScoreModel, ByVal the_label As Label)
            MyBase.new(score_model)
            m_Label = the_label
        End Sub

        ' Display the data in the label.
        Protected Overrides Sub m_ScoreModel_DataModified(ByVal index As Integer)
            Dim txt As String = ""
            For i As Integer = 0 To ScoreModel.MaxValue
                txt &= m_ScoreModel.Value(i).ToString & " "
            Next i
            m_Label.Text = txt
        End Sub
    End Class
```

This class declares a variable `m_Label` to store a reference to the label control where it will display values. The class's constructor calls the base class's constructor to save a reference to the `ScoreModel` and it initializes `m_Label`.

When it receives a `DataModified` event, the object concatenates all of the model's values into a single string and displays the result in the label. This is the label shown at the bottom of Figure 7-6.

The following code shows the `ScoreGraphView` class that displays the model's data in a graph:

```
' Displays score data in a graph.
Public Class ScoreGraphView
    Inherits ScoreView

    ' The PictureBox we draw on.
    Private WithEvents m_Canvas As PictureBox

    ' Save the ScoreModel and Label.
    Public Sub New(ByVal score_model As ScoreModel, _
     ByVal picture_box As PictureBox)
        MyBase.new(score_model)
        m_Canvas = picture_box
    End Sub

    ' Display the data in a graph.
    Protected Overrides Sub m_ScoreModel_DataModified(ByVal index As Integer)
        m_Canvas.Invalidate()
    End Sub

    ' Draw the graph.
    Private Sub m_Canvas_Paint(ByVal sender As Object, _
     ByVal e As System.Windows.Forms.PaintEventArgs) Handles m_Canvas.Paint
        e.Graphics.Clear(m_Canvas.BackColor)
        Dim dx As Integer = m_Canvas.ClientSize.Width \ (ScoreModel.MaxValue + 1)
        Dim hgt As Integer = m_Canvas.ClientSize.Height
        For i As Integer = 0 To ScoreModel.MaxValue
            e.Graphics.DrawRectangle(Pens.Black, i * dx, _
                hgt - m_ScoreModel.Value(i) - 1, dx, hgt)
        Next i
    End Sub
End Class
```

The class declares a variable to store a reference to the picture box where it will draw.

This class declares a variable `m_Canvas` to store a reference to the picture box control where it will draw the graph. The class's constructor calls the base class's constructor to save a reference to the `ScoreModel` and it initializes `m_Canvas`.

When the class receives a `DataModified` event, it invalidates the picture box to make it generate a `Paint` event. The class's `Paint` event handler then redraws the graph.

The following code shows the `ScoreGraphViewController` class, which acts as both a view and a controller. The class declares references to the `ScoreGraphView` and `ScoreController` classes, and delegates much of its work to them. See the Delegation pattern described earlier in this chapter for more background on delegation.

```
' Acts as a ScoreGraphView and a ScoreController.
Public Class ScoreGraphViewController
    Private m_ScoreGraphView As ScoreGraphView
    Private m_ScoreController As ScoreController

    ' We need to catch MouseDown events on the graph.
    Private WithEvents m_Canvas As PictureBox

    ' Save the ScoreModel and Label.
    Public Sub New(ByVal score_model As ScoreModel, _
     ByVal picture_box As PictureBox)
        m_Canvas = picture_box
        m_ScoreGraphView = New ScoreGraphView(score_model, picture_box)
        m_ScoreController = New ScoreController(score_model)
    End Sub

    ' The index we are changing.
    Private m_Index As Integer = -1

    ' Change the clicked value.
    Private Sub SetValue(ByVal y As Integer)
        If y < 1 Then y = 1
        If y > m_Canvas.ClientSize.Height Then y = m_Canvas.ClientSize.Height
        m_ScoreController.Value(m_Index) = m_Canvas.ClientSize.Height - y
    End Sub
    Private Sub m_Canvas_MouseDown(ByVal sender As Object, _
     ByVal e As System.Windows.Forms.MouseEventArgs) Handles m_Canvas.MouseDown
        Dim dx As Integer = m_Canvas.ClientSize.Width \ (ScoreModel.MaxValue + 1)
        m_Index = e.X \ dx
        If m_Index > ScoreModel.MaxValue Then m_Index = ScoreModel.MaxValue

        SetValue(e.Y)
    End Sub
    Private Sub m_Canvas_MouseMove(ByVal sender As Object, _
     ByVal e As System.Windows.Forms.MouseEventArgs) Handles m_Canvas.MouseMove
        If m_Index < 0 Then Exit Sub
        SetValue(e.Y)
    End Sub
    Private Sub m_Canvas_MouseUp(ByVal sender As Object, _
     ByVal e As System.Windows.Forms.MouseEventArgs) Handles m_Canvas.MouseUp
        m_Index = -1
    End Sub
End Class
```

The class also declares its own `m_Canvas` variable to store a reference to the picture box where the graph is drawn. The class's constructor saves a reference to the picture box, and initializes the `ScoreGraphView` and `ScoreController` objects.

The class's `SetValue` subroutine uses the `ScoreController` object to modify a value in the model.

The `MouseDown`, `MouseMove`, and `MouseUp` event handlers track mouse movements in the picture box. If you click and drag on the graph, the `MouseDown` and `MouseMove` event handlers use the subroutine `SetValue` to update the model's data. That makes the model raise its `DataModified` event. The

ScoreGraphViewController's ScoreGraphView object catches the event and redraws the graph. The result is the graph updates in real-time as you drag the mouse.

The MouseUp event handler resets the m_Index value used by the MouseMove event handler, so future MouseMove events are ignored until you press the mouse down again.

The ScoreGraphViewController class acts as both a controller and a view for a graph. Similarly, the ScoreTextViewController class acts as a controller and view for a text box. It uses a similar approach, delegating much of its work to controller and view objects.

The following code shows the ScoreTextBoxView class used as a view for text boxes:

```
' Displays score data in a label.
Public Class ScoreTextBoxView
    Inherits ScoreView

    ' The TextBox where we display data.
    Private m_TextBox As TextBox

    ' The index of the value we display.
    Private m_Index As Integer

    ' Save the ScoreModel and TextBox.
    Public Sub New(ByVal score_model As ScoreModel, ByVal text_box As TextBox, _
     ByVal index As Integer)
        MyBase.new(score_model)
        m_TextBox = text_box
        m_Index = index
    End Sub

    ' Display the data in the TextBox.
    Protected Overrides Sub m_ScoreModel_DataModified(ByVal index As Integer)
        If m_Index <> index Then Exit Sub
        m_TextBox.Text = m_ScoreModel.Value(index).ToString
    End Sub
End Class
```

The class's constructor saves references to the ScoreModel and the text box where the object will display data. It also saves the index of the data item that this object will display. Unlike the ScoreLabelView and ScoreGraphView classes, which display every value, this class displays only a single value in its text box.

When the model's data changes, the class's DataModified event handler compares the index of the changed data to the index that the object is tracking. If the changed data is at the index of interest, the object displays the new value in its text box.

The following code shows the ScoreTextViewController class that acts as a text box view and controller. It delegates most of its work to ScoreTextBoxView and ScoreController objects.

```
' Acts as a ScoreTextView and a ScoreController.
Public Class ScoreTextViewController
    Private m_ScoreTextBoxView As ScoreTextBoxView
```

```
    Private m_ScoreController As ScoreController

    ' We need to catch TextChanged events in the TextBox.
    Private WithEvents m_TextBox As TextBox

    ' The index of the value in the model that we control.
    Private m_Index As Integer

    ' Save the ScoreModel and Label.
    Public Sub New(ByVal score_model As ScoreModel, ByVal text_box As TextBox, _
     ByVal index As Integer)
        m_TextBox = text_box
        m_Index = index
        m_ScoreTextBoxView = New ScoreTextBoxView(score_model, text_box, index)
        m_ScoreController = New ScoreController(score_model)
    End Sub

    ' Change the value.
    Private Sub m_TextBox_TextChanged(ByVal sender As Object, _
     ByVal e As System.EventArgs) Handles m_TextBox.TextChanged
        If IsNumeric(m_TextBox.Text) Then
            m_ScoreController.Value(m_Index) = CInt(m_TextBox.Text)
        End If
    End Sub
End Class
```

The following code shows how the main program uses these classes:

```
Public Class Form1
    ' This object holds the score data.
    Private m_ScoreModel As ScoreModel

    ' Create models, views, and controllers.
    Private Sub Form1_Load(ByVal sender As System.Object, _
     ByVal e As System.EventArgs) Handles MyBase.Load
        ' Make the model.
        m_ScoreModel = New ScoreModel(picGraph.ClientSize.Height)

        ' Make a ScoreLabelView.
        Dim label_view As New ScoreLabelView(m_ScoreModel, lblValues)

        ' Make the ScoreGraphViewController.
        Dim graph_view_controller As _
            New ScoreGraphViewController(m_ScoreModel, picGraph)

        ' Make ScoreTextViewControllers.
        Dim tvc As ScoreTextViewController
        tvc = New ScoreTextViewController(m_ScoreModel, txtValue0, 0)
        tvc = New ScoreTextViewController(m_ScoreModel, txtValue1, 1)
        tvc = New ScoreTextViewController(m_ScoreModel, txtValue2, 2)
        tvc = New ScoreTextViewController(m_ScoreModel, txtValue3, 3)
        tvc = New ScoreTextViewController(m_ScoreModel, txtValue4, 4)
        tvc = New ScoreTextViewController(m_ScoreModel, txtValue5, 5)
        tvc = New ScoreTextViewController(m_ScoreModel, txtValue6, 6)
```

```
        tvc = New ScoreTextViewController(m_ScoreModel, txtValue7, 7)
        tvc = New ScoreTextViewController(m_ScoreModel, txtValue8, 8)
        tvc = New ScoreTextViewController(m_ScoreModel, txtValue9, 9)

        ' Set some data.
        Dim rand As New Random
        For Each ctl As Control In Me.Controls
            If TypeOf ctl Is TextBox Then
                Dim txt As TextBox = DirectCast(ctl, TextBox)
                txt.Text = rand.Next(10, picGraph.ClientSize.Height).ToString()
            End If
        Next ctl
    End Sub
End Class
```

The program declares variables to hold a `ScoreModel`. When the form loads, the program initializes the `ScoreModel`, using the picture box's height as the largest allowed data value.

The program creates new `ScoreLabelView` and `ScoreGraphViewController` objects attached to the `ScoreModel`. It then makes a series of `ScoreTextViewController` objects to manage the program's text boxes.

Finally, the program generates some random data for its text boxes. When it sets a text box's value, the corresponding `ScoreTextViewController` object acts as a controller and updates the model. The model raises its `DataModified` event to notify the views and the views update their displays.

> *Notice that the program doesn't keep global references to any of its views or controllers. Because the variables declared for those objects are local to the form's* `Load` *event handler, you might wonder why garbage collection doesn't destroy them. Those objects are registered to receive events from various controls so they are still accessible to the program and are, therefore, not candidates for garbage collection.*
>
> *In some programs, you may want to disable a view or controller so that it can no longer participate in the pattern. In that case, you would need to keep references to the objects around so that you can set variables declared using the* `WithEvents` *keyword to* `Nothing` *to disable their event handlers.*

This example shows how a single form can display multiple views of the same data, and provide several ways for the user to modify the data. Some programs use the MVC pattern to allow different forms to provide views of the same data, or to allow the user to modify the same data from different forms.

Property Procedure

You might argue that a *property procedure* is not a pattern because it doesn't involve classes working together. You might also think it's too obvious to be included as a pattern. However, I see code all the time that doesn't use property procedures so, as is the case with Abstract Base Class, I'm going to err on the side of including too much information rather than not enough. Besides, it's short.

The Property Procedure pattern specifies a standard method for implementing properties. The technique is to not store property values in public variables. Instead, a class should store property values in private variables, and provide public methods to get and set the value.

The following code shows part of a Person class used by example program PropertyProcedures:

```
Public Class Person
    Private Sub ShowValues()
        Debug.WriteLine("[" & FirstName & "|" & LastName & "|" & _
            Street & "|" & City & "|" & State & "|" & Zip & "]")
    End Sub

    Private m_FirstName As String
    Public Property FirstName() As String
        Get
            Return m_FirstName
        End Get
        Set(ByVal value As String)
            m_FirstName = value
            ShowValues()
        End Set
    End Property

    ' Code omitted...

End Class
```

Subroutine ShowValues displays the object's property values in the Debug window for debugging purposes.

The FirstName property value is stored in the private variable m_FirstName. Property procedures allow the program to get and set this value.

There are a couple of reasons why you should write a property procedure instead of using a public variable. First, it isolates the rest of the program from the way in which the object stores its data. In this example, the FirstName property is stored in a string. Suppose you later need to change the way the Person object stores its data so that it reads and writes its values from a database. If the rest of the program accesses the values through property procedures, you will not need to modify that code. This makes the Person class encapsulate its data more tightly, and reduces coupling between the Person class and the code that uses it.

Another benefit of property procedures is that you can place diagnostic code in the property procedures. Suppose some part of the application is corrupting an object's FirstName value. Then you can place code in the FirstName property set procedure to look for suspicious values. The example problem calls the ShowValues routine in its property set procedures to display the Person object's current values. You can use similar code to see how and when the property values change.

Notice that the ShowValues subroutine displays the results of the property procedures (for example, FirstName), not the values in the object's private variables (m_FirstName). That provides an additional test that the property get procedures are working correctly.

Finally, you can set breakpoints in the property procedures. If you know that a certain piece of code is corrupting a FirstName value, you can set a breakpoint in the property set procedure and examine the value as it is set.

Building property procedures for every variable is a bit cumbersome. In fact, this book and most other Visual Basic books usually make property variables public so that the code is simpler and easier to read. However, property procedures give you a lot of flexibility, so you should always use them rather than public variables.

Snapshot

A *Snapshot* is a representation of an object's internal state. The object should be able to generate a Snapshot and later use a previously saved Snapshot to restore itself to its earlier state.

The details of the Snapshot are known to the class whose state it represents, but not to other classes. For example, the main program could take a Snapshot of an object and later use it to restore the object, but it would not know anything about the Snapshot's internal structure. Hiding the Snapshot's details from the main program makes it easier to use, tightens the Snapshot's encapsulation, and decreases coupling between the program and the class that the Snapshot represents.

The following code shows a `Person` class that can save and restore snapshots:

```
Public Class Person
    Public FirstName As String
    Public LastName As String
    Public Street As String
    Public City As String
    Public State As String
    Public Zip As String

    ' Save or restore a snapshot.
    Public Property Snapshot() As Object
        Get
            Dim person_snapshot As New PersonSnapshot
            person_snapshot.FirstName = FirstName
            person_snapshot.LastName = LastName
            person_snapshot.Street = Street
            person_snapshot.City = City
            person_snapshot.State = State
            person_snapshot.Zip = Zip
            Return person_snapshot
        End Get
        Set(ByVal value As Object)
            Dim person_snapshot As PersonSnapshot = _
                DirectCast(value, PersonSnapshot)
            FirstName = person_snapshot.FirstName
            LastName = person_snapshot.LastName
            Street = person_snapshot.Street
            City = person_snapshot.City
            State = person_snapshot.State
            Zip = person_snapshot.Zip
        End Set
    End Property

    ' This class is visible only within the Person class.
    Private Class PersonSnapshot
```

```
        Public FirstName As String
        Public LastName As String
        Public Street As String
        Public City As String
        Public State As String
        Public Zip As String
    End Class
End Class
```

The `Person` class stores information about a person in public variables. Its `Snapshot` property gets or sets a `PersonSnapshot` object.

The property get procedure makes a new `PersonSnapshot` object, saves the Person's data into the object's fields, and returns the object.

The property set procedure takes an object as a parameter. It converts the object into a `PersonSnapshot` and copies the object's property values into the `Person` object's fields.

Example program `SnapshotPerson` shown in Figure 7-7 uses this code to save and restore snapshots. Enter values in the text boxes and click the `Take Snapshot` button to add a snapshot to the list on the right. Click a snapshot in the list to restore the `Person` object to its corresponding saved state.

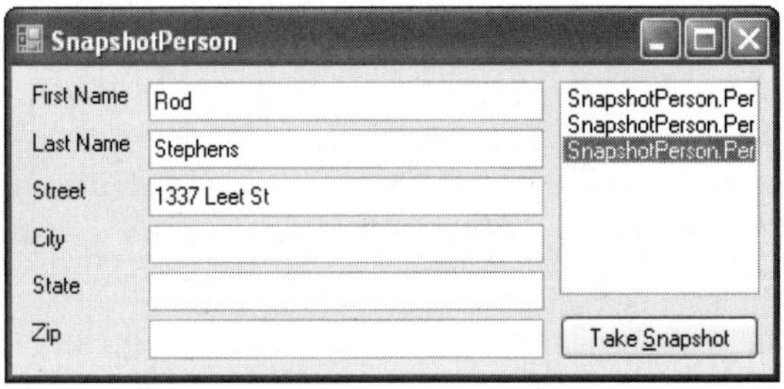

Figure 7-7: Example program `SnapshotPerson` saves and restores snapshots of a `Person` object.

The following code shows the most relevant parts of the `SnapshotPerson` program's code:

```
Private m_Person As New Person

' Save a snapshot.
Private Sub btnTakeSnapshot_Click(ByVal sender As System.Object, _
 ByVal e As System.EventArgs) Handles btnTakeSnapshot.Click
    lstSnapshots.Items.Add(m_Person.Snapshot)
End Sub

' Restore a snapshot.
Private Sub lstSnapshots_SelectedIndexChanged(ByVal sender As System.Object, _
 ByVal e As System.EventArgs) Handles lstSnapshots.SelectedIndexChanged
    m_Person.Snapshot = lstSnapshots.SelectedItem

    txtFirstName.Text = m_Person.FirstName
```

```
        txtLastName.Text = m_Person.LastName
        txtStreet.Text = m_Person.Street
        txtCity.Text = m_Person.City
        txtState.Text = m_Person.State
        txtZip.Text = m_Person.Zip
    End Sub
```

The program declares a `Person` variable named `m_Person`. When you click the Take Snapshot button, the program saves the `Person` object's `Snapshot` property in the list box.

When you click an item in the list box, the program sets the `Person` object's `Snapshot` property to the snapshot you selected. It then copies the `Person` object's values into text boxes so that you can see them. Corresponding code that copies the values you type into the `Person` object is not shown.

The `PersonSnapshot` class is declared privately within the `Person` class, so code outside of the class cannot see the class, its properties, or its methods. This effectively hides the implementation of the `PersonSnapshot` class from the entire application, except for the `Person` class. Unfortunately, it also means the `Person` class's `Snapshot` property must have the generic `Object` data type instead of a more specific data type.

You can fix this problem by putting the `Person` and `PersonSnapshot` classes in their own assembly, making the `PersonSnapshot` class public, and then declaring its properties and methods with the `Friend` keyword. Then, only code in the same assembly (in this case, that's just the `Person` class) can access the `PersonSnapshot`'s properties and methods. Code outside of the assembly can see the `PersonSnapshot` class because it is declared public, but cannot use its properties and methods. Unfortunately, this solution requires that you make a separate assembly.

You can make several variations on the Snapshot pattern. Rather than making the `Person` class's Snapshot property procedures save and restore object data, you could give the `PersonSnapshot` class `SaveSnapshot` and `RestoreSnapshot` methods to let it do all the work. This makes the `Person` class simpler, but it also requires that the `PersonSnapshot` class have access to all of the `Person` class's properties. In this example, that's not a problem. In a more general example, the `Person` class might need to save and restore the values of private variables, and the `PersonSnapshot` class could not access them. One solution to this dilemma is to again move the `Person` and `PersonSnapshot` classes into a separate assembly, and then change the visibility of the `Person` class's private properties to `Friend` so the `PersonSnapshot` class can see them.

The following code shows another variation that can simplify snapshots for classes such as `Person` that are serializable:

```
<Serializable()> _
Public Class Person
    Public FirstName As String
    Public LastName As String
    Public Street As String
    Public City As String
    Public State As String
    Public Zip As String
End Class

Public Class PersonSnapshot
```

```
    Private m_PersonSerialization As String

    ' Save the Person's serialization.
    Public Sub New(ByVal the_person As Person)
        Dim xml_serializer As New XmlSerializer(GetType(Person))
        Using string_writer As New StringWriter()
            xml_serializer.Serialize(string_writer, the_person)
            m_PersonSerialization = string_writer.ToString()
        End Using
    End Sub

    ' Return an object from this serialization.
    Public Function RecreatePerson() As Person
        Dim xml_serializer As New XmlSerializer(GetType(Person))
        Dim string_reader As New StringReader(m_PersonSerialization)
        Return DirectCast(xml_serializer.Deserialize(string_reader), Person)
    End Function
End Class
```

The `PersonSnapshot` class's constructor takes as a `Person` object as a parameter and saves the object's serialization in a private variable. The `RecreatePerson` method uses the saved serialization to return a new `Person` object.

Because the `RecreatePerson` method returns a new `Person` object rather than initializing an existing one, the code using the snapshot must assign the result of the `RecreatePerson` function to a new variable rather than using the snapshot to reset an existing object.

The following code shows how the `SnapshotPersonSerialization` example program uses this version of the `PersonSnapshot` class:

```
Private m_Person As New Person

' Save a snapshot.
Private Sub btnTakeSnapshot_Click(ByVal sender As System.Object, _
 ByVal e As System.EventArgs) Handles btnTakeSnapshot.Click
    lstSnapshots.Items.Add(New PersonSnapshot(m_Person))
End Sub

' Restore a snapshot.
Private Sub lstSnapshots_SelectedIndexChanged(ByVal sender As System.Object, _
 ByVal e As System.EventArgs) Handles lstSnapshots.SelectedIndexChanged
    Dim snapshot As PersonSnapshot = _
        DirectCast(lstSnapshots.SelectedItem, PersonSnapshot)
    m_Person = snapshot.RecreatePerson()

    txtFirstName.Text = m_Person.FirstName
    txtLastName.Text = m_Person.LastName
    txtStreet.Text = m_Person.Street
    txtCity.Text = m_Person.City
    txtState.Text = m_Person.State
    txtZip.Text = m_Person.Zip
End Sub
```

When you click the Take Snapshot button, the program saves a new `PersonSnapshot` object in its list box.

When you select an item from the list, the program uses the selected `PersonSnapshot` object to create a new `Person` object. It then copies the `Person` object's values into text boxes so that you can see them. Corresponding code that copies the values you type into the `Person` object is not shown.

If you compare this code to the previous version, you will see that the differences are relatively small.

Snapshots let you save and restore an object's state. If the object holds all of the application's state information, then this gives you a way to implement Undo and Redo functions. See the section "Undo and Redo" in Chapter 5, "User-Interface Design," for information.

Strategy

In the *Strategy pattern*, you create classes to represent different strategies or algorithms. You can create instances of the classes and pass them to routines that apply them without needing to know which strategy the objects represent. Each of the strategies should inherit from the same base class, or implement a common interface so the routines that use them can handle them uniformly.

Visual Basic uses this pattern in several places, including for defining sort orders. The `List` class's `Sort` method can take as a parameter an object that implements the `IComparer` interface. That interface indicates that the object should provide a `Compare` function that takes two objects as parameters and returns –1, 0, or 1 to indicate whether the first object should be considered less than, equal to, or greater than the second. To sort the objects it contains, the `List` class calls the `IComparer` object's `Compare` method to see whether items should go before or after each other.

Example program `Strategy` demonstrates strategies by using `IComparer` classes. The following code shows the simple `Person` class used by the program:

```
Public Class Person
    Public FirstName As String
    Public LastName As String

    Public Sub New(ByVal first_name As String, ByVal last_name As String)
        FirstName = first_name
        LastName = last_name
    End Sub

    Public Overrides Function ToString() As String
        Return FirstName & " " & LastName
    End Function
End Class
```

The following code shows two strategy classes. The `PersonSorterFirstLast` class sorts `Person` objects by first name followed by last name. The `PersonSorterLastFirst` class sorts `Person` objects by last name followed by first name.

```
Public Class PersonSorterFirstLast
    Implements IComparer(Of Person)

    Public Function Compare(ByVal x As Person, ByVal y As Person) As Integer
Implements System.Collections.Generic.IComparer(Of Person).Compare
```

```
        Dim x_name As String = x.FirstName & " " & x.LastName
        Dim y_name As String = y.FirstName & " " & y.LastName
        Return x_name.CompareTo(y_name)
    End Function
End Class

Public Class PersonSorterLastFirst
    Implements IComparer(Of Person)

    Public Function Compare(ByVal x As Person, ByVal y As Person) As Integer
Implements System.Collections.Generic.IComparer(Of Person).Compare
        Dim x_name As String = x.LastName & " " & x.FirstName
        Dim y_name As String = y.LastName & " " & y.FirstName
        Return x_name.CompareTo(y_name)
    End Function
End Class
```

The following code shows how the example program sorts its `Person` objects:

```
Dim m_People As New List(Of Person)

' Display the items in their current order.
Private Sub ShowPeople()
    lstPeople.Items.Clear()
    For Each per As Person In m_People
        lstPeople.Items.Add(per.ToString())
    Next per
End Sub

' Sort by first name/last name.
Private Sub radFirstLast_CheckedChanged(ByVal sender As System.Object, _
 ByVal e As System.EventArgs) Handles radFirstLast.CheckedChanged
    Dim sorter As New PersonSorterFirstLast()
    m_People.Sort(sorter)
    ShowPeople()
End Sub

' Sort by last name/first name.
Private Sub radLastFirst_CheckedChanged(ByVal sender As System.Object, _
 ByVal e As System.EventArgs) Handles radLastFirst.CheckedChanged
    Dim sorter As New PersonSorterLastFirst()
    m_People.Sort(sorter)
    ShowPeople()
End Sub
```

The program stores the `Person` objects in the `m_People` list. Subroutine `ShowPeople` copies the `Person` objects into the `lstPeople` list box in the order in which they are stored in the `m_People` list.

When you click the "FirstName, LastName" radio button, the program calls the list's `Sort` method passing it a new `PersonSorterFirstLast` strategy object. It then calls `ShowPeople` to redisplay the list.

When you click the "LastName, FirstName" radio button, the program calls the list's `Sort` method passing it a new `PersonSorterLastFirst` strategy object. It then calls `ShowPeople` to redisplay the list.

For More Information

This chapter has covered only the handful of design patterns that I've found most useful in the applications I've worked on. Design patterns is a large and growing field, and there are lots of other patterns available that you may find useful, depending on your project. For more information on "classic" design patterns, see a book about them such as *Design Patterns* by Gamma et. al (Boston: Addison-Wesley, 1995) or *Visual Basic Design Patterns* by Mark Grand and Brad Merrill (Indianapolis: Wiley, 2005).

There have also been some books written about "anti-patterns." These describe common unhealthy situations that projects often blunder into and ways to fix them. For example, see the book *Anti Patterns, Refactoring Software, Architectures, and Projects in Crisis* by William Brown, et. al (Indianapolis: Wiley, 1998).

Finally, there are many Web sites that discuss design patterns, and some include implementations in various programming languages. For example, Microsoft's Patterns and Practices home page at `msdn.microsoft.com/practices` covers a large assortment of topics including Web Services, data access, exceptions, testing, .NET and J2EE interoperability, and more.

Summary

Design patterns are recipes for implementing common solutions that are common in many applications. The following lists summarize the patterns described in this chapter, as well as their purposes.

Following are Creation patterns:

- *Clone* — Make a shallow or deep copy of an object.
- *Factory* — Allow code to create one of several types of objects without knowing the details about how the type is picked.

Following are Relation patterns:

- *Adapter* — Allow two classes that have incompatible interfaces to work together.
- *Facade* — Provide a simple interface to a collection of classes.
- *Interface* — Decouple classes so they can be written, debugged, and maintained independently.

Following are Behavior patterns:

- *Abstract Base Class* — Define behavior for derived classes.
- *Chain of Responsibility* — Apply a series of actions to an item until one of them handles it.
- *Chain of Events* — Apply a series of event handlers to an event until one of them handles it.
- *Command* — Encapsulate an action in an object so that you can pass it around and use it later without knowing the details of what the action is.
- *Delegation* — Make an object use other objects to implement its behavior. Can simulate multiple inheritance.

- *Model, View, Controller (MVC)*—Use simple classes to let the user view and edit data in complex ways.
- *Property Procedure*—Make debugging a property easier.
- *Snapshot*—Save and restore an object's state.
- *Strategy*—Encapsulate a technique in an object so you can apply one of several techniques without knowing about their internal details.

The chapters up to and including this one deal with pre-development preparation. They cover various aspects of application design and planning.

The chapters in the next part of the book cover "meta-development"—writing code that you will later use to write other code. This includes techniques that actually generate or execute code (such as add-ins, code snippets, and scripting). It also includes methods for making later development easier (such as building custom controls and property editors, and properly using code attributes).

Chapter 8, "Snippets, Macros, and Add-ins," describes methods for writing code that generates other code. Snippets use a fairly simple find-and-replace strategy to build pieces of code that differ in simple ways. Macros and add-ins let you build and manipulate code in more sophisticated ways. They let you write code that can manufacture just about any kind of code you can imagine.

Part II
Meta-Development

In this Part:

8

Snippets, Macros, and Add-ins

Visual Studio provides many tools that make writing code easier. This chapter describes three tools that you can use to automatically generate code: snippets, macros, and add-ins.

Snippets let you copy a piece of code into an application. After you insert the code, snippet-editing tools let you make simple systematic replacements to customize the new code.

Macros let you record actions you perform in a code editor and replay them later. By itself, that would only be useful if you needed to repeat the exact same series of operations. By editing the recorded macro, however, you can generate new code in very complicated ways.

Like macros, add-ins let you generate complicated pieces of code. Add-ins have the additional advantage that they are compiled, so you can write an add-in for developers while not allowing them to view or modify it. Because an add-in is a Visual Studio project in its own right, it can take advantage of the full power of the development environment.

Snippets

An *IntelliSense code snippet* (or just *snippet*) is a piece of code stored in a special XML format, so it is easy to insert into your applications. Visual Studio comes with several hundreds of pre-built snippets that you can use to generate code for such tasks as activating a running application, clearing the console window, creating a sorted dictionary, or calculating the sine of an angle:

Many of the pre-built snippets are quite simple. For example, the following code shows the snippet that calculates the sine of an angle:

```
Dim radians As Double = 120 * Math.PI / 180
Dim sin As Double = Math.Sin(radians)
```

When you insert this snippet, the code's "120" is highlighted by a green box and the cursor is positioned there. This is a replacement area. You should replace the default angle `120` with the angle you're interested in. If you hover the mouse over the replacement area, a tooltip gives you a hint about what you are supposed to do by saying, "Replace with the measurement in degrees."

Snippets can help you remember how to write the code for common programming tasks. They can automate tedious, repetitive chores, and can help you remember the little details that are so easy to forget. For example, they can automatically add the appropriate `Imports` statements when you use routines that require them. They build the pieces of property procedures, including the procedures themselves, the private variables that store procedure values, attributes to give descriptions of the procedures and categories in the Properties window, and even comments.

Snippets can even help you standardize your code. For example, suppose you have a standard comment block that you want every developer on the project to use at the beginning of every file. This block might include a copyright statement, the name of the module, the name of the developer who created the file, and places for revision history. You can help developers follow the standard by creating a snippet that contains the comment template. If developers insert the snippet into their modules, all of the files will have module-level comments in exactly the same format. The snippet's replacement areas even help the developers insert the module's name and the name of the developer who created the file.

The following section describes in greater detail how to insert snippets. The sections after that one explain how to write your own snippets.

Using Snippets

To insert a snippet into your code, right-click where you want to insert and select the Insert Snippet command. Visual Studio displays a cascading pop-up list, similar to the one shown in Figure 8-1.

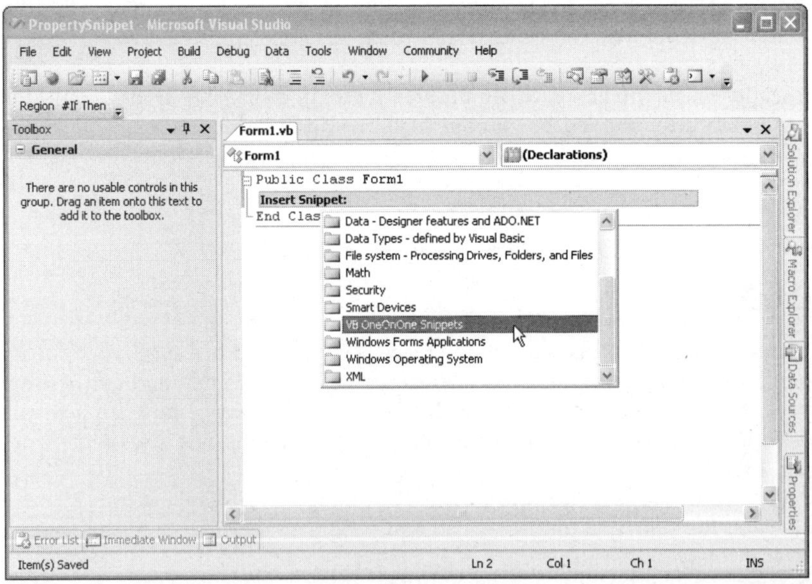

Figure 8-1: The Insert Snippet command lets you insert snippets from snippet folders.

Scroll down to the folder that contains the snippet you want and double-click it. In some cases, the initial snippet folder will contain subfolders. Continue delving into the snippet folders until you find a list of actual snippets similar to the one shown in Figure 8-2. Then double-click the snippet you want to insert.

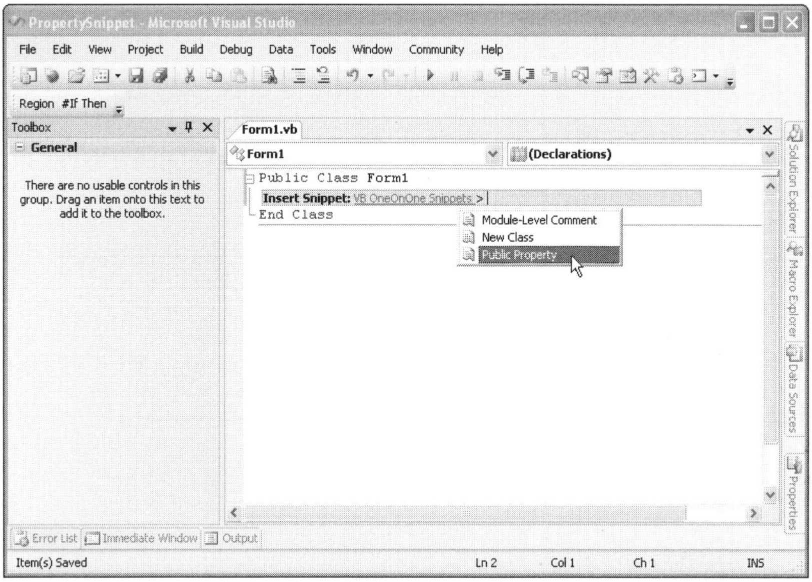

Figure 8-2: Double-click the snippet that you want to insert.

Figure 8-3 shows the code inserted by the Public Property snippet. Colored boxes indicate values that you should replace. In this example, the replacement values include the strings `FirstName`, `String`, and `Misc`. They also include blank values inside the quotes in the code's `Description` and `DefaultValue` attributes.

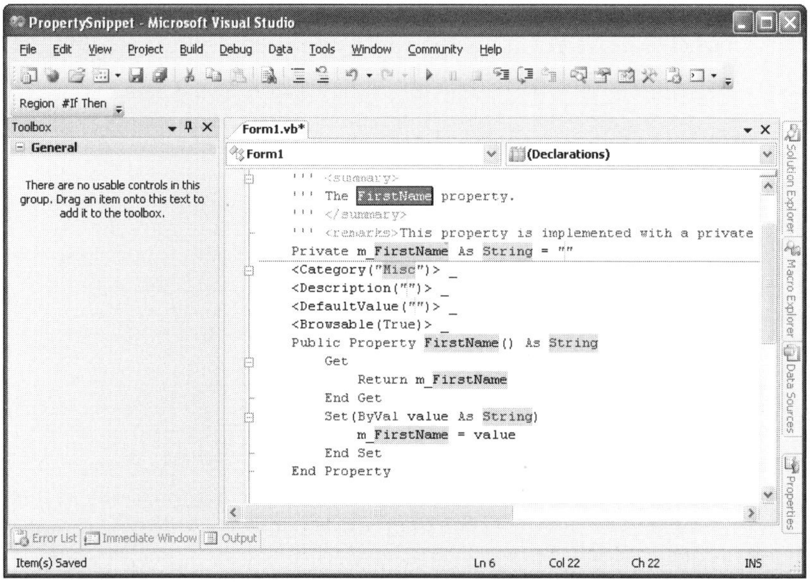

Figure 8-3: Make replacements in the snippet as necessary.

If you hover the mouse over a replacement area, a tooltip tells you what value you should put there.

Initially, the first replacement area for `FirstName` is highlighted. Enter the name you want to give this property. When you press the Tab key, the value you entered is copied to all of the `FirstName` replacement fields and the next replacement area is highlighted. Continue making replacements until you have replaced all of the values.

If there is a shortcut assigned to a snippet, then you can use it to insert the snippet more quickly. Type the first several letters in the shortcut, followed by a question mark (?), and press Tab. Visual Studio displays a pop-up list of snippets with the one matching the string you entered selected. Figure 8-4 shows the list displayed when I typed "propertysn?"

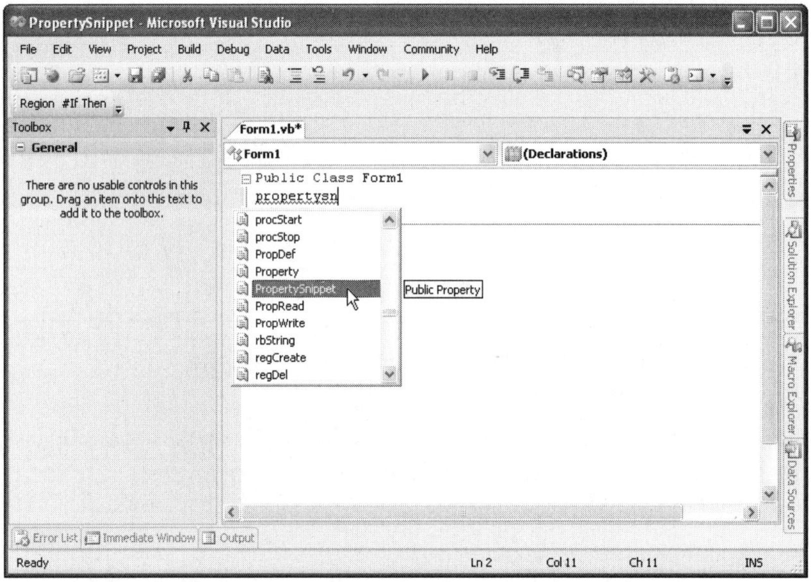

Figure 8-4: Using snippet shortcuts you can insert snippets very quickly.

If you use a snippet frequently, it will be faster to insert it using its shortcut than by navigating through the snippet folders.

Making Snippets

Snippets are stored in XML files with specific tags that identify the snippet's name, code, replacement values, and so forth.

To create a snippet, make a Visual Studio project. Open the Project menu and select Add New Item. Pick the XML File template, give the file a descriptive name with a `.snippet` extension, and click OK. For example, you might name a property snippet's file `Property.snippet`.

Actually, snippets are just text files in XML format, so you could write them using any text editor. However, when the Visual Studio IDE opens a snippet, it uses a special XML editor that makes editing the files easier. For example, it knows which tags should be allowed at different points. If you type "<"

inside a `Literal` *element, the editor displays a pop-up that lists the allowed sub-items: !-- (for comments),* `?` *(for XML processor instructions),* `Default`, `Function`, `ID`, `ToolTip`, *and* `Type`. *The editor also flags XML errors such as unclosed tags, mismatched open and close tags, and so forth.*

Double-click the file to open it. Initially, the file only contains an XML declaration. After the declaration, you must add a series of XML tags to define the snippet. Rather than wading through all of the ugly details, take a look at the following example. The text that follows describes the key sections that you need to modify:

```
<CodeSnippets>
  <CodeSnippet>
    <Header>
      <Title>Public Property</Title>
      <Shortcut>PropertySnippet</Shortcut>
    </Header>
    <Snippet>
      <Imports>
        <Import>
          <Namespace>System.ComponentModel</Namespace>
        </Import>
        <Import>
          <Namespace>System.Windows.Forms</Namespace>
        </Import>
      </Imports>
      <References>
        <Reference>
          <Assembly>System.Windows.Forms.dll</Assembly>
        </Reference>
      </References>
      <Declarations>
        <Literal>
          <ID>name</ID>
          <ToolTip>The property's name.</ToolTip>
          <Default>FirstName</Default>
        </Literal>
        <Literal>
          <ID>data_type</ID>
          <ToolTip>The property's data type.</ToolTip>
          <Default>String</Default>
        </Literal>
      </Declarations>
      <Code Language="VB">
        <![CDATA[
    ''' <summary>
    ''' The $name$ property.
    ''' </summary>
    ''' <remarks>This property is implemented with property procedures.</remarks>
    Private m_$name$ As $data_type$ = "$default$"
    <Browsable(True)> _
    Public Property $name$() As $data_type$
        Get
            MessageBox.Show("In $name$.Get")
            Return m_$name$
        End Get
        Set(ByVal value As $data_type$)
```

```
                MessageBox.Show("In $name$.Set")
                m_$name$ = value
            End Set
        End Property
        ]]>
          </Code>
        </Snippet>
      </CodeSnippet>
    </CodeSnippets>
```

Within the `Header` section, the `Title` value gives the title displayed in the cascading snippet menus shown in Figure 8-2. The `Shortcut` value gives the snippet's shortcut. If you type the first several letters from the shortcut followed by a question mark and a tab, Visual Studio displays a list of snippets with this one selected.

The `Snippet` section contains several key subsections. The `Imports` section contains information about imports that the code in the snippet requires. This example contains one import: `System.ComponentModel`. When you use this snippet, if the module does not already have an `Imports` statement for this namespace, the snippet adds it at the top of the module. In this example, the statements would be as follows:

```
Imports System.ComponentModel
Imports System.Windows.Forms
```

This example needs the `System.ComponentModel` namespace because it uses the `Browsable` attribute. It needs the `Systems.Windows.Forms` namespace to use the `MessageBox` class.

The `References` section contains references that the snippet's code needs. If the project doesn't already have a reference to the indicated assembly, the snippet adds it. This example requires a reference to `System.Windows.Forms.dll` because that library contains the `MessageBox` class.

The `Declarations` section defines replacement variables. Each `Literal` tag defines a word in the snippet code that the developer can replace. This example's first `Literal` defines a token called "`name`." The snippet code indicates a replacement value by enclosing the token's ID in dollar signs, as in `$name$`. Tags within the `Literal` give the tooltip to display and the item's default value. You should give a `Literal` a default value whenever possible, because it makes the value easier for the developer to see.

The `Declarations` section can also contain `Object` tags to define replacements representing objects that are usually defined outside of the snippet's code.

Finally, the `Code` tag contains the snippet's actual code. In this example, the tag's `Language` attribute indicates that this is a Visual Basic snippet. The `<![CDATA[` string allows an XML file to contain just about any text, including white spaces and carriage returns, until reaching the corresponding `]]>`.

Microsoft has produced a free snippet editor that lets you avoid the details of writing an XML file. Download it at `http://msdn.microsoft.com/vbasic/downloads/tools/snippeteditor`.

Installing Snippets

After you create a snippet file, put it in a directory where you want to store snippets. The cascading snippet menus shown in Figures 8-1 and 8-2 display the directory's name, so give the directory a meaningful name.

Next, open Visual Studio's Tools menu and select the Code Snippets Manager command to display the tool shown in Figure 8-5. Click the Add button, browse to your snippets directory, and click Open. Back in the Code Snippets Manager, click OK.

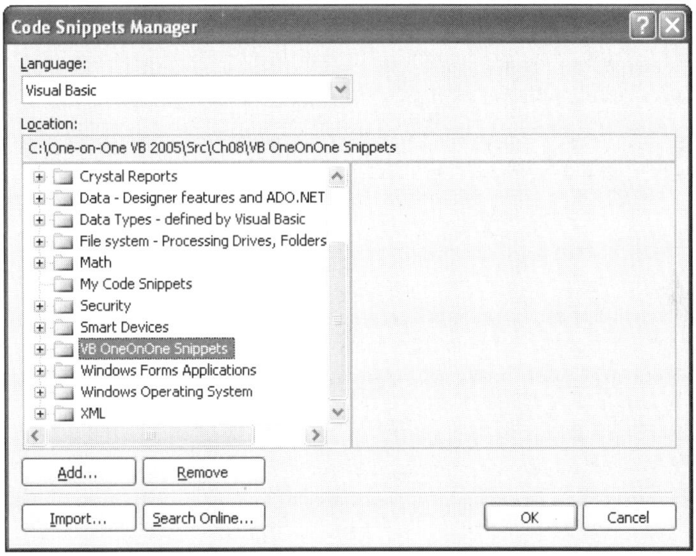

Figure 8-5: Use the Code Snippets Manager to add and remove snippet directories.

Now, Visual Studio is ready to use the snippets in that directory. When you right-click in a code editor and select the Insert Snippet command, you should see the directory and any snippets defined in `.snippet` files within the directory.

Sharing Snippets

Because snippets are plain old text files, they are easy to share. You can email them to other developers, or post them on your Web site. You can put them in a shared snippet directory to ensure that every developer on your project uses the same snippets so that they get the benefit of consistency.

You can also search the Web for snippets. You can download code snippets for Visual Studio at `http://msdn.microsoft.com/vstudio/downloads/codesnippets`. As of this writing, these are the snippets that come with Visual Studio 2005, so they should already be installed on your system. This is probably a good place to check for updates, however.

You can search this book's snippet library at www.vb-helper.com/snippets.html. If you come up with a good snippet that you'd like to share, send it to me at RodStephens@vb-helper.com and I'll add it to the library.

Macros

Snippets are a fantastic way to automate building certain chunks of code in a fixed format, while allowing you to make simple replacements. By using snippets, you can simplify moderately complicated tasks and add some useful consistency to a development project.

Although snippets are easy, they are fairly limited. They use a "design by example" approach, where you write code and then turn it into a snippet. This approach is extremely simple, but it's not very flexible. For example, the previous example that creates property procedures won't work if you want to add a parameter to the property, as shown in the following code:

```
' Get or set a test score.
Private m_Scores(0 To 9) As Double
Public Property Score(ByVal test_number As Integer) As Double
    Get
        Return m_Scores(test_number)
    End Get
    Set(ByVal value As Double)
        m_Scores(test_number) = value
    End Set
End Property
```

Snippets also only create code; they don't modify it or the Visual Studio IDE.

Macros give you much greater flexibility. They let you write new code, modify existing code, and control the development environment.

Visual Studio lets you record, write, edit, debug, and play back macros later, much as the Microsoft Office applications do (although the Microsoft Office applications use VBA as their macro language, whereas Visual Basic 2005 uses Visual Basic 2005 for macros). You can use macros to automate tasks that you need to perform frequently, such as the following:

- Writing a series of Visual Basic statements that are mostly the same
- Performing an action on similar code entities (for example, commenting functions or printing code documents)
- Altering the project's structure (for example, adding files to it)
- Modifying the Visual Studio environment

The following sections briefly describe how to record, edit, and use macros in Visual Studio.

Recording Macros

To record a macro, open the Tools menu, go to the Macros submenu, and select the Record `TemporaryMacro` command. Visual Studio displays the Macro Recorder shown in Figure 8-6, and starts recording a macro.

Figure 8-6: The Macro Recorder lets you pause, stop, or cancel macro recording.

While the Macro Recorder is running, you can add, edit, and delete code. Unfortunately, the Macro Recorder does not capture any changes to a form's properties and controls, so you may as well stay in a code editor.

When you have finished recording, click the Stop Recording button in the middle of the Macro Recorder. Visual Studio stores the new macro in a macro module. To see the macro, open the Tools menu, go to the Macros submenu, and the select the Macro Explorer command to display the Macro Explorer shown in Figure 8-7.

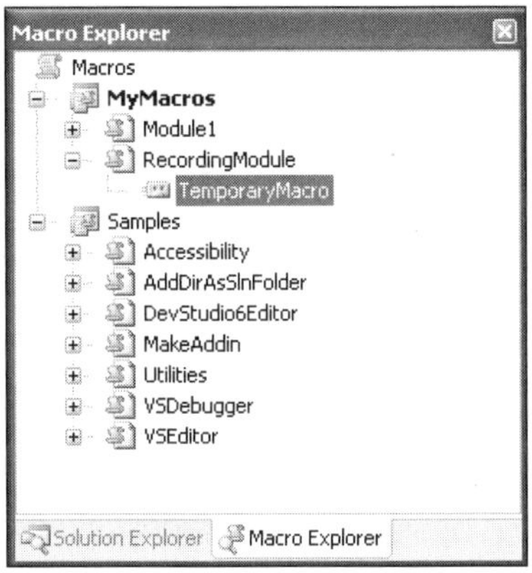

Figure 8-7: The Macro Explorer lets you view, edit, and run macros.

The new macro is the `RecordingModule` and is named `TemporaryMacro`. To execute the macro, double-click it, or right-click it and select Run from the context menu.

If you record a new temporary macro, the previous one is overwritten. If you want to save a temporary macro for later use, right-click it in Macro Explorer, select Rename, and give the macro a new name. Now, if you record a new macro, it is named `TemporaryMacro` and your old macro is saved.

Editing Macros

To edit a macro, right-click it in Macro Explorer, and select Edit to make Visual Studio open the Macro IDE shown in Figure 8-8.

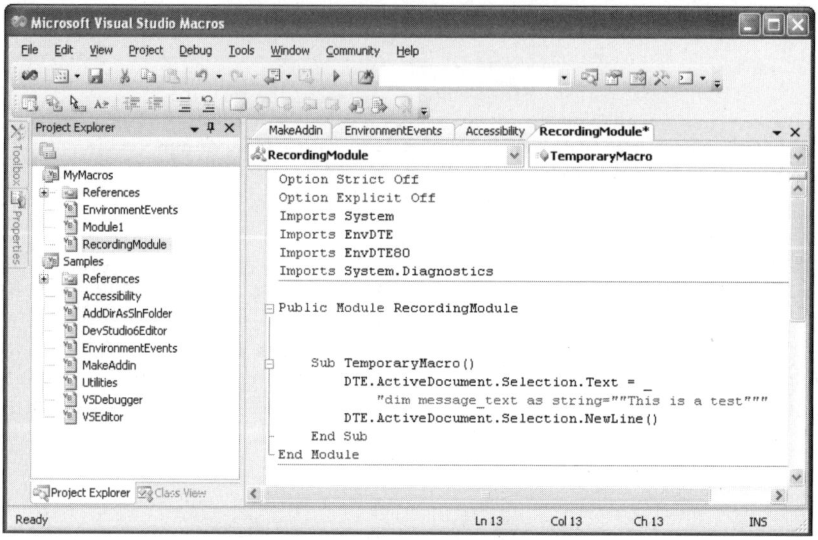

Figure 8-8: Visual Studio lets you edit macros much as it lets you edit Visual Basic projects.

You can modify the macro's code in the code editor shown in Figure 8-8 much as you can modify Visual Basic code in the Visual Studio IDE. You can even set breakpoints in the editor, and step through the code to debug it.

To organize your macros, you can use the Project Explorer shown on the left in Figure 8-8. Right-click and add folders and modules to the projects. Then you can copy the renamed temporary macro into one of those modules.

Modifying Macros

Unfortunately, recorded macros are often not very useful because they perform exactly the same steps that you performed already. If you need to perform an extremely repetitive and mechanical task, you might get some mileage out of repeating the same sequence of commands again and again.

Usually, it's more useful to do something *similar to* the recorded macro, and not repeat exactly the same steps each time. Start by recording a macro that is as similar as possible to what you need to do. Then edit the macro to suit your needs.

For example, suppose you have 16 `TextBox` controls named `TextBox0`, `TextBox1`, ..., `TextBox15` arranged in a grid on a form, and you want to set references to them in a two-dimensional array. You could record a macro while typing the following code:

```
m_TextBoxes(0, 0) = TextBox0
```

The following code shows the recorded macro:

```
Sub TemporaryMacro()
    DTE.ActiveDocument.Selection.Text = "m_TextBoxes(0, 0) = TextBox0"
    DTE.ActiveDocument.Selection.NewLine()
End Sub
```

DTE stands for "development tools environment." The `DTE` *object sits at the top of the Visual Studio extensibility object model. It is similar to the* `Application` *object used by some other programs such as the Microsoft Office applications.*

`ActiveDocument` *is an object that represents the currently active editor document, in this case the code in the code editor.* `Selection` *is a property of the* `ActiveDocument` *that represents the currently selected text. The previous code sets this text and then adds a new line to it.*

The extensibility object model is enormous, so there will barely be time to introduce it here. Look in the online help for "DTE" for more information.

You don't want to repeat exactly this statement 16 times, but it's easy to modify the recorded code. The following code loops through the four rows and columns, adding code for each control. Notice how it adds to the code the values of the row and column variables and the number in the control's name.

```
Sub SaveTextBoxes()
    For r As Integer = 0 To 3
        For c As Integer = 0 To 3
            DTE.ActiveDocument.Selection.Text = "m_TextBoxes(" & _
                r.ToString() & ", " & c.ToString() & _
                ") = TextBox" & (r * 4 + c).ToString()
            DTE.ActiveDocument.Selection.NewLine()
        Next c
    Next r
End Sub
```

The following code shows the result added to the form's `Load` event handler, plus the code that defines the `m_TextBoxes` array:

```
Public Class Form1
    Private m_TextBoxes(0 To 4, 0 To 4) As TextBox

    Private Sub Form1_Load(ByVal sender As System.Object, _
     ByVal e As System.EventArgs) Handles MyBase.Load
        m_TextBoxes(0, 0) = TextBox0
        m_TextBoxes(0, 1) = TextBox1
        m_TextBoxes(0, 2) = TextBox2
        m_TextBoxes(0, 3) = TextBox3
        m_TextBoxes(1, 0) = TextBox4
        m_TextBoxes(1, 1) = TextBox5
        m_TextBoxes(1, 2) = TextBox6
        m_TextBoxes(1, 3) = TextBox7
        m_TextBoxes(2, 0) = TextBox8
        m_TextBoxes(2, 1) = TextBox9
        m_TextBoxes(2, 2) = TextBox10
        m_TextBoxes(2, 3) = TextBox11
        m_TextBoxes(3, 0) = TextBox12
```

```
        m_TextBoxes(3, 1) = TextBox13
        m_TextBoxes(3, 2) = TextBox14
        m_TextBoxes(3, 3) = TextBox15
    End Sub
End Class
```

You could certainly type all of this code by hand. If you use copy and paste judiciously, it might even be faster than recording and modifying a macro, although it would still be a lot of work if you had a 10 by 10 grid of controls.

Although this example can save you a little work, you can get some serious power out of macros if you edit them to take advantage of the other capabilities offered by the extensibility object model — the classes that represent the IDE and the project you are editing.

For example, the following code comments out a selected section of code by placing it in an `#If ... #End If` block. It first prompts you for the name of the variable to use in the `#If` statement. It composes the block by concatenating the `#If` statement, the currently selected text, and the `#End If` statement. It then uses the current selection object's `Insert` method to replace the selected text with the block.

```
' Surround the selected code with an #If ... #End If block.
Public Sub PoundIfOut()
    ' Get the variable name.
    Dim variable_name As String = InputBox("Variable Name", "Variable Name", "")
    If variable_name.Length < 1 Then Exit Sub

    Dim sel As EnvDTE.TextSelection = DTE.ActiveDocument.Selection
    Dim txt As String = "#If " & variable_name & " Then" & vbCrLf & sel.Text
    If Not txt.EndsWith(vbCrLf) Then txt &= vbCrLf
    txt &= "#End If ' " & variable_name & vbCrLf

    ' Replace the selected text with the result.
    sel.Insert(txt, vsInsertFlags.vsInsertFlagsContainNewText)
End Sub
```

The following code shows a sample result. Here I selected the two lines used by the `MessageBox` statement, ran the macro, and entered the variable name `SHOW_MESSAGES` when prompted.

```
#If SHOW_MESSAGES Then
        MessageBox.Show("I've been commented out!", "Commented", _
            MessageBoxButtons.OK, MessageBoxIcon.Exclamation)
#End If ' SHOW_MESSAGES
```

In this example, it wouldn't have been hard to just type in the `#If` and `#End If` statements, but this is a handy macro when you want to quickly comment out a large block of code. Simply select the code, run the macro, and enter a variable name.

The following macro uses a similar technique to place code in a new region. It starts by prompting you for the region's name. It concatenates a `#Region` statement, the selected code, and an `#End Region` statement, and then inserts the result into the code.

```
' Put the selected code in a region.
Public Sub MakeRegion()
```

```
        ' Get the region name.
        Dim region_name As String = InputBox("Region Name", "Region Name", "")
        If region_name.Length < 1 Then Exit Sub

        ' Compose the new text.
        Dim sel As EnvDTE.TextSelection = DTE.ActiveDocument.Selection
        Dim txt As String = _
            "#Region """ & region_name & """" & vbCrLf & _
            sel.Text
        If Not txt.EndsWith(vbCrLf) Then txt &= vbCrLf
        txt &= "#End Region ' " & region_name

        ' Replace the selected text with the result.
        sel.Insert(txt, vsInsertFlags.vsInsertFlagsContainNewText)
    End Sub
```

The following macro shows how you can loop through an array of names to make property procedures for each. Writing each of these by hand, even using copy and paste or code snippets, would be tiresome.

```
    ' Make a series of property procedures for contact information.
    Public Sub MakeContactInfoProperties()
        Dim property_names() As String = { _
            "FirstName", "LastName", "Street", "Street2", "City", "State", "Zip", _
            "WorkPhone", "HomePhone", "Email", "WebPage"}
        Dim txt As String = ""

        For Each property_name As String In property_names
            txt &= "Private m_" & property_name & " As String = """"" & vbCrLf
            txt &= "Public Property " & property_name & "() As String" & vbCrLf
            txt &= vbTab & "Get" & vbCrLf
            txt &= vbTab & vbTab & "Return m_" & property_name & vbCrLf
            txt &= vbTab & "End Get" & vbCrLf
            txt &= vbTab & "Set(ByVal value As String)" & vbCrLf
            txt &= vbTab & vbTab & "m_" & property_name & " = value" & vbCrLf
            txt &= vbTab & "End Set" & vbCrLf
            txt &= "End Property" & vbCrLf & vbCrLf
        Next property_name

        ' Replace the selected text with the result.
        Dim sel As EnvDTE.TextSelection = DTE.ActiveDocument.Selection
        sel.Insert(txt, vsInsertFlags.vsInsertFlagsContainNewText)
    End Sub
```

When a macro inserts code, the code editor does not automatically reformat the code to fix its indentation. These macros finish with the new code selected. If you press the Tab key immediately after running the macros, the code editor will fix the code's indentation.

Unfortunately, the extensibility object model is enormous (too big to cover here), extremely complicated, and not very well-documented. Look in the online help's index for "extensibility" for information about the classes that represent the IDE and the loaded project.

Though the documentation isn't great, Microsoft has provided a large number of sample macros that you can study when designing your own macros.

Using Sample Macros

Notice the `Samples` project in the Project Explorer shown in Figure 8-8 and in the Macro Explorer shown in Figure 8-7. That project contains sample macros provided by Microsoft that demonstrate rather advanced techniques. The samples demonstrate various techniques for manipulating the development environment. For example, they show how to:

- Change the code editor's font size
- Change the code editor's colors
- Add the files in a directory sub-tree to a solution
- Print all open documents
- Comment out C++ code with `#ifdef` statements
- Save and restore window layouts
- Turn line numbers and word wrap on and off
- Catch events raised by the project, documents, windows, the task list, and so forth
- Convert a macro project into an add-in
- Add comments to all functions in a file
- List macros, breakpoints, modified files, and so forth
- Evaluate an expression
- Dump all threads' stacks
- List the languages that the debugger supports (Visual Basic, C#, C++, VJ#, and so on)
- Save a backup of the current document

To learn more about the samples in the online help, look in the index for "macros [Visual Studio Macros]" and select the sub-topic "samples."

Customizing Visual Studio

Special-purpose macros (such as `MakeContactInfoProperties` shown earlier in this chapter) are macros you will probably run only once or twice. In those cases, it's easy enough to run the macro by double-clicking it in the Macro Explorer, or by opening it in the Macro IDE and selecting the Debug menu's Run command.

Other macros (such as `PoundIfOut` and `MakeRegion`) can be useful on many occasions. In those cases, you may want to make the macro more accessible by customizing Visual Studio.

In Visual Studio, select the Tools menu's Customize command to display the Customize dialog shown in Figure 8-9. On the Toolbars tab, you can click the New button to make a toolbar to hold buttons for launching your macros.

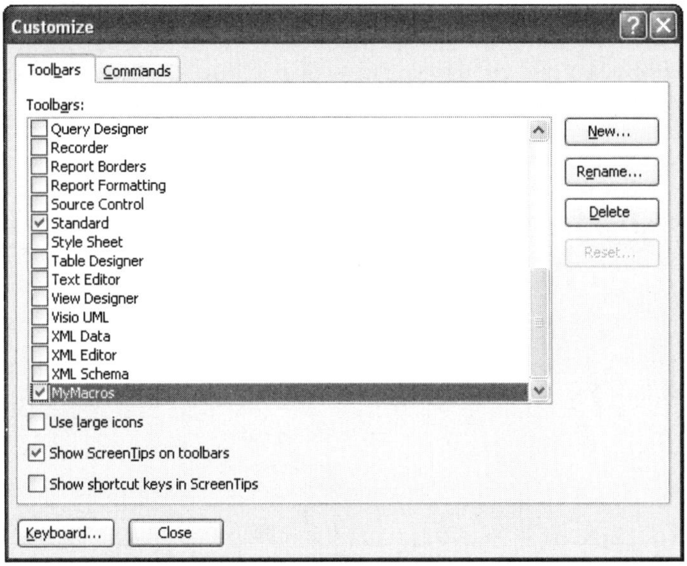

Figure 8-9: You can use the Toolbars tab's New button to make a new toolbar to provide easy access to macros.

On the Commands tab shown in Figure 8-10, scroll the list on the left down and select the Macros entry. Then, click and drag macros from the list on the right onto menus and toolbars.

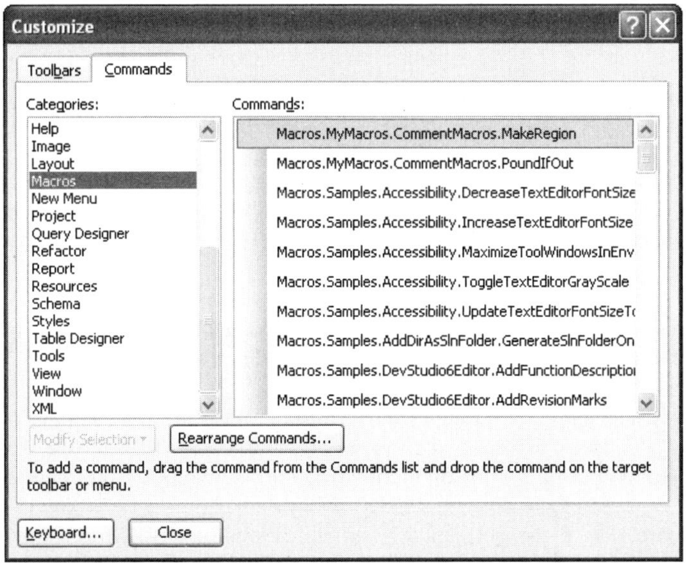

Figure 8-10: The Commands tab lets you drag commands (including macros) onto menus and toolbars.

Initially, the new menu or toolbar item is labeled with the full name of the macro. For example, the `MakeRegion` macro is given the unwieldy name `Macros.MyMacros.CommentMacros.MakeRegion`. You can right-click the new item and use the context menu to change the item's name to something more reasonable such as `Region`.

You can also right-click the item and make it display text, text and an icon, or just an icon. Figure 8-11 shows the context menu selecting the Text Only (Always) style. That style, which is the default, makes the item only display a textual label.

Figure 8-11: The context menu lets you determine whether the item displays text, an icon, or both.

The Text Only (in Menus) option makes the item display a text label only if it's in a menu, and an icon only if it's in a toolbar. The Image and Text option makes the item display both an icon and text in either a menu or toolbar. Finally, the Default style (which ironically isn't the default) displays an icon in toolbars and an icon plus text in menus.

You can use other commands in the context menu shown in Figure 8-11 to select, copy, and edit the item's icon.

To assign a shortcut to the macro, open the Customize dialog shown in Figure 8-10 and click the Keyboard button to display the Options dialog shown in Figure 8-12.

Initially, the list of macros in the middle right contains all of the hundreds of available macros. To narrow the list down a bit, enter text that forms part of the name of the macro you want to use. In Figure 8-12, I entered **Region** and the list narrowed down to the two macros `MakeRegion` and `CommentRegion`.

Select the macro you want to assign, click the text box below the label "Press shortcut keys," and press the keys that you want to assign to the macro. In this example, I pressed Alt+R.

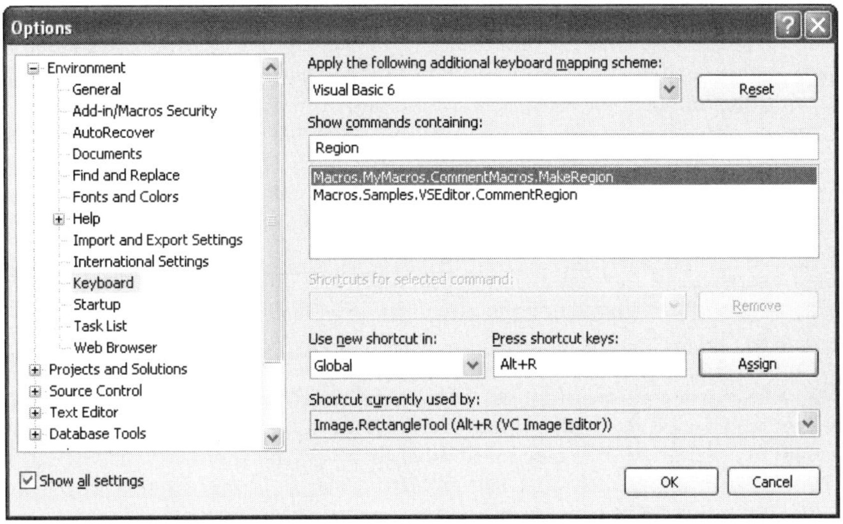

Figure 8-12: Use the Options dialog to assign keyboard shortcuts to macros.

The drop-down list below the "Shortcut currently used by" label lists any conflicts with existing shortcut assignments. Visual Studio assigns a huge number of key combinations, so you are likely to find collisions. In this example, the drop-down only lists the single conflict shown here. I don't need to run the `MakeRegion` macro while editing images, so this isn't a problem.

If you want a general scheme to keep all of your macro shortcuts separate from pre-assigned shortcuts, you'll need to use a more complicated key combination such as Ctrl+Shift+Alt+R or Alt+M, Alt+R. Then you can replace the final key R with other keys for other macros.

Sharing Macros

Sharing macros is relatively straightforward. To save a macro module in a text file, open the Macro IDE and find the module that you want to export in the Project Explorer. Right-click the module and select the Export command. Enter the name of the file you want to save and click Save.

Having saved the macro code into a file, you can share it with other developers, just as you can share any other file. You can email the file to other developers, put them in a shared library, or post them on the Web.

To use a macro module that someone sent you, open the Macro IDE. In the Project Explorer, right-click the project that you want to contain the new module, open the Add submenu, and select the Add Existing Item command. Select the new macro file and click Add.

Before you execute any macro, you should open it in a text editor and take a look at it to verify that it is safe and doesn't contain viruses or other nasty surprises. Use WordPad or another text editor to examine the module before you add it to your project.

Add-ins

Macros have greater flexibility than code snippets, but they still have some restrictions. The Macro IDE doesn't provide the full power of Visual Studio, and you cannot add as many different kinds of objects to a macro project. In particular, a macro module cannot contain forms.

Add-ins let you combine the ability to manipulate the Visual Studio IDE provided by macros with the power of Visual Studio itself.

An *add-in* is a compiled DLL that runs in the Visual Studio IDE. Like a macro, the add-in's code has access to all of the extensibility objects that control the Visual Studio session and the project that is currently loaded.

Because an add-in is compiled, you have more control over how the add-in's code is modified. You can distribute an add-in that contains proprietary code without giving away the details to users. The fact that the add-in is compiled also makes it more difficult for developers to modify the add-in. This is useful if you want to use the add-in to help bring consistency to your project.

Of course, the fact that the add-in is compiled also means that you cannot look at its code. If you receive an add-in from someone else, you must trust that it does not contain damaging code (such as a virus or code that damages your system).

Because the code is compiled into IL, it's fairly easy to read, even in its compiled form. Any determined developer can read the IL to see what the macro does. Compiling it will stop casual snoopers and those who might make careless changes, but if you really want to hide the details, you need to use an obfuscator to make the compiled code more difficult to read.

Making an Add-in

To make an add-in, open Visual Studio and select the File menu's New Project command. In the Project Types tree view, open the Other Project Types branch and select Extensibility. Select the Visual Studio Add-in template, as shown in Figure 8-13. Enter a meaningful name for the template project and click OK.

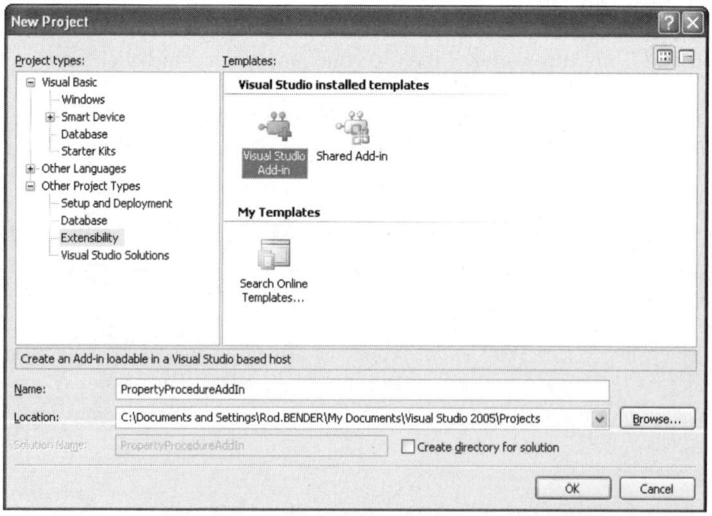

Figure 8-13: To make an add-in, select the Visual Studio Add-in template.

When you start a new add-in project, Visual Studio displays the Add-in Wizard shown in Figure 8-14. The wizard gathers basic information about the add-in you want to build, and then creates a lot of important (but tedious) code for connecting the add-in to the Visual Studio environment and interacting with the IDE.

When you click Next, the wizard displays the page shown in Figure 8-15 to let you specify the language you want to use to write the add-in. Select the Visual Basic option and click Next.

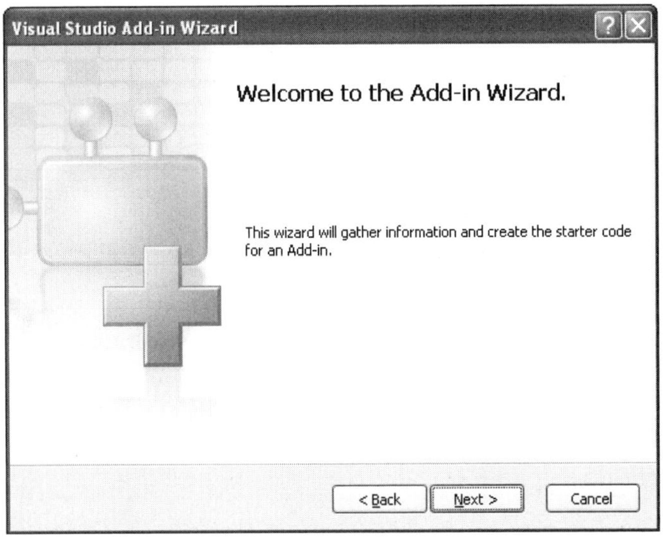

Figure 8-14: The Add-in Wizard helps.

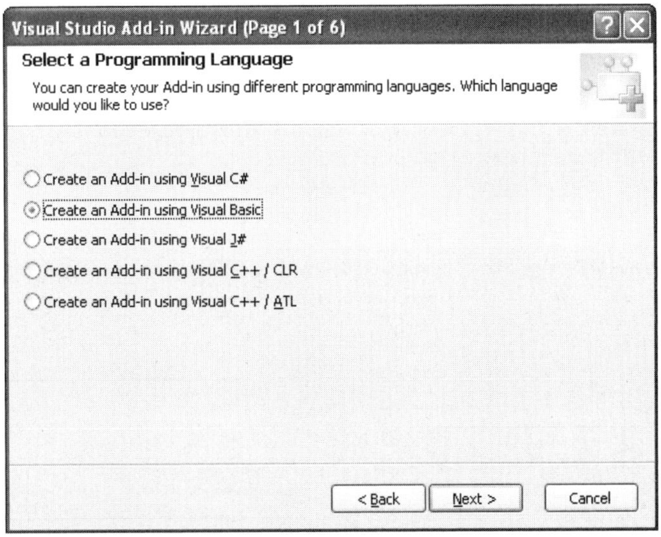

Figure 8-15: Select Visual Basic to write the add-in using Visual Basic.

The wizard's next page, shown in Figure 8-16, lets you pick the applications that will run the add-in. Your choices include the Visual Studio IDE and the Macro IDE. Unless you really get into writing macros, you will normally build add-ins for the Visual Studio IDE.

Check the IDEs that should run the add-in and click Next to display the page shown in Figure 8-17. Enter a name and description for your add-in. These are displayed by the Add-in Manager described shortly.

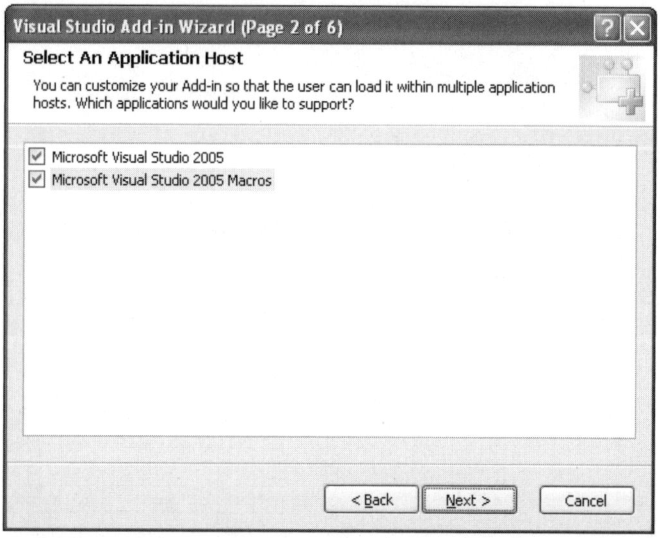

Figure 8-16: Check the IDEs that should run the add-in.

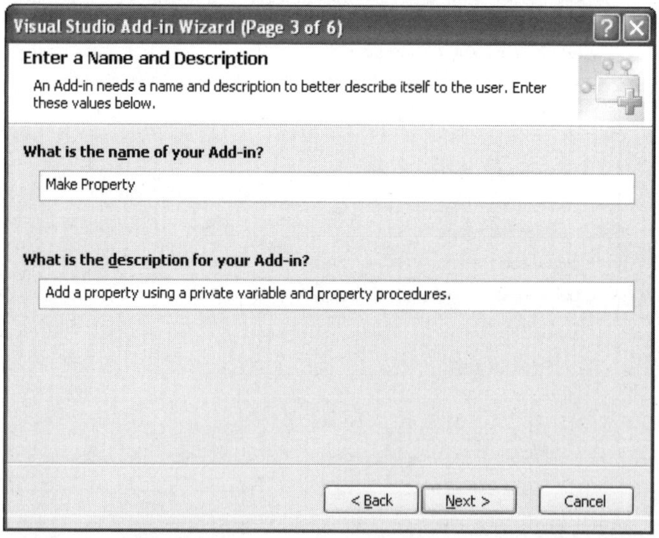

Figure 8-17: Enter the name and description that the Add-in Manager should use for your add-in.

When you click Next, the wizard displays the page shown in Figure 8-18. Check the first box if you want the wizard to automatically add a button for your add-in to the Tools menu. If you don't do this, then you'll need to use the Add-in Manager to add the button. You'll also need to add extra code manually to the add-in's `OnConnection` method. It's easier to just check the box.

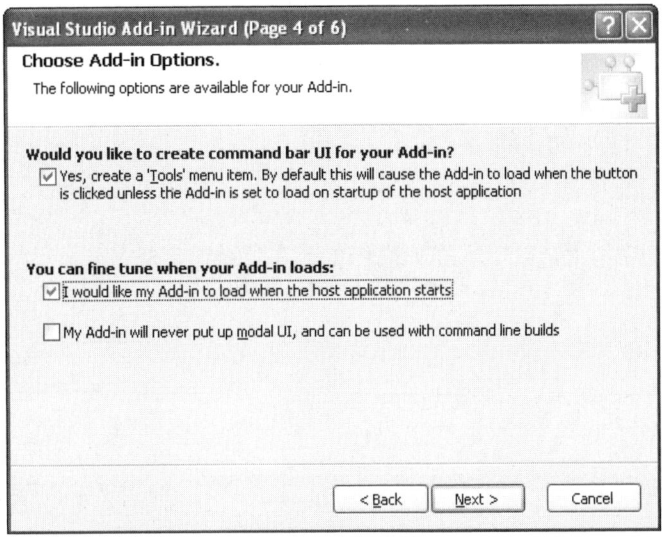

Figure 8-18: Select options for creating the add-in's toolbar button and loading the add-in.

If you check the second box, the add-in is loaded when the environment starts. The third checkbox indicates that the add-in never displays a modal dialog to prompt the user for input. If the add-in doesn't display any modal dialogs, then it can run unattended from the command line.

Click Next to display the page shown in Figure 8-19. If you want to include information about the add-in, check the checkbox and enter support information in the text box. The wizard stores this information (along with other information gathered by the wizard) in a file named after the add-in with an `.AddIn` extension. For example, if your add-in is named `MakeProperty`, then this file is called `MakeProperty.AddIn`.

If you check the box on this page and enter About information, Visual Studio displays this information in its About dialog. Open Visual Studio's Help menu and select the About Microsoft Visual Studio command to display the dialog shown in Figure 8-20. If you scroll down and select your add-in, you should see the About information in the "Product details" section.

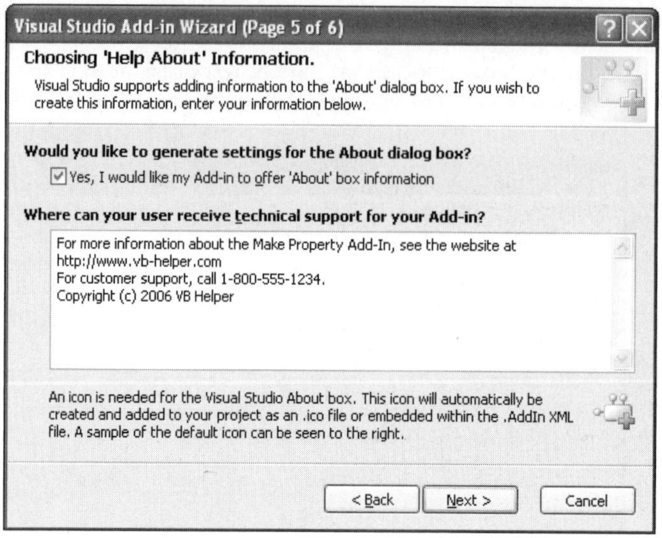

Figure 8-19: Enter About information.

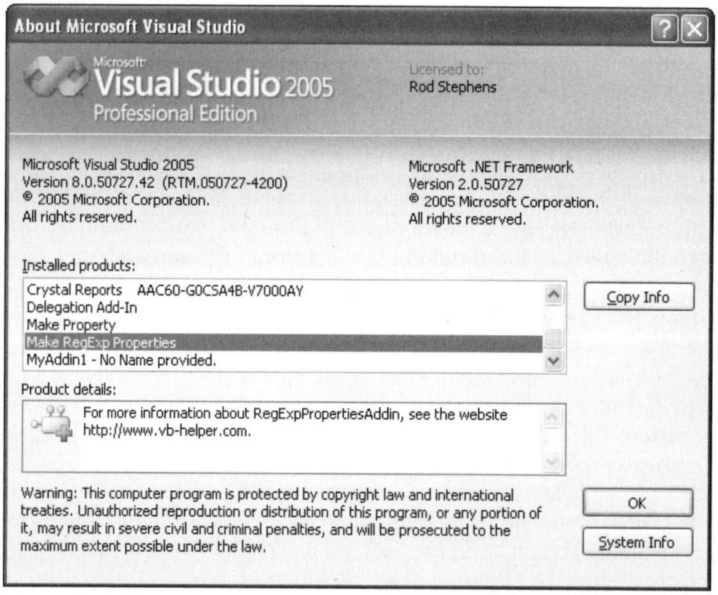

Figure 8-20: Visual Studio displays add-in information in its About dialog.

When you click the Next button, the Add-in Wizard displays a final page summarizing your selections. Verify the settings that the wizard will use, and click Finish to create the add-in project.

Adding Add-in Code

The Add-in Wizard generates a bunch of code that performs tasks such as connecting the add-in to the Tools menu, responding to events, and accessing the IDE object hierarchy. Most of this work is done in the module `Connect.vb`.

To modify the add-in, open `Connect.vb` and find the `OnConnection` subroutine. Inside the `Try Catch` block, find the `AddNamedCommand2` statement that is similar to the following. In `Connect.vb`, this statement is all on one line, but I've broken it here into multiple lines to make it easier to read:

```
'Add a command to the Commands collection:
Dim command As Command = commands.AddNamedCommand2(_addInInstance, _
  "PropertyProcedureAddIn", "PropertyProcedureAddIn", _
  "Executes the command for PropertyProcedureAddIn", True, 59, _
  Nothing, CType(vsCommandStatus.vsCommandStatusSupported, Integer) + _
    CType(vsCommandStatus.vsCommandStatusEnabled, Integer), _
  vsCommandStyle.vsCommandStylePictAndText, _
  vsCommandControlType.vsCommandControlTypeButton)
```

This statement creates the button that appears on the Tools menu when Visual Studio displays the add-in. Change the statement to give the button a better display name and tooltip, as shown in the second and third lines of the following statement:

```
Dim command As Command = commands.AddNamedCommand2(_addInInstance, _
  "PropertyProcedureAddIn", "Add Property", _
  "Add a property using a private variable and property procedures", True, 59, _
  Nothing, CType(vsCommandStatus.vsCommandStatusSupported, Integer) + _
    CType(vsCommandStatus.vsCommandStatusEnabled, Integer), _
  vsCommandStyle.vsCommandStylePictAndText, _
  vsCommandControlType.vsCommandControlTypeButton)
```

Next, find the `Exec` subroutine. Inside the `If` statement, place the code that the add-in should execute. To keep the automatically generated parts of the code as simple as possible, just place a call here to another subroutine that does all of the work. The following code shows how the `PropertyProcedureAddIn` project calls subroutine `MakeProperty`:

```
Public Sub Exec(ByVal commandName As String, _
 ByVal executeOption As vsCommandExecOption, ByRef varIn As Object, _
 ByRef varOut As Object, ByRef handled As Boolean) Implements IDTCommandTarget.Exec
    handled = False
    If executeOption = vsCommandExecOption.vsCommandExecOptionDoDefault Then
        If commandName = "PropertyProcedureAddIn.Connect.PropertyProcedureAddIn" _
        Then
            '*** Make the property.
            MakeProperty()

            handled = True
            Exit Sub
        End If
    End If
End Sub
```

The `PropertyProcedureAddIn` uses subroutine `MakeProperty` to create property procedures. It displays the dialog shown in Figure 8-21 to let you enter a comment, the property's accessibility (`Public`, `Private`, `Friend`, and so forth), modifier (`blank`, `ReadOnly`, or `WriteOnly`), name, and data type.

Figure 8-21: Enter values to describe the property procedure that you want to create and click OK.

The following code shows subroutine `MakeProperty` that is invoked by the `Exec` subroutine:

```
' Make the property.
Private Sub MakeProperty()
    ' Get the selection point.
    Dim sel As TextSelection = _
        CType(_applicationObject.ActiveDocument.Selection, TextSelection)
    If sel Is Nothing Then
        MessageBox.Show( _
            "Place the cursor inside a class before you use this add-in.", _
            "Not In Class", MessageBoxButtons.OK, MessageBoxIcon.Exclamation)
        Exit Sub
    End If

    ' Get the class containing the selection point.
    Dim code_class As CodeClass2 = _
        CType(sel.ActivePoint.CodeElement(vsCMElement.vsCMElementClass), _
            CodeClass2)
    If code_class Is Nothing Then
        MessageBox.Show( _
            "Place the cursor inside a class before you use this add-in.", _
            "Not In Class", MessageBoxButtons.OK, MessageBoxIcon.Exclamation)
        Exit Sub
    End If

    ' Display the dialog.
    Dim dlg As New dlgMakeProperty
    If dlg.ShowDialog() = System.Windows.Forms.DialogResult.OK Then
        ' Compose the code text.
        Dim txt As String = PropertyCode( _
```

```
                dlg.txtName.Text, _
                dlg.cboType.Text, _
                dlg.cboAccessibility.Text, _
                dlg.cboModifier.Text, _
                dlg.txtComments.Text)

            ' Add the code.
            Dim text_point As TextPoint = _
                code_class.GetStartPoint(vsCMPart.vsCMPartBody)
            Dim edit_point As EditPoint = text_point.CreateEditPoint()
            edit_point.Insert(txt)
        End If
    End Sub

    ' Make a property at this EditPoint.
    Private Function PropertyCode(ByVal property_name As String, _
     ByVal data_type As String, Optional ByVal accessibility As String = "", _
     Optional ByVal modifier As String = "", Optional ByVal comments As String = "") _
     As String
        Dim txt As String = ""

        ' Compose the code text.
        If comments.Length > 1 Then
            txt &= vbTab & "' " & comments.Replace(vbCrLf, vbCrLf & vbTab & "' ") & _
                vbCrLf
        Else
            txt &= vbTab & "' The " & property_name & " property." & vbCrLf
        End If

        ' Declare the private variable.
        txt &= vbTab & "Private m_" & property_name & " As " & data_type & vbCrLf

        ' Make the property statement.
        txt &= vbTab & accessibility        ' Public/Private/etc.
        txt &= modifier                     ' ReadOnly/WriteOnly.
        txt &= "Property " & property_name & "() As " & data_type & vbCrLf

        ' Property Get.
        If Not modifier.ToLower().Contains("writeonly") Then
            txt &= vbTab & vbTab & "Get" & vbCrLf
            txt &= vbTab & vbTab & vbTab & "Return m_" & property_name & vbCrLf
            txt &= vbTab & vbTab & "End Get" & vbCrLf
        End If

        ' Property Set.
        If Not modifier.ToLower().Contains("readonly") Then
            txt &= vbTab & vbTab & "Set(ByVal value As " & data_type & ")" & vbCrLf
            txt &= vbTab & vbTab & vbTab & "m_" & property_name & " = value" & vbCrLf
            txt &= vbTab & vbTab & "End Set" & vbCrLf
        End If

        txt &= vbTab & "End Property" & vbCrLf & vbCrLf

        Return txt
    End Function
```

The routine starts by getting a `TextSelection` object representing the current selection in the code editor. If there is no selection, then the developer doesn't have a code editor open.

Next, the routine gets a `CodeClass2` object representing the class containing the selection. If that object is `Nothing`, then the selection is not inside any class.

If the code gets this far, it presents the dialog shown in Figure 8-21. If the user clicks OK, the code calls function `PropertyCode`, passing it the values entered by the user. Function `PropertyCode` returns a string containing the appropriate property procedures. `MakeProperty` gets a `TextPoint` representing the start of the class containing the selection and uses it to get an `EditPoint` object. Finally, it inserts the property procedure text in the `EditPoint`.

Function `PropertyCode` composes the property procedure code in a relatively straightforward manner so I won't describe it in detail. You can step through the code on your own.

Making a Better Add-in

The `PropertyProcedureAddIn` is little more than a complicated snippet. Sure, it displays a nice dialog where you can specify the property procedure's accessibility, modifiers, data type, and so forth, but it's basically doing simple substitutions that you could easily handle in a much simpler snippet.

However, it does provide a model for implementing some more useful add-ins. The `RegExpProperties Addin` project displays the dialog shown in Figure 8-22. In this dialog, you can enter names, data types, and regular expressions to validate any number of properties. When you click OK, the add-in generates code for all of the properties at once. This is much faster than using the `PropertyProcedureAddIn`, plus it adds code to validate the properties by using the regular expressions you entered.

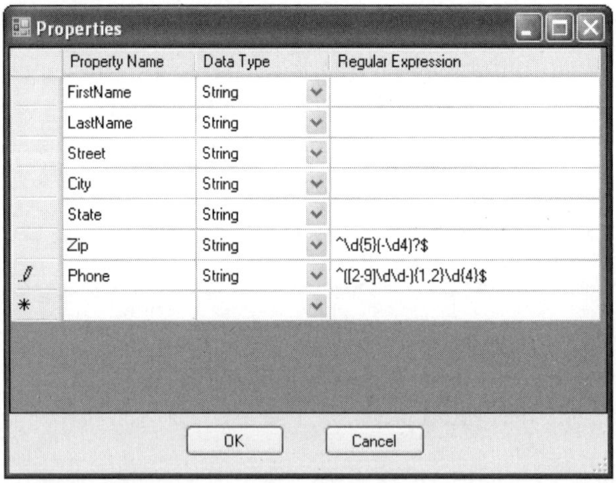

Figure 8-22: Enter the names, data types, and validation regular expressions for properties.

The following code shows the code generated for the `Phone` property using the values shown in Figure 8-22. Notice how the code uses the regular expression to validate new values passed into the `Phone` property Get procedure.

```
' The Phone property.
Private m_Phone As String
Public Property Phone() As String
    Get
        Return m_Phone
    End Get
    Set(ByVal value As String)
        If Not Regex.IsMatch(value, "^([2-9]\d\d-){1,2}\d{4}$") Then
            Throw New FormatException("Property Phone does not have the " & _
                "required format '^([2-9]\d\d-){1,2}\d{4}$'")
        End If
        m_Phone = value
    End Set
End Property
```

For rows with blank regular expressions in Figure 8-22, the resulting property procedures don't include validation code.

The code for this add-in is similar to the code for the previous one. This example just loops through the grid, generating code for each property. When it has generated code for each property, it adds the code at the start of the class containing the selection position. Download the example program from the book's Web site to see the details.

This example doesn't handle every possible situation. For example, it doesn't deal with indexed properties. It does handle my property creation needs most of the time, and should get you started if you need to handle something more elaborate.

Learning About Other Objects

The `DelegationAddIn` project uses more information than the inputs you enter. This add-in gathers information from the current project to let you easily make one class delegate to another.

For more information on delegation, see the Delegation design pattern described in Chapter 7, "Design Patterns."

When you run the add-in, it displays the dialog shown in Figure 8-23. It searches the current project and lists all of the top-level classes it finds in the combo box at the top of the dialog. When you select a class, the add-in lists its properties, methods, and events in the checked list box below. Check the properties and methods that you want to delegate to the class you selected and click OK.

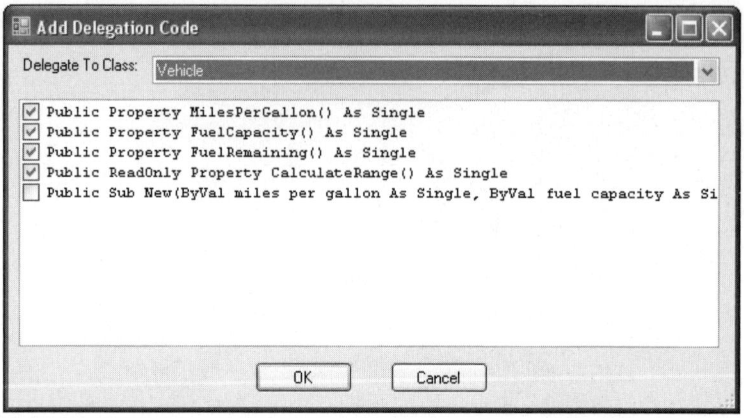

Figure 8-23: When you select a class in the combo box, this dialog lists its properties, methods, and events.

The add-in generates code to declare a private variable of the type of the class that you selected. It then makes code for the properties, methods, and events you selected, delegating each to the variable it declared. When it has finished, the add-in inserts the new code at the beginning of the class that contains the current selection.

The following code fragment shows some of the code generated for the `Vehicle` class selected in Figure 8-23. In this example, the code editor's selection point was inside the `MotorHome` class:

```
Public Class MotorHome

#Region "Delegated to m_Vehicle"
    Private WithEvents m_Vehicle As Vehicle

    Public Property MilesPerGallon() As Single
        Get
            Return m_Vehicle.MilesPerGallon
        End Get
        Set(ByVal value As Single)
            m_Vehicle.MilesPerGallon = value
        End Set
    End Property
    ' Code omitted...

    Public ReadOnly Property CalculateRange() As Single
        Get
            Return m_Vehicle.CalculateRange
        End Get
    End Property

#End Region ' Delegated to m_Vehicle

End Class
```

The automatically generated code lies inside a region named "Delegated to m_Vehicle." It declares a variable named m_Vehicle of type Vehicle. The code declares the variable with the WithEvents keyword, so the code can catch the object's events if necessary.

Next, the add-in generated the public MilesPerGallon property. Notice how it delegates the property to the m_Vehicle object's MilesPerGallon property.

The region includes some other properties not shown here, and finishes with the ReadOnly CalculateRange property.

Much of the DelegationAddIn's code generates code for properties, methods, and events. It's somewhat interesting, but handles many special cases, and is fairly long, so I won't reproduce all of it here. I will, however, explain some of the code that searches the project for information about the available classes.

The following code shows how the add-in displays a list of available classes. When the dialog loads, its Load event handler looks at the application object's Solution property, which represents the currently loaded solution. It loops through the solution's Projects collection to examine all of the loaded projects.

```
' Prepare the dialog.
Private Sub dlgAddDelegationCode_Load(ByVal sender As System.Object, _
 ByVal e As System.EventArgs) Handles MyBase.Load
    ' Loop through all solutions.
    For Each proj As Project In ApplicationObject.Solution.Projects
        ' Loop through project items in the project.
        For Each project_item As ProjectItem In proj.ProjectItems
            ' See if this project item has a code model.
            ' (For example, My Project does not.)
            If project_item.FileCodeModel IsNot Nothing Then
                ' Loop through the project item's code elements.
                Dim fcm As FileCodeModel2 = _
                    DirectCast(project_item.FileCodeModel, FileCodeModel2)
                For Each code_element As CodeElement2 In fcm.CodeElements
                    ' See if it's a class.
                    If code_element.Kind = vsCMElement.vsCMElementClass
                        cboClass.Items.Add(New NameValuePair(code_element.Name, _
                            code_element))
                    End If
                Next code_element
            End If
        Next project_item
    Next proj
End Sub
```

For each project, the code loops through the project's ProjectItems, which represent items in the Project Explorer.

For each ProjectItem, the code determines whether the item has a code model. If the item has no code model, then it is something that doesn't contain code, such as My Project.

If the ProjectItem has a code model, the add-in loops through its CodeElements collection. It checks each element's Kind property and, if the element is a class, the code adds its name to the dialog's combo box.

`NameValuePair` is a simple class that records a name and a value. Its `ToString` function returns the name so that the combo box can display it meaningfully. The program can later retrieve the value from the `NameValuePair` object when it needs to.

When you select an item in the dialog's combo box, the add-in uses the following code to list the properties, methods, and events provided by the selected class:

```
' Display properties and methods provided by this class.
Private Sub cboClass_SelectedIndexChanged(ByVal sender As System.Object, _
 ByVal e As System.EventArgs) Handles cboClass.SelectedIndexChanged
    btnOk.Enabled = True

    ' Get the selected object.
    Dim name_value_pair As NameValuePair = _
        DirectCast(cboClass.SelectedItem, NameValuePair)
    Dim class_element As CodeElement2 = _
        DirectCast(name_value_pair.Value, CodeElement2)

    ' See what items this class provides.
    lstItems.Items.Clear()
    For Each code_element As CodeElement2 In class_element.Children()
        Dim txt As String = ""

        ' Only list Public and Friend items.
        Select Case code_element.Kind
            Case EnvDTE.vsCMElement.vsCMElementEvent
                Dim code_event As CodeEvent = DirectCast(code_element, CodeEvent)
                txt = DeclarationEvent(code_element)

            Case EnvDTE.vsCMElement.vsCMElementFunction
                Dim code_function As CodeFunction2 = _
                    DirectCast(code_element, CodeFunction2)
                If code_function.Type.TypeKind = vsCMTypeRef.vsCMTypeRefVoid Then
                    txt = DeclarationSub(code_function)
                Else
                    txt = DeclarationFunction(code_function)
                End If

            Case EnvDTE.vsCMElement.vsCMElementProperty
                Dim code_property As CodeProperty2 = _
                    DirectCast(code_element, CodeProperty2)
                txt = DeclarationProperty(code_property)

            Case EnvDTE.vsCMElement.vsCMElementVariable
                Dim code_variable As CodeVariable2 = _
                    DirectCast(code_element, CodeVariable2)
                txt = DeclarationVariable(code_variable)
        End Select

        ' Ignore any that are not Public or Friend.
        If txt.Length > 0 Then
            lstItems.Items.Add(New NameValuePair(txt, code_element))

            ' Don't check constructors.
            If code_element.Name <> "New" Then
```

```
                lstItems.SetItemChecked(lstItems.Items.Count - 1, True)
            End If
        End If
    Next code_element
    End Sub
```

The code starts by enabling the dialog's OK button. It then finds the `NameValuePair` corresponding to the combo box's selection. It then retrieves the code element stored in the `NameValuePair`'s value field. That code element represents a class discovered by the dialog's `Load` event handler.

The add-in clears its list box, and loops through the element's `Children` collection. The code uses a `Select Case` statement to examine the child item's kind, and handles those that are events, functions, properties, or variables.

For each of the handled item kinds, the code converts the object into a more specific class type, and then calls a function to generate an appropriate declaration. See the declarations shown in the list box in Figure 8-23 for examples.

The add-in converts objects representing events into `CodeEvent` objects and calls function `DeclarationEvent` to generate the event's declaration.

The add-in converts objects representing functions into `CodeFunction2` objects. It then checks the function's return type and calls `DeclarationSub` if it is a subroutine (has a `void` return type) or `DeclarationFunction` if the function has some other return type.

The add-in converts objects representing properties into `CodeProperty2` objects and calls `DeclarationProperty` to generate their declarations.

Finally, the add-in converts objects representing variables into `CodeVariable2` objects, and calls `DeclarationVariable` to generate their declarations.

The various declaration functions return empty strings if the code item is not declared `Public` or `Friend`. Usually, you cannot delegate an item that is declared `Private` or `Protected`, so the add-in ignores those items.

Finally, the code adds a `NameValuePair` to the list box using the declaration as its name, and saving the code element representing the item as the `NameValuePair` object's value. If the element is not a constructor, the code checks it in the list box.

When you click the dialog's OK button, the add-in builds the region and declares a private variable of the appropriate type. It then loops through the items in the list that you checked. For each item, it calls an appropriate function to generate code to delegate the item. After it has generated the code for each checked item, the code closes the region and adds the code to the class that currently contains the selection. This code is fairly long, but reasonably straightforward, so it's not shown here. Download the example program and look it over.

Like the previous add-in, this add-in doesn't handle every possible situation. For example, it keeps the same visibility provided by the delegating class. Because the `Vehicle` *class's* `CalculateRange` *property is* `ReadOnly` *and* `Public`*, the delegated* `CalculateRange` *property is also* `ReadOnly` *and* `Public`*. Under some circumstances, you might want to make the new property* `Protected` *or* `Private`*. This example handles the most common, straightforward delegation chores, however. If necessary, you can modify the code after the add-in handles the basics.*

You will also need to add some additional code. For example, you'll need to initialize the delegation object (`m_Vehicle`*) somewhere. You might do that in delegating class's constructor. You could use the* `New` *keyword in the* `m_Vehicle` *variable's declaration and initialize it there.*

Summary

Code snippets let you copy and insert pieces of saved code, and make fairly straightforward replacements. Because creating and using snippets is so easy, they are the best method for automating code generation when they can handle the job.

For more complicated code generation, you can use macros. Recorded macros are so specific that they are rarely useful in their original recorded form, but you can often use a recorded macro as the basis for a new macro that you write yourself to perform more complicated tasks. Macros are somewhat restricted in the elements they can use (for example, the Macro IDE doesn't let you build forms), but they have full access to the Visual Studio IDE and the currently loaded project. Being plain code text, they are also easy to share.

Like macros, add-ins have full access to the Visual Studio IDE and the currently loaded project. They also provide all of the features available to any Visual Studio application, so, for example, they can use forms and dialogs that you build. Add-ins are compiled DLLs, so they can contain code that you don't want developers to view or modify.

To get the most out of macros and add-ins, you need to use Visual Studio's extensibility object model to manipulate the Visual Studio IDE and the currently loaded project. Unfortunately, this object model is enormous, extremely complicated, and not very well-documented. Look in the online help's index for "extensibility" for information about the classes that represent the IDE and the loaded project. You may also find some help in the book *Developing Visual Studio .NET Macros and Add-Ins* by Jeff Cogswell (Indianapolis: Wiley, 2003).

You can also look for samples on the Web that show how to automate various tasks in Visual Studio. On Microsoft's Web site, go to `www.microsoft.com/downloads` and search for "Visual Studio 2005 Automation Samples."

This chapter explains ways you can automatically generate code to add to the application at design time. Chapter 9, "Scripting," explains how you can use scripts to add code to the application at run-time. In some applications, you can use the same techniques to allow the user to execute code as well.

9

Scripting

There are many ways you can make a program extensible at run-time. For example, Chapter 22, "Reflection," shows how you can provide add-in functionality by loading compiled DLLs at run-time.

One of the most flexible methods for extending an application at run-time is scripting. By allowing the program to execute new code at run-time, you can enable it to do just about anything that you could do had you written the code ahead of time, at least in theory.

This chapter describes several techniques that you can use to add scripting to your applications. It explains how a program can execute SQL statements or Visual Basic .NET code, and how a program can parse and evaluate arithmetic expressions at run-time.

Scripting Safely

Scripting is an extremely flexible and powerful way to add functionality to an application. However, like many other powerful and flexible tools, scripting comes with a certain degree of danger. If you give users the ability to destroy the application or its data, you may very well need to deal with them doing exactly that. Sooner or later you'll get a call from a customer who has dropped a key table from the application's database, used a script to set foreground and background colors to black, or removed key objects from the application's object model, and wants you to make everything better. Even worse, a disgruntled or dishonest user might modify the data to damage the application or for fraudulent reasons, and you may need to sort out the mess.

To reduce the frequency of these types of calls, you should consider the users' needs and programming skill level. Then you should carefully select the scripting capabilities that you provide to match.

For example, if the users only need to make configuration changes such as setting colors and options, you can provide configuration dialogs to make that easier and safer. Provide a "Reset to Default" button to let them undo any really bad changes. In this example, scripting isn't really necessary.

Many users understand or can easily learn the basics of SQL. Querying the database is generally safe, so many of the applications I've written allow the users to execute ad hoc SQL queries. This gives the user an easy way to find particular records and to generate quick one-off reports without requiring the developers to build new reports into the system. Most users don't need to be able to perform more dangerous SQL statements that would let them drop tables, add or delete records, and remove indexes.

Even with queries, however, there are occasions when an application cannot allow the users unlimited freedom. If the application's data is sensitive, perhaps containing financial or medical information, all of the users may not be allowed to see all of the data. For example, in a medical application, you might want to allow receptionists to see only appointment and insurance information, and not medical records. In that case, you could not allow the users to write their own SQL queries.

Actually, if the database provides security at a sufficiently fine-grained level, you might be able to let users write their own queries. Some databases let you define column-level permissions for particular users. Then, if a user tries to select data that he or she is not allowed to see, the database will raise an error, and the script will fail safely.

You can make SQL scripting easier for the users if you provide some means to store and execute predefined queries. In some applications I've written, supervisors and more experienced users wrote queries for other users to execute. If you only allow the users to execute predefined queries stored in a database or a shared directory that only the supervisors have permission to edit, then you have pretty good control over what the users can do.

Another great place to store predefined queries is as stored procedures. That gives you a lot of control over who can create, modify, and view the queries. Stored procedures are saved in the database, so you can modify them without recompiling the application. Only developers who have the proper tools and permissions can view or modify stored procedures, so they are relatively protected. Often, databases can give better performance when executing stored procedures than they can when performing queries composed by the application's code. All in all, stored procedures are a great place to store database tools for the users to execute.

If the users are less sophisticated, you may want to build tools that help the user compose queries. The section "Generating Queries" later in this chapter shows one such tool.

Users rarely have the skills needed to modify the database safely, so you probably shouldn't give them the ability to execute non-query SQL commands such as `DROP TABLE`. That doesn't mean there's no point in executing these scripts, however. Sometimes it is useful to give supervisors or application administrators tools for performing database maintenance tasks. To protect the database, you may want to allow the users to execute only predefined scripts created by the developers.

Stored procedures are a great place to store these maintenance scripts, too.

These sorts of database modification tasks can also be extremely useful for developers. Many applications that I've worked on modify their data so that you cannot easily perform the same operations repeatedly without resetting the database. A script that inserts test data into the database can make development and testing much easier.

Scripts that manipulate the application's object model are usually a bit easier to safeguard than SQL scripts. If you expose an object model that only allows users to do what they can do by using the user interface, you don't need to worry as much about the user's permissions.

This approach does have some design consequences, however. It means that you cannot rely solely on the user interface to control the user's access to application features. For example, suppose supervisors should be able to modify work assignments, but clerks should only be able to view them. When a clerk starts the application, you can hide the menu items that allow the user to edit work assignments, but if the object model contains functions to do this, the clerk may be able to use a script to change assignments anyway.

To prevent this sort of flanking maneuver, the object model's sensitive methods must always verify the current user's privileges, even though they might normally be protected by the user interface.

If the users don't have the skills to write their own scripts, or if letting them write scripts is just too dangerous, you can still use scripts behind the scenes to provide new functionality. You can store scripts written by supervisors or developers in a database or protected directory, and then allow the program to execute them without the user ever seeing the details. You might provide a Scripts menu that lists the names of the scripts and then executes whichever scripts the user selects.

If you store the scripts in a database, you have good control over who can look at them. If you store the scripts in text files, you can encrypt them if you really don't want the users peeking.

As a final word of caution, consider how users might inadvertently or intentionally subvert a script, even if your code actually writes the code. For example, suppose an application stores user names and passwords in the `Users` table. Many programs use code similar to the following to build this query and verify the user's password:

```
' Verify the user name and password.
Private Sub btnVerify_Click(ByVal sender As System.Object, _
 ByVal e As System.EventArgs) Handles btnVerify.Click
    ' Compose the query.
    Dim user_name As String = txtUserName.Text
    Dim password As String = txtPassword.Text
    Dim query As String = _
        "SELECT COUNT(*) FROM Users " & _
        "WHERE UserName = '" & user_name & "'" & _
        "  AND Password = '" & password & "'"
    Debug.WriteLine(query)

    ' Execute the query.
    Try
        m_Connection.Open()
        Dim cmd As New OleDbCommand(query, m_Connection)
        Dim result As Integer = CInt(cmd.ExecuteScalar())
        m_Connection.Close()

        If result > 0 Then
            MessageBox.Show("User verified")
        Else
            MessageBox.Show("Invalid user")
        End If
```

```
    Catch ex As Exception
        MessageBox.Show(ex.Message, "Query Error", _
            MessageBoxButtons.OK, MessageBoxIcon.Exclamation)
    Finally
        If m_Connection.State = ConnectionState.Open Then m_Connection.Close()
    End Try
End Sub
```

This code creates and executes a query similar to the following:

```
SELECT COUNT(*) FROM Users
WHERE UserName = 'Rod'
  AND Password = 'VbGeek'
```

If this query returns a value greater than 0, the program assumes the user has a valid password.

Now, consider what happens if the user enters the name **Rod** and the bizarre password shown in the following code:

```
' OR True OR Password = '
```

When the code runs, it produces the following enigmatic SQL statement:

```
SELECT COUNT(*) FROM Users
WHERE UserName = 'Rod'
  AND Password = '' OR True OR Password = ''
```

This `WHERE` clause always evaluates to `True`, so the select statement always returns `1` (assuming there is one record with the user name Rod) and the program accepts the user name even though the password is incorrect.

Breaking into a database in this way is called a "SQL injection attack," and is a fairly common exploit on Web sites.

There are even cases where a user can innocently wreak havoc in the SQL query. If the user's name is O'Toole, for example, the code produces the following query:

```
SELECT COUNT(*) FROM Users
WHERE UserName = 'O'Toole'
  AND Password = '1337'
```

Here the extra apostrophe inside the user name confuses the database and the query fails.

One solution is to change the code to replace each apostrophe in the input strings with two apostrophes:

```
Dim user_name As String = txtUserName.Text.Replace("'", "''")
Dim password As String = txtPassword.Text.Replace("'", "''")
```

Now, the SQL injection attack creates the following SQL query:

```
SELECT COUNT(*) FROM Users
WHERE UserName = 'Rod'
  AND Password = ''' OR True OR Password = '''
```

Now, the database correctly reads the weird password entered by the user and is not fooled.

The program now creates the following query for user O'Toole:

```
SELECT COUNT(*) FROM Users
WHERE UserName = 'O''Toole'
  AND Password = '1337'
```

The database correctly places an apostrophe inside the user name and there's no problem.

Example program `ValidateUser` demonstrates both the safe and unsafe version of this code.

Scripting is a powerful technique, but it's not completely without risk. Carefully consider the users' needs, skill levels, and permissions. Then, you can pick a scripting strategy that gives the most additional flexibility with a reasonable level of risk.

Executing SQL Statements

Structured Query Language (SQL) is a relatively easy-to-learn language for interacting with databases. It includes commands for creating, reading, editing, and deleting data.

SQL also includes commands that manipulate the database itself. Its commands let you create and drop tables, add and remove indexes, and so forth.

Visual Studio provides objects that interact with databases by executing SQL statements, so providing scripting capabilities is fairly easy.

The following section explains how a program can execute queries written by the user. The section after that shows how a program can provide a tool that makes building queries easier and safer. The final section dealing with SQL scripts shows how a program can execute more general SQL statements to modify and delete data, and to alter the database's structure.

Note that these sections provide only brief coverage of database programming as it applies to scripting in Visual Basic, and they omit lots of details. For more in-depth coverage of database programming, see a book about database programming in Visual Basic .NET, such as my book *Visual Basic .NET Database Programming* (Indianapolis: Que, 2002).

Running Queries

Executing a SQL query is fairly easy in Visual Basic. The following code shows a minimalist approach for executing a query and displaying the results in a `DataGridView` control:

```
' Open the connection.
m_Connection.Open()

' Select the data.
Dim data_table As New DataTable("Books")
Dim da As New OleDbDataAdapter(query, m_Connection)

' Get the data.
```

```
da.Fill(data_table)

' Display the result.
dgvBooks.DataSource = data_table

' Close the connection.
m_Connection.Close()
```

The code starts by opening the connection object named `m_Connection`. It creates a `DataTable` object to hold the selected data, and makes an `OleDbDataAdapter` to execute the query on the connection. It then uses the adapter to fill the `DataTable`. The code finishes by setting the `DataGridView` control's `DataSource` property to the `DataTable` and closing the database connection.

Example program `UserSqlQuery` uses similar code to execute ad hoc queries. It provides some additional error-handling code, and does some extra work to format the `DataGridView`'s columns (for example, it right-justifies numbers and dates). Download the example to see how the code works. Figure 9-1 shows the program in action.

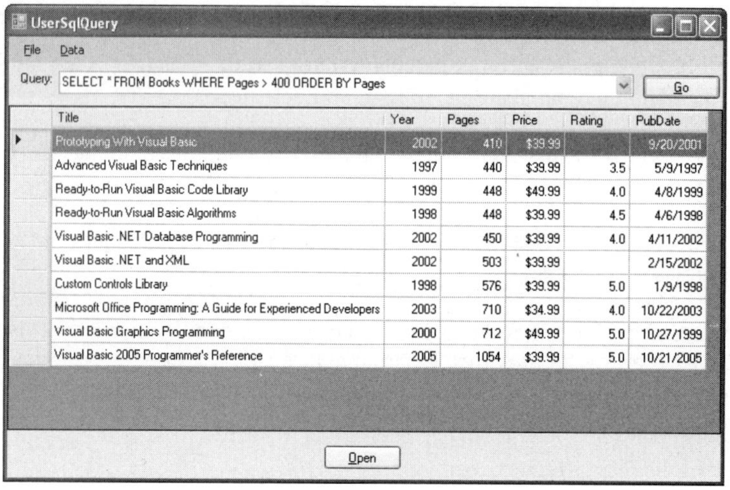

Figure 9-1: Program `UserSqlQuery` lets the user execute ad hoc SQL queries.

The program uses a combo box to let the user enter a query, or select from a list of previously defined queries. When the code successfully executes a query, the program saves it in the combo box's list and in the Registry so that it will be available to the user later.

Program `UserSqlQuery` also allows the user to select the fields displayed by the `DataGridView` control. When you select the Data menu's Select Fields command, the program displays the dialog shown in Figure 9-2. The dialog lists the fields returned by the query, and lets the user select the ones that should be visible in the grid.

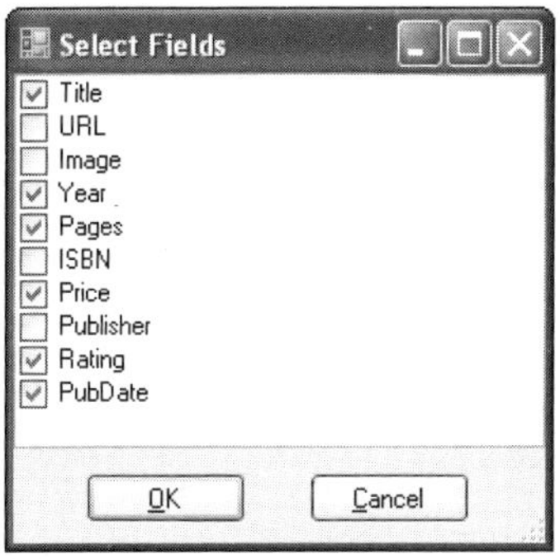

Figure 9-2: Program `UserSqlQuery` **lets the user select the fields it displays in its grid.**

The following code shows how the Select Fields dialog works:

```
Imports System.Data.OleDb

Public Class dlgSelectFields
    ' The DataGridView on the main form.
    Public TheDataGridView As DataGridView = Nothing

    ' Load the list of database fields.
    Private Sub dlgSelectFields_Load(ByVal sender As Object, _
     ByVal e As System.EventArgs) Handles Me.Load
        ' Make sure TheDataGridView has been initialized.
        Debug.Assert(TheDataGridView IsNot Nothing, "TheDataGridView is Nothing")

        ' Set properties. (Done here so it's easier to find.)
        clbFields.CheckOnClick = True

        ' Fill the checked list box with the fields.
        clbFields.Items.Clear()
        For i As Integer = 0 To TheDataGridView.Columns.Count - 1
            clbFields.Items.Add(TheDataGridView.Columns(i).HeaderText)
            Dim checked As Boolean = TheDataGridView.Columns(i).Visible
            clbFields.SetItemChecked(i, checked)
        Next i
    End Sub

    ' Apply the user's selections to the DataGridView.
    Private Sub btnOk_Click(ByVal sender As System.Object, _
     ByVal e As System.EventArgs) Handles btnOk.Click
        For i As Integer = 0 To TheDataGridView.Columns.Count - 1
            TheDataGridView.Columns(i).Visible = clbFields.GetItemChecked(i)
        Next i
    End Sub
End Class
```

The main program sets the form's `TheDataGridView` variable to a reference to the `DataGridView` control before displaying the form.

When the dialog loads, the code loops through the grid's `Columns` collection, adding each column's header text to the dialog's `CheckedListBox` control `clbFields`. It checks an item if the corresponding grid column is currently visible.

If the user clicks the OK button, the dialog again loops through grid's columns, this time setting a column's `Visible` property to `True` if the corresponding item is checked in the dialog's list box. (You can download this example at `www.vb-helper.com/one_on_one.htm`.)

Generating Queries

Ad hoc queries are great for users who know their way around SQL. For many users, however, even simple queries can be intimidating.

Example program `SelectCriteria` uses the dialog shown in Figure 9-3 to let the user specify selection criteria in a simpler manner. The user selects a database field in the left column, picks an operator (`>`, `>=`, `IS NULL`, `LIKE`, and so forth) in the middle column, and enters a value string in the right column.

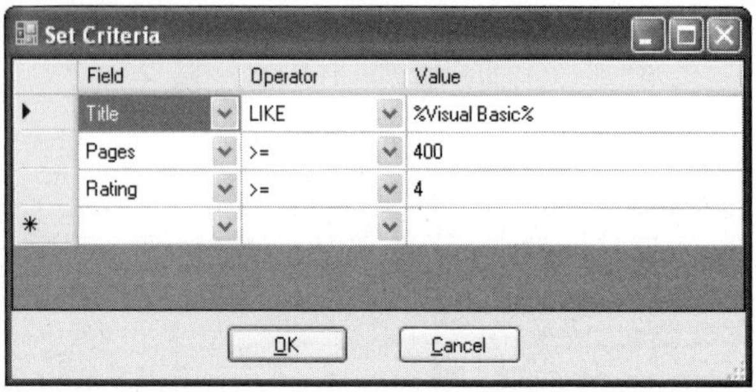

Figure 9-3: Program `SelectCriteria` uses this dialog to build SQL queries.

When the user clicks OK, the program uses the selections on the dialog to build a SQL query. The selections shown in Figure 9-3 generate the following SQL statement:

```
SELECT * FROM Books
WHERE Title LIKE '%Visual Basic'
  AND Pages >= 200
  AND Rating >= 4
ORDER BY Title
```

The program also saves the criteria in the Registry so that the program can use them the next time it starts.

The following code shows how the Set Criteria dialog works:

```
Imports System.Data.OleDb

Public Class dlgCriteria
    ' The DataGridView on the main form.
```

```
Public TheDataGridView As DataGridView = Nothing

' The collection of criteria.
Public TheCriteria As Collection = Nothing

' Delimiters for the field choices.
Private m_Delimiters As Collection

' Load the list of database fields.
Private Sub dlgSelectFields_Load(ByVal sender As Object, _
 ByVal e As System.EventArgs) Handles Me.Load
    ' Make sure TheDataGridView and TheCriteria have been initialized.
    Debug.Assert(TheDataGridView IsNot Nothing, "TheDataGridView is Nothing")
    Debug.Assert(TheCriteria IsNot Nothing, "TheCriteria is Nothing")

    ' Get the cell's template object.
    Dim dgv_cell As DataGridViewCell = dgvCriteria.Columns(0).CellTemplate
    Dim combo_cell As DataGridViewComboBoxCell = _
        DirectCast(dgv_cell, DataGridViewComboBoxCell)

    ' Make a list of the fields.
    combo_cell.Items.Clear()
    m_Delimiters = New Collection
    For i As Integer = 0 To TheDataGridView.Columns.Count - 1
        ' Add the name to the combo cell.
        Dim field_name As String = TheDataGridView.Columns(i).Name
        combo_cell.Items.Add(field_name)

        ' Get an appropriate delimiter for the data type.
        Dim delimiter As String = ""
        If TheDataGridView.Columns(i).ValueType Is GetType(String) Then
            delimiter = "'"
        ElseIf TheDataGridView.Columns(i).ValueType Is GetType(Date) Then
            ' Note that you need to handle dates differently in SQL Server.
            delimiter = "#"
        End If
        m_Delimiters.Add(delimiter, field_name)
    Next i

    ' Display current criteria.
    dgvCriteria.RowCount = TheCriteria.Count + 1
    For r As Integer = 0 To TheCriteria.Count - 1
        Dim condition As Criterion = DirectCast(TheCriteria(r + 1), Criterion)

        dgvCriteria.Rows(r).Cells(0).Value = condition.FieldName
        dgvCriteria.Rows(r).Cells(1).Value = condition.Op
        dgvCriteria.Rows(r).Cells(2).Value = condition.Value
    Next r
End Sub

' Create the new Criteria collection.
Private Sub btnOk_Click(ByVal sender As System.Object, _
 ByVal e As System.EventArgs) Handles btnOk.Click
    ' Verify that each row has a field and operator.
    For r As Integer = 0 To dgvCriteria.RowCount - 2
```

```
            If dgvCriteria.Rows(r).Cells(0).Value Is Nothing Then
                MessageBox.Show( _
                    "You must select a field for every row", _
                    "Missing Field", _
                    MessageBoxButtons.OK, _
                    MessageBoxIcon.Exclamation)
                dgvCriteria.CurrentCell = dgvCriteria.Rows(r).Cells(0)
                dgvCriteria.Select()
                Me.DialogResult = Windows.Forms.DialogResult.None
                Exit Sub
            End If
            If dgvCriteria.Rows(r).Cells(1).Value Is Nothing Then
                MessageBox.Show( _
                    "You must select an operator for every row", _
                    "Missing Field", _
                    MessageBoxButtons.OK, _
                    MessageBoxIcon.Exclamation)
                dgvCriteria.CurrentCell = dgvCriteria.Rows(r).Cells(1)
                dgvCriteria.Select()
                Me.DialogResult = Windows.Forms.DialogResult.None
                Exit Sub
            End If
        Next r

        ' Make the new criteria collection.
        TheCriteria = New Collection
        For r As Integer = 0 To dgvCriteria.RowCount - 2
            Dim field_name As String = _
                DirectCast(dgvCriteria.Rows(r).Cells(0).Value, String)
            Dim delimiter As String = _
                DirectCast(m_Delimiters(field_name), String)
            Dim op As String = _
                DirectCast(dgvCriteria.Rows(r).Cells(1).Value, String)
            Dim value As String = _
                DirectCast(dgvCriteria.Rows(r).Cells(2).Value, String)

            TheCriteria.Add(New Criterion(field_name, op, value, _
                delimiter))
        Next r
    End Sub
End Class
```

When the dialog loads, it gets the template cell for the dialog's first grid column. This cell acts as a template to define other cells in the column so that when the program defines the field names in its drop-down list, it defines the values for every drop-down in this column.

The program loops through the main program's `DataGridView` columns, adding each column's name to the drop-down list. It saves a corresponding delimiter (apostrophe for strings, # for dates, an empty string for other data types) for the column in the `m_Delimiters` collection.

The allowed operators (<, <=, =, >=, >, `LIKE`*,* `IS NULL`*, and* `IS NOT NULL`*) were set for the second column at design time.*

The program then loops through the collection named `TheCriteria`, which contains `Criterion` objects representing the program's current selection criteria. It uses the objects' properties to set field names, operators, and values in the dialog's grid.

When the user clicks the dialog's OK button, the program first verifies that every entered row has a non-blank field name and operator. It then loops through the grid's rows, builds `Criterion` objects for each, and adds them to a new `TheCriteria` collection.

The following code shows the `Criterion` class. Its main purpose is just to store a field name, operator, and delimiter. It includes a couple of constructors to make creating objects easier. The `ToString` function makes it easier to save objects in the Registry.

```
' Represent a condition such as FirstName >= 'Stephens'.
Public Class Criterion
    Public FieldName As String
    Public Op As String
    Public Value As String
    Public Delimiter As String

    Public Sub New(ByVal new_field_name As String, ByVal new_op As String, _
     ByVal new_value As String, ByVal new_delimiter As String)
        FieldName = new_field_name
        Op = new_op
        Value = new_value
        Delimiter = new_delimiter
    End Sub

    ' Initialize with tab-delimited values.
    Public Sub New(ByVal txt As String)
        Dim items() As String = txt.Split(CChar(vbTab))
        FieldName = items(0)
        Op = items(1)
        Value = items(2)
        Delimiter = items(3)
    End Sub

    ' Return tab-delimited values.
    Public Overrides Function ToString() As String
        Return FieldName & vbTab & Op & vbTab & Value & vbTab & Delimiter
    End Function
End Class
```

Like `UserSqlQuery`, example program `SelectCriteria` lets the user select the columns that should be displayed in the main program's `DataGridView` control. (You can download this example at `www.vb-helper.com/one_on_one.htm`.)

Running Commands

Though executing ad hoc queries is handy for users, developers need more powerful tools. Often, it's handy to execute more general SQL commands that add, modify, or delete data, or that modify the database's structure. Fortunately, Visual Basic's database tools make this relatively straightforward.

The `ExecuteNonQuery` function shown in the following code executes a SQL command and returns a success or failure message. It simply creates an `OleDbCommand` object associated with the command and the database connection and then executes it.

```
' Execute a non-query command and return a success or failure string.
Public Function ExecuteNonQuery(ByVal conn As OleDbConnection, _
 ByVal txt As String) As String
    Try
        ' Make and execute the command.
        Dim cmd As New OleDbCommand(txt, conn)
        cmd.ExecuteNonQuery()
        Return "> Ok"
    Catch ex As Exception
        Return "*** Error executing command ***" & vbCrLf & ex.Message
    End Try
End Function
```

The following code shows a function that executes a query. It creates an `OleDbCommand` object for the query and calls its `ExecuteReader` command to run the query and get a data reader to process the results. It loops through the reader's columns, adding their names to a result string. It then uses the reader to loop through the returned rows and adds the rows' field values to the result string.

```
' Execute a query command and return
' the results or failure string.
Public Function ExecuteQuery(ByVal conn As OleDbConnection, _
 ByVal query As String) As String
    Try
        ' Make and execute the command.
        Dim cmd As New OleDbCommand(query, conn)
        Dim reader As OleDbDataReader = cmd.ExecuteReader()

        ' Display the column names.
        Dim row_txt As String = ""
        For c As Integer = 0 To reader.FieldCount - 1
            row_txt &= ", " & reader.GetName(c)
        Next c

        ' Remove the initial ", ".
        Dim txt As String = "-----" & vbCrLf & _
            row_txt.Substring(2) & vbCrLf & "-----" & vbCrLf

        ' Display the results.
        Do While reader.Read()
            row_txt = ""
            For c As Integer = 0 To reader.FieldCount - 1
                row_txt &= ", " & reader.Item(c).ToString()
            Next c

            ' Remove the initial ", ".
            txt &= row_txt.Substring(2) & vbCrLf
        Loop
        reader.Close()
        Return txt
    Catch ex As Exception
        Return "*** Error executing SELECT statement ***" & vbCrLf & _
```

```
            ex.Message
        End Try
    End Function
```

Example program `ExecuteSqlScript` uses these functions to run general SQL scripts. It uses the following to break a script apart and call functions `ExecuteNonQuery` and `ExecuteQuery` to process the pieces.

```
    ' Execute the SQL script.
    Private Sub btnRun_Click(ByVal sender As System.Object, _
     ByVal e As System.EventArgs) Handles btnRun.Click
        ' Open the connection.
        m_Connection.Open()

        ' Break the script into semi-colon delimited commands.
        Dim commands() As String = Split(txtScript.Text, ";")

        ' Execute each command.
        Dim results As String = ""
        For i As Integer = 0 To commands.Length - 1
            ' Clean up the command to see if it's non-blank.
            Dim cmd As String = _
                commands(i).Replace(vbCr, " ").Replace(vbLf, " ").Trim()

            ' Execute only non-blank commands.
            If cmd.Length > 0 Then
                Debug.WriteLine(commands(i))

                ' Display the command.
                results &= commands(i) & vbCrLf

                txtResults.Text = results
                txtResults.Select(results.Length, 0)
                txtResults.ScrollToCaret()
                txtResults.Refresh()

                ' See if this is a SELECT command.
                If cmd.ToUpper.StartsWith("SELECT") Then
                    ' Execute the query.
                    results = results & ExecuteQuery(m_Connection, commands(i))
                Else
                    ' Execute the non-query command.
                    results = results & ExecuteNonQuery(m_Connection, commands(i))
                End If

                results &= vbCrLf & "==========" & vbCrLf
                txtResults.Text = results
                txtResults.Select(results.Length, 0)
                txtResults.ScrollToCaret()
                txtResults.Refresh()
            End If
        Next i

        ' Close the connection.
```

```
        m_Connection.Close()

        results &= "Done" & vbCrLf
        txtResults.Text = results
        txtResults.Select(results.Length - 1, 10)
        txtResults.ScrollToCaret()
    End Sub
```

The code starts by opening a database connection. It reads the script in the `txtScript` text box and splits it into semicolon-delimited commands.

For each command, the program removes carriage returns and line feeds, and decides whether the command is blank. If the command is not blank, the code determines whether the command begins with the `SELECT` keyword and calls function `ExecuteNonQuery` or `ExecuteQuery` as appropriate. As it executes each command, it displays the command and its results in an output text box so that the user can see the results as work progresses.

Figure 9-4 shows the program in action. The upper text box shows the bottom of a script that drops the `Books` table, creates a new `Books` table, inserts several records, and then selects the records. The bottom text box shows the results.

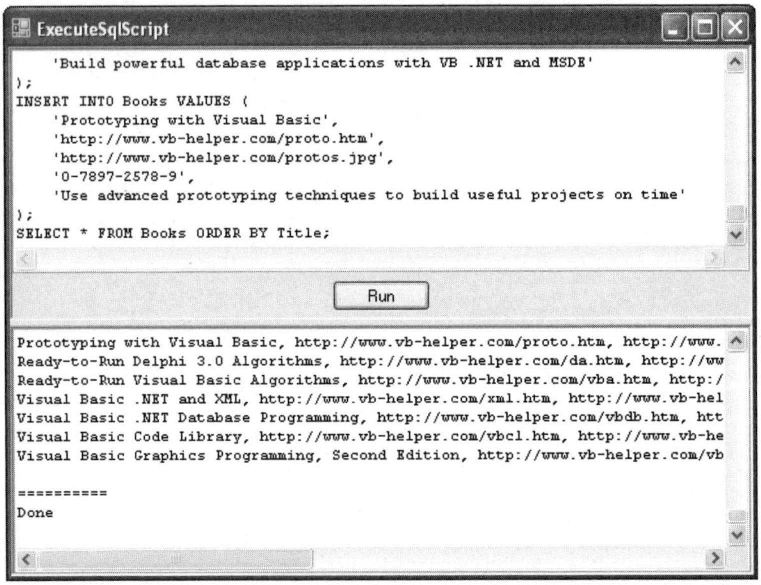

Figure 9-4: Program `ExecuteSqlScript` lets you execute SQL scripts.

(You can download this example at `www.vb-helper.com/one_on_one.htm`.)

You may never want to give this sort of functionality to users, but you may find it useful during development and testing.

Executing Visual Basic Code

Programs such as Microsoft's Word, Excel, and Visual Studio applications allow the user to record, edit, and run macros to automate repetitive tasks. Similarly, you can add some scripting support to your applications.

One approach to this kind of scripting is to use objects in the `System.CodeDom` and `System.Reflection` namespaces to load, compile, and run Visual Basic .NET script code at run-time. If you're reading this, however, you undoubtedly know that writing Visual Basic code is a significant undertaking. Even if you are an experienced developer, writing out a script without the Visual Studio IDE is a dubious proposition. No matter how much care you take, any non-trivial script is likely to contain bugs, and debugging the script without the IDE can be slow and painful.

If you want to integrate your application with Visual Studio, you should look into Microsoft's Visual Studio Industry Partner (VSIP) program. You can learn more at `msdn.microsoft.com/vstudio/partners/default.aspx`.

Another alternative is to write and debug scripts by writing code in Visual Studio with your project loaded. Then copy the resulting code into a script file and execute it later. Using this approach, users are unlikely to successfully write anything but the simplest scripts, but at least developers can easily extend the application by providing scripts for the users to load and run.

Running Code

The basic approach to running code compiled at run-time is to use a code provider to compile the code. The program can then use reflection to examine the compiled assembly, find the code it wants to execute, and invoke it. The `CodeRunner` class shown in the following code shows how to do this:

```
Imports System.CodeDom.Compiler
Imports System.Text
Imports System.Reflection

Public Class CodeRunner
    ' Errors generated by the last run.
    Public CompilerErrors As New CompilerErrorCollection

    ' Array of references needed by the code.
    Public References As New Collection

    Public Function Run(ByVal vb_code As String) As Object
        ' Prepare the compiler parameters.
        ' Add any needed references.
        Dim compiler_params As CompilerParameters = New CompilerParameters
        For Each reference As String In References
            compiler_params.ReferencedAssemblies.Add(reference)
        Next reference

        ' Generate a library in memory.
        compiler_params.CompilerOptions = "/t:library"
        compiler_params.GenerateInMemory = True

        ' Compile the code.
```

```
            Debug.WriteLine(vb_code)
            Dim code_provider As VBCodeProvider = New VBCodeProvider
            Dim compiler_results As CompilerResults = _
                code_provider.CompileAssemblyFromSource(compiler_params, vb_code)
            code_provider.Dispose()

            ' Check for errors.
            CompilerErrors = compiler_results.Errors
            If compiler_results.Errors.Count > 0 Then
                ' There were errors.
                Throw New CompilerException("Compile Errors")
            Else
                ' There were no errors. Try to execute the code.
                ' Get the assembly.
                Dim the_assembly As System.Reflection.Assembly = _
                    compiler_results.CompiledAssembly

                ' Make a MainClass object.
                Dim main_object As Object = _
                    the_assembly.CreateInstance("MainNamespace.MainClass")

                ' Get the MainClass's type.
                Dim main_object_type As Type = main_object.GetType

                ' Get the MainClass's Main method.
                Dim run_method_info As MethodInfo
                run_method_info = main_object_type.GetMethod("Main")

                ' Execute the method and return the result.
                Return run_method_info.Invoke(main_object, Nothing)
            End If
        End Function
    End Class
```

This class provides a public `CompilerErrors` collection to let the main program know about any errors that occur when it compiles the code. The `References` collection lets the program list the libraries that the code needs to reference.

The class's `Run` method compiles and executes the script code. First, it makes a `CompilerParameters` object and adds any needed references to it. It sets the object's `CompilerOptions` and `GenerateInMemory` properties to indicate that it wants to compile a library in memory (as opposed to writing the compiled result into a DLL file).

The code then makes a `VBCodeProvider` object and uses its `CompileAssemblyFromSource` method to compile the script source code. If there are errors, the code throws a `CompilerException` error. `CompilerException` is a simple class that I derived from `ApplicationException` to let the main program know that the compilation failed.

If the script compiled, the program gets a reference to the compiled result's `Assembly` object. It then creates an instance of the class named `MainClass` in the namespace named `MainNamespace`. It uses the object's `GetType` method to get type information about `MainClass`, and then uses the type's `GetMethod` function to get information about the `Main` subroutine. Finally, the code uses the `Main` method's information to invoke the `Main` method for the `MainClass` object it created earlier.

Note that all of this assumes that the script contains a namespace named `MainNamespace` containing the class `MainClass`, which defines a `Main` routine that takes no parameters. The following code shows a simple script that this code can run:

```
Imports System.Windows.Forms ' Contains MessageBox.

Namespace MainNamespace
  Class MainClass
    Public Function Main() As Object
      MessageBox.Show("Hello")
      MessageBox.Show("Goodbye")
      Return("Done")
    End Function
  End Class
End Namespace
```

This script starts by importing the `System.Windows.Forms` namespace so that it can use the `MessageBox` class. The `Main` function displays messages that say Hello and Goodbye, and then returns the string `"Done"`.

The following code shows how example program `ExecuteClassCode` (which you can download at `www.vb-helper.com/one_on_one.htm`) uses the `CodeRunner` class to execute a script:

```
Private Sub btnRun_Click(ByVal sender As System.Object, _
 ByVal e As System.EventArgs) Handles btnRun.Click
    ' Set references.
    Dim code_runner As New CodeRunner
    code_runner.References.Add("system.dll")
    code_runner.References.Add("system.windows.forms.dll")

    ' Run the code.
    Try
        Dim result As Object = _
            code_runner.Run(txtCode.Text)
        If result IsNot Nothing Then
            If TypeOf result Is String Then
                MessageBox.Show(DirectCast(result, String))
            End If
        End If
    Catch ex As CompilerException
        Dim txt As String = "Compiler error:" & vbCrLf & vbCrLf
        For Each compiler_error As CompilerError In code_runner.CompilerErrors
            txt &= vbTab & "Line " & compiler_error.Line.ToString() & _
                ": " & compiler_error.ErrorText & vbCrLf
        Next compiler_error
        MessageBox.Show(txt, _
            "Compiler Error", _
            MessageBoxButtons.OK, _
            MessageBoxIcon.Exclamation)
    Catch ex As Exception
        Dim txt As String = "Runtime error:" & vbCrLf & vbCrLf
        txt &= ex.Message & vbCrLf & vbCrLf
        txt &= ex.InnerException.Message
        MessageBox.Show(txt, _
```

```
                "Runtime Error", _
                MessageBoxButtons.OK, _
                MessageBoxIcon.Exclamation)
        End Try
    End Sub
```

This code creates a new `CodeRunner` object and adds the `system.dll` and `system.windows.forms.dll` libraries to the object's references collection. It then calls the `CodeRunner`'s `Run` function, passing it the script in the text box `txtCode`. If the function returns a string (the sample script returns `"Done"`), the program displays it in a message box.

If the code doesn't compile, the `CodeRunner` throws a `CompilerException`. The main program loops through the `CodeRunner`'s `CompilerErrors` collection, adding each error's line number and message to a result string. When it is finished, the code displays the string. For example, if you omit the closing parenthesis in the `Return` statement, the code displays the message "`Line 9: ')' expected.`"

If the code compiles but generates a run-time error, the `CodeRunner`'s call to `Invoke` throws the fairly generic error "`Exception has been thrown by the target of an invocation.`" The exception object's `InnerException` property provides more detailed information about the error that actually occurred within the script code.

For example, suppose you add the following statements at the beginning of the `Main` function in the previous script:

```
    Dim i As Integer = 1
    i = i / 0
```

This causes a divide-by-zero error in the script, and the `ExecuteClassCode` example program displays the message shown in Figure 9-5.

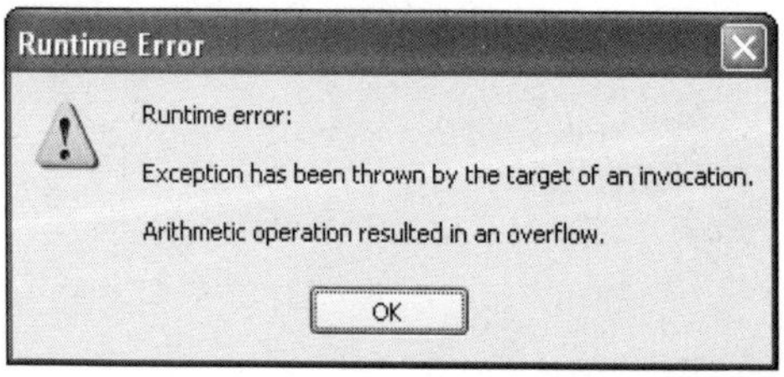

Figure 9-5: If the script throws an error at run-time, the exception's `InnerException` property provides useful details.

Exposing an Object Model

The example script in the previous section is fairly simplistic in that it only uses objects provided by Visual Studio and the .NET Framework. It's quite limited because it doesn't interact with any other parts of the application. Normally, a script would interact with the application's object model. For example, a macro or add-in you write to customize Visual Studio could modify code, print the current document, or close all open windows.

Example program ExecuteObjectModel uses a new version of the CodeRunner class that allows scripts to access its object model. This version of CodeRunner is similar to the one described in the previous section, except that it provides a public property named MainParameter. The main program should set this to an object that should be passed into the Main subroutine.

The CodeRunner's Run method works almost exactly as before. The only difference is in the call to the script's Main function. The new version makes an array of objects containing the values stored in the MainParameter variable, and then passes the array into the call to Invoke as shown in the following code:

```
' Execute the method and return the result.
Dim params() As Object = Nothing
If MainParameter IsNot Nothing Then
    params = New Object() {MainParameter}
End If
Return run_method_info.Invoke(main_object, params)
```

This program defines two classes, Picture and Segment, that let it draw simple pictures. The Picture class holds a collection of Segment objects. The Segment class stores the coordinates of a line segment's end points.

The main ExecuteObjectModel program defines a variable m_Picture from the Picture class. This object stores and draws the program's picture.

When you execute a script, the program sets the CodeRunner's MainParameter property to m_Picture so the script's Main function can manipulate this object.

The following script adds new segments to the Picture object. The Main function calls the object's Clear method to remove any existing Segments. It then uses a series of calculations to generate a series of points, and uses the object's AddSegment method to make new Segments connecting them. Notice that the script defines two private functions for its own use.

```
Imports System
Imports System.Math
Imports System.Windows.Forms

Namespace MainNamespace
  Class MainClass
    Public Function Main(ByVal the_picture As Object) As Object
        Const cx As Integer = 125
        Const cy As Integer = 125
        Dim t As Single = 0
        Dim dt As Single = 0.1
        Dim x1, y1, x2, y2 As Integer

        the_picture.Clear()
        x2 = cx + X(t)
        y2 = cy + Y(t)
        t += dt
        Do While t < 14 * PI
            x1 = x2
            y1 = y2
            x2 = cx + X(t)
```

```
            y2 = cy + Y(t)
            the_picture.AddSegment(x1, y1, x2, y2)
            t += dt
        Loop
        x1 = cx + X(0)
        y1 = cy + Y(0)
        the_picture.AddSegment(x1, y1, x2, y2)

        Return the_picture.Segments.Count
    End Function

    Private Function X(ByVal t As Single) As Integer
        Return CInt((2000 * (27 * Cos(t) + 15 * Cos(t * 20 / 7)) / 42) / 20)
    End Function

    Private Function Y(ByVal t As Single) As Integer
        Return CInt((2000 * (27 * Sin(t) + 15 * Sin(t * 20 / 7)) / 42) / 20)
    End Function
  End Class
End Namespace
```

In this example, the main program displays the number of segments returned by the `Main` function in the form's title bar. Figure 9-6 shows the program after it has executed the script.

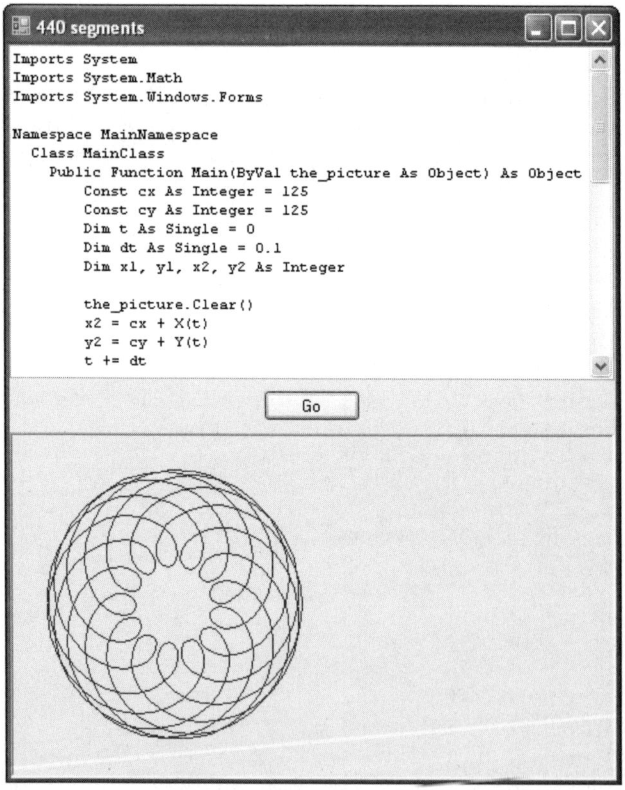

Figure 9-6: Program `ExecuteObjectModel` scripts can draw with a `Picture` object.

Even this example is fairly straightforward, passing a single relatively simple object to the `Main` function. You could pass an array of objects to the function. You may find it simpler, however, to have a single top-level object provide references to any other objects that the script may need.

You could call this top-level class something similar to `Application`. *I suggest that you pick a different name, perhaps* `TopObject`, *or name it after the application, so you don't confuse it with the* `Application` *object provided by Visual Basic, the Microsoft Office applications, and other programs.*

Simplifying Scripting

The previous examples show how an application can execute Visual Basic script code. Unfortunately, over the years, Visual Basic has grown less and less basic. Although many users have at least some knowledge of Visual Basic for Applications (VBA), few know more than a smattering of Visual Basic .NET. Many will be immediately lost when they see the `Imports`, `Namespace`, and `Class` statements that the script needs.

You can simplify scripting somewhat by building some of the necessary code for the user. Example program `ExecuteSimplerCode` uses the following `SimplerCodeRunner` class to execute code. This class adds the `Imports` statement and wraps the script in a `Namespace`, `Class`, and `Main` function.

```
Imports System.CodeDom.Compiler
Imports System.Text
Imports System.Reflection

Public Class SimplerCodeRunner
    ' Errors generated by the last run.
    Public CompilerErrors As New CompilerErrorCollection

    ' Array of references needed by the code.
    Public References As New Collection

    ' Object to be passed to the Main function.
    Public MainParameter As Object

    Public Function Run(ByVal vb_code As String) As Object
        ' Prepare the compiler parameters.
        ' Add any needed references.
        Dim compiler_params As CompilerParameters = New CompilerParameters
        For Each reference As String In References
            compiler_params.ReferencedAssemblies.Add(reference)
        Next reference

        ' Generate a library in memory.
        compiler_params.CompilerOptions = "/t:library"
        compiler_params.GenerateInMemory = True

        ' Indent the entered code to make it easier to read.
        vb_code = "        " & vb_code.Replace(vbCrLf, vbCrLf & "        ").Trim()

        ' Insert the code inside a class and function.
        vb_code = _
            "Imports System" & vbCrLf & _
            "Imports System.Math" & vbCrLf & _
```

```
            "Imports System.Windows.Forms" & vbCrLf & vbCrLf & _
            "Namespace MainNamespace" & vbCrLf & _
            "  Class MainClass" & vbCrLf & _
            "    Public Function Main(ByVal the_picture As Object) As Object" & _
              vbCrLf & _
            vb_code & vbCrLf & _
            "    End Function" & vbCrLf & _
            "  End Class" & vbCrLf & _
            "End Namespace"

        ' Compile the code.
        Debug.WriteLine(vb_code)
        Dim code_provider As VBCodeProvider = New VBCodeProvider
        Dim compiler_results As CompilerResults = _
            code_provider.CompileAssemblyFromSource(compiler_params, vb_code)
        code_provider.Dispose()

        ' Check for errors.
        CompilerErrors = compiler_results.Errors
        If compiler_results.Errors.Count > 0 Then
            ' There were errors.
            Throw New CompilerException("Compile Errors")
        Else
            ' There were no errors. Try to execute the code.
            ' Get the assembly.
            Dim the_assembly As System.Reflection.Assembly = _
                compiler_results.CompiledAssembly

            ' Make a MainClass object.
            Dim main_object As Object = _
                the_assembly.CreateInstance("MainNamespace.MainClass")

            ' Get the MainClass's type.
            Dim main_object_type As Type = main_object.GetType

            ' Get the MainClass's Main method.
            Dim run_method_info As MethodInfo
            run_method_info = main_object_type.GetMethod("Main")

            ' Execute the method and return the result.
            Dim params() As Object = Nothing
            If MainParameter IsNot Nothing Then
                params = New Object() {MainParameter}
            End If
            Return run_method_info.Invoke(main_object, params)
        End If
    End Function
End Class
```

The following code shows a script that draws the picture shown in Figure 9-6. This version is somewhat simpler than the previous one, although it's still fairly complicated. The picture is complex, so the code that generates it is complex. At least more of the complexity is because of the nature of the script, rather than the Visual Basic syntax.

```
Const cx As Integer = 125
Const cy As Integer = 125
Dim t As Single = 0
Dim dt As Single = 0.1
Dim x1, y1, x2, y2, xt, yt As Integer

the_picture.Clear()
xt = CInt((2000 * (27 * Cos(t) + 15 * Cos(t * 20 / 7)) / 42) / 20)
yt = CInt((2000 * (27 * Sin(t) + 15 * Sin(t * 20 / 7)) / 42) / 20)
x2 = cx + xt
y2 = cy + yt
t += dt
Do While t < 14 * PI
    x1 = x2
    y1 = y2
    xt = CInt((2000 * (27 * Cos(t) + 15 * Cos(t * 20 / 7)) / 42) / 20)
    yt = CInt((2000 * (27 * Sin(t) + 15 * Sin(t * 20 / 7)) / 42) / 20)
    x2 = cx + xt
    y2 = cy + yt
    the_picture.AddSegment(x1, y1, x2, y2)
    t += dt
Loop
t = 0
xt = CInt((2000 * (27 * Cos(t) + 15 * Cos(t * 20 / 7)) / 42) / 20)
yt = CInt((2000 * (27 * Sin(t) + 15 * Sin(t * 20 / 7)) / 42) / 20)
x1 = cx + xt
y1 = cy + yt
the_picture.AddSegment(x1, y1, x2, y2)

Return the_picture.Segments.Count
```

Even with this simplification, you may decide that scripting is too difficult for the users. In that case, you may need to write scripts for them and let the users load and run. (You can download this example at `www.vb-helper.com/one_on_one.htm`.)

Evaluating Expressions

Many applications need to evaluate arithmetic expressions. Sometimes these are as simple as multiplying cost times quantity times tax rate to get total cost. Other times, these equations can be quite complex. I've seen applications evaluate expressions to perform least-square curve fitting, three-dimensional surface graphing, and cost calculations involving dozens of parameters.

Over the years, I've written several expression evaluators in Visual Basic and other languages. They make an interesting challenge, but they're a lot of work. It's much easier to write code that generates a script that evaluates the function for you.

The `EvaluateExpression` example program (available for download at `www.vb-helper.com/one_on_one.htm`) uses this technique to evaluate expressions involving five variables named `A`, `B`, `C`, `D`, and `E`. Initially the expression it evaluates is as follows:

```
3*(A-3)^2+(1.2+Cos(B/A))^1.4+2*B^3*Sin(D/E)-4*Cos(D+E)
```

The following code shows the script the program builds for this expression:

```
Imports System
Imports System.Math
Imports System.Windows.Forms
Namespace MainNamespace
  Class MainClass
    Public Function Main(ByVal A as Double, ByVal B as Double, ByVal C as Double, _
     ByVal D as Double, ByVal E as Double) As Object
       Return 3*(A-3)^2+(1.2+Cos(B/A))^1.4+2*B^3*Sin(D/E)-4*Cos(D+E)
    End Function
  End Class
End Namespace
```

If you need to execute this expression once, you can use the methods described in the previous sections. However, some programs need to execute the same expression many times, but with different parameter values. In that case, you can save a lot of time by compiling the code only once, and then passing it different parameter values.

Program `EvaluateExpression` executes the script code for a number of trials that you can specify. The following code shows the code that program `EvaluateExpression` uses to execute the script for a large number of trials:

```
' Make the parameters array.
Dim params(0 To 4) As Object

' Get the variable values.
Dim A As Double = Double.Parse(txtValue1.Text)
Dim B As Double = Double.Parse(txtValue2.Text)
Dim C As Double = Double.Parse(txtValue3.Text)
Dim D As Double = Double.Parse(txtValue4.Text)

' Evaluate the expression.
Dim num_trials As Long = Long.Parse(txtNewTrials.Text)
Dim result As Double
Try
    For i As Double = 1 To num_trials
        params(0) = A
        params(1) = B
        params(2) = C
        params(3) = D
        params(4) = i
        result = CDbl(run_method_info.Invoke(main_object, params))
    Next i
Catch ex As Exception
    MessageBox.Show(ex.Message)
End Try
```

This code allocates a parameter array and reads some parameter values from text boxes. It then reads the number of trials it performs and enters a loop. During each loop, the code saves the parameter values into the `params` array and invokes the `Main` function, passing it the array.

Not recompiling the script each time through the loop lets the code run quite quickly. My 2.0 GHz Athlon 64 computer can evaluate the expression 500,000 times in about 4 seconds, or about 125,000 times per second.

With a lot of hard work, you can write an expression evaluator that runs a little faster than invoking a script but it's probably not worth the extra effort. (If you're interested in seeing expression evaluator code, email me at `RodStephens@vb-helper.com` and I'll send some to you.)

Summary

Scripting provides a method for adding new features to your application at run-time. By using SQL script, you can let users perform ad hoc queries. If your users are not experienced with SQL, you can build tools that let them compose queries more easily.

More-powerful SQL scripts can perform actions such as creating tables, making indexes, and modifying data. These more-powerful SQL scripts are generally too dangerous to give to any but the most experienced users, but they can be very handy for developers.

By using the objects in the `System.CodeDom` and `System.Reflection` namespaces, your application can execute Visual Basic scripts at run-time. Though most users may have trouble writing these scripts from scratch, you may be able to supply them with predefined scripts that they can run to perform new tasks that you didn't originally build into the application.

Scripts encapsulate new features in the sense that the users can execute them without needing to know how they work. Another way to encapsulate complex functionality at design time rather than at run-time is to use custom controls. While scripts deliver new features to users, custom controls package functionality for other developers. Chapter 10, "Custom Controls and Components," explains how to build custom controls that let developers provide complex functionality without needing to know all of the details about how the controls work internally.

10

Custom Controls and Components

Perhaps the most important benefit of object-oriented programming is encapsulation. *Encapsulation*, or information hiding, protects the internal details of a class from prying eyes. It insulates the rest of the program from changes to the class's internals.

Probably the biggest benefit of all is that encapsulation lets developers working with a class ignore the details of the class. You can use an object without needing to keep track of how the class works so that you can focus on other things. Imagine trying to keep all of the details of a 100,000-line program in your head at the same time! You need to be able to ignore as much of the program as possible while you focus on the part you are writing.

Controls and components provide excellent encapsulation. They can encapsulate complicated behavior and allow developers to interact with them only through properties, methods, and events.

If the controls are compiled rather than included within the main program, then the encapsulation is fairly tight. It's not as easy for developers to peek inside a compiled control or component and take advantage of its internals, possibly tying themselves to a particular implementation of the control.

Controls and components are also extremely common items in Visual Basic development. Even a relative novice knows how to use a control's properties, methods, and events.

Controls and components provide such tight encapsulation, they work particularly well when your project involves developers at different locations. One developer can build a control and other developers can use it. The separation of the control's code and the main program's code helps keep the developers' work decoupled, and creates a design-by-contract atmosphere almost all by itself. I've used this approach on a couple of projects very successfully.

Of course, controls and components are just special kinds of libraries, so you can gain similar advantages by using compiled libraries, but the ability to assign properties at design time in the Properties window seems to foster the feeling of separation.

This chapter explains how to build custom controls and components. It describes three main approaches: deriving controls and components from existing classes, building controls based on the `UserControl` class, and building controls and components from scratch.

Building Derived Controls

If an existing control does almost what you need, it would be a waste of time for you to build the control from scratch. Instead, you can derive a control from the existing one, and then modify its behavior to suit your needs.

To derive a control or component from an existing class, you simply use the `Imports` statement. Then you can override and shadow existing features of the parent class, and add new features of your own.

For example, suppose you want to build a better `ListBox` control. Visual Basic's `ListBox` control provides the ability to draw items with different images, fonts, colors, and other graphical effects, but it doesn't make the process easy. The example described here lets you easily assign images, colors, and fonts to list items at design time.

To build the controls, start by creating a new Windows Controls Library project. Remove the `UserControl` created by default and add a new class. Name the class `StyledListBox` and make it inherit from the `ListBox` class. Now, add code to this class to allow it to store and display list items.

You could add new properties to the control to let the user define a series of images, fonts, and colors. Then the control would need to match up the entries in those lists with the control's items to draw them. Unfortunately, this means you must match up several different lists of properties. That's rather cumbersome, and makes it hard for the developer to keep the properties synchronized. For example, if you remove an entry from the beginning of the item list, you also need to remove corresponding items from the color, font, and image lists.

Instead of this approach, I decided to make a new class `StyledListBoxItem` to store the information about a list box entry. The following code shows how the class stores an entry's color, text, font, and image values:

```
<Serializable()> _
Public Class StyledListBoxItem
    ' The Color property.
    Private m_Color As Color
    Public Property Color() As Color
        Get
            Return m_Color
        End Get
        Set(ByVal value As Color)
            m_Color = value
        End Set
    End Property

    ' The Text property.
```

```
    Private m_Text As String
    Public Property Text() As String
        Get
            Return m_Text
        End Get
        Set(ByVal value As String)
            m_Text = value
        End Set
    End Property

    ' The Font property.
    Private m_Font As Font
    Public Property Font() As Font
        Get
            Return m_Font
        End Get
        Set(ByVal value As Font)
            m_Font = value
        End Set
    End Property

    ' The Image property.
    Private m_Image As Image
    Public Property Image() As Image
        Get
            Return m_Image
        End Get
        Set(ByVal value As Image)
            m_Image = value
        End Set
    End Property

    ' Display the object's text.
    Public Overrides Function ToString() As String
        Return Me.Text
    End Function
End Class
```

Note that this class is serializable. Visual Basic needs the class to be serializable so that it can save and restore values set at design time.

The following code shows the `StyledListBox` class:

```
Public Class StyledListBox
    Inherits ListBox

    ' Create a new strongly typed Items property so
    ' the Properties Window can provide an editor for it.
    ' Delegate it to the inherited Items property.
    Public Shadows Property Items() As StyledListBoxItem()
        Get
            Dim item_list(0 To MyBase.Items.Count - 1) As StyledListBoxItem
            For i As Integer = 0 To MyBase.Items.Count - 1
                item_list(i) = DirectCast(MyBase.Items(i), StyledListBoxItem)
            Next i
```

```
            Return item_list
        End Get
        Set(ByVal value() As StyledListBoxItem)
            MyBase.Items.Clear()
            For Each styled_item As StyledListBoxItem In value
                MyBase.Items.Add(styled_item)
            Next styled_item
        End Set
    End Property

    ' Specify OwnerDraw mode.
    Public Sub New()
        MyBase.New()
        MyBase.DrawMode = Windows.Forms.DrawMode.OwnerDrawVariable
    End Sub

    ' Set the size for an item.
    Private Const ITEM_MARGIN As Integer = 2

    Private Sub StyledListBox_MeasureItem(ByVal sender As Object, _
     ByVal e As System.Windows.Forms.MeasureItemEventArgs) Handles Me.MeasureItem
        If e.Index < 0 Or e.Index >= MyBase.Items.Count Then Exit Sub

        ' Convert the item into a StyledListBoxItem.
        Dim the_item As StyledListBoxItem = _
            DirectCast(MyBase.Items(e.Index), StyledListBoxItem)
        ' Debug.WriteLine("Measure: " & the_item.Text)

        ' See how much room it will need.
        Dim hgt As Integer = 0
        Dim wid As Integer = 0

        ' Allow room for the image if present.
        If the_item.Image IsNot Nothing Then
            wid = the_item.Image.Width + 2 * ITEM_MARGIN
            hgt = the_item.Image.Height + 2 * ITEM_MARGIN
        End If

        ' Measure the text.
        If (the_item.Text IsNot Nothing) AndAlso (the_item.Text.Length > 0) Then
            Dim the_font As Font = the_item.Font
            If the_font Is Nothing Then the_font = Me.Parent.Font
            Dim item_size As SizeF = _
                e.Graphics.MeasureString(the_item.Text, the_font)

            Dim txt_hgt As Integer = CInt(item_size.Height + 2 * ITEM_MARGIN)
            If txt_hgt > hgt Then hgt = txt_hgt

            wid += CInt(item_size.Width + 2 * ITEM_MARGIN)
        End If

        e.ItemWidth = wid
        e.ItemHeight = hgt
    End Sub

    ' Draw the item.
```

```
    Private Sub StyledListBox_DrawItem(ByVal sender As Object, _
     ByVal e As System.Windows.Forms.DrawItemEventArgs) Handles Me.DrawItem
        If e.Index < 0 Or e.Index >= MyBase.Items.Count Then Exit Sub

        ' Convert the item into a StyledListBoxItem.
        Dim the_item As StyledListBoxItem = _
            DirectCast(MyBase.Items(e.Index), StyledListBoxItem)
        ' Debug.WriteLine("Draw: " & the_item.Text)

        ' Clear the item's drawing area.
        e.DrawBackground()
        If Me.SelectedIndex = e.Index Then e.DrawFocusRectangle()

        ' Draw the image if present.
        Dim x As Integer = ITEM_MARGIN
        If the_item.Image IsNot Nothing Then
            Dim y As Integer = _
                e.Bounds.Top + (e.Bounds.Height - the_item.Image.Height) \ 2

            e.Graphics.DrawImage(the_item.Image, x, y)
            x = the_item.Image.Width + 2 * ITEM_MARGIN
        End If

        ' Draw the text if present.
        If (the_item.Text IsNot Nothing) AndAlso (the_item.Text.Length > 0) Then
            Dim the_font As Font = the_item.Font
            If the_font Is Nothing Then the_font = Me.Parent.Font
            Dim item_size As SizeF = _
                e.Graphics.MeasureString(the_item.Text, the_font)

            Dim y As Integer = _
                e.Bounds.Top + CInt((e.Bounds.Height - item_size.Height) / 2)

            Using the_brush As New SolidBrush(the_item.Color)
                e.Graphics.DrawString(the_item.Text, the_font, the_brush, x, y)
            End Using
        End If
    End Sub

End Class
```

The control starts by inheriting from the `ListBox` class.

It then defines a new `Items` property that shadows the one provided by `ListBox`. The new version is an array of `StyledListboxItem` objects. Exposing this array lets the Properties window and other designers manage the items as `StyledListboxItem` objects.

Some developers might add a new property to the control instead of shadowing the existing one. That could lead to confusion when other developers using the control tried to figure out which property to use. The control is intended to display a single list of items, so it should have a single `Items` *property. Shadowing the original property lets the control manage its list more directly while avoiding possible confusion.*

This also lets the control delegate to the existing `Items` *property so it saves some coding.*

Figure 10-1 shows the Properties window displaying a `StyledListBox` control's `Items` property. The entry is expanded to show the items in the array.

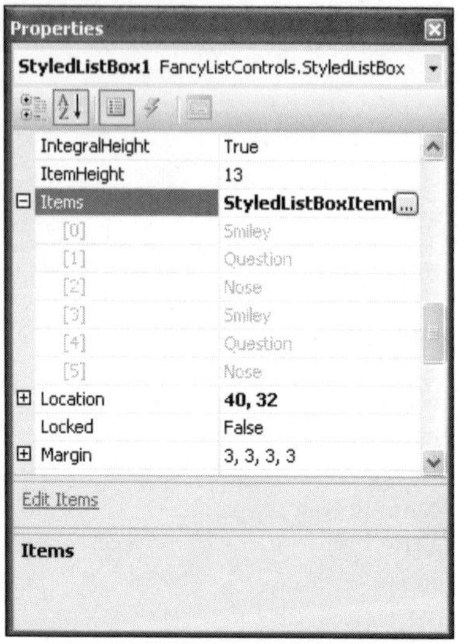

Figure 10-1: The Properties window lists the objects in the `Items` property.

The values displayed in the array are those returned by the `StyledListBoxItem` class's `ToString` method. If you don't provide an overridden version of this function, the Properties window uses the object's default `ToString` method, which makes every item display the value "`FancyListControls.StyledListBoxItem`."

If you click on the ellipsis to the right of the `Items` property, Visual Studio displays the collection editor shown in Figure 10-2. Click the Add button to make a new `StyledListBoxItem`. Then use the property grid on the right to set the item's properties. Visual Studio automatically provides this editor because the `Items` property is an array of serializable objects.

The `Items` property procedures delegate their responsibilities to the `ListBox` class's `Items` property. The actual `StyledListboxItem` objects are stored in the `ListBox` class's `Items` property. These property procedures simply move the items in an out of an array of `StyledListboxItem`.

The control's constructor invokes its parent class's constructor. It then sets the control's `DrawMode` property to `OwnerDrawVariable`. This tells the control that the program will draw its items and that they will not all be the same size.

When the control needs to display an item, it raises a `MeasureItem` event. The `StyledListBox_MeasureItem` event handler catches this event and sets the size needed to draw the item currently being considered.

The event handler retrieves the item of interest and converts it from a generic `Object` into a `StyledListBoxItem`. It then calculates the space needed by the item. This program allows room for the item's image and text, plus a 2-pixel margin around each. If the developer has not assigned a font to the item, the code uses the list box's parent's font.

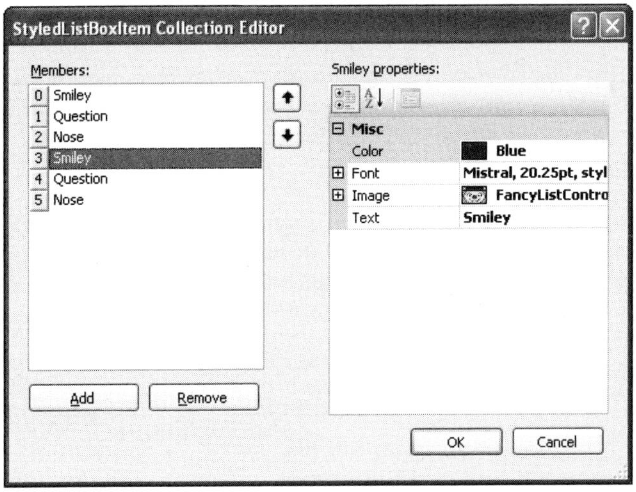

Figure 10-2: Visual Studio automatically provides this collection editor for the `Items` property.

When the control needs to draw an item, it raises a `DrawItem` event. The `StyledListBox_DrawItem` event handler follows steps similar to those taken by `StyledListBox_MeasureItem`, except that it draws the item rather than just measuring it.

The `e` parameter's `DrawBackground` method draws the item's background in a color that depends on whether the item is currently selected. If the item is selected, the event handler calls the `e` parameter's `DrawFocusRectangle` to draw a focus rectangle around the item.

Next, the event handler draws the item. The `e` parameter's `Bounds` property gives the area on which this item should be drawn. The code draws the item's image and text centered vertically within the bounds.

Figure 10-3 shows the `StyledListBox` control in action. The first `Question` and second `Smiley` items are selected, so they display a darker background. The `DrawItem` event handler provides the appropriate background when it calls the `DrawBackground` method. (You can download this example at `www.vb-helper.com/one_on_one.htm`.)

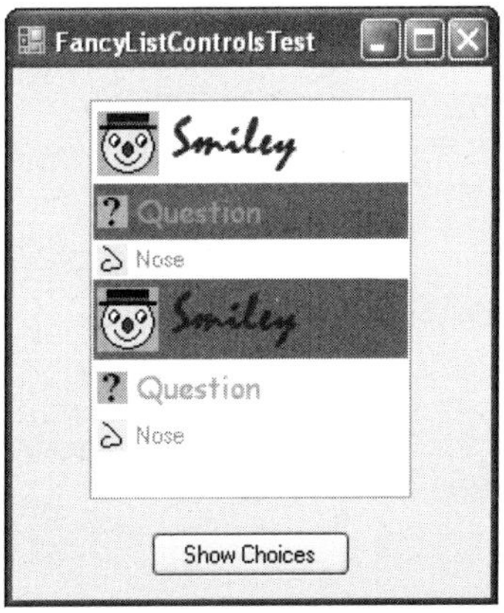

Figure 10-3: The `StyledListBox` control displays items with images, different fonts, and different colors.

Setting Toolbox Bitmaps

By default, icons that you make display a little gear in the control toolbox. It's a cute icon, but it wouldn't be very informative if you have dozens of controls that all display the same icon, particularly if you don't use the toolbox's list view so the icons and tooltips are the only tools you have for finding the controls you want.

Unfortunately, setting a control's toolbox bitmap is rather tricky. To set the bitmap, you add a `ToolboxBitmap` attribute to the control's class. This attribute has a couple of different constructors. The simplest gives the complete path to the control's 16_16–pixel bitmap file. The following code shows this type of attribute for the `StyledListBox` control:

```
<ToolboxBitmap("C:\StyledListBox\Resources\tbxStyledListBox.bmp")> _
Public Class StyledListBox
...
```

This version of the `ToolboxBitmap` attribute is simple and reliable. Unfortunately, it ties the code to a specific location. If you later move the toolbox bitmap, the statement no longer works.

To avoid this problem, you can just leave the control and its files in the location where you initially build them. Another solution is to place all of your toolbox bitmaps in a directory somewhere and never move them. These solutions work, but restrict what you can do with the control's project. For example, if you email the project to someone else, they must modify the attribute's constructor so it can find the bitmap on the new computer.

Another constructor provided by the `ToolboxBitmap` attribute takes as parameters the type of a class contained in an assembly, and then the name of a bitmap resource in that assembly. The following code shows this version of the attribute for the `StyledListBox` control:

```
<ToolboxBitmap(GetType(StyledListBox), "tbxStyledListBox")> _
Public Class StyledListBox
...
```

This code tells Visual Basic to look in the assembly containing the `StyledListBox` class for the resource named `tbxStyledListBox`.

In theory, this is a nice solution that lets the attribute find the bitmap resource even if you move the project. In practice, getting this to work can be tricky.

First, add a 16_16–pixel bitmap resource to the project and draw the image you want to display in the toolbox. Next, select the bitmap file in the Solution Explorer. In the Properties window, set the bitmap's `Build Action` property to `Embedded Resource`.

If all goes well, the control will get the correct toolbox bitmap. Unfortunately, if there's any kind of problem (for example, if Visual Basic cannot find the file or the class), you won't see an error message and the control gets the default gear icon.

If you change the control's icon and still see the wrong icon in the toolbox, click the control in the toolbox, press the Delete key, and confirm that you want to remove the control from the toolbox. Next, right-click the toolbox and select Choose Items. Click the Browse button and find the compiled control's `DLL` or EXE file. When you select the file and click Open, the dialog adds the controls contained in that file to its list and selects them. Click the control's entry to preview its toolbox bitmap. If you see the gear bitmap (which you may be getting sick of by this point), click Cancel so you don't add the control to the toolbox (so you don't have to remove it again) and try again.

Testing Controls

Eventually, you may want to compile your control into a DLL or EXE and distribute it to others. They can right-click in the control toolbox, select Choose Items, and select the compiled control library to use the control.

While you're building the control, however, you need a way to test it in the debugger. The easiest way to do that is to load the control's project, open the File menu, select the Add item, and pick New Project. Add a new Windows Application project to the solution.

In the Project Explorer, right-click the new project and select "Set as StartUp Project" so that Visual Studio will run this new project instead of the control project when you execute the solution.

Now you can add the control to the new project and test it. You can set breakpoints in the control's code and debug it.

> *Debugging controls can be fairly tricky, particularly when you're trying to debug drawing code. If you set a breakpoint inside a* `Paint` *event handler, the control immediately receives another* `Paint` *event when you resume execution. This is a problem with other kinds of projects, too, but is particularly common when you are building controls.*
>
> *Avoid interrupting* `Paint` *event handlers with breakpoints. Use* `Debug.WriteLine` *statements or write debugging information into a text file instead.*

If you build a `UserControl` (described shortly), you can also test the control in the Test Container. If you execute the project, the Test Container shown in Figure 10-4 appears.

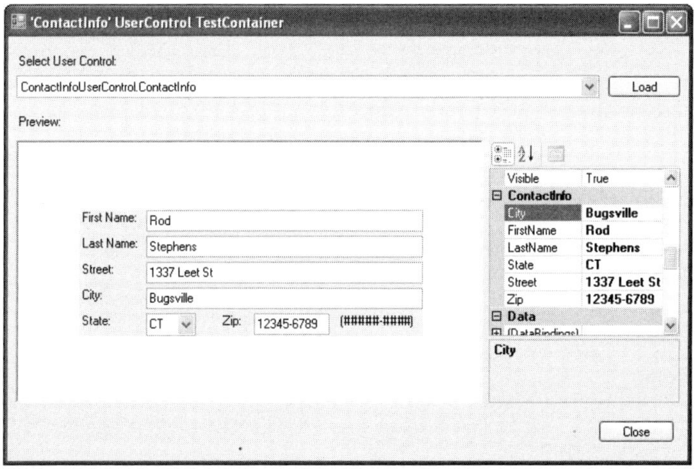

Figure 10-4: The `TestContainer` lets you test a `UserControl`.

While you are running in the Test Container, you can interact with the control just as you could if it were running in an application. You can also set properties in the property grid on the right, and the control immediately updates itself. The reverse is not true, however. If you manipulate the control and its properties change, the property grid on the right does not automatically display the new values. If you click a property, the grid refreshes its display for that property and shows the new value.

If the control project contains more than one control, you can select the control that you want to test from the drop-down list at the top.

To debug the control, you can set breakpoints and step through the code as you interact with it in the Test Container.

Building UserControls

`UserControl` is a class that can act as a container for new controls. It acts as a container where you can place other *constituent* controls to build a self-contained package. Figure 10-4 shows the Test Container displaying a `UserControl` that contains seven labels (six prompts and a completion aid giving the ZIP code format), five text boxes, and a combo box.

`UserControl` also provides support for the Test Container, so you can use the Test Container to test your control. The Test Container acts pretty much as any other form that contains an instance of the `UserControl` and provides a property grid to manipulate the `UserControl`'s properties.

Building controls by using a `UserControl` is easy. If you start a new Windows Control Library project, Visual Studio adds a `UserControl` to the project by default. You can then simply drop controls onto the `UserControl`, set their properties, give them event handlers, and do everything else you normally do to controls on a form.

The `UserControl` represents the group of controls that you place on it as a single entity. It does not provide direct access to those controls, so you need to add whatever properties, methods, and events you think appropriate to provide access to the controls.

For example, the `ContactInfo` `UserControl` shown in Figure 10-4 provides property procedures to get and set the control's `FirstName`, `LastName`, `Street`, `City`, `State`, and `Zip` values. The `UserControl` delegates these properties to its constituent controls. The following code shows how it delegates its `FirstName` property to the `txtFirstName` control. It handles its other properties similarly.

```
<Category("ContactInfo")> _
Public Property FirstName() As String
    Get
        Return txtFirstName.Text
    End Get
    Set(ByVal value As String)
        txtFirstName.Text = value
    End Set
End Property
```

This `UserControl` also provides a public `DataChanged` event that it raises when any of the values displayed by its controls changes. The following code shows how the `ConstituentDataChanged` subroutine catches events for all of the controls and raises the `UserControl`'s `DataChanged` event:

```
Public Event DataChanged()

' If any data changes, raise the DataChanged event.
Private Sub ConstituentDataChanged(ByVal sender As System.Object, _
 ByVal e As System.EventArgs) Handles txtFirstName.TextChanged, _
 txtLastName.TextChanged, txtStreet.TextChanged, txtCity.TextChanged, ...
    RaiseEvent DataChanged()
End Sub
```

Finally, the `UserControl` provides a `ToString` function to return a textual version of all of the control's properties:

```
' Return a textual representation of the data.
Public Overrides Function ToString() As String
    Return txtFirstName.Text & " " & txtLastName.Text & ", " & txtStreet.Text & ",
" & txtCity.Text & "  " & cboState.Text & "  " & txtZip.Text
End Function
```

Figure 10-5 shows the `RGBColorSelector UserControl` running in the Test Container.

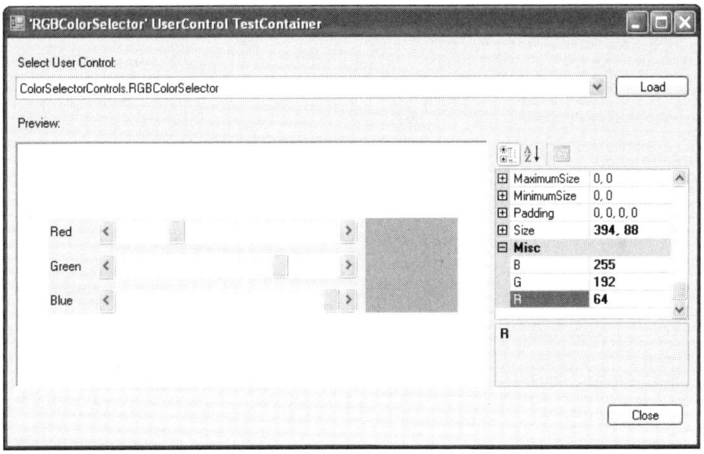

Figure 10-5: The `RGBColorSelector UserControl` lets the user set a color's red, green, and blue components.

This `UserControl` delegates its `R`, `G`, and `B` property values to its three horizontal scroll bars. The following code shows how the control works:

```
Public Class RGBColorSelector
    Public Event ColorChanged()

    Private Sub hbarColor_Scroll(ByVal sender As System.Object, _
```

```
        ByVal e As System.Windows.Forms.ScrollEventArgs) Handles _
        hbarRed.Scroll, hbarGreen.Scroll, hbarBlue.Scroll
            ShowSample()
        End Sub
        Private Sub hbarColor_ValueChanged(ByVal sender As Object, _
        ByVal e As System.EventArgs) Handles hbarRed.ValueChanged, _
        hbarGreen.ValueChanged, hbarBlue.ValueChanged
            ShowSample()
        End Sub

        Private Sub ShowSample()
            picSample.BackColor = Color.FromArgb(255, hbarRed.Value, _
                hbarGreen.Value, hbarBlue.Value)
            RaiseEvent ColorChanged()
        End Sub

        Public Property R() As Byte
            Get
                Return CByte(hbarRed.Value)
            End Get
            Set(ByVal value As Byte)
                hbarRed.Value = value
            End Set
        End Property
        Public Property G() As Byte
            Get
                Return CByte(hbarGreen.Value)
            End Get
            Set(ByVal value As Byte)
                hbarGreen.Value = value
            End Set
        End Property
        Public Property B() As Byte
            Get
                Return CByte(hbarBlue.Value)
            End Get
            Set(ByVal value As Byte)
                hbarBlue.Value = value
            End Set
        End Property
    End Class
```

The `hbarColor_Scroll` and `hbarColor_ValueChanged` event handlers catch `Scroll` and `ValueChanged` events for all three scroll bars. Those routines just call subroutine `ShowSample`.

Subroutine `ShowSample` displays the currently selected color in the sample picture box named `picSample` and then raises the control's `ColorChanged` event.

The rest of the code shows how the control delegates its `R`, `G`, and `B` properties to its scroll bars. (You can download this example at `www.vb-helper.com/one_on_one.htm`.)

Controls such as the `RGBColorSelector` provide a somewhat useful selection mechanism that you might want to add to many different applications. It might make sense to compile that project into a control library and use it in several applications.

The `ContactInfo` control, however, has a much more specific use, so it might not make sense to use it in many applications. Sometimes you might build a similar control with other information such as account numbers and customer IDs that is so specific that it would be useless in other applications. In that case, it would make sense to build the `UserControl` into the application that needs it, rather than making a separate control library.

To do that, create the main Windows Application project. Then open the Project menu and select Add User Control. Now the control is part of the main project and not in its own library.

This may seem like an awkward way to provide the controls contained in the `ContactInfo UserControl`. After all, you could simply add those labels and text boxes directly to the program's forms. Using a control lets you provide consistency in different parts of the application, however. The control can also include validation and error-handling code that you won't need to repeat if you need to gather the same information on several forms. Finally, the control encapsulates these controls so developers working on a particular form don't need to deal with any details hidden within the control.

I have seen applications where developers built `UserControls` that were used a single time. For example, imagine a form with several tabs that display different kinds of information about a customer. One might display basic contact information, another might show orders pending, and a third might show an order history. You could build a `UserControl` that holds all of the controls for each of these tabs, and then place a single instance of the controls on the pages of a `TabControl`.

It doesn't seem like there's much benefit to building these `UserControls` that are used only once. They contain all of the code you would need to add to the form if you had placed the constituent controls directly inside the `TabControl`'s pages. In fact, they contain extra code because you need to provide property procedures to let the program get values in and out of the controls.

However, all of this code is localized to the controls and not in the form that uses them, so that form's code is much simpler. It may be better to write a few extra lines of code in exchange for simplifying what would otherwise be a much more complex form. You may even be able to have separate developers work on the controls and the form that uses them.

Building Controls from Scratch

Derived controls and `UserControls` make building certain kinds of controls fairly easy.

If you want to make a control that does almost what an existing control does, you can derive your control from the existing control. If you need a control composed out of other controls, the `UserControl` makes building the control easy.

Both of these methods come with some extra overhead, however. When you derive a control from an existing control, you carry along all of the baggage of the existing control. When you build a `UserControl`, you not only carry the load of the features provided by the `UserControl` itself, but you also bring along everything included by all of the controls that you place on the `UserControl`. If you don't need all of these extras, you may be better off building your control from scratch.

To make a control from scratch, start a new Windows Control Library project and delete the initial `UserControl` that Visual Studio creates. Next, use the Project menu's Add New Item command to add a new Custom Control to the project. This makes Visual Studio create a new class that inherits from `System.Windows.Forms.Control`. If you look at the designer-generated code, you can see the class's `Inherits` statement.

The following shows the code initially created for you to modify. If the control is to display anything visibly, you need to implement the `Paint` event handler, so Visual Studio makes one for you.

```
Public Class CustomControl1

    Protected Overrides Sub OnPaint( _
     ByVal pe As System.Windows.Forms.PaintEventArgs)
        MyBase.OnPaint(pe)

        'Add your custom paint code here
    End Sub

End Class
```

For an example, look at Figure 10-6. The `MapViewFinder` control on the upper right lets the user drag a rectangular "thumb" around on a small image of a map. The program displays a full-scale version of the area selected by the thumb on the picture box on the left. (You can download this example at `www.vb-helper.com/one_on_one.htm`.)

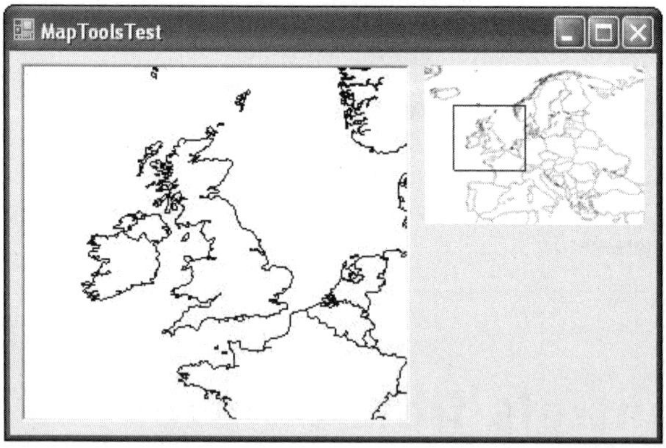

Figure 10-6: The `MapViewFinder` control on the right lets the user select an area in a larger map to view.

Building a view finder such as this one would involve some fairly confusing code, so it's probably worth moving out of the main program and into a control just for the encapsulation value. It might also be useful in other applications, so making it a control will make the code more easily reusable.

Of course, this is a chapter about writing controls, so it's a foregone conclusion that this will be built as a control. In real development, however, it's worth taking a few seconds to decide whether it's worth the extra hassle of building a special-purpose control.

You could derive this control from the `PictureBox` class. Probably the only feature of the `PictureBox` class that this control would use would be the `Image` property to display the small map image, so this approach won't help you too much.

You could also build this as a `UserControl`. It doesn't require a group of constituent controls, however. You would either end up placing a single `PictureBox` on the `UserControl`, or drawing directly on the `UserControl`'s surface. This approach wouldn't help you much and would add the extra overhead imposed by the `UserControl`.

The key to this control is to make a graphical transformation to make working in the original map's coordinate system easier. In general, a transformation scales, translates, and rotates points from one coordinate system to another. This control uses a transformation that maps points in the map's coordinate system onto the control's surface so that the map fills the control without distortion.

The control provides two public properties. `MapImage` is a picture of the program's map at full scale. In this example, it's a map of Europe that you can see at reduced size in the view finder in Figure 10-6. The map's coordinates are measured in pixels on the original map image.

The `ThumbLocation` property is a `Rectangle` that gives the location and size of the thumb within the map in the map's coordinate system.

The `MakeTransformation` subroutine shown in the following code builds the control's transformation:

```
' Make a transformation to display the map on our surface.
Private Sub MakeTransformation()
    ' Do nothing if we have no map image.
    If m_MapImage Is Nothing Then Exit Sub
    If Me.Width < 1 Then Exit Sub
    If Me.Height < 1 Then Exit Sub

    ' Find the scales needed to shrink the map
    ' to fit vertically and horizontally.
    Dim scale_horz As Double = (Me.Width - 1) / m_MapImage.Width
    Dim scale_vert As Double = (Me.Height - 1) / m_MapImage.Height

    ' Use the smaller scale.
    Dim the_scale As Double = Math.Min(scale_horz, scale_vert)

    ' Make the transformation to map
    ' the map image onto our surface.
    Dim scaled_map_wid As Double = m_MapImage.Width * the_scale
    Dim scaled_map_hgt As Double = m_MapImage.Height * the_scale
```

```
    Dim x0 As Double = (Me.Width - 1 - scaled_map_wid) / 2
    Dim y0 As Double = (Me.Height - 1 - scaled_map_hgt) / 2
    Dim pts() As PointF = { _
        New PointF(CSng(x0), CSng(y0)), _
        New PointF(CSng(x0 + scaled_map_wid), CSng(y0)), _
        New PointF(CSng(x0), CSng(y0 + scaled_map_hgt)) _
    }
    m_Transformation = _
        New Matrix(m_MapImage.GetBounds(GraphicsUnit.Pixel), pts)

    ' Save the inverse transformation.
    m_InverseTransformation = m_Transformation.Clone()
    m_InverseTransformation.Invert()

    ' Redraw.
    Me.Invalidate()
End Sub
```

The code exits if the control doesn't yet have a map image or a size. It then determines the factor by which it would need to scale the map image to make it fit within the control vertically and horizontally. It picks the smaller of the two values for its scale so that the image fits, but is not stretched or squashed.

The code then determines the size of the shrunken map image and calculates where it needs to put the map's upper-left corner to center the image.

Next, the program makes an array of `PointF` structures that define the upper-left, upper-right, and lower-left corners of the rectangle where the shrunken map should be drawn. The code then uses a constructor that creates a transformation that maps a source rectangle onto the rectangle defined by those points. If it uses this transformation, the program can draw using the map image's coordinates, and the transformation will automatically convert the coordinates so that they fit properly on the control's surface.

More generally, the points can define a parallelogram that is not necessarily rectangular, but that's not needed for this control. A non-rectangular parallelogram would distort the map.

The code makes a copy of the transformation and inverts it to get a transformation that maps points from the control's surface back to the map's coordinate system. The code described shortly uses the inverse transformation to tell where the user clicks and drags on the map.

The `MakeTransformation` subroutine finishes by invalidating the control so that it generates a `Paint` event. The following code shows how the control draws itself:

```
Protected Overrides Sub OnPaint(ByVal pe As System.Windows.Forms.PaintEventArgs)
    MyBase.OnPaint(pe)

    'Add your custom paint code here
    DrawControl(pe.Graphics)
End Sub

' Draw the control.
Private Sub DrawControl(ByVal gr As Graphics)
    ' Do nothing if we have no image or transformation.
```

```
    If (m_MapImage Is Nothing) Then
        gr.DrawLine(Pens.Blue, 0, 0, Me.Width, Me.Height)
        gr.DrawLine(Pens.Blue, 0, Me.Height, Me.Width, 0)
        Exit Sub
    End If

    ' Set the transformation.
    gr.Transform = m_Transformation

    ' Draw the image.
    gr.InterpolationMode = Drawing2D.InterpolationMode.High
    gr.DrawImage(m_MapImage, 0, 0, m_MapImage.Width, m_MapImage.Height)

    ' Draw the thumb.
    If (m_ThumbLocation.Width > 0) AndAlso (m_ThumbLocation.Height > 0) Then
        Using foreground_pen As New Pen(Me.ForeColor)
            gr.DrawRectangle(foreground_pen, m_ThumbLocation)
        End Using
    End If
End Sub
```

The `OnPaint` subroutine calls the `Control` base class's `OnPaint` method and then calls the `DrawControl` subroutine.

If the control doesn't yet have a map image, the `DrawControl` subroutine draws an X on the control and exits. If the control does have a map image, the code sets the `Graphics` object's transformation to the one created by subroutine `MakeTransformation`. It then draws the map image and thumb onto the control. The code uses the map's coordinate system, and the transformation translates onto the control's surface.

The final interesting piece of code lets the user click and drag the thumb. The following code shows the mouse event handlers that deal with this:

```
' MouseDown. See if we are within the thumb.
Private Sub MapViewFinder_MouseDown(ByVal sender As Object, _
 ByVal e As System.Windows.Forms.MouseEventArgs) Handles Me.MouseDown
    ' Transform the mouse's position into map coordinates.
    Dim pts() As Point = {New Point(e.X, e.Y)}
    m_InverseTransformation.TransformPoints(pts)

    ' See if this is within the thumb.
    If Not m_ThumbLocation.Contains(pts(0)) Then Exit Sub

    ' It's inside the thumb. Start dragging.
    m_Dragging = True
    m_PrevX = pts(0).X
    m_PrevY = pts(0).Y
End Sub

' Continue dragging.
Private Sub MapViewFinder_MouseMove(ByVal sender As Object, _
 ByVal e As System.Windows.Forms.MouseEventArgs) Handles Me.MouseMove
```

```
        ' See if we are dragging the thumb.
        If Not m_Dragging Then Exit Sub

        ' Transform the mouse's position into map coordinates.
        Dim pts() As Point = {New Point(e.X, e.Y)}
        m_InverseTransformation.TransformPoints(pts)

        ' Get the thumb's new position.
        Dim new_x As Integer = m_ThumbLocation.X + pts(0).X - m_PrevX
        Dim new_y As Integer = m_ThumbLocation.Y + pts(0).Y - m_PrevY

        ' Save the new position.
        m_PrevX = pts(0).X
        m_PrevY = pts(0).Y

        ' Make sure the thumb stays within the map's bounds.
        If new_x < 0 Then new_x = 0
        If new_y < 0 Then new_y = 0
        If new_x > m_MapImage.Width - m_ThumbLocation.Width - 1 Then
            new_x = m_MapImage.Width - m_ThumbLocation.Width
        End If
        If new_y > m_MapImage.Height - m_ThumbLocation.Height - 1 Then
            new_y = m_MapImage.Height - m_ThumbLocation.Height - 1
        End If

        ' See if it moved.
        If (new_x = m_ThumbLocation.X) AndAlso _
           (new_y = m_ThumbLocation.Y) Then Exit Sub

        ' Move the thumb.
        m_ThumbLocation.X = new_x
        m_ThumbLocation.Y = new_y

        ' Redraw.
        Me.Invalidate()

        ' Raise the ThumbScroll event.
        RaiseEvent ThumbScroll()
    End Sub

    ' Stop dragging.
    Private Sub MapViewFinder_MouseUp(ByVal sender As Object, _
     ByVal e As System.Windows.Forms.MouseEventArgs) Handles Me.MouseUp
        ' See if we are dragging the thumb.
        If Not m_Dragging Then Exit Sub

        m_Dragging = False

        ' Raise the ThumbScrollComplete event.
        RaiseEvent ThumbScrollComplete()
    End Sub
```

The `MouseDown` event handler makes an array of `Point` structures containing the mouse's location. It uses the inverse transformation created by subroutine `MakeTransformation` to map the point from the control's coordinate system back to the map's coordinate system. It then compares the transformed point with the thumb's location to see if the point lies within the thumb. If the point is inside the thumb, the program sets the variable `m_Dragging` to `true` and saves the transformed point.

When the mouse moves, the `MouseMove` event handler again uses the inverse transformation to map the mouse's position into map coordinates. It calculates the thumb's new position and saves the new mouse position. It then ensures that the thumb is completely within the map area. If the corrected new location is different from the thumb's current location, the code moves the thumb, invalidates the control to generate a `Paint` event, and raises its `ThumbScroll` event.

When the user releases the mouse, the `MouseUp` event handler sets `m_Dragging` to `False` and raises the `ThumbScrollComplete` event.

The following code shows how the `MapToolsTest` program uses a `MapViewFinder` control:

```
Public Class Form1
    ' Make the MapViewFinder's thumb fit the window.
    Private Sub Form1_Load(ByVal sender As System.Object, _
     ByVal e As System.EventArgs) Handles MyBase.Load
        Me.MapViewFinder1.ThumbLocation = New Rectangle(0, 0, _
            picWindow.ClientSize.Width, picWindow.ClientSize.Height)

        ' Draw the initial image.
        DisplaySelectedWindow()
    End Sub

    ' The user is scrolling the MapViewFinder's thumb.
    Private Sub MapViewFinder1_ThumbScroll() Handles MapViewFinder1.ThumbScroll
        DisplaySelectedWindow()
    End Sub

    ' The user finished scrolling the MapViewFinder's thumb.
    Private Sub MapViewFinder1_ThumbScrollComplete()_
     Handles MapViewFinder1.ThumbScrollComplete
        DisplaySelectedWindow()
    End Sub

    ' Display the part of the map selected by the MapViewFinder.
    Private Sub DisplaySelectedWindow()
        Dim bm As New Bitmap( _
            picWindow.ClientSize.Width, _
            picWindow.ClientSize.Height)
        Using gr As Graphics = Graphics.FromImage(bm)
            gr.DrawImage(My.Resources.europe, _
                picWindow.ClientRectangle, _
                MapViewFinder1.ThumbLocation, _
                GraphicsUnit.Pixel)
        End Using

        picWindow.Image = bm
    End Sub
End Class
```

When the form loads, the program sets the `MapViewFinder`'s `ThumbLocation` property to a rectangle that is the same size as the area inside the `picWindow` control (the `PictureBox` on the left in Figure 10-6). It then calls subroutine `DisplaySelectedWindow` to draw that part of the map.

When the `MapViewFinder` control raises a `ThumbScroll` or `ThumbScrollComplete` event, the program also calls `DisplaySelectedWindow` to draw the selected part of the map. If you comment out the code in the `ThumbScroll` event handler, the program only displays the selected area after the user finishes dragging the thumb. This may improve performance if it takes awhile to draw the map.

Subroutine `DisplaySelectedWindow` makes a `Bitmap` to fit the `picWindow` control and makes a `Graphics` object associated with the `Bitmap`.

It uses the `Graphics` object's `DrawImage` method to draw a piece of the map. The first parameter to `DrawImage` is the map of Europe stored in the program's resources. The second parameter is a destination rectangle that covers the `picWindow` control's whole client surface.

The third parameter gives the source rectangle that should be copied from the image. The `MapViewFinder` control's `ThumbLocation` property gives the area that the thumb has currently selected in the map's coordinate system.

The final parameter to `DrawImage` indicates that the units used are pixels.

Sometimes you can save time and trouble by deriving a control from an existing control, or by adding controls to a `UserControl`. When neither an existing control nor a `UserControl` offers much help, you can build your own control from scratch.

Building Components

Components are basically like controls that are invisible at run-time. At design time, they appear as labeled icons in the *component tray* below the form's main design area. Figure 10-7 shows a form containing `Timer`, `ErrorProvider`, `EventLog`, `FileSystemWatcher`, and `PerformanceCounter` components. These are standard components that come with Visual Basic.

To create a component, start a new Class Library project and remove the class it initially contains. Then select the Project menu's Add Component command and add a Component Class to the project.

Alternatively, you can make a class and make it inherit from System.ComponentModel.Component.

If you open the Project Explorer and double-click a component, the Component Designer opens. Initially, the designer displays a message that says:

To add components to your class, drag them from the Toolbox and use the Properties window to set their properties.

To Create methods and events for your class, click here to switch to code view.

As the message says, you can drag components from the Toolbox and drop them on the Component Designer. You can also drag controls from the Toolbox onto the Component Designer.

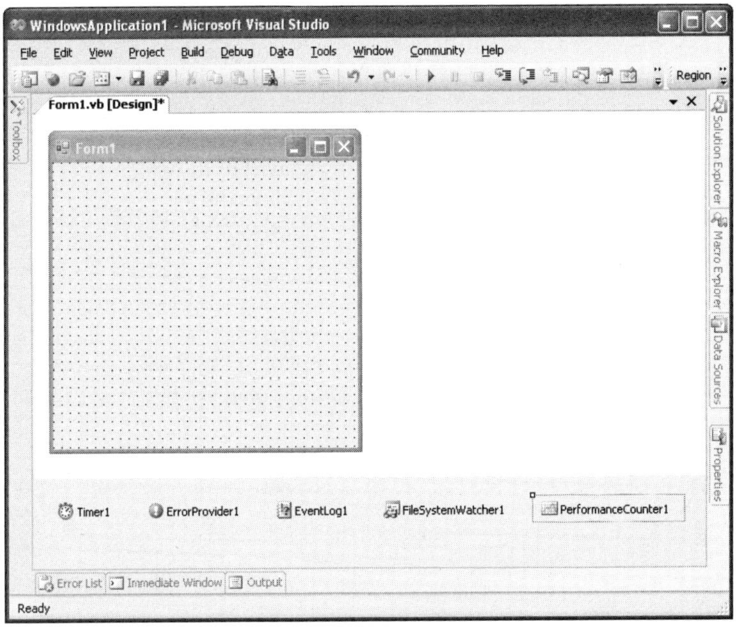

Figure 10-7: At design time, components appear in the component tray below a form.

If you made the component by selecting the Project menu's Add Component command, a hidden file contains designer-generated code to support the Component Designer. If you added a generic class to the project and made it inherit from the Component class, the Component Designer adds an InitializeComponent subroutine to the class. The following code shows a component after I dragged a Label onto the Component Designer:

```
Public Class Class1
    Inherits System.ComponentModel.Component

    Private Sub InitializeComponent()
        Me.Label1 = New System.Windows.Forms.Label
        '
        'Label1
        '
        Me.Label1.AutoSize = True
        Me.Label1.Location = New System.Drawing.Point(0, 0)
        Me.Label1.Name = "Label1"
        Me.Label1.Size = New System.Drawing.Size(100, 23)
        Me.Label1.TabIndex = 0
        Me.Label1.Text = "Label1"

    End Sub
    Friend WithEvents Label1 As System.Windows.Forms.Label
End Class
```

Notice that this code doesn't actually call the `InitializeComponent` subroutine. If you want to use the control you dragged onto the Component Designer, you need to call this routine, probably in a constructor.

If you used the Project menu's Add Component command, all of this code is placed in a hidden designer-generated file, so you don't have to worry about it. You won't have quite as much control over exactly what code is in the class, but you'll have less to maintain, so this is probably the better option.

After you create the component and add any necessary constituent controls and components to it, add code as usual to make the component do whatever it needs to do.

The following code shows a simple `TickOnce` component that works much as a `Timer` does, except that it generates a single `Tick` event after a specified time period and then disables itself. I created this class by adding a component to the project, so the extra Component Designer support code is hidden in a designer-generated code module. I also added `Timer` component named `tmrTicker` to this component in the Component Designer.

```
Public Class TickOnce

    ' Delegate the Interval and Enabled properties,
    ' and to tmrTicker.
    Public Property Interval() As Integer
        Get
            Return tmrTicker.Interval
        End Get
        Set(ByVal value As Integer)
            tmrTicker.Interval = value
        End Set
    End Property
    Public Property Enabled() As Boolean
        Get
            Return tmrTicker.Enabled
        End Get
        Set(ByVal value As Boolean)
            tmrTicker.Enabled = value
        End Set
    End Property

    ' Reraise the event and disable the timer.
    Public Event Tick()
    Private Sub tmrTicker_Tick(ByVal sender As Object, _
     ByVal e As System.EventArgs) Handles tmrTicker.Tick
        tmrTicker.Enabled = False
        RaiseEvent Tick()
    End Sub
End Class
```

The code delegates the component's `Interval` and `Enabled` properties to the `tmrTicker` constituent component. When that component raises a `Tick` event, the `TickOnce` component disables `tmrTicker` and then raises its own `Tick` event. (You can download this example at `www.vb-helper.com/one_on_one.htm`.)

Note that you could have derived this particular component from the `Timer` class, as shown in the following code:

```
Public Class TickOnce
    Inherits System.Windows.Forms.Timer

    ' Disable the control and process the Tick event.
    Protected Overrides Sub OnTick(ByVal e As System.EventArgs)
        Me.Enabled = False
        MyBase.OnTick(e)
    End Sub
End Class
```

Two common and very useful types of components are extender providers and dialogs. The following section describes extender providers. The rest of this section explains how you can make a component that displays a dialog.

While a component is invisible at design time, it can display forms that are visible. The basic idea is to add a form to the dialog component's project, and then give the component a method that displays the form.

To make your dialog components as consistent with those provided by Visual Studio (such as the `ColorDialog`, `OpenFileDialog`, and `SaveFileDialog`), give the component a `ShowDialog` method that returns a value of type `DialogResult`. Usually, this result will be `OK` or `Cancel`. To make this a little easier, the component's `ShowDialog` method can simply call the form's `ShowDialog` method and return its result.

The `AHlsColorDialog` component (available for download at `www.vb-helper.com/one_on_one.htm`) displays a color selection dialog that lets the user pick a color using the hue, lightness, saturation (HLS) color model. It also lets the user select an alpha value to define the color's transparency.

Figure 10-8 shows the dialog in action. The color wheel on the left lets the user set the color's hue and saturation (the amount of the color's "pureness"). The smoothly shaded slider lets the user select the color's brightness. The user can also use the scroll bars at the bottom to set the hue, lightness, and saturation. The checkered slider lets the user set the color's alpha value. Values near the bottom represent very transparent colors (alpha near 0), so the checkerboard shows through. Values near the top give very opaque colors (alpha near 255), so the selected color covers the checkerboard.

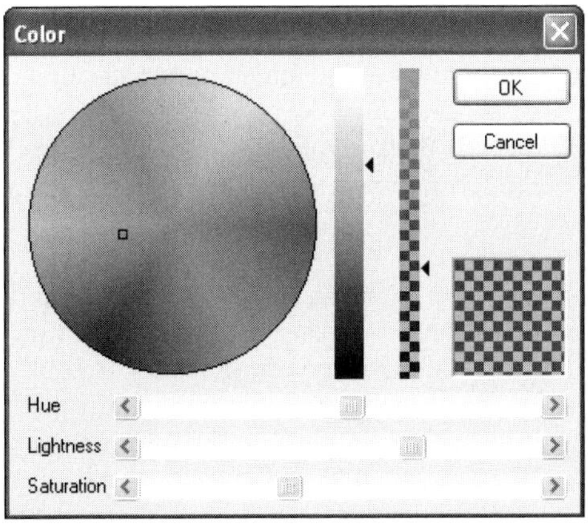

Figure 10-8: The `HlsColorDialog` component displays this control to let the user select a color.

The following code shows how the `HlsColorDialog` component displays its color selection dialog:

```
<ToolboxBitmap(GetType(HlsColorDialog), "tbxHlsColorDialog")> _
Public Class HlsColorDialog
    Inherits System.ComponentModel.Component

    Private m_Dialog As New HlsColorDialogForm

    ' Delegate the Color property to m_Dialog.
    Public Property Color() As Color
        Get
            Return m_Dialog.Color
        End Get
        Set(ByVal Value As Color)
            m_Dialog.Color = Value
        End Set
    End Property

    ' Display the HLS color dialog.
    Public Function ShowDialog(Optional ByVal show_rgb As Boolean = False) _
     As DialogResult
        ' Size the form to show the desired scroll bars.
        Dim desired_client_height As Integer
        If Not show_rgb Then
            desired_client_height = m_Dialog.panHLS.Top + _
                m_Dialog.panHLS.Height + 8
        Else
            desired_client_height = m_Dialog.panRGB.Top + _
                m_Dialog.panRGB.Height + 8
        End If
        m_Dialog.Height += desired_client_height - m_Dialog.ClientSize.Height

        ' Display the dialog.
        Return m_Dialog.ShowDialog()
    End Function
End Class
```

The component includes a variable of type `HlsColorDialogForm`. This is the actual form that the component displays. The component delegates its `Color` property to this form's `Color` property.

The component's `ShowDialog` method takes a Boolean parameter that indicates whether the form should display scroll bars to let the user adjust the selected color's red, green, and blue components. The routine sizes the form to show or hide these scroll bars accordingly. In Figure 10-8, these scroll bars are hidden off the bottom edge of the form. `ShowDialog` then calls the form's `ShowDialog` method and returns the result.

At design time, I set the OK button's `DialogResult` property to `OK` and the Cancel button's `Dialog Result` property to `Cancel`. That means if the user clicks either button, the form automatically hides, and its `ShowDialog` method returns the corresponding result.

The dialog component delegates its `Color` property to the form's `Color` property, and the form's code delegates its `Color` property to its constituent controls.

The following code shows how the ColorPickerControlsTest application uses an AHlsColorDialog component named AHlsColorDialog1. It sets the component's Color property to the value stored in variable m_SampleColor. It then calls the component's ShowDialog method. If the result is OK, the code saves the new value of m_SampleColor and invalidates the picSample PictureBox to raise a Paint event.

```
Private Sub btnPickColorWAlpha_Click(ByVal sender As System.Object, _
 ByVal e As System.EventArgs) Handles btnPickColorWAlpha.Click
    AHlsColorDialog1.Color = m_SampleColor
    If AHlsColorDialog1.ShowDialog() = Windows.Forms.DialogResult.OK Then
        m_SampleColor = AHlsColorDialog1.Color
        picSample.Invalidate()
    End If
End Sub
```

The following code shows the picSample control's Paint event handler. It draws the image in the face resource onto the control. It then fills a rectangle covering the image with the selected color m_Sample Color. If this color is transparent, the image shows through.

```
Private Sub picSample_Paint(ByVal sender As System.Object, _
 ByVal e As System.Windows.Forms.PaintEventArgs) Handles picSample.Paint
    e.Graphics.DrawImage(My.Resources.face, 0, 0)

    Dim br As New SolidBrush(m_SampleColor)
    e.Graphics.FillRectangle(br, picSample.ClientRectangle)
    br.Dispose()
End Sub
```

The dialog shown in Figure 10-8 includes a lot of other interesting code, but it's long and not essential to this discussion, so it's not shown here. It includes code for building the HsColorWheel, LightnessBar, and AlphaBar controls that were built from scratch (as opposed to being derived from other controls, or being based on UserControls) and used on the dialog's form. It also includes an HlsColorDialog component that is similar to the AHlsColorDialog, but doesn't let the user set an alpha value. Download the code from the book's Web page www.vb-helper.com/one_on_one.htm and examine the code for yourself.

Building Extender Providers

An *extender provider* is a component that adds new properties to other components. For example, the ErrorProvider component that comes with Visual Basic is an extender provider. Suppose you add an ErrorProvider named ErrorProvider1 to a form. Then all of the controls on the form magically receive a new property called "Error on ErrorProvider1." If you set this property to a non-blank value, the ErrorProvider displays a little error icon (a red circle with a white exclamation point in it) next to the corresponding control. If the user hovers the mouse over the icon, a tooltip appears displaying the error text. Figure 10-9 shows an ErrorProvider displaying its icon and an error tooltip.

> *Note that the* ErrorProvider *component only provides this service for controls. Because it displays a graphical icon and message, it wouldn't make sense for an* ErrorProvider *to provide this service for a non-visual component such as a* Timer *or* FileOpenDialog*. Each* ExtenderProvider *can decide the kinds of objects that it will support.*

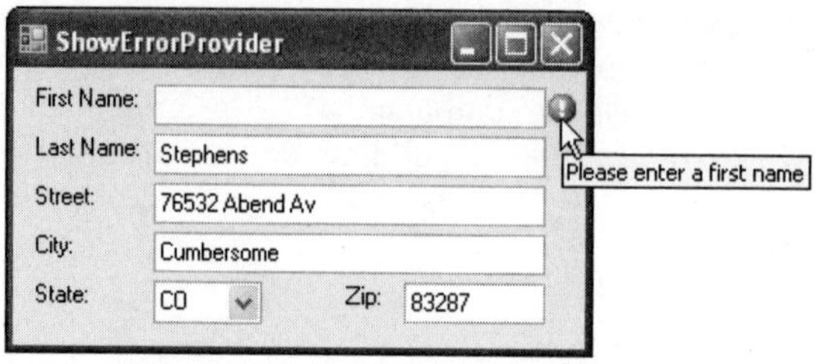

Figure 10-9: The `ErrorProvider` component displays error messages for a control.

The most obvious purpose of `ExtenderProviders` is to provide additional properties to components, but they can also manipulate those components in other ways. For example, when the program sets a value for the extender's property, the extender can manipulate the client component. It can examine the component's properties, call its methods, and even give it new event handlers so that the provider can take action when the client raises certain events.

For example, the `ErrorProvider` uses the properties of its client control to figure out where it should display the error icon. The `ToolTip` component catches a client's mouse events to decide when and where to display a tooltip.

`ExtenderProviders` are very powerful and provide excellent encapsulation benefits, but they are underused by most Visual Basic developers for a couple of reasons. First, they're relatively new. Long-time Visual Basic developers are not used to them, so they are usually overlooked as a useful tool.

Second, it's not always obvious when and how an `ExtenderProvider` might be useful. Instead of thinking about adding new properties to a component, think about adding new features to components. That not only includes new properties, but it also includes new event handlers and behaviors. An `ExtenderProvider` can provide a new channel for the program to interact with its client controls. It can interact directly with some or all of the controls that use it. For example, an `EnabledProvider` could enable or disable client controls as a group.

Finally, building `ExtenderProviders` isn't easy. The `ExtenderProvider` must use attributes to identify the properties it will provide, it must implement the `IExtender` interface and provide the `CanExtend` function that the interface requires, it must provide `Get` and `Set` routines for the properties, and it must save and manage information about each client and its properties.

Though building `ExtenderProviders` is sometimes difficult, it's often well worth the effort. A good `ExtenderProvider` encapsulates a new feature that you can easily add to other components at design time without any new coding.

Figure 10-10 shows a program that uses two `ExtenderProviders` that use regular expressions to validate text. The text boxes on the left use the `RegexValidationProvider` component. When the user moves out of a field, the component uses an `ErrorProvider` to display an error icon if the text doesn't match the control's assigned regular expression. (You can download this example at `www.vb-helper.com/one_on_one.htm`.)

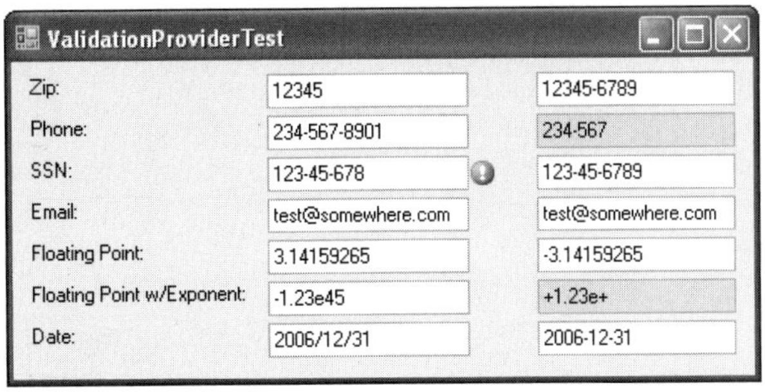

Figure 10-10: The `RegexValidationProvider` **and** `RegexHighlightProvider` **components use regular expressions to validate text.**

The text boxes on the right use the `RegexHighlightProvider` component. Whenever a text box's text changes, the component determines whether the text matches the control's regular expression and, if the text doesn't match the expression, the provider makes the control's background yellow.

In Figure 10-10, the left `SSN` field displays an error icon because its value isn't a valid Social Security number. In the right-hand column, the phone number and floating-point value with exponent have invalid formats, so they have yellow backgrounds.

A Simple Example

Before discussing these more complicated `ExtenderProviders`, consider the simpler `ExtraTagProvider`. This component adds a new string property called `ExtraTag` to `Label` and `TextBox` controls.

To build the `ExtraTagProvider`, I used the Project menu's Add Component command. In addition to making a new class for the provider, Visual Basic also made a hidden designer-generated module containing code to support the Component Designer.

The following code shows how `ExtraTagProvider` works:

```
<ToolboxBitmap(GetType(ExtraTagProvider), "tbxExtraTagProvider")> _
<ProvideProperty("ExtraTag", GetType(Control))> _
Public Class ExtraTagProvider
    Implements IExtenderProvider

    ' Hold controls' extra tags.
    Private m_ExtraTags As New Generic.Dictionary(Of Control, String)

    ' We extend Labels and TextBoxes.
    Public Function CanExtend(ByVal extendee As Object) As Boolean _
     Implements System.ComponentModel.IExtenderProvider.CanExtend
        Return (TypeOf (extendee) Is Label) OrElse (TypeOf (extendee) Is TextBox)
    End Function

    ' Return a control's ExtraTag value.
```

```
    Public Function GetExtraTag(ByVal client_control As Control) As String
        If m_ExtraTags.ContainsKey(client_control) Then
            Return m_ExtraTags.Item(client_control)
        Else
            Return ""
        End If
    End Function

    ' Set a TextBox's ExtraTag value.
    Public Sub SetExtraTag(ByVal client_control As Control, _
     ByVal extra_tag As String)
        If extra_tag Is Nothing Then extra_tag = ""
        If extra_tag.Length = 0 Then
            ' Remove it.
            If m_ExtraTags.ContainsKey(client_control) Then
                m_ExtraTags.Remove(client_control)
            End If
        Else
            ' Add it.
            m_ExtraTags.Item(client_control) = extra_tag
        End If
    End Sub
End Class
```

The code begins with a ToolboxBitmap attribute that defines the component's toolbox icon.

It then uses a ProvideProperty attribute to tell Visual Basic that this ExtenderProvider provides the ExtraTag property for Control objects. The CanExtend function (described shortly) refines this, so the provider only supports Labels and TextBoxes.

Next, the provider includes a generic Dictionary that matches String values with Control objects. This Dictionary holds the ExtraTag values for the client controls.

Next the code provides the CanExtend function that is required by the IExtenderProvider interface. This function examines an object and returns True if the provider can extend that object. In this example, the function returns True if the object is a Label or TextBox.

To actually implement the new property, the provider must include two routines named "Get" and "Set", followed by the name of the property. For the ExtraTag property, these routines must be called GetExtraTag and SetExtraTag.

Function GetExtraTag takes as a parameter an object and returns the object's ExtraTag value. In this code, the function looks for the object in the m_ExtraTags Dictionary and returns its stored value if it is present or Nothing if the object is not in the Dictionary.

Subroutine SetExtraTag takes as parameters an object and the ExtraTag value that it should have. If the new ExtraTag value is blank, the subroutine removes the object from the m_ExtraTags Dictionary. If the new value is not blank, the subroutine sets the object's ExtraTag value in the Dictionary. (You can download this example at www.vb-helper.com/one_on_one.htm.)

A More Useful Example

The `ExtraTagProvider` component described in the previous section is not spectacularly useful. You can use it to give `Labels` and `TextBoxes` an `ExtraTag` property at design time. At run-time, the program can use the `ExtraTagProvider`'s `GetExtraTag` and `SetExtraTag` methods to get and set values for `Labels` and `TextBoxes`. That's about all this component can do. This section explains how the much more useful `RegexValidationProvider` and `RegexHighlightProvider` components work.

To build the `RegexValidationProvider`, I used the Project menu's Add Component command. In addition to making a new class for the provider, Visual Basic also made a hidden designer-generated module containing code to support the Component Designer. After adding the component, I used the Component Designer to give the component an `ErrorProvider` named `errRegex`.

The following code shows how the `RegexValidationProvider` works:

```
<ToolboxBitmap(GetType(RegexValidationProvider), "tbxRegexValidationProvider")> _
<ProvideProperty("RegexPattern", GetType(TextBox))> _
<ProvideProperty("RegexMessage", GetType(TextBox))> _
<ProvideProperty("RegexAllowBlank", GetType(TextBox))> _
Public Class RegexValidationProvider
    Implements IExtenderProvider

    ' Store a control's regular expression pattern and error message.
    Private Const ALLOW_BLANK_DEFAULT As Boolean = True
    Private Class RegexInfo
        Public Pattern As String = ""
        Public Message As String = ""
        Public AllowBlank As Boolean = ALLOW_BLANK_DEFAULT
        Public Function IsBlank() As Boolean
            Return (Pattern.Length = 0) AndAlso _
                   (Message.Length = 0) AndAlso _
                   (AllowBlank = ALLOW_BLANK_DEFAULT)
        End Function
    End Class

    ' Hold information about controls and their regular expressions.
    Private m_RegexInfos As New Generic.Dictionary(Of TextBox, RegexInfo)

    ' Extend only TextBoxes.
    Public Function CanExtend(ByVal extendee As Object) As Boolean _
     Implements System.ComponentModel.IExtenderProvider.CanExtend
        Return (TypeOf extendee Is TextBox)
    End Function

#Region "RegexPattern Property"
    ' Return a TextBox's RegexPattern value.
    Public Function GetRegexPattern(ByVal client_control As TextBox) As String
        If m_RegexInfos.ContainsKey(client_control) Then
            Return m_RegexInfos.Item(client_control).Pattern
        Else
            Return ""
        End If
```

```
    End Function

    ' Set a TextBox's RegexPattern value.
    Public Sub SetRegexPattern(ByVal client_control As TextBox, _
     ByVal new_pattern As String)
        If new_pattern Is Nothing Then new_pattern = ""

        ' Get the client's RegexInfo object or make a new one.
        Dim regex_info As RegexInfo = GetOrMakeRegexInfo(client_control)

        ' Save the new pattern.
        regex_info.Pattern = new_pattern

        ' Add or remove the entry if necessary.
        AddOrRemoveIfNecessary(client_control, regex_info)
    End Sub
#End Region ' RegexPattern Property

    ' Code for the RegexMessage and RegexAllowBlank properties omitted.
    ' ...

    ' Return the client's RegexInfo or make a new one.
    Private Function GetOrMakeRegexInfo(ByVal client_control As TextBox) _
     As RegexInfo
        If m_RegexInfos.ContainsKey(client_control) Then
            Return m_RegexInfos.Item(client_control)
        Else
            Return New RegexInfo
        End If
    End Function

    ' Add or remove the entry if necessary.
    Private Sub AddOrRemoveIfNecessary(ByVal client_control As TextBox, _
     ByVal regex_info As RegexInfo)
        ' See if it's all blank.
        If regex_info.IsBlank() Then
            ' Remove the TextBox from the expression dictionary.
            If m_RegexInfos.ContainsKey(client_control) Then
                m_RegexInfos.Remove(client_control)
                RemoveHandler client_control.Validating, _
                    AddressOf Client_Validating
            End If
        Else
            ' Add or update the control's expression.
            m_RegexInfos.Item(client_control) = regex_info
            AddHandler client_control.Validating, AddressOf Client_Validating
        End If
    End Sub

    ' A client is being validated. See if it matches its expression.
    Private Sub Client_Validating(ByVal sender As Object, _
     ByVal e As System.ComponentModel.CancelEventArgs)
        ' Get the TextBox and its information.
        Dim text_box As TextBox = DirectCast(sender, TextBox)
        If Not m_RegexInfos.ContainsKey(text_box) Then Exit Sub
```

```
        Dim regex_info As RegexInfo = m_RegexInfos(text_box)

        ' Validate the expression.
        If regex_info.AllowBlank And text_box.Text.Length = 0 Then
            ' Blank is okay. Clear any error.
            errRegex.SetError(text_box, "")
        ElseIf Regex.IsMatch(text_box.Text, regex_info.Pattern, _
            RegexOptions.IgnoreCase) _
        Then
            ' It matches. Clear any error.
            errRegex.SetError(text_box, "")
        Else
            ' It doesn't match. Display the error message.
            If regex_info.Message.Length = 0 Then
                errRegex.SetError(text_box, "Invalid format")
            Else
                errRegex.SetError(text_box, regex_info.Message)
            End If
        End If
    End Sub
End Class
```

The code begins with a `ToolboxBitmap` and `ProvideProperty` attributes much as the `ExtraTagProvider`'s code does. Note that this code uses three `ProvideProperty` attributes to define three different properties: `RegexPattern`, `RegexMessage`, and `RegexAllowBlank`.

The `ExtraTagProvider` stored a single string for its client controls in a `Dictionary`. This provider must store three properties for its clients. You could store the values in three separate `Dictionaries` or some other data structure. This code stores the values in a single `Dictionary` containing `RegexInfo` objects.

The `RegexInfo` class includes three public fields: `Pattern`, `Message`, and `AllowBlank`. Its `IsBlank` function returns `True` if these fields all have default values.

This provider's `CanExtend` function returns `True` only if the client control is a `TextBox`.

The next two routines implement the `RegexPattern` property. Function `GetRegexPattern` looks in the `Dictionary` to see if the client control is present. If the `Dictionary` has an entry for the control, the function returns the entry's `Pattern` value. If the `Dictionary` has no entry for the control, the function returns an empty string for the `RegexPattern` property.

Subroutine `SetRegexPattern` stores a new pattern value for a client control. It calls the `GetOrMakeRegexInfo` function described shortly to get the client's `RegexInfo` object, or to make a new one. It sets the object's new `Pattern` value and calls subroutine `AddOrRemoveIfNecessary`, also described shortly, to update the `Dictionary`.

The code that handles the `RegexMessage` and `RegexAllowBlank` properties is similar, so it's not shown here. Download the example program from the book's Web page to see the details.

Function `GetOrMakeRegexInfo` looks for an object's entry in the `Dictionary`. If it finds the item, the function returns its `RegexInfo` object. If the function does not find the object, it creates a new `RegexInfo` object and returns it.

Subroutine AddOrRemoveIfNecessary saves or removes a client control's RegexInfo. If the new RegexInfo contains only default values (blank Pattern and Message, and AllowBlank is True), the routine removes the object from the Dictionary if it is present. If the new RegexInfo does not hold only default values, the routine saves it in the Dictionary.

As it adds or removes objects from the Dictionary, subroutine AddOrRemoveIfNecessary also adds and removes an event handler to catch the TextBoxes' Validating event. When one of the TextBoxes raises its Validating event at run-time, the Client_Validating routine executes.

This routine retrieves the TextBox and the text it contains. If the control allows blanks and contains no text, the routine uses the errRegex constituent ErrorProvider component's SetError method to clear the control's error.

If the control doesn't allow blank values or its text isn't blank, the subroutine uses the Regex regular expression class's shared IsMatch method to see if the TextBox's text matches the RegexPattern. If the text matches, the routine again uses the errRegex component's SetError method to clear the TextBox's error.

A complete discussion of regular expressions is outside of the scope of this book. You can get more information from the online help and from regular expression Web sites. You can also download a PowerPoint presentation that I gave to the Denver Visual Studio User's Group at www.vb-helper.com/handy_namespaces.html. *That presentation provides an introduction to the* Xml, Regex, *and* Crypto *namespaces.*

You should also be aware that there are a couple of different regular expression languages, so examples you find on some Web sites may not work correctly with the Regex *class.*

Finally, if the control's text doesn't match RegexPattern, the routine uses the errRegex component's SetError method to display the text in the control's RegexMessage property.

The RegexHighlightProvider is very similar to the RegexValidationProvider. The main differences are that it provides different properties (HighlightPattern, HighlightAllowBlank, and HighlightInvalidColor) and that it catches the client controls' TextChanged event instead of the Validating event. Otherwise, the two are very similar. You can download the example code at www.vb-helper.com/one_on_one.htm and look at RegexHighlightProvider yourself.

The RegexValidationProvider and RegexHighlightProvider components let you add sophisticated error-validation code to your application extremely easily. Simply drop one of the providers on a form, set a few properties for the controls you want validated, and you're ready to go.

Summary

Controls and components provide a nice, clean, easy-to-understand interface for developers to use at design time and run-time. They encapsulate features tightly so that developers don't need to worry about the objects' internal details.

By building your own controls and components, you can bring the same benefits to your code. You can provide easy-to-use tools that make different parts of the application more powerful and consistent, while allowing developers to focus on their own work without constantly reinventing common program features such as field validation.

This chapter explains how to build controls derived from existing controls, how to make `UserControls`, and how to build controls from scratch. It also tells how to make components, and focuses on dialog components and `ExtenderProviders`.

Chapter 11, "Property Support," explains how to provide additional support for your custom controls and components. It shows how you can provide extra support for properties to make editing them at design time easier and safer from errors.

11

Property Support

Visual Studio developers take the Properties window for granted, but it's actually a pretty remarkable tool. When you click a control on a form, the window displays the control's properties and lets you edit them in ways that are appropriate for the different property data types. It lets you enter text for properties that are strings or simple values such as numbers, it lets you select files and colors from dialogs, and it lets you pick choices from a drop-down list for enumerated values. If a property is a collection of objects, you can click an ellipsis to the right of the property to open a collection editor where you can add and remove objects, and edit their properties.

When you build a custom control, you get all of this functionality for free. In many cases, this default behavior is more than enough to let developers use your controls.

In fact, if you are developing controls for in-house use, I would recommend that you try to live with the capabilities provided by the Properties window for you. Additional features (such as custom property editors) make developing with controls easier, but they are fairly tricky to implement. Unless you will be spending a *lot* of time working with the properties, it may not be worth the additional effort of writing customized tools.

In contrast, if you are building controls that will be used by developers outside of your project, it may be worthwhile providing some of these extra capabilities. You may also need to build some of these tools if your controls' properties will be directly accessible to end users. For example, the `PropertyGrid` control lets users view and modify object properties at run-time. If you use that control, you may need to streamline your properties so that they are easier for the users to understand and manage.

Unfortunately, controls (and code, in general) often live far longer than was originally intended. The control that you plan to use only once may be adopted by other projects, and you may end up supporting it practically forever. To avoid unwelcome work, you should make your controls (and all of your code) as bulletproof as possible, but you can still avoid adding gratuitous extras. Make the control's property procedures validate their data so developers cannot push bad data into the control. You don't necessarily need to give every property fancy property editors until you're certain there's a need for them.

This chapter describes some of the ways you can add design-time support for custom controls and their properties. It shows how to add drop-down and dialog editors to the Properties window, how to add smart tags to a control, and how to build property sheets.

Some of the attributes, interfaces, and classes used by the examples in this chapter require that you add a reference to `System.Design` *and* `System.Windows.Forms.Design` *namespaces. Double-click My Project, select the References tab, and check the namespaces in the list. If one of the namespaces (probably* `System.Design`*) is missing from the list, click the Add button and select the namespace there.*

Customizations Overview

This chapter describes several ways that you can enhance Visual Basic's design time for custom controls. To demonstrate most of these enhancements, this chapter uses an example control named `ScribbleControl`. This control displays a hand-drawn image. At design time, you can both see and edit the image. At run-time, the user can view the image. If the control's `Enabled` property is `True`, the user can also edit the image at run-time.

Figure 11-1 shows the control at design time displaying an image.

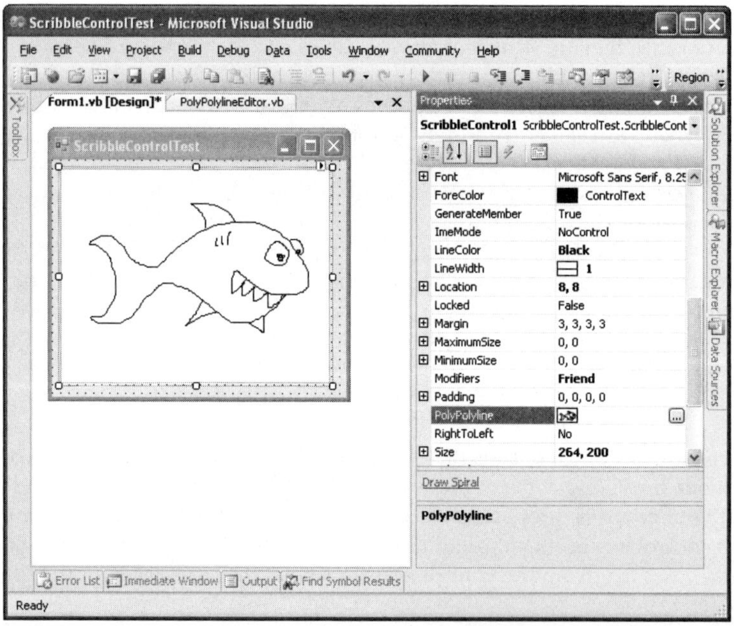

Figure 11-1: The `ScribbleControl` displays a hand-drawn image at design time and run-time.

This control represents its drawing as a series of *polylines,* where a polyline is a series of connected points. The control's `PolyPolyline` property contains a reference to a `PolyPolyline` object. That object contains an array of `Polyline` objects, each of which contains an array of `Points`. Each of these classes has support methods that perform such tasks as drawing a `Polyline` or `PolyPolyline`.

Figure 11-1 shows several enhancements to Visual Basic's design-time support for the `ScribbleControl` class. Because the `PolyPolyline` property is an array of objects, the Properties window would normally display a collection editor to allow the developer to add, remove, and modify `Polyline` objects. That's not a very useful way to specify a drawing, however, so the control overrides this behavior.

If you click the ellipsis shown on the right of the `PolyPolyline` property in Figure 11-1, Visual Basic displays the editor dialog shown in Figure 11-2. On this editor, you can click the left mouse button and drag to draw new polylines. If you click the right mouse button, the editor clears the picture. When you are finished, you can click OK to save the new `PolyPolyline` property, or Cancel to leave the control's `PolyPolyline` property unchanged.

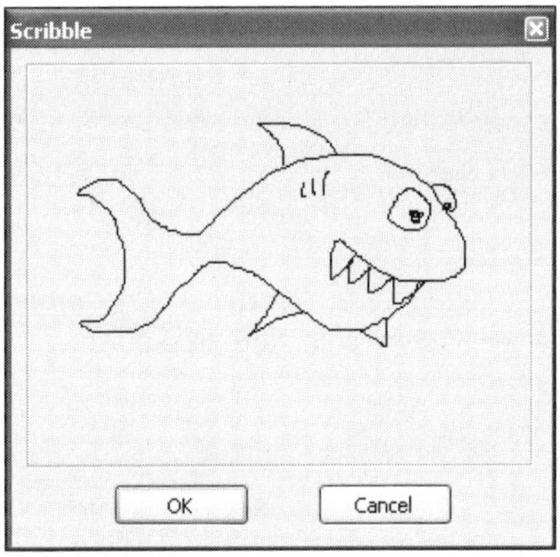

Figure 11-2: You can edit a `ScribbleControl`'s picture at design time.

Notice also that the Properties window displays a tiny image of the drawing in the `PolyPolyline` property's entry.

The `ScribbleControl` provides several other custom properties. The `LineColor` property determines the color that the control uses to draw its polylines. In this control, however, `LineColor` isn't just any old color. Instead, it must be one of red, orange, yellow, green, blue, indigo, violet, black, or white.

You can see in Figure 11-1 that the `LineColor` entry in the Properties window displays the name of the currently selected color. If you select that property, the window displays a drop-down arrow on the right as it normally would for a color property. If you click this arrow, however, you don't see a normal color selection dialog. Instead, you see the color selection drop-down shown in Figure 11-3.

The `LineWidth` property determines the thickness of the lines that the control draws. The Properties window displays `LineWidth` by showing a sample of the line and the line's width in pixels. Like the `LineColor` property, `LineWidth` displays a custom drop-down when you click its drop-down arrow. Figure 11-4 shows the `LineWidth` drop-down.

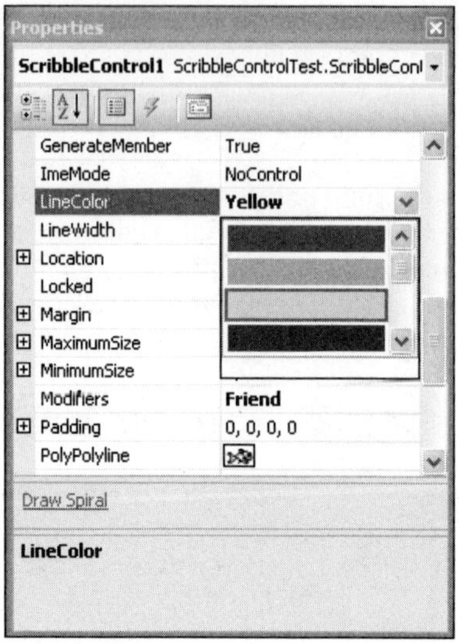

Figure 11-3: The `LineColor` property displays a custom selection drop-down.

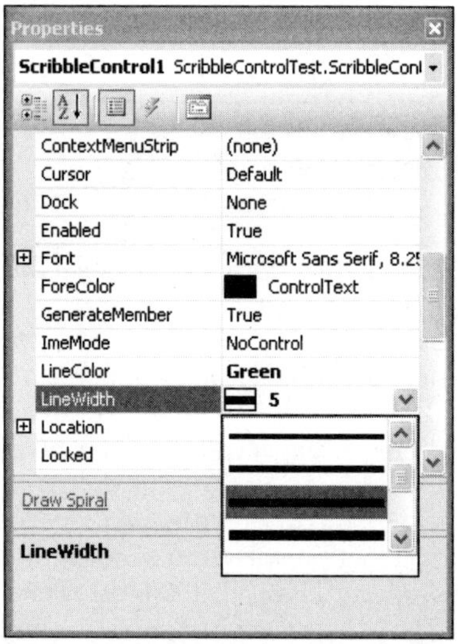

Figure 11-4: The `LineWidth` property displays a custom selection drop-down.

Below the properties in the Properties window in Figure 11-1, you can see a link labeled "Draw Spiral." This is a command verb supported by the `ScribbleControl` class. If you click this link, the control clears its picture and draws a spiral. More generally, a *command verb* can take any action that is appropriate to configure or modify the control. While the entries in the Properties window affect only a single property, these verbs can perform any action on the control.

The `ScribbleControl` in the form designer is selected in Figure 11-1. If you look closely near the control's upper-right corner, you'll see a small box holding a little rightward-pointing triangle. This is called a *smart tag*. If you click a smart tag, a panel of actions pops up that lets you configure the associated control.

If you click the smart tag for the `ScribbleControl`, you'll see the smart tag panel shown in Figure 11-5. Controls on this panel let you set the `ScribbleControl`'s `BackColor`, `LineColor`, and `LineWidth` properties.

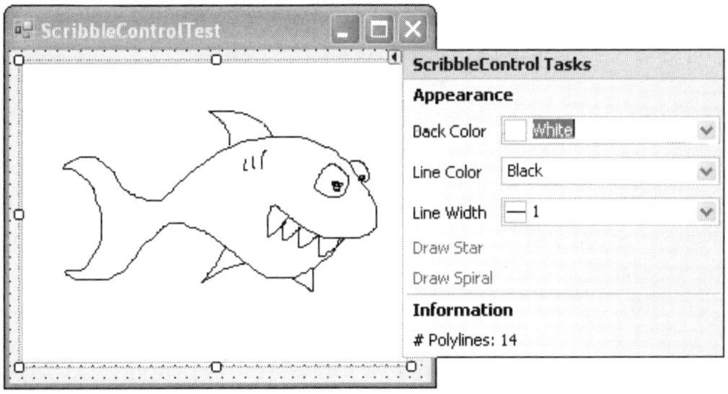

Figure 11-5: The `ScribbleControl`'s smart tag lets you configure the control.

The smart tag's Draw Star command clears the control's picture and draws a star. Figure 11-6 shows the control after clicking this command.

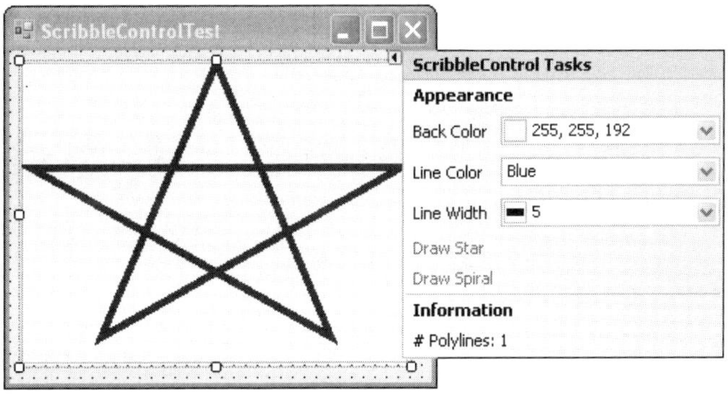

Figure 11-6: The Draw Star command draws a star.

The Draw Spiral command clears the control's picture and draws the spiral shown in Figure 11-7. The Draw Spiral command is the same command displayed as a link below the properties in the Properties window.

The bottom of the smart tag's panel contains an Information area that displays the number of `Polylines` in the current drawing. In Figure 11-5, this area shows that the shark drawing contains 14 `Polylines`.

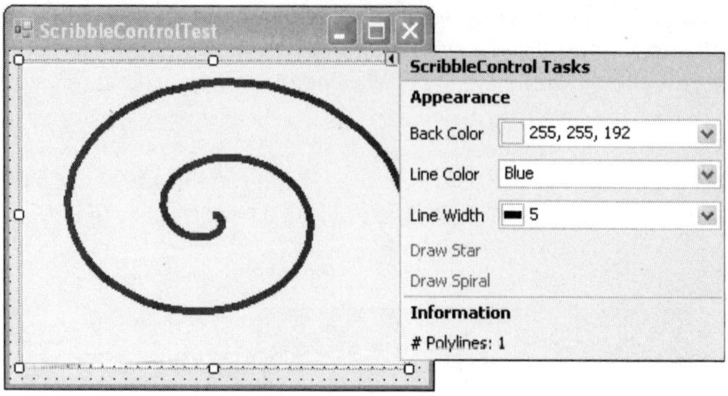

Figure 11-7: The Draw Spiral command draws a spiral.

Finally, the `ScribbleControl` also provides property pages. These have gone somewhat out of fashion since Visual Basic .NET was released, but they are still useful for manipulating a control in very complex ways. Like the smart tag panel, property sheets let you change all of the control's properties in one place. They can also provide more complex commands such as the Draw Star and Draw Spiral tools.

While the smart tag pop-up must display all of its tools at once, property sheets can include many pages. In some very complex controls (such as graphing and charting controls), property sheets may contain pages to set basic properties (colors, line types, point symbols), chart style (line graph, bar graph, pie chart), data, axis labels, and so forth.

If you right-click the `ScribbleControl` and select Properties, Visual Basic displays the property sheets shown in Figure 11-8. (Normally, right-clicking and selecting Properties displays the Properties window. But if the control has property pages, Visual Basic displays those instead.) You can also display the property sheets by clicking the property pages button at the top of the Properties window. You can see this button in Figure 11-4 to the right of the lightning bolt button that displays the control's `Events`.

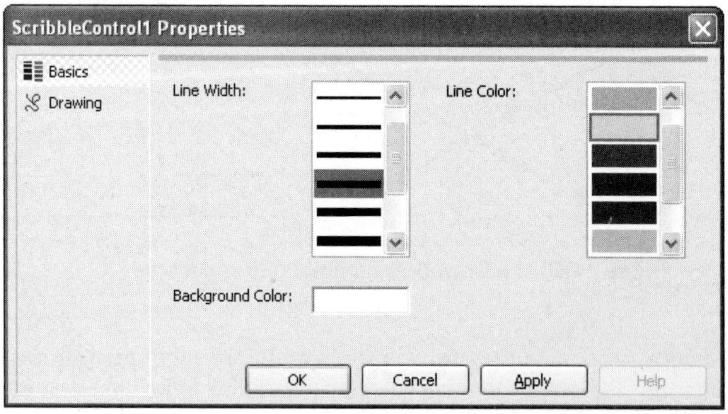

Figure 11-8: Property sheets let you manipulate a control in complex ways.

The column on the left shows icons and names for the pages contained by the property sheet. The rest of the dialog contains controls that manipulate the control you right-clicked in the form designer. Figure 11-8 shows the first property page, which lets you set the control's basic properties.

If you click the Drawing item in the left-hand column, you'll see the second property page shown in Figure 11-9. This page lets you use the mouse to draw a new picture.

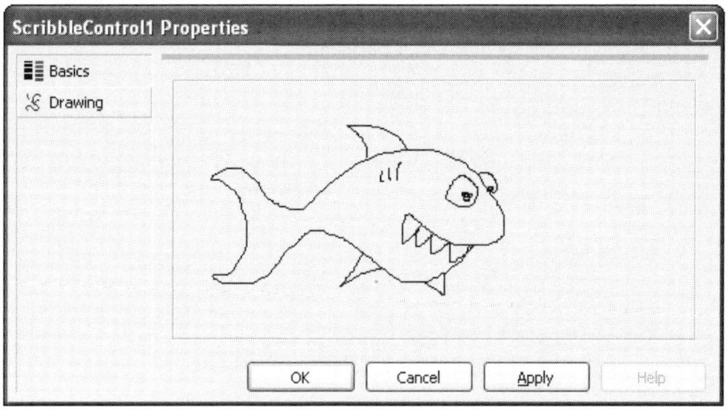

Figure 11-9: This property sheet lets you draw pictures with the mouse.

When you make a change to any of the controls on the property pages, the Apply button is enabled. If you click Apply, the property sheet applies all of the changes to the `ScribbleControl` that you originally right-clicked in the form designer. If you click OK, the dialog applies the changes and closes. If you click Cancel, the dialog closes and leaves the `ScribbleControl` unchanged.

The following sections explain in detail how to implement each of these design-time features. This control contains a lot of code for performing such chores as adding `Polyline` objects to the control's `PolyPolyline` property, adding points to a `Polyline`, and drawing the control's image. This code isn't central to creating the design-time customizations, so most of this code has been omitted to save space. Download the example project from `www.vb-helper.com/one_on_one.htm` to see the details.

> *Important Note: When you build the editors and other classes that provide the design-time support, some of them seem to get cached or linked tightly to Visual Studio. If you make a change to the editor class and recompile, Visual Studio may continue using the old version.*
>
> *To make Visual Studio relinquish its hold on the older editor, save your changes, close Visual Studio, delete the project's* `bin` *and* `obj` *directories, restart Visual Basic, and rebuild the application.*
>
> *Note also that Visual Studio sometimes gets confused if you load a form containing a control that you have modified. For example, suppose you save a form containing a* `ScribbleControl`*, close the form, and then remove the control's* `LineWidth` *property. When you reopen the form, the form designer tries to reload the control's properties from the form's resources. Unfortunately, those resources include a* `LineWidth` *property, so the form designer will probably become confused. You may need to manually edit the resource file (which is just XML text) and remove the offending property.*
>
> *One way to avoid this problem is to not save forms containing the controls you are currently building. Open the application and then open a test form. Place a control on it and test the design-time features you are working on. Then close the form without saving changes. Modify the control as needed, and then, when you reopen the form, you can add a new control.*

The chapter finishes by discussing another common scenario: providing design-time support for properties that are references to objects. It shows how you can allow developers to view and modify the object's sub-properties.

Displaying and Editing LineWidth

To display a property in a special format and to allow custom editing in the Properties window, you need to associate the property with a *property editor class*. For example, the following code shows how the `ScribbleControl` declares its `LineWidth` property:

```
' The thicknesses of the lines.
Private m_LineWidth As Integer = 1
<EditorAttribute(GetType(LineWidthEditor), GetType(UITypeEditor))> _
Public Property LineWidth() As Integer
    Get
        Return m_LineWidth
    End Get
    Set(ByVal value As Integer)
        If value < 1 Then value = 1
        If value > 10 Then value = 10
        m_LineWidth = value
        Me.Invalidate()
    End Set
End Property
```

The `EditorAttribute` attribute indicates that the `PolyPolylineEditor` class provides support for editing the `PolyPolyline` property in the Properties window. It provides that support with the `LineWidthEditor` class.

The `LineWidthEditor` class uses a `LineWidthListBox` object. The `LineWidthEditor` and `Line WidthListBox` classes are described in the following sections. (You can download these examples at `www.vb-helper.com/one_on_one.htm`.)

LineWidthEditor

The `LineWidthEditor` class performs two tasks. First, it lets the user edit a `LineWidth` property by selecting an item from a drop-down list. Second, it displays a sample line with the right thickness in the Properties window. Figure 11-4 shows both the editing drop-down and the sample line drawn in the Properties window.

The following code shows the `LineWidthEditor` class perform these tasks:

```
Imports System.Drawing.Design

Public Class LineWidthEditor
    Inherits System.Drawing.Design.UITypeEditor

    ' Indicates that this editor displays a dropdown.
    Public Overloads Overrides Function GetEditStyle( _
     ByVal context As System.ComponentModel.ITypeDescriptorContext) _
     As System.Drawing.Design.UITypeEditorEditStyle
        Return UITypeEditorEditStyle.DropDown
    End Function

    ' Edit a line width.
    Public Overloads Overrides Function EditValue(_
```

```
    ByVal context As System.ComponentModel.ITypeDescriptorContext, _
    ByVal provider As System.IServiceProvider, ByVal value As Object) As Object
        ' Get an IWindowsFormsEditorService.
        Dim editor_service As IWindowsFormsEditorService = _
            CType(provider.GetService(GetType(IWindowsFormsEditorService)), _
                IWindowsFormsEditorService)

        ' If we failed to get the editor service, return the value.
        If editor_service Is Nothing Then Return value

        ' Convert the generic value into a line width value.
        Dim line_width As Integer = DirectCast(value, Integer)

        ' Make the editing control.
        Dim editor_control As New LineWidthListBox(line_width, editor_service)

        ' Display the editing control.
        editor_service.DropDownControl(editor_control)

        ' Save the new results.
        Return editor_control.SelectedIndex + 1
    End Function

    ' Indicate that we draw a representation for the Properties window's value.
    Public Overrides Function GetPaintValueSupported(_
     ByVal context As System.ComponentModel.ITypeDescriptorContext) As Boolean
        Return True
    End Function

    ' Draw a representation for the Properties window's value.
    Public Overrides Sub PaintValue(_
     ByVal e As System.Drawing.Design.PaintValueEventArgs)
        e.Graphics.FillRectangle(Brushes.White, e.Bounds)

        Dim line_width As Integer = DirectCast(e.Value, Integer)
        Dim y As Integer = e.Bounds.Y + e.Bounds.Height \ 2
        Using line_pen As New Pen(Color.Black, line_width)
            e.Graphics.DrawLine(line_pen, _
                e.Bounds.Left + 1, y, _
                e.Bounds.Right - 1, y)
        End Using
    End Sub
End Class
```

`LineWidthEditor` inherits from the `UITypeEditor` class. That class provides basic support for the Properties window.

The editor overrides its inherited `GetEditStyle` function to return `UITypeEditorEditStyle.DropDown`, indicating that the editor provides a drop-down property editor.

The `EditValue` function actually does the editing. It casts the value it should edit into an `Integer` `LineWidth` value. It then makes a `LineWidthListBox` control (described in the following section) and uses an `IWindowsFormsEditorService` object to display the control. The function finishes by returning the line width selected by the control. The Properties window sets the `LineWidth` property of the `ScribbleControl` it is editing to this value.

The `LineWidthEditor`'s `GetPaintValueSupported` function returns `True` to indicate that the class can draw a special representation of the `LineWidth` property. Subroutine `PaintValue` does the drawing. It clears a rectangle inside the bounds where it should draw, and then draws a line with the appropriate thickness.

See Figure 11-4 to see the result. Notice that the Properties window displays a textual representation of the `LineWidth` in addition to the sample line.

LineWidthListBox

To edit a `LineWidth` value, the `LineWidthEditor` class displays a `LineWidthListBox` control. This control should be a single control that the Properties window can display as a drop-down.

The following code defines the `LineWidthListBox` control:

```
Imports System.ComponentModel

<ToolboxItem(False)> _
Public Class LineWidthListBox
    Inherits ListBox

    ' The editor service displaying us.
    Private m_EditorService As IWindowsFormsEditorService

    ' A margin around the image in the list box.
    Private Const ITEM_MARGIN As Integer = 2

    Public Sub New(ByVal line_width As Integer, _
     ByVal editor_service As IWindowsFormsEditorService)
        MyBase.New()
        m_EditorService = editor_service

        ' Give the list some items.
        For i As Integer = 0 To 9
            Me.Items.Add(i)
        Next i
        Me.SelectedIndex = line_width - 1
        Me.DrawMode = Windows.Forms.DrawMode.OwnerDrawFixed
        Me.ItemHeight = 16 + 2 * ITEM_MARGIN
    End Sub

    ' Close the dropdown.
    Private Sub LineWidthEditorDropdown_Click(ByVal sender As Object, _
     ByVal e As System.EventArgs) Handles Me.Click
        If m_EditorService IsNot Nothing Then m_EditorService.CloseDropDown()
    End Sub

    ' Draw a menu item.
    Private Sub LineWidthEditorDropdown_DrawItem(ByVal sender As Object, _
     ByVal e As System.Windows.Forms.DrawItemEventArgs) Handles Me.DrawItem
```

```
        ' Clear the background background.
        e.DrawBackground()

        ' Decide where to draw.
        Dim x1 As Integer = e.Bounds.X + ITEM_MARGIN
        Dim x2 As Integer = e.Bounds.Right - ITEM_MARGIN
        Dim y As Integer = e.Bounds.Y + e.Bounds.Height \ 2

        ' Draw the appropriate line.
        Using line_pen As New Pen(Color.Black, e.Index + 1)
            e.Graphics.DrawLine(line_pen, x1, y, x2, y)
        End Using

        ' Draw the focus rectangle if appropriate.
        If e.State = DrawItemState.Selected Then e.DrawFocusRectangle()
    End Sub
End Class
```

The control begins with a `ToolboxItem` attribute with the value `False`. That prevents the control from appearing in the form designer's toolbox. This control is used only by the `ScribbleControl`'s design-time support classes, so application developers don't need to use it.

The control inherits from the `ListBox`, so it's basically a list control that draws its items.

The control's constructor adds items to represent line widths from 1 to 10 to its `Items` collection and selects the appropriate item. It sets its `DrawMode` property to indicate that the control's code will draw the items and that they will all have the same size. It sets `ItemHeight` to 16 plus a margin to indicate that the items will have this height.

When the user selects an item from the control's list, the `Click` event handler calls the editor service's `CloseDropDown` method. This tells the service that the user has finished using the drop-down. At that point the `LineWidthEditor` object's call to the service's `DropDownControl` method returns, so the `LineWidthEditor` can save the new `LineWidth` value.

The `LineWidthListBox` control's `DrawItem` event handler is invoked when the drop-down must draw an item. The control simply draws a sample line within the bounds on the Properties window. Then, if the item it is drawing is currently selected in the list, the control draws a focus rectangle around it.

Displaying and Editing LineColor

The `ScribbleControl` handles its `LineColor` property much as it does its `LineWidth` property. The following code shows how the `ScribbleControl` declares its `LineColor` property:

```
' The color we use for the lines.
Public Enum LineColors
    Red
    Orange
    Yellow
    Green
    Blue
```

```
        Ingido
        Violet
        Black
        White
    End Enum
    Public Const NumLineColors As Integer = 9

    Private m_LineColor As LineColors = LineColors.Black
    <EditorAttribute(GetType(ColorIndexEditor), GetType(UITypeEditor))> _
    Public Property LineColor() As LineColors
        Get
            Return m_LineColor
        End Get
        Set(ByVal value As LineColors)
            m_LineColor = value
            Me.Invalidate()
        End Set
    End Property
```

The `LineColors` enumerated type lists the values that are allowed for the property and the property has type `LineColor`.

The property's `EditorAttribute` attribute indicates that the `ColorIndexEditor` class provides editing features for the property. This class is similar to the `LineWidthEditor` class, except that it displays a `ColorIndexListBox` control instead of a `LineWidthListBox` control.

Like `LineWidthListBox`, the `ColorIndexListBox` control inherits from the `ListBox` control and draws its own items. The only important difference is that `ColorIndexListBox` draws samples of colors rather than sample lines.

Unlike the `LineWidthEditor`, the `ColorIndexEditor` control does not provide an implementation of its inherited `GetPaintValueSupported` and `PaintValue` routines. That means the class does not display a sample of the color in the Properties window. It displays a drop-down, just as the control does for editing `LineWidth`, but it doesn't show a sample of the color in the Properties window.

Instead the Properties window automatically generates a textual representation from the enumerated type. Figure 11-3 shows the color drop-down that lets you pick a color value. The Properties window shows the textual equivalent Yellow above it.

Displaying and Editing PolyPolyline

The `ScribbleControl`'s `PolyPolyline` property also provides support for special display and editing. This property is different from `LineWidth` and `LineColor` in a couple of respects. First, it wouldn't make much sense to display a textual representation of the property in the Properties window (what string would represent the fish drawing?). To prevent confusion, the code overrides this behavior and displays a blank string in the Properties window.

Second, this property provides the modal dialog editor shown in Figure 11-2 instead of a drop-down editor.

The following code shows how the `ScribbleControl` defines its `PolyPolyline` property:

```
' The points we draw.
Private m_PolyPolyline As PolyPolyline = New PolyPolyline
<TypeConverter(GetType(PolyPolylineConverter))> _
<EditorAttribute(GetType(PolyPolylineEditor), GetType(UITypeEditor))> _
Public Property PolyPolyline() As PolyPolyline
    Get
        Return m_PolyPolyline
    End Get
    Set(ByVal value As PolyPolyline)
        m_PolyPolyline = value
        Me.Invalidate()
    End Set
End Property
```

The `TypeConverter` attribute tells Visual Studio that the `PolyPolylineConverter` class can convert a `PolyPolyline` object into other data types. The Properties window uses this converter to translate the `PolyPolyline` property to and from strings.

The `EditorAttribute` attribute indicates that the `PolyPolylineEditor` class provides support for editing the `PolyPolyline` property in the Properties window.

PolyPolylineConverter

By default, the Properties window would display this property as a collection of `Polyline` objects and would let the user edit the value by using a collection editor. Each of the `Polyline` objects would have a `Points` property that was a collection of `Point` objects. Viewing and editing the `PolyPolyline` by using these collection editors would be ridiculously difficult.

It also wouldn't be very meaningful to display a `PolyPolyline` object in a string representation. You could display a list of X and Y coordinates separated by commas, parentheses, and brackets. This might be useful for code loading and saving data, but it would be no more meaningful to the developer than a series of collection editors.

To avoid displaying these useless representations, the `PolyPolylineConverter` class converts a `PolyPolyline` object into a blank string. The Properties window then displays the blank string instead of a collection of `Polylines` or a sequence of coordinates.

The following code shows how the `PolyPolylineConverter` class works:

```
' Displays a blank string for a PolyPolyline property.
' Cannot convert from anything.
Imports System.ComponentModel

Public Class PolyPolylineConverter
    Inherits TypeConverter

    ' We can convert into String.
    Public Overrides Function CanConvertTo( _
     ByVal context As System.ComponentModel.ITypeDescriptorContext, _
     ByVal destinationType As System.Type) As Boolean
```

```
        If destinationType Is GetType(String) Then Return True
        Return MyBase.CanConvertTo(context, destinationType)
    End Function

    ' Convert into a blank String.
    Public Overrides Function ConvertTo(_
     ByVal context As System.ComponentModel.ITypeDescriptorContext, _
     ByVal culture As System.Globalization.CultureInfo, _
     ByVal value As Object, ByVal destinationType As System.Type) As Object
        If destinationType Is GetType(String) Then
            Return ""
        Else
            Return MyBase.ConvertTo(context, culture, value, destinationType)
        End If
    End Function
End Class
```

The class inherits from `TypeConverter`. It overrides the inherited `CanConvertTo` function to return `True` if the destination data type is `String`. This tells Visual Studio that the class can convert to a `String`.

The `ConvertTo` function returns a blank string if the destination type is `String`. This is what the Properties window displays.

The class does not override its inherited `CanConvertFrom` and `ConvertFrom` methods, so the control cannot convert other types such as `String` into a `PolyPolyline`. If you wanted to allow the user to enter new textual values for the property in the Properties window, you would override these routines to translate `Strings` into `PolyPolylines`.

PolyPolylineEditor

The `PolyPolylineEditor` class provides editing and display capabilities for the `PolyPolyline` property in the Properties window. When you click the ellipsis to the right of the property in the Properties window, Visual Studio displays the dialog shown in Figure 11-2. It also draws the tiny image of the drawing shown in Figure 11-1.

The following code shows the first half of the `PolyPolylineEditor` class. This is the code that provides the editing dialog.

```
' This is an editor for a PolyPolyline property.
' It displays a ScribbleControl in a modal dialog.
Imports System.Drawing.Design

Public Class PolyPolylineEditor
    Inherits System.Drawing.Design.UITypeEditor

#Region "Value Editing Code"
    ' Indicates that this editor displays a modal dialog.
    Public Overloads Overrides Function GetEditStyle( _
     ByVal context As System.ComponentModel.ITypeDescriptorContext) _
     As System.Drawing.Design.UITypeEditorEditStyle
        Return UITypeEditorEditStyle.Modal
```

```
    End Function

    ' Edit a PolyPolyline.
    Public Overloads Overrides Function EditValue(_
     ByVal context As System.ComponentModel.ITypeDescriptorContext, _
     ByVal provider As System.IServiceProvider, ByVal value As Object) As Object
        ' Get an IWindowsFormsEditorService.
        Dim editor_service As IWindowsFormsEditorService = _
            CType(provider.GetService(GetType(IWindowsFormsEditorService)), _
                IWindowsFormsEditorService)

        ' If we failed to get the editor service, return the value unchanged.
        If editor_service Is Nothing Then Return value

        ' Convert the generic value into a PolyPolyline.
        Dim ppline As PolyPolyline = DirectCast(value, PolyPolyline)

        ' Make the editing dialog.
        Dim editor_dialog As New PolyPolylineEditorDialog()
        editor_dialog.PolyPolyline = ppline
        editor_dialog.EditorService = editor_service

        ' Display the editing dialog.
        editor_service.ShowDialog(editor_dialog)

        ' Save the new results.
        If editor_dialog.DialogResult = DialogResult.OK Then
            ' Return the new PolyPolyline.
            Return editor_dialog.PolyPolyline
        Else
            ' Return the old PolyPolyline.
            Return ppline
        End If
    End Function
#End Region ' Value Editing Code
```

Like the `LineWidthEditor` and `LineColorEditor` classes, this class inherits from `UITypeEditor`. Whereas the other classes override their `GetEditStyle` functions to return `UITypeEditorEditStyle.DropDown`, this class returns `UITypeEditorEditStyle.Modal` to indicate that it displays a modal editor dialog.

In the previous classes, the `EditValue` function displays a drop-down. In this class, `EditValue` displays the modal editor. First, it casts the value that it is editing into a `PolyPolyline` object. It then makes a new `PolyPolylineEditorDialog`. This is a form defined in the `ScribbleControl` project, and is the form shown in Figure 11-2. You can download the example program to see all of the dialog's code.

The `PolyPolylineEditorDialog` contains a `ScribbleControl` with the `Enabled` property set to `True` so you can click the control's surface to draw a new `PolyPolyline`.

The editor form has a public `PolyPolyline` property. When the `PolyPolylineEditor` object sets the form's `PolyPolyline` property, the form copies the `PolyPolyline` into its `ScribbleControl`.

After setting the dialog's `PolyPolyline` property, the `PolyPolylineEditor` displays the dialog modally. If the user clicks the OK button, the `EditValue` method returns the dialog's new `PolyPolyline` property. If the user clicks Cancel, the function returns the original `PolyPolyline` value so the control's property is unchanged.

The following code shows the second half of the `PolyPolylineEditor` class. This is the code that lets the Properties window display the miniature image of the `ScribbleControl`'s drawing shown in Figure 11-1.

```
#Region "Property Display Code"
    ' Indicate that we draw a representation for the Properties window's value.
    Public Overrides Function GetPaintValueSupported(_
     ByVal context As System.ComponentModel.ITypeDescriptorContext) As Boolean
        Return True
    End Function

    ' Draw a representation for the Properties window's value
    ' by converting the scribble into a tiny image.
    Public Overrides Sub PaintValue(_
     ByVal e As System.Drawing.Design.PaintValueEventArgs)
        ' Get the points.
        Dim ppline As PolyPolyline = DirectCast(e.Value, PolyPolyline)
        If (ppline IsNot Nothing) Then
            ' Find the points' bounds.
            Dim ppline_rect As Rectangle = ppline.Bounds()
            ppline_rect.Inflate(CInt(ppline_rect.Width * 0.1), _
                CInt(ppline_rect.Height * 0.1))

            ' Make a bitmap to hold a small image of the scribble.
            Dim pts_wid As Integer = ppline_rect.Width
            Dim pts_hgt As Integer = ppline_rect.Height
            Dim bm_wid As Integer = e.Bounds.Width - 2
            Dim bm_hgt As Integer = e.Bounds.Height - 2
            Dim x_scale As Double = bm_wid / pts_wid
            Dim y_scale As Double = bm_hgt / pts_hgt
            Dim scale As Single = CSng(Math.Min(x_scale, y_scale))

            Dim bm As New Bitmap(bm_wid, bm_hgt)
            Using gr As Graphics = Graphics.FromImage(bm)
                Dim x0 As Integer = CInt(ppline_rect.X +  _
                    (ppline_rect.Width - bm_wid / scale) / 2)
                Dim y0 As Integer = CInt(ppline_rect.Y +  _
                    (ppline_rect.Height - bm_hgt / scale) / 2)
                gr.TranslateTransform(-x0, -y0)
                gr.ScaleTransform(scale, scale, Drawing2D.MatrixOrder.Append)
                gr.SmoothingMode = Drawing2D.SmoothingMode.AntiAlias
                ppline.Draw(gr, Pens.Black)
            End Using

            ' Copy the little bitmap onto the drawing surface.
            e.Graphics.InterpolationMode = Drawing2D.InterpolationMode.High
            e.Graphics.DrawImage(bm, e.Bounds.X + 1, e.Bounds.Y + 1)
        End If
```

```
    End Sub
#End Region ' Property Display Code

End Class
```

The class overrides its inherited `GetPaintValueSupported` function, so it returns `True` to indicate that this class can draw a `PolyPolyline`'s value in the Properties window.

The `PaintValue` subroutine draws the value. It converts its `e.Value` parameter into the `PolyPolyline` value that it must draw. It uses the `PolyPolyline` object's `Bounds` property to get a bounding box for the drawing, and inflates the bounds to include a small margin around the drawing.

Next, `PaintValue` make a `Bitmap` that fits the bounds where the Properties window needs the image drawn. It builds a graphical transformation that translates and scales the image so that it fits on the `Bitmap` and draws the image. Finally `PaintValue` draws the `Bitmap` onto the Properties window.

Displaying Smart Tags

To display a smart tag, you use the `Designer` attribute to associate the control with a designer. The following code shows the `Designer` attribute that associates the `ScribbleControl` class with the `ScribbleControlDesigner` class. You'll see this `Class` statement with a bit more context later in this chapter.

```
...
<Designer(GetType(ScribbleControlDesigner))> _
...
Public Class ScribbleControl
    ...
End Class
```

The `ScribbleControlDesigner` class is relatively simple. The following shows the class's code:

```
' Designer for the ScribbleControl.
' This lets the control display a smart tag.
Public Class ScribbleControlDesigner
    Inherits ControlDesigner

    Private lists As DesignerActionListCollection

    Public Overrides ReadOnly Property ActionLists() _
     As DesignerActionListCollection
        Get
            If lists Is Nothing Then
                lists = New DesignerActionListCollection()
                lists.Add(New ScribbleActionList(Me.Component))
            End If
            Return lists
        End Get
    End Property
End Class
```

`ScribbleControlDesigner` inherits from the `ControlDesigner` designer class and overrides its inherited `ActionLists` function. This function returns a `DesignerActionListCollection` that contains a list of classes that represent the lists of actions that the smart tag should contain. This example uses the single action list class named `ScribbleActionList`.

The `ScribbleActionList` class is longer, but it's not too complicated. The following code shows how the class works:

```
' This is the action list displayed by the ScribbleControl's smart tag.
Imports System.ComponentModel.Design
Imports System.Drawing.Design
Imports System.Math

Public Class ScribbleActionList
    Inherits DesignerActionList

    ' The control we are manipulating.
    Private m_Scribble As ScribbleControl

    Private m_DesignerService As DesignerActionUIService = Nothing

    ' Save a reference to our control.
    Public Sub New(ByVal component As IComponent)
        MyBase.New(component)

        m_Scribble = DirectCast(component, ScribbleControl)

        ' Save a reference to DesignerActionUIService we can refresh it.
        m_DesignerService = _
            CType(GetService(GetType(DesignerActionUIService)), _
                DesignerActionUIService)
    End Sub

#Region "Smart Tag Items"

    ' LineColor.
    <EditorAttribute(GetType(ColorIndexEditor), GetType(UITypeEditor))> _
    Public Property LineColor() As ScribbleControl.LineColors
        Get
            Return m_Scribble.LineColor
        End Get
        Set(ByVal value As ScribbleControl.LineColors)
            SetControlProperty("LineColor", value)
        End Set
    End Property

    ' BackColor.
    Public Property BackColor() As Color
        Get
            Return m_Scribble.BackColor
        End Get
        Set(ByVal value As Color)
            SetControlProperty("BackColor", value)
        End Set
```

```
End Property

' LineWidth.
<EditorAttribute(GetType(LineWidthEditor), GetType(UITypeEditor))> _
Public Property LineWidth() As Integer
    Get
        Return m_Scribble.LineWidth
    End Get
    Set(ByVal value As Integer)
        SetControlProperty("LineWidth", value)
    End Set
End Property

' Make a star Polyline.
Public Sub DrawStar()
    ' Make a new PolyPolyline containing a star.
    Dim ppline As New PolyPolyline
    ppline.Clear()
    ppline.AddPolyline()

    Dim cx As Integer = m_Scribble.ClientSize.Width \ 2
    Dim cy As Integer = m_Scribble.ClientSize.Height \ 2
    Dim dtheta As Double = 2 * PI * 2 / 5
    For i As Integer = 0 To 6
        Dim x As Integer = CInt(cx + Cos(i * dtheta - PI / 2) * cx)
        Dim y As Integer = CInt(cy + Sin(i * dtheta - PI / 2) * cy)
        ppline.AddPoint(x, y)
    Next i

    ' Save the new property.
    SetControlProperty("PolyPolyline", ppline)

    ' Refresh the smart tag list to show the new Polyline count.
    Me.m_DesignerService.Refresh(Me.Component)
End Sub

' Make a spiral Polyline.
Public Sub DrawSpiral()
    ' Make a new PolyPolyline containing a star.
    Dim ppline As New PolyPolyline
    ppline.Clear()
    ppline.AddPolyline()

    Dim cx As Integer = m_Scribble.ClientSize.Width \ 2
    Dim cy As Integer = m_Scribble.ClientSize.Height \ 2
    Dim theta As Double = 0
    Const NUM_POINTS As Integer = 100
    Dim dtheta As Double = 4 * PI / NUM_POINTS
    Dim rx As Double = 0
    Dim drx As Double = cx / NUM_POINTS
    Dim ry As Double = 0
    Dim dry As Double = cy / NUM_POINTS
    For i As Integer = 0 To NUM_POINTS - 1
        Dim x As Integer = CInt(cx + Cos(theta) * rx)
        Dim y As Integer = CInt(cy + Sin(theta) * ry)
```

```
            ppline.AddPoint(x, y)
            theta += dtheta
            rx += drx
            ry += dry
        Next i

        ' Save the new property.
        SetControlProperty("PolyPolyline", ppline)

        ' Refresh the smart tag list to show the new Polyline count.
        Me.m_DesignerService.Refresh(Me.Component)
    End Sub

    ' Set a property value for the control.
    ' You could just set the property directly
    ' as in m_ScribbleControl.LineWidth = 1 but then
    ' the IDE's undo/redo feature doesn't work properly and
    ' the form is not marked as modified in the IDE.
    Private Sub SetControlProperty(ByVal property_name As String, _
     ByVal value As Object)
        TypeDescriptor.GetProperties(m_Scribble)(property_name). _
            SetValue(m_Scribble, value)
    End Sub

#End Region ' Smart Tag Items

    ' Return a collection representing the smart tag items.
    Public Overrides Function GetSortedActionItems()_
     As DesignerActionItemCollection
        Dim items As New DesignerActionItemCollection()

        ' Define section headers.
        items.Add(New DesignerActionHeaderItem("Appearance"))
        items.Add(New DesignerActionHeaderItem("Information"))

        ' Appearance entries.
        items.Add( _
            New DesignerActionPropertyItem( _
                "BackColor", _
                "Back Color", _
                "Appearance", _
                "Sets the background color."))
        items.Add( _
            New DesignerActionPropertyItem( _
                "LineColor", _
                "Line Color", _
                "Appearance", _
                "Sets the line drawing color."))
        items.Add( _
            New DesignerActionPropertyItem( _
                "LineWidth", _
                "Line Width", _
                "Appearance", _
                "Sets the line thickness."))
```

```
        ' The DrawStar subroutine.
        items.Add( _
            New DesignerActionMethodItem( _
                Me, _
                "DrawStar", _
                "Draw Star", _
                "Appearance", _
                "Draws a star.", _
                False))

        ' The DrawSpiral subroutine.
        ' Also appears in the context menu.
        items.Add( _
            New DesignerActionMethodItem( _
                Me, _
                "DrawSpiral", _
                "Draw Spiral", _
                "Appearance", _
                "Draws a spiral.", _
                True))

        ' Information entries.
        Dim txt As String = "# Polylines: " & _
            m_Scribble.PolyPolyline.Polylines.Length
        items.Add( _
            New DesignerActionTextItem( _
                txt, _
                "Information"))

        Return items
    End Function

End Class
```

The `ScribbleActionList` class inherits from `DesignerActionList`. It has private variables to refer to the `ScribbleControl` that the smart tag is editing, and to the designer service it is using. The class's constructor saves references to those objects.

The class then contains a series of properties to represent values that it can manipulate. It delegates the properties to the `ScribbleControl` it is editing.

One oddity here is the way the property set routines work. These routines could just set the control's property directly. For example, the `LineColor` property set routine could use the following statement:

```
m_ScribbleControl.LineColor = value
```

Unfortunately, this method doesn't work well for three reasons. First, it doesn't make the smart tag update the control, so the control doesn't show any changes. In this case, that means it wouldn't redraw to use the new `LineColor`. (You could fix this by invalidating the control, but there are other problems.)

Second, this doesn't integrate with the IDE's undo and redo features, so undo and redo won't work properly.

Finally, this method doesn't flag the form as modified. If you open a form in the form designer, use the smart tag to change a property, and then close the form, the IDE doesn't realize that you made a change, so it doesn't save the new property value.

To work around all of these problems, the property set procedures call helper subroutine `SetControlProperty`. That routine uses a `TypeDescriptor` to get the control's property information, and then calls the `SetValue` method to set the property's new value. This makes the IDE properly aware of the change.

Notice that the `LineColor` and `LineWidth` properties use `EditorAttribute` attributes to associate the properties with the same `ColorIndexEditor` and `LineWidthEditor` classes used by the `ScribbleControl` itself. This allows the smart tag panel to use the associated editor controls to display and edit the properties just as the Properties window does. Figure 11-10 shows the smart tag panel displaying its `LineWidth` editor.

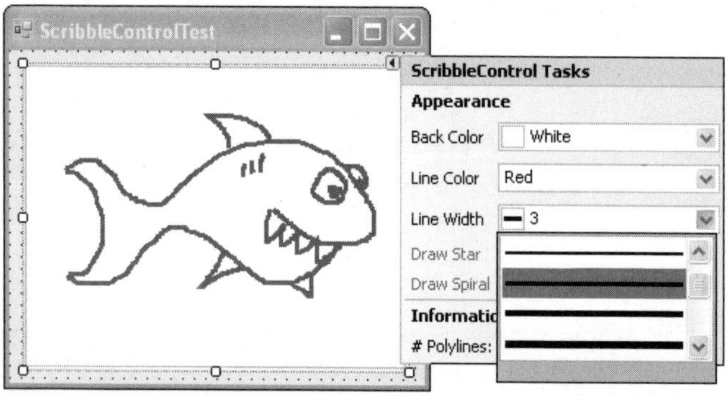

Figure 11-10: The smart tag panel can use `UITypeEditors`, too.

The `LineColor`, `BackColor`, and `LineWidth` properties are relatively straightforward. The `DrawStar` and `DrawSpiral` subroutines are almost as simple. They each create a new `PolyPolyline` object and add points to it to make a star or spiral. They then use the `SetControlProperty` subroutine to set the `ScribbleControl`'s `PolyPolyline` property to the new object.

The routines finish by calling the designer service's `Refresh` method to make the smart tag panel refresh itself. In this example, that updates the `Polyline` count displayed on the panel.

After the properties and action subroutines, the `ScribbleActionList` class overrides its inherited `GetSortedActionItems` function. This function provides instructions for laying out the smart tag panel. If you omit this function, the panel includes the properties and action subroutines in alphabetical order. Usually, you will want to override `GetSortedActionItems` to group related items in sections, and to give them a more meaningful order.

In this example, the function creates a new `DesignerActionItemCollection`. It then adds two section headers that display the text `Appearance` and `Information`.

Next, the function adds objects to the `DesignerActionItemCollection` to determine how the items are arranged. For a property, the code adds a `DesignerActionPropertyItem` object. The object's constructor specifies the property's name, the text that should be displayed on the smart tag panel, the section that should include it (`Appearance` or `Information` in this example), and a tooltip.

For the DrawStar and DrawSpiral subroutines, the code adds a DesignerActionMethodItem object. The constructor includes the object providing the method, the method's name, the text that should be displayed on the smart tag panel, the section that should include it, a tooltip, and a Boolean indicating whether the item should also be displayed as an action verb below the Properties window. This example sets this Boolean to False for the DrawStar method and True for the DrawSpiral method, so only DrawSpiral appears below the Properties window in Figure 11-1.

Finally, the GetSortedActionItems function adds a DesignerActionTextItem to the DesignerActionItemCollection. This item displays some static text; in this case, showing the number of Polylines drawn by the ScribbleControl. When the DrawStar or DrawSpiral subroutine calls the designer service's Refresh method, the GetSortedActionItems function is called again so this value is updated. (You can download this example at www.vb-helper.com/one_on_one.htm.)

Displaying Property Sheets

The final design-time enhancement provided by the ScribbleControl is support for property sheets. To display property sheets, you use an EditorAttribute statement to associate the control class with an editor class. The following code shows how the ScribbleControl class is associated with the ScribbleControlEditor class:

```
<ToolboxBitmap(GetType(ScribbleControl), "tbxScribble")> _
<Designer(GetType(ScribbleControlDesigner))> _
<EditorAttribute(GetType(ScribbleControlEditor), GetType(ComponentEditor))> _
Public Class ScribbleControl
    Inherits Control
...
End Class
```

The following code shows how the ScribbleControlEditor class works:

```
' The editor that displays the component editor pages.
' when you right-click the control at design time
' and select Properties.
Public Class ScribbleControlEditor
    Inherits System.Windows.Forms.Design.WindowsFormsComponentEditor

    ' Return an array containing the types of the component editor pages
    ' to display.
    Protected Overrides Function GetComponentEditorPages() As Type()
        Return New Type() { _
            GetType(ScribbleControlEditorBasicsPage), _
            GetType(ScribbleControlEditorPolyPolylinePage) _
        }
    End Function

    ' Return the index of the first page to display.
    Protected Overrides Function GetInitialComponentEditorPageIndex() As Integer
        Return 0
    End Function
End Class
```

The `ScribbleControlEditor` class inherits from `WindowsFormsComponentEditor`. It overrides its inherited `GetComponentEditorPages` function to return an array containing type information describing the classes that implement the editor's property pages. This example uses two property page classes named `ScribbleControlEditorBasicsPage` and `ScribbleControlEditorPolyPolylinePage`.

The `ScribbleControlEditor` class also overrides its `GetInitialComponentEditorPageIndex` function to return the index of the property page that should initially be displayed. This example simply returns `0` to display the first page.

The following code shows the `ScribbleControlEditorBasicsPage` class:

```
' The property editor's basic property page.
<ToolboxItem(False)> _
Public Class ScribbleControlEditorBasicsPage
    Inherits System.Windows.Forms.Design.ComponentEditorPage

    Private m_ScribbleControl As ScribbleControl

    Friend WithEvents lblLineWidth As System.Windows.Forms.Label
    Friend WithEvents lwlLineWidthEditorListBox As LineWidthListBox
    Friend WithEvents lblBackColor As System.Windows.Forms.Label
    Friend WithEvents picBackColor As System.Windows.Forms.PictureBox
    Friend WithEvents dlgBackColor As System.Windows.Forms.ColorDialog
    Friend WithEvents lblLineColor As System.Windows.Forms.Label
    Friend WithEvents cilColorIndexListBox As ColorIndexListBox

    ' Initialize the page.
    Public Sub New()
        Me.Size = New Size(400, 200)
        Me.Text = "Basics"
        Me.Icon = My.Resources.icoScribbleBasics

        Me.lblLineWidth = New System.Windows.Forms.Label
        Me.lblLineWidth.AutoSize = True
        Me.lblLineWidth.Location = New System.Drawing.Point(8, 8)
        Me.lblLineWidth.Name = "lblLineWidth"
        Me.lblLineWidth.Size = New System.Drawing.Size(61, 13)
        Me.lblLineWidth.TabIndex = 0
        Me.lblLineWidth.Text = "Line Width:"

        Me.lwlLineWidthEditorListBox = New LineWidthListBox(1, Nothing)
        Me.lwlLineWidthEditorListBox.Location = New System.Drawing.Point(112, 8)
        Me.lwlLineWidthEditorListBox.Name = "lwdLineWidthEditorDropdown"
        Me.lwlLineWidthEditorListBox.Size = New System.Drawing.Size(72, 134)
        Me.lwlLineWidthEditorListBox.TabIndex = 1

        ' Other control creation code omitted...

        Me.dlgBackColor = New System.Windows.Forms.ColorDialog

        Me.Controls.AddRange(New Control() { _
            lblLineWidth, lwlLineWidthEditorListBox, _
            lblBackColor, picBackColor, _
```

```
                lblLineColor, cilColorIndexListBox _
            })
        End Sub

        ' The LoadComponent method is raised when the ComponentEditorPage is displayed.
        Protected Overrides Sub LoadComponent()
            m_ScribbleControl = DirectCast(Me.Component, ScribbleControl)
            picBackColor.BackColor = m_ScribbleControl.BackColor
            lwlLineWidthEditorListBox.SelectedIndex = m_ScribbleControl.LineWidth - 1
            cilColorIndexListBox.SelectedIndex = _
                CType(m_ScribbleControl.LineColor, Integer)
        End Sub

        ' Save the selected LineWidth and BackColor.
        Protected Overrides Sub SaveComponent()
            m_ScribbleControl.LineWidth = lwlLineWidthEditorListBox.SelectedIndex + 1
            m_ScribbleControl.BackColor = picBackColor.BackColor
            m_ScribbleControl.LineColor = _
                CType(cilColorIndexListBox.SelectedIndex, ScribbleControl.LineColors)
        End Sub

        ' Let the user select a color from a ColorDialog.
        Private Sub picBackColor_Click(ByVal sender As Object, _
         ByVal e As System.EventArgs) Handles picBackColor.Click
            If dlgBackColor.ShowDialog() = Windows.Forms.DialogResult.OK Then
                picBackColor.BackColor = dlgBackColor.Color

                ' Let the editor know that the user changed a property value.
                Me.SetDirty()
            End If
        End Sub

        ' Let the editor know that the user changed a property value.
        Private Sub lwlLineWidthEditorListBox_SelectedIndexChanged(_
         ByVal sender As Object, ByVal e As System.EventArgs) _
         Handles lwlLineWidthEditorListBox.SelectedIndexChanged
            Me.SetDirty()
        End Sub

        ' Let the editor know that the user changed a property value.
        Private Sub cilColorIndexListBox_SelectedIndexChanged(ByVal sender As Object, _
         ByVal e As System.EventArgs) Handles cilColorIndexListBox.SelectedIndexChanged
            Me.SetDirty()
        End Sub
    End Class
```

This class includes a `ToolboxItem` attribute with value set to `False` so the page does not appear in the form designer's toolbox. It makes little sense to allow developers to place the property page on a form.

The `ScribbleControlEditorBasicsPage` class inherits from `ComponentEditorPage`. It declares a reference to the control it is editing. It then declares `WithEvents` variables to represent the controls it will display.

The class's constructor creates those controls and sets their properties such as name, position, size, and text.

Rather than trying to design the form by hand using properties in this manner, you may want to make a new form and arrange the controls you need on it. Then, open the designer-generated code, and copy and paste what you need into the class.

This section of code creates `LineWidthListBox` and `LineColorListBox` controls to let the developer edit the `ScribbleControl's` `LineWidth` and `LineColor` properties. If you look back at Figure 11-8, you can see those controls. These are the same controls used by the property editors to provide drop-down lists in the Properties window and in the smart tag panel. The `ScribbleControl` code makes these controls serve triple duty.

The constructor finishes by calling the class's `Controls.AddRange` method to add the controls to the page.

The class overrides its inherited `LoadComponent`. This routine is called when the property sheet loads information for a control. The routine copies property values from the `ScribbleControl` into the controls displayed on the property page.

If the developer makes changes to some properties and then clicks the property sheet's Apply or OK button, the property sheet calls the property page's `SaveComponent` subroutine. This class overrides this method to copy the property values from its controls back to the `ScribbleControl` that it is editing.

The property page handles the `BackColor` property specially. When the developer clicks the `picBackColor` `PictureBox` control, the code displays a `ColorDialog`. If the developer selects a color and clicks OK, the code sets the `PictureBox's` `BackColor` property to the selected color. The code also calls the property page's `SetDirty` method. This tells the property sheet that a value has been modified by the developer. That makes the property sheet enable its Apply button, and tells it that it should call the page's `SaveComponent` method if the user clicks Apply or OK.

Finally, the page's code catches any `SelectedIndexChanged` events raised by its `LineWidthListBox` or `ColorIndexListBox` controls. The event handlers also call the page's `SetDirty` method to tell the property sheet that the developer has changed a property. (You can download this example at `www.vb-helper.com/one_on_one.htm`.)

Displaying Object Properties

Most control properties are relatively simple values that determine a single aspect of the control's behavior. They determine the control's background color, image, text, or visibility. Occasionally, however, a property is a reference to another object. For example, the `Font` property used by most controls that display text refers to a `Font` object that has its own properties and methods.

To examine object properties such as these, this section uses a new example. Figure 11-11 shows a form containing a `UserControl` named `ContactViewer`. This control has two object properties: `Contact` and `Address`.

The `Contact` class has `FirstName`, `LastName`, and `Phone` properties. The `Address` class provides `Street`, `City`, `State`, and `Zip` properties. The `ContactViewer` simply displays the values in those properties in its `Label` controls.

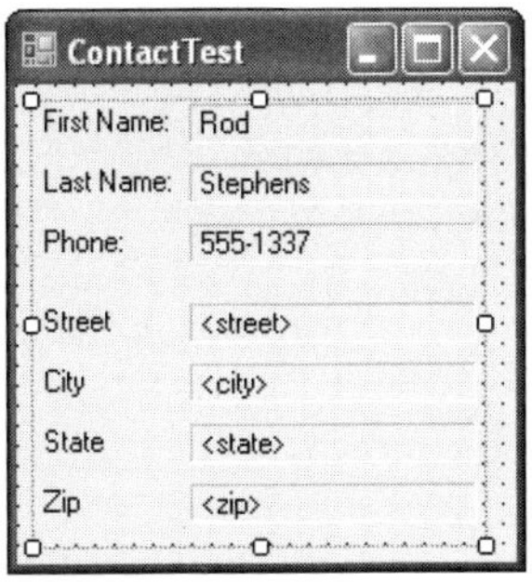

Figure 11-11: The `ContactViewer` `UserControl` has `Contact` and `Address` properties that are objects.

Left to its own devices, the Properties window displays an object reference property by using the value returned by its `ToString` function. `ToString` is inherited from the `Object` class so every class has one. The default implementation provided by `Object` returns the object's class name, which is seldom very useful.

For example, in the example program `ContactTest`, the Properties window displays the `ContactViewer` control's `Address` property as "`ContactTest.Address`." You can see this value near the top of the Properties window shown in Figure 11-12.

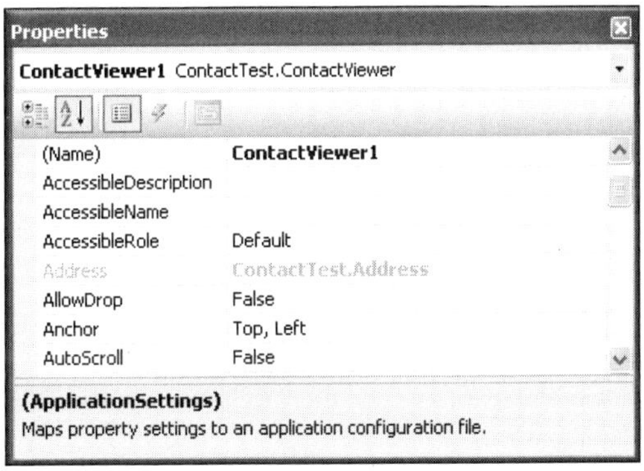

Figure 11-12: By default, the Properties window displays the `Address` property's class name.

It's not hard to override the `ToString` method to make an object property display something more meaningful. The following code makes `ToString` return a concatenated version of the `Address` object's properties:

```
' Display the Address fields.
Public Overrides Function ToString() As String
    Return Street & ", " & City & ", " & State & ", " & Zip
End Function
```

Figure 11-13 shows the Properties window displaying the value returned by `ToString`.

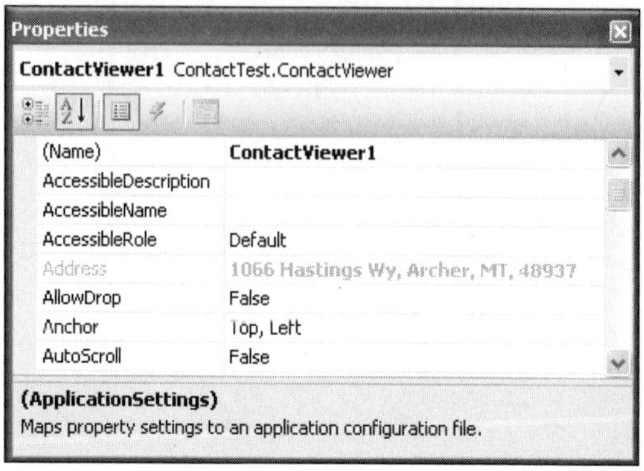

Figure 11-13: The Properties window displays the result of an object's `ToString` function.

This is better, but it's still not perfect. The value displayed for the property is grayed out and not editable. The Properties window also doesn't display the object property's sub-properties, and it doesn't let the user edit them the way it does for other standard property types such as `Point`, `Size`, and `Font` properties.

To allow the developer to view and edit sub-properties, you must provide a type converter for the property's class. The following code shows how this example's `Contact` class is defined. It includes a `TypeConverter` attribute to make the `ContactConverter` class this class's type converter.

```
Imports System.ComponentModel

<TypeConverter(GetType(ContactConverter))> _
Public Class Contact
...
End Class
```

The following code shows how the `ContactConverter` class works:

```
Imports System.ComponentModel

Public Class ContactConverter
    Inherits ExpandableObjectConverter

    ' We can convert from String.
    Public Overrides Function CanConvertFrom( _
     ByVal context As System.ComponentModel.ITypeDescriptorContext, _
     ByVal sourceType As System.Type) As Boolean
        If sourceType Is GetType(String) Then Return True
        Return MyBase.CanConvertFrom(context, sourceType)
    End Function

    ' Convert from String.
    Public Overrides Function ConvertFrom(_
```

```
        ByVal context As System.ComponentModel.ITypeDescriptorContext, _
        ByVal culture As System.Globalization.CultureInfo, ByVal value As Object) _
        As Object
            If TypeOf (value) Is String Then
                Try
                    Dim new_contact As New Contact
                    Dim txt As String = DirectCast(value, String)
                    Dim name_phone() As String = txt.Split(New Char() {"("c, ")"c})
                    new_contact.Phone = name_phone(1).Trim
                    Dim first_last() As String = name_phone(0).Split(","c)
                    new_contact.FirstName = first_last(0).Trim()
                    new_contact.LastName = first_last(1).Trim()
                    Return new_contact
                Catch ex As Exception
                    Throw New ArgumentException("Error converting '" & _
                        CStr(value) & "' into a Contact object")
                End Try
            Else
                Return MyBase.ConvertFrom(context, culture, value)
            End If
        End Function

        ' We can convert into String.
        Public Overrides Function CanConvertTo(_
         ByVal context As System.ComponentModel.ITypeDescriptorContext, _
         ByVal destinationType As System.Type) As Boolean
            If destinationType Is GetType(String) Then Return True
            Return MyBase.CanConvertTo(context, destinationType)
        End Function

        ' Convert into a String.
        Public Overrides Function ConvertTo(_
         ByVal context As System.ComponentModel.ITypeDescriptorContext, _
         ByVal culture As System.Globalization.CultureInfo, ByVal value As Object, _
         ByVal destinationType As System.Type) As Object
            If (destinationType Is GetType(String)) AndAlso _
               (TypeOf value Is Contact) _
            Then
                Dim the_contact As Contact = DirectCast(value, Contact)
                Return the_contact.FirstName & ", " & _
                    the_contact.LastName & " (" & _
                    the_contact.Phone & ")"
            Else
                Return MyBase.ConvertTo(context, culture, value, destinationType)
            End If
        End Function
    End Class
```

`ContactConverter` inherits from the `ExpandableObjectConverter` class. This class provides support for converting objects to and from strings containing property values. In this example, the class will convert a `Contact` object to and from a string containing the object's `FirstName`, `LastName`, and `Phone` values in the format "Rod, Stephens (555-1337)".

The ContactConverter overrides its inherited CanConvertFrom method to return True if the desired format is String. This indicates that the converter can convert a String into a Contact object.

The ConvertFrom function performs the conversion. It creates a new Contact object, uses Split to break the string into pieces separated by the "(" and ")" characters, and uses the second of those pieces as the new object's Phone value. It uses Split again to break the first piece of the string into comma-separated pieces, and saves the new object's FirstName and LastName values. It finishes by returning the new object.

The class also overrides its inherited ConvertTo function to return a string representing the Contact object in the desired format.

Figure 11-14 shows the result. The Properties window displays the string version of the Contact object. It also lets you expand the object to view and modify its properties separately.

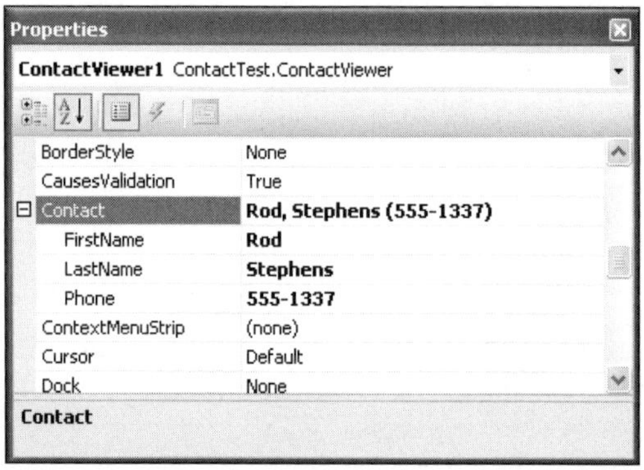

Figure 11-14: A type converter lets you edit an object's properties separately.

Building the ContactConverter class and using the TypeConverter attribute to associate it with the Contact class is almost all you need to do to make the property work as expected in the Properties window. The final trick is making the Properties window and the control update their displays when properties change.

If you edit the string representation of the Contact property in Figure 11-14, the sub-properties update automatically. However, if you change one of the sub-properties' values, the combined string representation does not update until you click it, and the UserControl on the form also does not update to display the new sub-property value.

To make the string representation automatically update, you can add the RefreshProperties attribute to the Contact class's property procedures. For example, the following code shows the Contact object's FirstName property procedure. The RefreshProperties attribute indicates that the Properties window should refresh the object's properties if the FirstName property changes.

```
Private m_FirstName As String = "<first name>"
<RefreshProperties(RefreshProperties.Repaint)> _
Public Property FirstName() As String
    Get
```

```
            Return m_FirstName
        End Get
        Set(ByVal value As String)
            m_FirstName = value
        End Set
    End Property
```

Now, the Properties window refreshes the `Contact` object's string representation when you change a sub-property value, but it still does not update the `UserControl` on the form.

One way to make the `UserControl` update its display is to add a `DataChanged` event to the `Contact` class and make class's property set procedures raise this event. The `UserControl` can then catch the event and display the new property values.

The following code fragment from the `Contact` class shows the `DataChanged` event's declaration and the way the `Phone` property set procedure raises the event:

```
' Let the owner know when data changes.
Public Event DataChanged()
...
Private m_Phone As String = "<phone>"
<RefreshProperties(RefreshProperties.Repaint)> _
Public Property Phone() As String
    Get
        Return m_Phone
    End Get
    Set(ByVal value As String)
        m_Phone = value
        RaiseEvent DataChanged()
    End Set
End Property
...
```

The following code shows how the `ContactViewer` `UserControl` handles the `DataChanged` event. The variable `m_Contact` refers to the `Contact` object used by the control to store data.

```
' Data has changed. Display the new values.
Private Sub m_Contact_DataChanged() Handles m_Contact.DataChanged
    lblFirstName.Text = m_Contact.FirstName
    lblLastName.Text = m_Contact.LastName
    lblPhone.Text = m_Contact.Phone
End Sub
```

Now, the `UserControl`, the property's string representation, and the property's sub-properties all keep each other up to date.

If a control's object property is `Nothing`*, the Properties window doesn't display any sub-properties for it. For example, suppose the* `ContactViewer` `UserControl` *initially set its* `Contact` *property to* `Nothing`*. Then the Properties window would display a blank string for the* `Contact` *property, but it would not allow you to expand the object to show its sub-properties. You would need to type in a valid string of the form "Rod, Stephens (987-6543)" for that property. At that point, Visual Studio would assign a new* `Contact` *object to the control's property. The Properties window would then allow you to expand the* `Contact` *property and see its sub-properties.*

To avoid having to type in a string representation of the object in the correct format from memory, don't initialize the control's object properties to `Nothing`*. Instead, initialize those properties to new objects. You can give the objects blank sub-property values or default values such as* `"<first name>,"`*, but ensure that the object properties always refer to a real object rather than* `Nothing`.

(You can download this example at `www.vb-helper.com/one_on_one.htm`.)

Summary

This chapter describes ways you can provide enhanced support for custom properties at design time. To help developers view and edit simple properties in the Properties window, you can use type converters and editors.

To allow developers to view and modify several properties all at once, add a smart tag to your control. You can use the smart tag to define commands that perform more complex actions on the control, possibly involving several properties and methods. You can also turn the actions into verbs that appear as links below the Properties window so that developers can invoke them with a single click.

For the most complex interactions with a control, you can define property sheets. Property sheets can include many pages to let developers set a control's properties, invoke the control's methods, and do just about anything else that Visual Basic code can do to a control.

The previous chapter explained how to build custom controls and components. This chapter explained how to add additional support for the properties of those controls and components. It shows how to make type converters and property editors that let the Properties window display and edit values. It explained how to provide smart tags and property sheets to let developers manipulate custom controls in complex ways at design time.

The techniques described in this chapter use attributes to associate one class with another. For example, the `EditorAttribute` statement associates an editor class with a property, and the `TypeConverter` attribute associates a type conversion class with a property.

Chapter 12, "Attributes and XML Comments," summarizes these and other useful attributes that you can add to your code. It also describes XML comments that you can add to your code to add further information about your code. Together, attributes and XML comments provide extra information about what your code does, and how it should be used.

12

Attributes and XML Comments

The Properties window and IntelliSense do a remarkable job of figuring out how your objects and their properties work. For example, suppose your program uses the following code to define the `JobTypes` enumerated values and the `AssignJob` subroutine:

```
Public Enum JobTypes
    Design
    Documentation
    Development
    Testing
    Debugging
End Enum

Private Sub AssignJob(ByVal job_type As JobTypes)
    ' ...
End Sub
```

If you type **"AssignJob("** in the code window, IntelliSense automatically displays all of the information shown in Figure 12-1. It shows the `AssignJob` subroutine's signature below the cursor, it displays the list of possible `JobTypes` values that you could use for the subroutine's first parameter, and it even displays the numeric value of the currently selected `JobTypes` value.

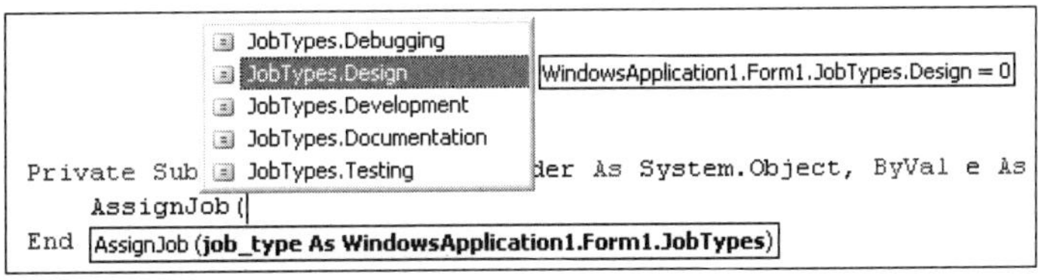

Figure 12-1: IntelliSense automatically displays a subroutine's signature and lists possible `JobTypes` values.

Similarly, the Properties window automatically discovers the types of the properties provided by a component, and supplies appropriate editors in many cases. For example, it automatically provides dropdowns for selecting colors or enumerated values, dialogs for selecting files or colors, and a combination of sub-properties and a dialog for selecting fonts.

Visual Studio provides all of this support automatically.

Although all of these tools are extremely useful, Visual Studio cannot deduce the intent of your code. IntelliSense can list the signature of the `AssignJobs` subroutine, but it cannot guess the routine's purpose. It can display a list of the possible values that you might use for the routine's parameter, but it doesn't know what the parameter is for.

By using attributes and XML comments, you can give additional information that IntelliSense and editors such as the Properties window can use to provide extra support for developers. In most cases, adding this support takes only a few seconds, but giving developers a better understanding of what the code is supposed to do can save you hours of frustrating debugging and maintenance.

This chapter is divided into two parts that describe some useful attributes and XML comments. (You can download examples demonstrating most of these attributes and XML comments at `www.vb-helper.com/one_on_one.htm`.)

Attributes

Visual Studio uses attributes to "decorate" code with extra information. This information is mostly used by code generators, editors, and other processes that manipulate the code itself. For example, the Properties window uses many attributes to decide how a particular item should be displayed and edited.

Run-time code can also examine attributes to learn more about a particular item. For example, XML serialization routines can examine an object's attributes to learn more about how the object should be serialized.

In fact, you can make your code examine an object's attributes. This is a relatively unusual need, however, so it's not described here. For more information, search the online help for "Retrieving Information Stored in Attributes," or look at `msdn.microsoft.com/library/en-us/cpguide/html/cpconretrievinginformationstoredinattributes.asp`.

Attributes can decorate many different kinds of programming entities, including modules, classes, structures, subroutines, functions, properties, fields, enumerated types, and method parameters. You can only apply an attribute to an item for which it was designed.

For example, the `Browsable` attribute determines whether a property or event should be visible in the Properties window. You can apply the `Browsable` attribute to a class, but it will be ignored.

To apply an attribute, you enclose a call to the attribute class's constructor inside pointy brackets before the code item. The following code fragment shows how you might add a `Description` attribute to a class's `FirstName` property:

```
Imports System.ComponentModel
...
<Description("The employee's first or given name")> _
Public Property FirstName() As String
    ...
End Property
```

The `Description` attribute class is contained in the `System.ComponentModel` namespace so the code imports `System.ComponentModel` to make using the attribute easier. The call to the `Description` attribute's constructor takes a single parameter giving the property's description. The call is enclosed in pointy brackets.

The attribute is followed by a line-continuation character, so the attribute is actually part of the same line of code as the property's declaration. Putting attributes on separate lines makes the code easier to read.

The class name for an attribute generally ends with the word "Attribute." In Visual Basic, you can omit this last part for convenience and to make the code less cluttered. For example, the class that provides the `Description` attribute is named `DescriptionAttribute`. Normally, you don't need to worry about this, but if you want to learn more about the class, you should search the online help for "DescriptionAttribute class."

You can include multiple attributes inside the pointy brackets to apply more than one attribute to a code item. The following code fragment applies the `Description`, `ReadOnly`, and `DefaultValue` attributes to the `FirstName` property:

```
<Description("The employee's first or given name"), _
 [ReadOnly](True), _
 DefaultValue("(missing)")> _
Public Property FirstName() As String
    ...
```

Notice square brackets around the `ReadOnly` attribute's name. This lets Visual Basic distinguish between the attribute name and Visual Basic's `ReadOnly` keyword.

An alternative technique is to include each attribute within its own set of pointy brackets, as shown in the following code. I prefer this version because it is a little easier to read, you don't need to worry about matching up the commas properly, and you can work with each attribute separately. For example, you could delete the line containing the `DefaultValue` attribute, or add a new attribute line without modifying the others.

```
<Description("The employee's first or given name")> _
<[ReadOnly](True)> _
<DefaultValue("(missing)")> _
Public Property FirstName() As String
    ...
```

The .NET Framework defines more than 300 attribute classes, so they are not all described here. Many are useful only under very specific circumstances, so there are many that you will probably never need to use.

The following sections described some of the attribute classes that I have found the most useful, grouped by the types of tasks they perform. They describe the attributes' purposes and the code items that are mostly likely to use the attributes. They also include a brief example.

Helping the Properties Window

These attributes help the Properties window do a better job. They tell the window how to display and edit properties and events.

AmbientValue

This attribute indicates that a property gets its value from another source unless it is overridden. For example, controls typically use the `Font`, `ForeColor`, and `BackColor` properties used by their parent controls unless you override them.

The following code makes the `BoxColor` property ambient:

```
<AmbientValue(GetType(Color), Nothing)> _
Public Property BoxColor() As Color
    Get
        If (m_BoxColor = Nothing) AndAlso (Me.Parent IsNot Nothing) Then
            Return Me.Parent.ForeColor
        Else
            Return m_BoxColor
        End If
    End Get
    Set(ByVal value As Color)
        m_BoxColor = value
    End Set
End Property
```

The property get procedure checks the `m_BoxColor` variable. If no value has been assigned to the variable, and if the control has a parent, then the procedure returns the parent's `ForeColor` property.

Browsable

This attribute determines whether a property or event is visible in the Properties window. This is useful if you want to make a property or event available at run-time but not at design time. For example, suppose you build a component with a `CurrentPrice` property that uses a Web Service to get a stock price at run-time. It might not make sense to display the stock price at design time.

The following code fragment hides the `CurrentPrice` property from the Properties window:

```
<Browsable(False)> _
Public Property CurrentPrice() As Single
...
```

Category

The `Category` property determines the category in which a property or event is grouped in the Properties window when you click the window's Categorized button. You don't need to do anything else to define a new category. Simply type a new category name into a `Category` attribute and the Properties window will make a new category for it.

```
<Category("Name Values")> _
Public Property FirstName() As String
...
```

DefaultProperty

This attribute indicates a component's default property. When you select a control in the form designer, the Properties window initially selects the same property that it already had selected. For example, if you have the `Text` property of a `Label` selected and then click a `TextBox`, the `Text` property is still selected.

If the newly selected control doesn't have the selected property, the Properties window selects the control's default property.

The following code sets the `UserControl1` class's default property to `DrawingFlags`:

```
<DefaultProperty("DrawingFlags")> _
Public Class UserControl1
...
```

DefaultValue

This attribute sets the default value for a property. If the developer right-clicks the property in the Properties window and selects Reset, Visual Studio sets the property's value to the default value.

Usually, you should set the property to the same default value when the object is initially created. The following code defines a constant to hold the default value for the `Title` property. It uses the private variable `m_Title` to hold the property's value, and it initializes the value to the default value in the variable's declaration. The `DefaultValue` attribute uses the same value, so if the developer resets the `Title` property, its value is set to "`Untitled`."

```
Private Const DEFAULT_TITLE As String = "Untitled"
Private m_Title As String = DEFAULT_TITLE
<DefaultValue(DEFAULT_TITLE)> _
Public Property Title() As String
...
```

Using the `DefaultValue` attribute is straightforward for simple data types such as strings and singles. For properties that are objects, you must use a different attribute constructor that includes the object's type and a string value that can be converted into that type.

Usually, you should reset object properties to `Nothing`. The following code shows how to do this for an `Image` property:

```
<DefaultValue(GetType(Image), Nothing)> _
Public Property StatusImage() As Image
...
```

Description

The `Description` attribute sets the text displayed below the Properties window when the property is selected. The following code places the `FirstName` property in the `"Name Values"` category and gives the property a description.

```
<Category("Name Values")> _
<Description("The employee's first or given name.")> _
Public Property FirstName() As String
    ...
```

Figure 12-2 shows the Properties window with the `FirstName` property selected. Notice the description at the bottom of the window. Notice also that the property is in the Property window's Name Values section.

Figure 12-2: The `Description` attribute determines the text displayed below the Properties window for a property.

Designer

This attribute associates a class with a designer class that is used to display smart tags on the form designer. The following code associates the `ScribbleControl` class with the `ScribbleControl Designer` class:

```
<Designer(GetType(ScribbleControlDesigner))> _
Public Class ScribbleControl
...
```

See the section "Displaying Smart Tags" in Chapter 11, "Property Support," for more information about this attribute.

DisplayName

This attribute specifies the name that the Properties window should display for a property. You should try to give properties names that are meaningful to the developers who will use them, but you can use this property if you must.

The following code makes the Properties window display the `RuntimeUser` property with the name `Customer`:

```
    <DisplayName("Customer")> _
    Public Property RuntimeUser() As Person
...
```

Editor

This attribute associates a property with an editor class that can edit the property. See the section "Displaying and Editing `LineWidth`" in Chapter 11 for more information about this attribute.

ReadOnly

This attribute determines whether the developer can modify a property in the Properties window. The following code allows the developer to see the `OutsideTemperature` property but not modify it:

```
<[ReadOnly](True)> _
Public Property OutsideTemperature() As Single
...
```

Figure 12-3 shows the Properties window displaying this property. The property's name and value are grayed out and the value is not editable.

Figure 12-3: The `ReadOnly` attribute makes the Properties window display a property grayed out and not editable.

Localizable

This attribute determines whether a property's value is saved in localized resource files. If this is `False` (the default), the property value is saved only once and is shared for all locales. If this is `True`, then when you design for different locales in the form designer, the property's localized values are saved into the appropriate resource files.

The following code makes the `ReportLanguage` property localizable:

```
<Localizable(True)> _
Public Property ReportLanguage() As String
...
```

NotifyParentPropertyAttribute

This attribute determines whether a parent property is notified when this child property is changed. For example, if a property is a `Structure` that contains other properties, you can use this attribute on the `Structure`'s properties.

The following code makes the `FirstName` property notify a parent property when it is changed:

```
<NotifyParentProperty(True)> _
Public Property Contact() As Contact
...
```

ParenthesizePropertyName

This attribute determines whether the property's name is surrounded by parentheses in the Properties window. When the Properties window sorts properties alphabetically, those with parentheses are shown at the top, so this can make key properties easier to find. When the Properties window is grouping items by category, the parenthesized properties appear at the top of their category.

The following code makes the Properties window display an `About` property with a parenthesized name. This is a dummy property that doesn't store or display any value. However, it has an associated editor class named `AboutEditor`. That makes the Properties window display an ellipsis to the right of the property's value. If you click the ellipsis, the `AboutEditor` displays a simple `About` dialog.

```
' A dummy property to display an About dialog.
<ParenthesizePropertyName(True)> _
<Editor(GetType(AboutEditor), GetType(UITypeEditor))> _
Public Property About() As String
    Get
        Return Nothing
    End Get
    Set(ByVal value As String)
    End Set
End Property
```

Download the `UseAttributes` example program and look at the code to see exactly how the `AboutEditor` class works. See the section "Displaying and Editing PolyPolyline" in Chapter 11 for more information on property editors.

PasswordPropertyText

This attribute tells the Properties window to hide the property's value with asterisks or some other password-masking character. The following code sets this attribute for the `DatabasePassword` property:

```
    <PasswordPropertyText(True)> _
    Public Property DatabasePassword() As String
...
```

You can see the `DatabasePassword` property in Figures 12-2 and 12-3.

Note that the property's value is still stored in plain text in the designer-generated code, so the value isn't completely hidden. It just doesn't jump out for people walking past the developer to see.

PropertyTab

This attribute associates a component class with a property tab class. The property tab class allows the Properties window to display an additional tab that can provide a customized view of the component's properties.

Figure 12-4 shows the Properties window displaying a tab named Test Properties. This tab displays only properties that are in the Test Properties category.

Figure 12-4: The Test Properties tab displays only properties in the Test Properties category.

The following code shows how the program associates the `UserControl1` class with the `TestPropertiesTab` class:

```
<PropertyTabAttribute(GetType(TestPropertiesTab), PropertyTabScope.Document)> _
Public Class UserControl1
...
```

The following code shows how the `TestPropertiesTab` class works:

```
Imports System.ComponentModel

' This tab lists only properties in the Test Properties category.
Public Class TestPropertiesTab
    Inherits PropertyTab

    ' Returns only the properties in the Test Properties category.
    Public Overloads Overrides Function GetProperties(ByVal component As Object, _
     ByVal attributes() As System.Attribute) _
     As System.ComponentModel.PropertyDescriptorCollection
        Dim props_in As PropertyDescriptorCollection
        If attributes Is Nothing Then
            props_in = TypeDescriptor.GetProperties(component)
        Else
            props_in = TypeDescriptor.GetProperties(component, attributes)
        End If

        Dim props_out As New PropertyDescriptorCollection(Nothing)
        Dim i As Integer
        For i = 0 To props_in.Count - 1
            If props_in(i).Category = "Test Properties" Then
                ' Create a PropertyDescriptor for this property.
                props_out.Add( _
```

```
                    TypeDescriptor.CreateProperty( _
                            props_in(i).ComponentType, _
                            props_in(i), _
                            Nothing) _
                )
            End If
        Next i
        Return props_out
    End Function

    Public Overloads Overrides Function GetProperties(ByVal component As Object) _
     As System.ComponentModel.PropertyDescriptorCollection
        Return Me.GetProperties(component, Nothing)
    End Function

    ' Provides the name for the property tab.
    Public Overrides ReadOnly Property TabName() As String
        Get
            Return "Test Properties"
        End Get
    End Property

    ' Provides an image for the property tab.
    Public Overrides ReadOnly Property Bitmap() As System.Drawing.Bitmap
        Get
            Return My.Resources.TestProperties
        End Get
    End Property
End Class
```

The parent class `PropertyTab` does most of the work.

The class overrides its inherited `GetProperties` method to return a collection of objects describing the properties that should be displayed on the tab. The routine loops through the components and adds those in the Test Properties category to the result collection.

The tab class's `GetProperties` function calls its `GetProperties` method and returns the result.

The read-only `TabName` property returns the name of the tab. This is the text displayed in the tooltip shown in Figure 12-4.

Finally, the read-only `Bitmap` property returns the bitmap displayed for the tab in the Properties window. In this example, the property returns the `Bitmap` stored in the `TestProperties` resource. (You can download this example at `www.vb-helper.com/one_on_one.htm`.)

RefreshPropertiesAttribute

This attribute determines how the Properties window refreshes its display when the property's value changes. The `ContactViewer` control described in Chapter 11 uses this attribute to update its property display. The control has a property of type `Contact`. The `Contact` class has `FirstName`, `LastName`, and `Phone` properties. The program uses a type converter to allow the Properties window to display these sub-properties. It also flags the `FirstName`, `LastName`, and `Phone` properties with the `RefreshPropertiesAttribute` to make the Properties window update the `Contact` property's display whenever one of its sub-properties changes.

The following code shows how the example applies this attribute to the `FirstName` property:

```
<RefreshProperties(RefreshProperties.Repaint)> _
Public Property FirstName() As String
...
```

See the section "Displaying Object Properties" in Chapter 11 for more information.

TypeConverter

This attribute associates a property with a type converter class. The type converter allows the Properties window to convert the property from its true data type to and from strings. The following code associates the `PolyPolyline` property with the `PolyPolylineConverter` class:

```
<TypeConverter(GetType(PolyPolylineConverter))> _
Public Property PolyPolyline() As PolyPolyline
...
```

See the section "Displaying and Editing PolyPolyline" in Chapter 11 for more information on this attribute.

Helping the Form Designer

The attributes described in the following sections provide extra help for the form designer.

DefaultEvent

This attribute specifies a class's default event. When you double-click the control in the form designer, the code editor opens an event handler for this event.

The following code sets the `UserControl1` class's default event to `ADefaultEvent`:

```
<DefaultEvent("ADefaultEvent")> _
Public Class UserControl1
...
```

Docking

This attribute indicates whether a control should automatically dock to fill its container if it is created in a container that holds no other controls.

The following code makes the `UserControl1` control dock to fill its container:

```
<Docking(DockingBehavior.AutoDock)> _
Public Class UserControl1
...
```

ToolboxBitmap

This attribute sets the bitmap displayed for a component in the toolbox. The following code sets the toolbox bitmap for the `UserControl1` control to the `tbxUserControl1` resource in the assembly containing the `UserControl1` class:

```
<ToolboxBitmap(GetType(UserControl1), "tbxUserControl1")> _
Public Class UserControl1
...
```

See the section "Setting Toolbox Bitmaps" in Chapter 10, "Custom Controls and Components," for more information about setting toolbox bitmaps.

ToolboxItem

This attribute determines the type of toolbox item displayed for a component, or whether a toolbox item is displayed at all. This is useful, for example, if you want to build a constituent control for use in another control, but you don't want to make the constituent control directly available to other developers.

The following code makes the `ToolNotInToolbox` component not appear in the toolbox:

```
<ToolboxItem(False)> _
Public Class ToolNotInToolbox
...
```

Helping the Code Editor

The attributes described in these sections help the code editor. They provide additional information about items so that the code editor can display them, and provide help appropriately at design time and while debugging.

AttributeUsage

If you define your own attribute class, this attribute indicates the types of items that can have your attribute. For example, you can specify that your attribute must be used on a class or property.

Building your own attribute classes is very application-specific because you also must write the code that reads and uses the attributes, so it's not described further here. For more information, see the online help.

ComClassAttribute

This attribute makes a class visible to COM so that Visual Basic 6 applications can use it. For more information on COM interoperability, search the online help for "Applying Interop Attributes," or go to `msdn2.microsoft.com/library/d4w8x20h.aspx`.

Conditional

This attribute can make the run-time system ignore calls to a method when the program executes. The following code demonstrates the `Conditional` attribute:

```
Public Class Form1
    Private Sub Form1_Load(ByVal sender As System.Object, _
     ByVal e As System.EventArgs) Handles MyBase.Load
```

```
        IfCondition1()
        IfCondition2()
    End Sub

    <Conditional("DEBUG")> _
    Private Sub IfCondition1()
        MessageBox.Show("IfCondition1")
    End Sub

    <Conditional("Condition2")> _
    Private Sub IfCondition2()
        MessageBox.Show("IfCondition2")
    End Sub
End Class
```

The code defines two conditional subroutines: `IfCondition1` and `IfCondition2`. `IfCondition1` is conditional on the `DEBUG` compilation constant, so it executes only if the program is running in debug mode.

`IfCondition2` is conditional on the `Condition2` compilation constant. To set this constant, double-click My Properties, select the Compile tab, and click the Advanced Compile Options button to display the dialog shown in Figure 12-5. Enter the constant's definition in the "Custom constants" text box.

Figure 12-5: You can use the Advanced Compiler Settings dialog to define compilation constants.

If a conditional method's condition is not defined as `True`, the method is compiled into the executable program, but calls to it are ignored at run-time.

DebuggerHidden

This attribute prevents the debugger from stepping into a method or a property's code. It also prevents you from setting a breakpoint inside the code. The following code shows how to use this attribute:

```
<DebuggerHidden()> _
Private Sub IsDebuggerHidden()
    ...
End Sub
```

DebuggerStepThrough

This attribute is similar to `DebuggerHidden`, except that you can apply it to a method or a class. If you apply it to a class, you cannot step into any of the class's code.

The following code prevents you from stopping execution n any code within the `DebuggerHiddenClass`:

```
<DebuggerStepThrough()> _
Public Class DebuggerHiddenClass
    ...
End Class
```

EditorBrowsable

This attribute determines when a property is visible to IntelliSense. You can set this to `Always` (appears in all IntelliSense tabs), `Advanced` (appears in the All tab, but not the Common tab), or `Never` (doesn't appear in either IntelliSense tab). The following code makes the `RuntimeUser` property appear in IntelliSense's All tab:

```
<EditorBrowsable(EditorBrowsableState.Advanced)> _
Public Property RuntimeUser() As Person
    ...
```

Flags

This attribute indicates that an enumerated type should be treated as a bit field that allows combinations of its values. To allow developers to make bitwise combinations of values, you should set the values to powers of 2: 1, 2, 4, 8, 16, and so forth. You should also create a `None` value set to `0`. If you like, you can define common combinations of values.

The following code defines values that tell a control whether to draw a box, X, or cross. The value `Spider` means both an X and a cross.

```
<Flags()> _
Public Enum DrawingFlagValues
    None = 0
    Box = 1
    X = 2
    Cross = 4
    Spider = X Or Cross
End Enum
```

HideModuleName

This attribute tells IntelliSense to hide a module's name. You can still type the module's name if you like, and IntelliSense will show the items inside the module. The following code hides the name of `HiddenModule` from IntelliSense:

```
<HideModuleName()> _
Module HiddenModule
    ...
```

ProvideProperty

This attribute gives the name of a property that an extender provider implements for its client controls. The following code indicates that the `ExtraTagProvider` class provides the `ExtraTag` property:

```
<ProvideProperty("ExtraTag", GetType(Control))> _
Public Class ExtraTagProvider
    ...
```

For more information on building extender providers, see the section "Building Extender Providers" in Chapter 10.

Obsolete

This attribute indicates that an item is obsolete. Optionally, you can provide a message for Visual Studio to display in the Error List window and as a tooltip when the developer hovers the mouse over the code that uses the obsolete item.

The following code marks the `SortCustomerArray` subroutine as obsolete. If the code uses this subroutine, Visual Studio displays the warning, "This method has been replaced with SortArray," as shown in Figure 12-6.

```
<Obsolete("This method has been replaced with SortArray")> _
Public Sub SortCustomerArray(ByVal customer_array() As Customer)
    MessageBox.Show("SortCustomerArray")
End Sub
```

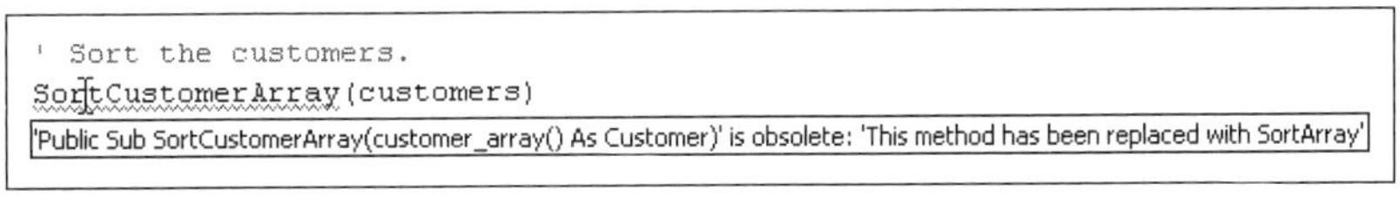
' Sort the customers.
SortCustomerArray(customers)
'Public Sub SortCustomerArray(customer_array() As Customer)' is obsolete: 'This method has been replaced with SortArray'

Figure 12-6: The code editor displays an error message if you use an obsolete subroutine.

This attribute can also indicate whether using the obsolete item should generate a warning or an error. For example, when you replace a subroutine in a new release of your software, you can make calls to the old version raise a warning so developers can find and fix them. In the next release of your code, you can make the old call cause an error so that developers who have not yet updated their code are forced to do so.

This attribute can also be a useful tool in managing your own code. If you want to replace a routine with a better version, you can mark the old version as obsolete. That gives you a little extra documentation on the routine, and Visual Studio will nag you about using the routine until you get around to removing it.

Helping Serialization

The attributes described in these sections help determine how objects are serialized and deserialized. These are a bit different from the attributes described so far, because they are used at run-time, whereas the previously described attributes are used by the Properties window, form designer, code editor, and other design-time tools.

The reason Visual Basic uses attributes here instead of some more run-time–oriented technique is that serializers use reflection at run-time to examine the objects they are serializing. Attributes decorate a class, property, or other item so that the serializer can learn about the attributes at run-time.

Serializable

This attribute indicates that a class is serializable. The following code marks the `Person` class as serializable:

```
<Serializable()> _
Public Class Person
...
```

OnDeserializing, OnDeserialized, OnSerializing, and OnSerialized

These attributes indicate that a class method should be executed during and after serialization or deserialization.

The following code fragment shows part of the `Person` class. The `OnSerializingMethod` subroutine has the `OnSerializing` attribute, so it is called when a `Person` object is serialized. In this example, the subroutine sets the `Person` object's `FirstName` property to `"OnSerializingMethod"`.

```
<Serializable()> _
Public Class Person
    ...
    <OnSerializing()> _
    Friend Sub OnSerializingMethod(ByVal context As StreamingContext)
        FirstName = "OnSerializingMethod"
    End Sub
    ...
End Class
```

The intent of this routine is to allow the class to modify an object's properties before they are serialized. For example, the class might refresh data in volatile properties.

The `OnDeserialized`, `OnSerializing`, and `OnSerialized` attributes work similarly. Download the `SoapSerializationTest` example from the book's Web site to see how these attributes work.

These attributes only affect SOAP and binary formatter serializations, not the `XmlSerializer` *class.*

OptionalField

This attribute indicates that a field is optional in a serialization. If a serialization is missing a field, a deserializer normally throws an exception. If the field is flagged as optional, the deserializer doesn't throw an error.

The following code marks the `Phone` field as optional:

```
<OptionalField()> _
Public Phone As String
...
```

You can use this attribute to provide some backward-compatibility with older serialization files. If you add a new `Phone` field to the class, the program can still read older serializations without the field if you make the field optional.

This attribute only affects SOAP and binary formatter serializations, not the `XmlSerializer` *class.*

XmlArray

This attribute indicates that an array property should be serialized as an XML element containing sub-elements holding an array's values. The following code indicates that the `Letters` property should be serialized as an XML array named `TheLetters` containing items named `ALetter`:

```
Private m_Letters() As String = {}
<XmlArray("TheLetters")> _
<XmlArrayItem("ALetter")> _
Public Property Letters() As String()
    Get
        Return m_Letters
    End Get
    Set(ByVal value() As String)
        m_Letters = value
    End Set
End Property
```

The following code shows this part of the serialization for a `Letters` property containing three letters:

```
<TheLetters>
  <ALetter>A</ALetter>
  <ALetter>B</ALetter>
  <ALetter>C</ALetter>
</TheLetters>
```

XmlArrayItem

This attribute gives the name of the sub-elements inside an XML array. See the description of the `XmlArray` attribute in the previous section.

XmlAttribute

This attribute indicates that a property should be serialized as an attribute of an XML element. The following code indicates that the `Address` class's `Street` and `City` fields should be serialized as attributes of the `Address` element. The second `XmlAttribute` statement indicates that the `City` value's attribute should be named `"Town"`.

```
<Serializable()> _
Public Class Address
    <XmlAttribute()> _
```

```
        Public Street As String

        <XmlAttribute("Town")> _
        Public City As String

        Public State As String

        Public Zip As String
        ...
    End Class
```

The following code shows the serialization for an `Address` object:

```
    <Address Street="1234 Elf St" Town="Bugsville">
      <State>CA</State>
      <Zip>98765</Zip>
    </Address>
```

XmlElement

This attribute indicates the name that an XML serialization should use for a property. The following code indicates that the `PersonType` property should be called `"TypeOfPerson"` in the serialization:

```
    <XmlElement("TypeOfPerson")> _
    Public Property PersonType() As PersonTypes
        ...
```

When you use this attribute on an array property, it indicates a type of object that might be included in the array. For example, the following code indicates that the `Things` array might contain objects of the types `Thing1` and `Thing2`:

```
    <XmlElement(GetType(Thing1))> _
    <XmlElement(GetType(Thing2))> _
    Public Property Things() As Object()
        ...
```

XmlEnum

This attribute indicates how an XML serialization should represent an enumerated value. The following code defines an enumerated type containing the values `None`, `Cust`, `Mgr`, and `Emp`. A serialization would represent those values as `Unknown`, `Customer`, `Manager`, and `Employee`.

```
    Public Enum PersonTypes
        <XmlEnum("Unknown")> None
        <XmlEnum("Customer")> Cust
        <XmlEnum("Manager")> Mgr
        <XmlEnum("Employee")> Emp
    End Enum
```

XmlIgnore

This attribute indicates that a property should not be serialized. This is useful for properties that are calculated from other properties' values, or that are generated at run-time.

For example, suppose a control's `OnlineStatus` property indicates whether the computer is connected to the network. It probably wouldn't make sense to save this value in a serialization, so the following code makes serializations ignore this property:

```
<XmlIgnore()> _
Public Property OnlineStatus() As String
    ...
```

XmlText

This attribute indicates that the property should be serialized as XML text inside an XML element. The following code indicates that the `Address` class's `State` property should be included as text:

```
<Serializable()> _
Public Class Address
    <XmlAttribute()> _
    Public Street As String

    <XmlAttribute("Town")> _
    Public City As String

    <XmlText()> _
    Public State As String

    Public Zip As String
    ...
End Class
```

The following text shows the result. Notice that the state `CA` is placed without any identification between the opening `Address` tag and the open `Zip` tag.

```
<Address Street="1234 Elf St" Town="Bugsville">CA<Zip>98765</Zip></Address>
```

XML Comments

Many of the attributes described so far have been around in previous versions of Visual Basic .NET. XML comments, however, were added in Visual Basic 2005 and were awaited eagerly by many experienced developers.

XML comments allow you to add a new type of documentation to your code. A comment begins with three single quotes (`'''`). Within the comment, XML tags define various sections of documentation. The comments must be well-formed XML code (ignoring the single quotes).

The following code shows XML comments for a `Person` class:

```
''' <summary>
''' Represents a customer or employee.
''' </summary>
''' <remarks>Use a Manager object for managers.</remarks>
Public Class Person
    ...
```

XML comments can go immediately in front of a wide variety of code elements, including classes, variable declarations, event declarations, subroutines, and functions.

If you move the text cursor to a blank line immediately before a code element and type three single quotes, Visual Basic automatically generates an XML comment for the element, complete with the XML tags that it thinks make sense for that element. The comment includes tags for any parameters the item might take, so you should define the parameters before you generate the comment.

For example, suppose you write a `PrintLetter` subroutine that takes parameters named `letter_text` and `priority`. If you then place the text cursor on a blank line above the subroutine declaration and type three single quotes, Visual Basic generates the following XML comment:

```
''' <summary>
'''
''' </summary>
''' <param name="letter_text"></param>
''' <param name="priority"></param>
''' <remarks></remarks>
Public Sub PrintLetter(ByVal letter_text As String, ByVal priority As Integer)
    ...
End Sub
```

You should enter appropriate text inside the XML tags to document the subroutine.

> *If you later modify your code, you must remember to also update the XML comments. For example, if you add a new parameter, you must add a corresponding* `param` *tag. If you define all of the parameters before you build the initial XML comment, Visual Basic automatically creates the correct* `param` *tags for you, so it's a bit easier to finish defining the routine before you make the comments.*

There are two reasons why using XML comments is worthwhile: automatic documentation and design-time support.

Automatic Documentation

To enable automatic documentation, double-click My Project, select the Compile tab, and check the "Generate XML documentation file" box at the bottom, as shown in Figure 12-7.

Now, when you compile the code, Visual Basic generates an XML document containing the XML comments. It places this file in the project's `bin` and `obj` directories in an appropriate subdirectory. For example, if you are working on a project named `PersonComments` in debug mode, it will create the file `bin/Debug/PersonComments.xml`.

The following code shows this file for a small example program containing XML comments only for the `Person` class's `PrintLetter` subroutine:

```
<?xml version="1.0"?>
<doc>
<assembly>
<name>
PersonComments
```

```
</name>
</assembly>
<members>
<member name="M:PersonComments.Person.PrintLetter(System.String,System.Int32)">
 <summary>
 Print a letter and envelope for this person.
 </summary>
 <param name="letter_text">The text of the letter to be printed.</param>
 <param name="priority">The letter's priority. 1 = Highest.</param>
 <remarks>Use this routine to generate a letter for a person.
 The routine prints the letter on the default printer and
 then waits for you to load an envelope in the manual feed before
 addressing the envelope.</remarks>
</member>
</members>
</doc>
```

The file begins with an XML declaration and a `doc` tag to hold the entire document. The `assembly` tag contains the name of the assembly.

The `members` tag contains information about the comments in the project.

Each `member` tag represents one item in the code. This example has a single `member` tag for the `PrintLetter` subroutine. This tag's name attribute gives the full path to the method (`M` means method, `PersonComments` is the root namespace, `Person` is the class, `PrintLetter` is the subroutine's name) and the data types of its parameters.

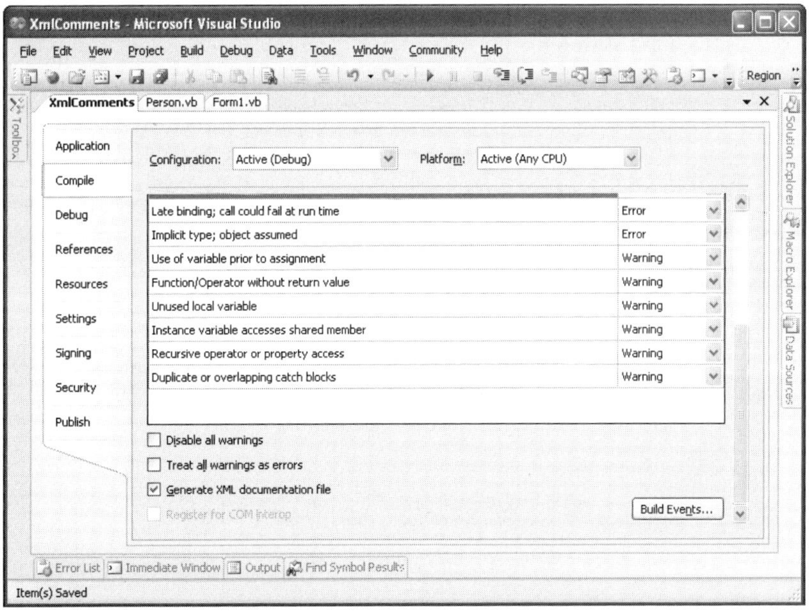

Figure 12-7: Check the "Generate XML documentation file" box to produce documentation automatically.

The `summary`, `param`, and `remarks` tags contain values that were entered manually in the code.

Having built this file, you can parse it to automatically generate readable documentation. Various XML tags define such documentation items as cross-references and "see also" references, so with some work, you can generate a reasonable document. Types of documents that you might want to generate include HTML or Microsoft Word representations.

Rather than writing your own XML processor, you may be able to find an existing tool on the Internet. For example, NDoc (`ndoc.sourceforge.net`) can convert XML comment files into Web pages or help files.

You probably shouldn't modify the resulting documentation manually because it will be rewritten if you recompile the application and process the XML file again.

Design-Time Support

The second reason to use XML comments is that they give more information that IntelliSense can use to make it easier for developers to understand your code.

When a routine appears in the IntelliSense list, a tooltip displays the routine's name and parameters, plus any information you entered in the `summary` XML tag. Figure 12-8 shows the IntelliSense tooltip for the `PrintLetter` method.

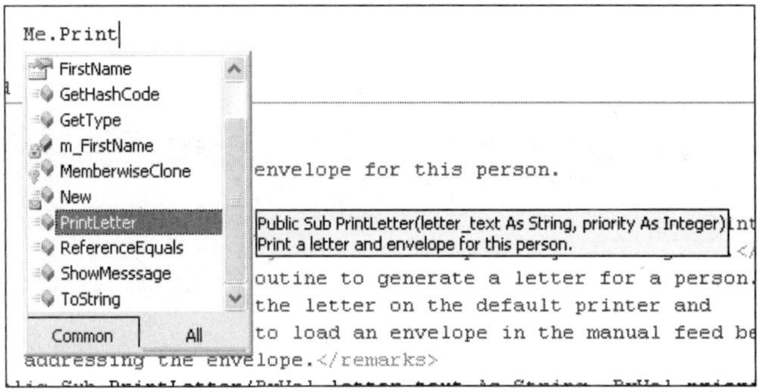

Figure 12-8: IntelliSense includes any text included in a routine's `summary` tag.

As you enter values for the method call's parameters, IntelliSense shows tooltips describing the parameters and including any information you typed into the corresponding `param` tags. Figure 12-9 shows the IntelliSense for the `PrintLetter` subroutine's `letter_text` parameter. It includes the signature of the call to `PrintLetter` and the `param` tag information for this parameter.

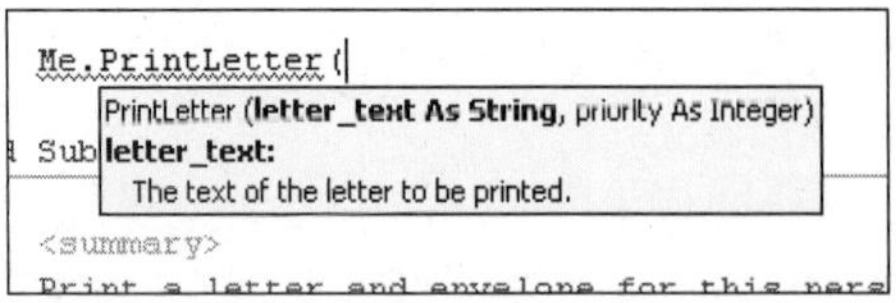

Figure 12-9: IntelliSense displays `param` tag information about parameters.

Recommended Tags

If you type three single quotes before a code element, Visual Basic fills in default XML tags that are appropriate for the element. You can enter other tags within the XML comment to provide additional information.

Visual Studio provides good support for adding new tags. If you type an opening pointy bracket, IntelliSense lists the tags that make sense at that point.

For example, suppose you add a new parameter named `address` to the `PrintLetter` subroutine. Next you move to the end of the last line of XML comment before the `PrintLetter` subroutine and press Enter. Visual Studio automatically adds three single quotes at the start of the new line to continue the XML comment. Now, if you type the opening bracket, IntelliSense displays the list of tags shown in Figure 12-10. The list includes a new `param` tag for the new address parameter.

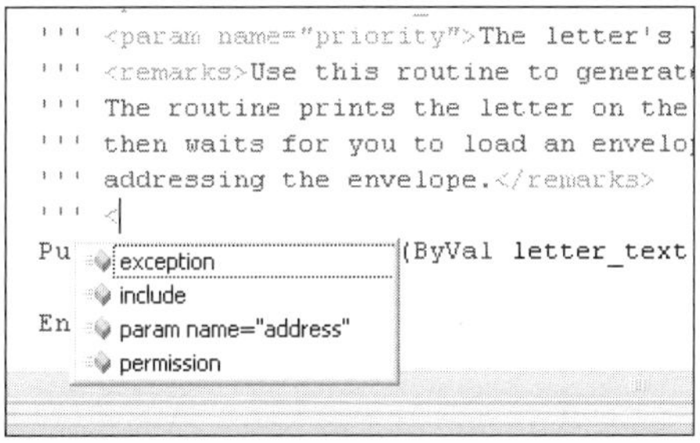

Figure 12-10: IntelliSense lists the tags that make sense at that point.

You can use the IntelliSense list as usual to pick a tag if you like. You can also type in any other tag, including tags that you invent yourself.

Visual Studio may flag some tags if it thinks they don't make sense. For example, it generally doesn't like to see two tags with the same name in the same comment block. If you enter two remarks tags, it ignores the second one. Visual Studio also displays a warning and ignores a `param` tag if the tag's `name` attribute doesn't match one of the routine's parameters.

> *Unfortunately, Visual Studio does not display a warning if there is a parameter without a corresponding* `param` *tag documenting it.*

When you type the closing bracket to end the opening tag, Visual Studio automatically fills in a corresponding ending tag. If you type **<custom_info>**, Visual Studio adds the `</custom_info>` closing tag for you. Now you just need to add whatever information you need between the two tags.

Some tags can also be contained within other tags. For example, the `<c>` tag indicates that the enclosed text is code. For example, you can use this information to format that text in a monospaced font in the final documentation.

The following text shows XML comments for an enumerated type. The `summary` tag for the `Enum` itself uses the `<c>` tag because the text "Low" is an enumeration value, so it should be typeset in a code style. The summary of the `Normal` value at the bottom uses the `<c>` tag to refer to the `Medium` enumeration value.

```
''' <summary>
''' Defines allowed letter qualities. The actual quality may depend on the printer.
''' For example, a fast printer may provide high-quality results even if
''' you select the <c>Low</c> setting.
''' </summary>
Public Enum LetterQualities
    ''' <summary>
    ''' Use the lowest possible letter quality. Suitable only for drafts.
    ''' </summary>
    Low

    ''' <summary>
    ''' Use a medium-level qualify suitable only for working copies.
    ''' </summary>
    Medium

    ''' <summary>
    ''' Use the highest quality possible. Suitable for giving to customers
    ''' or producing final documentation.
    ''' </summary>
    High

    ''' <summary>
    ''' Use the default quality, usually <c>Medium</c>.
    ''' </summary>
    Normal
End Enum
```

The following table describes standard tags that Microsoft recommends you use with Visual Basic. You can use these tags for their intended purposes or other purposes of your own. You can even invent your own tags, but following these recommendations as much as possible will make it easier to find existing tools for translating your XML comments into documentation.

Tag	Purpose
`<c>`	The enclosed text should be styled as code.
`<code>`	The enclosed text should be styled as code. Similar to `<c>`, but intended for multi-line code.
`<example>`	The enclosed text is an example.
`<exception>`	Describes an exception that the code may throw. Using a `cref` attribute indicates the exception that may be thrown. Use a separate `exception` tag for each exception. For example, the following code indicates that a routine might throw a `DivideByZeroException` or an `ArgumentException`.

Tag	Purpose
	''' <exception cref="DivideByZeroException"> ''' Thrown if the total of the weights equals 0. ''' </exception> ''' <exception cref="ArgumentException"> ''' Thrown if the number of values is different ''' from the number of weights. ''' </exception>
<include>	Includes tags from an external XML file in the XML documentation. The following code opens the file external_comments.xml. It looks inside the FormTags root element for a Sub tag with name attribute equal to SayHi. It then inserts everything inside that Sub tag in the resulting XML documentation. ''' <include file="external_comments.xml" ''' path="FormTags/Sub[@name='SayHi']/*"></include>
<list>	Defines a definition list as a two-column table, a bulleted list, or a numbered list. The following code defines a table: ''' <remarks> ''' Here's what the routine does: ''' <list type="table"> ''' <listheader> ''' <term># Inputs</term> ''' <description>Result</description> ''' </listheader> ''' <item> ''' <term>1</term> ''' <description>The input</description> ''' </item> ''' <item> ''' <term>2</term> ''' <description>The ave of the inputs</description> ''' </item> ''' <item> ''' <term>> 2</term> ''' <description>The middle value</description> ''' </item> ''' </list> ''' </remarks>
<para>	Indicates the enclosed text should be formatted as a paragraph.
<param>	Describes a parameter. The following code sets a description for the min_x parameter: ''' <param name="mix_x">The minimum X coordinate.</param> IntelliSense displays the description when a developer is entering the parameter. The Object Browser also displays this information, as shown in Figure 12-11.

Table continued on following page

Tag	Purpose

<paramref>	This tag's `name` attribute gives the name of a parameter, so the documentation program can display the parameter in a distinct font. The following code indicates that the word `"top_pen"` should be formatted as a parameter:
	`''' <remarks>`
	`''' The <paramref name="top_pen" /> parameter gives the pen`
	`''' that the routine should use to draw the rectangle.`
	`''' </remarks>`

<permission>	Indicates a permission that the code needs to work.
<remarks>	Gives additional remarks describing the code. This isn't shown by IntelliSense, but is shown in the Object Browser, as shown in Figure 12-11.
<returns>	Gives text describing the return value. This isn't shown by IntelliSense, but is shown in the Object Browser, as shown in Figure 12-11.
<see>	Describes a link to another code item. For example, it might refer to another subroutine or function in the current class.
<seealso>	Describes a link that should appear in a "See Also" section at the end of the item's documentation.
<summary>	Gives a summary of the item. IntelliSense displays this when a developer is selecting this item, as shown in Figure 12-8. The Object Browser also displays this information, as shown in Figure 12-11.

<typeparam>	Describes a `type parameter` for generic code. This text is not used by IntelliSense, but is displayed by the Object Browser. The following code defines a generic `Quadtree` class:
	`''' <summary>`
	`''' A quadtree node to store geographic data.`
	`''' </summary>`
	`''' <typeparam name="T">`
	`''' The data that should be stored in the quadtree.`
	`''' Must implement IHasPosition.`
	`''' </typeparam>`
	`''' <remarks></remarks>`
	`Public Class Quadtree(Of T As IHasPosition)`
	`  ...`
	`End Class`

<value>	Describes a property's value.

Figure 12-11 shows the Object Browser displaying information about the `Form1` class's `DisplayMessage` function. Unfortunately, the Object Browser doesn't understand XML comments such as `<include>`, `<list>`, or `<para>`, so the sections can sometimes be poorly formatted.

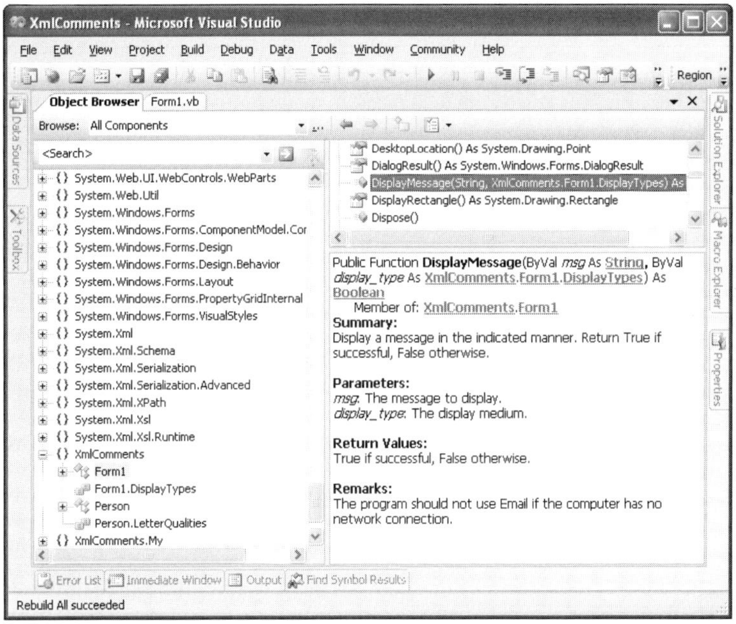

Figure 12-11: The Object Browser displays text from the `summary`, `param`, `returns`, and `remarks` tags.

Recommendations

With so many attributes and XML comments available, it's easy to forget which ones are the most useful. The following table lists the attributes that I find most useful, together with a brief note explaining why.

Attribute	Notes
`AmbientValue`	Ambient values make it easier for developers to use properties consistently. Be sure to provide a `DefaultValue` so the developer can reset the property.
`Browsable`	Use this to hide properties that should not be viewed or set at design time.
`Category`	Use this to group properties. If you add only a few new properties, you can put them all in a group so they don't get mixed in with standard properties such as `Location` and `Size`.
`DefaultProperty`	This is nice, but not essential.
`DefaultValue`	Use this for properties that are references to objects.
`Description`	Include this for all properties.

Table continued on following page

Attribute	Notes
`Designer`	This is a lot of work. Don't bother for simple controls, controls that will only be used a few times, and controls for your own use. Provide this if the control is complicated, and setting its properties is easier in property pages rather than one at a time.
`Editor`	This is a lot of work. Don't bother for controls that will only be used a few times and controls for your own use. Provide this if the control will be used many times by different developers.
`ReadOnly`	Use this if appropriate. Usually, developers don't need to see values that are not editable and, in that case, you can hide the property completely by using `Browsable`.
`Localizable`	Use if appropriate.
`PasswordPropertyText`	Use for sensitive information.
`RefreshProperties Attribute`	Use if needed.
`TypeConverter`	All properties should display something useful in the Properties window or nothing at all. If the developer doesn't need to set a property at design time, hide it by using `Browsable`. Otherwise, provide a type converter for complex types.
`DefaultEvent`	This is not essential, but it's nice and easy to provide, so use it.
`ToolboxBitmap`	Use this to provide a meaningful toolbox bitmap.
`ToolboxItem`	Use this to hide controls that you use as a constituent control or as editors.
`ComClassAttribute`	Use if you want to expose a method for COM (Visual Basic 6).
`EditorBrowsable`	Only use this if the control will be used by many developers with differing skill levels, and you want to display the property only in IntelliSense's All tab.
`Flags`	Use this for enumerated types that are bit fields. Use values that are powers of 2 and set None = 0.
`ProvideProperty`	Use for extender providers.
`Obsolete`	Use if you write routines used by other developers. If you are the only one who uses a routine, simply replace the old call with the new one.
`Serializable`	Use only if you actually need to serialize a class.
`OptionalField`	Use to provide compatibility if you use SOAP or binary formatters.
Other XML Attributes	Use as appropriate only if you actually need to serialize a class.

The following table lists the XML comment tags that I find most useful, together with a brief note explaining why. My preferences are based on the tags' usefulness during development, rather than for producing documentation. Their usefulness in producing documentation depends on the tool you use to convert the automatically generated XML documentation into other formats.

Comment Tag	Notes
`<example>`	Provide an example if the call is confusing.
`<exception>`	List expected or common exceptions only.
`<param>`	Always provide this for every parameter so that IntelliSense and the Object Browser can display it.
`<remarks>`	Don't bother with this unless you add more than is already in the `<summary>`. This isn't displayed by IntelliSense, so it's often non-essential. It appears in the Object Browser, so it's useful if your code will be used by many other developers.
`<returns>`	Don't bother with this unless you add more than is already in the `<summary>`. This isn't displayed by IntelliSense, so it's often non-essential. It appears in the Object Browser, so it's useful if your code will be used by many other developers.
`<summary>`	Always provide this for every parameter so that IntelliSense and the Object Browser can display it.
`<typeparam>`	Always provide this for generic classes.

Summary

Attributes and XML comments let you give extra information about your code to editors and other programming environment objects. Those objects can then provide additional support for developers. They can provide new display and editing capabilities for the Properties window, property sheets, IntelliSense support, and automatic documentation.

Though these features are undeniably cool, and many are even useful, some of them are fairly difficult to implement. Property pages and smart tags can give developers sophisticated ways to manipulate a control's properties, but they require some effort to build. Before you start frenetically cranking out code for editors, type converters, and property tabs, you should determine whether these advanced features will really be worth the effort. If you are building top-of-the-line controls that provide complex visualization tools for hundreds or thousands of customers, it may well be worth the extra struggle to implement these advanced features. If you are writing a simple control that you will use only once or twice, you can probably skip much of this and save yourself a lot of time and trouble.

This chapter (and the four before it) dealt with meta-development. These are topics that deal with tools that help developers perform their tasks. They provide assistance for other programmers, not end users.

The chapters in the next section of the book are more user-oriented. They cover development practices that bring better features and more stable applications to end users.

This chapter discussed XML comments that you can use to automatically generate XML files that describe the code. Chapter 13, "Documentation," continues this topic by showing how you can write Visual Basic code that transforms this XML data into HTML files or Word documents.

Part III
Development

In this Part:

13

Documentation

Chapter 12, "Attributes and XML Comments," explains how you can use attributes and XML comments to provide some automatic documentation for an application. That provides a nice starting point, but the result is hardly ready for customers to use. The XML comments are combined into an XML document that includes the XML comments surrounded by tags to indicate their purposes. You still need to do a lot of work to turn this into a user-friendly resource.

There are also many kinds of documentation that don't naturally fit in XML comments. Because they are in the code, XML comments tend to explain what the code does and how it works, rather than how the user can use the application.

This chapter complements Chapter 12 by discussing kinds of documentation that you should provide for an application. It explains in high-level terms the types of documentation that you should provide. It also explains how you can automatically turn the collected XML documentation into a more usable form.

Documentation Timing

Many developers leave documentation for the very end. They write and debug the application, often going past their original scheduled release date, and then slap together some documentation at the last minute. The result is usually poorly organized, badly written, and incomplete.

It is also too late to allow enough time for training. If the application is complicated, users may need a week or more of training. If the number of users is large, or if all of the users can't drop what they're doing for training at the same time, you may need to run several training sessions at different times, so the whole process may take a month or more. The trainers leading the training sessions will probably also need several weeks to learn the system well enough to teach the users, and to develop training materials.

With this last-minute approach, even if you finish writing code on time, the users may not be able to actually use the application until a month or two later.

Many developers and project managers are happy enough to meet their deadlines and send an application to the users, even if it doesn't have documentation. In the short term, meeting deadlines is important, but if the result is an angry mob of unhappy customers, your reputation as a builder of high-quality software can be irreparably damaged. Even in the short term, you may not gain much by releasing a program without documentation if you are then flooded with technical support calls.

A much better approach is to write documentation continually throughout application development. The initial project specification forms the start of the documentation. As system and other high-level designs are written, they are added to the body of documentation. Use cases, Unified Modeling Language (UML) diagrams, lower-level design, and other development documents are also added, so the amount of documentation grows as development progresses.

Visual Studio lets you associate documentation with a programming project. Open the Project menu, select Add Existing Item, and select the documentation file that you want associated with the project. Now you can double-click the file in Project Explorer to open it.

If the project is large, it will probably be broken into pieces so that developers can work on different pieces at the same time. Associating the appropriate documentation with each piece makes it easier for a developer to find the relevant files to read about the design or to update the documentation. You'll still need to store higher-level documentation that deals with more than one piece of the application separately, but this technique works well for lower-level developer documentation.

Many of these documents are used by developers to guide programming, so writing them not only lays the foundation for good user documentation later, but it can also have big payoffs during development. Good documentation gives the developers a common vision that they can use to guide development. It allows developers to make the same assumptions so that they can work on their pieces of code while staying in synch with other programmers.

As the work continues, developers will find mistakes in the designs and correct them. That will mean that the documentation will also need to be updated. To preserve the project's history, you should place the documentation in a revision control system such as Visual Source Safe (VSS) just as you do with code. When the documentation is modified, you should check the appropriate document out of the revision control system, update it, and check in your changes.

If, for some reason, you don't have a revision control system, you can save snapshots of the documentation each time you make a change. One way to do that is to email the revised documentation to yourself or to a special documentation account. This is less efficient than using a revision control system because those systems typically only save the differences between different versions of a file, rather than the entire new version, but disk space is relatively inexpensive these days.

You may also want to use revision marks when you modify the documentation so that you can see what has changed from version to version. If you follow this approach, you may also want to accept all changes when you create a new version of a file so that you only see the changes since the previous version. It's pretty hard to find a particular change if a document contains hundreds of changes made over a one-year period.

If you use iterative prototyping or another development approach that requires frequent changes to the design, the project's documentation will change a lot during development. Continually revising the documentation can seem frustrating to developers who would rather be writing code. However, revising the documentation provides another opportunity for developers to mentally review the design. Often, reformulating the design in documentation can help developers discover unanticipated problems, and it can lead to a better design.

Sometimes large projects have dedicated technical writers who specialize in writing user documentation and training materials. Writing documentation early and keeping it up-to-date can help technical writers immensely. This is particularly true for military projects, government projects, and projects in other organizations that have rigidly defined development processes.

Frequent changes to the documentation can be even more frustrating to technical writers than it is to developers, partly because the writers may not see the need for some changes. You may need to remind them that the changes are driven by customer requirements and design needs, and that they are not as arbitrary as they may seem.

Translating changes in the developer documentation into changes in the user documents and training materials is much easier if you use a revision control system. Then you can compare revision dates to see which design documents have changed since the user documents and training material were revised. Revision control systems such as VSS can also display the changes to a document so that you can figure out what has changed in the documents and make the corresponding changes.

> *Word processing applications such as Microsoft Word also have revision tracking capabilities. In Word, you can turn revision tracking on by selecting the Tools menu's Track Changes command. Then you can easily see the document's entire history and find changes quickly. Unfortunately, Word shows all changes, not just those since a specific date, so it can be hard to find the most recent changes in a document that changes frequently. If you save new copies of the document after each change, perhaps in your revision control system, then you can use a difference tool to see what has changed between two versions. To compare to documents in Word, select the Tools menu's Compare and Merge Documents command.*

In some development approaches such as staged delivery and some agile methods, development may never end. Instead, the program keeps evolving to adapt to new conditions and requirements. In those situations, the documentation must also evolve to match.

The short cycle times often used by these approaches can make it hard to keep the documentation up-to-date. If an agile project releases a new version of the program every three to four weeks, the time needed to update the documentation can be a significant fraction of the total time for each release.

Although keeping the documentation current is difficult in these sorts of frequent-release projects, it is particularly important. If the application's features change monthly, the users must have reliable documentation so that they can figure out how things should work on their current version of the program.

It is also important that you label the documentation so it is obvious that it matches the current release. You should use the same numbering system for the documentation and the program. Program version 2.1.12 should come with documentation 2.1.12. The users should also be able to easily find the program and documentation version numbers so that they know they are working with the right documentation. It's extremely frustrating to be doing exactly what the documentation says, but still get the wrong result because you have the wrong version of the documentation.

If users may be working with different versions of the software, matching numbering systems will greatly simplify support. When a user calls with a question, the support engineer can ask for the program's version number, and then use the corresponding documentation to find the problem.

Documentation Types

An application should include several different kinds of documentation. You can group them according to their target audience: users and developers.

User Documentation

User documentation is intended for use by the application's eventual users. This includes those who will actually use the program on a regular basis, and those who are involved in specifying and designing the application. It includes the executives who approve and monitor the project, and the "power users" who help determine its functionality. It also includes trainers who will teach the users and support engineers who will answer the users' questions when they use the program.

The following sections describe some of the types of user documentation that a typical project might need. What the project actually needs varies, depending on such factors as how large the application is, the number of users, and how formal the development effort is.

For example, I've worked on simple projects designed for two or three users where the user manual was good enough for training. I've also worked on projects designed for use with several hundred users where trainers developed a full-blown curriculum.

Overview

The *overview document* provides a high-level description of the program's purpose and operation. An executive summary describes the program as succinctly as possible. More detailed sections describe the application's environment, other systems that it interacts with, who the users are, and so forth.

This document should focus on high-level ideas, rather than the program's specific implementation and usage. Typically, this is a relatively short document of one to ten pages.

Sometimes the overview is included in the specification, but it's also useful to be able to pull it out to give to executive-level readers who don't need all of the detail provided by the specification.

Specification

The *specification* provides a detailed description of exactly what the program should do. It focuses on how the program helps the users perform their tasks without explaining how the program works. This document is updated throughout application development, so it is often called a "living specification."

Specifications are often extremely detailed and can be very long. If you use iterative or agile techniques, the specification usually grows over time, so it can be quite long by the time the application is finished.

I've worked on projects with specifications ranging from one or two pages to several hundred pages.

Use Cases

These are scenarios that describe how the program lets a user perform a specific task. They describe the task, expected inputs and results, and the exact steps that the user needs to perform to accomplish the task.

Often, use cases are included in the specification and help define the application's requirements. It is also useful to be able to pull them out so that users, developers, and testers can test the growing application to see whether it handles the use cases.

User Manual

The *user manual* describes every part of the application from the user's point of view. It may include tutorials that introduce new users to the application and tutorials (or "How-To's") that explain how to perform specific tasks, possibly those described by the use cases.

The user manual should use an instructional approach, much as a textbook does, so that the user can read the chapters in order to learn about different parts of the system. The user should not need to jump around to read about specific topics. After reading the manual, a typical user should be able to use the program reasonably competently. The manual may also include sections describing advanced concepts and techniques.

Usually, the user manual should not include the full detail provided by the specification. The specification is designed to let developers and customers decide whether the application does what it should. The user manual is designed to help end users learn how to perform their day-to-day tasks.

Help Files

The *help files* explain parts of the system to the users while they are running the application. The help should describe each form and dialog in the application. Ideally, the forms and dialogs should provide a way for the user to open the corresponding help page.

The help for a form or dialog should explain the purpose of every control that it contains. Obvious controls such as a First Name text box only take a short sentence to describe. Though it may seem excessive to document every name, address, and phone number field, it's easy to write descriptions of these, and it's easy for the users to skip them if those fields don't confuse them. A simple statement such as "The customer's billing address street number" can also be quite helpful when the user can't figure out whether an address is for billing, shipping, the customer contact, or something else.

Controls that are more complicated or confusing need longer descriptions. A good description of a complex topic can save you technical support calls.

Don't be afraid of describing seemingly obvious facts in some detail. Users only look at the help when they are confused and they don't find the form obvious. Users are rarely offended by help that is too descriptive. They are much more irritated by incomplete help.

An annotated screen shot of a form or dialog can tie controls to their descriptions concisely.

Often, the user manual is included in the help system so that the user can easily review its material and search for tutorials that show how to perform specific tasks. It may still be useful to provide a separate printed version of the user manual, however, so users can read it away from their computers.

Context-Sensitive Help

Context-sensitive help provides help based on the controls with which the user is interacting. For example, if the focus is in a street address field, the user might press F1 to view the help for that field either in a help file or in a popup window. This information is probably duplicated in the main help file describing the form containing the field.

In Visual Basic, you can display a help button in the form's title bar. When the user clicks this button, the cursor changes to an arrow with a question mark. If the user then clicks a control, Visual Basic raises the control's `HelpRequested` event and the program can display appropriate help for the control.

A control's `HelpRequested` event is also raised if the user presses F1 while focus is in that control.

Figure 13-1 shows the `HelpButton` example application. You can see the question mark arrow cursor hovering over the First Name text box.

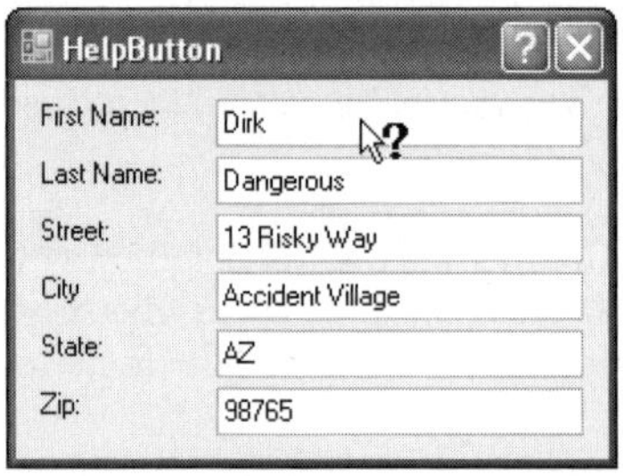

Figure 13-1: When you click the help button in the title bar, the cursor changes to a question mark arrow.

The following code shows how this example works. This example stores a control's help string in its `Tag` property. When the form loads, the program sets a `HelpRequested` event handler for each of the form's controls. The `HelpRequested` event handler simply displays the control's `Tag` property.

```
Public Class Form1
    ' Add a HelpRequested event handler to every control.
    Private Sub Form1_Load(ByVal sender As System.Object, _
     ByVal e As System.EventArgs) Handles MyBase.Load
        For Each ctl As Control In Me.Controls
            AddHandler ctl.HelpRequested, AddressOf Control_HelpRequested
        Next ctl
    End Sub

    ' Display help for the clicked control.
    Private Sub Control_HelpRequested(ByVal sender As Object, _
     ByVal hlpevent As System.Windows.Forms.HelpEventArgs)
        ' Get the control.
        Dim ctl As Control = DirectCast(sender, Control)

        ' Display the control's Tag property.
        Dim txt As String = DirectCast(ctl.Tag, String)
        If (txt Is Nothing) OrElse (txt.Length = 0) Then
            MessageBox.Show( _
```

```
                "Sorry, there's no help for control " & ctl.Name, _
                "Help", MessageBoxButtons.OK, MessageBoxIcon.Information)
        Else
            MessageBox.Show( _
                txt, _
                "Help", MessageBoxButtons.OK, MessageBoxIcon.Information)
        End If
    End Sub
End Class
```

Example program `ResourceContextHelp` *(available for download at* `www.vb-helper.com/one_on_one.htm`*) shows another approach that stores help strings in the project's resources.*

When the user clicks the help button and then clicks one of the controls, the event handler builds the name of the resources that should contain the control's help string. It uses `My.Resources.ResourceManager` to get the resource string and displays it if it exists.

Unfortunately, Visual Basic ignores the form's `HelpButton` *property if either the* `MinimizeBox` *or* `MaximizeBox` *property is* `True`*. That means you can only display the help button on forms that cannot be minimized or maximized. In many applications, that basically means the dialogs.*

Pressing F1 while a control has the focus still raises its `HelpRequested` *event even if the help button is hidden, so you can still provide this kind of help on forms that have Minimize or Maximize buttons.*

The `HelpProvider` component provides another way to display context-sensitive help. Figure 13-2 shows the `HelpProvider` example program using as `HelpProvider` component. In this figure, I clicked the help button and then clicked the State text box. The `HelpProvider` component displays the help in a popup.

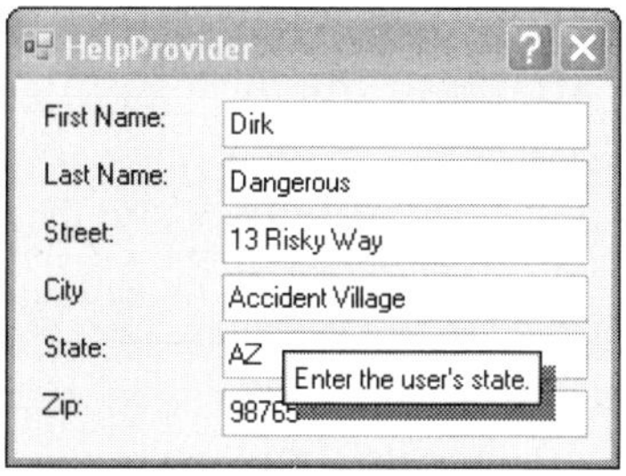

Figure 13-2: The `HelpProvider` component displays help in a popup.

To use a `HelpProvider`, add a `HelpProvider` component to the form. To display a simple string for a control, set the control's `HelpString` property that is added by the component. For example, if you give the `HelpProvider` the name `hlpFields`, each control on the form gets a new property called `HelpString on hlpFields`. If you set this string, the `HelpProvider` automatically displays it when the user requests help.

For other features provided by the `HelpProvider` component, see the online help.

Tooltips

Tooltips provide a tiny amount of additional documentation for the user. They are unobtrusive, so experienced users can ignore them easily. If you forget what a field is for, you can hover the mouse over the field to see the tooltip.

To give a control a tooltip, add a `ToolTip` component to the form and then set the control's `ToolTip` property added by the component. For example, if you give the `ToolTip` component the name `tipFields`, every control on the form gets a new property named `ToolTip on tipFields`.

After you set the controls' `ToolTip` properties, the `ToolTip` component displays the tooltips automatically. Figure 13-3 shows example program `TooltipHelp` displaying a tooltip for the City text box.

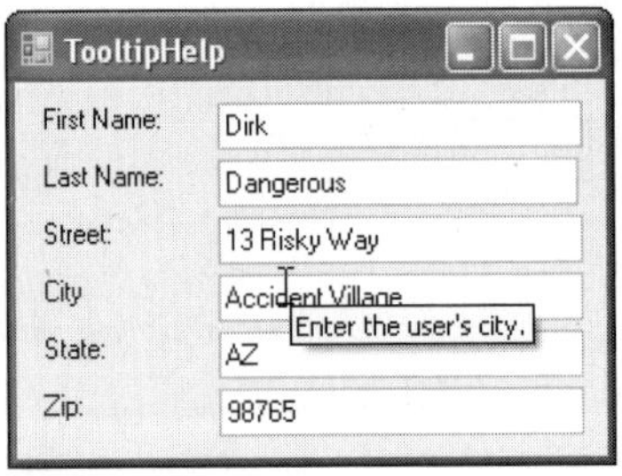

Figure 13-3: The `ToolTip` component displays tooltips for controls.

Users who have vision impairments rely heavily on tooltips. The screen readers used by these users depend on tooltips to help the user understand the application better.

Training Materials

The type and amount of *training materials* needed for a project vary widely, depending on the complexity of the project and the number and types of users. A simple project designed for use by one or two users won't need much in the way of training materials. The user manual and an hour's time with the project manager may be enough. For a complicated project intended for use by many users, training may involve a week or more of detailed instruction and hands-on study with handouts, slide shows, demonstrations, catering, and hotel rooms.

Often, the training materials will cover much of the same material included in the user manual. It should include an overview, basic instructions for using the application, and some specific examples. It may include hands-on exercises that let the users experiment with the application on their own with the instructor present to lend a helping hand.

You can make that sort of hands-on training easier if you plan for it from the beginning. In particular, you should try to design the application so that it can easily work with test data that students can destroy without affecting real operations. Training users on live production systems can be difficult and dangerous.

While the training materials may be based largely on the user manual, much of the material may need to be rewritten to work in a classroom setting.

Building effective training materials is an art in its own right. Unless you have a special talent for teaching, or you have a fairly simple application and small user population, you'll probably be better off leaving this to a dedicated instructor.

Support Materials

Support materials include tools used by support engineers to help users solve problems. For a simple application, this may be nothing more than the user manual and some additional notes. For a more complex application, it might include tables of steps to follow when trying to resolve a problem, or even a separate application that helps guide troubleshooting.

Historical Documentation

In a long or complicated project, customers, managers, designers, and developers make a huge number of decisions. Sometimes the same issues are faced repeatedly. To avoid wasted time making the same decisions over and over again, possibly in contradictory ways, you should keep a project history that documents every decision made during the project's lifespan.

You should update the project specification to record important decisions, but it's important to have a record somewhere of all of the little decisions, too. One method for storing this information is to copy all project emails into a special History account. Later, if you face the same problem again, you can search that account's emails for messages that deal with the same subject.

Developer Documentation

User documents are often used by developers, too. For example, the specification determines what the program should do, so it guides the design. The use cases describe how the program should handle specific scenarios, so they guide development and provide tests that developers can use to see if the program does what it should.

In addition to the user documentation, developers need extra documentation that is geared toward development tasks. These are described more fully in Chapter 2, "Lifecycle Methodologies," so they are described only briefly here.

Specification

Although I listed the *specification* as a user-oriented document earlier in this chapter, it's so important to developers that I'm listing it again here, too. The specification is the final word in what the application should do, so developers should be very familiar with it. If the program doesn't do what the specification says it should, either the program must be fixed, or the specification revised.

High-Level Design

High-level design documentation describes how the major pieces of the application fit together. It includes architectural and platform decisions, and describes the application's biggest systems.

System-Level Documentation

Whereas high-level design explains how the application's major systems fit together, *system-level design* explains how the systems work. This may include UML diagrams, flowcharts, and other process modeling diagrams, as well as text.

Often, each system can be built as a separate Visual Basic project. For example, the main user interface might be one project that links to the other system built as separate DLLs. In that case, you may be able to link each system's documentation to its project as described earlier in this chapter by using the Project menu's Add Existing Item command.

Module-Level Documentation

Module-level documentation describes a particular source code module. This includes descriptions of routines that are accessible outside of the module, and descriptions of the code used within the module.

If you use the design-by-contract methods described in Chapter 3, "Agile Methodologies," you should describe the contracts satisfied by the routines in the module.

Higher-level documentation for the module can be included in separate documents. This might include an index of public routines available within the module and the contracts they provide.

Other more-detailed documentation is usually included as comments within the module's code. Different development organizations often have standard formats that they want for this type of documentation. The following code shows a standard format for describing the module as a whole:

```
' **************************************************
' File:
' Copyright:
'
' Revision History:
'   Date        By          Reason
'   ----------  ----------  ----------
'
'
' Purpose:
'
' Entry Points:
'
' Dependencies:
'
' Issues:
'
' Method:
'
' ************************************************
' Global Definitions
' ----------------------------
' Global API Declarations
' ----------------------------

' ----------------------------
' Global Types
' ----------------------------

' ----------------------------
' Global Enums and Constants
' ----------------------------
```

```
' ----------------------------
' Global Variables
' ----------------------------

' ************************************************
' Private Definitions
' ----------------------------
' Private API Declarations
' ----------------------------

' ----------------------------
' Private Types
' ----------------------------

' ----------------------------
' Private Constants and Enums
' ----------------------------

' ----------------------------
' Private Variables
' ----------------------------
```

The following code shows a format for a routine comment:

```
' ************************************************
' Purpose:      $purpose$
'
' Method:
'
' Inputs:
'
' Outputs:
'
' Errors:
'
' Asserts:
'
' Revision History:
'   Date        By          Reason
'   ----------  ----------  ----------
'   $date$      $creator$   Initial creation
'
' ************************************************
```

To make using the comments easier, you can turn them into code snippets as described in Chapter 8, "Snippets, Macros, and Add-ins." You can download text and snippet versions of these comments at the book's Web page.

Inline Comments

In the long term, one of the most important kinds of documentation for developers is the *inline comment*. Comments give extra context to help developers understand what the code is doing. Developers who don't understand precisely what the code is doing before making changes are very likely to break the code, so this kind of documentation is absolutely essential.

During the time I've been programming, I've seen many projects with insufficient comments. On one project that I helped write, we added extensive comments to the code to explain exactly what the code was doing. We placed comments on key lines to give developers general information. Then we added additional comments to almost every line explaining exactly what the code was doing in excruciating detail. These extra comments were far to the right, so they were not normally visible; you could only see them if you scrolled to the right.

After writing this application, we transferred the code to another corporate organization for long-term maintenance. That organization had the philosophy that any comment that wasn't essential to understanding the code must be distracting, so they removed all of our secondary comments and some of the main comments. A few months later, they discovered that they couldn't maintain the code because they couldn't understand it. Somehow, they never made the connection that they didn't understand it because the comments were gone.

That same organization determined a project's budget based on the number of lines of code. Because the count didn't include comments, it implicitly discouraged their use. A developer was rewarded for writing inefficient code that used lots of extra unnecessary steps, but not for writing comments that were critical for maintaining the software.

Since then, I've met other developers who shared this "if it isn't necessary, it's distracting" philosophy. The problem with this idea is that most code is obvious when you understand it. If the code and its comments are well-written, it should be obvious how the code works. At that point, it's easy to think the comments are unnecessary and remove them. Unfortunately, when someone else reads the code, or when you look at it again later, the code may be far less obvious and the lack of comments can be disastrous. It's much better to have too many comments and then ignore them when you don't need them.

Another project I worked on included about 65,000 lines of Visual Basic code and practically no comments. The application was several years old and pieces of it had been written, rewritten, and rewritten again in everything from Visual Basic 3 to Visual Basic 6. The many rewrites and the lack of comments made huge sections of the code practically incomprehensible. The only way to figure out how some routines worked was to step through them in the debugger. Making even simple changes to the code sometimes took a week or more, and had a high probability of introducing a new bug.

Add extensive comments to your code. Add more comments than you think are really necessary. Of course, you don't need to be intentionally stupid about it. The following comment doesn't add anything to a developer's understanding of the code:

```
index += 1    ' Increment the index.
```

Add plenty of comments, but try to add a new perspective that isn't blindingly obvious from the code itself.

One technique that I often use to comment code is to write the comments first. Start with the specification for a routine and break it down into a series of steps that you need to perform to accomplish the routine's tasks. Then break those steps into smaller steps. Continue the process until it's easier to write the code than to further refine the steps. Now, place apostrophes in front of the text you've written to make them comments and fill in the code.

This type of code reads very differently from code written with the more typical comment-last approach. With the usual approach, you read the code and then use the comments to try to figure out what the code is doing. With the comment-first approach, you read the comments and then verify that the code does what the comment says it does. Just as it's easier to select a command from a menu than it is to type in a command from memory, it's easier to verify that code does what it should than it is to decipher code with insufficient context.

XML Documentation

Chapter 12 explains how you can add a new type of comments to your code. An XML comment begins with three single quotes (`'''`). Within the comment, XML tags define various sections of documentation. The comments must be well-formed XML code (aside from the single quotes).

The following code shows XML comments for a `Person` class:

```
''' <summary>
''' Represents a customer or employee.
''' </summary>
''' <remarks>Use a Manager object for managers.</remarks>
Public Class Person
    ...
```

When it builds an application, Visual Basic automatically gathers these comments and puts them in an XML file. The following code shows the resulting XML code for these comments:

```
<?xml version="1.0"?>
<doc>
<assembly>
<name>
PersonComments
</name>
</assembly>
<members>
<member name="M:PersonComments.Person.PrintLetter(System.String,System.Int32)">
 <summary>
 Print a letter and envelope for this person.
 </summary>
 <param name="letter_text">The text of the letter to be printed.</param>
 <param name="priority">The letter's priority. 1 = Highest.</param>
 <remarks>Use this routine to generate a letter for a person.
 The routine prints the letter on the default printer and
 then waits for you to load an envelope in the manual feed before
 addressing the envelope.</remarks>
</member>
</members>
</doc>
```

Visual Basic understands certain predefined XML comment tags and provides extra support for them. For example, if you type three single quotes on the line before a subroutine, Visual Basic enters the tags that it thinks are appropriate for the routine. This includes `summary` and `remarks` tags, and `param` tags for any parameters that the routine takes. See Chapter 12 for more information. The section "Recommended Tags" toward the end of Chapter 12 lists tags that Microsoft recommends that you use in XML comments.

Custom XML Tags

In addition to predefined tags, you can add tags of your own to the XML comments. That means you can store all of the information described earlier in this chapter in XML comments instead of normal comments. For example, you can add history tags to record changes to a module.

The following code shows the XML comments on the `Employee` class. The `History` tags include three `Change` elements that record some changes.

```
''' <summary>
''' Represents an employee.
''' </summary>
''' <remarks>Inherits from Person.</remarks>
''' <SeeAlsoSection>
'''   <seealso cref="Person">Person parent class</seealso>
''' </SeeAlsoSection>
''' <scope>Public</scope>
''' <History>
'''   <Change By="Rod Stephens" Date="4/1/2007">Initial creation.</Change>
'''   <Change By="Rod Stephens" Date="4/3/2007">Added comments.</Change>
'''   <Change By="Zaphod" Date="4/13/2007">Deleted confusing stuff.</Change>
''' </History>
Public Class Employee
    ...
End Class
```

Though the XML document produced by Visual Basic doesn't do anything special with these custom tags, it does include them. (Two options for processing the XML document are to use available programs such as NDoc and Sandcastle to convert the file into something more readable, and to write your own program to process the file. The following sections say more about these approaches.)

Example program `XmlTestClasses` (available for download at `www.vb-helper.com/one_on_one.htm`) uses several new tags to store additional information. The following list shows some of these new tags, plus some others that you might want to use:

- `History`—Contains a series of `Change` tags recording changes.
- `Scope`—Gives the item's scope (`Public`, `Private`, and so forth). The XML document does not include this information by itself.
- `SeeAlsoSection`—Makes a section to hold `seealso` tags. You can include `seealso` tags in any other XML comment section, but Microsoft hasn't defined a specific section to hold them. The intent of `SeeAlsoSection` is to give you a place to put the `seealso` tags, probably at the end of the other comments.
- `Method`—Explains how a routine works.
- `Inputs`—Describes a routine's input parameters.
- `Outputs`—Describes a routine's output parameters.
- `Errors`—Describes errors that a routine might generate.
- `Exceptions`—Describes exceptions that the routine might throw and how to fix them.

- `ToDo` — Lists changes that should be made to the code later.
- `Asserts` — Describes preconditions that the code asserts.
- `EntryPoints` — Describes the public properties, methods, and events provided by a class or module for external use. This would probably include `see` or `seealso` tags linking to those properties, methods, and events.
- `Dependencies` — Lists other pieces of code on which this one depends. This would probably include `see` or `seealso` tags linking to the dependent code.

Using XML Documentation

Once you've inserted XML comments and compiled the application, you need a way to use the resulting XML documentation.

One option is to use existing tools such as NDoc (`ndoc.sourceforge.net`) to convert the XML documentation into Web pages or help files. NDoc uses reflection to gather extra information about the code that is not included in the XML documentation. For example, it discovers the inheritance hierarchy of the classes it is documenting and adds that information to its output.

Figure 13-4 shows an NDoc help page for one of the `Person` class's two constructors.

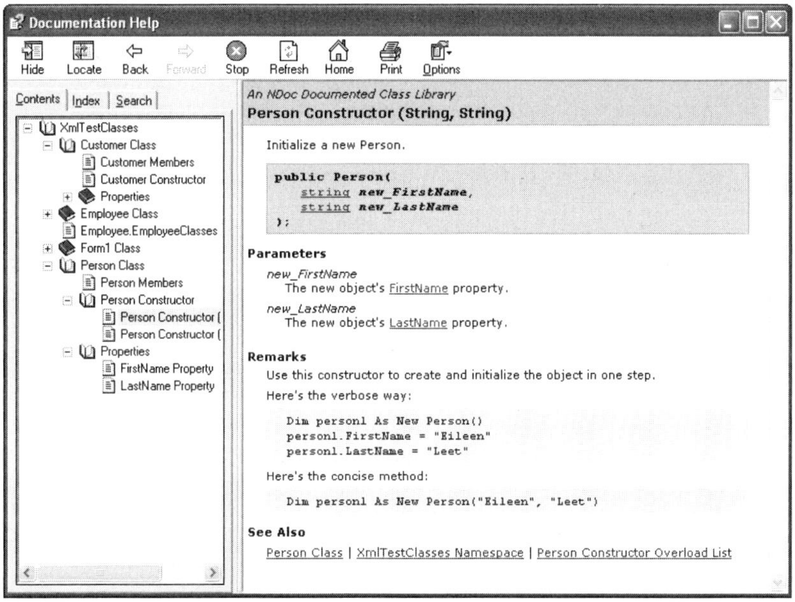

Figure 13-4: NDoc uses reflection and XML documentation to build Web and help pages.

NDoc provides a high-quality result with very little effort on your part, so if its results are sufficient for your needs, you should use it. However, NDoc only handles tags that are predefined by Visual Studio. As you might expect, it doesn't have a clue about what to do with a `History`, `Exceptions`, or `Asserts` tags.

The West Wind HTML Help Builder (`west-wind.com/wwhelp`) can help you build HTML help in a similar manner, although, unlike NDoc, it's not free.

Microsoft has also written a tool code named Sandcastle that compiles the XML documentation file into compiled help (CHM) files. It is not quite ready for release as of this writing, although it should be available in Microsoft's Download Center (`http://www.microsoft.com/downloads`) by the time you read this. Currently, it is described as similar to NDoc.

Although these tools are useful and convenient, if you want to use custom tags in your XML comments, you need to process the documentation yourself. There are a couple of ways you might do this, but none is easy.

You could write Extensible Stylesheet Language (XSL) to transform the original XML documentation into other formats such as HTML or WordML, which you could then import into Microsoft Word. Unfortunately, XSL is a pretty complicated language, so this would be fairly difficult unless you already have extensive experience with it.

Another option is to load the XML document into a Visual Basic application and process it. The `XmlDocToText` example program, available at `www.vb-helper.com/one_on_one.htm` and described in the following section, does that. It uses the XML documentation to produce a textual representation of the code.

Program XmlDocToText

Program `XmlDocToText` reads an XML document file and produces the display shown in Figure 13-5. This figure shows that the `XmlTestClasses` assembly contains a public class named `Employee`. That class includes a public type (`Enum`) named `EmployeeClasses` that defines values `Developer`, `ProjectManager`, and `VicePresident`. The class has two private fields (variables) called `m_EmployeeClass` and `m_Office`, and two public properties called `EmployeeClass` and `Office`.

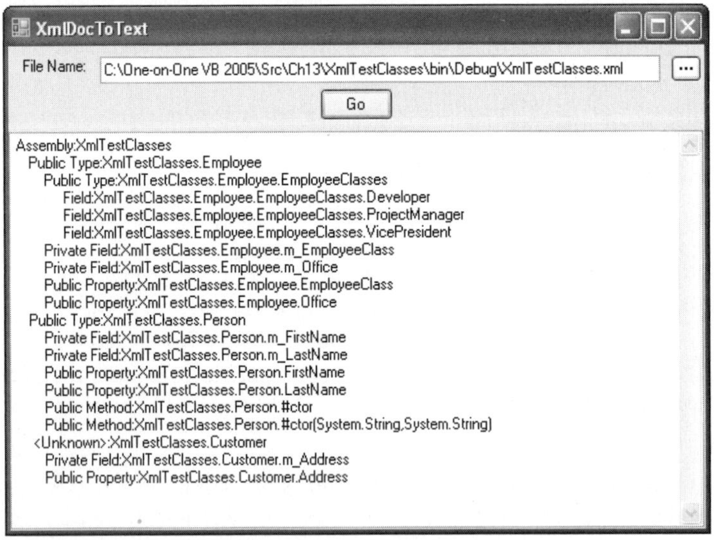

Figure 13-5: Program `XmlDocToText` displays a project's code hierarchy.

You can examine Figure 13-5 to learn more about the code hierarchy. The value `<Unknown>` means the program could not figure out a code item's type or scope because they were not documented in the XML comments. The XML documentation uses the name `#ctor` to refer to a class's constructor.

To understand how the program works, you need to know a bit more about the XML documentation file. This file contains a series of `member` tags that contain information about code elements. For example, the following code shows the `member` tag for the `Employee` class, slightly reformatted to make it easier to read:

```
<member name="T:XmlTestClasses.Employee">
    <summary>
    Represents an employee.
    </summary>
    <remarks>Inherits from Person.</remarks>
    <SeeAlsoSection>
        <seealso cref="T:XmlTestClasses.Person">Person parent class</seealso>
    </SeeAlsoSection>
    <scope>Public</scope>
    <History>
        <Change By="Rod Stephens" Date="4/1/2007">Initial creation.</Change>
        <Change By="Rod Stephens" Date="4/3/2007">Added comments.</Change>
        <Change By="Zaphod" Date="4/13/2007">Deleted confusing stuff.</Change>
    </History>
</member>
```

The "`T`" before the name in the `member` tag indicates that this is a type (in this case, a class). The code includes standard tags such as `summary` and `remarks` in addition to custom tags such as `scope` and `History`.

The following code shows the `member` tag for the `Employee` class's `Office` property. The "`P`" in front of the name means this is a property.

```
<member name="P:XmlTestClasses.Employee.Office">
    <summary>
    The Employees's building and office number.
    </summary>
    <value>The Employee's office number.</value>
    <returns>An employee's office number.</returns>
    <remarks>Used in mailing addresses.</remarks>
    <scope>Public</scope>
</member>
```

Unfortunately, the XML documentation doesn't contain any of the code's hierarchical information. In the previous example, notice that the XML code does not contain tags indicating that the `Office` item is contained in the `Employee` item. The only clue about the hierarchy is in the item's name: `XmlTestClasses.Employee.Office`. You can use that name to try to locate other objects in the XML documentation that are related. For example, you can look for `XmlTestClasses.Employee` to find the class that contains the property.

Unfortunately, the documentation only includes tags for items that have XML comments. If you don't add any XML comments to the `XmlTestClasses.Employee` class, the document won't contain a `member` tag for that class.

NDoc uses reflection to work around this limitation. It examines the assembly to determine the class containing the property. That's a more effective method than the one used by program `XmlDocToText`, *but it's more work.*

Program `XmlDocToText` uses a `DocNode` class to represent the code elements described by the XML documentation. This class has variables that represent the object's element in the XML document file, full name (as in `XmlTestClasses.Employee.Office`), short name (as in `Office`), and type (`assembly`, `type`, `property`, `constructor`, and so forth). It also stores the item's scope if defined by a `scope` tag and a collection of `DocNode` objects representing the item's children. For example, the `XmlTestClasses.Employee` class's `DocNode` object has the `XmlTestClasses.Employee.Office` `DocNode` object as a child.

Program `XmlDocToText` uses the following code to read the XML file:

```
' Parse the XML document.
Private Function ParseXmlDocument(ByVal file_name As String) As DocNode
    ' Load the XML file.
    Dim xml_doc As New XmlDocument()
    xml_doc.Load(file_name)

    ' Find the <assembly> node.
    Dim assembly_node As XmlNode = xml_doc.DocumentElement.Item("assembly")

    ' Get the <name> value.
    Dim root As New DocNode(assembly_node, _
        assembly_node.Item("name").InnerText.Trim, "A")

    ' Add the <members> to the root node.
    Dim members_node As XmlNode = xml_doc.DocumentElement.Item("members")
    For Each member As XmlNode In members_node.ChildNodes
        ' Make the child node.
        Dim full_name As String = member.Attributes("name").Value
        Debug.Assert(full_name.Contains(":"), _
            "Member node's name does not contain ':'")
        Dim type_code As String = full_name.Substring(0, full_name.IndexOf(":"))
        full_name = full_name.Substring(full_name.IndexOf(":") + 1)
        Dim child_node As New DocNode(member, full_name, type_code)

        ' Add the child to the root node.
        root.AddChild(child_node)
    Next member

    Return root
End Function
```

The code creates a new `XmlDocument` object and loads the file. The object's `DocumentElement` property returns a reference to the XML root element. The code uses that object's `Item` method to get the `assembly` element that contains information about the code assembly. It gets the `InnerText` value from the assembly node's `name` element and uses it to create a new `DocNode` object. It passes the `DocNode` constructor the XML node representing the assembly, the assembly's name, and the character `A` to indicate that this is an assembly node. The code uses this `DocNode` as the root of a tree of `DocNode` objects.

Next, the code gets the document's `members` element, which contains the `member` elements. It loops through those elements, creating `DocNode` objects for each. It calls the root `DocNode`'s `AddChild` method to add the new node to the `DocNode` tree.

The following code shows how the `DocNode` class's `AddChild` method works:

```
' Add a child to this node's Children collection.
Public Sub AddChild(ByVal new_child As DocNode)
    ' See if the new child has our full name.
    If new_child.FullName = Me.FullName Then
        ' The child has information that belongs in our node.
        ' Save the XML node and type code, and discard the new child.
        Me.XmlDocNode = new_child.XmlDocNode
        Me.TypeCode = new_child.TypeCode
        Me.TypeName = new_child.TypeName
        Me.ScopeName = new_child.ScopeName
    Else
        ' Get the next piece of the child's name.
        ' Remove the first part.
        Dim name_piece As String = _
            new_child.FullName.Substring(Me.FullName.Length + 1)
        ' Remove the last part.
        Dim paren_pos As Integer = name_piece.IndexOf("(")
        If paren_pos < 0 Then paren_pos = name_piece.Length
        If name_piece.LastIndexOf(".", paren_pos) >= 0 Then
            name_piece = name_piece.Substring(0, name_piece.IndexOf("."))
        End If

        ' See if we have a child with this short name.
        If Children.Contains(name_piece) Then
            ' We have this child. Get it.
            Dim child_node As DocNode = _
                DirectCast(Children.Item(name_piece), DocNode)

            ' Put the new child inside this child.
            child_node.AddChild(new_child)
        Else
            ' We don't have the needed child. Make it.
            Dim child_node As New DocNode(Nothing, _
                Me.FullName & "." & name_piece, "?")
            Me.Children.Add(child_node, name_piece)

            ' Put the new child inside this child.
            child_node.AddChild(new_child)
        End If
    End If
End Sub
```

This code first compares the current `DocNode` object's full name with the new child's name. If they match, the child's information belongs here, so the code copies it into the current object.

If the names don't match, the program pulls off the next piece of the child's name. For example, suppose the current `DocNode` has name `XmlTestClasses.Employee` and the child has name `XmlTestClasses.Employee.Office.Phone`. The code removes the current node's name from the child's name to get `Office.Phone`.

Next, the program removes everything after the first period, in this case giving `Office`. The code must perform some extra tests to ensure that it doesn't remove parameters provided for a constructor. For example, the `Person` class in the test application has a constructor that takes two string parameters that the XML documentation file names `#ctor(System.String,System.String)`.

Next, the program checks the current `DocNode`'s `Children` collection to see if it contains a child with this name. If it does, the program calls that child's `AddChild` method to place the new data in that part of the tree. If the collection does not contain a child with this name, the program creates one, and then calls its `AddChild` method to add the new data.

The process continues moving the new `DocNode` data down into the tree until it reaches a node that represents it. When it has finished, the program has a tree structure built from `DocNodes` corresponding to the XML document's nodes.

Note that the code creates intermediate `DocNode` objects as necessary to build the complete tree. For example, suppose the XML document contains a `member` element for `XmlTestClasses.Customer.Address` but not for `XmlTestClasses.Customer`. The code creates a `DocNode` object for that class anyway, but it doesn't contain information about the class's scope and type because that information is missing from the XML document. In Figure 13-5 you can see that the program displayed this class's scope as `<Unknown>` and it doesn't show a type.

After it loads the `DocNode` tree, the program calls the root node's `SortChildren` method. This routine, shown in the following code, copies the node's children into an array, uses the `Array.Sort` method to sort the nodes by their names, and then copies the sorted array back into the `Children` collection. The routine then recursively calls the child nodes' `SortChildren` methods so that all of the nodes in the tree sort their children.

```
Public Sub SortChildren()
    ' Copy the children into a temporary array.
    Dim new_children(0 To Children.Count - 1) As DocNode
    For i As Integer = 0 To Children.Count - 1
        new_children(i) = DirectCast(Children.Item(i + 1), DocNode)
    Next i

    ' Sort the array.
    Dim doc_node_comparer As New DocNodeComparer()
    Array.Sort(Of DocNode)(new_children, doc_node_comparer)

    ' Copy the sorted children back into the Children collection.
    Children = New Collection
    For i As Integer = 0 To new_children.Length - 1
        Children.Add(new_children(i), new_children(i).ShortName)
    Next i
```

```
    ' Recursively sort the children.
    For Each child_node As DocNode In Children
        child_node.SortChildren()
    Next child_node
End Sub
```

This code uses a `DocNodeComparer` object to sort the children. This class compares two `DocNode` objects and returns a value indicating which should come first. It arranges items so that they are arranged by scope (`Public`, `Private`, and so forth), type (`assembly`, `constructor`, `type`, `field`, and so forth), and name. Download the example program and look at the code for details about this class.

After loading and sorting the `DocNode` tree, the program calls the root node's `PrefixOrder` method shown in the following code. This routine builds a string starting with some spaces for indentation and then containing the `DocNode`'s description. It then recursively calls the `PrefixOrder` method of each of the node's children, increasing the indentation by four spaces.

```
' Display the node's data.
Public Function PrefixOrder(Optional ByVal indent As Integer = 0) As String
    Dim result As String = Space(indent) & ShortDescription & vbCrLf

    For Each child_node As DocNode In Children
        result &= child_node.PrefixOrder(indent + 4)
    Next child_node
    Return result
End Function
```

The program displays the result of the call to the root node's `PrefixOrder` method, as shown in Figure 13-5.

Program XmlDocToHtml

Example program `XmlDocToText` (available for download at `www.vb-helper.com/one_on_one.htm`) is fairly simple. It displays the scope, type, and names of objects in a hierarchical display, but it doesn't display any of the other information contained in XML comments.

Example program `XmlDocToHtml` is much more ambitious. It builds a collection of Web pages describing the assembly. It includes an index page outlining the code hierarchy. Links lead to information about the objects in the hierarchy. The pages describing those objects include summary, remarks, links, and other information provided by the solution's XML comments.

Figure 13-6 shows the index page for the solution used in Figure 13-5. The left column holds the objects' short names and links to detail pages. The right column displays the objects' summary information.

If you click the Person link in Figure 13-6, you'll see the detail page shown in Figure 13-7. The page contains sections giving the item's signature (scope, type, and name), and the summary and remarks data contained in the XML comments. The Members link at the top leads to a page describing the `Person` class's properties, methods, and events. The other links at the top lead to sections on this page.

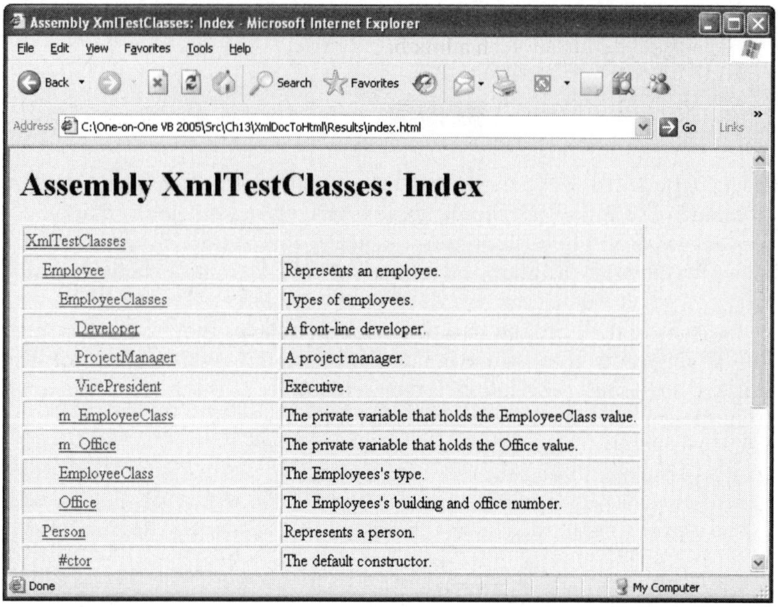

Figure 13-6: Program `XmlDocToHtml` builds this index page from an XML document.

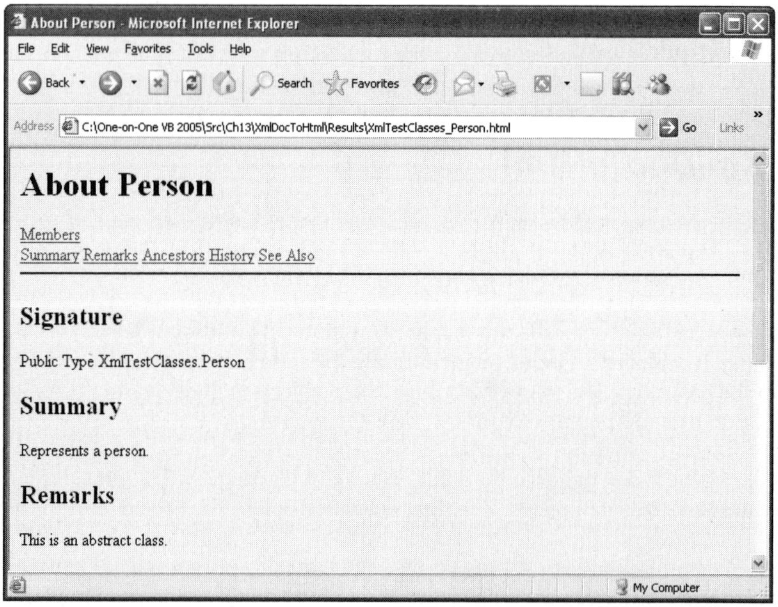

Figure 13-7: Program `XmlDocToHtml` builds this detail page for the `Person` class.

Figure 13-8 shows the bottom half of this page. The `XmlDocToHtml` program uses the structure of the `DocNode` tree to display links to the `Person` class's ancestors. The `History` section shows information contained in `History` XML comments. The `See Also` section contains links defined by `seealso` tags in the XML comments. The page ends with a link back to the hierarchy index shown in Figure 13-6.

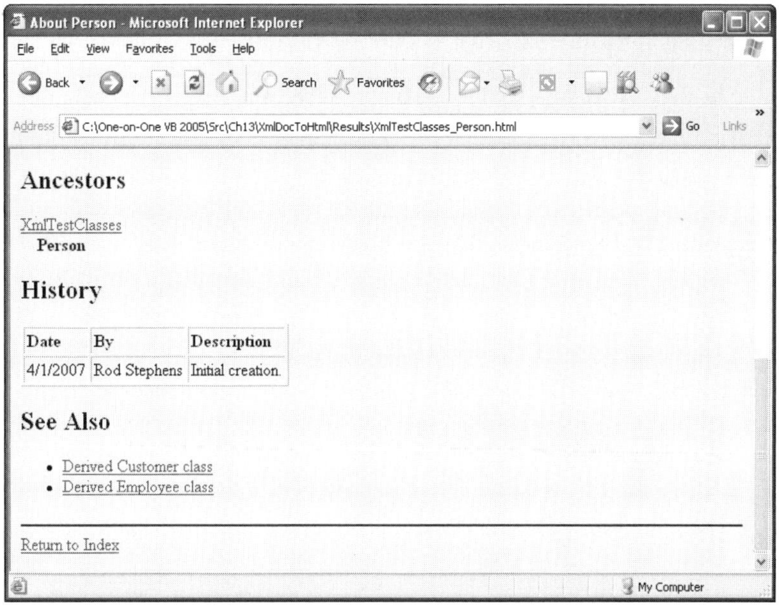

Figure 13-8: The bottom of the `Person` class's Web page displays ancestor and history data.

Program `XmlDocToHtml` is much longer than program `XmlDocToText`, so only a little of it is shown here. You can download the project and look at the code to see the details.

The basic idea behind the two programs is similar, however. Program `XmlDocToHtml` builds a `DocNode` tree much as program `XmlDocToText` does. It then traverses the tree to generate output. Unlike program `XmlDocToText`, however, this program saves its output in HTML files.

The following code shows how the program generates the index page:

```
' Make the index page.
Private Sub MakeIndex(ByVal root_node As DocNode, ByVal output_dir As String, _
 ByVal assembly_title As String)
    ' Make the file's title.
    Dim txt As String = My.Resources.IndexTemplate
    txt = txt.Replace("@TITLE@", assembly_title & ": Index")

    ' Make the file's body.
    Dim lines As String = root_node.PrefixOrder(True, False, False, False, True)
    lines = lines.Replace(vbTab, "    ")
    txt = txt.Replace("@BODY@", lines)

    ' Write the file.
    My.Computer.FileSystem.WriteAllText(output_dir & "index.html", txt, False)
End Sub
```

Subroutine MakeIndex starts by copying a template file from the IndexTemplate resource into a string. This resource is a text file containing a skeleton for an HTML page. It uses tokens such as @BODY@ to represent parts of the skeleton that should be replaced to build the final Web page.

The subroutine replaces the @TITLE@ token with the assembly's name. It then calls the root DocNode's PrefixOrder method to build a string describing the items in the DocNode tree. This version of PrefixOrder is similar to the version described in the previous section and used by program XmlDocToText, except it takes more parameters and can produce differently formatted results. This code passes the method parameters indicating that it needs the results to look like the rows in the table shown in Figure 13-8.

The program replaces tab characters used by PrefixOrder to indent item names with HTML non-breaking spaces, and inserts the result in the Web page template. It finishes by writing the result into the file index.html.

Other routines in program XmlDocToHtml similarly build other Web pages. Subroutine MakeWebPages, shown in the following code, builds the Web pages for a DocNode and its descendants:

```
' Make a Web page describing this object.
Public Sub MakeWebPages(ByVal output_dir As String)
    Dim txt As String = My.Resources.ObjectPageTemplate
    txt = txt.Replace("@TITLE@", "About " & Me.ShortName)
    txt = txt.Replace("@DESCRIPTION@", _
        Me.Description(False, True, True, True, False))

    ' Insert the members section.
    txt = txt.Replace("@MEMBERSMENU@", Me.MembersLink(output_dir))

    ' Insert the summary.
    txt = txt.Replace("@SUMMARY@", Me.Summary())

    ' Insert the parameters.
    Dim parameters_text As String = Me.Parameters()
    txt = txt.Replace("@PARAMETERS@", parameters_text)

    ' If the Parameters section is not empty,
    ' then insert a local link to it.
    If parameters_text.Length > 0 Then
        txt = txt.Replace("@PARAMETERSMENU@", _
            "  <A HREF=""#parameters"">Parameters</A>")
    Else
        txt = txt.Replace("@PARAMETERSMENU@", "")
    End If

    ' Insert the remarks.
    txt = txt.Replace("@REMARKS@", Me.Remarks())

    ' Insert the ancestor hierarchy.
    txt = txt.Replace("@ANCESTORS@", Me.Ancestors())

    ' Insert the revision history.
    txt = txt.Replace("@HISTORY@", Me.History())
```

```
        ' Insert the See Also section.
        Dim seealso_text As String = Me.SeeAlso()
        txt = txt.Replace("@SEEALSO@", seealso_text)

        ' If the See Also section is not empty,
        ' then insert a local link to it.
        If seealso_text.Length > 0 Then
            txt = txt.Replace("@SEEALSOMENU@", "  <A HREF=""#seealso"">See Also</A>")
        Else
            txt = txt.Replace("@SEEALSOMENU@", "")
        End If

        ' Save the result.
        My.Computer.FileSystem.WriteAllText(output_dir & _
            Me.FullName.Replace(".", "_") & ".html", _
            txt, False)

        ' Recursively make children.
        For Each child_node As DocNode In Children
            child_node.MakeWebPages(output_dir)
        Next child_node
    End Sub
```

This code starts with the Web page template stored in the `ObjectPageTemplate` resource. It adds the object's name to the page's title and inserts the object's description, which includes the item's scope, type, and name. This description appears in the Web page's `Signature` section.

The code inserts the item's summary, parameter information, remarks, ancestors, history, and `See Also` section. When it finishes, the code saves the result in an HTML file, and then recursively calls the `MakeWebPages` method of the current item's children.

For a sample of how these other routines work, see the `Parameters` function shown in the following code. This function returns text that builds an HTML table describing information in `param` tags in an item's XML comments.

```
    ' Return the object's parameters.
    Private Function Parameters() As String
        If Me.XmlDocNode Is Nothing Then Return ""

        ' Get all param nodes that are children of this node.
        Dim parameter_nodes As XmlNodeList = Me.XmlDocNode.SelectNodes("./param")
        If parameter_nodes.Count = 0 Then Return ""

        ' Process the parameter nodes.
        Dim txt As String = "<H2><A NAME=""parameters"">Parameters</A></H2>" & vbCrLf
        txt &= "<TABLE BORDER=""1"" CELLPADDING=""2"">" & vbCrLf
        txt &= "  <TR><TH ALIGN=""Left"">Parameter</TH>" & _
            "<TH ALIGN=""Left"">Description</TH></TR>" & vbCrLf
        For Each parameter_node As XmlNode In parameter_nodes
            txt &= "  <TR>"
            txt &= "<TD>" & parameter_node.Attributes("name").Value & "</TD>"
            txt &= "<TD>" & ProcessXml(parameter_node) & "</TD>"
            txt &= "</TR>" & vbCrLf
```

```
        Next parameter_node
        txt &= "</TABLE>" & vbCrLf

        Return txt
    End Function
```

The function uses the XML node associated with its `DocNode` object. It uses the node's `SelectNodes` method to find all XML elements named `param`. If it finds any `param` elements, the code starts the HTML table and loops through those elements.

The following code shows the format of two `param` elements:

```
    ''' <param name="new_FirstName">
    ''' The new object's <see cref="FirstName">FirstName</see> property.
    ''' </param>
    ''' <param name="new_LastName">
    ''' The new object's <see cref="LastName">LastName</see> property.
    ''' </param>
```

For each `param` element, the code adds the element's name attribute to the HTML table's first column. It calls the `ProcessXml` function described shortly to evaluate the text inside the `param` element, and adds the result to the HTML table's second column.

Figure 13-9 shows the resulting table.

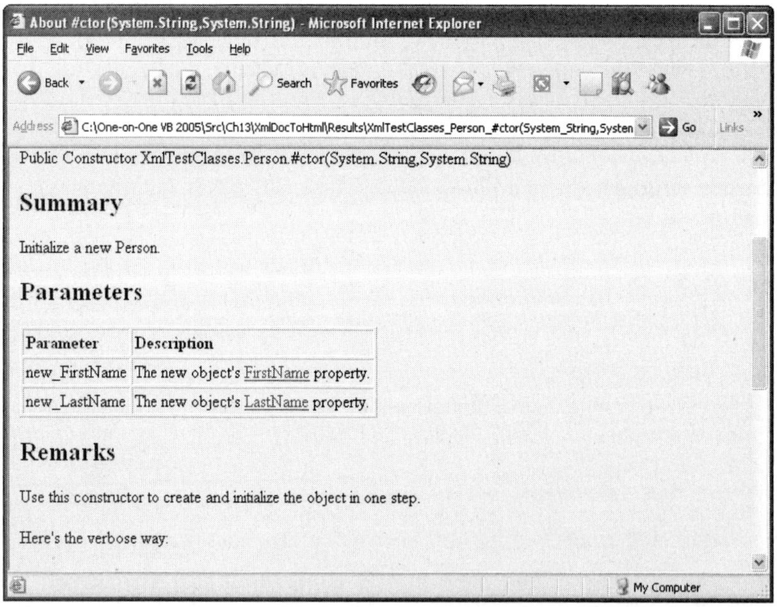

Figure 13-9: `DocNode` **function** `Parameters` **builds an HTML table built from** `param` **tags.**

Function `ProcessXml` shown in the following code converts a piece of the XML document into HTML code. It replaces `see`, `seealso`, `list`, and other XML comment elements with appropriate HTML code.

```
' Return HTML text representing this node's contents.
Private Function ProcessXml(ByVal xml_node As XmlNode) As String
    ' Process the children.
    Dim txt As String = ""
    For Each child_node As XmlNode In xml_node.ChildNodes
        Select Case child_node.Name
            Case "#text"    ' Just some text.
                txt &= child_node.Value
            Case "para"     ' Insert a paragraph.
                txt &= "<P>"
            Case "list"     ' Make a table.
                txt &= MakeTable(child_node)
            Case "see"      ' Make an inline link.
                txt &= "<A HREF=""" & _
                    MakeHtmlLink(child_node.Attributes("cref").Value) & """>"
                txt &= ProcessXml(child_node)
                txt &= "</A>"
            Case "c"        ' Format as inline code <TT>.
                txt &= "<TT>"
                txt &= ProcessXml(child_node)
                txt &= "</TT>"
            Case "code"     ' Format as code <PRE>.
                txt &= "<PRE>"
                Dim code_text As String = ProcessXml(child_node)

                ' Trim off leading carriage returns and line feeds.
                Dim crlf() As Char = New Char() { _
                    Microsoft.VisualBasic.ControlChars.Cr, _
                    Microsoft.VisualBasic.ControlChars.Lf _
                }
                code_text = code_text.TrimStart(crlf)

                ' Trim all trailing whitespace.
                code_text = code_text.TrimEnd()

                txt &= code_text
                txt &= "</PRE>"
            Case "seealso"
                ' These are not displayed here. Instead they
                ' are are collected in the See Also section.
            Case Else
                ' Handle other cases here.
        End Select
    Next child_node

    Return txt
End Function
```

The function examines the child nodes of the XML element that it is examining. It checks each child's name to see what kind of XML comment made it. The following list shows the types of elements that the function can handle and the actions it takes for them:

- `#text` — This is a text value field. The function simply adds its value to the result.
- `para` — The function adds an HTML paragraph break `<P>`.
- `list` — The function calls function `MakeTable` to convert this child and its descendants into an HTML table. Download the application to see how function `MakeTable` works.
- `see` — This is an inline link. The function calls `MakeHtmlLink` to build an HTML anchor element. The XML node's `cref` attribute gives the link's destination URL. When it creates the XML document, Visual Studio inserts the complete path to the object here. For example, if the XML comment indicates a link to `Employee.Office`, the XML document would indicate a link to `XmlTestClasses.Employee.Office`. Function `ProcessXml` calls itself recursively to evaluate the text that it should display inside the HTML anchor element.
- `c` — This is inline code. The function calls itself recursively to evaluate the code it should display and places the result in a `<TT>` HTML element.
- `code` — This is paragraph-formatted code. The function calls itself recursively to evaluate the code it should display. It trims off leading carriage returns and line feeds (but not spaces), and removes all trailing whitespace. It places the result in a `<PRE>` HTML element.
- `seealso` — This function ignores `seealso` elements. Function `SeeAlso` handles these. See the code for details.

This code ignores all other cases. You could extend the code to handle additional elements by adding more `Case` statements.

`ProcessXml` is an important function. It is used wherever an element in the XML document might contain embedded tags such as `para`, `c`, `code`, or `see`.

Download the example program from the book's Web site `www.vb-helper.com/one_on_one.htm` to learn more about how the code works.

Summary

There are several kinds of documentation that are aimed at different audiences, and sometimes may take many forms. User documentation is designed for an application's end users and may include user manuals, online help, context-sensitive help, tooltips, and training materials.

Developer documentation includes the project specification, high- and low-level designs, and inline comments.

Comments within modules provide a good place to store module-level documentation, because the documentation is guaranteed to remain with the module. Use standard comment templates to ensure that all developers follow the same documentation practices. You can store these templates in code snippets to make them easier to use.

XML comments provide some additional capabilities. As described in Chapter 12, IntelliSense gets information from some of them. Visual Studio can also generate XML documentation from these comments. You can then transform the XML documentation into other forms such as Word documents or Web pages.

You can use available programs such as NDoc to convert XML documentation into other forms, or you can write programs of your own. Though building your own program is a lot more work, it also gives you more flexibility. It allows you to create new XML comments of your own to store information that is not handled by NDoc.

Writing documentation is an ongoing process. In many projects, developers neglect documentation until after all of the code is written. That often leads to hastily assembled documentation that is incomplete and poorly arranged. If the project is behind schedule, the documentation may be skipped entirely.

Working on documentation throughout the project improves both the documentation and the code. At the higher levels, the specification, high-level designs, and use cases guide development. At this level, writing carefully crafted documentation before programming is complete can uncover design flaws that might otherwise not be noticed until much later when they are more difficult to correct.

At the lower levels, module-level design and inline comments guide future development and maintenance work. It is much easier and safer to debug and enhance code if detailed comments give you a good understanding of how the code works. If you write comments as you write the code, while it is still fresh in your mind, you'll produce better documentation.

In fact, comment-first design can make reading the comments even easier. When you write the comments before the code, later developers usually only need to verify that the code does what the comments say, rather than trying to decipher what the code does. This is largely a philosophical approach to commenting code. The fundamental result is the same whether you write the comments first or last: code with interspersed comments. The different approaches make the comments read quite differently, however, and can have a big impact on how maintainable the code is.

Chapter 14, "Development Philosophy," describes other philosophical approaches that you can use to make development easier. These ideas allow you to write code more quickly with fewer bugs in the short term, and to maintain code more easily in the long term.

14

Development Philosophy

When I started writing this chapter, I reviewed my list of developer tips, looked over some other lists posted on the Web, skimmed through my collection of development books, and put together a list of my 50 or so favorite pieces of advice. Because I didn't want this chapter to be a huge list of bullet points, I spent quite a while grouping and compressing the ideas into about a dozen key concepts.

At that point, I realized that there's really only one main theme that covers them all: avoiding unnecessary work. When you develop an application, you really have three goals:

- Build an application that works.
- Build it on time.
- Build it within budget.

If you assume that it is possible to build something that does the job correctly (admittedly, not always a valid assumption), the rest is largely a matter of avoiding unnecessary work. If you perform more work than necessary, you'll finish late and over budget. You'll also end up spending more time maintaining the code and fixing bugs in the long term.

At this point, I also realized that many of the techniques used by the agile programming methods described in Chapter 3, "Agile Methodologies," address these issues. For example, the idea that you should make frequent stable builds fits naturally with such ideas as programming for people, keeping the user in charge, and making sure code works before moving on to the next task.

This chapter describes some of the most important ideas that you should keep in mind while you are working on a project. Some ideas are most useful during specific stages of development. For example, it is important to assign people to the tasks for which they are best suited early in the project. Other ideas apply to the whole development process. For example, whether you are building a high-level design, writing code, testing changes, or writing documentation, you should do the best job possible before moving to new things. You will be more productive if you can move forward with confidence, instead of planning to go back and test and fix things later.

Program for People

Chapter 1, "Language Selection," briefly mentions that programs are written for people and not for computers. If you were writing only for the computer, you would use 0s and 1s, or at least some form of assembly language rather than a high-level language such as Visual Basic. The computer doesn't care what language you use. It's all 0s and 1s when the CPU executes it. The reason you use a high-level language is to make programming, understanding, debugging, and maintaining the code easier *for people.*

At some later date, you or someone else will try to read the code. Unfortunately, reading code is harder than writing code. When you are writing code, you have a mental model of what the code is supposed to do and how it will do it. You just need to type it into the IDE. Depending on how good a programmer you are, the model may be a bit fuzzy or incomplete, and you may need to flesh it out as you go.

However, when you try to read someone else's code, or even your own code at a later date, you don't yet have a mental model of the code. You need to study the code to decide what it does. As your model develops, you will find places where it conflicts with what the code actually does. Then you need to revise your model to match the code, a process that can sometimes be difficult. If you don't update your model appropriately, you won't properly understand the code, and any changes you make may lead to bugs.

I've worked on several existing applications where the developers clearly had no clue about how to make the code readable. They used cryptic variable names, no comments, and stacks of very deep subroutine calls (some more than 30 calls deep). Some applications have included dead code that is no longer accessible from any other place in the system. Some have been completely without design documentation. Some of this code was so bad that even developers who had been working on the system for more than 10 years could spend more than a week trying to figure out how one part of the system worked or how to fix a relatively simple bug.

Once I was brought in to fix a large Excel application. The developer previously maintaining the program had quit unexpectedly, and the client thought the program needed about three days to repair. Unfortunately, the application had been written over a period of a few years by several different developers, and it contained no comments or other documentation. After spending a day digging through the code, I concluded that the code might only need a few days' worth of work, but it would take a few months to get to the point where anyone could do the work. The code was so complicated and hard to read that it would have needed a lot of study to fix any bugs without causing others.

Anything you do that makes it easier for a reader to build a mental model of your code makes it easier to understand, modify, and maintain. Whereas code is relatively hard to read, prose is relatively easy. You will probably read this section of the book in just a few seconds, and will understand most of it with little difficulty, although it will take me several minutes to write it.

To take advantage of this fact, add enough comments to your code to describe in prose what the code is doing. When you need to understand the code later, the comments can help you build a correct mental model of what the code does. At that point, you only need to verify that the code does what you think it does, instead of trying to decipher the code's purpose.

To help the reader more, give your variables nice long meaningful names that follow naming conventions. (Chapter 15, "Coding Standards," has more to say about naming conventions.) Later, when you encounter a variable named `selected_products`, you can fit it neatly into your mental model without wasting extra thought figuring out what the variable does. Each time you see the variable, it reinforces your understanding of it. In contrast, if the variable were named `selprods`, each time you saw it you would need to re-evaluate your mental model to see if your idea of the variable's purpose matches its latest use.

As you write code, keep the idea in mind that you are writing code for people to read, not the com puter. Anything that you can do to make the code easier for people to read makes it more stable and maintainable.

Agile methods don't emphasize the idea of programming for people but it's absolutely critical for agile teams. Because agile development relies on frequent small releases, the same code must be modified again and again. That makes it essential that developers can understand the code as quickly as possible so that they can make the necessary changes without introducing time-consuming bugs.

Some agile approaches also promote the notion that the code is owned by the team, rather than by individual programmers. You may work on a routine one day, but someone else may need to work on it the next. In that case, it's particularly important that the code be easy to understand. You can't rely on your memory of how the code works, because you may not be the next person who modifies it.

Unfortunately, frequent releases may pressure developers into skimping on comments and other documentation. If you adopt agile methods, you must fight this at all costs. If the code becomes unreadable, you may make the current release on time, but you'll soon find that future releases take longer and longer as developers struggle to understand the code.

Keep the User in Charge

For some applications, the goal is to have the program do all of the work without any user intervention. Unfortunately, writing a program that is perfectly autonomous is extremely difficult in practice. Often, when you try to make a program run completely without help, you run into the 80/20 problem: 80 percent of the code is needed to handle the trickiest 20 percent of the functionality.

In addition to taking up a lot of room, that 80 percent of the code usually includes the code that's the most complicated, confusing, bug-prone, and trouble to maintain. In many cases, the situation is even worse and trying to exhaustively handle every conceivable situation that the program might encounter is prohibitively difficult.

Rather than trying to handle every possible situation without user intervention, it's usually much easier to build a program that handles the most common cases but lets the user deal with the really strange situations. If the program handles 80 percent of the load automatically, you may be able to cut out much of the 80 percent of the code that would otherwise be necessary to handle the remaining 20 percent.

> *One project I worked on was a dispatch system that assigned jobs to repair people. Twice during the pilot testing period, the system assigned someone to work at his ex-wife's house. In each case, the repairmen recognized the address and called the dispatcher to request a different job. The system was flexible enough that the dispatcher was able to assign the job to someone else.*
>
> *To handle this special case automatically, the program would have had to include some sort of table listing customers that each employee could not visit. We would also have needed to ask the employees to list everyone whose house they couldn't visit. It would have been possible, but it would have been a large amount of work to handle a very rare situation.*

In deciding what tasks to leave to the user, you need to weigh the benefits and costs. If a task is very easy for the user, but difficult for the program, let the user handle it. If a task is time-consuming for the user, or there's some reason why the computer can do a better job than the user, the program should handle it.

This approach may not only save you a huge amount of work, but it can also help the user feel empowered and in charge. Design the application as a tool that helps the user handle the majority of the work, instead of as an independent application replacing the user.

In some applications, you can take these ideas even further and actually make the user do your work for you. If you let the program execute scripts, Visual Basic code, and SQL scripts, the users can write some of the code for you. If you move database operations into scripts or stored procedures kept inside the database, you can move some of the work out of the application. Chapter 9, "Scripting," has more to say about some of these kinds of scripting.

Scripting is particularly useful when the program must handle a large number of relatively simple tasks. Instead of building all of the code in the application itself, you may be able to train the users to write the scripts for you.

One indication that scripting may be helpful is if you find the users cannot agree on the application's functionality, or if the required features change a lot during specification and early development. If different groups of users think they need different features, you may be able to satisfy them all by allowing them to write macros to suit their individual needs.

Agile methods don't require that you leave the user in control of the application. You could use agile methods to develop a program that runs completely independently.

However, agile methods do fit in well with this notion. Agile development requires frequent small releases that implement only part of the application's functionality. If the program cannot handle absolutely every possible situation that it may encounter, you either need to release a program that is incomplete, or you need to allow the user to deal with the cases that it cannot handle. If you take the second approach, you can initially focus on the most common 80 percent of the cases. In later releases, you can expand the program's coverage to include less-typical cases if necessary. At some point, if the difficulty of handling special cases outweighs the benefits, you can stop development.

Make the Program Find Errors

For many years, programmers have been told to program defensively — to make the code bulletproof so no matter what weird data is thrown at it, the program won't crash. One classic technique is to always include an `Else` block in a series of `If` statements, or in a `Select Case` statement so the program does *something* no matter what data it sees.

For example, the following code calls various routines to set a program's privileges based on the user's type. If the user's type isn't one of `Supervisor`, `Clerk`, or `HelpDesk`, the code's `Case Else` statement calls subroutine `SetHelpDeskPrivileges` to give the user the fewest privileges possible.

```
Select Case user_type
    Case Supervisor
        SetSupervisorPrivileges()
    Case Clerk
        SetClerkPrivileges()
    Case HelpDesk
        SetHelpDeskPrivileges()
    Case Else
        SetHelpDeskPrivileges()
End Select
```

The problem with this code is that it hides an unexpected condition. Though this code will run and is reasonably safe, giving users of unknown type the least privileges possible, some other part of the program may later be confused by this. Perhaps some other part of the program will try to perform an action only allowed to supervisors and will crash. Perhaps the unknown `user_type` value came from a corrupted data file that contains other problems that are more difficult to correct.

Instead of programming defensively, program offensively. Make the code aggressively inspect its data and complain loudly if it finds something suspicious. Then you can fix the problem and move on without worrying that the issue will cause trouble later.

Some developers object to this approach by saying that it is better for the user if the program continues even with something wrong than it is to crash. Fortunately, you can have the best of both worlds. Inside the `Else` case, use a `Debug.Assert` statement to validate the data and follow that by the defensive code. When you make a debug build, the `Debug.Assert` statement will catch the error so that you can fix it. When you make a release build and give it to a customer, the `Debug.Assert` statement is ignored, and the defensive code keeps the program running so the user doesn't crash.

The following code shows the previous `Select Case` statement rewritten to catch problems with the `user_type` value:

```
Select Case user_type
    Case Supervisor
        SetSupervisorPrivileges()
    Case Clerk
        SetClerkPrivileges()
    Case HelpDesk
        SetHelpDeskPrivileges()
    Case Else
        Debug.Assert(False, "Unknown user_type")
        SetHelpDeskPrivileges()
End Select
```

Make it Work First

Many developers waste untold hours optimizing code that doesn't need optimization. Optimizing code is challenging and interesting, and programmers are trained to write complex optimized code, so many developers try to implement the "perfect" solution for every problem.

However, completely optimal code is rarely necessary. In the vast majority of code, a simple solution will provide good enough performance. Modern computers are extremely fast, so it's often not worth the time it takes to write the perfect piece of code. Though a custom-built, balanced, red-black tree might provide an elegant solution, Visual Basic's built-in `Collection` and `Hashtable` classes are more than fast enough for most applications. Instead of spending a couple of weeks coding and debugging your tree structure, just try a `Collection` or `Hashtable` and see if the performance is good enough. You will not only save time now, but you'll also greatly reduce maintenance later.

After the program is working correctly, use a performance analysis tool to find the parts of the application that take the most time. Then you can optimize those pieces and skip the code that is good enough.

> *One project with around 60,000 lines of Visual Basic 6 code had some serious performance problems. After a few hours with a performance profiler, I discovered that more than 90 percent of the time was spent in a few routines. While loading a few thousand pieces of data, some routines were being executed millions of times.*
>
> *It took me about a week to tighten up the code that was causing the problems. It was only a few hundred lines out of more than 60,000 that really needed optimization.*

If the application doesn't work properly, it doesn't matter how fast it is. No one is going to use a blindingly fast program that produces incorrect results. Focus on making the application work correctly first. Deferring optimization will not only save you time, but it will keep the code simpler so that making it work properly will be easier. After the program is working, then you can look for performance bottlenecks and only fix the code that really needs fixing.

The "defer optimization until proven necessary" rule has a few immediate corollaries:

- *Don't be clever* — Use the simplest possible solution so that other developers can read the code easily. Later, if you do need to optimize code, use lots of comments to make the code easy to understand.
- *Don't generalize until you know you must* — When you write a routine that calculates taxes for your state, don't generalize it for other states, unless you are sure you will need it. You can rewrite the routine later when it proves necessary.
- *Don't internationalize if it's not necessary* — Internationalization is basically another form of generalization. If you are writing an application for use in your country, don't provide support for every language in Europe and the Pacific Rim. You can internationalize later when you find that you have a huge market in other countries. At that point, you should have a working application, so you can add support for other locales relatively easily without worrying about a huge number of bugs at the same time.

Note that none of this means you need to be intentionally stupid. If you are pretty certain that a particular routine will be a performance bottleneck or will need generalization later, go ahead and do it right the first time. If you know that you'll need to support multiple locales, then do some upfront planning for different date, time, and currency formats.

Agile approaches require frequent builds (as many as several per day) and many small releases. To make all of these small releases quickly, you cannot include every optimization and extravagant feature in the first build. Instead you should use the simplest, most straightforward solution possible. Later, if you discover that the simplistic approach isn't good enough, you can optimize the code and add extra features in a later release.

Agile methods also require that you fix problems as soon as they are discovered, rather than plugging ahead with scheduled tasks even when bugs have been discovered. Keeping the code as simple as possible makes it less likely to contain bugs, and makes bugs easier to fix when they are found.

Look Before You Leap

Take the time to thoroughly plan each step of development before you actually start. A multitude of studies have shown that bugs are more expensive to find and fix the longer they are present before they are discovered. If you introduce a bug early in the development process, it is much easier to fix right away than it is at development's end.

I've worked on a couple of applications that were developed over a very long period of time. One project had pieces of code written in Visual Basic 3 through Visual Basic 6. There may once have been a strategy, but as the years passed, changes were added incrementally without any real design and planning. The end result was an application that was completely unmaintainable.

I have heard some proponents of extreme programming argue that excessive planning restricts development. I have actually seen postings such as the following:

> **"'Think hard before you code' is called up-front design and that is against the spirit of agile development."**

That is completely incorrect. The point of agile programming is not to save time by skipping planning. The point is to make many small incremental releases so that you can respond to changing and refined requirements quickly. The idea is not to start throwing code around and see what pops out.

After each small release cycle, an agile development team should take the time to plan the next cycle. They must decide what new features to add and what bugs to fix in the next release. Far from discouraging planning, agile methods require very frequent planning.

Some agile methods also add extra planning to fine-tune the development process itself. The Crystal Clear methodology adds a reflective improvement step where developers make a list of the practices that are working and those that are not, and adjust future development accordingly.

The more design you do before starting development, the better you'll understand what you need to do, and the better will be the resulting code. You certainly shouldn't spend four weeks planning for a release if your extreme programming release cycle is only five weeks long, but neither should you just start slapping code together.

The same principle also applies to other development tasks. Before you start writing test code, think about what you need to test. What are the unusual and unexpected cases that might give the code problems? What are the typical cases that the application must handle every day? You must write random tests, too, but a few carefully thought-out tests can often uncover most of the code's bugs.

Similarly, a little thought about a bug can make pinpointing the bug easier. When you know something isn't working, think about what the program is trying to do and what might lead to the results you see. Step through the code to see exactly what it's doing and figure out why things are going wrong. I have seen developers jump to some conclusion about what's wrong with the code and start making fixes right away. Often, the first guesses are wrong, and they not only must figure out the cause of the original bug but they also need to figure out why their fixes don't work.

When you're ready to make a change, think about the change's consequences so that you don't introduce new bugs.

Take a few minutes to plan your actions before taking them. A few minutes of thought usually saves you time in the long run. As Augustus Caesar reportedly said, "Hasten slowly."

Do a Good Job; Then Move On

It's amazing how many developers release code without testing it even superficially. You might expect untested code to appear on Internet discussion groups where the participants are not getting paid for their time, but all too often professional developers add code to an application without even stepping through the code in the debugger.

It's natural to assume that your code works. After all, you just wrote it and the ideas are fresh in your mind. If you knew the code didn't work, you would have fixed it as you wrote it. Unfortunately, your natural intuition is misleading at this point. Bugs do appear in code and wishing it wasn't so doesn't make them disappear.

After you write a piece of code, test it thoroughly. Assume the code contains bugs that are hiding from you, and try to flush them out. Don't use any code that you have not tested thoroughly.

Test the code with expected and unexpected inputs. Test it with randomly generated data. Step through the code in the debugger, and make sure all of the code is actually executed.

Write test routines to exercise the code. Then save those routines so you can test the code again later. When you make changes to the code, run the test routines again. It's a lot easier (and thus a lot more likely) to thoroughly test the code after you make changes if you already have test routines built.

After you test the code thoroughly, you can move on with some confidence that it works. You should have the feeling that success is inevitable, not that you are adding additional layers to a house of cards.

Test at all levels. As soon as you write a routine, test it. Later, as you assemble routines into larger subsystems, test them. Only after you have tested the application's pieces separately should you test the system as a whole.

Agile methods rely heavily on thoroughly tested code. They require frequent releases of a stable program. Regular builds help uncover bugs but thorough testing is even better.

Test-driven development requires you to write the tests before writing the code. That allows you to design the tests with fewer preconceptions about how the code works, so you are less likely to avoid cases that you "know" the code can handle. After you write the code, however, add more tests to focus on specific cases that you know may give the code problems.

Use Object-Oriented Principles

Object-oriented techniques were originally billed as the final word in development that would enable ordinary programmers to quickly build fantastically complicated applications, increase productivity while reducing bug counts, effortlessly reuse code, guarantee world peace, and leap tall buildings in a single bound. Like most development methodologies, object-oriented techniques were over-hyped, but they do contain some very important innovations if you take advantage of them.

The three classic features of object-oriented programming are inheritance, encapsulation, and polymorphism.

Inheritance means an object inherits the properties, methods, and events provided by its parent class. For example, an `Employee` object can do everything a `Person` object can because `Employee` inherits from `Person`. Inheritance lets you reuse code; you don't need to rewrite the `Person` code for the `Employee` class because `Employee` inherits that code. The benefit is greater if several classes inherit from the same ancestor class. If `Employee`, `Supervisor`, and `Customer` all inherit from `Person`, you get to use the same `Person` code in all four classes while needing to write and maintain it once.

Polymorphism means an object can behave as if it were an object from its parent class. If a subroutine takes a `Person` object as a parameter, you can also pass it an `Employee` because an `Employee` can do everything that a `Person` can. Like inheritance, polymorphism provides a form of code reuse. It allows a single routine to handle both `Person` and `Employee` objects, so you don't need to write, debug, and maintain two routines.

Writing code at the highest level that makes sense gives you the best opportunity for reuse. Adding code to the `Person` class lets you reuse the code in the derived classes. However, don't put code artificially high in the inheritance hierarchy if it doesn't make sense. If the `Employee` and `Supervisor` classes can share a `ScheduledVacation` property, but the `Customer` class cannot, putting that routine in the `Person` class will cause unnecessary confusion. Instead, put the code in the `Employee` class and derive `Supervisor` from it, or create a new class that both `Employee` and `Supervisor` can inherit.

Encapsulation means a class hides the details of its inner workings from code outside of the class as much as possible. If the program needs to generate an invoice for a customer, it calls a `Customer` object's `MakeInvoice` method without needing to know how that routine works.

Usually, the main benefit of encapsulation is taken to be flexibility. You can change the way the `Customer` class implements the `MakeInvoice` method without changing any of the code that calls that method. While that is a nice benefit, a potentially greater benefit lies in the fact that encapsulation reduces the programmer's cognitive load. A developer who calls the `MakeInvoice` method doesn't need to think about how the method works. He doesn't need to know how to get the customer's account balance, doesn't need to know how to format the invoice, doesn't need to know how to send the invoice to the right printer, and doesn't care. Instead, the developer can focus completely on the code he or she is currently writing: the code that calls the `MakeInvoice` method.

Encapsulation breaks the program into smaller, manageable pieces. It compartmentalizes the application so that you can consider the pieces separately without worrying too much about how they interact, at least on a daily basis. No one can keep all of the code in a large application in mind at all times, so it's only by breaking it up that you have a chance of making it work.

Breaking an application into compartmentalized pieces isn't a new idea. It's been around since long before object-oriented principles were formalized. Object-oriented languages such as Visual Basic, C++, and Java just make encapsulation more formal and easier.

Still, many developers don't take encapsulation as far as they might. They make properties and methods public when they don't need to be. They use global variables that let routines interact across modules in unpredictable ways. They use module-level variables to store values between subroutine calls when a static variable inside the routine would work just as well.

To get the greatest benefit from encapsulation, use local variables when you can, module-level variables only when you must, and global variables as a last resort. Restrict access to everything as much as possible by declaring variables and subroutines `Private` so that only code within the class can access it. Later, when you discover that you really need to use a routine outside of a class, you can widen its scope to `Protected`, `Friend`, or `Public` to allow a wider audience of routines to have access.

Take Advantage of Visual Studio

Visual Studio provides a lot of tools that many developers ignore. IntelliSense makes using long, descriptive variable and routine names easy, but only if you let it. Give your variables meaningful names and then use IntelliSense to avoid typing them.

If you write some code and then decide that a variable's name doesn't match its purpose, rename it. Right-click the variable and use the Rename command to give it a new name. This is quick, easy, and safer than using a find-and-replace command that may change the text in the comments and other code.

Use consistent code standards. If you name variables consistently, IntelliSense can help you remember the variables' names. For example, if, like most Visual Basic developers, you always name text box controls with a `txt` prefix you can easily discover the name of any text box. Simply type "**txt**" and then press Ctrl+Space to make IntelliSense display a list of variables with names starting with "txt," and picking the right one should be easy.

Use XML comments to describe routines and their parameters so that IntelliSense can remind you and other programmers about them. You may have no trouble remembering a subroutine's name and purpose now, but will you remember in a week? In a year? Many applications remain in use long after the original developers thought they would be (remember the Y2K bug?), so you or someone else may need to read the code decades from now.

Visual Studio automatically formats code, providing consistent indentation and capitalization. You can take advantage of these features by intentionally *not* indenting and capitalizing your code. If the syntax is correct, Visual Studio will update your code so it formats correctly. If you make a syntax error, it will be obvious because Visual Studio will not reformat it.

Visual Basic also highlights syntax errors and suspicious pieces of code with wavy underlines. Don't ignore these. If you see some code with a wavy underline, hover the mouse over it to see what Visual Basic thinks is wrong and fix it.

When Visual Basic displays a warning that is not necessarily an error, rewrite the code to eliminate the warning. For example, the following code builds a SQL `SELECT` statement. Because the second line uses the variable query before it is assigned a value, Visual Basic flags that line with a warning.

```
Dim query As String
query &= "SELECT " & field_names
query &= "FROM " & table_names
query &= where_clause
```

Figure 14-1 shows the warning popup displayed for this code.

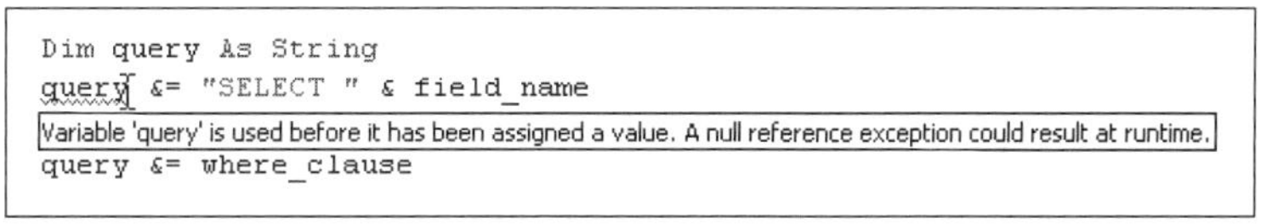

Dim query As String
query &= "SELECT " & field_name
Variable 'query' is used before it has been assigned a value. A null reference exception could result at runtime.
query &= where_clause

Figure 14-1: Visual Basic displays a popup describing errors and warnings.

Experienced Visual Basic developers know that a string variable is initialized to an empty string, so this code works perfectly well. If you ignore this warning, however, it will be more difficult for you to notice other warnings that indicate real problems such as an object variable that is not initialized before it is used, leading to an uninitialized object exception.

Fix the code like this to remove the warning:

```
Dim query As String = ""
query &= "SELECT " & field_names
query &= "FROM " & table_names
query &= where_clause
```

Now, any warnings or errors that appear in the Error List window are meaningful, and you know not to ignore any of them.

Beware of the Weakest Link

The rapid pace of innovation in software development makes it a ripe field for "silver bullet" solutions. Managers are always looking for the ultimate tool that will allow them to develop effective software on time and under budget. Over the years, an endless series of solutions destined to revolutionize programming have paraded across developers' desks. These technologies have included the following:

- Fundamental language and design concepts such as block-structured languages, modular programming, abstract data types, top-down structured programming, event-driven design, artificial intelligence, and object-oriented programming
- Design methodologies such as the waterfall model, successive prototyping, and extreme programming
- Best practices such as patterns, anti-patterns, refactoring, design by contract, test-driven development, and comment-first programming
- Tools for performing specific tasks such as database access (SQL, DAO, RDO, ADO, ADO.NET) and inter-process communication (pipes, Winsock, OLE, DDE)

Many of these initially claimed to be the final solution that would henceforth allow developers to build reliable systems on time and under budget, but all have fallen short of their promises for two reasons.

First, as tools improve, the types of problems developers try to solve become more complex. At one time, a simple checkbook-balancing application would have been considered state-of-the-art. After spreadsheets were invented, that sort of simple number-crunching application seems like no big deal. For all practical purposes, spreadsheets solved this sort of problem, so developers turned to more complex applications. If anyone ever does create a "silver bullet" application that makes development foolproof, developers will start working on new even more complicated applications that the application cannot handle.

The second reason why these technologies fall short is that they are only as good as the developers who use them. No matter how good the tools are, you won't be able to build quality software on time and within budget if developers use them incorrectly.

It is well-known that there is a huge difference between the productivity of the best developers and average developers. A good developer can build a stable system effectively using any set of languages and tools. Somehow, developers in the 1960s, 1970s, and 1980s built large applications that performed important tasks before Visual Basic, extreme programming, and object-oriented concepts.

Conversely, a poor developer will always build buggy code no matter how good the tools are. A well-maintained computer will work properly for years, or at least until it is replaced by something faster. A properly managed source code control system safeguards your code and data. A top-of-the-line database can provide a very high level of availability.

Unfortunately, though you can fill out a purchase requisition for a bigger hard drive, you cannot fill out a requisition for a top-notch developer. All too often, the developers on a project have a mix of skills and aptitudes, and you're stuck with them.

That doesn't mean some developers are worthless. The trick isn't to get rid of the weakest programmers (although, in extreme cases, that sometimes helps). Instead, you need to find the best fit for each developer. Some developers are good at programming, some are good at debugging, some are good at documentation, and some are good at breaking things. Ideally, you can assign each of these developers to tasks that suit their abilities. Let the best programmer program, the developer who breaks things test the code, and the good debugger fix the problems that arise.

> *I once worked with a developer who was a brilliant coder. He knew the operating system inside and out, and knew how to make it stand up and dance. However, he was interrupt-driven. Whenever anyone asked him to do something, he would immediately drop what he was working on and start on the new task. As often as not, another task would appear to interrupt him before he finished that one, and by the end of the day, he wouldn't have finished anything. This developer was a huge asset to any project, but he needed to be put in the right role. He had the skills to be a team lead, but he didn't have the focus. In the end, he made a great toolsmith, and was even able to support more than one project at a time with quick tools and utilities, although the team leaders did need to check on him once in awhile to be sure he didn't get distracted. He was a good example of an excellent programmer, but not a great developer, at least without supervision.*

Another developer I worked with took a very low-level view of any system. She was miserable at seeing the big picture and wasn't very good at designing or implementing software. However, she had been building relational databases for twenty years and was extremely good at it. With a little guidance on what the project needed, she was like a database-building savant.

I've worked with developers on several projects who had a very narrow view of their tasks. They could write their own pieces of code competently, but they could not step outside of their box and help someone else. If a task fell outside their assigned area, they had a great deal of trouble shifting gears and working on the new material. In one case, when pushed, one of these developers flatly refused to take on anything new. It's not that he had too much work to do or that he couldn't understand the new material, he just didn't feel that it was his part of the project. I've seen project managers rant, rave, and browbeat developers such as this one into expanding his role, but often that leads to low-quality code on both his original piece of the project and anything new.

Assign developers to the roles that suit them best. If the developers work in the tasks for which they are best suited, the work will be easier and of better quality.

Agile methods address the weakest link issue in several ways. For example, osmotic communication helps developers share information easily, personal safety allows developers to take risks in pursuit of improved code, and pair programming lets developers support each other.

Save Everything

Keep a record of everything. Use a source control system to track how the code changes over time. You never know when you might discover that some code you removed months ago will be useful after all.

Back up frequently, and make the backups easily available. Developers can work with greater confidence if they know that their work is safe.

About once every year or two, a typical developer accidentally does something that damages a big chunk of code. He might accidentally delete a routine or make a long series of changes that turn out to be incorrect. If you can quickly restore a recent backup, you may be able to save the developer a day or two of work.

One time, a project I was on had an entire operating system accidentally destroyed. We were able to rebuild the system and restore the previous days' backup in a few hours.

Another time, a malicious user tried to delete all of our project's source code. He failed, but even if he had succeeded, it would have taken only about an hour to restore the previous night's backup.

If you have limited disk space, go buy a new disk for source code control and backups. External disk drives today are so cheap (in a quick search I just found a 250GB external drive for $60 after rebates), it doesn't make sense to skimp on source control and backups.

Another easy way to back up critical files is to get a free email account from a Web site. Then you can encrypt the file and email it to your free account. You should still keep a copy safe in case the free account's servers lose the file, but this gives you an extra copy stored offsite in case something disastrous happens such as a fire destroying all of your servers.

Just as you should use source control and backups to protect source code, you should use similar methods to safeguard documentation. Keep copies of proposals, specifications, use cases, and design documents. Use source control or an archive to remember how those documents change over time.

Keep every memo and note written about the project, particularly those that record decisions.

On one project, we created a special email account named History and copied every email to that account. Whenever we had a phone conversation with a customer, we wrote it up and emailed the summary to the project team, History, and the customer. The project manager wrote up meeting notes and also emailed them to everyone.

Later, when customers had questions about why something was done a particular way, we could easily search the email database to find the message that recorded the decision. That must have saved our team dozens, if not hundreds, of hours that might otherwise been spent rehashing the same decisions again and again. For example, we were probably asked once a month for a year why we were programming in C instead of COBOL.

Agile methods don't focus much on this issue, but any time you make decisions fast and frequently it makes sense to document them. Producing a new release every six weeks doesn't do you much good if waffling decisions make you add and remove the same features with each new release.

Avoid the Bleeding Edge

Working with cutting-edge tools is fun and interesting. Unfortunately, the "cutting edge" is right next to the "bleeding edge," the point where the newness of a tool makes it dangerous to use. Trying new things is exciting, but it also often means that you get to help debug the new tool. Getting your application to work correctly is a lot easier if you only need to worry about fixing your own code and not someone else's product.

Most vendors know that customers don't like to use the first, buggiest versions of their products, so some first editions are not labeled version 1.0. Often, a vendor will initially release a product with version 3 or use the year it was released as in MeetingPlanner 2007 to give you the impression that the product is well-established. Do some additional research to determine whether the product has really been around as long as it implies.

Of course, if no one ever uses a new product, the vendor cannot fix any problems it might have. If you are building a mission-critical application with short deadlines, let someone else be the guinea pig and debug new products. However, if you are building a proof-of-concept prototype, you may be able to use the latest gadgets. They may not work perfectly, but they may be good enough for your temporary needs. You can give useful feedback so that the vendor can improve the product, and you may be able to use it in your final implementation. And, occasionally, vendors do produce a useful, stable product right from the start.

New tools may also interact with other tools that you are using. Installing a new archive tool may break the database tool that you have been using. When the database upgrade is available, your report-generation tool may stop working.

Sometimes it can be difficult to figure out which of a web of interrelated products is the one causing a bug, and product vendors are generally only of marginal help as they point fingers at each other. In extreme cases when you are using several interrelated tools, it can take quite a while before you find a working combination of product versions.

> *I know of one project manager who uses a program written in Visual Basic 3 to manage a production facility. Because Visual Basic 3 builds 16-bit executables, he has to use an older 16-bit operating system such as Windows 3.1. Because it's a 16-bit operating system, he can only use versions of database tools and other products that are ancient and no longer supported.*
>
> *But it all works. If he tried to upgrade any of his components (for example, the operating system), he would need to upgrade them all and rewrite his entire application in a newer version of Visual Basic. While that might be an interesting exercise, it wouldn't buy him any new functionality that he needs to keep his operation running. Instead, he keeps a small reserve of old computers on hand. If his production computer breaks, he swaps it out, copies a disk image of his software onto the new system, and is up and running again in a few minutes.*
>
> *His situation is a bit extreme, but it's fairly common for businesses to spend a lot of time and money upgrading their entire operation simply to get the latest version of one particular piece of the system (such as the operating system) or to use the latest version of Visual Basic.*

Avoid adopting new products until someone else has debugged them first. Unless a tool provides a clear benefit to your project, stick with more established tools whenever possible.

Use the Agile Smorgasbord

The goal of agile programming is to allow development to respond rapidly to changes or refinements in requirements. This can allow development to zero in on a usable application quickly and with high-quality code.

Chapter 3, "Agile Methodologies," describes agile methods in detail. Various agile methods use a variety of techniques and guidelines. For example, extreme programming (XP) includes such elements as frequent delivery, small releases, continuous integration, pair programming, and test-driven development.

I have seen it argued that the XP techniques only work if you adopt all of them. That may be true of XP as a complete methodology, but there's no reason why you can't take advantage of some of these techniques while using another development methodology.

For example, suppose you are using an iterative prototyping approach. You might not have the very short cycle times used in XP, but you might still benefit from continuous integration and test-driven development. Both of these techniques force you to test your code frequently so that you find bugs earlier when they are easier to fix.

Any development effort may benefit from pair programming and code reviews, particularly if you pair experienced and novice developers. Those techniques make more programmers view each piece of code, so you have more chances to catch mistakes.

The "reflective improvement" that Crystal Clear uses to continually improve its development cycle can also benefit any type of development. It makes no sense to continue using methods that aren't working out, yet many development organizations do exactly that. They stick to organizational rules and standards, even if they are crushing a particular project. Even if you are using a waterfall model with long time frames, it makes sense to sit back every now and then and ask yourself which development activities are working and which are not.

Putting all of the agile techniques together gives you a powerful combination, but there's no reason to avoid a particular technique just because you cannot adopt them all. Take advantage of any tools you can.

Summary

You can search the Web for hundreds of tips that make development easier. This chapter summarizes some of the most important ideas that I find helpful, but that many developers ignore. Other developers apply these ideas incompletely, following them sometimes, but not others. To really get the greatest benefit from these ideas, you need to make them part of your development philosophy so that they are in the back of your mind at all times.

The single overriding concept in this chapter is avoiding work. The following list summarizes how each of the points described in this chapter can help you achieve the "lazy developer's" philosophy:

- Writing code for people and not for computers makes it easier to read, debug, and maintain the code later.
- Letting the user handle special cases lets you avoid writing code to make the program handle them.
- Programming offensively makes the program find bugs so that you don't have to.
- Deferring optimization and extra features until they are proven necessary lets you skip writing features that are never needed.
- Thinking and planning ahead before taking action lets you do your work more effectively. It also often lets you avoid false starts and dead ends that lead to unnecessary work.
- Doing a thorough job and testing your code before moving on lets you work on future tasks with confidence. It helps you fix problems while they are easy to solve, rather than risking compounding them with new code based on buggy programming.
- The object-oriented principles of inheritance and polymorphism let you reuse code. Encapsulation makes code easier to understand and, thus, reduces the number of bugs and the time it takes to fix them.
- Visual Studio provides tools such as IntelliSense and warnings that make writing and debugging code easier.
- Assigning developers to the tasks they are best at makes the work easier for them and makes everyone happier.

- Keeping a history of all design, code, emails, memos, and other documentation allows you to easily restore lost materials, and quickly review decisions without needing to rehash the same old issues.
- Avoiding the "bleeding edge" lets you avoid the work of debugging a vendor's product. Unless a new technology can save you more effort than you will spend integrating it with other possibly incompatible products, let someone else be the guinea pig.
- Using the techniques described by agile and other development methods can save you plenty of time and trouble. Although the agile methods may seem wild and uncontrolled, many of the specific techniques are based on long experience and sound development practice. Even if you don't jump completely on the agile bandwagon, you should examine what these methods have to offer and adopt those that make sense to you.

This chapter describes some fairly high-level ideas that make development easier and, thus, faster and cheaper. The following chapters describe more specific techniques for following some of these principles. Chapter 15, "Coding Standards," describes rules you can follow to make code more consistent and easier to read. Chapter 16, "Bug Proofing," explains ways you can make the code identify errors in debug builds, and recover gracefully when it encounters errors in release builds.

15

Coding Standards

Coding standards are rules that developers follow to make their code more consistent. Consistent code is easier to read, so developers can understand and modify it more quickly with less chance of introducing new errors.

For example, suppose I build an application that uses a First Name text box. My particular set of standards says the text box should be named `txtFirstName`, the associated label should be named `lblFirstName`, and, if I need to copy the text entered in the text box into a variable, the variable should be named `first_name`. If I see any of those items (`txtFirstName`, `lblFirstName`, or `first_name`) in the code, I know exactly what they are. Similarly, if I see items such as `txtStreet`, `lblBillingCity`, or `cboState`, I immediately know what the values are for, even without studying the code in detail. That makes my understanding of the code faster and more accurate.

> *The object names in the previous paragraph use standard prefixes to indicate the types of objects that they represent. These are* `txt` *for* `TextBox`, `lbl` *for* `Label`, *and* `cbo` *for* `ComboBox`. *The section "Component Names" later in this chapter lists other object prefixes.*

It is important that all of the programmers on your project follow the same coding standard so that they can more easily read and understand each other's code. It is less important, however, what standard you adopt. Consistency is the important thing, not whether you name variables using "Pascal case" (`FirstName`), "camel case" (`firstName`), or lowercase with underscores (`first_name`). The important thing is that all of the developers follow the same rules.

Standards are also useful for preventing arguments. As strange as it seems, some developers can become quite heated when discussing the merits of Hungarian notation, camel casing, and the other niceties of coding conventions. Having a well-defined standard can defuse some of these arguments before they start.

> *I've never worked on a project where these sorts of arguments were much of an issue. If someone found a situation that wasn't covered by the standard, we took a quick poll to see what the developers preferred and added it to practice.*

In fact, that's the approach I suggest you take for dealing with unexpected items. If you don't have a rule to cover the situation, create one. It doesn't matter much what decision you make, as long as you make one.

This chapter describes my particular set of coding standards. It also describes some standards recommended by Microsoft developers and others. After you study the different standards, you can use their ideas to write your own standard that best suits your needs.

Names

Most Visual Basic statements include the names of subroutines, functions, variables, modules, enumerated types, and other program items defined by the user. Because programmers spend so much time reading these items, their names must be as easy to understand as possible. If the reader must spend even a tiny amount of extra time remembering what a name means, it can take a lot longer to understand the code.

Picking good names can have a large impact on how easy it is to understand and maintain code, so developers have spent a lot of time and effort on naming conventions. The following sections describe some of the rules I use when naming variables.

Hungarian Notation

Hungarian notation is a system where you add characters to the beginning of a variable's name to give extra information about its data type and scope. For example, the variable `mblnReady` would be a module-scope (`m`) Boolean (`bln`) variable, and `gaintCustomerIds` would be a global (`g`) array (`a`) of integers (`int`).

The idea behind Hungarian notation was to make up for lenient compilers. A loosely typed language such as Visual Basic 6 will let you assign an integer variable to a string value, or vice versa. For that matter, it will let you put an integer or string value in a form variable, and it won't tell you there is a potential problem until the code actually tries to make the assignment at run-time.

If you use proper Hungarian notation, you should notice the problem as you write the code. For example, in the following code, that fact that the variable on the left is a form (`frm`) and the value on the right is an integer (`int`) should raise a warning flag for you:

```
mfrmPlaces = intOrderCenters
```

If you take Hungarian notation to the extreme, you should never have variables in the same assignment statement that have different data types. You should not even assign an integer value to a long integer variable without explicitly using a conversion operator such as `CLng` or `CType`.

Although the motivation behind Hungarian notation is reasonable, I have rarely seen type and scope mismatches cause problems. However, I have often seen developers greatly confused by badly named variables. If you give variables good enough names, it is easier for the reader to remember what they represent. In many cases, the name can help the reader remember the data type as well.

For example, if the integer variable in the previous example were named `num_order_centers`, it would be fairly obvious that it was a number and should not be assigned to a form variable.

The Visual Basic .NET environment has also become much better at warning you when you try to make suspicious assignments. For example, it will raise an error if you try to assign an integer to a form variable. This makes Hungarian notation less important than it was in the past and, in fact, the Visual Basic documentation explicitly recommends that you not use it.

> *In fact, I wish Visual Basic were even stricter than it is. For example, it won't let you implicitly assign a long integer value to an integer variable because the long value might be too big to fit in an integer (this is called a "narrowing conversion" because the long is bigger or wider than the integer). However, it will let you assign an integer value to a long variable (a "widening conversion"). I would rather at least see an error message so that I have to think about the assignment and explicitly use* `CLng` *to make the conversion safely.*
>
> *Some developers would flag these issues as warnings instead of as errors. But if you ignore a bunch of warnings, it's difficult to sift out the ones that are important from those that aren't. I would rather fix every such instance with* `CLng`, `CType`, `DirectCast`, *or other conversion statements and not see a warning or error again. My goal is always to have no warnings or errors ever.*

For all of these reasons, I recommend that you don't use Hungarian notation. It adds clutter to variable names and doesn't really help all that much. Instead, focus on making the rest of the name as descriptive as possible so that the reader can remember what the variable means. The following sections give some tips on making variable names easy to remember.

Component Names

Components are different from other variables used in the code because you do not declare them yourself in your code. Instead, they are created on a form and the code can then refer to them. The fact that they are declared in this special manner gives them a slightly different status than variables declared within the code.

Components are also very important to Visual Basic programs, and code often sets a variable's value equal to some property of a component. To make the link between a component and its corresponding variable obvious, you should give them names that are similar. For example, you might store the text value taken from the `txtFirstName` `TextBox` in the variable `first_name`.

Visual Basic developers often use three-letter prefixes to indicate a component's type. For example, standard abbreviations include `txt` for `TextBox`, `lbl` for `Label`, `btn` for `Button`, and so forth.

The more recent versions of Visual Basic have added new controls that don't have intuitive three-letter abbreviations. For example, in Visual Basic 6, the Common Dialog Control's methods allowed the user to select a color, font, file for saving, or file for loading. It also provided methods for displaying help or a print dialog. The prefix for this control in Visual Basic 6 was `dlg`.

Visual Basic 2005 uses separate components to handle these tasks: `ColorDialog`, `FontDialog`, `OpenFileDialog`, `SaveFileDialog`, `HelpProvider`, and `PrintPreviewDialog`. You could give them obscure prefixes such as `cd`, `fd`, `ofd`, `sfd`, `hp`, and `ppd`, but it would probably take awhile to grow accustomed to them.

Instead, I prefer to use slightly longer abbreviations that are easier to read. For these controls, I prefer these prefixes: `dlgcolor`, `dlgfont`, `dlgopen`, `dlgsave`, `hlp`, and `dlgppv`. The leading "`dlg`" on all of them (except the `HelpProvider`) makes it obvious that the component is a dialog. The rest of the prefix helps you remember which kind of dialog.

If you really want to save a few keystrokes, you can abbreviate the abbreviations to `dlgclr`, `dlgfnt`, `dlgopn`, `dlgsav`, `hlp`, *and* `dlgppv`. *I prefer to keep the names a little easier to read and let IntelliSense do the typing for me.*

The following table lists some suggested prefixes for the most common Windows forms components.

Component	Abbreviation	Component	Abbreviation
BackgroundWorker	bw	ImageList	il
BindingNavigator	nav	Label	lbl
BindingSource	bsrc	LinkLabel	llbl
Button	btn	ListBox	lst
CheckBox	chk	ListView	lvw
CheckedListBox	clb	MaskedTextBox	msk
ColorDialog	dlgcolor	MenuStrip	mnu
ComboBox	cbo	MessageQueue	que
ContextMenuStrip	ctx	MonthCalendar	mcal
DataGridView	dgv	NotifyIcon	nico
DataSet	ds	NumericUpDown	nud
DateTimePicker	dtp	OpenFileDialog	dlgopen
DirectoryEntry	dir	PageSetupDialog	dlgpage
DirectorySearcher	srch	Panel	pan
DomainUpDown	dud	PerformanceCounter	pc
ErrorProvider	err	PictureBox	pic
EventLog	log	PrintDialog	dlgprint
FileSystemWatcher	fsw	PrintDocument	pdoc
FlowLayoutPanel	flo	PrintPreviewControl	ppv
FolderBrowserDialog	dlgfolder	PrintPreviewDialog	dlgppv
FontDialog	dlgfont	Process	proc
GroupBox	grp	ProgressBar	pbar
HelpProvider	hlp	PropertyGrid	pgrid
HScrollBar	hbar	RadioButton	rad

Component	Abbreviation	Component	Abbreviation
ReportViewer	rpt	TextBox	txt
RichTextBox	rch	Timer	tmr
SaveFileDialog	dlgsave	ToolStrip	ts
SerialPort	port	ToolStripContainer	tscon
ServiceController	serv	ToolTip	tip
Splitter	split	TrackBar	tbar
StatusStrip	ss	TreeView	tvw
TabControl	tab	VScrollBar	vbar
TableLayoutPanel	tpan	WebBrowser	wbr

You can find many lists of name prefixes on the Web. Microsoft has a fairly large one at `support.microsoft.com/kb/q173738`.

Constant Names

For constants, I use uppercase words separated by underscores, as in the following example:

```
Const MAX_USERS As Integer = 10
```

This makes it obvious that a value is a constant. Unfortunately it doesn't indicate the constant's scope. A constant looks the same whether it is declared within a subroutine, at the module level, or globally. I have rarely found this to be a problem, however, at least partly because constants make up such a small fraction of the symbols in a typical application. It's just not that hard to track down a constant on those rare occasions when you need to know where it was declared.

Routine Variable Names

I declare variables within a subroutine using lowercase with underscores separating words, as shown in the following example:

```
Dim num_items As Integer
Dim total_cost As Decimal
Dim sales_tax As Decimal
```

Parameters to a routine are declared within the context of the routine, so I treat them as routine-level variables and also declare them using lowercase with underscores separating words. For example, in the following code, the `file_path` and `file_title` parameters follow this naming convention:

```
Public Sub LoadData(ByVal file_path As String, ByVal file_title As String)
    ...
End Sub
```

Other Names

For names that are not constants and that are not declared within routines, I use Pascal case (with the first letter in each word capitalized). For example, a method that generates a new invoice might be called `GenerateNewInvoice`.

Items whose names appear in Pascal case include namespaces, modules, classes, properties, methods, events, Enums, Enum values, module-level variables, global variables, events, and interfaces.

I prefix module-level variables with "`m_`" and global variables with "`g_`" to indicate their scope. For example, the following code declares a variable for use within a class:

```
Private m_DataIsDirty As Boolean
```

Public variables declared with a class have normal Pascal case names with no leading scope indicator.

Using scope indicators is a common technique used by many Visual Basic developers, but I've seen some strange uses. On one large project that had been running for a very long time, some of the developers clearly didn't understand what the `m_` *meant, and you could find variables declared inside subroutines that began with* `m_`*. Because the rule wasn't applied consistently, it was almost useless.*

Like most developers, I add the letter "`I`" before an interface name. For example, an interface for drawable objects might be called `IDrawable`.

I do not add a "`C`*" before class names as in* `CEmployee` *or* `CCustomer`*, although many developers do this. Microsoft recommends that you do not.*

When I define an enumerated type, I add "`Types`" to the end of the name. That lets me use the same name (minus the "`s`" in "`Types`") as the name of a property having that type. For example, the following code uses the `ShapeTypes` enumeration that defines some shape types. The `ShapeType` property has type `ShapeTypes`.

```
Public Enum ShapeTypes
    Line
    Ellipse
    Rectangle
    Polygon
End Enum

Private m_ShapeType As ShapeTypes

Public Property ShapeType() As ShapeTypes
    Get
        Return m_ShapeType
    End Get

    Set(ByVal value As ShapeTypes)
        m_ShapeType = value
    End Set
End Property
```

The code implements this property by using a private variable named m_ShapeType. This variable has the same name as the property with the m_ scope indicator to show that it is private to this class.

Boolean Names

When you declare something that has a Boolean data type, give it a name that includes a form of the verb "to be." Use normal capitalization rules to indicate the item's type and scope as usual (for example, is_running, is_dirty, WasHandled, or m_WillBePrinted).

The name should sound like a statement of truth and not a question. If the value does not refer to the "current" object, you may need to put the form of "to be" inside the name, rather than at the beginning if you want it to sound like a statement.

For example, in the Order class the IsDirty property indicates that the Order's data has changed. The property applies to the current Order object, so the statement IsDirty makes sense for that object.

If an Order object's code refers to several printers, it might use the variables printer1_is_ready, printer2_is_ready, and so forth, to refer to their readiness. The names is_printer1_ready, is_printer2_ready, and so on, sound more like questions than statements.

The final test is to try the name out in a Boolean expression. The following statement is fairly easy to read:

```
If printer1_is_ready Or printer2_is_ready Then ...
```

The following statement is more awkward:

```
If is_printer1_ready Or is_printer2_ready Then ...
```

This version is harder to read, so it will take longer to read and is more likely to lead to misunderstanding.

Abbreviations

Ideally, you would avoid all abbreviations in names. Spelling out words makes names easier to understand, and if you use IntelliSense properly, it doesn't really take more time to type.

Abbreviations can also lead to inconsistencies among developers. For example, different developers might name a variable that holds the number of employees as number_of_employees, num_employees, num_emps, or no_emps.

In practice, however, some abbreviations are extremely common. The .NET Framework uses min and max to mean "minimum" and "maximum" in several places, so those seem like safe abbreviations. Many developers also use num for "number" so that also seems reasonably safe.

In some applications, it may also make sense to use industry-specific abbreviations. When I was working at a GTE Laboratories, abbreviations such as pots (Plain Old Telephone Service) and mark (referring to another application, Mechanized Assignment and Record Keeping) were common.

To keep things consistent, make a list of allowed abbreviations and add to it when necessary. Try to spell words out and use IntelliSense to make typing them easier. However, if everyone in the office already uses certain abbreviations, it sometimes makes the code more consistent and easier to read to use them in the program as well.

Escaped Names

Visual Basic allows you to use keywords in names by surrounding the name in square brackets. The following code shows a function named `Sub` that takes a parameter named `New`. The code uses brackets to differentiate these names from the Visual Basic keywords `Sub` and `New`.

```
Private Function [Sub](ByVal [New] As Integer) As Integer
    If [New] < 10 Then [New] = 10
    If [New] > 100 Then [New] = 100
    Return [New]
End Function
```

If this code is contained in a class, other code within the class could invoke the function using either of the following statements:

```
Debug.WriteLine([Sub](1))
Debug.WriteLine(Me.Sub(1))
```

This code is confusing and difficult to read. Don't use escaped names unless absolutely necessary.

The only situation I know of when you really need to use escaped names is when you are using a library or other tool that uses Visual Basic keywords for names. For example, C# does not have the `ReDim` keyword, so it is possible that someone writing a library in C# might create a class named `ReDim`. To use that class in Visual Basic, you must surround the name with brackets, as in the following statement:

```
Dim redimmer As New [ReDim]
```

Even then you could use the library's fully qualified name, as in this version:

```
Dim redimmer As New ReDimLib.ReDim
```

The `ReDimLib` example solution available for download at `www.vb-helper.com/one_on_one.htm` includes a C# library that defines a simple `ReDim` class and a Visual Basic program that uses it.

I've never heard a plausible reason why you would need to use keywords for names in code that you write.

Class Names

Use nouns or noun phrases for class names. Classes define objects, which are things, so their names should be things as well. Some good class names include `Customer`, `Report`, `StartTime`, and `DispatchStrategy`.

Note that some names such as `Customer` and `Report` are in some sense tangible, whereas others such as `StartTime` and `DispatchStrategy` are not.

Property Names

Make the names of properties nouns or noun phrases such as `TextColor`, `LineWidth`, or `Straightness`. A property is a characteristic of an object, and these names sound like characteristics.

Microsoft recommends that you consider naming properties after their data types, if that makes sense. For example, if a class needs a font property, you could name it `Font`. The following code shows how a class might declare a `Font` property of type `Font`:

```
Private m_Font as Font

Property Font() As Font
    Get
        Return m_Font
    End Get

    Set(ByVal value As Font)
        m_Font = value
    End Set
End Property
```

This can sometimes lead to confusion (particularly because it's not as easy to make a property named after an enumerated type that you create within the class), so I usually prefer to change the name slightly. For example, you could change this property's name to `TextFont`.

Method Names

A subroutine makes an object do something, so its name should reflect that by indicating an action. Give subroutines names that are verbs or verb phrases. For example, some good subroutine names include `PrintInvoices`, `DeleteItem`, and `Execute`.

Avoid names that could be interpreted as either nouns or verbs. For example, don't use the name `Color` for a subroutine that colors a shape, because someone reading the code might read `Color` as a noun and assume it is a property rather than a subroutine.

Usually, you can avoid this issue by adding an extra word. In this case, you could change the subroutine's name to `ColorShape`.

A function is similar to a subroutine except that it returns a value. Because a function returns a value, it is usually more natural to treat the function as a noun instead of a verb. For example, the following code calls the `driving_map` object's `BestForeColor` function and saves the result in a form's `ForeColor` property:

```
Me.ForeColor = driving_map.BestForeColor()
```

In cases such as this one, there is practically no difference between a function and a read-only property. Both make the most sense with names that are noun phrases, both return a value, and you cannot assign a value to either.

Sometimes it's difficult to decide whether to implement a feature as a function or a property. The following list gives some reasons why you might want to choose one or the other:

- If the action is a conversion function such as `ToString`, Microsoft recommends that you use a function.
- If the action takes a long time, use a function. Properties are expected to be fast.
- If the action has side effects, use a function. Properties should not have side effects.
- If the action returns an array, use a function. Properties that return arrays can be confusing.
- If you want to serialize the value, use a property.
- If you want to display values in a `PropertyGrid` or other property editor, use a property. This is most useful if the developer must set the value at design time, or if the user must set it at run-time.
- If you want to notify the program when the value changes, use a property and an associated property changed event. For example, if the program might need to know when the `MinimalPathLength` value changes, make it a read-only property and raise the `MinimalPathLengthChanged` event when it changes. It is more natural and traditional to associate an event with a property than with a function.

Event Names

For events that occur before the code takes some action, end the event's name with the "ing" form of a verb, as in `Clicking`, `Changing`, `Moving`, or `Canceling`. For events that occur after the code takes some action, end the event's name with a verb in the past tense, as in `Clicked`, `Changed`, `Moved`, or `Canceled`.

Make the rest of the name explain the thing to which the verb applies — for example, `SeatClicked`, `CustomerChanged`, `DrawingObjectMoved`, or `JobSchedulingCanceled`.

Microsoft recommends that you add `EventHandler` to the end of event handler names, as in the following code:

```
Public Delegate Sub SeatClickedEventHandler(ByVal seat_clicked As Seat)
```

This makes sense when you are declaring a delegate. Later, when you declare a variable with the delegate's type, the name makes it easier to understand that this is an event handler.

```
Dim clicked_event_handler As SeatClickedEventHandler
```

In Visual Basic, it is traditional to name an event handler by using the name of the object raising the event, followed by an underscore and then the name of the event. The Visual Basic code editor names events this way if you use the drop-downs to build an event handler. The event handler name is the same as the name in the `Handles` clause, except the dot is replaced with an underscore.

The following code shows how the code editor would name the `SeatClicked` event raised by an object named `m_SeatingChart`:

```
Public Sub m_SeatingChart_SeatClicked(ByVal seat_clicked As Seat) _
   Handles m_SeatingChart.SeatClicked
...
End Sub
```

Sometimes you might want to create an event handler yourself without using the code editor's drop-downs. For example, suppose you create several `Drawable` objects at run-time, and you want to use `AddHandler` to associate them all with an `ObjectMoved` event handler. To make the event handler's name consistent with the code editor's naming style, end the name with an underscore and the event name.

Start the name with a phrase that describes the objects that raised the event. For example, if the program keeps the objects in a collection or array, you could use the collection or array's name. The following shows an example:

```
Public NetworkObjects As List(Of Drawable)

Private Sub NetworkObjects_DrawableMoved(ByVal sender As Drawable)
    MessageBox.Show(sender.Name)
End Sub

Private Sub Form1_Load(ByVal sender As System.Object, _
 ByVal e As System.EventArgs) Handles MyBase.Load
    Dim new_drawable As Drawable
    For i As Integer = 1 To 10
        new_drawable = New Drawable
        AddHandler new_drawable.DrawableMoved, _
            AddressOf NetworkObjects_DrawableMoved
    Next i
End Sub
```

The code starts by declaring a list of `Drawable` objects. The event handler that catches the objects' `DrawableMoved` events is named `NetworkObjects_DrawableMoved`. The name consists of the name of the list `NetworkObjects` followed by an underscore and the name of the event: `DrawableMoved`.

The form's `Load` event handler adds some `Drawable` objects to the list and uses `AddHandler` to associate the `NetworkObjects_DrawableMoved` event handler with the objects' `DrawableMoved` events.

Declaring Variables

In Visual Basic 6 and earlier versions, it was common practice to declare all variables at the beginning of a routine. If you were reading code and needed to remember how a variable was declared, you could easily find it at the beginning of the routine.

In Visual Basic .NET, the custom has shifted to declaring variables as close as possible to the place where they are used. Often, that means you can see the variable's declaration whenever you are reading the code that uses it. There are still plenty of times where a long piece of code uses variables that were declared much earlier, but at least some of the time you can keep the declaration in view while the variable is used.

Placing variables close to where they are used fits well with newer statements that allow you to declare variables inside a more limited scope. For example, the `For` statement can declare its looping variable so that the variable only exists within the loop. Similarly `For Each`, `Using`, `Catch`, and other statements let you define variables that only exist within their blocks.

Declarations in Visual Basic .NET also allow you to initialize variables when they are declared. This is a good practice because it ensures that the variable is initialized before it is used (and it avoids Visual Basic warning you about a possibly uninitialized variable). Initializing all variables at the beginning of a routine often seems strange because the value you use for the initialization doesn't make much sense (and, in fact, may not exist) until later when the variable is used.

Many developers still prefer the older system of declaring variables at the beginning of the routine, and I can't say with certainty that they're wrong. I've used both methods for a long time, and I prefer the newer "declare when needed" style, but both systems can work. You should try them both and decide what works best for you and your development team.

If you can't see a variable's declaration, you can right-click it and select Go To Definition to jump to the variable's declaration.

As an added tip, insert an @ character in the code before you jump to the declaration. Then, if the declaration is in the same file, you can press Ctrl+Z to undo the insertion of the @ and get back where you started. If moving to the declaration made you switch modules, Ctrl+Z won't undo changes in the module where you started, but you can find the @ character in Visual Studio's Error List.

Declaring variables close to the code that uses them helps restrict their scope so that you don't need to worry about what the variable is for in other code. An even better way to restrict scope is to declare variables within a block of code. For example, a variable declared inside a `For` loop, `Do` loop, `If Then` block, `Case` block, `Try Catch` block, or other block of code is visible only within that code. That means you don't need to think about the variable outside of the block, you don't need to worry about code outside of the block modifying the variable, and you can even reuse the variable name in other blocks of code.

The following code declares the variables `test_seat` and `seat_status` within the `For` loop so that they are only visible within the loop. You don't need to worry about what those variables do and what values they contain while you are looking at the code outside of the loop.

```
' Examine the seats.
For seat_num As Integer = 0 To num_seats - 1
    Dim test_seat As Seat = AllSeats(seat_num)
    Dim seat_status As SeatStatus = test_seat.Status
    ...
Next seat_num ' End examining the seats.
```

When you write a `For` loop, the looping variable is often an index and has little real purpose other than controlling the loop. The variable doesn't mean anything by itself, so it usually has a non-descriptive name such as `i`, `j`, or `x`. Whenever possible, declare these variables in the `For` statement. That restricts the variable's scope to the loop, while still allowing you to reuse the variable in other loops.

The following code declares the variable `i` in the `For` statement:

```
' Print the employees' work assignments.
For i As Integer = 0 To num_employees - 1
    ' Print this employee's work assignment.
    ...
Next i
```

The `Using` statement introduced in Visual Basic 2005 takes this idea a step further. Visual Basic not only makes variables declared in a `Using` statement local to the block, but it also automatically calls the variables' `Dispose` method when the block ends. Of course, that means the variables must represent objects that have a `Dispose` method such as a `Pen`, `Brush`, `Control`, or `Form` object.

When the code is done with an object, calling `Dispose` *makes it free resources that it is using, and makes garbage collection more efficient. It is not strictly necessary, but improves performance and limits the variable's scope, so it's worthwhile.*

The following code draws a thick ellipse on a form. The `Using` statement creates a `Pen` object that is blue and 15 pixels thick. Inside the `Using` block, the code draws an ellipse within the form's client rectangle.

```
Private Sub Form1_Paint(ByVal sender As Object, _
 ByVal e As System.Windows.Forms.PaintEventArgs) Handles Me.Paint
    Using thick_pen As New Pen(Color.Blue, 15)
        e.Graphics.DrawEllipse(thick_pen, Me.ClientRectangle)
    End Using
End Sub
```

When the `Using` block ends, the `Pen` is `Disposed` and the variable is destroyed.

If the `Using` block is long, add a comment at the end reminding the user of the variables created by the `Using` statement and of the block's purpose.

Another feature introduced in Visual Basic .NET is the ability to initialize variables in their declarations. The following code fragment declares two `Customer` object variables. It sets the first one to a new `Customer` object and explicitly sets the second to `Nothing`. The code then declares an `Integer` that it sets to `10` and a `String` that it sets to an empty string.

```
Dim test_customer As New Customer("Carson", "Repins")
Dim new_customer As Customer = Nothing
Dim max_allowed_items As Integer = 10
Dim order_summary As String = ""
```

Experienced developers know what values Visual Basic uses to initialize variables by default and sometimes take advantage of this fact. For example, they know that object variables, such as the two `Customer` variables in the previous code, are initialized to `Nothing`. They also know that `Integer` variables are initialized to 0. It's less obvious that string variables are initialized to `Nothing` rather than an empty string.

Though you may know the values that Visual Basic uses to initialize variables, it's much less obvious to someone reading the code later, whether you knew those values and were relying on them, or whether you just missed something. To avoid possible confusion, always initialize variables explicitly and do so in their declarations, if possible. That way, a variable's value is explicitly set in the code as soon as the variable is declared, so there can be no surprises.

Overloading and Optional Parameters

Microsoft recommends that you overload methods rather than using optional parameters, because optional parameters are not allowed by the CLR. Unfortunately, using overloaded versions of a method in place of optional parameters has several problems.

To keep the code as simple as possible, don't use optional parameters or write overloaded versions of a method unless you know that you must. Start with a simple version of the method and make parameters optional, or overload it only after you discover that it is really necessary.

First, this fills IntelliSense with different versions of the method that may actually be identical. If the parameters really are intended to be optional, you need to scroll through a list of different method signatures to find the one you want. Finding the right version to read the IntelliSense information can be difficult.

This is particularly a problem if the method has a couple of truly different versions in addition to versions that differ only in "optional" parameters. For example, suppose you build a `Customer` class that has two types of constructors. The first type takes as a parameter an integer giving the customer's ID in a database. The second form comes in seven overloaded versions, allowing the program to specify some or all of the new customer's first name, last name, street, city, state, and ZIP code. In this case, IntelliSense buries the constructor that takes an integer as a parameter among all of the other constructors.

In contrast, if you declare the seven overloaded constructors as a single method with optional parameters, you only need to look at one IntelliSense entry to see all of the parameters at once. Only versions that are truly different appear in IntelliSense. In this example, that would be the constructor that takes a customer ID as a parameter, and one other constructor that takes any or all of the name and address parameters.

A second problem with overloaded methods is that they lead to more code to debug and maintain. Rather than having a single version of the method, you need to have one for each overloaded version. Each routine can call the next version in the series to perform most of its work, but there's still more code and more changes to make mistakes.

The `CustomerWithOverloads` class shown in the following code includes a series of seven overloaded constructors. Notice how each version calls the next more complicated version, passing in a default value (in this example blank) for the missing parameter.

```
Public Class CustomerWithOverloads
    Public FirstName As String
    Public LastName As String
    Public Street As String
    Public City As String
    Public State As String
    Public Zip As String

    Public Sub New()
        Me.New("")
    End Sub
```

```
    Public Sub New(ByVal new_FirstName As String)
        Me.New(new_FirstName, "")
    End Sub

    Public Sub New(ByVal new_FirstName As String, ByVal new_LastName As String)
        Me.New(new_FirstName, new_LastName, "")
    End Sub

    Public Sub New(ByVal new_FirstName As String, ByVal new_LastName As String, _
     ByVal new_Street As String)
        Me.New(new_FirstName, new_LastName, new_Street, "")
    End Sub

    Public Sub New(ByVal new_FirstName As String, ByVal new_LastName As String, _
     ByVal new_Street As String, ByVal new_City As String)
        Me.New(new_FirstName, new_LastName, new_Street, new_City, "")
    End Sub

    Public Sub New(ByVal new_FirstName As String, ByVal new_LastName As String, _
     ByVal new_Street As String, ByVal new_City As String, _
     ByVal new_State As String)
        Me.New(new_FirstName, new_LastName, new_Street, new_City, new_State, "")
    End Sub

    Public Sub New(ByVal new_FirstName As String, ByVal new_LastName As String, _
     ByVal new_Street As String, ByVal new_City As String, _
     ByVal new_State As String, ByVal new_Zip As String)
        FirstName = new_FirstName
        LastName = new_LastName
        Street = new_Street
        City = new_City
        State = new_State
        Zip = new_Zip
    End Sub
End Class
```

Ideally, you would use the `Description` attribute to describe each constructor. Each constructor's method would be slightly different, describing a different set of parameters, so you couldn't even copy and paste them without some modification.

You would also ideally use XML comments with a `param` tag to describe each of the parameters for all of the methods. Because each overloaded version has different parameters, these won't be quite the same either.

The following code shows the code with the `Description` attribute and XML comments for one of the constructor's versions. Download the `Overloads` example program to see the other versions.

```
''' <summary>
''' Create a new Customer with a given first and last name, and a default address.
''' </summary>
''' <param name="new_FirstName">The new customer's first name.</param>
''' <param name="new_LastName">The new customer's first name.</param>
''' <remarks></remarks>
```

```
<Description("Create a new Customer with a given name, and a default address")> _
Public Sub New(ByVal new_FirstName As String, ByVal new_LastName As String)
    Me.New(new_FirstName, new_LastName, "")
End Sub
```

The `CustomerWithOptional` class shown in the following code uses a single constructor with optional parameters. This code needs only one set of `Description` attributes and XML comments.

```
Public Class CustomerWithOptional
    Public FirstName As String
    Public LastName As String
    Public Street As String
    Public City As String
    Public State As String
    Public Zip As String

''' <summary>
''' Create a new Customer with a given first and last name, and a default address.
''' </summary>
''' <param name="new_FirstName">The new customer's first name.</param>
''' <param name="new_LastName">The new customer's first name.</param>
''' <param name="new_Street">The new customer's street address.</param>
''' <param name="new_City">The new customer's city.</param>
''' <param name="new_State">The new customer's state.</param>
''' <param name="new_Zip">The new customer's 5-digit ZIP code.</param>
''' <remarks></remarks>
    Public Sub New(Optional ByVal new_FirstName As String = "", _
     Optional ByVal new_LastName As String = "", _
     Optional ByVal new_Street As String = "", _
     Optional ByVal new_City As String = "", _
     Optional ByVal new_State As String = "", _
     Optional ByVal new_Zip As String = "")
        FirstName = new_FirstName
        LastName = new_LastName
        Street = new_Street
        City = new_City
        State = new_State
        Zip = new_Zip
    End Sub
End Class
```

A third problem with overloaded methods is that the user cannot omit one parameter without omitting all of the following parameters. If you wanted to create a `CustomerWithOverloads` object without specifying a `LastName` parameter, you could not specify any address values. In contrast, the following code shows how you could create a `CustomerWithOptional` object while setting only its first name and street address parameters:

```
Dim cust As New CustomerWithOptional("Rod", , "1337 Leet St")
```

Optional parameters also allow you to use named parameters. The following code shows another way you can make a new `CustomerWithOptional` object while specifying only the first name and street address:

```
Dim cust As New CustomerWithOptional( _
    new_FirstName:="Rod", new_Street:="1337 Leet St")
```

Overloaded methods don't let you use named parameters in a particularly useful way. You can use them, but you must provide values for all of the parameters in the version that you are using.

Overloaded methods do have some advantages, however. A developer can omit any combination of optional parameters, but by using overloaded methods, you can prevent certain combinations.

To continue the previous example, you might want to allow the code to include or omit the customer's first and last names as a pair, but not to use one without the other. If you make the parameters optional, a developer could create a customer object with only a first name or only a last name. Similarly, it might make sense to require all or none of the address fields. It probably doesn't make a lot of sense for the code to create a customer with only a street address and state while omitting the city and ZIP code.

In this case, it would make sense to use overloaded constructors. One would take no parameters; another would require first and last names; and a third would take first and last names, plus all of the address fields.

If you do use overloaded methods, keep similar parameters in the same order. Don't make one version take first name and last name parameters, and have another version start with street address followed by first name and last name. Keeping the parameter lists consistent makes them easier to read.

I've seen code where overloaded methods rearranged parameters to give different signatures so that Visual Basic could tell them apart. For example, suppose a method draws some text. The first version of the method takes some text (a string) and a font size (an integer) as parameters, while a second version takes the desired height of the text (an integer) and some text (a string) as parameters. The order of the parameters is switched solely because Visual Basic will not allow you to make two versions of a routine that have the same parameter types.

Similarly, I've seen overloaded methods where the data type of a parameter has been changed to distinguish the different method versions. For example, one version might take an integer parameter while another uses a long integer. This is fine if the two versions do more or less the same thing, just with different parameter types. However, it can be very confusing if the type has been changed simply to create two different versions of the routine that do something different.

Overloaded versions of a method should have the same purpose and do the same thing. If you want different versions of the method to do different things, make them two separate methods with different names. Using the same name for multiple purposes is confusing.

> *My favorite example of this in Visual Basic 6 was the* `Line` *method. Depending on the parameters you passed to it, it could draw a line or a rectangle, filled or unfilled, with the first corner measured either at an absolute position or relative to the last point drawn, and the opposite corner either measured at an absolute position or relative to the first corner. This single routine did way too much. It should at least have been split into* `Line` *and* `Rectangle` *methods, and probably into separate absolute and relative versions. Visual Basic .NET's* `Graphic's` *class solves this problem by providing separate* `DrawLine` *and* `DrawRectangle` *methods, and not allowing relative positions.*

If you want optional parameters, use optional parameters instead of overloaded methods. Use overloaded methods if you want to use parameters that can be included or omitted as a group. Also use overloaded methods if you have a good reason for allowing different versions of a method to take different parameters (as opposed to rearranging parameters to provide versions that do different things).

ParamArrays

You can use the `ParamArray` keyword to allow a method to take an unknown number of parameters. For example, the following code shows a `Sum` function that returns the sum of its parameters:

```
' Return the sum of the numbers.
Private Function Sum(ByVal ParamArray args() As Integer) As Integer
    Dim total As Integer = 0
    For i As Integer = 0 To args.Length - 1
        total += args(i)
    Next i
    Return total
End Function
```

Note that the program can always pass the routine the value `Nothing`, as shown in the following statement:

```
total = Sum(Nothing)
```

In this case, the `args` parameter is `Nothing` inside the function, so you cannot use it for anything. In this case, the previous `Sum` function crashes when it tries to evaluate `args.Length`. To protect against this error, the function should check that its parameter is not `Nothing` before continuing.

The program can also call the function without passing it any parameters, as shown in the following code:

```
total = Sum()
```

In this case, the parameter `args` exists in the function, it just contains no items. The previous version of the `Sum` function works correctly and returns `0`.

An alternative to `ParamArrays` is to make the method take a parameter that is an array. The following code shows a version of the `Sum` function that takes this approach:

```
' Return the sum of the numbers.
Private Function Sum(ByVal args() As Integer) As Integer
    Dim total As Integer = 0
    For i As Integer = 0 To args.Length - 1
        total += args(i)
    Next i
    Return total
End Function
```

The following code shows how the program might call this version:

```
total = Sum(New Integer(){ 1, 2, 3}))
```

This is a bit more complicated than simply passing in a series of values as in `Sum(1, 2, 3)` as you can with a `ParamArray`.

The program cannot call this version of the function without passing it anything, although it can still pass the function `Nothing`.

Some methods that take a variable number of parameters need to take them in groups. For example, you could write a `WeightedAverage` function that takes a weighted average of a series of numbers. The function would multiply each number by a weight, and then divide the total by the sum of the weights.

You could implement this function by using a `ParamArray` where half of the array's items are values and half are weights. Unfortunately, that requires the program to use the correct number of parameters in the proper order. Without looking at the function, you can't tell whether the values should come first followed by the weights, whether the weights should come first, or whether values and weights should alternate.

A better solution is to use two parameters that are arrays, as shown in the following code:

```
' Calculate the weighted average of a series of numbers.
Private Function WeightedAverage(ByVal values() As Single, _
 ByVal weights() As Single) As Single
    Dim total_values As Single = 0
    Dim total_weight As Single = 0
    For i As Integer = 0 To values.Length - 1
        total_values += values(i) * weights(i)
        total_weight += weights(i)
    Next i
    Return total_values / total_weight
End Function
```

Now it is obvious (and IntelliSense makes it clear) that the values come first followed by the weights. The program can still call the function with a different number of values and weights, but at least IntelliSense gives you more information than it would with a `ParamArray`.

Be cautious when using `ParamArrays`. If the arguments are identical in type and meaning, as they are with a simple `Sum` function, a `ParamArray` can make using the function easier. If the parameters have different purposes, as the values and weights do in the previous example, use parameters that are arrays instead of a `ParamArray`.

If Then and Select Case

If a series of `If Then ElseIf` statements should cover every possible case, include an `Else` statement to catch any missing cases. The following code examines the variable `user_type` for various values. If it doesn't find any of the expected values, it uses a `Debug.Assert` statement to throw an exception.

```
If user_type = UserTypes.Clerk Then
    ...
ElseIf user_type = UserTypes.Supervisor Then
    ...
ElseIf user_type = UserTypes.Manager Then
    ...
Else
    Debug.Assert(False, "If Then series does not cove all possibilities")
End If
```

Include the `Else` clause even if you are certain that the `If` tests should catch every possibility. In this example, the `UserTypes` enumerated type might only include the three values `Clerk`, `Supervisor`, and `Manager`, so you might know for a fact that the `Else` code will never execute.

However, someone may later add another value to the enumeration. In that case, the `Else` code will tell you if you don't add a corresponding `ElseIf` statement to the code.

For similar reasons, you should always include a `Case Else` section to a `Select Case` statement, as shown in the following code:

```
Select Case user_type
    Case UserTypes.Clerk
        ...
    Case UserTypes.Supervisor
        ...
    Case UserTypes.Manager
        ...
    Case Else
        Debug.Assert(False, "If Then series does not cove all possibilities")
End Select
```

To make reading `If Then` and `Select Case` code easier, put the shortest cases first. Then, when the user reads them, the original `If` or `Select` statement will still be visible above.

If the code in a series of `If` statements is long (more than a few lines of code), or a `Select Case` statement contains many cases, use comments to tell the reader how the series began. The following code shows a series of long `If Then` statements. Comments after each `ElseIf` and `Else` remind the reader about what the series is doing.

```
' Set options based on user type.
If user_type = UserTypes.Clerk Then
    ... A long block of code ...
ElseIf user_type = UserTypes.Supervisor Then    ' Set options based on user type.
    ... A long block of code ...
ElseIf user_type = UserTypes.Manager Then       ' Set options based on user type.
    ... A long block of code ...
Else                                            ' Set options based on user type.
    Debug.Assert(False, "If Then series does not cove all possibilities")
End If   ' Set options based on user type.
```

The following code shows similar comments for a `Select Case` statement:

```
' Set options based on user type.
Select Case user_type
    Case UserTypes.Clerk                              ' Set options based on user type.
        ...
    Case UserTypes.Supervisor                         ' Set options based on user type.
        ...
    Case UserTypes.Manager                            ' Set options based on user type.
        ...
    Case Else
        Debug.Assert(False, "If Then series does not cove all possibilities")
End Select    ' Set options based on user type.
```

Block Endings

Add a comment at the end of blocks of code that are more than a few lines long to tell the reader what is ending. The previous section included comments at the end of `If Then` and `Select Case` blocks. You should also add comments at the end of subroutines, functions, classes, modules, regions, and other long blocks of code so that the reader can tell what code is ending.

The following code shows a module that contains a region holding some functions. Comments at the end of each of these give the name of the block they are ending.

```
Module Geometry
    ...
#Region "Convex Hull Code"
    Private Function FindConvexHull(ByVal points() As Point) As Point()
        ...
    End Function ' FindConvexHull

    Private Function CullHull(ByVal points() As Point) As Point()
        ...
    End Function ' CullHull
    ...
#End Region ' Convex Hull Code
    ...
End Module ' Geometry
```

It's a shame that Visual Basic doesn't automatically add some kind of hint at the end of a block of code, either as a keyword (for example, `End Function CullHull`*), a comment, or even as an IntelliSense popup when you hover over the* `End` *keyword. If you have a lot of long routines, knowing which one is ending can make finding your way through the code a lot easier.*

When you write a `For` loop in Visual Basic, the `Next` statement can optionally repeat the name of the looping variable. Always include that name to make it easier for the reader to remember what loop is ending. This is particularly important when you have a complicated series of nested loops.

If the variable's name alone isn't enough to help the reader remember what the loop does, add a comment. The following example shows nested `For` loops with the looping variable name repeated in the `Next` statement. It also includes comments describing the loops.

```
For e As Integer = 0 To num_employees - 1
    For j As Integer = 0 To num_jobs - 1
        ' See if employee e can work job j.
        ...
    Next j ' End looping over jobs.
Next e ' End looping over employees.
```

Similarly, if a `Do` loop uses a control variable, include its name in a comment after the `Loop` statement.

If a `Do` loop performs its test at the beginning, include a comment after the `Loop` statement to remind the user about what the loop does. If the loop performs its test at the end, add a comment at the beginning describing the loop. (Actually, you should usually add a comment at the beginning in any case.)

```
' Process existing jobs.
Do While num_jobs > 0
    ' Process a job and remove it from the queue.
    ...
Loop ' End processing jobs and removing them from the queue.

' Get new jobs.
Do
    ' Get a new job and add it to the queue in the proper position.
    ...
Loop While num_new_jobs > 0 ' End queueing new jobs.
```

In these small examples, the comments seem a bit excessive. If the code represented by ellipses (...) is several pages long, however, the reader needs these comments to help remember the loop's purpose.

Exit Points

Some developers suggest that a routine should only have one exit point. If a routine has only a single exit point, you can easily set a breakpoint there to check values before the routine exits. A routine would contain at most one `Return` or `Exit` statement placed at the end of the routine.

By using the right combination of Boolean variables and `If` tests, you can always make a routine exit at a single point, but sometimes it makes the code a lot harder to read. You can simplify the code by moving complicated tests into subroutines or functions, but this is still sometimes awkward.

`Exit Sub` and `Exit Function` statements are not allowed inside the routine. Not only do they make it more difficult to find the place where the executing code is leaving the routine, but they also make the code more confusing because they break the normal flow of program execution. They are essentially "go to" statements that can break the normal rules of program control flow and jump out of the routine at any point.

I don't follow this rule rigorously, but I do try to make a routine's exit points as obvious as possible. I often allow a routine to begin with validation and error-checking code, and the code can exit if the validations fail. After that, the routine should have a single exit point, if possible.

The following code shows the event handler for a new user dialog's OK button. The code begins by validating the user's inputs. If any of the inputs is invalid, the code displays a message and exits the routine. After checking all of the inputs, the routine creates a new `User` object, and then sets the dialog's `DialogResult` property to `OK` to make the dialog hide itself. The routine's final exit point is the `End Sub` statement.

```
Public Class dlgNewUser
    Private Sub btnOk_Click(ByVal sender As System.Object, _
     ByVal e As System.EventArgs) Handles btnOk.Click
        ' Validate the user's entries.
        If txtFirstName.Text.Length = 0 Then
            MessageBox.Show("Please enter a first name", _
                "Missing First Name", _
                MessageBoxButtons.OK, _
                MessageBoxIcon.Exclamation)
            txtFirstName.Focus()
            Exit Sub
        End If

        If txtLastName.Text.Length = 0 Then
            MessageBox.Show("Please enter a last name", _
                "Missing last Name", _
                MessageBoxButtons.OK, _
                MessageBoxIcon.Exclamation)
            txtLastName.Focus()
            Exit Sub
        End If

        ' Create the new User.
        ' ...

        ' The exit point is here.
        Me.DialogResult = Windows.Forms.DialogResult.OK
    End Sub
End Class
```

This example has more than one exit point, but it follows a standard format. Validation code at the beginning can exit the subroutine. If the data passes validation, the routine must continue to its single exit point at the end.

Exit For, Exit Do, and Continue

Just as an `Exit Sub` or `Exit Function` statement breaks the normal rules of program control flow, the `Exit For`, `Exit Do`, and `Continue` statements break the normal rules for moving through a loop.

Just as you can rewrite code to avoid using `Exit Sub` and `Exit Function`, you can rewrite code to avoid using these statements, but, as is the case with `Exit Sub` and `Exit Function`, you may make the code less readable.

A reasonable compromise is to only use these statements at the start or end of the loop. For example, a `For` loop might begin with a series of tests and use an `Exit For` statement if any of them fails. A `Do` loop might include tests at the beginning or end of the loop. Usually these tests can immediately follow the statements that modify the looping variable.

End

Don't stop a program by using the `End` statement. The `End` statement immediately halts the program without giving it a chance to clean up its mess. For example, any forms that are running do not raise their `FormClosing` events, so any code in those routines to perform housekeeping chores (such as updating a database, closing files, saving settings in the Registry, and so forth) is not called. `End` also prevents the application's `Shutdown` event handler from executing if one is defined.

Similarly the `Environment.Exit` method, which ends the application and returns a status code to the environment that started the program, also prevents forms from raising their `FormClosing` events.

Stop the application by closing all forms and exiting from the startup subroutine if there is one. Then forms and other elements have a chance to shut down gracefully.

Example program `ExitAndEnd`, which is available for download at `www.vb-helper.com/one_on_one.htm`, demonstrates these three methods for stopping a program.

Summary

A list of specific programming tips could go on practically forever. This chapter describes some of the rules I've adopted that seem to give the greatest benefit.

To be useful, a programming language must be flexible. Unfortunately, flexibility leads to ambiguity, and that leads to confusion, lack of understanding, and bugs. Coding standards add consistency to code to reduce ambiguity and confusion, while allowing the programmer to take advantage of the language's flexibility.

Use prefixes to identify component types, but don't use Hungarian notation. Avoid abbreviations. Use a form of "to be" in Booleans (as in `IsReady` or `WasScheduled`). Use nouns for properties, verbs for methods, and "ing" or "ed" verbs for events (as in `Assigning` or `Assigned`).

Declare a variable as close to the position where it is used as possible, and initialize it right away. Declare variables inside code blocks to minimize their scope. Use the `Using` statement.

Microsoft prefers overloaded methods to optional parameters, but I think it makes IntelliSense more confusing. `ParamArrays` are confusing, so you're usually better off passing arrays of objects instead.

Always provide a default `Else` or `Select Else` statement in long `If Then` or `Select Case` blocks. Use comments at the end of code blocks, including `If Then` and `Select Case` statements, to remind the reader about the block's purpose.

While I don't recommend requiring that all methods have a single exit point, restrict the number and position of exit points. Usually, it's sufficient to begin a routine with validation code that may use `Exit Sub`, `Exit Function`, or `Exit Property` statements, and then have only one other exit point at the end. Similarly, restrict `Exit For`, `Exit Do`, and `Continue` statements.

Finally, don't stop a program with the `End` statement. Instead, unload all forms and end the `Main` subroutine so that forms and other objects have a chance to perform housekeeping chores.

> *A good place to get more information about coding standards recommended by Microsoft is its Web page ".NET Framework General Reference, Design Guidelines for Class Library Developers" at* `http://msdn.microsoft.com/library/en-us/cpgenref/html/cpconNETFrameworkDesignGuidelines.asp`.

One of the less-obvious rules in my coding standards is to always provide `Else` and `Case Else` blocks for long `If Then` and `Select Case` statements. If you don't expect those cases to occur, then the code should use `Debug.Assert` to throw an exception so that you will know if the unexpected happens. This is a bug-proofing technique that makes the code find bugs for you.

Chapter 16, "Bug Proofing," describes other methods you can use to make your code more robust. It shows how to use application-level events to catch errors that might otherwise cause a program to crash, and how to work around the shortcomings of `Try Catch` blocks.

16

Bug Proofing

Any non-trivial application is extremely likely to contain bugs. If you write more than a few hundred lines of code, bugs are practically inevitable. Even after a program is thoroughly tested and has been in use for awhile, it probably still contains bugs waiting to appear later.

Although bugs are nearly guaranteed, you can take steps to minimize their impact on the application. Careful design and planning can reduce the total number of bugs that are introduced into the code to begin with. "Offensive programming" techniques that emphasize bugs rather than hiding them and verified design by contract (DBC) can detect bugs quickly after they are introduced. Thorough testing can detect bugs before they affect customers.

Together, these techniques can reduce the probability of a user finding a bug to an extremely small level. No matter how small that probability, however, users are likely to eventually stumble across the improbable conditions that bring out the bug.

This chapter discusses some of the techniques you can use to make an application more robust in the face of bugs. It shows how a program can detect bugs when they reveal themselves at runtime, and explains the actions that you might want the program to take in response.

Catching Bugs

Suppose you have built a large application and tested repeatedly until you can no longer find any bugs. Chances are there are still bugs in the code; you just haven't found them yet. Eventually a user will load the right combination of data, perform the right sequence of actions, or use up the right amount of memory with other applications and a bug will appear. Just about any resource that the program needs and that lies outside of your code can cause problems that are difficult to predict.

Modern networked applications have their own whole set of unique problems. If the network is heavily loaded, requests may time out. If a network resource such as a Web site or a Web Service is unavailable or just plain broken, the program won't be able to use it. These sorts of situations can be quite difficult to test. How do you simulate a heavy load or an incorrect response from the Google or TerraServer Web Services?

When that happens, how does the program know that a bug has occurred? Many applications have no idea when an error is occurring. They obliviously corrupt the user's data or display incorrect results. They continue blithely grinding the user's data into garbage, if they don't crash outright. Only the user can tell if a bug occurred, and, if the bug is subtle, the user may not even notice.

There are two ways a program can detect bugs: it can wait for bugs to come to it or it can go hunting for bugs.

Waiting for Bugs

One way to detect bugs is to wait for a bug that is so destructive that it cannot be ignored. These bugs are so severe that the program must handle them or crash. They include such errors as division by zero, accessing array entries that don't exist, invoking properties and methods of objects that are not allocated, trying to read beyond the end of a file, and trying to convert an object into an incompatible object type.

A program can protect against these kinds of bugs by surrounding risky code with a `Try Catch` block. Experience and knowledge of the kinds of operations that the code performs tell you where you need to put this kind of error trapping. For example, if the program performs arithmetic calculations that might divide by zero or tries to open a file that may not exist, the program needs protection.

But it is assumed that you cannot know exactly every place that an error might occur. After all, if you could predict every possible error, you could protect against them and there would be no problem. So, how can you trap every conceivable error? The answer lies in how Visual Basic handles errors.

When an error occurs, Visual Basic looks for an active error handler in the currently executing routine. If there is no active `Try Catch` block or `On Error` statement, control moves up the call stack to the routine that called this one. Visual Basic then looks for an active error handler at that level. If that routine also does not have an active error handler, control moves up the call stack again.

Control continues moving up the call stack until Visual Basic finds an active error handler, or until control pops off the top of the stack and the program crashes. At that point, Visual Basic deals with the error by displaying a usually cryptic error message and then sweeping away the program's wreckage. If an error handler catches the error at any time while climbing up the call stack, the program can continue running. One way you can be certain to catch all errors is to put `Try Catch` blocks around every routine that might be at the top of the call stack.

Because Visual Basic is event-driven, there are only two kinds of routines that can start code running, and that can be at the top of the call stack: event handlers and `Sub Main`.

That observation leads to a way for catching every possible error: put a `Try Catch` block around every event handler and `Sub Main` (if it exists). Now, any time a bug rears its ugly head, the routine at the top of the call stack catches the error in its `Try Catch` block and saves the program from crashing.

Example program `CrashProof` uses the following code to protect three event handlers from crashing. The code in each event handler is contained in a `Try Catch` block. If the code fails, the program displays an error message and continues running.

```
' Cause a divide by zero error.
Private Sub btnDivideByZero_Click(ByVal sender As System.Object, _
 ByVal e As System.EventArgs) Handles btnDivideByZero.Click
    Try
        Dim i As Integer = 1
        Dim j As Integer = 0
        i = i \ j
    Catch ex As Exception
        MessageBox.Show("Error performing calculation" & _
            vbCrLf & ex.Message, "Calculation Error", _
            MessageBoxButtons.OK, MessageBoxIcon.Exclamation)
    End Try
End Sub

' Cause an error by trying to read a missing file.
Private Sub btnOpenMissingFile_Click(ByVal sender As System.Object, _
 ByVal e As System.EventArgs) Handles btnOpenMissingFile.Click
    Try
        Dim txt As String = My.Computer.FileSystem.ReadAllText( _
            "Q:\Missing\missingfile.xyz")
    Catch ex As Exception
        MessageBox.Show("Error reading file" & _
            vbCrLf & ex.Message, "File Error", _
            MessageBoxButtons.OK, MessageBoxIcon.Exclamation)
    End Try
End Sub

' Cause an error by accessing an out of bounds index.
Private Sub btnIndexError_Click(ByVal sender As System.Object, _
 ByVal e As System.EventArgs) Handles btnIndexError.Click
    Try
        Dim values(0) As Integer
        values(1) = 1
    Catch ex As Exception
        MessageBox.Show("Error setting array value" & _
            vbCrLf & ex.Message, "Array Error", _
            MessageBoxButtons.OK, MessageBoxIcon.Exclamation)
    End Try
End Sub
```

The `CrashProof` program (available for download at `www.vb-helper.com/one_on_one.htm`) also contains unprotected versions of these event handlers so that you can see what happens if the `Try Catch` blocks are missing.

All of this leads to a common development strategy:

- Start by writing code with little or no error handling.
- Add `Try Catch` blocks in places where you expect errors to occur. This is usually where the program interacts with some external entity such as a user, file, or Web Service that might return an

invalid result. These are really not bugs in the sense that the code is doing the wrong thing. Instead, it is where invalid interactions with external systems lead to bad behavior.

- Test the application. Whenever you encounter a new bug, add appropriate error handling.

At this point, some developers declare the application finished and ship it. More-thorough developers add `Try Catch` blocks to every event handler and `Sub Main` that doesn't already contain error handling to make the application crash-proof.

Global Error Handling

One problem with this wait-for-the-bug technique is that it requires that you add a lot of error-handling code when you don't know that an error might occur. Not only is that a lot of work, but it also makes the code more cluttered and more difficult to read.

To help with this problem, some Visual Basic 6 products could automatically add error handling to every routine that did not already have it. You would write code to protect against predictable errors such as invalid inputs and missing files, and then the product would automatically protect every other routine in the application.

Visual Basic 2005 helped with this problem by adding the ability to make an application-level error handler. Instead of adding a `Try Catch` block to every unprotected event handler and `Sub Main`, you can create a single event handler to catch unhandled exceptions.

To do that, open Solution Explorer and double-click My Project. Scroll to the bottom of the application's property page and click the View Application Events button shown in Figure 16-1.

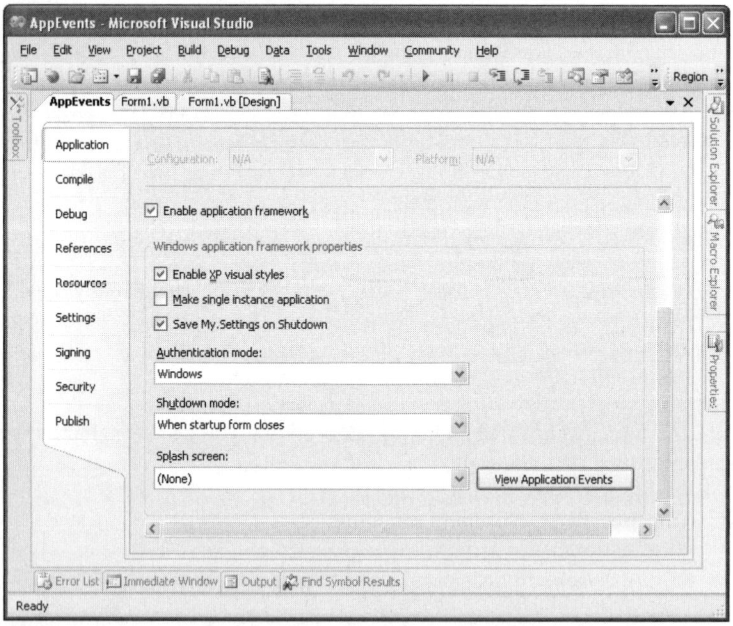

Figure 16-1: Use the View Application Events button to catch unhandled errors.

This opens a code editor for application-level event handlers. In the code editor's left drop-down, select "(MyApplication Events)." Then in the right drop-down, select `UnhandledException`. Now you can add code to handle any exceptions that are not caught by `Try Catch` blocks elsewhere in your code.

The following code shows the application module containing an `UnhandledException` event handler with some automatically generated comments removed to make the code easier to read:

```
Namespace My
    Partial Friend Class MyApplication
        Private Sub MyApplication_UnhandledException(ByVal sender As Object, _
         ByVal e As Microsoft.VisualBasic.ApplicationServices. _
         UnhandledExceptionEventArgs) Handles Me.UnhandledException
            MessageBox.Show("Unexpected error" & _
                vbCrLf & vbCrLf & e.Exception.Message & _
                vbCrLf & vbCrLf & e.Exception.StackTrace.ToString(), _
                "Unexpected Error", _
                MessageBoxButtons.OK, _
                MessageBoxIcon.Exclamation)
            e.ExitApplication = False
        End Sub
    End Class
End Namespace
```

The event handler code displays a message box showing the exception's message and a stack trace. It then sets `e.ExitApplication` to `False` so that the program continues running.

Now, the program is "crash-proof," but you don't need to clutter the code with a huge number of precautionary `Try Catch` blocks.

Note that the event handler must itself be crash-proof. If the `UnhandledException` *event handler throws an exception, the program crashes. Use* `Try Catch` *blocks to protect the event handler.*

This technique is fairly effective, but it has some drawbacks. First, by preventing the application from exiting, this particular example can lead to an infinite loop. When the program fails to crash, it may execute the same code that caused the initial problem. The program may become trapped in a loop throwing an unexpected error, catching it in the `UnhandledException` error handler, setting `e.ExitApplication` to `False`, and then throwing the same error again.

A second problem is that the `UnhandledException` event handler is normally disabled when a debugger is attached to the program, as is normally the case when you run in the Visual Basic IDE. That makes it easier to find and handle new bugs. You run the program in the IDE and, when a bug occurs, you can study it in the debugger and add code to handle the situation properly.

Unfortunately, this also makes testing the `UnhandledException` event handler more difficult because errors won't invoke this routine in the IDE. One way to test your global error-handling code is to move it into another routine that you can then call directly.

The following code shows how you can rewrite the previous example. The `UnhandledException` event handler simply calls subroutine `ProcessUnhandledException`, which does all the work. Both of these routines are contained in the `MyApplication` class inside the `ApplicationEvents.vb` module where you would normally create the `UnhandledException` event handler.

```
Private Sub MyApplication_UnhandledException(ByVal sender As Object, _
 ByVal e As Microsoft.VisualBasic.ApplicationServices. _
 UnhandledExceptionEventArgs) Handles Me.UnhandledException
    ProcessUnhandledException(sender, e)
End Sub

' Deal with an unhandled exception.
Public Sub ProcessUnhandledException(ByVal sender As Object, _
 ByVal e As Microsoft.VisualBasic.ApplicationServices. _
 UnhandledExceptionEventArgs)
    e.ExitApplication = _
        MessageBox.Show("Unexpected error. End application?" & _
            vbCrLf & vbCrLf & e.Exception.Message & _
            vbCrLf & vbCrLf & e.Exception.StackTrace.ToString(), _
            "Unexpected Error", _
            MessageBoxButtons.YesNo, _
            MessageBoxIcon.Question) = DialogResult.Yes
End Sub
```

Example program `GlobalErrorHandler` (available for download at `www.vb-helper.com/one_on_one.htm`) uses the following code to directly call subroutine `ProcessUnhandledException` to test that routine:

```
' Directly invoke the global error handler simulating a divide by zero.
Private Sub btnInvokeErrorHandler_Click(ByVal sender As System.Object, _
 ByVal e As System.EventArgs) Handles btnInvokeErrorHandler.Click
    ' Make a divide by zero exception.
    Try
        Dim i As Integer = 1
        Dim j As Integer = 0
        i = i \ j
    Catch ex As Exception
        ' Make the unhandled exception argument.
        Dim unhandled_args As New _
          Microsoft.VisualBasic.ApplicationServices.UnhandledExceptionEventArgs( _
          True, ex)

        ' Call ProcessUnhandledException directly.
        My.Application.ProcessUnhandledException(My.Application, unhandled_args)

        ' End the application if ExitApplication is True.
        If unhandled_args.ExitApplication Then End
    End Try
End Sub
```

The code uses a `Try Catch` block that contains code that causes an error. It makes an `UnhandledExceptionEventArgs` object for the resulting exception and passes it to the `ProcessUnhandledException` subroutine.

When `UnhandledException` executes, the application ends automatically if the code sets `ExitApplication` to `True`. This version of `ProcessUnhandledException` does not automatically end the application, so the code here ends the program if `ExitApplication` is `True`.

A second problem with this code is that the message displayed to the user is difficult to understand. The `UnhandledException` event handler doesn't really know much about what is going on at the time of the error, so it can't easily give the user meaningful information about what caused the problem. The exception information does include a stack trace, so a developer might be able to guess what was happening, but it would be difficult to tell the user how to fix the problem.

It would be much better to catch the error closer to where it occurred. There the program has a better chance of knowing what is happening and can give the user more constructive suggestions for fixing the problem.

To move the error handling closer to the point of the actual error, make the `UnhandledException` event handler store the error information somewhere for developers to look at later. It might note the error in a log file or email the information to developers. Later, the developers can look at the saved stack trace, figure out what code caused the problem, and then add appropriate error-handling code so the error doesn't make it all the way to `UnhandledException`.

The program would then display a more generic message to the user simply explaining that an unexpected error occurred, that the developers have been notified, and that the program is continuing (if it can). The program might also ask the user for information about what the program was doing when it encountered the error to give developers extra context.

This solution helps address the problem of the error being caught far from the code that threw the exception. A subtler problem occurs when the code that throws the exception is far from the code that is responsible for causing the error. For example, suppose one subroutine calculates a customer ID incorrectly. Much later, the program tries to access the customer and crashes when it finds that the customer doesn't exist.

In this case, the `UnhandledException` event handler will catch the error, display a message, and log information telling what code tried to access the customer. Unfortunately, the real error occurred earlier when the program incorrectly calculated the customer ID. By the time the problem becomes apparent, figuring out where the incorrect ID was calculated may be difficult.

Sometimes, invalid values hide in the system for hours before causing trouble. If invalid or corrupt data is stored in a database, problems may arise months later when it's too later to re-create the original data.

One solution to this problem of incorrect conditions causing problems later is to go hunting for bugs rather than letting them come to you.

Hunting for Bugs

A basic problem with error handlers is that they only catch severe errors. Visual Basic knows when the code tries to access an object that doesn't exist, or tries to convert a `SalesReport` object into an integer. By itself, Visual Basic has no way of knowing that a particular value should be a 7 instead of a 14, or that the program will later need access to a `HotelReservation` object when the code sets it to `Nothing`.

Those are restrictions on the data imposed by the application rather than the Visual Basic language, so Visual Basic cannot catch them by itself. Instead, you should add extra tests to the code to look for these sorts of invalid conditions and catch them as soon as they occur.

If you detect invalid conditions as soon as they arise, you can display meaningful error messages and log useful information about where the problem lies. That makes fixing the problem much easier than it is if you only have a record of where the problem makes itself obvious.

Most of the trickiest bugs in C and C++ programming involve memory allocation. In those languages, the program explicitly allocates and frees memory for objects. The code can crash if you access an object that has no memory allocated for it, if you try to access an object that has been freed, or if you try to free the same memory more than once. The real problem (for example, freeing an object that you will need later) can occur long before you notice the problem (when you try to access the freed object). To make matters worse, sometimes you can access the freed object and the program doesn't crash.

These kinds of delayed memory problems are so difficult to debug that developers have written many memory management systems that add an extra layer to the memory-allocation system to watch for these sorts of things. Some go so far as to keep a record of every memory allocation and deallocation so that later, when you try to read memory that has been freed, you can figure out where it was freed.

Luckily for us, Visual Basic doesn't use this sort of memory-allocation system, so this kind of bug cannot occur. The problem of invalid conditions caused in one routine only appearing later in another routine is still an issue, however, and can cause bugs that are very difficult to track down.

The "design by contract" (DBC) approach described in Chapter 3, "Agile Methodologies," hunts for bugs proactively instead of waiting for them to occur and then responding. In DBC, the program's subsystems explicitly verify pre- and post-conditions on the data. Comments describe the state that the data must have before a routine is called, and the state the data will be in when the routine exits. The code performs tests to verify those conditions and, if the one of the conditions fails, the code immediately stops so that you can fix the error.

Normally, the code tests these conditions with `Debug.Assert` statements. If a condition is not satisfied and the program is running in the debugger, the program stops execution so that you can figure out what's going wrong. If the user is running the program in release mode, the `Debug.Assert` statement is ignored and execution continues. The idea is to thoroughly test the application in the debugger so that the assertions should not fail after you release the program to the end users.

Sometimes, however, these sorts of bugs will slip through into the final application. In that case, the `Debug.Assert` statements don't help you because they are deactivated. You can make them more powerful by performing the tests in your own Visual Basic code, rather than with `Debug.Assert` statements. Then you can perform the tests in the release version of the application in addition to the debug version.

The following code shows a `ReleaseAssert` subroutine that you can use to perform assertions in the program's release version. The routine takes as parameters a Boolean condition to check and an optional message to display, much as `Debug.Assert` does.

```
' If the assertion is False, display a message and a stack trace.
Public Sub ReleaseAssert(ByVal assertion As Boolean, _
 Optional ByVal message As String = "Assertion Failed")
    If Not assertion Then
        ' Get a stack trace.
        Dim stack_trace As New StackTrace(1, True)
```

```
            ' Log the message appropriately
            My.Application.Log.WriteEntry( _
                vbCrLf & Now & vbCrLf & _
                message & vbCrLf & _
                stack_trace.ToString() & _
                "**********" & vbCrLf)

            ' Add a prompt and the stack trace.
            message &= vbCrLf & vbCrLf & _
                "Do you want to try to continue running anyway?"
            message &= vbCrLf & vbCrLf & stack_trace.ToString()

            ' Display the message.
            If MessageBox.Show( _
                message, _
                "Failed Assertion", _
                MessageBoxButtons.YesNo, _
                MessageBoxIcon.Exclamation) = DialogResult.No _
            Then
                End
            End If
        End If
    End Sub
```

If the assertion fails, the subroutine makes a `StackTrace` object representing the application's current state. The parameter `1` makes the trace skip the topmost layer of the stack, which is the call to subroutine `ReleaseAssert`.

The subroutine writes the current date and time, the message, and the stack trace into the program's log file. By default, this file is stored with a name having the following format:

```
base_path\company_name\product_name\product_version\app_name.log
```

Here the `company_name`, `product_name`, and `product_version` come from the assembly information. To view or change that information, open Solution Explorer, double-click My Project, and click the Assembly Information button.

The `base_name` is typically something similar to the following:

```
C:\Documents and Settings\user_name\Application Data
```

For example, the log file for the `Assertions` example program (which is available for download at `www.vb-helper.com/one_on_one.htm`) is stored on my system at the following location:

```
C:\Documents and Settings\Rod.BENDER\
    Application Data\TestCo\TestProd\1.2.3.4\Assertions.log
```

Subroutine `ReleaseAssert` then displays a message to the user describing the problem and asking if the user wants to continue running anyway. If the user clicks No, the program ends.

When one developer's code calls routines written by another developer (or even a routine written by the same developer at a different time), there is a chance that the two developers had a different understanding of the data's conditions, and that makes routine calls a productive place to put these sorts of DBC assertions. However, those are not the only places where it makes sense to perform these kinds of tests. Though the DBC philosophy only requires that you validate data during calls between routines, there's no reason you can't make similar assertions at any point where you think a problem may creep into the data.

Worthwhile places to inspect the data for correctness include the following:

- Places where data is created. Was it created correctly?
- Places where data is transformed. Was it transformed correctly?
- Places where data is moved from one place to another (between a database and the program, between an XML file and the program, between one subsystem and another). Was the data transferred correctly? Is there redundant data now left in the old location? Is there a way to ensure that they are synchronized?
- Places where data is discarded. Are you sure you won't need it later?

In one project, an algorithm developer was trying to decide where to put some error-checking code. He was loading data from a database and needed to know that the data was clean. When he asked whether we should put error-checking code on the routines that saved the data into the database or on the algorithm code, the project manager and I simultaneously answered, "Both." No matter how hard you try, errors eventually sneak into the data. It may happen when new types of data slip past obsolete filters, or it may be when a developer makes an incorrect change to validation code. The only defense is to verify all of the data as often as is practical.

In places such as these, it makes sense to use `Debug.Assert` to verify correctness. If it won't impact performance too much, it may also make sense to use a routine similar to `ReleaseAssert` to verify correctness in the program's release version.

Many developers resist extra data validation as inefficient. They argue that the program doesn't need to recheck the data, so you can leave these tests out to improve performance. In most applications, however, performance is relative. The application should be responsive enough for the users to get their jobs done, but most programs are much faster than necessary. Is it really important to shave a few milliseconds off of the application's time so the idle process can use 99 percent of the CPU? In some applications, it may even make sense to have a background thread wandering through the data looking for trouble while nothing else is happening.

I often add code to check inputs and outputs for every routine in an entire application. Noted author and expert developer John Mueller (`www.mwt.net/~jmueller`) does the same. If you ask around, I suspect you'll find that a lot of top-notch developers check inputs and outputs practically to the point of paranoia. It sounds like a lot of work, but it usually only takes a few minutes, and can easily catch bugs that might require hours or even days to find.

Don't wait for bugs to find you through `Try Catch` blocks. Use contract verification to validate data between routine calls. Add extra condition checks whenever the data might become corrupted. If the tests don't take much time, use `ReleaseAssert` to keep them in the program's release version. The first time you discover a data problem near its source instead of hours and thousands of lines of code later, you'll realize the extra work was worth the effort.

Try Catch Blocks

`Try Catch` blocks are the basic method for catching errors in Visual Basic .NET. Unlike the `On Error` statements used in Visual Basic 6, they are nice, block-oriented structures that make it easy to tell when the code is protected in an error handler and when an error has occurred. Unfortunately, they still have a few drawbacks.

One problem with `Try Catch` blocks is that they are difficult to use to ignore errors. The following code shows some Visual Basic 6 code that performs a series of steps and ignores any errors that occur. The `On Error Resume Next` statement makes the code continue executing, even if one of the subroutines raises an error.

```
On Error Resume Next
Step1
Step2
Step3
```

The following code shows the Visual Basic .NET equivalent. Each subroutine call must be contained in its own `Try Catch` block so that any errors it generates can be ignored.

```
Try
    Step1
Catch ex As Exception
End Try

Try
    Step2
Catch ex As Exception
End Try

Try
    Step3
Catch ex As Exception
End Try
```

One solution to this problem is to mix the old and new styles of error handling. Inside the three subroutines, you can use the newer `Try Catch` block while the calling routine uses `On Error Resume Next`.

Visual Basic will not let you mix the two error-handling styles in the same routine.

Another approach is to use a `Do` loop to repeatedly execute the steps until they are all complete. The loop uses the variable `next_step` to keep track of the next step that it should perform. Each time through the loop, the code uses a `Try Catch` block to ignore errors. Inside the `Try` section, it uses a `Select Case` statement to execute the next step. After the `Try Catch` block, the program increments `next_step` so that it performs the next step during the next trip through the loop.

```
Dim next_step As Integer = 0
Do
    Try
        Select Case next_step
            Case 0
                Step1()
            Case 1
                Step2()
            Case 2
                Step3()
        End Select
    Catch ex As Exception
    End Try

    next_step += 1
Loop While next_step >= 0
```

In both of these solutions, using `On Error Resume Next` or using a `Do` loop, the code will be simpler if you group related steps into a single subroutine call. For example, suppose the code should open a text file, read its contents, and then append to it. If you can consider this as an atomic operation that either succeeds or fails as a unit, you can move the code into a subroutine and simplify the code that tries to ignore any errors.

> *Personally, I find* `On Error Resume Next` *simpler and easier to read. If parts of the code could use a* `Try Catch` *block, move that code into a subroutine so you can use the block. Visual Basic won't let you mix* `Try Catch` *with* `On Error` *statements in the same routine, so you need to move the two styles into separate subroutines.*

Another disadvantage to `Try Catch` blocks is that they are relatively inefficient. When an exception occurs, it takes awhile for the application to build the proper exception object and invoke the error handler.

If you can predict the kinds of errors that might occur, it is usually much more efficient to check for those conditions, rather than allowing a `Try Catch` block to handle the problem after the fact. For example, if you need to divide by a number, it is much faster to check whether the number is zero than to let a `Try Catch` block deal with the error if the value is zero. Similarly, if you need to read from a file, it is faster to use `My.Computer.FileSystem.FileExists` to see whether the file exists before you try to read the file.

Example program `ExceptionSpeeds` shown in Figure 16-2 demonstrates these errors. Enter a number of trials and click the Divide By Zero button to make the program use a `Try Catch` block to catch a divide-by-zero error. Click the Check For Zero button to make the program check whether the denominator is zero before performing the division. Click the Missing File button to make the program try to read a missing file. Click Check For File to make the program use `My.Computer.FileSystem.FileExists` and skip reading the file if the file doesn't exist.

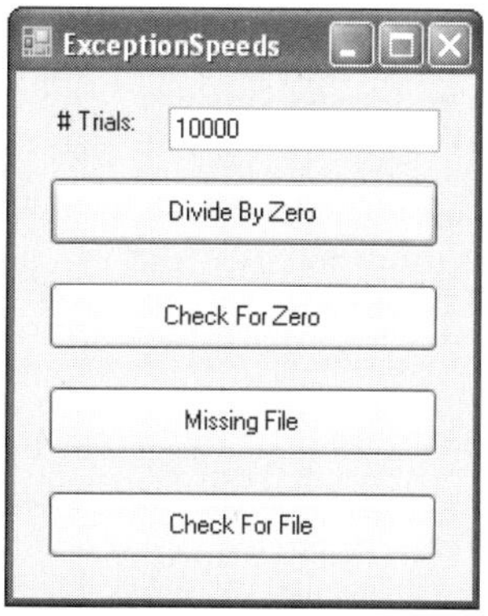

Figure 16-2: Program `ExceptionSpeeds` shows it's faster to check for dangerous conditions than to let `Try Catch` handle the resulting errors.

In one set of tests, program `ExceptionSpeeds` (available for download at `www.vb-helper.com/one_on_one.htm`) took slightly more than 4 seconds to divide by zero 100,000 times. It took no noticeable time to realize that the denominator was zero and avoid the division. Similarly, the program took about 9.25 seconds to fail to read a missing file 100,000 times, while it took only 0.8 seconds to realize that the file was missing and skip trying to read it 100,000 times.

Exceptions are for exceptional situations (hence the name), so don't use them needlessly. Anticipate predictable errors and avoid them. Don't throw your own exceptions to indicate a predictable condition; use a variable or function return value as a status flag instead.

Don't throw exceptions to simply exit from a routine and unwind part of the call stack. It may be tempting to use an exception to jump several layers up the call stack to the closest error handler, but that kind of code can be confusing and extremely difficult to debug.

Using `Try Catch` to protect against unexpected conditions is fine but using it to protect the program against predictable error situations is not. It is much better to look for possible problems and avoid throwing an exception than it is to rely on exception handling to validate the program's data.

Responding to Bugs

Suppose you apply all of the bug-proofing techniques at your disposal: good design, pair programming, code reviews, offensive programming, verified DBC, and thorough testing. Now, when the program detects an error at run-time, what should it do?

In part, the action the program should take depends on the kind of error. If the error is one that you expected, the program may be able to fix it. For example, suppose the program asks the user to enter a file name but the file doesn't exist. The program can tell the user that there is no such file and ask for a new name. In this case, no further action is needed.

On the other hand, an error may be completely unexpected. In that case it is unlikely that the program can correct the problem even with the user's help. To allow developers to fix the problem later, the program should make relevant information available.

To do that, the program can ask the user to record the information. Unfortunately, the information the developer needs (such as the exact error description and the state of the call stack) means less than nothing to the user so the user is unlikely to record the right information accurately.

A better solution is for the program to make the necessary information directly available to the developers. The section "Hunting for Bugs" earlier in this chapter includes code that writes error information into a log file. The program might also ask the user for a brief description of what the program was doing when the error occurred, and add that to the log so that the developers know what the user was trying to do.

Another approach is to email the information to the developers. The `SendEmail` subroutine shown in the following code sends an email message. A program can use similar code to send error messages to developers.

```
' Send an email message.
Public Sub SendEmail(ByVal mail_server As String, ByVal mail_from As String, _
 ByVal mail_to As String, ByVal mail_subject As String, ByVal mail_body As String)

    Using mail_message As New MailMessage(mail_from, mail_to, _
     mail_subject, mail_body)
        ' Make the SMTP mail client to send the message.
        Dim mail_client As New SmtpClient(mail_server)

        ' Use the user's Windows credentials.
        mail_client.UseDefaultCredentials = True

        ' Send the message to the mail server.
        mail_client.Send(mail_message)
    End Using
End Sub
```

Unfortunately, when an error occurs, the application may be unstable. For example, if the user's system is running out of memory, the program may throw an `OutOfMemoryException`. If memory is that scarce, the program may not be able to obtain enough resources to write to a log file or email a message to developers. If the computer's file system is having trouble (for example, if it has run out of space), the event handler may be unable to write log entries. If the computer is having network problems, it may be unable to email error information to developers.

Use `Try Catch` blocks to protect the event handler from these conditions. If the event handler encounters its own errors, it can fall back on simpler methods for reporting the problem.

The `ErrorFallback` example program (available for download at `www.vb-helper.com/one_on_one.htm`) uses the following `UnhandledException` event handler to deal with errors. It tries to save the most detailed information for developers in the most convenient way possible. If one method fails, it tries a simpler method that is more likely to succeed.

```
Private Sub MyApplication_UnhandledException(ByVal sender As Object, _
 ByVal e As Microsoft.VisualBasic.ApplicationServices. _
 UnhandledExceptionEventArgs) Handles Me.UnhandledException
    Dim msg As String = ""

    ' Try to make a message with a stack trace.
    Try
        Dim stack_trace As New StackTrace(1, True)
        msg = vbCrLf & Now & vbCrLf & stack_trace.ToString()
    Catch ex As Exception
    End Try

    ' Try making a simpler message.
    If msg.Length = 0 Then
        Try
            msg = vbCrLf & Now & "Unable to save stack trace."
        Catch ex As Exception
        End Try
    End If

    ' Try to email the message.
    Dim email_worked As Boolean = False
    Try
        SendEmail("mailserver", _
            "myapplication@somewhere.com", _
            "developers@somewhere.com", _
            "Automated Error Report", _
            msg)
        email_worked = True
    Catch ex As Exception
    End Try

    ' Try writing to a log file.
    ' Note: You may want to do this even if the email works.
    Dim log_worked As Boolean = False
    If Not email_worked Then
        Try
            My.Application.Log.WriteEntry(msg)
            log_worked = True
        Catch ex As Exception
        End Try
    End If

    ' See if we succeeded.
    If email_worked Then
        ' Tell the user that we emailed a message to the developers.
        e.ExitApplication = _
            MessageBox.Show("Unexpected error: " & vbCrLf & _
                e.Exception.Message & vbCrLf & vbCrLf & _
                "Automatically emailed a report to the developers." & _
                vbCrLf & vbCrLf & "Do you want to end the application?", _
                "Unexpected Error", _
                MessageBoxButtons.YesNo, _
                MessageBoxIcon.Question) = DialogResult.Yes
```

```
        ElseIf log_worked Then
            ' Tell the user that we saved a log entry.
            e.ExitApplication = _
                MessageBox.Show("Unexpected error: " & vbCrLf & _
                    e.Exception.Message & vbCrLf & vbCrLf & _
                    "Automatically saved a log entry." & _
                    "Please notify the developers." & vbCrLf & vbCrLf & _
                    "Do you want to end the application?", _
                    "Unexpected Error", _
                    MessageBoxButtons.YesNo, _
                    MessageBoxIcon.Question) = DialogResult.Yes
        Else
            ' We did not save any information.
            ' Ask the user to call support.
            MessageBox.Show("Unexpected error: " & vbCrLf & _
                e.Exception.Message & vbCrLf & vbCrLf & _
                "Unable to save error information." & _
                "Please call the developers immediately." & vbCrLf & vbCrLf & _
                "After talking to the developers, " & _
                "click OK to close the application.", _
                "Unexpected Error", _
                MessageBoxButtons.OK, _
                MessageBoxIcon.Exclamation)
            e.ExitApplication = True
        End If
    End Sub
```

The code first tries to make a message string that contains a stack trace. If that fails, it makes a simpler string that says the program cannot save a stack trace.

If the program cannot make the stack trace, something is seriously wrong. For example, the program may be so low on memory that it cannot make a string big enough to hold a stack trace, which admittedly may be fairly verbose. You could try unloading some data structures to free some memory before building the stack trace, particularly if you're planning to end the application anyway.

You could also try unloading some forms, although at this point you don't know whether the current stack trace passes through those forms. If you unload a form containing code that is in the call stack, the program crashes.

After creating the message, the code calls subroutine `SendEmail` to send the message to the developers.

If subroutine `SendEmail` fails (for example, if the network is unavailable), the code writes the message into a log file. You may want to perform this step even if the email message works so that you have a permanent record of the message in case the email gets lost.

Finally, the code tells the user whether it sent email or made a log entry, and asks whether it should exit the application. If neither the email nor the log entry worked, the program asks the user to call the developers to report the problem.

Instead of asking the user to call Technical Support, you could ask the user to go to a Web site to report the problem online. This has the advantage of the user being able to do it any time of the day or night, without dragging the developers out of their beds. It has the disadvantages of the user not being able to get an immediate reply from developers, it relies on the user entering useful and accurate information, and it assumes that the user will take the trouble to enter any information at all. It also assumes that the user's system is still stable enough to run a Web browser.

At this point, there are no perfect solutions. If the program cannot send email and write log files, there's probably something very wrong with the user's system, and the program's options are probably very limited.

Summary

Start with a clean design and well-defined architecture so that all developers have a good understand of what the different pieces of code should do. Use agile techniques such as pair programming, code reviews, DBC, and test-driven development to reduce the number of bugs that slip into the code in the first place.

When you know that the code may contain bad data, look for it rather than letting an error handler catch the problem. For example, if the program must open a file, see if the file exists before trying to open it. Treat these predictable situations as validation issues rather than errors.

Add extra validation code to check data at key points throughout the code. Examine data when it is created, modified, or transferred between parts of the application. Don't wait for bugs severe enough to crash the program; go looking for them.

As you test the code, identify new errors and add appropriate error-handling code.

When you can find no other bugs, make an `UnhandledException` event handler to catch any unexpected errors that arise. Make that event handler call another routine that does all the work so that you can test your error handling. Be sure the global error-handling code is robust. If this code fails, you'll learn nothing about the error and won't be able to stop it from happening again.

This chapter discusses ways you can catch and handle errors. It tells where you should put error-handling code, how you can catch otherwise unhandled errors, and what you might want to do when those unhandled errors occur.

Chapter 17, "Testing," explains advanced debugging and testing techniques. It explains how you can devise tests to uncover bugs and how to track down bugs while the code is executing.

17

Testing

Previous chapters have mentioned testing in passing, but have not really explained what kinds of tests are possible and what kinds of tests you should perform. For example, the section on test-drive development in Chapter 3, "Agile Methodologies," assumes that you write tests for code before you write the actual code, but it doesn't explain how to do that.

This chapter provides some additional information about testing. It describes the kinds of tests you can perform and their purposes. It explains when you should test different parts of an application, and what you should do when tests detect a problem.

Testing Philosophy

The way you think about testing shapes the application's progress. Too many developers think of testing as an annoying, half-unnecessary process that should be performed at the end of development and only as time permits. The result is an application full of known and unknown bugs that may be shipped to meet some preset deadline. The users develop an unfavorable perception of your development team, and believe the application is frustrating and has low quality. (I'm sure you can think of a few major commercial applications that satisfy that description.)

To produce a stable application, programmers must have the idea from the start that testing is an important, necessary, and helpful part of development that occurs throughout the application lifecycle. They should understand that testing happens for a reason: to find bugs before the users do.

Bugs found by tests are generally much easier to fix than those found by users. A well-designed test can give you much better information about what was happening when the error occurred than the user can. A test can often lead you directly to the code that caused the error, whereas a user has no idea what the code is doing internally when the problem surfaces.

Finding a bug with a test not only saves you time; it saves your users the time they would otherwise spend reporting and tracking bugs. It also improves their perception that your development team builds solid applications and that you consider the users' time and needs important.

Agile methods require frequent builds, and help promote early and frequent testing. Very few developers would release a program with absolutely no testing whatsoever. If you plan for a new release every four weeks, you know that at least at a system level the code is tested every month.

That's a start, but it's not sufficient. If the pressure to make a new release every month leads you to defer testing until the monthly build, you may end up with bugs that are deeply embedded in the code. You will only have added at most four weeks' work on top of the bug, but digging through that code can put you significantly behind schedule. Remember that the next build is due in only another four weeks.

In any development effort, you need to build on a solid foundation. You need to check every piece of code thoroughly so that you can move on with confidence to the next phase of development. Agile methods emphasize this because incomplete testing leads so quickly to big problems, but the same is true no matter what development approach you use.

Frequent system-level testing is good, but you need to do more.

Test Early and Often

Testing should begin as soon as there is something to test. Whenever programmers write a piece of code that does something well-defined, they should write tests to prove that it works. No code should be treated as working until it has been tested. After you have done a thorough job of testing the code, you can move on confidently without having to wonder if the code is stable.

Developers naturally have a difficult time following this advice. After they write a small piece of code, they often feel that the code is too simple to need testing. They don't know of any problems in the code (after all, if they knew of problems they would fix them), so they assume there are none.

Developers continue writing code until they have a big enough piece that it won't easily fit inside their heads. At that point, it is much easier to believe that there may be bugs in the code, so it's more natural to start testing (assuming developers don't face time pressures that make it easy to put off testing even longer).

Unfortunately, at this point, it's also much more difficult to find any bugs. Because the developer cannot keep the whole body of code easily in mind, it's much more difficult to understand what might be causing a bug once you find it. If the code is so complex that you think it's worth looking for bugs, then it's too complex to easily find the bugs.

If you had tested the code in smaller pieces as each was written, the same bug would still be there. I'm not talking about changing the way you write code at this point, so you presumably would have made the same mistake. It just would have been easier to find.

Instead of thinking of a small piece of code as too simple to test, you should think of it as being easier to test. You don't need to write as many test cases to cover all of the paths through a small piece of code. You don't need to worry about complex interactions among lots of pieces of code if you're only working on one piece.

Later, after you test the pieces individually, you can test them together. At that point, you should find fewer bugs, because you have already shaken them out during the lower-level tests.

Frequent testing often changes the structure of your code. If you test everything in small pieces, you will tend to break the code into small pieces. Instead of writing a single long routine, you can write a smaller routine that calls several other small, closely related routines that you write and test individually.

Test Everything

No piece of code is too small or too simple to test. Looked at in tiny pieces, particularly right after you have written it, most code is simple, straightforward, and obviously correct. I have probably seen hundreds of pieces of code that were so simple they could not possibly be wrong, and yet they contained a bug.

Test everything, no matter how simple it seems. You'll flush out bugs while they are easy to catch and before other developers have a chance to find them. Simple code is easy to test, so you can get a feeling of accomplishment with little extra effort.

Save Tests Forever

When code is later modified, you need to test it again to see if the modifications broke the code. You should also test the rest of the application's code (or at least any code that could possibly have been affected by the changes) to see if the changes broke that code, as well. Retesting old code to see if new changes broke it is called *regression testing*.

Testing the modified code is a lot easier if you still have the original test code lying around. If the changes should not have affected the code's behavior, you can rerun the tests as they are. If the modifications were intended to change the code's results, you can modify the tests accordingly. You may also need to add new tests, but testing the altered code will be easier starting from the old tests than it would be if you had to write new tests from scratch.

Regression testing other code is practically trivial if you save the original tests. You start by rerunning those tests. You may need to add new tests to exercise new features in the code, but if the modifications are not supposed to change a piece of code's behavior, you can use its old tests as they are.

Writing tests can take as much time as writing any other kind of code, so you should treat it accordingly. Save the test code with the code it tests in a source-code control system. Then, if you need to retrieve an older version of the code, you can also retrieve its tests.

Chapter 3 says a bit more about testing in its section titled "Test-Driven Development." A point worth repeating here is that you must ensure that the test is correct. If the test is wrong, it may report that the code contains a bug, when really the bug is in the testing code. Usually, the bug really is in the code, but it's worth keeping this issue in the back of your mind. If it's taking more time than you think it should to find the bug, take a look at the testing code.

It's also important to remember that tests can rarely guarantee that the code is correct. A test cannot say the code is perfect; the test can only say that it did not find any problems.

Don't Shoot the Messenger

Each developer should test his or her own code as soon as it is written. Usually, a developer will also test his or her own code when it is integrated into other pieces of code written by the same developer. At some level, however, the application's code must be tested in larger pieces that contain code written by more than one developer. At that point, egos sometimes step in and make testing argumentative and hostile.

When another developer finds a bug in your code, it's hard not to take it personally. You wrote the code and created the bug, so it's natural to feel as if your skills are being questioned. Instead of becoming defensive, focus on the end result. Someone else who finds a bug in your code saves you the embarrassment of having a user find the bug. Though a user finding a bug may feel less personal (the user doesn't know who added the bug to the code), it reflects badly on the development team as a whole.

Thank other developers who find your bugs because they're doing your work for you. Fix the bug, and try to think of ways you could have caught it earlier. Add new tests to the code's test suite so that bug would be caught in the future, and try to apply the lesson to future code.

Kinds of Tests

There are several kinds of tests you should make during different stages of development. You can group these according to the scope of the code that you are testing:

- Sub-unit level testing looks at the smallest pieces of code that you can effectively test.
- Unit-level testing covers the smallest self-contained subsystems in the application.
- Integration tests study the ways units interact.
- System tests look at the application as a complete tool as the user sees it.

Sub-Unit Tests

Sub-unit tests look for bugs in the smallest units of code that are executable. They test intermediate results that may not be intended for use by larger parts of the application. These are typically helper routines used to implement tools that are used by other parts of the application.

For example, suppose you are writing a dispatch application that routes repair trucks to service calls. The assignment module will need helper routines that match trucks with jobs they can work (does a job need special equipment or skills?), calculate distances between repair trucks and the service calls through the street network (who is closest?), track appointment windows (when will the customer be available?), and so on. Those routines will need other helper routines that build the street network, find shortest paths, check for street restrictions (such as a 10-ton limit on certain a bridge), track employee assignments (who is driving which truck), and so forth.

Ideally, you will have sub-unit tests for every routine that you write. As soon as you write one of these routines, you write a test routine and verify that the routine works. (Or, if you're using test-driven development, you may write the tests first.) You write a routine to load a street network and then test it. Next you write a routine that checks employee assignments and merges employee skills with the trucks' equipment, and then test it. You write a shortest-path function and test it. By the time you've written the main assignment module, all of the routines that make it up should be tested.

In practice, most developers skip testing at this level. Instead, they write all of the routines that make up a higher-level unit of code and then test at the unit level. There are two problems with that technique. First, if the unit test discovers a problem, it may be more difficult to trace back to the sub-unit routine that caused the problem. If the helper routines work relatively independently, it may not be too difficult to track the problem. If the helper routines have complex interactions, then figuring out which one is broken can take considerable time and effort.

The second problem with relying on unit-level testing is that it can be difficult to ensure that you have tested every code path through every helper routine.

For example, suppose a major code unit uses five helper routines that can each take five paths of execution. If you test the 5 routines separately, you need to use at least 5 * 5 = 25 sets of inputs to follow every possible path of execution. It may take some thinking, but it shouldn't be too difficult to come up with inputs to test each of those paths.

In contrast, suppose you only test the five routines together in their larger unit. In that case, there are a total of 5^5 = 3,125 possible combinations of routes through the 5 routines. Manually designing enough test cases to cover all of these possible combinations would be very difficult. If you can easily generate sets of inputs randomly, you can perform 3,125 test cases easily enough, but there's no guarantee that the random cases will follow every possible path of execution. Even if the helper routines operate independently so that you only need to cover the 25 possible paths through the individual routines and not the 3,125 combinations, there's no guarantee that you will hit them all. Later, when you make a change to the code, there's no guarantee that the random tests will exercise the modified code, so a new bug can remain hidden until much later.

If possible, test at the sub-unit level before you test at the unit level. You should be able to cover each possible path of execution at least once a lot more easily than you can at the unit level.

Unit Tests

Unit tests look for bugs in relatively self-contained pieces of code. Typically, these are subsystems, libraries, and other tools used by various parts of an application. They should generally be written in separate modules, possibly in separate class or control libraries.

Whenever you have built a self-contained part of a code unit, you should test it. The sooner you test the code, the simpler it will be, so the easier it will be to fix any problems that you find.

If you test the unit frequently as you add to it and modify it, you can focus on the code that has changed since the last tests when you encounter a bug. Suppose you add 20 lines to a library containing 10,000 lines, test it, and find a new bug that wasn't there before. Chances are good that the new bug is in the most recent 20 lines. In contrast, suppose you add 300 new lines before testing. Then, if you find a new bug, you have a lot more code to study to isolate the bug.

Unit testing is usually your final chance to find any bugs before the other members of the development team find them and embarrass you at the next staff meeting.

And they can embarrass you! I know of one project where they tacked a rubber chicken to the door of anyone who broke the weekly system build. The follow-on project used a stuffed skunk. In a third project, a developer named Fred was so well-known for breaking the weekly build that the other developers eventually spoke of "defredding" the code every Friday afternoon.

Do a thorough job of testing the unit as it was intended to be used, covering as many different situations as possible. Also, test it with abnormal and missing data. Sooner or later, another developer will pass the wrong kind of data to your code and you must be prepared to handle it. If your public routines do a good job of validating inputs, throwing well-described exceptions when the data is incorrect, then other developers will understand that their code is causing the problem and they can fix it without bothering you. Some projects spend a lot of time on finger-pointing competitions that are easy to avoid if you check the inputs to your code carefully.

Integration Tests

Unit tests try to find problems in a single, more-or-less independent unit. *Integration tests* look for bugs when two or more system units interact.

An integration test should make one unit call code in another, and then use the results in some meaningful way. Ideally, the units contain lots of input and output validation, so the called unit validates its inputs, calculates a result, validates the result, and returns the result to the caller. The caller then validates the results to ensure that they make sense. If you have done a really good job of unit testing and performed extensive validations, you should find no surprises during integration testing.

One way to think of integration testing is as the process of integrating one unit with the rest of the application. That may not be strictly accurate, because integration tests often cover changes to one or more units, rather than newly adding a unit to the system, but the idea of focusing on a single unit for testing is useful.

Aside from random bugs that should have been caught by more thorough unit testing, the most common kind of problem discovered by integration testing occurs when two developers have different ideas about what the interfaces between the units should look like. If everyone is doing proper input and output validation, one unit rejects another's input or output. The developers who wrote the two units must then (hopefully amicably) decide which set of assumptions is correct, and make whatever changes are needed to bring the code into line.

System Tests

System tests look for problems with the application as a whole. If you have run a rigorous set of sub-unit, unit, and integration tests, you should find very little at this stage.

Any bug that you do find should be caused by unexpected interactions among the application's units. For example, you may need to follow a long and very specific set of steps to put the data into a state that causes an error. Any simple operations that cause errors should have been caught during integration testing.

During system testing, you should step through all of the use cases defined by the specification. You should also try variations on the test cases, because it is likely that users will use those variations either intentionally or accidentally. If possible, try executing the same steps in different orders to see what happens. The results should match the expected results defined by the use cases.

Try everything that the users will try, and all of the things they shouldn't try. Run tests with missing and invalid inputs, illegal orders of operations, and anything else you can think of that the users might do wrong. Make sure the program doesn't crash, and gives the user enough information to fix the problem.

The system tests are your last chance to catch bugs before the users find them. Your credibility suffers when the users catch bugs that you should have caught during system testing. Customer-reported bugs also usually come with an extra level of management, requiring additional bug tracking, formal reporting, and possibly definition and approval by a change committee before you can fix them. Catch bugs before they reach the users to make things nice and simple.

Regression Tests

A *regression test* repeats previously executed tests to see if any of the application's behavior has changed after you have made changes to the code. A user reports a bug, you fix the offending code, and then you perform regression tests to see if the fix worked and if it broke anything else.

Ideally, you would rerun every test ever written for the application to look for new problems. If you have a well-designed automated testing system, you may actually be able to do that. More often, however, developers only run system-level tests that exercise the feature that was modified.

Whenever you make a change to the code, you should step through the code in the debugger to verify that the change actually works. It is amazing how many developers change some code and perform a few system-level tests that don't actually execute all of the new code. Developers also often verify that the modified code fixes the immediate problem, but don't run enough tests to be certain that it doesn't break some previously working scenario. Then the bug reappears at a later date in a new guise, and you need to debug the same code again. Do a good job of regression testing the first time so that you don't have to waste time fixing it again.

Whenever you find a bug in the code, you should add new tests at every level possible to catch that bug in the future. You should add new validation tests to the code using `Debug.Assert`. You should add new sub-unit and unit-level tests to your existing library of testing routines. If a bug in one unit is visible from another unit, you should add integration tests to detect it. Finally, if you have automated system tests, you should add a new test to look for the bug. If you cannot detect the bug manually, you should add new scenarios to the system's use cases to look for the bug. If you add all of these tests, this bug should never go undetected again.

Test Techniques

Many developers perform an ad hoc sort of testing. They write some code, throw some obvious sets of data at it, and if no errors occur, they assume that the code is correct. Though you should not ignore your instincts about what data is likely to flush out errors, there are some specific techniques that you can use to make finding any bugs more likely. These techniques test the code with typical and atypical values, values that are very large and very small, and values that don't make any sense.

Exhaustive Testing

In *exhaustive testing*, you feed every possible combination of data into a routine and you validate the result. For example, suppose your application monitors five input queues, finds the item with the highest priority, and processes it. If the items in the queues might have priorities ranging from 1 to 10, there are at most 10^5 = 100,000 combinations of priorities. In that case, you could write a test that loops through every possible combination of priorities, runs the code that picks out the highest-priority item, and then verifies that it selected the right item.

Exhaustive testing guarantees that the code works correctly. If you try every possible input and always produce a correct output, you have proven that the code works. Unfortunately, in practice it's often impossible to exhaustively test every possible input to a routine.

Suppose you have a shop-scheduling problem where you have a number of jobs that can be performed on different pieces of equipment. You know how long it takes to change a machine's setup from one configuration to another, and you want to know the best order in which to work the jobs to minimize setup time. If you only have 5 jobs, you can try all 5 factorial (or 5! = 120) possible combinations to see if your code has picked the best one. If you have 10 jobs, you can still check all of the 3.6 million or so possible combinations. If you might have up to 20 jobs, however, there would be more than 2.4E18 possible combinations, and exhaustive verification is impossible. Even if you could examine 1 million combinations per second, it would take you more than 77,000 years to try every possibility.

Although exhaustive testing provides the best proof that a routine works, it's usually impractical. In that case, you need to use another method such as black box or white box testing.

Black Box Testing

In *black box testing*, you treat the routine that you are testing as an opaque black box. You put inputs in one side and results pop out the other. Because the box is black, you can't see what's going on inside. All you can do it enter inputs and see if the result is correct.

When you design black box tests, you can use information about the types of inputs and outputs that the application will actually need. For example, suppose you have a routine that gives bonuses to employees based on the number of sales they make during a year. You may know from experience that salespeople generally sell between $1 million and $10 million worth of products per year. In that case, you could test a selection of values between 1 million and 10 million. You might expand the range to cover values between 10 thousand and 100 million just to be sure you cover all of the reasonable inputs.

You should also test weird cases that are unlikely to ever occur to make sure that the program raises an appropriate error. In this example, you could see what the program does if you enter $1, $0, $-10, or $1 trillion. You should also see what the code does if you call the routine passing it no inputs at all (if that is possible for the routine).

These tests cover the normal, expected values, plus strange values that the code might not handle properly, but picking them didn't require any knowledge of how the code works. If you know how the code works, you can look for more bugs by using white box testing.

White Box Testing

White box testing is similar to black box testing, except that now you get to use information about how the code works to pick inputs that are likely to cause problems.

Suppose you know that the code in the previous example uses a `Select Case` statement to calculate bonuses that increase when a salesperson sells $1 million, $2 million, $5 million, and $10 million. In that case, you could test the code at these breakpoint values and at values one penny greater or less.

Random Testing

Random testing is exactly what it sounds like: trying the code with an assortment of randomly generated values. Because you have no way of knowing how likely a random value is to detect a bug, you usually need to run a lot of random tests to have much assurance that the code works correctly.

For example, consider the previous sales bonus example and suppose the code has trouble with values that are less than one dollar below the cutoff values $1 million, $2 million, $5 million, and $10 million. If you generate random dollar amounts between $0 and $100 million, you will have about a 4 in 100 million chance of randomly picking a value that will uncover the bug. If you run 100 thousand tests, you will only have about a 33 percent chance of detecting the bug. You'll need to run around 1 million tests to have a 98 percent chance of finding this bug.

Random testing is not a substitute for black box and white box testing. It simply gives you a chance to catch bugs using inputs that you didn't know would cause problems. The best strategy is to use all three methods: black box, white box, and random testing. Test the most typical inputs, strange inputs that might give the code problems, and a large number of random inputs.

Testing Mechanics

To test a routine, you can make another routine that calls it with various inputs and verifies that the outputs are correct. To make tracking the test routines easier, use a simple naming convention so that they are easy to find. For example, suppose you have a `ComplexNumber` class. You could put the routines that test that class in a module named `Test_ComplexNumber.vb`.

You can embed the test routines in the main application, or you can make an external testing application.

Testing Inside the Application

To embed test routines in the main application, simply create new testing modules in the application. To run the tests, add one or more testing forms to the project. Give these forms meaningful names that are similar to the test module names so that they're also easy to find. For example, you might call a test form `frmTest_ComplexNumber`.

If the test form can set up the tests easily by itself, you can change the program's startup form to the test form and run the program. Open Solution Explorer, double-click My Project, click the Application tab, and select the form in the "Startup form" drop-down, as shown in Figure 17-1. Now, when you run the application, the test form starts and you can perform the tests.

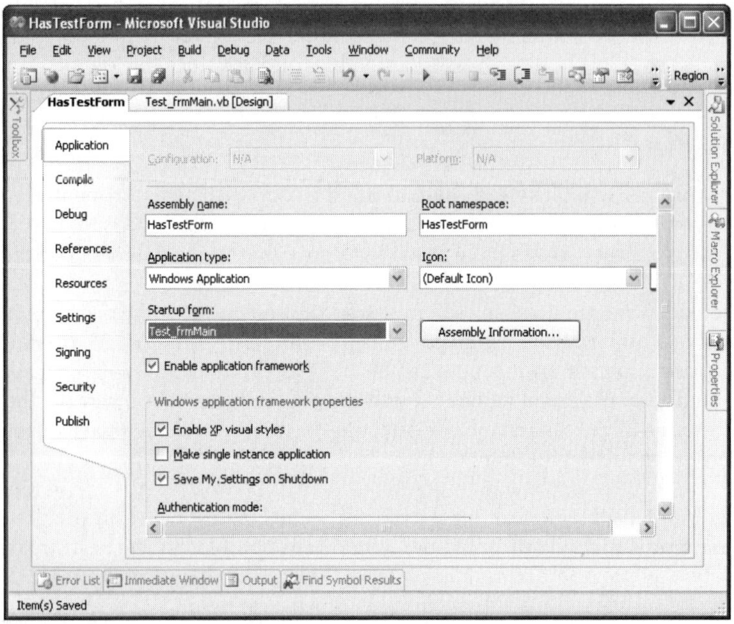

Figure 17-1: Use the "Startup form" drop-down to select the test form.

When you are finished testing, use the "Startup form" drop-down again to change the startup form back to the application's main form.

Sometimes setting up the data to run the tests is difficult. It may take you quite a while working through the application's normal forms before you get the data in a state where you can test it. In that case, it may be easier to display the test form after you have worked the application into the proper state. Add a menu item or secret key sequence that displays the test form, and hide this shortcut from the users.

One way to hide the test menu is to use a custom constant. In Solution Explorer, double-click My Project, click the Compile tab, and click the Advanced Compile Options button to display the dialog shown in Figure 17-2. Enter custom constants in the indicated text box. The dialog in Figure 17-2 sets the `SHOW_TEST_MENU` constant to `True`.

> *Rather than creating your own constant, you can use the pre-defined constant* `DEBUG`*. Then, the application will show the test menu in debug builds and not in release builds.*

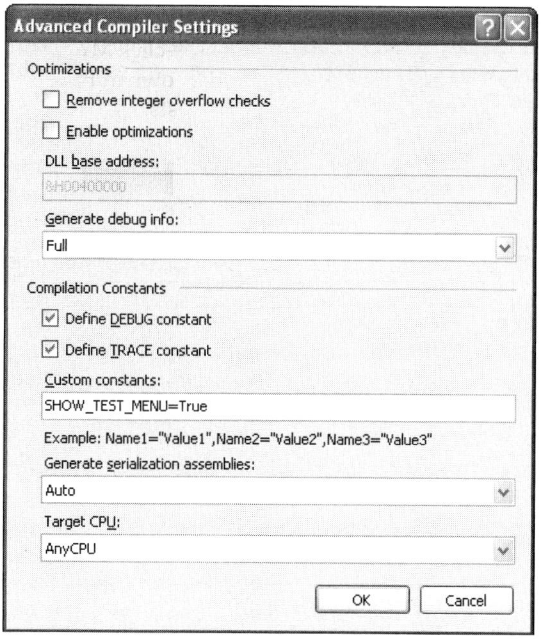

Figure 17-2: Enter custom constants in the Advanced Compiler Settings dialog.

Now, write code to check the constant and show or hide the test menu. The following code shows the `HasTestForm` example program's main form `Load` event handler. (You can download this example at `www.vb-helper.com/one_on_one.htm`.) If the `SHOW_TEST_MENU` constant is `True`, the program makes the menu `mnuTests` visible and enabled. If the constant is missing or `False`, it hides and disables the menu.

```
Private Sub frmMain_Load(ByVal sender As System.Object, _
 ByVal e As System.EventArgs) Handles MyBase.Load
    ' Hide the Tests menu unless the SHOW_TEST_MENU
    ' command line argument is defined.
#If SHOW_TEST_MENU Then
    mnuTests.Visible = True
    mnuTests.Enabled = True
#Else
    mnuTests.Visible = False
    mnuTests.Enabled = False
#End If
End Sub
```

The following code shows how the program displays the test form when you select the `Test` menu's `Main Test Form` command. It simply displays the test form modally. The code is contained in an `#If` block, so it is omitted when the `SHOW_TEST_MENU` constant is undefined or `False`.

```
' Display the test form.
Private Sub mnuTestsMainTestForm_Click(ByVal sender As System.Object, _
 ByVal e As System.EventArgs) Handles mnuTestsMainTestForm.Click
#If SHOW_TEST_MENU Then
    Dim frm As New Test_frmMain
    frm.ShowDialog()
#End If
End Sub
```

Now, you can use the application until you have created the conditions you need for testing and then display the test form.

Eventually, you will probably want to remove the testing code from the application to send the final program to the users. First, save a copy of the program with the testing code included so that you can modify and test it later.

Because you used a naming convention for the test modules and forms (for example, starting each with `Test`), you can easily find and remove those modules from the project. The only remaining references to the testing modules should be in the code that displays the test form. In the previous example, that code is contained in the `mnuTestsMainTestForm_Click` event handler. You can hide the code by setting the `SHOW_TEST_MENU` constant to `False`.

Over time, references from the main program to the testing often sneak into the code, so removing the testing code isn't as easy as you would hope. You can prevent those sorts of dependencies by periodically going through the exercise of removing the testing code to see if you can build the application without it. If you make this build fairly regularly, you won't have to make many changes when you need to build a release for the users.

Testing Outside the Application

If you test from within the application, you must be able to hide the test code from users. For example, you may need to hide and disable testing menus. You will also eventually want to remove the testing from the finished application.

Another approach is to make a separate testing application to exercise the code. This works best if you break your code into separate class libraries. Make a new executable application and add a reference to one or more of the libraries. Now, add whatever code you need to test the routines in the libraries.

Because the test application lies outside of the libraries, it can only call their public methods, so it can only perform tests at the unit level and higher. It cannot see the methods private to the libraries, so it cannot perform sub-unit level testing.

The test program also cannot see code placed in the application's main form, `Sub Main`, and other code that is not contained in libraries. This encourages you to put as much code as possible in libraries. That helps decouple the different parts of the application, so that usually gives you a more robust design in the end.

This also encourages you to separate the application's code from its user interface. That also generally leads to more modular designs that are easier to implement, test, and debug. The result is a thin user interface sitting on top of a rich set of libraries.

If you add the test application and the main program to the same Visual Studio solution, you can easily build them both in the same place. To run the test program, open Solution Explorer, right-click the test program, and select Set as Startup Project. To run the user application, open Solution Explorer, right-click the user program, and select Set as Startup Project.

A Testing Example

The `ExpressionLib` library available for download at `www.vb-helper.com/one_on_one.htm` contains a `CompiledExpression` class that lets a program evaluate mathematical expressions at run-time. The program builds a `CompiledExpression` object, passing the constructor an expression. It then calls the object's `Evaluate` method, passing it a `Dictionary` giving the names and values of variables in the expression.

For more information on how the code works, see the Microsoft Word document that comes with the download.

Figure 17-3 shows the `CompileExpression_Test` program included in the same solution. Enter an expression in the first text box, and a series of variables and their values in the second text box. When you click Evaluate, the program builds a `CompiledExpression` and evaluates the expression.

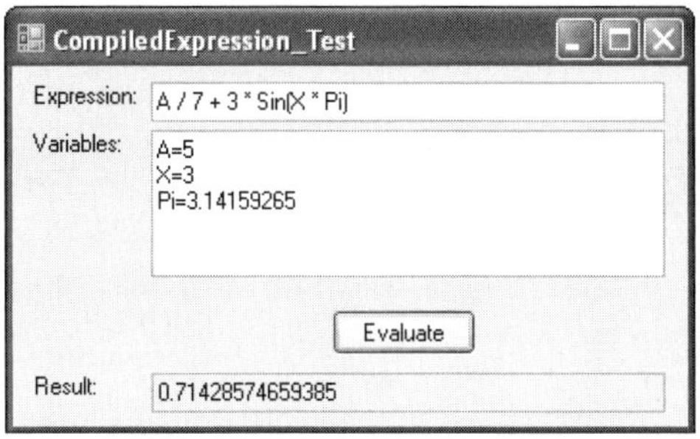

Figure 17-3: Program `CompiledExpression_Test` lets you interactively test the `CompiledExpression` class.

The `CompileExpression_Test` program provides a simple interactive user interface for the `CompiledExpression` class. It lets you evaluate expressions one at a time, but using it to thoroughly test the class would be difficult because you would need to enter a whole bunch of test expressions by hand one at a time.

The `CompileExpression_RunTests` program, also included in the same solution, automatically runs a series of tests. The code executes a series of tests to give the `CompiledExpression` class a more thorough workout.

I won't show the program's code here because it's fairly long and not central to the chapter's main ideas, but the idea is fairly simple. The `RunTest` subroutine takes as parameters an expression to evaluate and a `Dictionary` containing parameters it should use. It makes a `CompiledExpression` object and uses it to evaluate the expression.

Next, the routine uses the techniques described in Chapter 9, "Scripting," to evaluate the expression. It composes a string containing a Visual Basic function that evaluates the expression and returns the result. It then uses the `CodeDom` to compile and execute the function.

Subroutine `RunTest` then compares the result it got using the `CompiledExpression` object with the result returned by the `CodeDom` and displays the outcome in a `ListBox`. It needs to perform a few special checks to ensure that the two evaluation methods also return the same result when an error occurs. For example, if the expression is `1\0`, both methods should throw a divide-by-zero exception.

Program `CompileExpression_RunTests` starts by calling subroutine `RunTest` for a series of black box tests. These are fairly simple tests that use each of the operators handled by the `CompiledExpression` class such as `+`, `-`, `*`, `Sin`, `Cos`, and `ATan`.

Next, the program performs a series of white box tests. It uses `RunTest` to evaluate expressions that I know from the design of the class exercise more complicated aspects of the class. For example, the expressions `2+3*4` and `2+(3*4)` test operator precedence and parentheses.

The program then uses `RunTest` to evaluate some weird expressions such as `1\0`, `Sqrt(-1)`, `(-1`, and `()`. Finally, the program builds and evaluates a number of random expressions.

Figure 17-4 shows the `CompileExpression_RunTests` program in action. In this test, the program evaluated 71 pre-defined tests and 100 random tests. This part of the output shows expressions that the test code generated randomly.

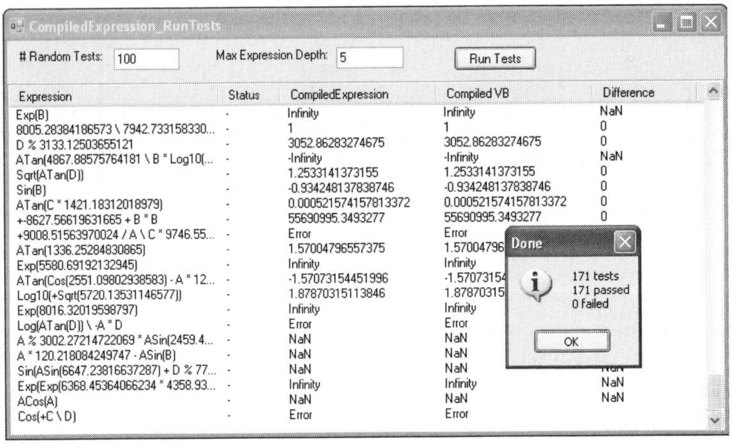

Figure 17-4: Program `CompiledExpression_RunTests` automatically performs hundreds of tests for the `CompiledExpression` class.

In the left column, you can see some of the odd equations the program evaluated. The `Status` column shows a dash if a test succeeded or `Failed` if a test failed, so finding failed tests is easy. The third and fourth columns show the results given by the `CompiledExpression` class and the `CodeDom`.

You can see that many expressions generate errors. For example, because `ASin` returns the inverse sine of a number, its input must be a valid sine value between –1 and 1, so the equation fourth from the bottom fails because it includes a call to `ASin` with an input greater than 1. While many expressions cause errors, notice that the `CompiledExpression` class and the `CodeDom` generate the same errors.

While running the tests, the program identified two bugs. First, the `CompileExpression` class was not evaluating numbers that begin with a decimal point. It only took a few minutes to track the error down and make it handle 0.1 and .1 in the same way.

The second error was a little trickier. The `CompiledExpression` class was returning the wrong result for the randomly generated expression `Tan(-(A)^-ATan(D))` where `A` = 123.456 and `D` = 2.235E+210. I added a new test to easily reproduce the error. I also added a test to evaluate the sub-expressions contained in the call to the `Tan` function and found that the inner expression `-(A)^-ATan(D)` was evaluated incorrectly, but that `-(A)` and `-ATan(D)` were calculated properly.

By simplifying the pieces that weren't working, I found that the `CompiledExpression` class returned `1` for the expression `-1^-2` while the `CodeDom` returned `-1`. Eventually, I realized that the code was not handling the unary `-` operator's precedence properly. The `CompiledExpression` class was treating the expression as `(-1)^(-2)` instead of `-(1^(-2))` as it should have.

A fairly small change to the code fixed this problem, so the class could evaluate the expression `-1^-2`. Because I had left all of the other tests in the code, including the original expression `Tan(-(A)^-ATan(D))`, I knew the fix worked for them as well. Because the test program still performs all of the other black box, white box, and random tests, regression testing is easy, and I know that the fix didn't break anything else. The lesson here is to keep all of the old tests for later use, and add new ones when you find a new bug.

The problem with the expression `-1^-2` and the others is that the `^` operator has higher precedence than the unary `-` operator. The `CompiledExpression` class was incorrectly deciding to evaluate `-1` and `-2` separately and then combine them with the `^` operator. This problem only occurred because the expression contained a unary `-` followed immediately by a `^` operator.

I initially didn't think of this unusual situation, so it wasn't covered by the black box and white box tests. It is also a pretty unlikely scenario, so it was only after several hundred random tests that the problem surfaced. The moral is that it is very difficult to think of every possible scenario, so using a large number of random tests can be very helpful.

Testing Tools

If you surf around the Web, you can find several automated testing tools that work with Visual Basic. One of the most popular (possibly because it's free) is NUnit. The current version of NUnit was written in C# and takes advantage of many of the features of the .NET Framework. It uses reflection to examine assemblies and discover classes that you build to implement tests. It then provides a simple mechanism for selecting and executing the tests, and determining whether tests succeeded or failed.

To use NUnit, download it from the NUnit Web site (`www.NUnit.com`) and install it on your system. It's a relatively small download and an easy installation.

Write the code that you want to test. Then, add a new class to test your code. Add a reference to the `nunit.framework` testing library to the test class's project. On my system, that library is at `C:\Program Files\NUnit-Net-2.0 2.2.8\bin\nunit.framework.dll`. Add an `Imports` statement to the beginning of the test module to make working with NUnit easier.

Add the `TestFixture` attribute to the test class so NUnit can tell that it should use the class for testing. The class should provide one or more public subroutines decorated with the `Test` attribute. NUnit locates those routines and runs them to test the code.

Optionally, the class can define setup and teardown routines to run before and after each test. Other attributes tell NUnit such things as whether to ignore a test, to expect a particular exception from a test (in case you want a test to throw an exception), and whether a test should be placed in a particular category.

The following code shows some of an `ExpressionLibTester` class that tests the `CompiledExpression` class much as the code described in the previous section does. The class imports the NUnit testing framework namespace, and some system namespaces that the test code uses. The `ExpressionLibTester` class is marked with the `TestFixture` attribute so that NUnit knows it is a testing class.

```
Imports NUnit.Framework
Imports System.CodeDom.Compiler
Imports System.Reflection
Imports System.Math

<TestFixture()> Public Class ExpressionLibTester
    Private m_Variables As Dictionary(Of String, Double)
    Private m_Random As New Random

    ' Create a new CompiledExpressionTest.
    Public Sub New()
        MyBase.New()
    End Sub

    ' Initialize. Prepare to run the tests.
    <TestFixtureSetUp()> Public Sub Init()
        ' Make some parameters.
        m_Variables = New Dictionary(Of String, Double)
        m_Variables.Add("A", 123.456)
        m_Variables.Add("B", 7463.218)
        m_Variables.Add("C", 0.000000367)
        m_Variables.Add("D", 2.235E+210)
    End Sub

    ' Run the basic tests.
    <Test()> Public Sub BasicTests()
        RunTest(".1", m_Variables)
        RunTest("0.1", m_Variables)
        RunTest("1234", m_Variables)
        RunTest("A", m_Variables)
        RunTest("(17)", m_Variables)
        RunTest("-13", m_Variables)
        ' Code omitted...
    End Sub
```

```
        ' This test fails.
        <Test()> Public Sub TestFails()
            RunTest("10 Mod 3", m_Variables)
        End Sub

        ' More code omitted...
    End Class
```

The class defines a dictionary to hold equation parameters, and makes a new `Random` object to use while generating random expressions.

The `TestFixtureSetUp` attribute on the `Init` subroutine tells NUnit to run the routine once before performing any tests. This routine adds some values to the expression argument dictionary.

The rest of the class contains code that tests the `CompiledExpression` class. Subroutine `BasicTests` calls the `RunTest` subroutine several times to evaluate several simple expressions. Subroutine `RunTest` uses a `CompiledExpression` object and the `CodeDom` to evaluate the expression and compares the results. If the results differ, the routine throws an exception, and NUnit reports the error. The exception's description contains the expression that caused the error, so it's easy to reproduce the problem and debug the `CompiledExpression` class.

Subroutine `TestFails` runs a test that the `CompiledExpression` cannot handle so that you can see how NUnit handles errors. The `CompiledExpression` class uses the `%` symbol to take a modulus rather than the `Mod` keyword, so it fails on the expression `10 Mod 3`.

The rest of the class contains helper routines such as subroutine `RunTest`. These aren't central to the discussion of NUnit, so they are not shown here. Download the example program to see how they work.

After you have built the testing class, you can run the NUnit graphical user interface. Use the File menu's New Project command to make a new NUnit project. Then open the Project menu, select Add Assembly, and add your compiled assembly. NUnit searches the assembly for classes marked with the `TestFixture` attribute and identifies their subroutines that are flagged with NUnit attributes. It then displays a hierarchical list of the assemblies it has examined, as well as the test classes and tests it has found.

Figure 17-5 shows NUnit after it has run a series of tests. Click an entry in the hierarchy on the left and click the Run button to execute the tests. NUnit displays a green circle next to tests that pass and a red circle next to those that fail.

In Figure 17-5, the `TestFail` subroutine is flagged with a red circle. The output window on the right shows that the test threw a `System.Exception` and that the exception's description is "Expression failed: 10 Mod 3."

NUnit works much as the code described in the previous section does. When you use the techniques described in the previous section, you must build a testing user interface to manage the tests. When you use NUnit, you can use specially designed test classes and attributes to allow NUnit to automatically provide a user interface to the tests. Otherwise, the two methods are similar and can perform the same tests.

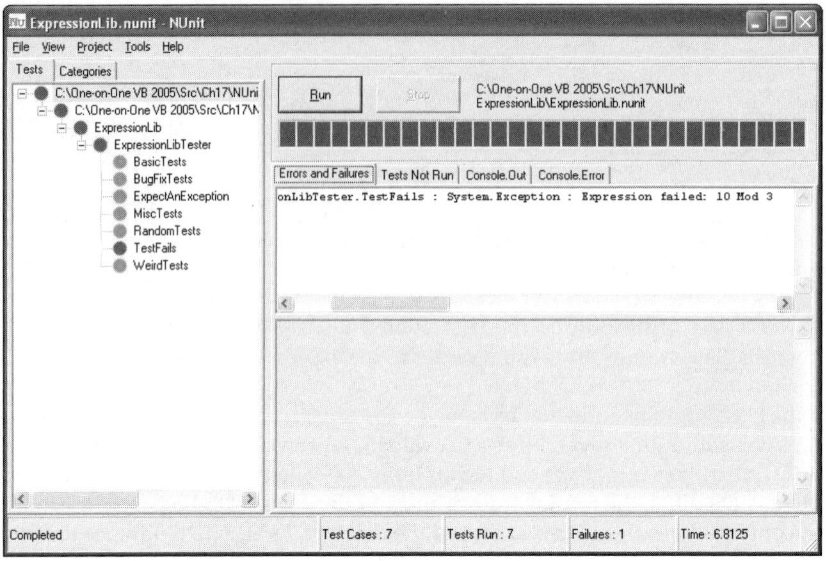

Figure 17-5: NUnit displays a red circle next to tests that fail.

Visual Studio Testing Tools

Microsoft's Visual Studio Team System (VSTS) editions include additional testing tools that are not provided in the other editions. VSTS includes several different products aimed at different types of developers. For example, Microsoft Visual Studio 2005 Team Edition for Software Testers is designed for use by developers who test software.

This edition of the product contains tools for building and managing several different types of testing, including tests similar to those described in the previous sections. For example, you can use Visual Studio to create a unit test project, and then use tools to create simple test classes marked with the `TestClass` attribute. Routines within the class marked with the `TestMethod` attribute contain the tests that the class can perform. The testing routines use `Debug.Assert` statements to throw exceptions if a test fails. All of this is very similar to the way NUnit works.

As you might expect, VSTS's testing tools are more closely integrated into the environment than NUnit. For example, in VSTS you can open Solution Explorer, right-click a test project, and select the Unit Test command. The new unit test defines a test class with initialization and cleanup methods, and a single test method, all with the appropriate attributes. The code doesn't really do anything, however, until you add some test code. Visual Studio marks key points in the code where you need to make changes with the `TODO` flag, so you can easily find them in the Task List window.

VSTS includes additional tools for performing Web tests, load tests, data-driven tests, and coverage analysis. It also allows you to create test lists so that you can group and manage tests more easily. For example, you can make lists of tests for different application subsystems.

The basic concepts of testing in VSTS are the same as those you follow in any case, so this chapter doesn't describe them in greater depth here. You can learn more about testing in Visual Studio by searching the online help for "unit test." On the Web, you can find a VSTS unit test overview at `msdn2.microsoft.com/library/ms182516.aspx`. The navigation frame on the left of this page provides links to other testing topics such as Web testing, load testing, and the Team Test API. You can learn more about VSTS at `msdn.microsoft.com/vstudio/teamsystem`.

GUI Testing

Graphical user interface (GUI) testing presents its own special problems. While you can use code to call subroutines and functions relatively easily, it's more difficult to programmatically move the mouse around, click controls, press and release the mouse buttons, and perform other GUI tasks as the user would.

The `mouse_event` API function lets your code move the mouse and click its buttons, but it's a cumbersome process requiring you to convert among form, screen, and mouse coordinate systems. The `MouseMoveClick` example program included in this chapter's download uses the `mouse_event` API function to move the mouse and click on a form.

Depending on the application, it may be quite difficult to simulate a user's actions. For example, suppose a program tracks the mouse as it moves across a form. You would need to make a series of `mouse_event` calls to gradually move the mouse, rather than simply moving it to its desired ending position.

Some commercial testing tools can capture and replay mouse movement and clicks so that you can simulate user interface actions. These tools can also take and compare form snapshots so, for example, you can require that a form have exactly the same appearance during subsequent tests. If you need that level of GUI testing, you should look into commercial testing tools.

No matter how you simulate GUI actions, you also implicitly make the assumption that the controls themselves work as you think they should. You might use `mouse_event` or a commercial capture and replay tool to simulate moving the mouse onto a control and clicking there. But what happens if the control has a different behavior if you click it in another position? If you're really paranoid, you would need to click every pixel on the control to see that it always behaves in the same way.

Usually, controls behave consistently, but that is not always the case. A user of one application I worked on was getting intermittent crashes. She would move the mouse around, click a few places, resize some panels, click some more, and sometimes the application crashed. It could happen after a few minutes, a few hours, or not at all. She was unable to figure out how to reliably reproduce the problem and I couldn't duplicate it.

Eventually, we both flew to the same place so I could watch her break the program. It took about 10 minutes (during which she began doubting her sanity). After I experimented with the program for a while, I found the problem. A particular window on one form was resizable. If you shrunk it so it disappeared, the program was fine. If you enlarged it so that it was two or more pixels tall, there was no problem. But if you happened to make the window exactly one pixel tall, the control crashed. We added some code to make the control at least two pixels tall and called the bug fixed.

This is an extremely difficult bug to find. Generally, you assume that controls work as intended and that they behave consistently. To find this particular problem through automated testing, you would have had to get unbelievably lucky, or you would have had to try making the control hundreds of different sizes. The application contained hundreds of other controls, too, so you would have to run millions of tests to catch this sort of thing in every conceivable situation. This level of testing is generally impractical, but it's worth keeping in mind that controls are not necessarily completely perfect, and that some amount of manually trying weird things is worthwhile.

A final lesson from this story is that you should take users' comments seriously, no matter how bizarre they may sound. Users may not always report exactly what they experience in precise technical terms, but if they say there is a problem, chances are good that something is wrong.

Another technique for simulating mouse events and other events caught by controls is to use the controls' "`OnEvent`" methods. For example, you can use a form's `OnMouseDown`, `OnMouseMove`, and `OnMouseUp` methods to send `MouseDown`, `MouseMove`, and `MouseUp` events to the form.

The `SimulateMouseDraw` sample program (available for download at `www.vb-helper.com/one_on_one.htm`) uses the following code to let you draw on its form. The `MouseDown` event handler saves the mouse's current position. The `MouseMove` event handler draws from the previous position to the mouse's new position. The `MouseUp` event handler sets `m_Drawing` to `False` to indicate that no more drawing is in progress.

```
Private m_Drawing As Boolean = False
Private m_LastPoint As Point = Nothing

' Start drawing.
Private Sub Form1_MouseDown(ByVal sender As Object, _
 ByVal e As System.Windows.Forms.MouseEventArgs) Handles Me.MouseDown
    m_Drawing = True
    m_LastPoint = New Point(e.X, e.Y)
    Dim gr As Graphics = Me.CreateGraphics()
    gr.Clear(Me.BackColor)
End Sub

' Continue drawing.
Private Sub Form1_MouseMove(ByVal sender As Object, _
 ByVal e As System.Windows.Forms.MouseEventArgs) Handles Me.MouseMove
    If Not m_Drawing Then Exit Sub
    Dim gr As Graphics = Me.CreateGraphics()
    gr.DrawLine(Pens.Blue, m_LastPoint, New Point(e.X, e.Y))
    m_LastPoint = New Point(e.X, e.Y)
End Sub

' Stop drawing.
Private Sub Form1_MouseUp(ByVal sender As Object, _
 ByVal e As System.Windows.Forms.MouseEventArgs) Handles Me.MouseUp
    m_Drawing = False
End Sub
```

Program `SimulateMouseDraw` uses the following code to programmatically simulate drawing:

```
' Simulate manual drawing by using mouse_event.
Private Sub btnSimulatedDraw_Click(ByVal sender As System.Object, _
 ByVal e As System.EventArgs) Handles btnSimulatedDraw.Click
    Dim cx As Integer = Me.ClientSize.Width \ 2
    Dim cy As Integer = Me.ClientSize.Height \ 2
    Dim radius As Integer = _
        Math.Min(Me.ClientSize.Width, Me.ClientSize.Height) \ 3

    ' MouseDown.
    Dim down_args As New MouseEventArgs( _
        Windows.Forms.MouseButtons.Left, _
        0, _
        CInt(cx + radius * Cos(0)), _
        CInt(cy + radius * Sin(0)), _
        0)
    Me.OnMouseDown(down_args)

    ' Move the mouse around in a randomized circle.
    Dim rnd As New Random
    For angle As Double = PI / 10 To 6 * PI Step PI / 10
        Dim move_args As New MouseEventArgs( _
            Windows.Forms.MouseButtons.Left, _
            0, _
            CInt(cx + radius * Cos(angle) + rnd.Next(-20, 20)), _
            CInt(cy + radius * Sin(angle) + rnd.Next(-20, 20)), _
            0)
        Me.OnMouseMove(move_args)
    Next angle

    ' Connect back to the first point.
    Me.OnMouseMove(down_args)

    ' MouseUp.
    Me.OnMouseUp(down_args)
End Sub
```

The code creates a `MouseEventArgs` object to hold information about the mouse's current position. It calls the form's `OnMouseDown` method to generate a `MouseDown` event. The event handler shown earlier handles the event as if the user had pressed the mouse's button down.

Next, the code generates a series of points, and uses the form's `OnMouseMove` method to simulate the user moving the mouse. The program's `MouseMove` event handler catches the events and draws.

Finally, the code uses the form's `OnMouseUp` method to simulate the user releasing the mouse.

This technique is much simpler than using the `mouse_event` API function.

The final approach to GUI testing described here is to make event handlers as thin as possible, and simply pass requests on to subroutines that implement the necessary behavior. The following code shows new versions of the drawing program's `MouseDown`, `MouseMove`, and `MouseUp` event handlers. They simply call the corresponding routines `DoMouseDown`, `DoMouseMove`, and `DoMouseUp`.

```
' Start drawing.
Private Sub Form1_MouseDown(ByVal sender As Object, _
 ByVal e As System.Windows.Forms.MouseEventArgs) Handles Me.MouseDown
    DoMouseDown(e.X, e.Y)
End Sub

' Continue drawing.
Private Sub Form1_MouseMove(ByVal sender As Object, _
 ByVal e As System.Windows.Forms.MouseEventArgs) Handles Me.MouseMove
    DoMouseMove(e.X, e.Y)
End Sub

' Stop drawing.
Private Sub Form1_MouseUp(ByVal sender As Object, _
 ByVal e As System.Windows.Forms.MouseEventArgs) Handles Me.MouseUp
    DoMouseUp()
End Sub
```

The following code shows the `DoMouseDown`, `DoMouseMove`, and `DoMouseUp` routines. They perform the same tasks as the event handlers in the earlier example.

```
' Start drawing.
Private Sub DoMouseDown(ByVal x As Integer, ByVal y As Integer)
    m_Drawing = True
    m_LastPoint = New Point(x, y)
    Dim gr As Graphics = Me.CreateGraphics()
    gr.Clear(Me.BackColor)
End Sub

' Continue drawing.
Private Sub DoMouseMove(ByVal x As Integer, ByVal y As Integer)
    If Not m_Drawing Then Exit Sub
    Dim gr As Graphics = Me.CreateGraphics()
    gr.DrawLine(Pens.Blue, m_LastPoint, New Point(x, y))
    m_LastPoint = New Point(x, y)
End Sub

' Stop drawing.
Private Sub DoMouseUp()
    m_Drawing = False
End Sub
```

Finally, the following code uses the new routines to simulate the user drawing. This code is somewhat simpler than the earlier version because it doesn't need to build `MouseEventArgs` objects. Instead, it calls the "`Do`" methods directly, passing them only the data they need instead of a more complicated `MouseEventArgs` object.

```
' Simulate manual drawing by using mouse_event.
Private Sub btnSimulatedDraw_Click(ByVal sender As System.Object, _
 ByVal e As System.EventArgs) Handles btnSimulatedDraw.Click
    Dim cx As Integer = Me.ClientSize.Width \ 2
    Dim cy As Integer = Me.ClientSize.Height \ 2
    Dim radius As Integer = Math.Min(Me.ClientSize.Width, Me.ClientSize.Height) \ 3
```

```
        ' MouseDown.
        DoMouseDown( _
            CInt(cx + radius * Cos(0)), _
            CInt(cy + radius * Sin(0)))

        ' Move the mouse around in a randomized circle.
        Dim rnd As New Random
        For angle As Double = PI / 10 To 6 * PI Step PI / 10
            DoMouseMove( _
                CInt(cx + radius * Cos(angle) + rnd.Next(-20, 20)), _
                CInt(cy + radius * Sin(angle) + rnd.Next(-20, 20)))
        Next angle

        ' Connect back to the first point.
        DoMouseMove( _
            CInt(cx + radius * Cos(0)), _
            CInt(cy + radius * Sin(0)))

        ' MouseUp.
        DoMouseUp()
    End Sub
```

Many developers argue that you should use this thin event-handler approach to separate the user interface from the implementation code in case you want to give the application a new user interface at some later date. The most obvious reason you might want to do this would be to make both desktop and Web versions of an application. The two environments are so different, however, that you may want to change other aspects of the application design instead of simply patching a new interface over the existing code.

I suggest that you initially keep the code as simple as possible. If you think it's easier to understand or test code with the extra "`Do`" routine layer, by all means add it. If it's easier for you to think of working with the event handlers directly and using the "`OnEvent`" methods to simulate GUI testing, omit the "`Do`" routine layer. You can add the extra layer relatively easily later if you need it.

Summary

Most developers leave testing for relatively late in the project. They write a bunch of code, perhaps test it superficially, and then wait until integration testing or even system testing before the code really gets a workout.

The later you detect a bug, the more difficult it is to fix, so it's well worth the extra effort to test code early and often. One of the big benefits of agile methods that require frequent releases is that the code must be tested often.

When you write a new piece of code, write a test to go with it (or even write the tests first). Do a thorough job of testing so that you can move on with confidence that the code won't break the first time it is called by another routine. Save all tests for later use in regression testing.

Whether you use the free NUnit tool, VSTS testing tools, or some other commercial testing product, you need to write the actual test code yourself. You'll be more than repaid in time saved later, however.

After you have written, debugged, and tested your application, you need to deploy it. The program won't do users any good until they install it on their systems. Chapter 18, "Deployment," explains some of the deployment strategies available for Visual Basic .NET applications. It describes ClickOnce deployment, Windows Installer deployment, and Xcopy deployment, and gives the advantages and disadvantages of each.

18

Deployment

When you build an application for yourself, you can simply run the executable created by Visual Basic. If you are building the application for others, however, you need to make it possible for them to install the program on their computers.

Visual Studio gives you a couple of options for building installation packages, including ClickOnce deployment, Windows Installer setup projects, `Xcopy`, and `RoboCopy` deployment.

> *The section "Xcopy" later in this chapter says more about* `Xcopy` *and* `RoboCopy` *deployment. In brief, however,* `Xcopy` *deployment simply means copying a program and all of the files that it needs to work onto the target computer. You don't need to register the executable, DLLs, or any other object, and you don't need to modify the Registry.* `RoboCopy` *is the next version of* `Xcopy` *provided in the Vista operating system.*

Before you start churning out deployment packages, however, it's worth taking a few minutes to consider deployment in the abstract. A clear idea of how and when you want to provide releases to users can make things easier for you and them.

Deployment Models

Before getting into the details about deployment options available for Visual Basic applications, it's worth thinking about deployment on a higher level. Before you plan a deployment strategy, you should decide what type of deployment is appropriate for your users. You should ask yourself how quickly users will want new releases, and how much effort they will be willing to spend downloading, installing, and configuring new releases.

User Types

When you pick a deployment method, you should think about the kinds of users that will be installing the application.

First consider the amount of emotional and monetary investment the users are putting into your application. If your application is a relatively small utility that is available for free on the Internet, then users will probably be unwilling to spend a huge amount of time downloading, installing, and configuring it. A user who clicks your download link and discovers that it will take 17 hours to finish will probably cancel the download and search the Web for another tool. Similarly, if users must spend an hour wading through complicated configuration screens before using the application, they may decide to search for a more user-friendly solution.

If users have little investment in your application, you must make download and installation as fast and painless as possible. ClickOnce deployment is extremely simple, although it is a relatively new technology, so many users may be unfamiliar with it. It is easy enough for novice computer users, however. `Xcopy` deployment is also fairly simple and is intuitive for those with some computer experience, so it also works well with these non-captive users.

Configuration must also be as simple as possible. The application should start with a default configuration that works in most situations. (It can provide more-advanced options for users who have special needs and, therefore, have a greater need for your program.)

These less-dedicated users don't register their product and don't install updates unless they contain something really useful. You have little hold over these casual users, so they will run at the first sign of trouble.

In contrast, if your application is a mission-critical tool that costs thousands of dollars, users will be willing to spend a lot more time and effort installing the application. They will wait for longer downloads, although many users who spend thousands on software also spend the few extra dollars per month needed to get high-speed Internet connections, so their download will be faster than the casual user working with a modem. They are often willing to wait for you to mail them the application on CD-ROM or DVD, and they often expect accompanying packaging and printed documentation.

For these more-committed users, it is still worthwhile to provide a default configuration that handles most situations, although many of them will customize their installations at some point. These users are more likely to register their products, read emails describing bug fixes and enhancements, and install updates.

Of course, there are many exceptions to these rules. There are non–mission-critical applications that have very dedicated users. For example, many game players will spend hours downloading the latest modifications and enhancements to their games even though they are not exactly mission-critical.

Though anti-virus and anti-spyware software doesn't cost thousands of dollars, it is mission-critical, and users have enormous incentives to keep these programs up-to-date.

Conversely, sometimes users have little incentive to update very important applications. Visual Basic itself provides an excellent example. I know many developers who still use Visual Basic 6, even though Visual Basic .NET is clearly a better platform. The reason many developers don't upgrade is that they have a large base of existing code that would cost a lot of time and money to rewrite. Their existing programs work well enough with Visual Basic 6, so they have little incentive to upgrade.

When thinking about your users, you must understand what motivates them. Does your application provide features that they will want badly enough to download and install the software? Do your upgrades provide features that will motivate the users? Does registration get the users notices of upgrades or other extra information that they will want enough to bother with registering?

While you ask yourself these questions, remember that initially you have no existing users. Once users have installed your program and they find out how useful it is, they may be willing to go to more trouble to install updates. Until users have installed your program for the first time, however, they have little invested in it.

Major and Minor Releases

A very common release strategy uses major and minor releases. Periodically, you release a major version of the application containing important new features, enhancements, and bug fixes. Usually vendors make customers pay for new major releases.

Between major releases, you release minor or "point" releases to fix bugs in the most recent major release.

In recent years, Microsoft has also added a third tier of release: the Service Pack. Microsoft provides minor releases to fix large numbers of bugs all at once, and Service Packs to fix individual bugs or smaller groups of bugs between point releases. Often, the Service Packs address security issues or incompatibilities among various products.

When I started programming under the VMS operating system, we got major releases about once per year, and one or two minor releases per year, which we sometimes didn't bother to install. Rarely did we get a high-priority security release. Lately, users have become accustomed to major releases every year or two with frequent point releases and, in Microsoft's case at least, very frequent Service Packs. It's not uncommon to have several high-priority Service Pack releases in the same week.

Just because users have become used to this, however, doesn't mean they like it. Overly frequent releases are annoying and disruptive. They take up the users' time and may make the application incompatible with other applications that they must then update. To minimize customer annoyance, you should try not to churn out releases too quickly.

This rule, too, has its exceptions. Critical operating system security patches and virus protection software often must be updated very frequently. Even then, however, users complain if they receive updates too often. Requiring mandatory security patches every day for a week (and I've seen it happen) is very annoying, and gives the impression that the software was poorly written in the first place.

For those programs that do provide frequent updates, most make the process as painless as possible. They check for updates automatically and give the user some options for installing them immediately, later, or not at all (if it's not mandatory).

Agile Releases

Agile development methods require frequent releases. Just because you build frequent releases, however, doesn't mean you need to give them to the users. A large part of the benefit of frequent releases in agile development is that they force you to bring the application into a consistent state and thoroughly test it. If you do this frequently, any new bugs cannot have been in the application for too long, so they are easier to find and fix. The point is to make the code more reliable, not to bury the users in a landslide of rapid releases.

Suppose you are working on an application that is used by several hundred corporate users. Every time you give them a new release, the users must spend some time learning about the new features. If you have 200 users and it takes them only 30 minutes to read about, try, and get comfortable with the new features (usually it takes longer), then every release costs the company 100 hours of lost productivity. Users also may become frustrated at the frequent changes, and they may not use the new features anyway. It's usually better to provide fewer releases with more substance than to hand out lots of little releases.

One approach to make moving to new features easier is to add new features without removing existing ones, at least initially. When the user accesses an older feature, the program displays a tooltip describing the new feature. As long as the user isn't forced to use the new feature, learning about new ones can be entertaining, rather than threatening.

Instead of inundating the users with a new release every month, you can skip releases and only give the users a new release when the program contains a nice assortment of new features. Alternatively, you can make the more frequent releases available, but make them point releases and let the users know that they are not mandatory. Tell users what new features are available in the point releases, and let them decide whether it's worth installing the new version.

Deployment Methods

There are three basic strategies for deploying Visual Basic applications: ClickOnce, Windows Installer, and `Xcopy`. ClickOnce deployment makes providing automatic updates relatively easy. Windows Installer provides greater flexibility than the other methods, although it requires more work and doesn't automatically check for needed libraries as ClickOnce deployment does. An `Xcopy` deployment simply copies the files in a project onto the target computer.

ClickOnce

ClickOnce deployment provides a lot of useful support for you automatically. It gives you a good deal of control over when the user is required to check for updates, and allows you to distribute only the modified pieces of an application to the user, rather than an entirely new application.

Because ClickOnce deployment allows simple updates and lets you specify when the user must update the application, it is a good choice for projects that must be updated frequently. As explained earlier in this chapter, however, frequent updates can take up a considerable amount of the users' time, and can annoy and frustrate the users, so you shouldn't abuse this power. You should only require updates when the new features are either essential (such as critical security patches) or transparent to the user.

To publish a ClickOnce application, open Solution Explorer and double-click the My Project entry to view the project's properties. Open the Publish tab, click the Publish Wizard button, and use the wizard to configure the installation.

Rather than rehashing the material available in the help files and on the Microsoft Web site, this section describes the options available for ClickOnce installation and updates, and discusses when they might be most appropriate. You can check the online help for more detailed instructions on selecting these options.

Installation Methods

You can pick from three methods for installing a ClickOnce application. First, you can install the application from a Web site or a network share. This method downloads the application's components as necessary from the installation location, and installs them on the user's computer. Because this downloads the application's components, it works best if the user is likely to have a fast Internet connection, or if the user will have access to a local network containing the installation package, as is often the case when you are writing an application for internal company use and you can deploy it on the company network.

The second installation method is to configure the application to start from a Web site or a network share. In this version, a link on the Web site or a shortcut on the network share leads to the application. When the user clicks the link or double-clicks the shortcut, the application is downloaded to the user's computer and executes, but the application is not permanently installed. The application is cached as Web pages are, so the user can run it again without downloading it if it is still in the cache. If the application has been removed from cache, clicking the link or double-clicking the shortcut downloads the application again.

Because downloading the application can take awhile, this approach works best if the user only needs to run the application very rarely, and when the user has a high-speed Internet connection or fast network.

If the user will use the application frequently, it makes more sense to use one of the other methods to install a copy of the application on the user's computer. Then, when the user runs the application, the system only needs to update modified components, rather than downloading the whole application again. Disk space is so inexpensive these days that it's not worth making the user wait to save a little disk space.

The third method for installing a ClickOnce application is from a CD-ROM, DVD, or other removable media. In this scenario, the user still needs access to a network or the Internet to look for updates, but the initial installation can be much quicker than it would be over a slow network connection. This can be a huge benefit for users who do not already have the .NET Framework installed. The first time they install a .NET application, the computer installs the massive Framework. Subsequent updates only need to install the relatively small changes to the application that you make. This type of installation is also useful if your program needs a large amount of data. If you are building a mapping application that comes with 5GB of map data, many users will prefer to receive the files in one or more DVDs instead of downloading them.

Many users prefer the instant gratification of downloading and installing an application directly from the Web, but this method is particularly useful for users with slower network connections. Even if you use the first option to let users install directly from the Internet, you may also want to make CD-ROMs or DVDs available for those with slower connections.

Update Methods

After a user initially installs an application, the program can automatically check for any updates that you make available. To set update options, open Solution Explorer, double-click the My Projects entry, open the Publish tab, and click the Updates button to display the dialog shown in Figure 18-1.

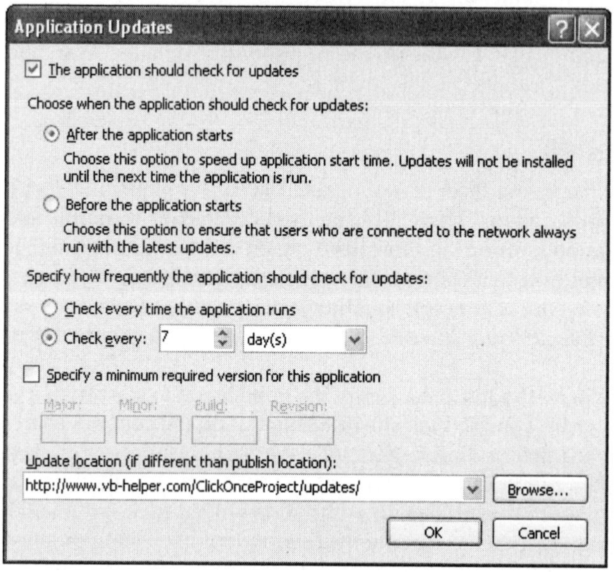

Figure 18-1: Use the Application Updates dialog to indicate when a ClickOnce application should check for updates.

Check the "The application should check for updates" box to make the application look for updates when it runs.

If you check the "After the application starts" radio button, the program looks for updates asynchronously when it starts. If it finds an update, it installs it the next time the application runs.

If you check the "Before the application starts" radio button, the program checks for updates before it runs. If an update is available, the system downloads and installs it before running the program.

Use the next two radio buttons to specify how often the program should check for updates. You can make the application look for updates every time it runs, or after a specified number of hours, days, or weeks.

Updates are not normally mandatory. If you want to require users to have a particular version installed, check the "Specify a minimum required version for this application" box and enter the required version information in the Major, Minor, Build, and Revision text boxes. If the user has an older version installed, the program requires an update before it will run. If you want to force users to keep up to date, you can set this to the most recent version every time you publish a build.

All of this is great if you have an always-on Internet connection. Automatic updates and mandatory versions are much more difficult to handle if you don't have a good network connection. They can also be difficult for users who work on a secure network with strong firewalls. Before you require mandatory version-checking and updates, consider your users. If you are writing software for use inside your company, and all of the users sit on the same side of the firewall, these sorts of updates may be no problem. If your users are scattered all over the Internet and may want to run your program on computers with no network connections, mandatory updates may prevent them from using your application.

CD-ROM Installation with Web Updates

A particularly useful deployment combination uses an initial installation from CD-ROM or DVD, followed by updates downloaded from the Web. The installation includes the application plus the 26+ MB required for the .NET Framework. The updates include only changes to the application, so they are much smaller.

To use this deployment scenario, open Solution Explorer, double-click the My Projects entry, and open the Publish tab shown in Figure 18-2. Select the "The application is available offline as well" radio button.

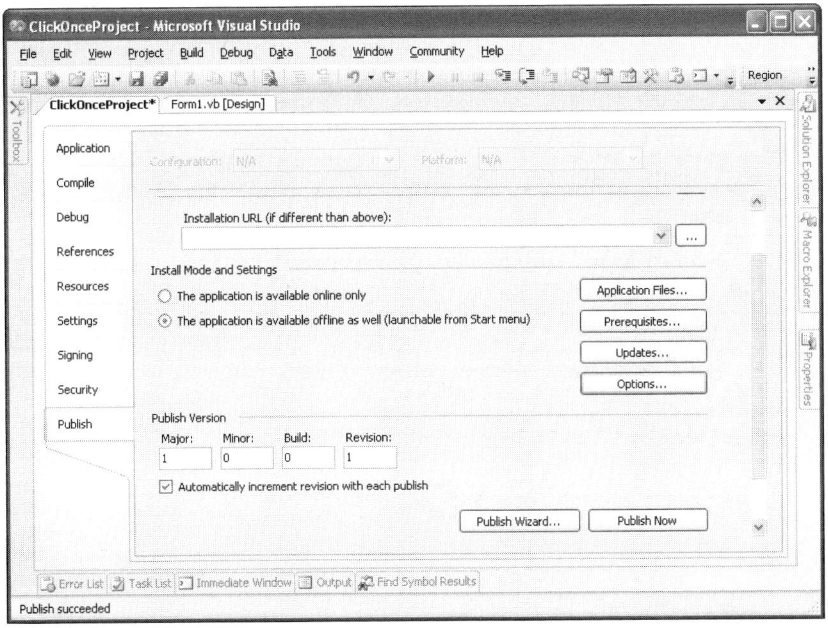

Figure 18-2: The Publish tab lets you set deployment options and publish the application.

To indicate that the .NET Framework should be included in the initial installation, click the Prerequisites button to display the dialog shown in Figure 18-3. Verify that the top checkbox and the .NET Framework checkbox are checked. Select the "Download prerequisites from the same location as my application" radio button and click OK.

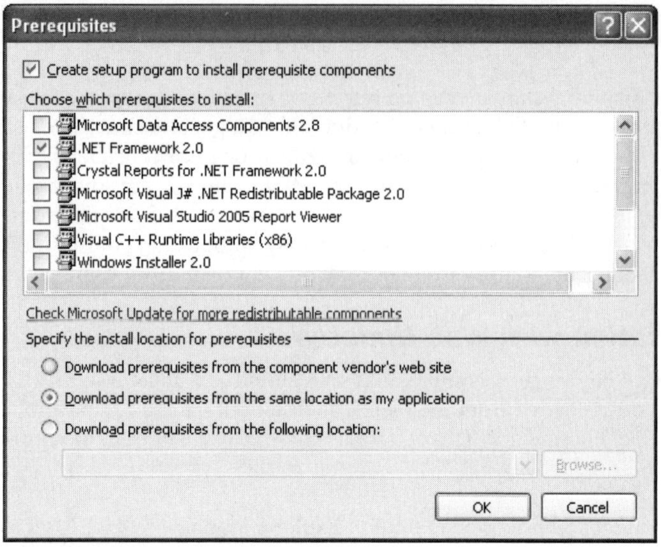

Figure 18-3: Use the Prerequisites dialog to include the .NET Framework in the installation.

Return to the Publish tab shown in Figure 18-2 and click the Publish Wizard button to display the wizard's first page shown in Figure 18-4. Enter the file path where you want to put the installation files. The default is `publish/`, which indicates a subdirectory inside the application's project directory.

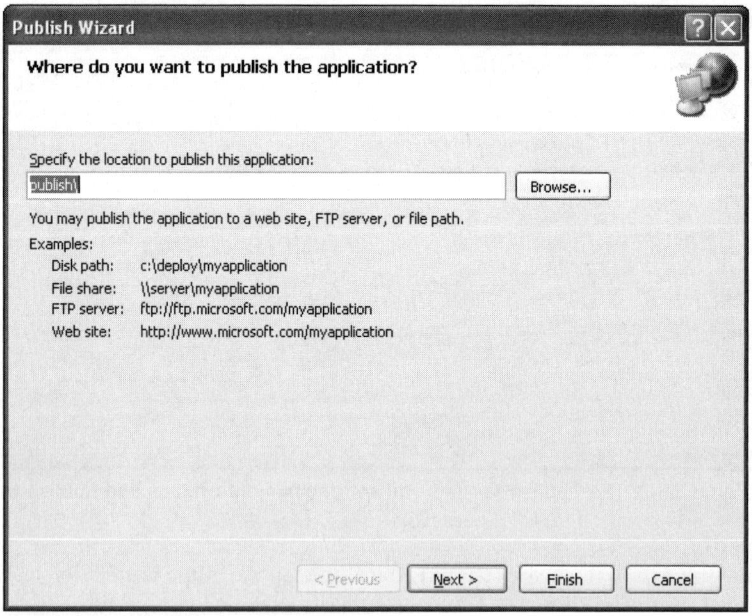

Figure 18-4: Enter the path where you want to put the installation files.

Click Next to display the Publish Wizard's second page shown in Figure 18-5. Select the "From a CD-ROM or DVD-ROM" option.

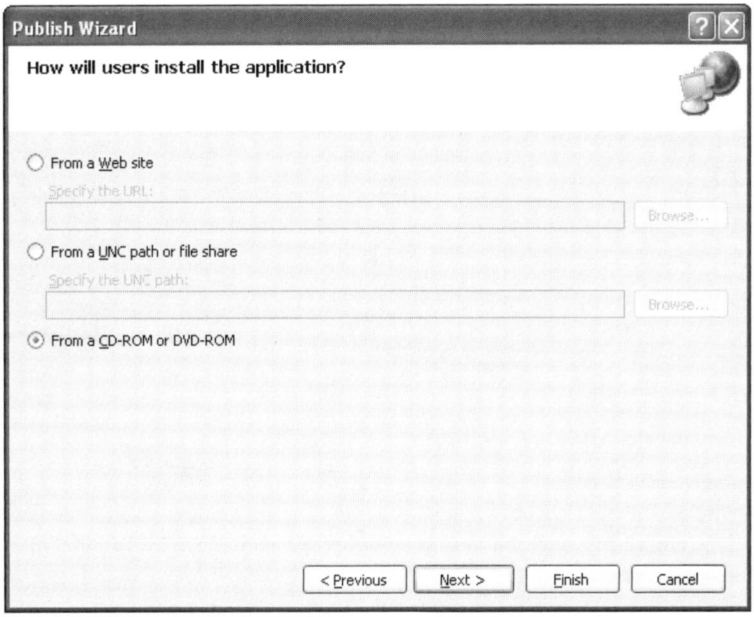

Figure 18-5: Use this page to specify where users will install the application.

Click Next to display the Publish Wizard's third page, shown in Figure 18-6. Select the first radio button and enter the URL where you will post updates.

Click Next to see a brief summary of the options you selected, or click Finish to build the installation package.

The Publish Wizard builds the installation directory. This directory contains a `setup.exe` program to begin the installation and some manifest files, which are XML files describing the application's setup. It also contains two directories.

The `ClickOnceProject_1_0_0_0` directory contains another manifest describing its contents and the actual application data. The directory's name includes the application's name (`ClickOnceProject`) and its version information (`1.0.0.0`).

The second subdirectory in the installation directory is called `dotnetfx`. It contains a Windows Installer application and the .NET Framework.

Copy the installation directory's contents onto a CD-ROM or DVD and give it to your users. When the user double-clicks `setup.exe`, the program installs the .NET Framework and your application. That could take a while, even from a CD-ROM or DVD. The program then installs your application, which should be much faster.

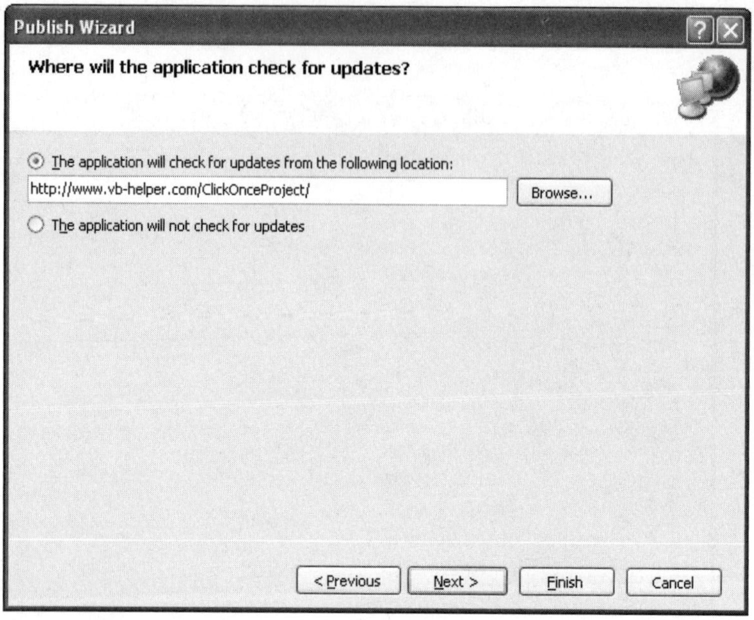

Figure 18-6: Select the first radio button and enter the URL where you will post updates.

To make an update, modify the program, build it, and test it. Then open the Publish tab and click the Publish Now button. Visual Studio will add new files to the publish directory for the new version. For this example, those files include new versions of the `ClickOnceProject.application` manifest and `setup.exe`. It also includes a completely new `ClickOnceProject_1_0_0_1` application manifest and `ClickOnceProject_1_0_0_1` project directory for the new version (assuming the new publish version is 1.0.0.1).

Copy the two new manifests and the `ClickOnceProject_1_0_0_1` directory to the update URL. Now, when a user runs your application, the program can find the update if necessary. When it does find an update, the program only needs to download the changes, not the huge .NET Framework or even the smaller `setup.exe` program.

Remember to set the update options you want in the Application Updates dialog shown in Figure 18-1. Testing is usually easiest if you make the application check for updates before it runs so that you can see the check each time you run the program.

Windows Installer

Like ClickOnce deployment, Windows Installer builds application installation packages. Windows Installer has some advantages and disadvantages compared to ClickOnce.

ClickOnce deployment installs an application and creates a shortcut for it at a default in the system's Start menu.

Windows Installer gives you much more freedom about where things are installed. It lets you put the application's output file (the executable or DLL) and other files in specific locations such as the installation directory, Desktop, `Common Files` folder, `Fonts` folder, `System` folder, and others. It also lets you create shortcuts in a specific location in the Start menu, in the Start menu itself, in special folders such as the `Desktop` or `System` folder, the Startup and Send To menus, and more.

Unlike ClickOnce, Windows Installer can also write to the Registry, install more than one product at a time, install services, install to the Global Assembly Cache (GAC), register COM components, and make an application available to multiple users. It even lets you execute code to perform custom actions after the installation is complete, so you can perform tasks that Windows Installer cannot handle for you.

Still, Windows Installer has some drawbacks. It's not as easy to program or use as ClickOnce. It also doesn't provide automatic update checking or mandatory updates, and it cannot require the application to run only while online.

For more information about the differences between ClickOnce and Windows Installer, see the article "Choosing Between ClickOnce and Windows Installer" (`http://msdn.microsoft.com/library/en-us/dndotnet/html/clickoncevsinstaller.asp`) by Michael Sanford. It contains a useful overview of both technologies and gives some advice about which to use in different circumstances. "Introduction to ClickOnce Deployment" (`http://msdn.microsoft.com/vbasic/learning/clickonce/`) also describes ClickOnce deployment and compares it with Windows Installer.

To make a Windows Installer application, open your project. Open the File menu's Add submenu and select New project. Expand the Other Project Types entry in the tree view on the left, and select the Setup Project template, as shown in Figure 18-7. Enter a project name and location, and click OK.

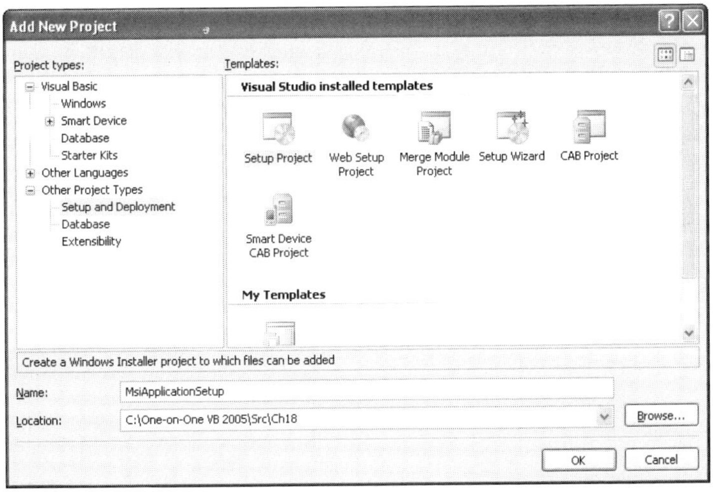

Figure 18-7: Use the Setup Project template to make a Windows Installer application.

Figure 18-8 shows a setup project. The left column shows locations on the target computer. Right-click the topmost File System on Target Machine entry and open the Add Special Folder context menu to add other folders to the list.

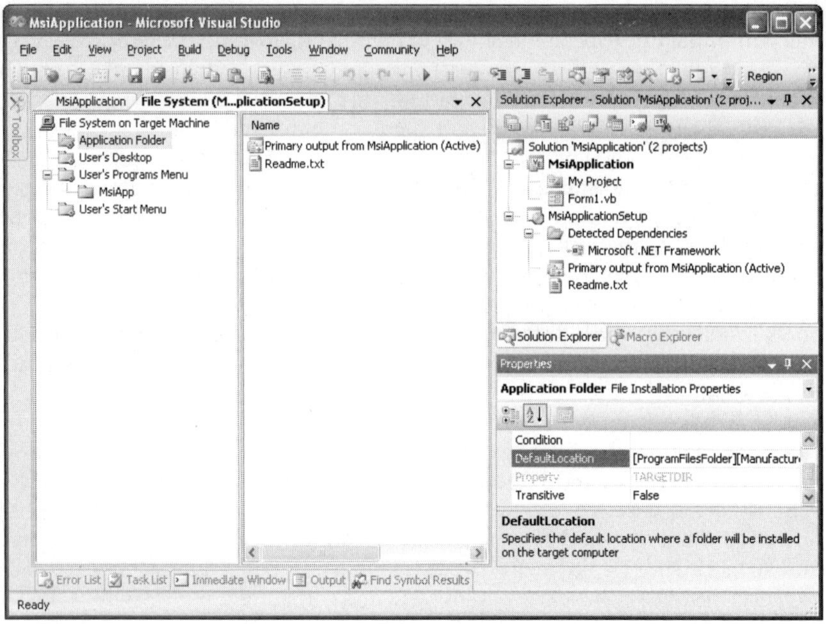

Figure 18-8: A setup project builds a Windows Installer `.msi` file.

Right-click on a folder to manage that folder. Open the Add submenu to add new items to the folder, such as a project output (for example, an executable or DLL), subfolder, file, or assembly.

The middle column shows items within the folder selected on the left. Right-click in this column and pick Create New Shortcut to add a new shortcut to the folder. The dialog shown in Figure 18-9 lets you select project items for the shortcut's target. In a typical example, you would put the application's output (the executable) in the Application Folder. Using the dialog shown in Figure 18-9, you can browse to that output and make a shortcut point to it.

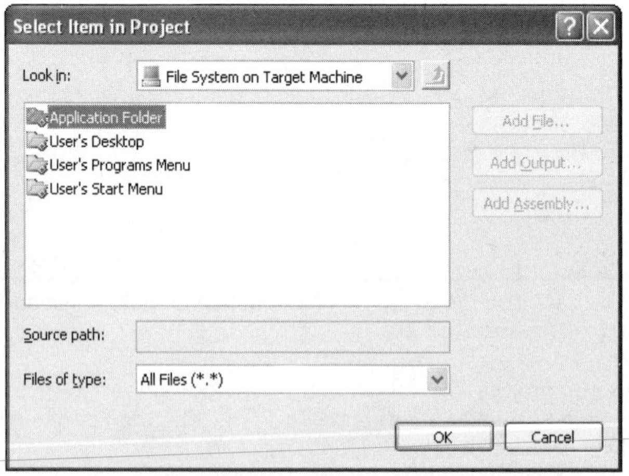

Figure 18-9: Use this dialog to select a shortcut's target.

The right column in Figure 18-8 shows the Solution Explorer and Properties windows. The Solution Explorer entry for the setup application shows any files that will be installed with this program. In this example, the project will install the output of the `MsiApplication` project and the file `Readme.txt` in the target computer's application folder.

Just as you may want to include prerequisite files such as the .NET Framework in a ClickOnce deployment, you may want to include the same files in a Windows Installer project. To make the project include prerequisite files, select the project in Solution Explorer. Select the Project menu's Properties command to display the project's property pages as shown in Figure 18-10.

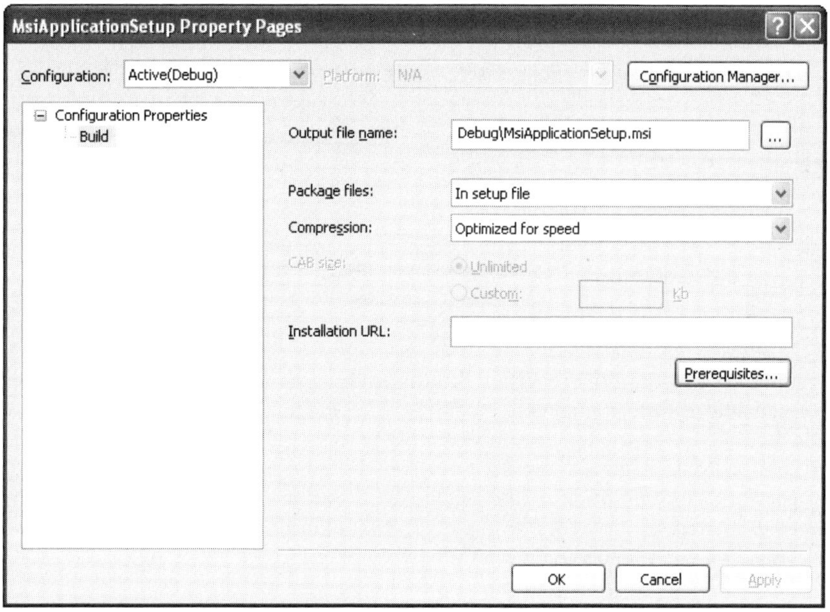

Figure 18-10: Click the Prerequisites button to make a Windows Installer project include prerequisite files.

Click the Prerequisites button to display the dialog shown in Figure 18-11.

Check the box at the top to make the project install the prerequisite files. Check the files you want to install in the middle list box. Use the radio buttons at the bottom to determine where the installer should get the files and click OK.

The options selected in Figure 18-11 make the setup project include the .NET Framework files in the installation. When you build the project, the solution includes an `.msi` file that tells Windows Installer what to do, and that includes the main program's code. The solution directory also includes a `dotnetfx` directory that includes executable files that the Installer will use to install the Framework.

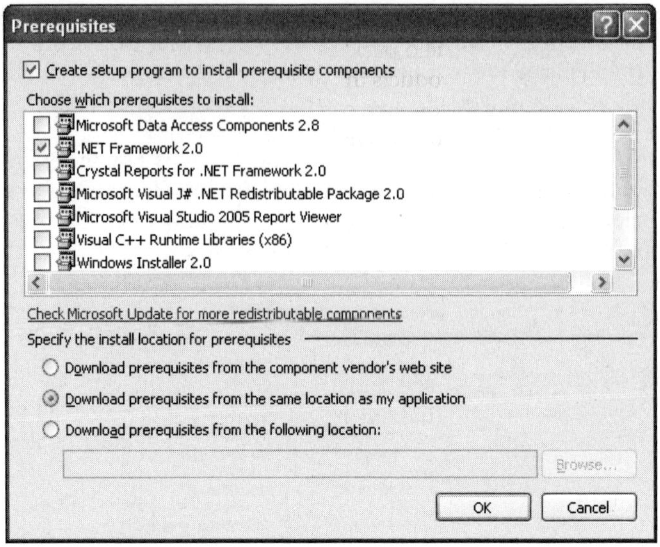

Figure 18-11: This dialog lets you indicate if and how the installation installs prerequisite files.

When you compile the setup project, Visual Studio produces an `.msi` file that guides Windows Installer and that contains the application you are installing. This file has a database-like format describing what the Installer should do, and the format of the dialogs it should display. Though you can't open the file using true database tools such as `OleDbConnection` objects or SQL Server, you can edit it if you must. The file's format and contents are described in the Windows Installer parts of the Platform SDK available at `www.microsoft.com/msdownload/platformsdk/sdkupdate`. The SDK includes an `.msi` file editor named Orca that you can use to view and modify the contents of an `.msi` file.

Other Solutions

Windows Installer includes several features that are not available in ClickOnce deployment, but it is more difficult to use. If you want the flexibility provided by Windows Installer, but want an easier interface, you should look into commercial installation products. Some of the more popular of the many products available include the following:

- InstallShield (`www.installshield.com`)
- Wise (`www.wise.com`)
- Zero G (`www.zerog.com`)
- Ghost Installer (`www.ethalone.com`)
- WinINSTALL (`www.ondemandsoftware.com`)

The InstallSite Web site (`www.installsite.org`) contains lots of information about creating Microsoft Windows Installer (MSI) and InstallShield packages. The page `www.installsite.org/en/msi/authoring.htm` describes about 30 products that build installation packages. The page `www.installsite.org/pages/eb/msi/comparison.htm` compares the features provided by Visual Studio itself, as well as various versions of InstallShield and Wise.

If you do a little Web surfing, you will also find a large number of freeware and shareware installation programs. Their features and ease of use vary widely, so you may need to do some extensive research to pick the one that best suits your needs.

Xcopy

The Windows `Xcopy` command copies files and directory hierarchies from one location to another. If you know that the target computer already has any required prerequisites such as the .NET Framework, database drivers, Registry entries, and so forth, then you only need to copy your executable file or DLL and any associated files that you need onto the target system.

Unfortunately, there are many ways this type of installation can go wrong. If the application tries to use incompatible library versions, fails to register needed components, or doesn't have a necessary prerequisite, then the application won't run correctly.

For example, the `XcopyExample` program available for download uses the following code to display a message when its form loads:

```
Dim welcome_getter As New WelcomeGetter
lblWelcome.Text = welcome_getter.GetWelcomeText(True)
```

The `WelcomeGetter` class shown in the following code is defined in a class library:

```
Public Class WelcomeGetter
    ' Return a welcome message.
    Public Function GetWelcomeText() As String
        Return "This program uses version 1 of GetWelcomeText"
    End Function
End Class
```

If you build this application and copy the executable and DLL onto a target computer that has the .NET Framework installed, then the executable should run.

If you make changes to the `GetWelcomeText` function, but don't change its signature (its parameters and return value), you can copy the compiled DLL onto the target computer and the program will still run. However, if you change `GetWelcomeText` so it takes a parameter and copy the new DLL over, the application will crash. Even if you don't change the function's signature, you probably haven't thoroughly tested the old version of the executable with the new version of the DLL, so they may be incompatible and cause unexpected behavior even if the program still runs.

Sometimes you can use `Xcopy` to replace a single file that has been modified in some small way, but it's usually better to let ClickOnce figure out what it needs to update.

`RoboCopy` is the next version of `Xcopy` that is included with the Vista operating system. It is generally similar to `Xcopy` with some additional features (such as the ability to copy only files that are newer in the source than in the destination, the ability to copy files within certain modification date or size ranges, and the ability to skip empty directories).

Summary

For really simple installations when you know the user already has the .NET Framework and any other prerequisites installed, `Xcopy` installation is quick and easy, particularly if the user is fairly experienced with computers.

If you are unsure whether the user has the prerequisites installed, or if you will want to provide updates of changed pieces of your application, ClickOnce provides a solution that is easy for you and the user. It also provides options for allowing the application to automatically check for updates and install them either synchronously or asynchronously.

If you need to perform more-extensive actions during installation (such as modifying the Registry, picking the installation directory, registering COM components, or executing post-installation code), you should use a Windows Installer setup project.

Finally, if you want more features in an easy-to-use tool, consider a commercial installation product such as InstallShield, Wise, Zero G, Ghost Installer, or WinINSTALL.

Up to this point, the chapters in this book have dealt with general concepts. While many of them include demonstration code and examples, their focus is on major ideas, rather than specific techniques.

The chapters in the remainder of the book describe specific techniques you can use to add useful features to your application. Chapter 19, "Splash Screens," tells how to add eye-catching and informative splash screens to your application.

Part IV
Specific Techniques

In this Part:

19

Splash Screens

The first thing a user sees of an application is its splash screen. As the adage says, "You only get one chance to make a first impression," so it's important that your splash screen represent your application appropriately. Though the user only gets one first impression of your application, the splash screen appears every time the application starts, so it's important that it has a positive impact each time the user sees it.

A typical splash screen displays some basic information about the application such as its name, version number, and copyright information. Splash screens often provide contact information so that users can get technical support if necessary.

In addition to giving the user a little information, a splash screen gives the user something to look at while the application loads. At this point, the application might look for all sorts of resources such as databases, files, special devices, network connections, remotely mounted drives, Web Services, and so forth. It can connect to databases and open files, parse XML data, and otherwise get ready for business. If a program takes several seconds to do all this, then a splash screen shows the user that something is happening. If it includes a progress bar or status animation, it can let the user know that the program is working and has not become stuck.

The application can also perform security checks while the splash screen is visible. It can try to open password-protected databases, check the user's credentials, and see if it can connect to the network through the user's firewall.

In some applications, I have included user name and password text boxes on the splash screen so that the user can use it to log in. The splash screen's code then checked a password database to verify that the user name and password were correct, and to see what kind of user this is (clerk, supervisor, manager, and so forth). The rest of the application used that information to configure itself, displaying or hiding menus and buttons as appropriate.

A well-crafted splash screen shows the users that you pay attention to details and makes an application look more professional. I usually build a splash screen for a new application as soon as development starts so that customers viewing prototypes can see it. In one application for the

State of Minnesota, I made a splash screen in the shape of the state's map. After the initial demonstration, the first question they asked was, "How did you make that cool splash screen?"

(The second question they asked was, "How long did it take?" They liked the splash screen but didn't want to waste money on frills. As you'll see in this chapter, making a shaped splash screen only takes a few minutes.)

This chapter explains how to build and use splash screens in Visual Basic. It tells how to add interesting and unusual features to a splash screen, such as a shaped form, rotated text, and text filled with a color gradient or pattern. Adding all of these features to every form in a project would probably make the application appear cluttered and distracting, but in a splash screen, they can make an otherwise utilitarian form more interesting.

Determining Splash Screen Contents

Figure 19-1 shows the splash screen displayed by the `ShapedSplashScreen` example application. (You can download this example at `www.vb-helper.com/one_on_one.htm`.) The form is shaped to fit an image on the left and has rounded corners. It displays the application's title `eJack` in outlined text that is filled with a color gradient shading from red to yellow to green (it looks much better on the screen than in this book). It displays the program's version, serial number, and copyright information. It also displays a progress bar to show the user how far the application has proceeded in loading its data.

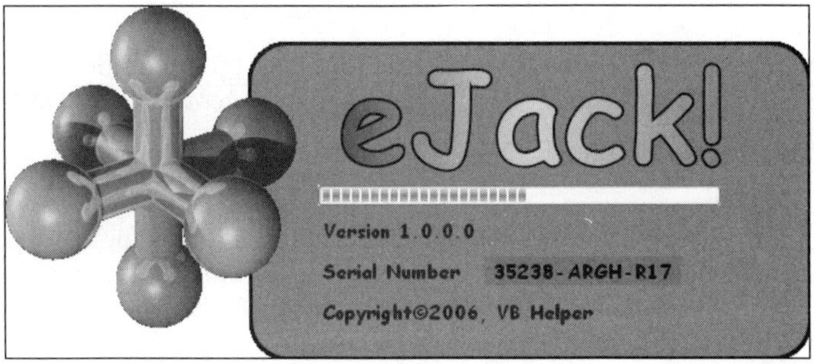

Figure 19-1: The `ShapedSplashScreen` program displays this splash screen when it starts.

The image on the left in Figure 19-1 was even generated by Visual Basic, specifically Visual Basic 6 code from my book, Visual Basic Graphics Programming: Hands-On Applications and Advanced Color Development, Second Edition (Indianapolis: Wiley, 1999).

A program's About dialog should also display the same information. It should display the program's name, version, serial number, and copyright statement. Because the About dialog contains the same information as the splash screen, it makes sense to use the same form for both.

Figure 19-2 shows the `ShapedSplashScreen` program displaying its About dialog. It is similar to the splash screen except that it doesn't display a progress bar. It also displays a rotated link to the support Web site `www.vb-helper.com` and an OK button so the user can close it. .

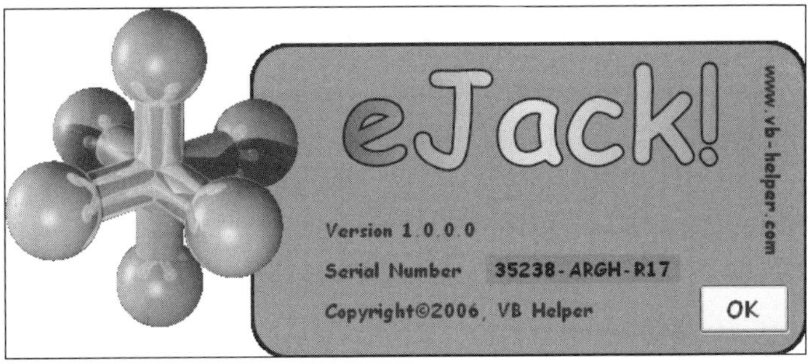

Figure 19-2: The About dialog displays much of the same information as the splash screen.

A splash screen should not display system information such as memory usage or disk space. To manage system resources, the user should use the operating system tools, not your application.

When a user needs help with an application, the technical support people usually need to know the program's serial number. These numbers are often quite long (my Visual Basic serial number has 20 digits plus embedded dashes), so, to make entering the serial number in an email easier, the About dialog displays it in a read-only text box. That allows the user to select the serial number, press Ctrl+C to copy it to the clipboard, and then press Ctrl+V to paste it into the email.

Many splash screens and About dialogs also contain hidden surprises, often called *Easter Eggs*. If you hover the mouse over a small area on the dot in the title's exclamation point, the mouse cursor changes to a crosshair. If you click that spot, the hidden screen shown in Figure 19-3 appears. Often, this kind of hidden screen displays extra non-critical information such as the names of the developers who worked on the application.

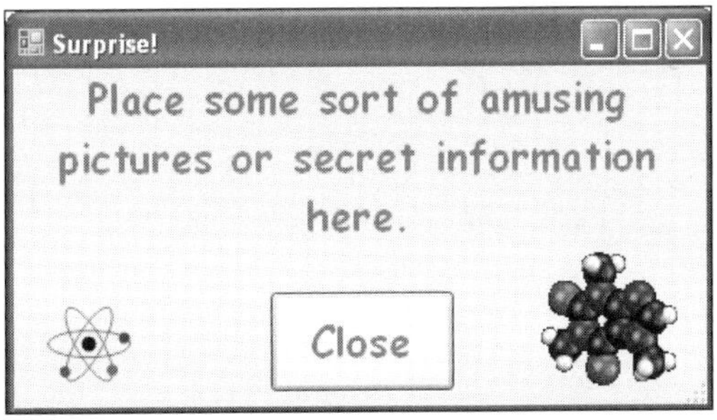

Figure 19-3: This surprise screen displays animations of an atom and caffeine molecule.

Some hidden screens are extremely elaborate. Some play music or make the developers' names appear in an amusing animation. I've even seen some that included complicated games that the user can play.

Whereas splash screens provide important information and feedback while the application is loading, hidden screens are definitely optional. They're usually fun and easy to build, however, so developers can add them in a spare moment without much wasted effort (complicated games notwithstanding).

Displaying Splash Screens

Visual Basic provides a way to automatically display a splash screen, although it's a little awkward and not very well-documented.

First, build the form you want to use as a splash screen. Then open Solution Explorer and double-click the My Project item. On the Application tab, scroll to the bottom and select the form in the "Splash screen" drop-down, as shown in Figure 19-4.

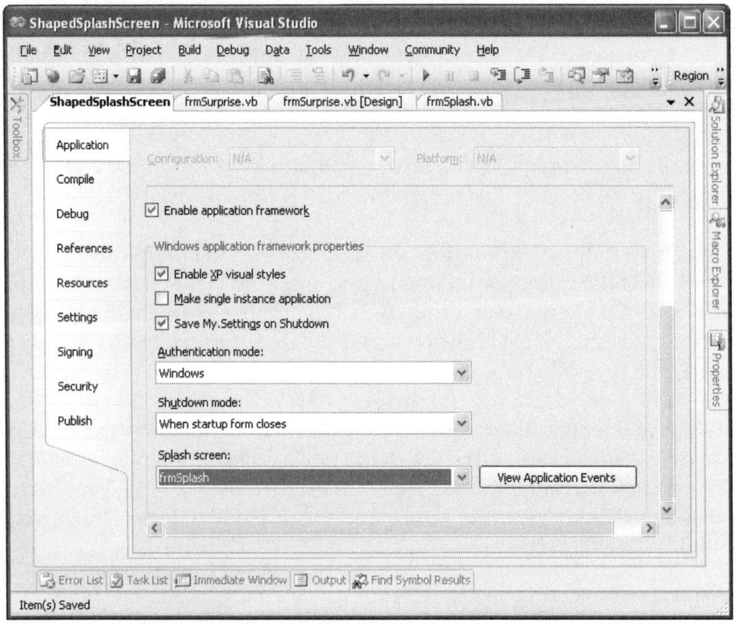

Figure 19-4: Select the splash screen's form from the drop-down list.

At this point, Visual Basic will automatically display the splash screen when the application starts. It displays the form until the program's main form has finished its startup sequence, or until a certain minimum amount of time has passed, whichever comes second. Unfortunately, changing the minimum amount of time or adding data loading code requires some extra work on your part.

To do either of these tasks, open Solution Explorer and double-click the My Project entry. On the Application tab, click the View Application Events button at the bottom, as shown in Figure 19-4.

To change the minimum amount of time the splash screen is displayed, add the following code to the `MyApplication` class to override the class's `OnInitialize` method. This code sets the application's `MinimumSplashScreenDisplayTime` property to 5 seconds (5,000 milliseconds) rather than its default value of 3 seconds. It then calls the base class's `OnInitialize` method so that the application can resume its startup procedure as normal.

```
' Override OnInitialize to set the splash screen's minimum display time.
Protected Overrides Function OnInitialize(ByVal commandLineArgs As _
```

```
 System.Collections.ObjectModel.ReadOnlyCollection(Of String)) As Boolean
    ' Display the splash screen for at least 3 seconds.
    Me.MinimumSplashScreenDisplayTime = 3000

    ' Continue initialization as usual.
    Return MyBase.OnInitialize(commandLineArgs)
End Function
```

The minimum amount of time that a splash screen should be visible is a matter of preference, but 2 or 3 seconds seems to work best. If the form vanishes after less than 2 seconds, the user doesn't really have a chance to see it. If the form sticks around for more than 5 seconds, it violates the "5-second rule" that says an interactive application should respond within 5 seconds whenever possible.

Visual Basic displays the splash screen for a minimum amount of time, or until the main form finishes its startup sequence. To get the most benefit from the splash screen, you should make the application load data, connect to databases, use Web Services to check for updates, and perform other lengthy startup actions during this time.

To perform actions while the form is starting up, open the application events module as you would to set the `MinimumSplashScreenDisplayTime` property. Open the code editor's left drop-down and select "(MyApplication Events)". Then, in the right drop-down, select the `Startup` event. Enter your initialization code in the `MyApplication_Startup` event handler.

The following code shows a dummy `Startup` event handler. It gets a reference to the application's splash screen form so that it can send status information to the form's progress bar (this is described further later in this chapter). It then uses some loops to waste some time before exiting. In a real application, you would load data, connect to databases, and perform other time-consuming setup chores instead of just waiting for a few seconds.

```
' Prepare the application to run:
' Connect to databases, load data, etc.
Private Sub MyApplication_Startup(ByVal sender As Object, _
 ByVal e As Microsoft.VisualBasic.ApplicationServices.StartupEventArgs) _
 Handles Me.Startup
    Dim splash_screen As frmSplash
    splash_screen = DirectCast(My.Application.SplashScreen, frmSplash)

    ' Wait one second three times.
    For progress As Integer = 0 To 100 Step 10
        ' Update the progress display.
        splash_screen.Progress = progress

        ' Wait a little while.
        Dim stop_time As Date = Now.AddSeconds(0.25)
        Do While Now < stop_time
            Application.DoEvents()
        Loop
    Next progress
End Sub
```

Displaying About Dialogs

Using a splash screen as an About dialog is easy. An About dialog displays most of the same information as a splash screen. In this example, the differences are that the About dialog does the following:

- Displays an OK button
- Displays a link to a support Web site
- Provides the hidden link to the surprise screen
- Does not display a progress bar

To make displaying the splash screen's form as an About dialog easy, the form provides the `ShowAbout` method shown in the following code. This code makes the OK button, surprise label, and Web site label visible. It hides the progress bar, and calls the form's `ShowDialog` method to display the form modally.

```
' Display as an About dialog.
Public Sub ShowAbout(ByVal owner As IWin32Window)
    btnOk.Visible = True
    lblSurprise.Visible = True
    pbarLoad.Visible = False
    lblUrl.Visible = True

    Me.ShowDialog(owner)
End Sub
```

The main program uses the following code to display the About dialog when the user selects the Help menu's About command:

```
' Display the About dialog.
Private Sub mnuHelpAbout_Click(ByVal sender As System.Object, _
 ByVal e As System.EventArgs) Handles mnuHelpAbout.Click
    Dim frm As New frmSplash
    frm.ShowAbout(Me)
End Sub
```

Providing Feedback

As the main form works through its startup chores, it provides feedback so that the splash screen can update its progress bar. Unfortunately, the main form's startup code and the splash screen's user interface run in separate threads. Code can only set a control's property if it is running in the thread that created the control, so the main startup code cannot simply set the `Value` property for the splash screen's `ProgressBar` control. Instead, the startup code sets the splash screen's `Progress` property as shown in the section "Displaying Splash Screens" earlier in this chapter. The splash screen then updates its own `ProgressBar` control.

The following code shows how the splash screen handles its `Progress` property:

```
' Set the progress.
Public Delegate Sub ShowProgressDelegate(ByVal progress As Integer)
Public Sub ShowProgress(ByVal progress As Integer)
```

```
        pbarLoad.Value = progress
    End Sub

    ' Get or set the progress indicator.
    Public Property Progress() As Integer
        Get
            Return pbarLoad.Value
        End Get
        Set(ByVal value As Integer)
            If Me.InvokeRequired Then
                Dim show_progress_delegate As ShowProgressDelegate
                show_progress_delegate = AddressOf ShowProgress
                Me.Invoke(show_progress_delegate, New Object() {value})
            Else
                ShowProgress(value)
            End If
        End Set
    End Property
```

The code starts by defining a delegate named `ShowProgressDelegate` to represent a subroutine that takes an integer parameter. It also defines a simple `ShowProgress` subroutine that sets the `pbarLoad` progress bar's `Value` property to the routine's integer parameter.

The form then defines the `Progress` property that the startup code sets to provide feedback. The `Get` procedure simply returns the `ProgressBar`'s `Value` property. The `Set` procedure calls `Me.InvokeRequired` to see if the current code is running on a different thread than the form's user interface thread. `Me.InvokeRequired` returns `True` if the code is running in a different thread than the form's controls and, therefore, cannot set the control's `Value` property directly.

If `Me.InvokeRequired` returns `True`, the code makes a `ShowProgressDelegate`, sets it equal to the form's `ShowProgress` method, and uses the `Invoke` method to run that method, passing it the new value that the `Progress` property should have. This starts a call to `ShowProgress` on the form's user interface thread, and that routine can set the `ProgressBar` control's `Value` property directly.

If `Me.InvokeRequired` returns `False`, code setting the form's `Progress` property is running in the user interface thread, so the code can manipulate the `ProgressBar` control directly. In that case, the code simply calls the `ShowProgress` method itself.

Calling across to the form's user interface thread is a bit awkward, but at least the details are encapsulated in the form, so the main program's call is straightforward. That code simply sets the form's `Progress` property and the splash screen form handles the rest.

Controlling Item Placement

The splash screen form used by this program draws several items in code. It uses code to shape the form, draw the application's title (`eJack!`), and display rotated text.

To make working with these items easier, this example uses objects created at design time to determine the size and placement of the items. For example, the `Panel` control `panTextArea` determines the location of the rounded rectangle on the right in Figures 19-1 and 19-2. Similarly the `lblTitle` and `lblUrl Label` controls determine where the program's title and Web link go.

Not only do these controls determine the items' placement, but they also give the items' colors and fonts. To change the items' positions, size, color, or font, you can change the corresponding properties of the controls at design time.

The `lblTitle` and `lblUrl` controls sit on top of the `panTextArea` control. When you work with the controls in the form designer, the designer tends to place the `Labels` inside the `Panel` control. That makes their X and Y position properties relative to the `Panel` control's origin. However, the routines that draw these items on the form work relative to the form's origin, not the `Panel`'s origin.

To make working with these controls easier, the program uses the following code to move the controls outside of the `Panel` control. The code first makes an array containing the controls that are inside the `Panel` control, and then loops through those controls. It changes each control's parent to the form, and moves the control to account for the offset provided by the `Panel`. That puts the controls in their original positions, but contained inside the form and not the `Panel`.

```
' Move controls out of panTextArea.
Dim ctls(panTextArea.Controls.Count - 1) As Control
panTextArea.Controls.CopyTo(ctls, 0)
For Each ctl As Control In ctls
    ctl.Parent = Me
    ctl.Left += panTextArea.Left
    ctl.Top += panTextArea.Top
Next ctl
```

Now the program can use these controls to position screen elements.

Shaping Forms

Making a shaped form in Visual Basic doesn't take many steps, but it is rather confusing.

Forms have a property `TransparencyKey` that tells Visual Basic what color to use to make parts of the form transparent. In theory, if a pixel's background color has this value, then Visual Basic does not draw that part of the form and lets whatever lies below the form show through. In practice, things are more confusing.

To make any of the form transparent, first set the form's `TransparencyKey` and `BackColor` properties to the same color. If you run the program now, Visual Basic will not draw the form's client area.

To make parts of the form visible again, make a `Bitmap` that contains the picture you want to display. Call the `Bitmap`'s `MakeTransparent` method to make pixels of a certain color transparent.

Now set the form's `BackgroundImage` property to the `Bitmap`. The form will be transparent in the places where the `Bitmap`'s pixels are transparent.

The following code shows the pieces of the splash screen's `Load` event handler that shape the form:

```
' Prepare the splash screen.
Private Sub frmSplash_Load(ByVal sender As System.Object, _
 ByVal e As System.EventArgs) Handles MyBase.Load
    ' Shape the form.
```

```
        ' Make a bitmap for our form image.
        Dim bm As New Bitmap(Me.ClientSize.Width, Me.ClientSize.Height)
        Dim gr As Graphics = Graphics.FromImage(bm)

        ' Draw smooth curves.
        gr.SmoothingMode = SmoothingMode.AntiAlias

        ' Make a rounded rectangle for the text area.
        Using rect_path As GraphicsPath = _
         RoundedRectanglePath(panTextArea.Bounds(), 30, 30)
            ' Draw the text area.
            Using br As New SolidBrush(panTextArea.BackColor)
                gr.FillPath(br, rect_path)
            End Using
            Using thick_pen As New Pen(Color.DarkBlue, 3)
                gr.DrawPath(thick_pen, rect_path)
            End Using
        End Using

        ' Make a Bitmap containing the Jack image.
        Dim jack_bm As New Bitmap(My.Resources.Jack)
        jack_bm.MakeTransparent(bm.GetPixel(0, 0))

        ' Draw the Jack image onto the form's Bitmap.
        gr.DrawImage(jack_bm, jack_bm.GetBounds(GraphicsUnit.Pixel))
        ...
        ' Make black areas transparent.
        Me.BackColor = Color.Black
        Me.TransparencyKey = Me.BackColor

        ' Use the result for the form's background image.
        Me.BackgroundImage = bm
        ...
    End Sub
```

The code starts by creating a `Bitmap` to fit the splash screen form. It then makes a `Graphics` object to draw on the `Bitmap`, and sets the object's `SmoothingMode` property to `AntiAlias` to give drawn shapes smooth edges.

The code then uses a `GraphicsPath` object that it gets from the `RoundedRectanglePath` method described shortly. It uses the `panTextArea Panel` control to determine the size and position of the rounded rectangle. In Figures 19-1 and 19-2, the rounded rectangle is the area on the right containing the text.

The program fills the rounded rectangle with the `Panel`'s background color, and then outlines it in dark blue.

Next, the code loads the `jack` bitmap from the program's resources and calls its `MakeTransparent` method to make pixels with the same color as the one in its upper-left corner transparent. It then uses the `Graphics` object's `DrawImage` method to copy the `jack` image onto the `Bitmap`.

The code sets the form's `BackColor` and `TransparencyKey` properties to black and sets the form's background image to the `Bitmap`. The result is a form shaped to include the rounded rectangle and the `jack` image on the left.

The `RoundedRectanglePath` function shown in the following code makes a `GraphicsPath` representing a rounded rectangle. This code makes a `GraphicsPath`, and adds arcs and line segments to make the rounded rectangle:

```
' Return a GraphicsPath object representing a rounded rectangle.
Public Function RoundedRectanglePath(ByVal x As Integer, ByVal y As Integer, _
 ByVal wid As Integer, ByVal hgt As Integer, _
 ByVal x_radius As Integer, ByVal y_radius As Integer) As GraphicsPath
    Dim graphics_path As New GraphicsPath
    graphics_path.AddArc(x, y, x_radius * 2, y_radius * 2, 180, 90)
    graphics_path.AddLine(x + x_radius, y, x + wid - x_radius, y)
    graphics_path.AddArc(x + wid - x radius * 2, y, x radius * 2, _
        y_radius * 2, -90, 90)
    graphics_path.AddLine(x + wid, y + y_radius, x + wid, y + hgt - y_radius)
    graphics_path.AddArc(x + wid - x_radius * 2, y + hgt - y_radius * 2, _
        x_radius * 2, y_radius * 2, 0, 90)
    graphics_path.AddLine(x + wid - x_radius, y + hgt, x + x_radius, y + hgt)
    graphics_path.AddArc(x, y + hgt - y_radius * 2, x_radius * 2, y_radius * 2, _
        90, 90)
    graphics_path.AddLine(x, y + hgt - y_radius, x, y + y_radius)

    Return graphics_path
End Function

Public Function RoundedRectanglePath(ByVal rect As Rectangle, _
 ByVal x_radius As Integer, ByVal y_radius As Integer) As GraphicsPath
    Return RoundedRectanglePath(rect.X, rect.Y, rect.Width, rect.Height, _
        x_radius, y_radius)
End Function
```

The second overloaded version (the one used by the form's shaping code) takes a `Rectangle` and the radii that it should use for the corner curves as parameters. It translates these values into the parameters needed by the first version of `RoundedRectanglePath` and calls that version.

Filling Text

The following code shows how the splash screen draws filled text. It begins by creating a new `GraphicsPath` object.

```
' Draw "Jack!"
Using jack_path As New GraphicsPath()
    ' Make a path for the text.
    Using string_format As New StringFormat
        jack_path.AddString( _
            lblTitle.Text, _
            lblTitle.Font.FontFamily, _
            lblTitle.Font.Style, _
            lblTitle.Font.Size, _
            lblTitle.Bounds(), _
            string_format)
    End Using

    ' Fill the text with a gradient.
```

```
    Using jack_br As New LinearGradientBrush( _
     jack_path.GetBounds(), Color.Red, Color.Lime, LinearGradientMode.Horizontal)
        Dim color_blend As New ColorBlend()
        color_blend.Colors = New Color() {Color.Red, Color.Yellow, Color.Lime}
        color_blend.Positions = New Single() {0.0, 0.5, 1.0}
        jack_br.InterpolationColors = color_blend

        gr.FillPath(jack_br, jack_path)
    End Using

    Using jack_pen As New Pen(Color.DarkBlue, 2)
        gr.DrawPath(jack_pen, jack_path)
    End Using
End Using
```

The code uses the `GraphicsPath` object's `AddString` to add a string to the path. It passes information taken from the `lblTitle` label control to the `AddString` method. This lets you easily move, resize, and change the font for the text without modifying the code.

Next, the program makes a `LinearGradientBrush` that shades horizontally from red to lime across the width of the text. The code defines a color blend for the brush that shades from red to yellow to lime, and then uses the `Graphics` object's `FillPath` method to fill the text with this brush.

> *You could use any other brush to fill the text. For example, you could fill the text with a background color to make it hollow, or you could use a* `TextureBrush` *to fill the text with an image.*

After it fills the text, the code uses the `Graphics` object's `DrawPath` method to outline the text in dark blue.

Rotating Text

When the form displays as an About dialog, it draws the program's support Web site `www.vb-helper.com` on the right in a rotated font. The following code shows how the program draws this text:

```
' Draw the URL rotated over lblUrl.
If lblUrl.Visible Then
    Const URL_TEXT As String = "www.vb-helper.com"
    gr.RotateTransform(90, MatrixOrder.Append)
    Dim url_size As SizeF = gr.MeasureString(URL_TEXT, lblUrl.Font, 1000)
    gr.TranslateTransform(lblUrl.Left + url_size.Height, lblUrl.Top, _
        MatrixOrder.Append)
    gr.DrawString(URL_TEXT, lblUrl.Font, Brushes.Blue, 0, 0)

    ' Move lblUrl under the text so we can catch its Click event.
    lblUrl.Width = CInt(url_size.Height)
    lblUrl.Height = CInt(url_size.Width)
    lblUrl.Text = ""
End If
```

The `Graphics` object provides several methods for translating, scaling, and rotating its output. The code starts by adding a rotation transformation to make the `Graphics` object rotate its output 90 degrees.

Next, the code measures the string it will display. It adds a translation to make the `Graphics` object move text drawn at the origin onto the `lblUrl Label` control. Notice that the code adds the text's height to the horizontal translation. After the text is rotated, its drawing origin is in the upper-right corner of where the text is drawn. To make the text lie above the `lblUrl` control, the code must move it this extra distance to the right, as shown in Figure 19-5.

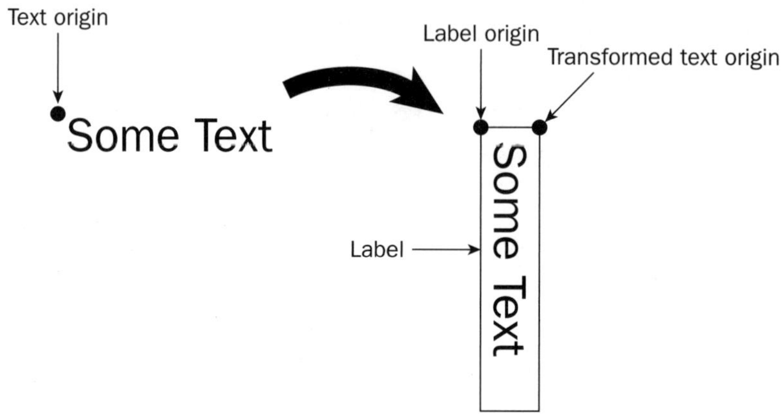

Figure 19-5: Text rotated 90 degrees must be translated an extra distance to make it line up over the `lblUrl` control.

You can use similar techniques to display text rotated at other angles, although exactly positioning the text can be even trickier than it is for text rotated 90 degrees.

The program clears the `lblUrl` control's text, so it is not seen. But the control is still present, so it can display a "hand" cursor and the user can click it. The following code shows how the program displays the VB Helper Web site when the user clicks the control. When the code uses `System.Diagnostics.Process` to "Start" the URL, the system opens the Web site in its default browser.

```
' Open the VB Helper Web site.
Private Sub lblUrl_Click(ByVal sender As Object, _
 ByVal e As System.EventArgs) Handles lblUrl.Click
    System.Diagnostics.Process.Start("http://www.vb-helper.com")
End Sub
```

Displaying Hidden Screens

The splash screen contains a tiny Label control named `lblSurprise`. The control's `Text` property is set to an empty string, so the user cannot see it. The control's `Cursor` property is set to `Cross`, so it displays a crosshair cursor when the user positions the mouse over it.

When the user clicks the `lblSurprise` control, the following event handler displays the surprise screen modally:

```
' Display a surprise form.
Private Sub lblSurprise_Click(ByVal sender As Object, _
 ByVal e As System.EventArgs) Handles lblSurprise.Click
```

```
        Dim frm As New frmSurprise
        frm.ShowDialog(Me)
    End Sub
```

The surprise form is mostly straightforward. It displays some text and an OK button that unloads the form. A `PictureBox` control in the lower right displays an animated `GIF` file showing a rotating caffeine molecule. The `PictureBox` animates the `GIF` automatically, so you don't need to do anything except set the control's `Image` property to the `GIF` file.

The only interesting code in the surprise form draws the animated atom in the lower left. The form contains a `Timer` control that fires its `Timer` event every one-tenth of a second. The following code shows how the event handler works. When the `Timer` event occurs, the code invalidates the `picAtom` `PictureBox` to force the control to repaint itself.

```
    Private Sub tmrAtom_Tick(ByVal sender As System.Object, _
     ByVal e As System.EventArgs) Handles tmrAtom.Tick
        picAtom.Invalidate()
    End Sub

    Private Sub picAtom_Paint(ByVal sender As Object, _
     ByVal e As System.Windows.Forms.PaintEventArgs) Handles picAtom.Paint
        Const DTHETA As Double = Math.PI / 5
        Static theta As Double = 0

        e.Graphics.Clear(picAtom.BackColor)
        e.Graphics.SmoothingMode = Drawing2D.SmoothingMode.AntiAlias
        theta += DTHETA

        Const E_RADIUS As Integer = 3
        Dim cx As Integer = picAtom.ClientSize.Width \ 2
        Dim cy As Integer = picAtom.ClientSize.Height \ 2
        Dim rx As Integer = CInt(picAtom.ClientSize.Width * 0.45)
        Dim ry As Integer = CInt(picAtom.ClientSize.Height * 0.15)
        Dim rect As New Rectangle(-rx, -ry, 2 * rx, 2 * ry)
        Dim x, y As Double
        e.Graphics.RotateTransform(60, Drawing2D.MatrixOrder.Append)
        e.Graphics.TranslateTransform(cx, cy, Drawing2D.MatrixOrder.Append)
        e.Graphics.DrawEllipse(Pens.Red, rect)
        x = rx * Cos(theta)
        y = ry * Sin(theta)
        e.Graphics.FillEllipse(Brushes.Red, _
            CInt(x - E_RADIUS), CInt(y - E_RADIUS), _
            2 * E_RADIUS, 2 * E_RADIUS)

        e.Graphics.ResetTransform()
        e.Graphics.RotateTransform(-60, Drawing2D.MatrixOrder.Append)
        e.Graphics.TranslateTransform(cx, cy, Drawing2D.MatrixOrder.Append)
        e.Graphics.DrawEllipse(Pens.Red, rect)
        x = rx * Cos(-theta * 0.9)
        y = ry * Sin(-theta * 0.9)
        e.Graphics.FillEllipse(Brushes.Green, _
            CInt(x - E_RADIUS), CInt(y - E_RADIUS), _
            2 * E_RADIUS, 2 * E_RADIUS)

        e.Graphics.ResetTransform()
```

```
        e.Graphics.TranslateTransform(cx, cy, Drawing2D.MatrixOrder.Append)
        e.Graphics.DrawEllipse(Pens.Red, rect)
        x = rx * Cos(theta * 0.8)
        y = ry * Sin(theta * 0.8)
        e.Graphics.FillEllipse(Brushes.Blue, _
            CInt(x - E_RADIUS), CInt(y - E_RADIUS), _
            2 * E_RADIUS, 2 * E_RADIUS)

        e.Graphics.ResetTransform()
        Const N_RADIUS As Integer = 4
        e.Graphics.FillEllipse(Brushes.Black, _
            cx - N_RADIUS, cy - N_RADIUS, _
            2 * N_RADIUS, 2 * N_RADIUS)
    End Sub
```

The control's `Paint` event handler clears the `PictureBox` and sets the `Graphics` object's `SmoothingMode` property to draw a smooth picture.

The code then calculates parameters to draw an ellipse centered at the origin. It uses the `Graphics` object's `RotateTransform` and `TranslateTransform` methods to draw the ellipse rotated 60 degrees and centered in the `PictureBox`. It then uses some trigonometry to figure out where to draw an electron on the ellipse. The program uses a static variable to keep track of the electron's angle around the ellipse so that it can move the electron to a new position next time the control repaints.

Next, the program resets the `Graphics` object's transformation and repeats the same steps to draw a new ellipse and electron rotated –60 degrees. It multiplies the angle it used to draw the previous electron by 0.9, so this electron rotates around its ellipse at a slower speed.

The program again resets the `Graphics` object's transformation and repeats the same steps to draw an ellipse and electron that is not rotated. This time, it multiplies the electron's angle by 0.8, so this electron moves even slower than the others.

Finally, the `Paint` event handler draws a nucleus in the center of the `PictureBox`.

Summary

This chapter describes some techniques you can use to make interesting and informative splash screens. Though they would be overly flashy in the body of most applications, they can add an extra dimension of interest to splash screens and About dialogs. These forms are displayed seldom enough that adding some extra sparkle won't hurt, and it gives you a chance to show some creativity in even the most staid application.

One of the purposes of a splash screen is to let the user know that the application is working while it performs initial setup. The version described in this chapter basically gives the user something interesting to look at while the program gets ready to run. While the splash screen is visible, the program can connect to databases, verify network connections, check user credentials, and otherwise prepare to work.

Another style of splash screen also lets the user know the program is running while displaying important information at the same time. This type of screen displays a message of the day, production note, or some other piece of information that the user can read while the program initializes. The screen acts more like an About dialog, and the user closes it after reading the latest message. You can still use the techniques described in this chapter to give the screen an interesting shape, shaded or rotated text, and a link to a support Web page, but because the user will spend more time on this type of screen, it should be a bit more conservative than the splash screen described here.

Visual Studio .NET changed the way you display splash screens. In Visual Basic 6, you needed to display the splash screen yourself and use a timer to remove it after a certain period of time, or after the application had finished loading, whichever came second.

Visual Basic .NET also greatly changed the way you send output to the printer. Visual Basic 6 included a `Printer` object that had methods that let you draw, print text, start a new page, and perform other printing operations in a straightforward, procedural way. Visual Basic .NET uses an event-driven approach where your code must respond to requests to generate output. Chapter 20, "Printing," describes Visual Basic .NET's event-driven printing model, and shows how you can build your own more procedural printing system.

20

Printing

Although many people try to make their offices as paperless as possible, some printing is inevitable. Whether you print documents to read while you are away from your computer, to put in printed reports, or to mail to customers, eventually you will probably need to print something.

Over the past few years, printing has gone from a tedious (but intuitive) process in Visual Basic 6 to a tedious (and non-intuitive) process in Visual Basic .NET. Visual Basic 6 used a procedural model for printing. You used the `Printer` object's properties and methods to generate output. You would call methods to write text, draw graphics, and generate new pages.

Visual Basic .NET takes an event-driven approach. Here, you start the printing process and then wait for events. A `PrintDocument` object raises events and asks you to generate the document's pages. The event handler includes a `Graphics` object, and you use its properties and methods to draw whatever output you want to print.

I find this approach rather unnatural, so I also devised a technique that uses metafiles to implement a more intuitive, procedural approach. This method lets you draw the entire printout all at once, rather than responding to events. It even lets you go back and modify earlier pages after you have drawn those that come later. For example, it lets you add page numbers of the form "Page 1 of 10" even if you don't know how many pages there are until after you have generated them.

This chapter describes Visual Basic .NET's basic event-driven model. It then explains the metafile-based, more intuitive procedural approach.

Event-Driven Printing

The basic idea behind event-driven printing is to create a `PrintDocument` object and tell it to start printing. Then you respond to the object's events to generate the pages of printout as the object needs them. The following list describes the object's key events:

- `BeginPrint` — This event occurs when the `PrintDocument` object is about to start printing the document. The code can use this event to prepare for printing by opening data sources, building fonts and brushes, setting a page number variable to `1`, and so forth.
- `QueryPageSettings` — This event occurs before the `PrintDocument` object starts printing a page. It gives the program a chance to change the page's settings before printing on it. For example, if you are printing a booklet, you might change the margins on odd and even numbered pages to allow a gutter on the side where the binding will go.
- `PrintPage` — This event occurs when the `PrintDocument` object needs to generate a printed page. The `e.Graphics` parameter gives the code a `Graphics` object on which to draw. The code should set the `e.HasMorePages` parameter to `True` if there are more pages to print or `False` if the program has printed the final page.
- `EndPrint` — This event occurs when the `PrintDocument` object is finished printing the last page. The program should perform cleanup tasks such as shutting down data sources, and disposing of fonts and brushes. Often, this event handler undoes actions taken in the `BeginPrint` event handler.

Example program `SimplePrint` (available for download at `www.vb-helper.com/one_on_one.htm`) prints and provides a print preview for a very simple document. It is stripped down to the bare minimum so that you can see how `PrintDocument` events work without becoming distracted by graphics details.

The program's form contains two non-visible components. The `pdocSimple` component is a `PrintDocument` object. It provides the events that generate the printout. The `pviewSimple` control is a `PrintPreviewDialog` control. It displays a preview of the printout.

The following code shows how the program works:

```
Public Class Form1
    ' Display a print preview.
    Private Sub btnPreview_Click(ByVal sender As System.Object, _
     ByVal e As System.EventArgs) Handles btnPreview.Click
        ' Set the print preview control's PrintDocument object.
        pviewSimple.Document = pdocSimple

        ' Display the preview.
        ' The PrintDocument object does the real work.
        pviewSimple.ShowDialog()
    End Sub

    ' Print.
    Private Sub btnPrint_Click(ByVal sender As System.Object, _
     ByVal e As System.EventArgs) Handles btnPrint.Click
        ' Use the PrintDocument to print.
        pdocSimple.Print()
```

```
    End Sub

#Region "Printing Code"
    Private m_NextPage As Integer
    Private m_Font As Font

    ' Prepare to print.
    Private Sub pdlgWrap_BeginPrint(ByVal sender As Object, _
     ByVal e As System.Drawing.Printing.PrintEventArgs) _
     Handles pdocSimple.BeginPrint
        ' Set the next page number.
        m_NextPage = 1

        ' Create the font we will use.
        m_Font = New Font("Times New Roman", 200, FontStyle.Bold, _
            GraphicsUnit.Point)
    End Sub

    ' Clean up.
    Private Sub pdocSimple_EndPrint(ByVal sender As Object, _
     ByVal e As System.Drawing.Printing.PrintEventArgs) _
     Handles pdocSimple.EndPrint
        ' Dispose of the font.
        m_Font.Dispose()
        m_Font = Nothing
    End Sub

    ' The PrintDocument needs a page. Print the next one.
    Private Sub pdlgWrap_PrintPage(ByVal sender As System.Object, _
     ByVal e As System.Drawing.Printing.PrintPageEventArgs) _
     Handles pdocSimple.PrintPage
        ' Draw the page number.
        e.Graphics.DrawString(m_NextPage.ToString, _
            m_Font, Brushes.Black, _
            e.MarginBounds.X, e.MarginBounds.Y)
        m_NextPage += 1

        ' Draw 5 pages.
        e.HasMorePages = (m_NextPage <= 5)
    End Sub
#End Region ' Printing Code
End Class
```

When you click the Preview button, the program sets the `pviewSimple` component's `Document` property to `pdocSimple`, and then calls the dialog's `ShowDialog` method. The dialog uses the `pdocSimple` object to generate the printout as necessary.

When you click the Print button, the program directly calls the `pdocSimple` object's `Print` method to make the object immediately generate and print the printout.

The printing section of the code includes some module-level variables that control printing and the `PrintDocument` object's event handlers. The `m_NextPage` variable tracks the number of the next page to print. The `m_Font` variable stores the font that the printing code uses.

When the PrintDocument's BeginPrint event fires, the event handler sets m_NextPage to 1 and creates a very large font to use when printing.

The PrintDocument's EndPrint event handler cleans up by disposing of the font.

The PrintPage event handler contains the most interesting code, although it's quite simple in this example. The code uses the e.Graphics object's DrawString method to display the current page number using the large font. It then increments the page number and sets e.HasMorePages to True if the program has not yet printed five pages.

After the PrintPage event handler exits, the PrintDocument object finishes generating the page and raises the event again if e.HasMorePages indicates that it must print more pages.

Figure 20-1 shows the PrintPreviewDialog displaying all five of the document's pages at the same time.

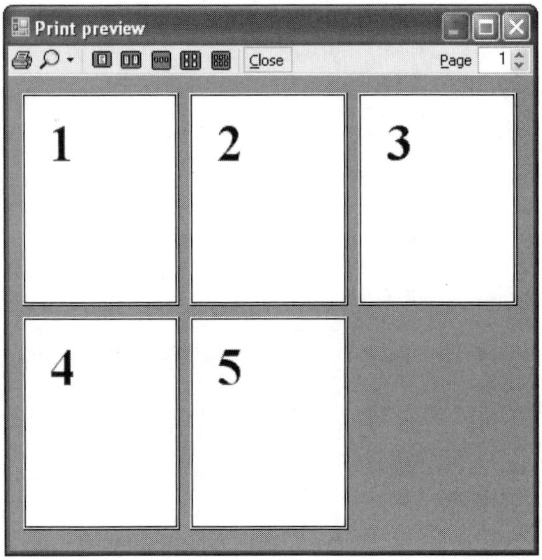

Figure 20-1: The PrintPreviewDialog control can display one, two, three, four, or six pages at a time. Here the dialog would display six pages, but the document has only five.

The SimplePrint example is easy enough to understand because it doesn't do much. Unfortunately printing a less-trivial document can be much more complicated. The following sections explain how you can handle other tasks that are more common and complex.

Printing Forms

Visual Basic 6 forms have a PrintForm method that immediately sends a bitmapped image of the form to the printer. The result is fairly grainy because the screen resolution is far lower than the printer's resolution, but this method is so simple that it is used heavily. It's a great way to produce a simple snapshot of a form, or to provide low-resolution printing until you have time to implement a higher-resolution version.

Here, "low-resolution" is a relative term. A typical monitor might provide between 72 and 130 pixels per inch (PPI). That's fine for a brightly lighted screen, but printers typically have much higher resolutions ranging from 300 to 1200 dots per inch (DPI). High-end inkjet printers have resolutions up to 9600 DPI. The difference in resolution between monitors and printers means that Visual Basic 6's `PrintForm` *method draws each screen pixel as a tiny square on the printer. The result looks a bit blocky.*

Unfortunately, Visual Basic .NET's forms don't have a `PrintForm` method, so you have to write your own. The first step is to use code similar to the following to get a bitmap representing the form's image:

```
Module PrintFormCode
    ' Return the form's image.
    Public Function GetFormImage(ByVal frm As Form, _
     ByVal include_borders As Boolean) As Bitmap
        ' Get the whole form.
        Dim wid, hgt As Integer
        wid = frm.Width
        hgt = frm.Height
        Dim bm As Bitmap = New Bitmap(wid, hgt)
        frm.DrawToBitmap(bm, New Rectangle(0, 0, wid, hgt))

        ' If we want the borders, return this bitmap.
        If include_borders Then Return bm

        ' Make a new bitmap to hold the image without the borders.
        Dim new_wid As Integer = frm.ClientSize.Width
        Dim new_hgt As Integer = frm.ClientSize.Height
        Dim new_bm As New Bitmap(new_wid, new_hgt)
        Dim new_gr As Graphics = Graphics.FromImage(new_bm)

        ' Get the client area's origin in screen coordinates.
        Dim origin As New Point(0, 0)
        origin = frm.PointToScreen(origin)

        ' See how far this is from the form's upper left corner.
        Dim x As Integer = origin.X - frm.Left
        Dim y As Integer = origin.Y - frm.Top

        ' Copy the form's client area image into the new bitmap.
        new_gr.DrawImage(bm, _
            New RectangleF(0, 0, new_wid, new_hgt), _
            New RectangleF(x, y, new_wid, new_hgt), _
            GraphicsUnit.Pixel)

        ' Return the client area image.
        Return new_bm
    End Function
End Module
```

The code starts by creating a bitmap big enough to hold the form's image. It then calls the form's `DrawToBitmap` method to make it draw itself into the bitmap. If the function's `include_borders` parameter is `true`, the function returns this bitmap.

If the `include_borders` parameter is `false`, the code makes a new bitmap that is the right size to hold the form's client area (the area inside the borders). It also makes a `Graphics` object for use when drawing on the smaller bitmap.

Next, the code makes a `Point` object holding the coordinates of the upper-left corner of the form's client area. It uses the form's `PointToScreen` method to translate that point into screen coordinates. The form's `Left` and `Top` properties give the coordinates of the form's upper-left corner in screen coordinates, so the difference between those values and the translated point gives the distance from the upper-left corner of the form to the upper-left corner of its client area.

The code uses those values to copy the part of the form's image corresponding to the client area into the smaller bitmap. It then returns the result.

Example program `PrintFormImage` (available for download at `www.vb-helper.com/one_on_one.htm`) uses function `GetFormImage` to get an image of the form. It then displays it in a `PrintPreviewDialog` or prints it directly. Checkboxes enable you to determine whether the program prints the image with or without borders, at normal size or scaled to fit the page, and in portrait or landscape orientation.

Figure 20-2 shows the program on the left. The Print preview dialog on the right displays the form's image with borders scaled to fill the page in landscape orientation.

Program `PrintFormImage` prepares its `PrintDocument` object and sets the `PrintPreviewDialog` object's `Document` property the same way program `SimplePrint` did in the previous section, "Event-Driven Printing."

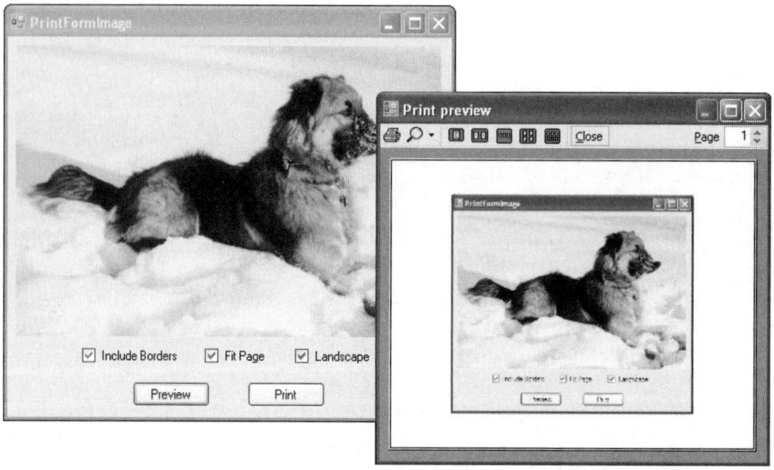

Figure 20-2: Program `PrintFormImage` can print an image with or without borders, at normal size or scaled to fit the page, and in portrait or landscape orientation.

The following code shows the `PrintDocument` event handlers that this program uses to display the form's image:

```
' Set landscape or portrait orientation.
Private Sub pdocForm_QueryPageSettings(ByVal sender As Object, _
 ByVal e As System.Drawing.Printing.QueryPageSettingsEventArgs) _
 Handles pdocForm.QueryPageSettings
    If cboLandscape.Checked Then
        ' Print in landscape.
        e.PageSettings.Landscape = True
```

```
        Else
            ' Print in portrait.
            e.PageSettings.Landscape = False
        End If
    End Sub

    ' Print the form's image.
    Private Sub pdocForm_PrintPage(ByVal sender As Object, _
     ByVal e As System.Drawing.Printing.PrintPageEventArgs) Handles pdocForm.PrintPage
        ' Get an image of the form.
        Dim bm As Bitmap = GetFormImage(Me, cboIncludeBorders.Checked)

        ' Prepare the Graphics object.
        PrepareGraphics(e, bm)

        ' Draw the image at the origin.
        e.Graphics.DrawImage(bm, 0, 0, bm.Width, bm.Height)

        ' There's only one page.
        e.HasMorePages = False
    End Sub

    ' Scale and translate the Graphics object appropriately.
    Private Sub PrepareGraphics(_
     ByVal e As System.Drawing.Printing.PrintPageEventArgs, ByVal bm As Bitmap)
        ' See how big the resulting image should be.
        Dim the_scale As Single
        If cboFitPage.Checked Then
            ' Scale to fit.
            Dim aspect1 As Double = bm.Width / bm.Height
            Dim aspect2 As Double = e.MarginBounds.Width / e.MarginBounds.Height
            If aspect1 > aspect2 Then
                ' The image is relatively wider and thinner than the page.
                ' Make it fit the page's width.
                the_scale = CSng(e.MarginBounds.Width / bm.Width)
            Else
                ' The image is relatively shorter and taller than the page.
                ' Make it fit the page's height.
                the_scale = CSng(e.MarginBounds.Height / bm.Height)
            End If

            ' Scale.
            e.Graphics.ScaleTransform(the_scale, the_scale)
        Else
            ' Use the image at its normal scale.
            the_scale = 1
        End If

        ' Translate to center the image.
        Dim wid As Single = bm.Width * the_scale
        Dim hgt As Single = bm.Height * the_scale
        Dim dx As Single = e.MarginBounds.X + (e.MarginBounds.Width - wid) / 2
        Dim dy As Single = e.MarginBounds.Y + (e.MarginBounds.Height - hgt) / 2
        e.Graphics.TranslateTransform(dx, dy, Drawing2D.MatrixOrder.Append)
    End Sub
```

The `QueryPageSettings` event handler checks the program's `cboLandscape` combo box. If the user has checked this box, the code sets the `PageSetting` object's `Landscape` property to `True` to make the printer use a landscape orientation. This also adjusts the `PrintDocument`'s margins so they work with the landscape setting.

The `PrintPage` event handler prints the form's image. It uses function `GetFormImage` to get a bitmap containing the form's image. It then calls subroutine `PrepareGraphics` to prepare the `Graphics` object to display the image properly scaled and centered. The routine uses the `e.Graphics` object's `DrawImage` method to draw the form's image at the position (`0, 0`) and sets `e.HasMorePages` to `False` to indicate that there are no more pages.

Subroutine `PrepareGraphics` starts by determining how big the form's image will be.

If the Fit Page combo box is checked, it compares the form's width-to-height ratio with the printed page's width-to-height ratio. If the form's ratio is greater than the page's ratio, the form image is relatively wider and shorter than the page, so the program picks a scale factor that makes the image fill the page horizontally. If the form's ratio is smaller than the page's ratio, the form image is relatively taller and thinner than the page, so the program picks a scale factor that makes the image fill the page vertically. The program then calls the `e.Graphics` object's `ScaleTransform` method to scale the result. When the program draws on the object, everything is scaled by this amount. The result is that the image will be scaled to fill the page.

After calculating the scale to use, the program determines the image's final size. It then calculates the translation it must use to center the scaled image on the form. It calls the `e.Graphics` object's `TranslateTransform` method to make this translation. Now, when the `PrintPage` event handler draws the image at position (`0, 0`), the image is scaled appropriately and translated, so it is centered.

Wrapping Text

Printing an image of a form is a fairly common task. Another everyday task is printing text. The `SimplePrint` example earlier in this chapter showed that printing a few numbers or letters is easy. Printing a lot of text that must wrap across pages is harder.

Example program `PrintWrap`, which is available for download at `www.vb-helper.com/one_on_one.htm`, prints text, wrapping lines at the margins and starting new pages as needed.

The program uses the following `ParagraphInfo` class to store information about paragraphs that it should print. The class's `FontNumber` property determines which of three program-defined fonts to use for each paragraph. The `Indent` property gives the amount to increase the paragraph's left margin. `SpaceAfter` indicates the amount of vertical space that should be added after the paragraph. Finally, the `Text` property gives the paragraph's text.

```
Public Class ParagraphInfo
    Public FontNumber As Integer
    Public Indent As Integer
    Public SpaceAfter As Integer
    Public Text As String

    Public Sub New(ByVal new_FontNumber As Integer, ByVal new_Indent As Integer, _
     ByVal new_SpaceAfter As Integer, ByVal new_Text As String)
```

```
        FontNumber = new_FontNumber
        Indent = new_Indent
        SpaceAfter = new_SpaceAfter
        Text = new_Text
    End Sub
End Class
```

The following code shows the `PrintDocument`'s `BeginPrint` and `EndPrint` event handlers:

```
' The lines we will print.
Private m_Paragraphs As List(Of ParagraphInfo)

' The number of the next page we will print.
Private m_NextPage As Integer

' The distance of the page number from the
' top and left edges of the margin area.
Private Const PAGE_NUM_MARGIN_X As Integer = 50
Private Const PAGE_NUM_MARGIN_Y As Integer = 50

' Fonts we use while printing.
Private m_Fonts(0 To 2) As Font

' Prepare to print.
Private Sub pdlgWrap_BeginPrint(ByVal sender As Object, _
 ByVal e As System.Drawing.Printing.PrintEventArgs) Handles pdocWrapped.BeginPrint
    ' Create the text to print.
    m_Paragraphs = New List(Of ParagraphInfo)
    m_Paragraphs.Add(New ParagraphInfo(0, 20, 20, _
        "19. Splash Screens"))
    m_Paragraphs.Add(New ParagraphInfo(1, 0, 20, _
        "The first thing a user sees of an application is its splash screen..."))
    ... Other lines omitted ...

    ' Make the fonts we need.
    m_Fonts(0) = New Font("Times New Roman", 22, FontStyle.Bold, _
        GraphicsUnit.Point)
    m_Fonts(1) = New Font("Times New Roman", 14, FontStyle.Regular, _
        GraphicsUnit.Point)
    m_Fonts(2) = New Font("Courier New", 10, FontStyle.Regular, _
        GraphicsUnit.Point)

    ' Set the next page number.
    m_NextPage = 1
End Sub

' Clean up.
Private Sub pdlgWrap_EndPrint(ByVal sender As Object, _
 ByVal e As System.Drawing.Printing.PrintEventArgs) Handles pdocWrapped.EndPrint
    ' Dispose of the printing fonts.
    For i As Integer = 0 To 2
        m_Fonts(i).Dispose()
        m_Fonts(i) = Nothing
    Next i
End Sub
```

Variable `m_Paragraphs` holds a list of `Paragraph` objects describing the text to print. Variable `m_NextPage` tracks the current page number. The `m_Fonts` array contains the three fonts that the program will use to print.

The `BeginPrint` event handler adds a series of `ParagraphInfo` objects to the `m_Paragraphs` list. It then creates three fonts: a large heading font, a smaller text body font, and a code font. It sets `m_NextPage` to `1` and exits.

The `EndPrint` event handler simply disposes of the fonts.

The following code shows the `PrintDocument`'s `PrintPage` event handler:

```
' The PrintDocument needs a page. Print the next one.
Private Sub pdlgWrap_PrintPage(ByVal sender As System.Object, _
 ByVal e As System.Drawing.Printing.PrintPageEventArgs) _
 Handles pdocWrapped.PrintPage
    ' Print the page number.
    Dim x As Single = e.MarginBounds.Right + PAGE_NUM_MARGIN_X
    Dim y As Single = e.MarginBounds.Top - PAGE_NUM_MARGIN_Y
    Dim string_format As New StringFormat
    string_format.Alignment = StringAlignment.Center
    string_format.LineAlignment = StringAlignment.Center
    e.Graphics.DrawString(m_NextPage.ToString(), _
        m_Fonts(1), Brushes.Black, x, y, string_format)
    m_NextPage += 1

    ' Start at the top.
    y = e.MarginBounds.Top

    ' Loop while we have paragraphs.
    Do While m_Paragraphs.Count > 0
        ' Get the next piece of text we need to print.
        Dim para As ParagraphInfo = m_Paragraphs(0)
        Dim txt As String = para.Text

        ' See how much room we have.
        Dim layout_area As New SizeF( _
            e.MarginBounds.Width - para.Indent, _
            e.MarginBounds.Bottom - y)

        ' Make the height at least 1 to avoid confusing MeasureString
        If layout_area.Height < 1 Then layout_area.Height = 1

        ' See how much of the text will fit.
        Dim characters_fitted As Integer
        Dim lines_filled As Integer
        string_format.Alignment = StringAlignment.Near
        string_format.LineAlignment = StringAlignment.Near
        string_format.Trimming = StringTrimming.Word
        string_format.FormatFlags = StringFormatFlags.LineLimit
        Dim text_size As SizeF = e.Graphics.MeasureString(txt, _
            m_Fonts(para.FontNumber), layout_area, string_format, _
```

```
                characters_fitted, lines_filled)

            ' See if any characters fit.
            If characters_fitted > 0 Then
                ' Draw the text that fits.
                Dim layout_rect As New RectangleF( _
                    e.MarginBounds.Left + para.Indent, _
                    y, _
                    text_size.Width, _
                    text_size.Height)
                e.Graphics.DrawString(txt, m_Fonts(para.FontNumber), _
                    Brushes.Black, layout_rect, string_format)

                ' Increase y.
                y += text_size.Height + para.SpaceAfter
            End If

            ' See how much of this paragraph is left.
            para.Text = para.Text.Substring(characters_fitted)

            ' If all of this paragraph fit, remove it.
            If para.Text.Length < 1 Then m_Paragraphs.RemoveAt(0)

            ' If we have any text left in the paragraph,
            ' then we have filled this page.
            ' End this page and go to the next one.
            If para.Text.Length > 0 Then Exit Do
        Loop

        ' See if we have any text left to print.
        e.HasMorePages = (m_Paragraphs.Count > 0)
    End Sub
```

The `PrintPage` event handler does the most interesting work. It begins by printing the page number outside of the page's margin. It uses a `StringFormat` object to center the number.

The program then sets variable `y` equal to the top margin. This variable keeps track of the upper edge of the area that has not yet been printed.

The code then enters a loop that continues as long as there are objects in the `m_Paragraphs` list. The code gets the paragraph's text. It then builds a `SizeF` object to represent the area available for printing. Initially, this is the whole page within the margins, but it shrinks as `y` increases.

Next, the program uses the `e.Graphics` object's `MeasureString` method to see how much of the current paragraph will fit in the available area. It uses a `StringFormat` object to indicate that the text will be printed aligned to the top left of the area, that lines should break at words, and that it should stop when no more lines will fit vertically (so that it doesn't print the top half of a line).

If any characters from the current paragraph fit, the code draws whatever text fits. It uses the same `StringFormat` object, so the `DrawString` method automatically wraps the text across lines and stops when it runs out of room. The code then increases `y` to move past the newly printed text.

It also adds the paragraph's `SpaceAfter` value to `y`. If the entire paragraph fit in the available area, then this is appropriate. If some of the paragraph did not fit, then the text goes to the bottom of the page, so adding `SpaceAfter` to `y` moves `y` past the bottom margin. As you'll see shortly, that makes the code start a new page.

The program then removes the printed text from the current paragraph's text. If the paragraph now has no text, the program removes the paragraph from the `m_Paragraphs` list.

If the current paragraph has any text remaining, the newly printed text must be at the bottom of the page, so the program exits its `Do` loop to end the page. If the current paragraph has no text, the `Do` loop continues to print the next paragraph.

The `Do` loop ends when the `m_Paragraphs` list is empty, or when a paragraph reaches the end of the page. The event handler sets `e.HasMorePages` to `True` if there are more paragraphs to print, and then exits.

Figure 20-3 shows program `PrintWrap`'s print preview dialog displaying the first three pages of the document. (You can download this example at `www.vb-helper.com/one_on_one.htm`.) Though you can't read the text, you can see that the first page contains a heading, some body text, a second heading, and more body text. The final paragraph continues on the second page. The third page contains body text, a heading, and some code text that is indented and drawn in a different font.

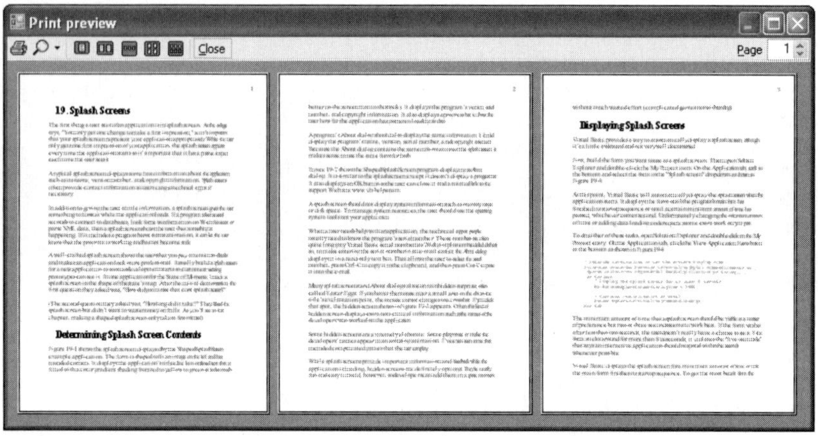

Figure 20-3: Program `PrintWrap` wraps text across lines and pages.

Flowing Text

Program `PrintWrap` described in the previous section is fairly useful if you only need to display text. A common task that this program cannot handle is displaying text interspersed with pictures. Program `PrintFlow`, shown in Figure 20-4, draws text that flows around pictures.

Figure 20-4: Program `PrintFlow` draws text that flows around pictures.

This program stores paragraph information in `ParagraphInfo` objects in the same way as program `PrintWrap` described in the previous section. It uses the following `PictureInfo` class to store information about pictures. This class stores the page number that should hold the picture, the picture's size and position, and the image to print.

```
Public Class PictureInfo
    Public PageNumber As Integer
    Public X As Integer
    Public Y As Integer
    Public Width As Integer
    Public Height As Integer
    Public Picture As Image

    Public Sub New(ByVal new_PageNumber As Integer, ByVal new_X As Integer, _
 ByVal new_Y As Integer, ByVal new_Width As Integer, _
 ByVal new_Height As Integer, ByVal new_Picture As Image)
        PageNumber = new_PageNumber
        X = new_X
        Y = new_Y
        Width = new_Width
        Height = new_Height
        Picture = new_Picture
    End Sub
End Class
```

Before looking at the code, it will be helpful to learn a bit about the program's basic approach. The general idea is to print the text one line at a time. For each line, the code builds a rectangle that represents the area that the line needs. Initially, this is a rectangle as tall as one line of text and spanning the width of the page's margins. The code puts this rectangle in a list of layout rectangles.

The code then compares the rectangles assigned to hold each picture to the layout rectangle. If the layout rectangle intersects with a picture rectangle, the program determines whether parts of the layout rectangle stick out beyond the sides of the picture rectangle. If the layout rectangle sticks out, the code breaks it into its left and right pieces, and adds them to the list of layout rectangles. It then continues comparing the remaining picture rectangles with the new pieces.

When it has finished, the list of layout rectangles represents the areas for this line of text that are not covered by pictures. The code loops through the rectangles, filling each with text, until it runs out of rectangles or text in the current paragraph.

Now that you understand the basic idea, you can look at the code. This program's `BeginPrint` and `EndPrint` event handlers are similar to those used by program `PrintWrap`, so they are not shown here. The following code shows the `PrintPage` event handler, which does the most interesting work:

```
' The PrintDocument needs a page. Print the next one.
Private Sub pdlgWrap_PrintPage(ByVal sender As System.Object, _
 ByVal e As System.Drawing.Printing.PrintPageEventArgs) _
 Handles pdocWrapped.PrintPage
    ' Make a list of rectangles that are reserved for pictures.
    Dim picture_rects As New List(Of Rectangle)

    ' Print any pictures for this page.
    For Each pic_info As PictureInfo In m_Pictures
        ' See if this picture belongs on this page.
        If pic_info.PageNumber = m_NextPage Then
            Dim pic_x As Integer
            If pic_info.X >= 0 Then
                ' Move right from left margin.
                pic_x = e.MarginBounds.Left + pic_info.X
            Else
                ' Move left from right margin.
                pic_x = e.MarginBounds.Right + pic_info.X
            End If
            Dim pic_y As Integer
            If pic_info.Y >= 0 Then
                ' Move down from top margin.
                pic_y = e.MarginBounds.Top + pic_info.Y
            Else
                ' Move up from bottom margin.
                pic_y = e.MarginBounds.Bottom + pic_info.Y
            End If

            ' Reserve this rectangle for the picture.
            Const PIC_MARGIN As Integer = 5
            Dim picture_rect As New Rectangle( _
                pic_x - PIC_MARGIN, pic_y - PIC_MARGIN, _
                pic_info.Width + 2 * PIC_MARGIN, _
                pic_info.Height + 2 * PIC_MARGIN)
            picture_rects.Add(picture_rect)

            ' Draw the picture.
            e.Graphics.DrawImage(pic_info.Picture, _
               pic_x, pic_y, pic_info.Width, pic_info.Height)
        End If
```

```
    Next pic_info

    ' Print the page number.
    Dim x As Single = e.MarginBounds.Right + PAGE_NUM_MARGIN_X
    Dim y As Single = e.MarginBounds.Top - PAGE_NUM_MARGIN_Y
    Dim string_format As New StringFormat
    string_format.Alignment = StringAlignment.Center
    string_format.LineAlignment = StringAlignment.Center
    e.Graphics.DrawString(m_NextPage.ToString(), _
        m_Fonts(1), Brushes.Black, x, y, string_format)
    m_NextPage += 1

    ' Start at the top.
    y = e.MarginBounds.Top

    ' Loop while we have paragraphs.
    Do While m_Paragraphs.Count > 0
        ' Get the next piece of text we need to print.
        Dim para As ParagraphInfo = m_Paragraphs(0)

        ' See how tall this paragraph's lines of text are.
        Dim line_hgt As Integer = m_Fonts(para.FontNumber).Height + 2

        ' Get the next area in which we can print.
        x = e.MarginBounds.Left + para.Indent
        Dim initial_rect As New Rectangle( _
            CInt(x), CInt(y), _
            CInt(e.MarginBounds.Right - x), line_hgt)

        ' Make the height at least 1 to avoid confusing MeasureString
        If initial_rect.Height < 1 Then initial_rect.Height = 1

        ' If the bottom of the layout region is below
        ' the bottom margin, then the page is full.
        If initial_rect.Bottom > e.MarginBounds.Bottom Then Exit Do

        ' Start the layout rectangle collection.
        Dim layout_rects As New List(Of Rectangle)
        layout_rects.Add(initial_rect)

        ' Intersect the layout rectangle with the picture rectangles.
        For Each pic_rect As Rectangle In picture_rects
            ' Copy new rectangles into this list.
            Dim new_layout_rects As New List(Of Rectangle)

            ' Compare this picture rectangle with each layout rectangle.
            For Each layout_rect As Rectangle In layout_rects
                ' See if the picture area intersects with the layout rectangle.
                If layout_rect.IntersectsWith(pic_rect) Then
                    ' They intersect.
                    ' See if there is any remaining
                    ' layout rectangle on the left.
                    If layout_rect.Left < pic_rect.Left Then
                        new_layout_rects.Add(New Rectangle( _
                            layout_rect.X, layout_rect.Y, _
```

```
                        pic_rect.Left - layout_rect.Left, _
                        layout_rect.Height))
                End If

                ' See if there is any remaining
                ' layout rectangle on the right.
                If layout_rect.Right > pic_rect.Right Then
                    new_layout_rects.Add(New Rectangle( _
                        pic_rect.Right, layout_rect.Y, _
                        layout_rect.Right - pic_rect.Right, _
                        layout_rect.Height))
                End If
            Else
                ' They don't intersect.
                ' Use the layout rectangle as it is.
                new_layout_rects.Add(layout_rect)
            End If
        Next layout_rect

        ' Save the new layout rectangles.
        layout_rects = new_layout_rects
    Next pic_rect

    ' Print in each layout rectangle until we run out of
    ' layout rectangles or text in this paragraph.
    For Each layout_rect As Rectangle In layout_rects
        ' See how much of the text will fit
        ' in this layout rectangle.
        Dim characters_fitted As Integer
        Dim lines_filled As Integer
        string_format.Alignment = StringAlignment.Near
        string_format.LineAlignment = StringAlignment.Near
        string_format.Trimming = StringTrimming.Word
        string_format.FormatFlags = StringFormatFlags.LineLimit
        Dim layout_size As New SizeF(layout_rect.Width, layout_rect.Height)
        Dim text_size As SizeF = e.Graphics.MeasureString(para.Text, _
            m_Fonts(para.FontNumber), layout_size, string_format, _
            characters_fitted, lines_filled)

        ' See if any characters fit.
        If characters_fitted > 0 Then
            ' Draw the text that fits.
            e.Graphics.DrawString(para.Text, m_Fonts(para.FontNumber), _
                Brushes.Black, layout_rect, string_format)
        End If

        ' See how much of this paragraph is left.
        para.Text = para.Text.Substring(characters_fitted)
        If para.Text.Length = 0 Then Exit For
    Next layout_rect

    ' Increase y for the next layout rectangles.
    y += line_hgt

    ' If all of this paragraph fit, remove it.
    If para.Text.Length = 0 Then
```

```
            m_Paragraphs.RemoveAt(0)
            y += para.SpaceAfter
        End If
    Loop

    ' See if we have any text left to print.
    e.HasMorePages = (m_Paragraphs.Count > 0)
End Sub
```

The event handler starts by looping through the list of `PictureInfo` objects. If a picture belongs on the current page, the program prints it in its desired location and adds a rectangle representing the picture to the `picture_rects` list. The code adds a small margin around the rectangle so that the text doesn't come too close to the picture.

The program provides a couple of special features for positioning pictures. If a picture's X coordinate is positive, the picture is drawn that distance inside the page's left margin. If the X coordinate is negative, the program draws the picture that distance to the left of the right margin. This makes it easy to align pictures on the left or right margins.

Similarly, the program draws the picture a given distance below the top margin or above the bottom margin, depending on the sign of the picture's Y coordinate.

`PrintPage` then draws and increments the page number, and sets variable `y` to the top margin much as the previous program `PrintWrap` did.

Also like program `PrintWrap`, this code enters a `Do` loop that lasts as long as the `m_Paragraphs` array is non-empty.

The program gets the next paragraph and sees how tall the paragraph's font is. It uses that height to build the initial layout rectangle for the line of text. If the rectangle extends below the page's bottom margin, the code exits the `Do` loop to end the current page.

The code adds the initial layout rectangle to the `layout_rects` list. It then loops through the picture rectangles and intersects each with the layout rectangle in the `layout_rects` list as described earlier.

After building the list of available layout rectangles for this line of text, the program loops through them. It uses the `e.Graphics` object's `MeasureString` method to see how much of the current paragraph fits inside each layout rectangle and draws whatever text will fit.

The code removes the newly printed text from the current paragraph. If the paragraph still contains text, the code continues its loop and writes text into the next layout rectangle.

After it has run out of layout rectangles or text, the program increases variable `y` to move to the next line. If the current paragraph is empty, it removes the paragraph from the `m_Paragraphs` list and adds in the paragraph's `SpaceAfter` value to `y`.

The `Do` loop continues printing until all of the paragraphs are gone or until an initial layout rectangle extends below the page's bottom margin and exits the loop.

After the `Do` loop ends, the program sets `e.HasMorePages` to `True` if there are still paragraphs to print.

Printing Procedurally

Visual Basic 6 has a simple procedural method for printing. You use the `Printer` object's properties and methods to tell the object to print something. You tell it to draw a line here, a rectangle there, and some text at some other position. Other methods tell the `Printer` object to start a new page, finish the document, or cancel printing.

Visual Basic .NET has an event-driven printing model that is non-intuitive for many developers. Rather than telling an object what to do, the program responds to requests to draw pages. Within a page, the code still uses an object's methods to draw, but the code cannot explicitly tell the program to move to the next page. Instead, it ends the `PrintPage` event handler and resumes work when the next `PrintPage` event fires.

However, by using metafiles, you can make Visual Basic .NET print procedurally. A *metafile* is a file that contains a series of drawing commands. The basic approach is to draw the document in a series of metafiles and then render them in the `PrintPage` event handler.

The following code shows how example program `PrintMetafile` uses metafiles to print procedurally:

```
' Metafiles representing the pages we will print.
Private m_Pages As List(Of Metafile)

' The number of the next page we will print.
Private m_NextPage As Integer

' Prepare to print.
Private Sub pdlgWrap_BeginPrint(ByVal sender As Object, _
 ByVal e As System.Drawing.Printing.PrintEventArgs) Handles pdocMetafile.BeginPrint
    ' Make the metafiles.
    MakeMetafiles(pdocMetafile.PrinterSettings.DefaultPageSettings)

    ' Start with the first page.
    m_NextPage = 0
End Sub

' The PrintDocument needs a page. Print the next one.
Private Sub pdlgWrap_PrintPage(ByVal sender As System.Object, _
 ByVal e As System.Drawing.Printing.PrintPageEventArgs) _
 Handles pdocMetafile.PrintPage
    ' Draw this page's metafile.
    e.Graphics.DrawImage(m_Pages(m_NextPage), 0, 0, _
        e.PageBounds.Width, e.PageBounds.Height)

    ' Move to the next page.
    m_NextPage += 1
    e.HasMorePages = (m_NextPage <= m_Pages.Count - 1)
End Sub
```

Variable `m_Pages` holds a list of metafiles. The `BeginPrint` event handler calls subroutine `MakeMetafiles` (described shortly) to initialize this list. It then sets `m_NextPage` to `0` and exits.

The `PrintPage` event handler simply uses the `e.Graphics` object's `DrawImage` method to draw the current page's metafile onto the page. It sets `e.HasMorePages` to `True` if there are more metafiles to draw.

The following code shows the `MakeMetafiles` subroutine. This is the code that does all the work of building the metafiles for later printing:

```
' Make the metafiles.
Private Sub MakeMetafiles(ByVal page_settings As PageSettings)
    ' Get a Graphics object representing the printer settings.
    Dim printer_settings As PrinterSettings = pdocMetafile.PrinterSettings
    Dim measure_gr As Graphics = printer_settings.CreateMeasurementGraphics()
    Dim hdc As IntPtr = measure_gr.GetHdc()

    ' Get the page's bounding rectangle in inches.
    ' Note that the PageSettings are in hundredths of inches.
    Dim page_rect As New RectangleF( _
        CSng(page_settings.Bounds.Left / 100), _
        CSng(page_settings.Bounds.Top / 100), _
        CSng(page_settings.Bounds.Width / 100), _
        CSng(page_settings.Bounds.Height / 100))

    ' Get a rectangle bounding the drawing area
    ' inside the margins in hundredths of inches.
    Dim xmin As Single = page_settings.Bounds.Left + page_settings.Margins.Left
    Dim ymin As Single = page_settings.Bounds.Top + page_settings.Margins.Top
    Dim xmax As Single = page_settings.Bounds.Right - page_settings.Margins.Right
    Dim ymax As Single = page_settings.Bounds.Bottom - page_settings.Margins.Bottom
    Dim wid As Single = xmax - xmin
    Dim hgt As Single = ymax - ymin
    Dim margin_rect As New RectangleF(xmin, ymin, xmax - xmin, ymax - ymin)

    ' Make a list of Graphics objects for the metafiles.
    Dim grs As New List(Of Graphics)

    ' Make the pages.
    m_Pages = New List(Of Metafile)
    For i As Integer = 0 To 3
        ' Make a new metafile for this page.
        Dim mf As New Metafile(hdc, _
            page_rect, _
            MetafileFrameUnit.Inch, _
            EmfType.EmfOnly)
        m_Pages.Add(mf)

        ' Make a Graphics object for the metafile.
        Dim gr As Graphics = Graphics.FromImage(mf)
        grs.Add(gr)

        ' Draw the page.
        Select Case i
            Case 0   ' Red ellipse.
                Using the_pen As New Pen(Color.Red, 5)
                    gr.DrawEllipse(the_pen, margin_rect)
                End Using
            Case 1   ' Green diamond.
                Dim cx As Single = (xmin + xmax) / 2
                Dim cy As Single = (ymin + ymax) / 2
                Dim pts() As PointF = { _
                    New PointF(cx, ymin), _
```

```
                    New PointF(xmax, cy), _
                    New PointF(cx, ymax), _
                    New PointF(xmin, cy) _
                }
                Using the_pen As New Pen(Color.Green, 10)
                    gr.DrawPolygon(the_pen, pts)
                End Using
            Case 2  ' Blue hexagon.
                Dim cx As Single = (xmin + xmax) / 2
                Dim cy As Single = (ymin + ymax) / 2
                Dim radius As Single = (xmax - xmin) / 2
                Dim theta As Single = -PI / 2
                Dim dtheta As Single = 2 * PI / 6
                Dim pts(0 To 5) As PointF
                For pt_num As Integer = 0 To 5
                    pts(pt_num) = New PointF( _
                        CSng(cx + radius * Cos(theta)), _
                        CSng(cy + radius * Sin(theta)))
                    theta += dtheta
                Next pt_num
                Using the_pen As New Pen(Color.Blue, 20)
                    gr.DrawPolygon(the_pen, pts)
                End Using
            Case 3  ' Orange star.
                Dim cx As Single = (xmin + xmax) / 2
                Dim cy As Single = (ymin + ymax) / 2
                Dim radius As Single = (xmax - xmin) / 2
                Dim theta As Single = -PI / 2
                Dim dtheta As Single = 2 * 2 * PI / 5
                Dim pts(0 To 4) As PointF
                For pt_num As Integer = 0 To 4
                    pts(pt_num) = New PointF( _
                        CSng(cx + radius * Cos(theta)), _
                        CSng(cy + radius * Sin(theta)))
                    theta += dtheta
                Next pt_num
                Using the_pen As New Pen(Color.Orange, 30)
                    gr.DrawPolygon(the_pen, pts)
                End Using
        End Select
    Next i

    ' Now that we know the page count, draw the page numbers.
    Dim string_format As New StringFormat
    string_format.Alignment = StringAlignment.Center
    string_format.LineAlignment = StringAlignment.Center
    Using big_font As New Font(Me.Font.FontFamily, 70, FontStyle.Bold, _
     GraphicsUnit.Pixel)
        Dim num_pages As Integer = m_Pages.Count
        Dim margin_rectf As New RectangleF(xmin, ymin, xmax - xmin, ymax - ymin)
        For i As Integer = 0 To m_Pages.Count - 1
```

```
                grs(i).DrawString("Page " & i + 1 & " of " & num_pages, _
                    big_font, Brushes.Black, _
                    margin_rectf, string_format)
                grs(i).Dispose()
            Next i
        End Using ' big_font

        ' Clean up.
        measure_gr.ReleaseHdc(hdc)
        measure_gr.Dispose()
    End Sub
```

The code starts by getting a `PrinterSettings` object that represents the printer pages. It gets a `Graphics` object associated with this object and gets a DC associated with it.

The program then creates a `RectangleF` to represent the page's printable area. The `page_settings.Bounds` measurements are in hundredths of inches, so the program divides by 100 to convert them into inches.

Next, the code creates a `RectangleF` to represent the page's area within its margins. The program will use this rectangle to draw, and a program draws on a metafile in hundredths of inches, so the units for this `RectangleF` are hundredths of inches.

The program makes a list to hold a `Graphics` objects for each of the metafiles. It then uses a loop to build the four metafiles it will print.

Inside the loop, the program creates a new metafile and adds it to the `m_Pages` list. It creates a `Graphics` object to work with the metafile and uses that object to draw a different picture for each page.

After it has generated all of the pages, the code adds text to each metafile giving the page number in the format "Page 3 of 4." This would be hard to do with Visual Basic .NET's normal event-driven printing. Because you must finish building one page before you build those that follow, you don't know how many pages you will print in total. With the metafile printing technique, you build every page before you print any of them, so you can go back and make changes such as this one to pages generated earlier.

Figure 20-5 shows program `PrintMetafile`'s print preview dialog displaying all four of the program's printed pages.

Not only do metafiles let you print procedurally, but they also give you a new way to export graphical data. The following code shows how you could modify the previous code to save each metafile in a file. Simply insert this line at the end of the `For` loop that adds the page numbers to the metafiles:

```
' Save the metafile.
m_Pages(i).Save(Application.StartupPath & "/page" & i & ".wmf", ImageFormat.Wmf)
```

Now you can open the pages' metafiles in many graphics applications, including CorelDRAW! and Windows Picture and Fax Viewer. You can even insert them into Microsoft Word documents.

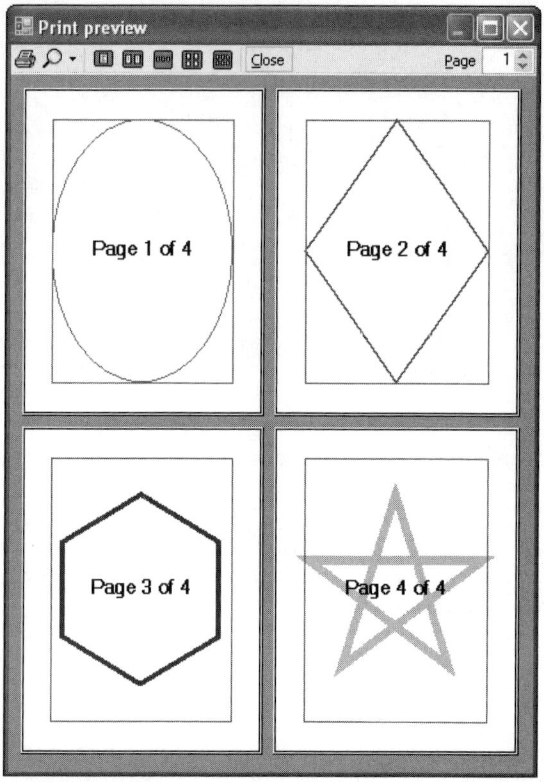

Figure 20-5: Program `PrintMetafile` draws pages onto metafiles before printing them.

Microsoft Paint can open metafiles, but the results are usually not very good. Microsoft Paint isn't really designed to work with metafiles.

Summary

The examples in this chapter show how to print form images and simple text in Visual Basic .NET. They show how to wrap text across lines and pages, and how to flow text around pictures. Program `PrintMetafile` shows how to print procedurally, rather than in an event-driven way.

However, this is far from the end of the story for printing. Even when printing text alone, you can add features for hyphenation, widow and orphan words and lines (for example, to prevent a paragraph from ending with a single word on the next page), indexing, building tables of contents, justification (left, right, center), tabs, multiple fonts within the same paragraph, and so forth. If you need all of these features, you are almost certainly better off using Visual Studio Tools for Office (VSTO) to dump your text into Microsoft Word and letting Word handle the typography. That will be a lot faster and easier than trying to rewrite Word yourself from scratch.

When a program prints a document, it actually only adds the document to a queue for printing later. The printing occurs asynchronously, so the program can move on to do other things without waiting for the queue to empty and for the relatively slow printer to finish its work.

Chapter 21, "Threading," describes other ways programs can perform tasks asynchronously. It shows how you can make your program perform more than one task at the same time. On computers with more than one CPU, this can truly make the application faster. Even on a single CPU system, however, multi-threading can make some applications simpler and more responsive to the user.

21

Threading

Most computers today have only a single central processing unit (CPU) that executes instructions. That means they can only do one thing at a time. Modern CPUs are pretty fast and can execute many millions or even billions of instructions per second. Most applications don't require that much speed, so the computer splits the CPU's time to let several different applications take turns running. The CPU is so fast that the switching takes place quickly enough to give the illusion that the computer is running more than one program at the same time. While the CPU can really only execute one instruction at a time, it appears as if the Windows operating system is running a whole bunch of applications simultaneously.

Each of the programs running on the computer is a separate *process*. Within a process, you can create multiple *threads of execution* that can also run simultaneously. Every program has at least one process and thread, but some create more. These threads are more closely related than the processes representing different applications, but the idea is similar. Like processes, the threads take turns running on the CPU so they give the illusion of running at the same time.

Typically, threads must communicate and work together to provide whatever application it is that they build as a group. To avoid confusion, the operating system imposes strict rules on how threads can communicate safely. It's easier for different threads to communicate than it is for different processes because they are more closely related, but there are still rules to follow.

For example, you could build a single application that monitors a stock quote Web site to track your favorite stocks. Separate threads could monitor each of several stocks and display their current prices on separate graphs within the same application. Each thread works separately, but they all interact with the main program's form to display their data.

This chapter describes some useful threading scenarios. It explains how to build applications that use threading to make the user interface more responsive, to perform tasks in the background while the user does other things, and to divide complex tasks into pieces.

Threading Pros and Cons

The technology used to build computer chips is reaching its physical limits, so the steady increases in CPU speed that developers have come to expect over the last few decades is starting to slow down. Because they are already using the fastest chips available, computer manufacturers cannot rely on even faster chips to improve performance. Instead, many computers now use multiple CPUs to improve performance. It is quite common these days to find computers using two CPUs, and it seems likely that the trend toward multiple CPUs will continue. Systems with up to eight processors will probably be available by the time you read this book.

The exact definition of these systems is sometimes a little fuzzy. Some "multi-core" systems have separate CPU chips, while others have multiple processors on a single chip. Some architectures have a central processor that controls several secondary processors. For the purposes of this chapter, all that matters is that the computer has more than one processor of some kind that can execute threads.

If you want to take full advantage of multi-CPU systems, you should know a bit about multi-threaded applications. The following sections describe some of the advantages and disadvantages of multi-threaded programming.

Advantages

Often, a multiple CPU system can execute different threads on different processors. In that case, if your code produces multiple threads, the program will run faster because each thread can run on a separate processor. The program probably won't run twice as fast, because there is some overhead in coordinating the threads, but it will probably run significantly faster than it would on a single CPU system.

Some multi-processor systems can automatically parallelize instructions and run pieces of the application in separate threads. For example, suppose a program must perform some calculations on some old values, read some new values from a file, and then combine the old and new values. The computer could start a thread running on one CPU to read values from the file, while another thread on a separate CPU performs the initial calculations. Then, the threads would need to synchronize so that they can combine the new and old values. Though the entire sequence cannot be split across two processors, some of the steps can be.

Even if the computer has a single processor, writing multiple threads can often make the application appear faster and more responsive to the user. For example, suppose a program must perform a very long series of calculations. In a single-threaded application, the program begins its calculation and cannot respond until it finishes. A well-written application provides feedback so that the user knows the program is still working. A poorly written application may appear stuck and might not even refresh its user interface. If the user covers and exposes the program, its form may not even redraw.

To keep the application responsive, you can start the long calculation on a separate thread. The system automatically switches control between this calculation thread and the application's user interface thread (*UI thread*) so that the user interface can update itself.

The user interface can also respond to user actions such as button clicks. In particular, the user may be able to click a button to cancel the long calculation.

A program can also control a thread's priority. The system gives precedence to higher-priority threads. You can make high-priority threads run important calculations, while lower-priority threads perform less-important tasks when the high-priority threads are idle. For example, you can perform long calculations or downloads on a lower-priority thread, so the user interface takes precedence. Because the user interface spends most of its time waiting for user input, that gives the lower-priority thread plenty of time to execute, but the user interface can still respond when the user does something to it.

Disadvantages

Despite the advantage of increased responsiveness (and possibly performance), threading has some serious drawbacks.

The biggest disadvantage to multi-threading is that it is confusing. Multi-threading code is more complicated and non-intuitive than code written for a single thread. It requires extra coordination among the threads and safe communications (particularly between other threads and the thread controlling the user interface). It requires additional work to ensure that the threads get access to the resources they need without wasting time competing for them.

These issues can lead to some very confusing bugs. Often, these bugs depend on the exact timing of a series of calculations. Execution timing is handled by the operating system and is out of your control so it can be very hard to reliably reproduce these bugs.

The two most problematic types of bugs caused by multi-threading issues are race conditions and deadlocks.

Race Conditions

For example, suppose a program uses two threads to calculate new values for a graph. The shared variables `old_x` and `old_y` record the coordinates of the last value plotted. When a thread receives a new Y value, it increments X, draws a line from the old point to the new one, and updates the `old_x` and `old_y` variables to hold the new point's coordinates. The following pseudocode shows how the threads work:

```
Get new_y
new_x = old_x + 1
Line (old_x, old_y)-(new_x, new_y)
old_x = new_x
old_y = new_y
```

Suppose `old_x` = 10 and `old_y` = 20. Suppose also that Thread A calculates a new Y value of 25 and Thread B calculates a new Y value of 30. The following timeline shows a normal expected execution for the threads where Thread A executes all of its statements before Thread B executes. The result is a line from (10, 20) to (11, 25) and another line from (11, 25) to (12, 30).

Thread A	Thread B
`1A: new_y = 25`	
`2A: new_x = 11`	
`3A: (10, 20)-(11, 25)`	
`4A: old_x = 11`	
`5A: old_y = 25`	
	`1B: new_y = 30`
	`2B: new_x = 12`
	`3B: (11, 25)-(12, 30)`
	`4B: old_x = 12`
	`5B: old_y = 30`

Now, consider the following timeline:

Thread A	Thread B
`1A: new_y = 25`	
`2A: new_x = 11`	
`3A: (10, 20)-(11, 25)`	
	`1B: new_y = 30`
	`2B: new_x = 11`
	`3B: (10, 20)-(11, 30)`
	`4B: old_x = 11`
	`5B: old_y = 30`
`4A: old_x = 11`	
`5A: old_y = 25`	

In this execution sequence, Thread A starts running its code, but the system interrupts it before it finishes. Thread A calculates its `new_y` and `new_x` values and draws a line from the old point (10, 20) to its new point (11, 25).

Now Thread B takes over. Because Thread A has not yet updated `old_x` and `old_y`, Thread B uses the original values 10 and 20, so it draws a line from (10, 20) to its new point (11, 30). Thread B updates `old_x` and `old_y` to the new coordinates (11, 30).

Thread A resumes and updates `old_x` and `old_y` again, setting them to the coordinates (11, 25). Future lines start at this point, not from the point (11, 30) saved by Thread B. The result is an extra line sticking up from the graph between points (10, 20) and (11, 30).

This type of bug is a type of *race condition*. A race condition occurs when two threads race toward a common piece of data, and the outcome depends on which thread gets there first. In this example, Thread B updates the `old_x` and `old_y` variables first, and then Thread A overwrites those values.

This problem would be confusing enough if the steps executed in the same order shown in the timeline every time, but, in general, you don't know when the operating system will decide that it's time to switch between Thread A and Thread B.

If you look carefully at the timeline, you can see that the problem occurs when Thread B executes between Thread A's steps 3A and 4A. Here, Thread A has drawn its line, but has not yet updated `old_x` and `old_y`. If Thread A contains about 100 lines of code, and given no other information, the odds that Thread B will start running between those steps is about 1 in 100. After testing the code 100 times, you would only have about a 63 percent chance of seeing the bug. You would need to test the code around 300 times to have a 95 percent chance of discovering the bug.

> *To calculate the probability of finding the bug in N trials, calculate 1 minus the probability of not finding the bug raised to the power N. In this case, 1 – 0.99 ^ 300 is approximately 0.95.*

At that point, you would know that a bug exists, but it would be very hard to reproduce. You cannot simply step through the code and see what it is doing the way you can with single-threaded code. You not only need to consider what the two threads are doing, but also the exact timing of their execution.

One way to avoid this kind of race condition is to make each thread "lock" a variable before using it. If the variable is locked by another thread, the code blocks until the other thread releases its lock before continuing.

The following table shows the previous timeline modified by making the threads lock the variables `new_x`, `new_y`, `old_x`, and `old_y`.

Thread A	**Thread B**
0A: Lock new_x, new_y old_x, old_y	
1A: new_y = 25	
2A: new_x = 11	
3A: (10, 20)-(11, 25)	
	0B: Lock new_x, new_y old_x, old_y
4A: old_x = 11	<blocked>
5A: old_y = 25	<blocked>
6A: Release locks	<blocked>
	1B: new_y = 30
	2B: new_x = 12
	3B: (11, 25)-(12, 30)
	4B: old_x = 12
	5B: old_y = 30
	6B: Release locks

In this version, when Thread B starts, it tries to lock the variables and blocks until Thread A releases its locks. That gives Thread A time to finish before Thread B resumes. When Thread B resumes, `old_x` and `old_y` have been updated, so the result is the same as if Thread A had run completely before Thread B started.

Deadlocks

Although locks can prevent race conditions, they lead to a new type of multi-threading bug called a deadlock. A *deadlock* occurs when one thread is blocked, waiting for another thread to release a lock while the other thread is waiting for the first thread to release a different lock.

For example, consider the following timeline. Here, Thread A tries to lock variable `X`, and then variable `Y`, while Thread B tries to lock `Y` and then `X`.

Thread A	**Thread B**
`1A: Lock X`	
	`1B: Lock Y`
	`2B: Lock X`
`2A: Lock Y`	`<blocked>`
`<blocked>`	`<blocked>`

In this example, Thread A locks `X` and Thread B locks `Y`. Then Thread B tries to lock `X` and blocks because Thread A already has that variable locked. Next, Thread A tries to lock `Y` and blocks, because Thread B already has it locked. Both threads are blocked waiting for each other, so execution stops.

You can fix this simple example by making the two threads try to lock `X` and `Y` in the same order, but in more complicated examples a solution isn't always obvious. For example, suppose Threads A, B, and C need to lock resources X, Y, and Z. Thread A starts and locks resource X before the CPU switches to run Thread B. Thread B locks resource Y and then is interrupted while Thread C takes over. Thread C locks resource Z and then tries to lock resources X and Y. Because all three resources are locked, all three of the threads are blocked.

Requiring the threads to lock the resources in a specific order works for the three-thread scenarios, as well. If all three threads try to lock the resources in the order X, Y, Z, then whichever thread locks resource X first gets access to the others. However, resources don't always have nicely ordered names, so it's not always clear what order would be best.

Suppose Thread A needs to perform a long task with resource X and short tasks with resources Y and Z. In that case, it makes sense for Thread A to use resource X first so that it keeps the other resources locked for the shortest time possible. Similarly, suppose Thread B must do a lot of work with resource Y, and Thread C must spend a lot of time working with resource Z. In this case, there are good reasons for the threads to grab the resources in different orders. If different developers are working independently on the code for the different threads, they need to coordinate carefully to avoid deadlocks.

To make matters worse, suppose the program has half a dozen threads accessing a dozen resources. Suppose some of the threads call library routines that might access the resources. You didn't write the library routines, so you can't dictate the locking order they use. To further confuse the situation, suppose the computer is running other applications that also need to use those resources. It would be very difficult to figure out how to coordinate all of these threads, library calls, and processes, some of which are out of your control, so they cannot deadlock.

A different approach to preventing deadlocks is to make lock attempts time out after awhile. In the previous example, if Thread B cannot lock variable `Y` within 1 second, it gives up, releases its lock on `X`, and tries again later. That lets Thread A get its lock on `Y` and continue. Later, Thread B tries again and, assuming Thread A has finished and released its locks, it can continue.

You can make time-outs a little more effective if they use random durations. In this example, it is possible that Thread A would also time out waiting for resource Y, just as Thread B times out waiting for resource X. Thread A then locks resource X again and is interrupted, while Thread B locks resource Y again. In practice, the operating system will be inconsistent enough to add a little randomness to the process, so this pattern is unlikely to repeat, but it is possible. You can reduce the chances slightly by introducing a bit of randomness to the time-out lengths. For example, Thread A might time out after 1.2 seconds, while Thread B times out after 0.9 seconds.

As is the case with race conditions, deadlocks depend on the exact execution timing. This example only causes problems if Thread B runs between steps 1A and 2A. Like race conditions, deadlocks are hard to reproduce, but they are a little easier to analyze when they occur because the threads stop running. A race condition leaves behind corrupt data and keeps running, but in a deadlock, you can at least tell which threads are stuck.

Performance Issues

Multi-threading can improve performance on multi-CPU systems and can improve responsiveness even on single-CPU systems, but it isn't free. The operating system needs to use extra resources to keep track of multiple threads. It also takes some time to switch from one thread to another.

This extra overhead actually slows down total execution, at least on single-CPU systems. If you run enough threads, the additional overhead may even slow down multi-CPU systems. If you have a lot of threads, the system may spend more time switching back and forth than running code.

Applications that typically benefit from multi-threading include those that combine relatively slow and relatively fast operations. For example, many applications spend most of their time waiting for the user to do something. The program sits idle until the user clicks a button, selects a menu item, or enters text. While the program is sitting idle, it could be running threads in the background to perform calculations.

Similarly, if the program spends a lot of time waiting for network downloads, disk access, Web Service calls, and other slow operations, other threads could do something more active at the same time.

One technique for dynamically deciding whether it's worth starting another thread is to check the system's CPU load. If the CPU is 50 percent used or less, another thread will probably provide a net gain in performance. If CPU usage is higher, such as 75 or 80 percent, adding another thread might degrade performance overall.

Use the `PerformanceCounter` *class to check the CPU load. You might want to look at a time average over several seconds because the CPU load can fluctuate quickly.*

Using Background Workers

To take advantage of multi-threading without stumbling into its pitfalls, it helps to keep things as simple as possible. Although Visual Basic provides tools for building extremely powerful multi-threaded applications, if you aren't careful, you can quickly build a program that is so complicated and confusing that you can't get it to work. If you use multi-threading in the simplest way that can get the job done, you can minimize your risks.

Visual Basic provides a `BackgroundWorker` component that makes threading easier and safer than it is if you use the underlying threading tools directly. `BackgroundWorker` provides events to perform work, provide the main program with progress reports, and notify the program when it has finished. Because they are safe and easy, most of the examples presented in this chapter use `BackgroundWorkers` to manage threading.

UI Threading

One of the most common reasons to use multiple threads is to allow the user interface (UI) to respond quickly while some longer task executes in the background. While a long download or calculation works in the background, the UI can still process button clicks and other user actions. In particular, it can handle the user's command to stop the background process.

I've run into two main problems with this kind of threading. First, the program may have trouble if the user interface can interact directly with the background process. For example, suppose clicking a Download button makes the program start a long calculation on a background thread. Now, suppose the user accidentally double-clicks this button. The program starts a new thread to perform the calculation and then starts another thread to perform the same calculation. At best, the two threads will split the CPU's cycles and cut performance in half. At worst, the two threads may interfere with each other, causing race conditions or a deadlock.

> *During beta testing on one project, we discovered exactly this problem. A user could launch a process by clicking a button. One tester found that if he quickly clicked the button again, he could start a second process, so he wrote it up as a bug report. He then found that if he clicked really quickly three times, he could make three processes run simultaneously, so he wrote that up separately. He went on to spend the afternoon reporting the same bug in about a dozen different ways. It probably wasn't the best use of his testing time, but at least we got to clear a lot of bug reports with a single fix.*

The easiest way to handle this sort of problem is to disable the user interface elements that launch the background thread while the thread is running. In this example, the program should disable the Download button before starting the thread. When the thread finishes, the program should re-enable the button.

The second major problem I've seen with UI threading is caused by the fact that a thread cannot directly interact with controls that it did not create. It would be perfectly natural for a thread that performs some calculation to display periodic progress messages and its final result on the main program's controls. Unfortunately, that isn't allowed.

Instead, the thread must use the `Invoke` method to call a routine defined on some control. `Invoke` passes the call to the thread that created the control so that it can execute the routine.

Usually a developer adds an update routine to the form and then uses `Invoke` to call that routine. The update routine can then access any control on the form.

Example program `BackgroundGraphs` (shown in Figure 21-1 and available for download at `www.vb-helper.com/one_on_one.htm`) uses four `BackgroundWorker` controls to display four graphs. Each `BackgroundWorker` uses `Invoke` to make the main UI thread update the corresponding graph.

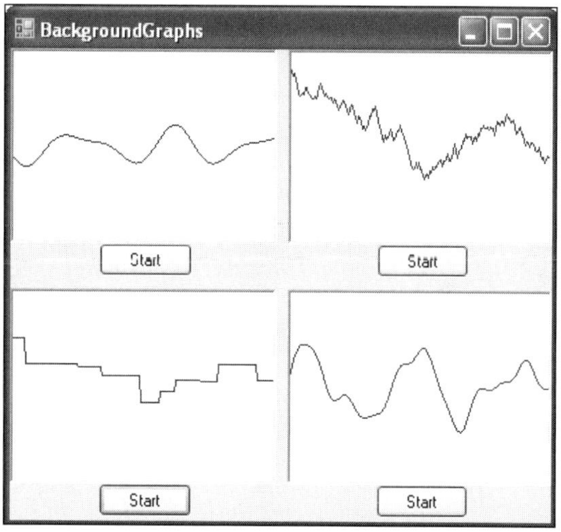

Figure 21-1: Program `BackgroundGraphs` displays four graphs with different shapes running at different speeds.

The following code shows how program `BackgroundGraphs` loads and starts its `BackgroundWorker` controls. (You can download this example at `www.vb-helper.com/one_on_one.htm`.) To make updating the graphs easier, the form's `Load` event handler saves references to their `PictureBoxes` in the `m_Graphs` array. It also makes `Bitmaps` to hold each graph's image. The code then sets initial data values for the four graphs and calls the `BackgroundWorkers'` `RunWorkerAsync` methods to make them start running asynchronously.

```
' The graphing PictureBoxes.
Private m_Graphs() As PictureBox

Private m_Wid As Integer
Private m_Hgt As Integer

' The graphs' images.
Private m_Bitmaps() As Bitmap
Private m_LastY() As Integer

Private Sub Form1_Load(ByVal sender As System.Object, _
 ByVal e As System.EventArgs) Handles MyBase.Load
    ' Save the PictureBoxes in an array.
    m_Graphs = New PictureBox() {picGraph0, picGraph1, picGraph2, picGraph3}

    ' Get the PictureBoxes' dimensions.
```

```
    m_Wid = picGraph0.ClientSize.Width
    m_Hgt = picGraph0.ClientSize.Height

    ' Make the bitmaps.
    Dim num_graphs As Integer = m_Graphs.Length
    ReDim m_Bitmaps(0 To num_graphs - 1)
    ReDim m_LastY(0 To num_graphs - 1)
    For i As Integer = 0 To 3
        m_Bitmaps(i) = New Bitmap(m_Wid, m_Hgt)
        Using gr As Graphics = Graphics.FromImage(m_Bitmaps(i))
            gr.Clear(Color.White)
        End Using
        m_Graphs(i).Image = m_Bitmaps(i)
    Next i

    ' Start the background workers.
    m_LastY(0) = Y0(0)
    bgwGraph0.RunWorkerAsync()

    m_LastY(1) = m_Hgt \ 2
    bgwGraph1.RunWorkerAsync()

    m_LastY(2) = m_Hgt \ 2
    bgwGraph2.RunWorkerAsync()

    m_LastY(3) = Y3(0)
    bgwGraph3.RunWorkerAsync()
End Sub
```

When the program calls a `BackgroundWorker`'s `RunWorkerAsync` method, the worker's `DoWork` event fires. The event handler should perform whatever task the worker is supposed to handle.

The following code shows how the first worker generates its graph. The other graphs work similarly, so their code isn't shown here.

```
' Draw graph 0.
Private Sub bgwGraph0_DoWork(ByVal sender As System.Object, _
 ByVal e As System.ComponentModel.DoWorkEventArgs) Handles bgwGraph0.DoWork
    ' Work at reduced priority.
    Thread.CurrentThread.Priority = ThreadPriority.BelowNormal

    Static X As Integer = 0
    Do
        ' Calculate the next point.
        X += 1

        ' Report the point to the UI thread.
        Me.Invoke(Me.m_PlotPointDelegate, 0, Y0(X))

        ' Pause a while.
        Thread.Sleep(1)

        ' See if we should cancel.
        If bgwGraph0.CancellationPending Then Exit Do
```

```
        Loop
    End Sub

    Private Function Y0(ByVal x As Integer) As Integer
        Return CInt(m_Hgt / 2 + 10 * Sin(x / 11) + 5 * Sin(x / 7))
    End Function
```

The code first reduces the priority for the new `BackgroundWorker`'s thread. That allows the UI thread to run at a higher priority, so it can respond quickly to user events.

This example also uses `Sleep` calls to allow the UI thread to make progress. If you don't lower the background threads' priority and you don't call `Sleep`, the threads hog the CPU, and the UI thread cannot respond to user events. For an interesting exercise, comment out the `Priority` and `Sleep` code and see what happens.

Next, the code enters a loop where it calculates graph values. It increments the graph's X coordinate, calculates the corresponding new Y value, and uses the form's `Invoke` method to call the `m_PlotPointDelegate` (described shortly). It passes this routine the index of the graph and the new Y coordinate.

The code then sleeps for 1 millisecond. This makes the system take control away from this thread. If you don't do this, the thread tends to hog the CPU, and the other threads don't make any headway. Eventually, the system decides the thread has had its share and runs another thread. The result is that one thread runs for awhile and the others are stuck. Then a new thread runs while the rest are stuck. The illusion of simultaneously running threads is lost.

You may get different results if your computer has multiple CPUs. For another interesting exercise, comment out the `Sleep` calls and see what happens.

Next, the `DoWork` event handler checks the `BackgroundWorker`'s `CancellationPending` property to see if the code has asked the worker to stop. If `CancellationPending` is `True`, the code exits its `Do` loop, so it stops drawing the graph.

The following code shows how the main UI thread updates the graphs. It first defines `PlotPointDelegate` to be a delegate referring to a subroutine that takes two integer parameters. Next, it declares variable `m_PlotPointDelegate` to be of this type and sets the variable to point to the `PlotPoint` subroutine.

```
    ' Plot a data point.
    Private Delegate Sub PlotPointDelegate(ByVal graph_num As Integer, _
        ByVal Y As Integer)

    Private m_PlotPointDelegate As PlotPointDelegate = AddressOf Me.PlotPoint

    Private Sub PlotPoint(ByVal graph_num As Integer, ByVal Y As Integer)
        ' Scoot the image over to the left.
        Dim bm As New Bitmap(m_Wid, m_Hgt)
        Using gr As Graphics = Graphics.FromImage(bm)
            gr.DrawImage(m_Bitmaps(graph_num), -1, 0)

            ' Clear the right edge.
            gr.DrawLine(Pens.White, m_Wid - 1, 0, m_Wid - 1, m_Hgt)

            ' Draw the new point.
```

```
            gr.DrawLine(Pens.Blue, m_Wid - 2, m_LastY(graph_num), m_Wid - 1, Y)
        End Using

        ' Save the new Y value.
        m_LastY(graph_num) = Y

        ' Refresh the graph.
        m_Bitmaps(graph_num) = bm
        m_Graphs(graph_num).Image = bm
    End Sub
```

When a `BackgroundWorker` invokes `m_PlotPointDelegate`, the main UI thread calls subroutine `PlotPoint`. That routine makes a new `Bitmap` for the appropriate graph. It copies the existing `Bitmap` onto the new one, shifting the image one pixel to the left. It erases the rightmost column of pixels and draws a line from the previous data point to the new one. It then saves the new data point and displays the new `Bitmap` in the appropriate `PictureBox`.

The last piece of code in program `BackgroundGraphs` lets the user start and stop a graph. The following code shows how the program starts and stops the first graph's `BackgroundWorker`. The program controls the others similarly.

```
    ' Stop a worker.
    Private Sub btnStop0_Click(ByVal sender As System.Object, _
     ByVal e As System.EventArgs) Handles btnStop0.Click
        ToggleWorker(btnStop0, bgwGraph0)
    End Sub

    Private Sub ToggleWorker(ByVal btn As Button, ByVal bgw As BackgroundWorker)
        If bgw.IsBusy Then
            bgw.CancelAsync()
            btn.Text = "Start"
        Else
            bgw.RunWorkerAsync()
            btn.Text = "Stop"
        End If
    End Sub
    End Class
```

When the user clicks the first graph's `Stop` button, the program calls subroutine `ToggleWorker`. That routine checks a `BackgroundWorker`. If the worker's `IsBusy` property indicates that it is running, the code calls its `CancelAsync` method to set the worker's `CancellationPending` property to `True`.

If you want to call a `BackgroundWorker`*'s* `CancelAsync` *method, you must set its* `WorkerSupportsCancellation` *property to* `True`*.*

If the worker's `IsBusy` property indicates that it is not running, the code calls the worker's `RunWorkerAsync` method to start it working again.

Following are the three main keys to this example:

- Lower the background workers' priority so that the user interface thread has precedence.
- Use `Sleep` to force the threads to give up control of the CPU so that they all get turns.
- Use `Invoke` to call back to the user interface thread.

Providing Feedback

The `BackgroundGraphs` program described in the previous section draws four graphs continuously. When a `BackgroundWorker` calculates a new graph point, it invokes the `PlotPoint` subroutine to display the new point. Constantly updating the graphs adds overhead to the application and slows the calculations considerably. This is appropriate in that example because the whole point is to display the graphs continuously. In other cases, however, it might make more sense to use a more concise progress report so that the calculation can continue as quickly as possible.

The `MandelbrotBackground` program (available for download at `www.vb-helper.com/one_on_one.htm`) draws the Mandelbrot Set. If you click the Full Scale button, or click and drag to select an area, the program zooms in on that part of the set. While it is building the new image, the program displays the percentage of the image that it has built in its title bar, as shown in Figure 21-2.

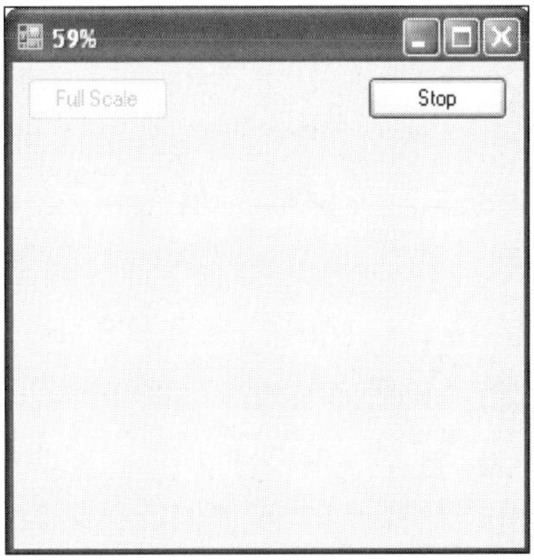

Figure 21-2: Program `MandelbrotBackground` displays the percentage of its image that it has generated in its title bar.

If you click the Stop button while the program is building an image, the program stops work and displays the parts of the image that it has built so far. Figure 21-3 shows the program after it has generated just over one-half of an image.

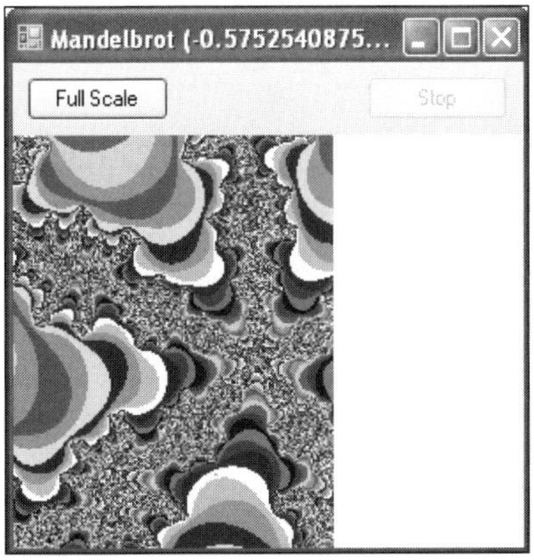

Figure 21-3: Program `MandelbrotBackground` lets you interrupt Mandelbrot Set calculations.

This example is actually fairly useful for navigating the Mandelbrot Set when you know that you want to zoom in on part of the image on the left. You can wait until the program has built part of the image, stop it, and zoom in on the piece it has finished.

Displaying a `BackgroundWorker`'s progress is relatively easy. When the worker wants to send progress notification to the main UI thread, it simply calls its `ReportProgress` method, passing it a value indicating the percentage complete. That raises the worker's `ProgresssChanged` event. The program can catch this event and display the progress in an appropriate way. This example displays the percentage complete in the form's title bar, but you might display it in a status bar or progress bar instead.

If you want to call a `BackgroundWorker`*'s* `ReportProgress` *method, you must set its* `WorkerReportsProgress` *property to* `True`.

This program allows you to stop the `BackgroundWorker` much as the previous example does. See the previous section, "UI Threading," for information about stopping `BackgroundWorkers`.

The following code shows an outline of the `BackgroundWorker`'s `DoWork` event handler. The details about how Mandelbrot Set calculations work isn't important for this discussion, so that code is omitted. Download the example program at `www.vb-helper.com/one_on_one.htm` to see the details. What's important here is that the calculations are fairly slow. The program must perform a series of fairly time-consuming calculations for every pixel in the image, so building a large Mandelbrot image can take quite awhile.

```
' Draw the Mandelbrot set.
Private Sub bgwMandelbrot_DoWork(ByVal sender As System.Object, _
 ByVal e As System.ComponentModel.DoWorkEventArgs) Handles bgwMandelbrot.DoWork
    ' Lower the thread's priority so the Stop button can fire.
    Thread.CurrentThread.Priority = ThreadPriority.BelowNormal

    ' Create the result bitmap.
    Dim bm As New Bitmap(picCanvas.ClientSize.Width, picCanvas.ClientSize.Height)
    e.Result = bm

    ' Create an associated Graphics object.
    Using gr As Graphics = Graphics.FromImage(bm)
        ' Clear the bitmap.
        gr.Clear(Color.White)

        ' Calculate the values.
        For i As Integer = 0 To wid - 1
            For j As Integer = 0 To hgt - 1
                ' Calculate and set the color for pixel (i, j).
                ' ...
            Next j

            If i Mod 10 = 0 Then
                ' Report our progress.
                Dim progress As Integer = CInt(100 * i / wid)
                bgwMandelbrot.ReportProgress(progress)

                ' See if we should cancel.
                'Thread.Sleep(1) ' Not needed if priority is lowered.
```

```
                If bgwMandelbrot.CancellationPending Then Exit Sub
            End If
        Next i
    End Using ' gr
End Sub
```

The code starts by reducing its priority so that the UI thread can respond quickly when necessary.

The code then creates a bitmap to hold the new image. It saves a reference to the bitmap in its `e.Result` parameter. When the routine finishes, this will be the result passed back to the main program via the worker's `RunWorkerCompleted` event.

The code then calculates the color for each pixel in the image. After every 10 columns of pixels, the worker calls its `ReportProgress` method to give the main program a status report. It also checks its `CancellationPending` property to see if it should stop building the image. If `CancellationPending` is `True`, the code exits its `Do` loop to stop building the image.

> *This code includes a commented out call to* `Thread.Sleep`*. You can use this instead of reducing the worker's priority to let the user interface thread take action when necessary.*

When this program's `BackgroundWorker` finishes building the new Mandelbrot image, its `DoWork` event handler exits and it raises its `RunWorkerCompleted` event. The main program uses the following code to catch this event and display the image built by the worker and contained in the `e.Result` parameter:

```
' The worker is done. Display the new image.
Private Sub bgwMandelbrot_RunWorkerCompleted(ByVal sender As Object, _
 ByVal e As System.ComponentModel.RunWorkerCompletedEventArgs) _
 Handles bgwMandelbrot.RunWorkerCompleted
    ' Get the result bitmap.
    Dim bm As Bitmap = DirectCast(e.Result, Bitmap)

    ' Display the bitmap.
    m_Bitmap = bm
    picCanvas.Image = m_Bitmap

    ' Discard any pending mouse events
    ' on picCanvas before we enable it.
    Application.DoEvents()

    ' Reset UI components.
    btnStop.Enabled = False
    btnFullScale.Enabled = True
    picCanvas.Cursor = Cursors.Cross
    Me.Cursor = Cursors.Default
    Me.Text = "Mandelbrot (" & _
        Format$(m_Wxmin) & ", " & _
        Format$(m_Wymin) & ")-(" & _
        Format$(m_Wxmax) & ", " & _
        Format$(m_Wymax) & ")"
End Sub
```

Providing Graphical Feedback

The BackgroundGraphs example described earlier in this chapter uses Invoke to call back to the UI thread to continuously update graphs. In contrast, example program MandelbrotBackground uses the ReportProgress method to tell the UI thread the percentage of its drawing that it has completed. It also uses the DoWork event handler's e.Result parameter to pass the final result image back to the UI thread.

Example program MandelbrotShowProgress (available for download at www.vb-helper.com/one_on_one.htm) updates the UI thread to show the new Mandelbrot Set as it is being constructed, as well as its percentage complete. Figure 21-4 shows the program when it has built 73 percent of the new image.

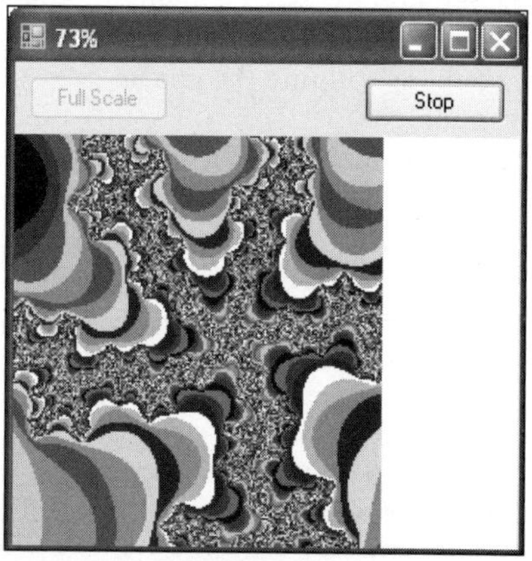

Figure 21-4: Program MandelbrotShowProgress **displays partial images as it builds them.**

This example works much as program MandelbrotBackground does. When its DoWork event handler calls the worker's ReportProgress method, however, it also passes in the partially completed bitmap bm, as shown in the following code:

```
my_worker.ReportProgress(progress, bm)
```

The following code shows how the UI thread handles the resulting ProgressChanged event. The code displays the percentage complete in the form's title bar. It then converts the e.UserState parameter into the Bitmap object passed by the call to ReportProgress, saves it in the m_Bitmap variable, and displays it in the picCanvas control.

```
' Display the progress.
Private Sub bgwMandelbrot_ProgressChanged(ByVal sender As Object, _
 ByVal e As System.ComponentModel.ProgressChangedEventArgs) _
 Handles bgwMandelbrot.ProgressChanged
    ' Display the progress percentage.
    Me.Text = e.ProgressPercentage & "%"

    ' Display the image so far.
```

```
        m_Bitmap = DirectCast(e.UserState, Bitmap)
        picCanvas.Image = m_Bitmap
    End Sub
```

The program's RunWorkerCompleted event handler uses similar code to display the final result.

This example spends some time updating its display, so, in theory, it should take longer than program MandelbrotBackground to draw an image. In practice, the difference isn't noticeable. Performance is similar to that of a program that draws the Mandelbrot Set on the main UI thread, but this version lets you stop the BackgroundWorker when you see as much of the Mandelbrot Set as you need.

Dividing Tasks

The previous sections explained how you can use BackgroundWorker components to perform calculations on background threads. The main goal was to keep the user interface responsive and indicate progress while you to stop and start those calculations.

Another reason to use multiple threads is to break a large task into pieces that can run on separate processors. If your computer has two or more CPUs and you break a task into two pieces, the pieces may be able to run simultaneously on different processors and reduce the total computation time.

Example program MandelbrotWorkers (available for download at www.vb-helper.com/one_on_one.htm) uses several BackgroundWorkers to build separate pieces of Mandelbrot Set images. The program uses the following WorkerInfo class to hold information about a particular worker's assignment. The xmin, xmax, ymin, and ymax properties tell the worker the coordinates of the image that it should build. dReaC and dImaC are parameters that the worker uses to move across the Mandelbrot Set. They essentially give the scale at which the image should be generated, and they are not described further here. The Result property refers to the bitmap that the worker is building.

```
' Information that describes the part of the
' Mandelbrot Set that a BackgroundWorker should build.
Public Class WorkerInfo
    Public MyForm As Form1
    Public xmin As Integer
    Public xmax As Integer
    Public ymin As Integer
    Public ymax As Integer
    Public dReaC As Double
    Public dImaC As Double
    Public Result As Bitmap

    Public Sub New(ByVal new_MyForm As Form1, ByVal new_xmin As Integer, _
     ByVal new_xmax As Integer, ByVal new_ymin As Integer, _
     ByVal new_ymax As Integer, ByVal new_dReaC As Double, _
     ByVal new_dImaC As Double)
        MyForm = new_MyForm
        xmin = new_xmin
        xmax = new_xmax
        ymin = new_ymin
        ymax = new_ymax
```

```
        dReaC = new_dReaC
        dImaC = new_dImaC
    End Sub
End Class
```

The following code shows how the program declares variables to manage its workers. It defines a constant `NUM_WORKERS` and then declares the `m_Workers` array to hold the required number of `BackgroundWorker` objects. The program uses the integer `m_NumWorkersRunning` to keep track of the number of background workers that are currently running.

```
' The BackgroundWorkers.
Private Const NUM_WORKERS As Integer = 2
Private m_Workers(0 To NUM_WORKERS - 1) As BackgroundWorker
Private m_NumWorkersRunning As Integer = 0
```

The following code fragment shows how the program creates its background workers. The code sets `dxmin` equal to the width of the vertical strip of image that each worker should draw. It then enters a loop where it creates a worker and adds event handlers for its `ProgressChanged`, `RunWorkerCompleted`, and `DoWork` event handlers. The program builds a `WorkerInfo` object to describe the worker's assignment, and starts the worker running by calling its `RunWorkerAsync` method, passing it the `WorkerInfo` object.

```
' Create the workers.
Dim xmin As Integer = 0
Dim dxmin As Integer = wid \ NUM_WORKERS
For i As Integer = 0 To NUM_WORKERS - 1
    ' Prepare the worker.
    m_Workers(i) = New BackgroundWorker
    m_Workers(i).WorkerReportsProgress = True
    m_Workers(i).WorkerSupportsCancellation = True

    ' Install the worker's event handlers.
    AddHandler m_Workers(i).ProgressChanged, _
        AddressOf Worker_ProgressChanged
    AddHandler m_Workers(i).RunWorkerCompleted, _
        AddressOf Worker_RunWorkerCompleted
    AddHandler m_Workers(i).DoWork, _
        AddressOf Worker_DoWork

    ' Get the bounds of the area that this worker will calculate.
    Dim xmax As Integer = xmin + dxmin - 1
    ' If it's the last worker, make it do the rest.
    If i = NUM_WORKERS - 1 Then xmax = wid - 1

    ' Prepare the worker's assignment.
    Dim worker_info As New WorkerInfo( _
        Me, xmin, xmax, 0, hgt - 1, dReaC, dImaC)

    ' Start the worker.
    m_Workers(i).RunWorkerAsync(worker_info)
    xmin += dxmin - 1
Next i
```

This version of the `DoWork` event handler is similar to the previous versions with one major difference. Because the program creates the `BackgroundWorkers` at run-time rather than at design time, it cannot use components to refer to the workers. There's no `bgwMandelbrot` component to use to control the worker.

To control itself, the worker uses the following code to convert the event handler's `sender` property into a `BackgroundWorker` object. Later, it uses this object to call its `ReportProgress` method.

```
' Get this BackgroundWorker.
Dim my_worker As BackgroundWorker = DirectCast(sender, BackgroundWorker)
```

One other major difference between this version and the previous ones lies in how the program updates its display. The previous version's code updates its display when it receives a `ProgressChanged` or `RunWorkerCompleted` event from its `BackgroundWorker` component. The worker raises these events one at a time, so there is little danger of multiple threads trying to access the final result image at the same time. In program `MandelbrotWorkers`, it's far more likely that more than one thread will try to modify an image at the same time.

Figure 21-5 shows program `MandelbrotWorkers` drawing an image. In this image, the program was using two `BackgroundWorker` components, and each has had some time to update the display.

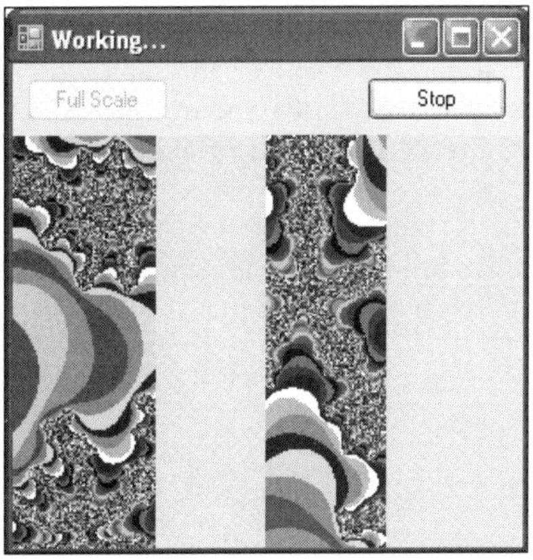

Figure 21-5: Program `MandelbrotWorkers` uses multiple `BackgroundWorkers` to draw Mandelbrot Sets.

If two threads try to set the colors of their bitmaps' pixels at exactly the same time, the program may encounter an error in the graphics subsystem. The top-level error discovered by the application is "Exception has been thrown by the target of an invocation." If you look at the inner exception, you'll find that the original error is "Object is currently in use elsewhere." Figure 21-6 shows the detail for the error with the `InnerException` property expanded.

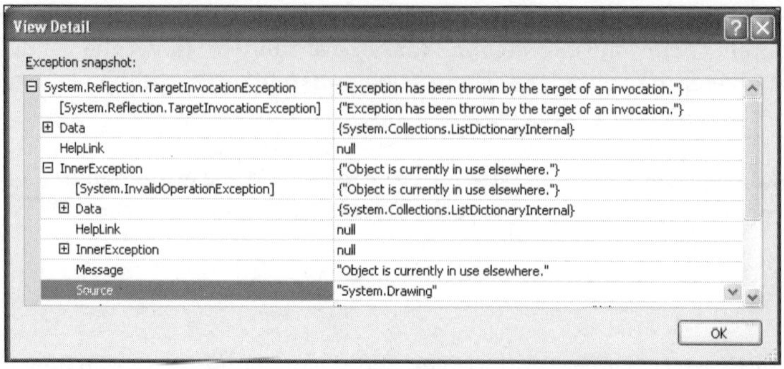

Figure 21-6: If multiple threads try to access bitmaps at the same time, the program may crash.

This is one of the kinds of errors that make debugging multi-threaded applications difficult. The error doesn't tell you what object is in use elsewhere, or where that is. It's also a hard bug to reproduce. You can run the program 100 times and not see the bug, only to have it appear during test number 101. If you do figure out how to fix the problem, you can test the program another 100 times and still wonder if the bug is really gone, or if you've just been lucky during those tests.

The `SyncLock` statement can prevent multiple threads from accessing particular pieces of code at the same time. `SyncLock` takes an object as a parameter and makes a thread wait until it has exclusive access to the object. If you add a `SyncLock` statement around the worker code that sets a pixel's color, then other workers cannot access that code until the executing thread reaches its corresponding `End SyncLock` statement.

The following code fragment shows how the worker now sets a pixel in its image. Note that the code must use an object for the `SyncLock` that is visible to all of the worker threads. This example uses the `m_Bitmap` object.

```
' Set the pixel's color.
SyncLock m_Bitmap
    bm.SetPixel(i - xmin, j - ymin, m_Colors(clr Mod m_NumColors))
End SyncLock
```

Understanding SyncLock

Unfortunately, the bug in program `MandelbrotWorkers` is extremely difficult to reproduce. If you comment out the `SyncLock` statement, the program may be able to generate dozens or even hundreds of images before it encounters the error. You need to run the program until the operating system switches the worker threads with precisely the right timing to make them try to update their bitmaps at the same time.

Example program `SyncLockTest` (shown in Figure 21-7 and available for download at `www.vb-helper.com/one_on_one.htm`) lets you experiment with the `SyncLock` statement. This program is more contrived than program `MandelbrotWorkers`, but it is much easier to understand.

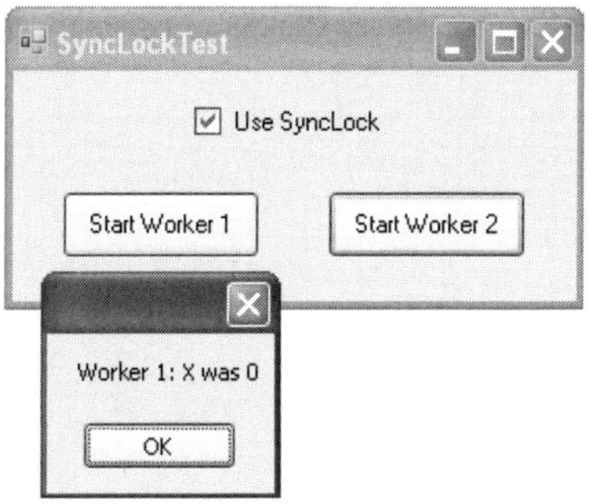

Figure 21-7: Program `SyncLockTest` lets you experiment with the `SyncLock` statement.

Click a button to start a `BackgroundWorker`. Each worker displays a message indicating that it is starting, displays the value of variable `X`, increments `X`, displays `X`'s new value, and displays a message indicating that it is done.

The following code shows how program `SyncLockTest` works. The buttons simply start their respective `BackgroundWorkers`.

```
Public Class Form1
    Private Sub btnStartWorker1_Click(ByVal sender As System.Object, _
     ByVal e As System.EventArgs) Handles btnStartWorker1.Click
        bgw1.RunWorkerAsync()
    End Sub
    Private Sub btnStartWorker2_Click(ByVal sender As System.Object, _
     ByVal e As System.EventArgs) Handles btnStartWorker2.Click
        bgw2.RunWorkerAsync()
    End Sub

    Private X As Integer = 0
    Private m_LockObject As New Object

    Private Sub bgw1_DoWork(ByVal sender As Object, _
     ByVal e As System.ComponentModel.DoWorkEventArgs) Handles bgw1.DoWork
        MessageBox.Show("Worker 1 Begin")
        If chkUseSyncLock.Checked Then
            SyncLock m_LockObject
                MessageBox.Show("Worker 1: X was " & X.ToString())
                X += 1
                MessageBox.Show("Worker 1: X now " & X.ToString())
            End SyncLock
        Else
            MessageBox.Show("Worker 1: X was " & X.ToString())
            X += 1
            MessageBox.Show("Worker 1: X now " & X.ToString())
        End If
        MessageBox.Show("Worker 1 End")
    End Sub

    Private Sub bgw2_DoWork(ByVal sender As Object, _
```

```
        ByVal e As System.ComponentModel.DoWorkEventArgs) Handles bgw2.DoWork
        MessageBox.Show("Worker 2 Begin")
        If chkUseSyncLock.Checked Then
            SyncLock m_LockObject
                MessageBox.Show("Worker 2: X was " & X.ToString())
                X += 1
                MessageBox.Show("Worker 2: X now " & X.ToString())
            End SyncLock
        Else
            MessageBox.Show("Worker 2: X was " & X.ToString())
            X += 1
            MessageBox.Show("Worker 2: X now " & X.ToString())
        End If
        MessageBox.Show("Worker 2 End")
    End Sub
End Class
```

Each `DoWork` event handler displays a start message. If the Use `SyncLock` box is checked, the code then uses a `SyncLock` statement to obtain exclusive access to an object. It doesn't really matter what object the code uses as long as both workers have access to it. This code creates a special `m_LockObject` solely for this purpose.

The code then displays the value of variable `X`, increments the value, displays the new value, and releases its lock.

If the Use `SyncLock` box is not checked, the code follows the same steps without the `SyncLock` and `End SyncLock` statements.

You can use the message boxes to control the exact flow of the two workers. For example, suppose `X` = 0 and you start worker 1 and close its starting message. It displays a message saying `X` is 1.

Now, start the second worker and close all of its message boxes. This worker shows messages indicating that `X` is 1 and then that `X` has been incremented to 2.

Now, return to the first worker and close its remaining message boxes. They will show you that `X` has been incremented to 2. From the first worker's point of view, `X` went from 0 to 2.

The following timelines shows this sequence of events.

Worker 1	**Worker 2**
`1: Starting`	
`2: Display X = 0`	
	`1: Starting`
	`2: Display X = 0`
	`3: Increment X, display X = 2`
	`4: Ending`
`3: Increment X, display X = 1`	
`4: Ending`	

Now, suppose you try to perform the same tasks with the Use `SyncLock` box checked. When you dismiss the first worker's starting message, the worker locks `m_LockObject` and displays `X`'s value as 0.

When you start the second worker, it displays its starting message. This time when you dismiss that message, the code tries to lock `m_LockObject` and blocks.

You must close the first worker's message showing `X` is 0 before the second worker can continue. When you close this message box, the first worker increments `X` and displays its new value 1. The second worker is still blocked until you close that message box.

At that point, the first worker releases its lock on `m_LockObject` so that the second worker can continue.

The following timeline shows this sequence of events. In this version, both workers see a consistent set of values for `X`. Both show a value for `X`, increment it, and the result is one greater than its original value.

Worker 1	**Worker 2**
`1: Starting`	
`2. SyncLock m_LockObject`	
`3: Display X = 0`	
	`1: Starting`
	`2. SyncLock m_LockObject`
`4: Increment X, display X = 1`	`<blocked>`
`5: End SyncLock`	`<blocked>`
	`3: Display X = 1`
	`4: Increment X, display X = 2`
	`5: End SyncLock`
	`6: Ending`
`6: Ending`	

Summary

Multi-threaded applications can be extremely difficult to write and debug. Often, their behavior depends on the exact timing and sequence of events that they experience at run-time. Sometimes, the code may need to execute hundreds or even thousands of times before precisely the right conditions occur to cause an error. That can make reproducing a bug, fixing it, and verifying that is has been fixed nearly impossible.

You can make threading much simpler by using the `BackgroundWorker` component. Use the component's `ReportProgress` method to give status information to the UI thread. Use the `RunWorkerCompleted` to let the UI thread process the worker's finished results. If the worker must interact with the form's controls directly, use `Invoke` to call back to the UI thread.

The .NET Framework contains other tools that you can use to coordinate among threads, but they are more difficult to use. For example, the `SyncLock` statement uses the `Monitor` class to lock objects. `Monitor` provides additional features such as the `TryEnter` method that times out if it cannot acquire a lock within a certain amount of time. `SyncLock` is much easier, however.

`SyncLock` also has some built-in safeguards. For example, whenever the code exits a `SyncLock` block, it automatically releases the underlying lock. If you use the `Monitor` class directly, you must ensure that the lock is always released, or the program may deadlock.

Often, multiple threads execute the same code, but with slightly different data. The `Mandelbrot Workers` example program uses a single set of worker subroutines for any number of workers. By examining the parameters it is passed, the `DoWork` event handler can figure out which worker it is, and what data it should use to produce a result.

Chapter 22, "Reflection," describes other ways a program can learn about itself. It explains some tricks you can use to learn more about the executing code, the properties, methods, and events provided by a class, and the values that are valid for enumerated data types.

22

Reflection

One of the most remarkable new features introduced by .NET was reflection. At its simplest, *reflection* is the process of allowing a program to discover information about code, possibly even about its own code. Reflection allows a program to learn about an assembly, either when it is running, or from its compiled DLL or executable code. It lets a program discover the types, properties, methods, and events defined by an assembly. It lets a program dynamically load the assembly, create instances of its types, and invoke its methods all at run-time. It even lets a program generate, compile, and execute new code completely from scratch.

Even if you don't expect your program to interact with other assemblies, you may find some reflection techniques useful. For example, if your application uses only its own modules, you may not think you need to use reflection to learn about what is contained in those modules. After all, you are writing the code, so you should know what it contains.

However, it may still be useful for the program to load assemblies at run-time. For example, the program can look in a tools directory to see what assemblies are available and load any tools that they define. Then, if you later decide to add, modify, or remove a tool, you only need to add, replace, or remove an assembly from this directory, and the program will automatically update itself the next time it runs. That makes distributing new tools to users quick and easy.

There isn't enough room in this chapter to cover all of the reflection tools provided by the .NET Framework, but there is enough room to cover some of the most useful of those tools. That should give you enough of a start that you can figure out how to use other tools as needed.

Exploring Assemblies

An obvious first task when using reflection is learning information about an assembly.

An assembly is the smallest unit of deployment in a .NET application. It is basically a piece of compiled code. Generally, that means a compiled `.exe` *or* `.dll` *file.*

Example program GetAssemblyInformation (available for download at www.vb-helper.com/one_on_one.htm) displays information about an assembly stored in a file. It's a long and involved program, but its basic operations are relatively simple when taken individually. The program doesn't even try to display all of the possible information about the assembly. Instead, it sticks to the most common and useful bits of information.

When you enter the path to an assembly and click the Go button, the program executes the following code:

```
' Display information about the assembly.
Private Sub btnGo_Click(ByVal sender As System.Object, _
 ByVal e As System.EventArgs) Handles btnGo.Click
    Dim assem As [Assembly] = [Assembly].LoadFrom(txtPath.Text)

    ' Display the assembly's full name.
    trvDetails.Nodes.Clear()
    trvDetails.Nodes.Add("Full Name: " & assem.FullName)
    trvDetails.Nodes.Add("Location: " & assem.Location)

    ' Display referenced assemblies.
    Dim ref_assem_node As TreeNode = trvDetails.Nodes.Add("Referenced Assemblies")
    For Each referenced_assembly As AssemblyName In assem.GetReferencedAssemblies()
        ref_assem_node.Nodes.Add(referenced_assembly.FullName)
    Next referenced_assembly

    ' Display the assembly's entry point.
    Dim entry_point As MethodInfo = assem.EntryPoint()
    trvDetails.Nodes.Add("Entry Point: " & entry_point.Name)

    ' Types.
    Dim types_node As TreeNode = trvDetails.Nodes.Add("Types")
    For Each exported_type As Type In assem.GetTypes()
        AddTypeData(types_node, exported_type)
    Next exported_type
End Sub
```

First, the code creates an Assembly object based on the assembly file you entered in the txtPath text box. It then clears the trvDetails TreeView control, where it will store its results, and adds the assembly's full name (name, version, culture, and token) and its location to the tree view.

The code then adds a node labeled Referenced Assemblies to the tree view. It loops through the values in the assemblies returned by the Assembly object's GetReferencedAssemblies function, adding each assembly's name to the tree view.

This code shows a common operation when exploring an assembly: the code finds an object and loops through an array representing items that are logically contained in the original object. In this case, the Assembly *object provides a list of referenced assemblies. Similarly, a* Type *object representing a class can have properties, fields, methods, events, and nested types.*

The code adds the assembly's entry point to the tree view, and then loops through the exported (public) types defined by the assembly. For each of these types, the code calls subroutine AddTypeData to add information about the type to the tree view. The following code shows subroutine AddTypeData:

```
' Return information about a type.
Private Sub AddTypeData(ByVal parent_node As TreeNode, ByVal the_type As Type)
    Dim txt As String = ""
    If the_type.IsPublic Then txt &= "Public "
    If the_type.IsInterface Then
        ' Skip MustInherit for Interfaces.
        txt &= "Interface "
    Else
        If the_type.IsAbstract Then txt &= "MustInherit "
    End If
    If the_type.IsClass Then txt &= "Class "
    If the_type.IsEnum Then txt &= "Enum "
    If the_type.IsValueType Then txt &= "Structure "

    Dim type_name As String = the_type.Name
    If the_type.ContainsGenericParameters Then
        ' Remove whatever comes after `.
        type_name = type_name.Substring(0, type_name.IndexOf("`"))

        ' Compose the generic parameters.
        Dim generic_params As String = ""
        Dim generic_type As Type = the_type.GetGenericTypeDefinition
        For Each arg_type As Type In generic_type.GetGenericArguments()
            generic_params &= ", " & arg_type.Name
        Next arg_type
        If generic_params.Length > 0 Then _
            generic_params = generic_params.Substring(2)
        type_name &= "(Of " & generic_params & ")"
    End If
    Dim type_node As TreeNode = parent_node.Nodes.Add(txt & type_name)

    If the_type.BaseType Is Nothing Then
        type_node.Nodes.Add("Inherits From: Nothing")
    Else
        type_node.Nodes.Add("Inherits From: " & the_type.BaseType.FullName)
    End If
    type_node.Nodes.Add("Attributes: " & the_type.Attributes.ToString)
    type_node.Nodes.Add("Qualified Name: " & the_type.AssemblyQualifiedName)

    ' See if it's an enum.
    If the_type.IsEnum Then
        ' It's an enum. List its values.
        Dim values_node As TreeNode = type_node.Nodes.Add("Values")
        For Each field_info As FieldInfo In the_type.GetFields()
            If field_info.IsStatic Then
                values_node.Nodes.Add(field_info.Name & " = " & _
                    CLng(field_info.GetValue(Nothing)))
            Else
                values_node.Nodes.Add(field_info.Name & " (non static)")
            End If
        Next field_info
    Else
        ' It's not an enum.
        ' Interfaces.
        Dim ifaces() As Type = the_type.GetInterfaces()
```

```
    If ifaces.Length > 0 Then
        Dim ifaces_node As TreeNode = type_node.Nodes.Add("Interfaces")
        For Each iface_type As Type In ifaces
            AddInterfaceData(ifaces_node, iface_type)
        Next iface_type
    End If

    ' Constructors.
    Dim constructor_infos() As ConstructorInfo = the_type.GetConstructors()

    ' If constructor_infos = Nothing,
    ' the type has only a default constructor.
    ' If constructor_infos is empty, it has no constructors.
    If constructor_infos Is Nothing Then
        ' It has no explicit constructors,
        ' only the default empty constructor.
        Dim constr_node As TreeNode = type_node.Nodes.Add("Constructors")
        constr_node.Nodes.Add("New " & type_name & "()")
    ElseIf constructor_infos.Length > 0 Then
        Dim constr_node As TreeNode = type_node.Nodes.Add("Constructors")
        For Each constructor_info As ConstructorInfo In constructor_infos
            AddConstructorData(constr_node, type_name, constructor_info)
        Next constructor_info
    End If

    ' Fields.
    Dim field_infos() As FieldInfo = the_type.GetFields()
    If field_infos.Length > 0 Then
        Dim fields_node As TreeNode = type_node.Nodes.Add("Fields")
        For Each field_info As FieldInfo In field_infos
            AddFieldData(fields_node, field_info)
        Next field_info
    End If

    ' Properties.
    Dim property_infos() As PropertyInfo = the_type.GetProperties()
    If property_infos.Length > 0 Then
        Dim properties_node As TreeNode = type_node.Nodes.Add("Properties")
        For Each property_info As PropertyInfo In property_infos
            AddPropertyData(properties_node, property_info)
        Next property_info
    End If

    ' Methods.
    Dim method_infos() As MethodInfo = the_type.GetMethods()
    If method_infos.Length > 0 Then
        Dim methods_node As TreeNode = type_node.Nodes.Add("Methods")
        For Each method_info As MethodInfo In method_infos
            AddMethodData(methods_node, method_info)
        Next method_info
    End If

    ' Events.
    Dim event_infos() As EventInfo = the_type.GetEvents()
    If event_infos.Length > 0 Then
```

```
                Dim events_node As TreeNode = type_node.Nodes.Add("Events")
                For Each event_info As EventInfo In event_infos
                    AddEventData(events_node, event_info)
                Next event_info
            End If

            ' Nested types.
            Dim nested_types() As Type = the_type.GetNestedTypes()
            If nested_types.Length > 0 Then
                Dim nested_types_node As TreeNode = type_node.Nodes.Add("Nested Types")
                For Each nested_type As Type In nested_types
                    AddTypeData(nested_types_node, nested_type)
                Next nested_type
            End If
        End If
    End Sub
```

Subroutine `AddTypeData` takes a `Type` object as a parameter. It checks the `Type`'s properties to determine whether the type is public, an interface, `MustInherit`, a class, an enumerated type, or a structure. It uses this information to build an appropriate declaration string for the type.

Next, the routine checks whether the type contains generic parameters, as in `Public Class TestClass(Of T1, T2)`. If it does, the code loops through the generic arguments to build an appropriate parameter list.

The code then adds a node to the tree view containing the type's basic declaration. The code adds any other tree view nodes for this type as descendants of this node.

The subroutine adds entries, giving the type from which this one inherits (note that interfaces don't inherit from anything), its attributes, and its fully qualified name. It then considers other items that are logically contained within the type.

If the type is an `Enum`, the code loops through its fields. If a field is static (has a constant value), the code displays its name and its value. If a field is not static, the code displays the field's name.

If the type is not an `Enum`, the subroutine loops through and displays information about the interfaces it implements. It then describes the type's constructors, fields, properties, methods, events, and nested types (for example, classes defined within this class).

For each of these more-complicated items, the `AddTypeData` subroutine calls other routines to provide additional information. For example, for a constructor, it calls subroutine `AddConstructorData`. For a nested type, subroutine `AddTypeData` calls itself recursively to describe the nested type.

The other routines used by the program are much simpler. Subroutine `AddConstructorData` shown in the following code adds a node to the tree view describing a constructor. It starts with the keyword `New` and uses function `ParameterList` to list its parameters.

```
    ' Return information about a type.
    Private Sub AddConstructorData(ByVal parent_node As TreeNode, _
     ByVal type_name As String, ByVal constructor_info As ConstructorInfo)
        ' Get the constructor's parameters.
        Dim txt As String = "New " & type_name & _
```

```
            ParameterList(constructor_info.GetParameters())
        parent_node.Nodes.Add(txt)
    End Sub
```

Function `ParameterList` loops through an array of `ParameterInfo` objects and calls `GetParameterData` to get a declaration for each.

```
    ' Return a string listing parameters from a collection.
    Private Function ParameterList(ByVal param_infos() As ParameterInfo) As String
        Dim params As String = ""
        For Each parameter_info As ParameterInfo In param_infos
            params &= ", " & GetParameterData(parameter_info)
        Next parameter_info
        If params.Length > 0 Then params = params.Substring(2)

        Return "(" & params & ")"
    End Function
```

Function `GetParameterData` examines a `ParameterInfo` object and builds its declaration as it would appear within a parameter list. This function is somewhat limited. For example, it doesn't try to completely interpret parameters that are of generic types as in `Sub Test(ByVal values As List(Of Boolean))`.

```
    ' Return information about a parameter.
    Private Function GetParameterData(ByVal parameter_info As ParameterInfo) As String
        Dim txt As String = ""
        If parameter_info.IsOptional Then
            txt &= "Optional "
        End If
        If parameter_info.IsOut Then
            txt &= "ByRef "
        Else
            txt &= "ByVal "
        End If
        txt &= parameter_info.Name
        If parameter_info.ParameterType.IsArray Then
            txt &= "()"
            txt &= " As " & parameter_info.ParameterType.GetElementType.Name
        Else
            txt &= " As " & parameter_info.ParameterType.Name
        End If
        If parameter_info.IsOptional Then
            If parameter_info.ParameterType.Name = "String" Then
                txt &= " = """ & parameter_info.DefaultValue.ToString() & """"
            ElseIf parameter_info.DefaultValue Is Nothing Then
                txt &= " = Nothing"
            Else
                txt &= " = " & parameter_info.DefaultValue.ToString()
            End If
        End If

        Return txt
    End Function
```

Subroutines `AddFieldData` and `AddPropertyData`, shown in the following code, examine `FieldInfo` and `PropertyInfo` objects to provide reasonable declarations for fields (public variables) and properties.

```
' Add information about a field.
Private Sub AddFieldData(ByVal fields_node As TreeNode, _
 ByVal field_info As FieldInfo)
    Dim txt As String = ""
    If field_info.IsPublic Then txt &= "Public "
    If field_info.IsPrivate Then txt &= "Private "
    If field_info.IsFamily Then txt &= "Protected "
    If field_info.IsStatic Then txt &= "Shared "
    txt &= field_info.Name
    txt &= " As " & field_info.FieldType.Name
    fields_node.Nodes.Add(txt)
End Sub

' Add information about a property.
Private Sub AddPropertyData(ByVal properties_node As TreeNode, _
 ByVal property_info As PropertyInfo)
    Dim txt As String = "Public "
    If property_info.CanRead AndAlso Not property_info.CanWrite Then
        txt &= "ReadOnly "
    ElseIf Not property_info.CanRead AndAlso property_info.CanWrite Then
        txt &= "WriteOnly "
    End If
    txt &= property_info.Name
    txt &= " As " & property_info.PropertyType.Name
    properties_node.Nodes.Add(txt)
End Sub
```

The following code shows how subroutine `AddMethodData` displays information about a method. It simply calls function `MethodSignature` to compose a description for a method. Function `MethodSignature` determines the method's visibility, and whether it is a subroutine or function. It adds the method's name and uses function `ParameterList` to add its parameters.

```
' Add information about a method.
Private Sub AddMethodData(ByVal methods_node As TreeNode, _
 ByVal method_info As MethodInfo)
    methods_node.Nodes.Add(MethodSignature(method_info))
End Sub

' Return a method's signature in a VB format.
Private Function MethodSignature(ByVal method_info As MethodInfo) As String
    Dim txt As String = ""
    If method_info.IsFamilyAndAssembly Then
        txt &= "Protected Friend "
    ElseIf method_info.IsFamily Then
        txt &= "Protected "
    ElseIf method_info.IsFamilyOrAssembly Then
        txt &= "Friend "
    ElseIf method_info.IsPrivate Then
        txt &= "Private "
    ElseIf method_info.IsPublic Then
```

```
            txt &= "Public "
        End If
        If method_info.IsFinal Then txt &= "NotOverridable "
        If method_info.IsHideBySig Then txt &= "Overrides "
        If method_info.IsAbstract Then txt &= "MustOverride "
        If method_info.IsStatic Then txt &= "Shared "
        If method_info.ReturnType.Name = "Void" Then
            txt &= "Sub "
        Else
            txt &= "Function "
        End If
        txt &= method_info.Name
        txt &= ParameterList(method_info.GetParameters())
        If method_info.ReturnType.Name <> "Void" Then
            txt &= " As " & method_info.ReturnType.Name
        End If

        Return txt
    End Function
```

Subroutine `AddEventData` simply adds an event's name to the tree view, and subroutine `AddInterfaceData` just adds the keyword `Implements` and the interface's name to the output.

```
    ' Add information about an event.
    Private Sub AddEventData(ByVal events_node As TreeNode, _
     ByVal event_info As EventInfo)
        events_node.Nodes.Add(event_info.Name)
    End Sub

    ' Add information about an implemented interface.
    Private Sub AddInterfaceData(ByVal ifaces_node As TreeNode, _
     ByVal iface_type As Type)
        ifaces_node.Nodes.Add("Implements " & iface_type.Name)
    End Sub
```

Figure 22-1 shows program `GetAssemblyInformation` in action. In this figure, the `Employee` class is open and displaying its interfaces, constructors, fields, and properties.

You can download the example program at `www.vb-helper.com/one_on_one.htm` and look at the `Employee` class it defines to see how it leads to the results shown in Figure 22-1.

Example program `GetMyAssemblyInformation` is almost the same as program `GetAssemblyInformation`, except it doesn't load an `Assembly` object from a file. Instead this program uses the following statement to get an `Assembly` representing itself as it is running:

```
    Dim assem As [Assembly] = [Assembly].GetExecutingAssembly()
```

This is reflection in a fairly literal sense. The code is actually examining at itself as if it were looking in a mirror.

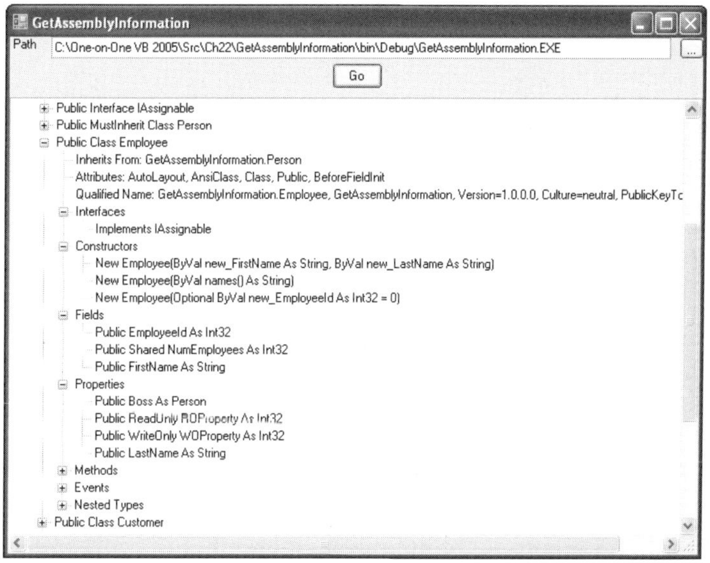

Figure 22-1: Program `GetAssemblyInformation` displays information about an assembly.

You may find program `GetAssemblyInformation` useful for exploring assemblies, but it's more important as an example showing how you can search through an assembly for particular information. For example, it shows how you can search an assembly to find the classes it defines. It also shows how to examine those classes to see which ones provide default constructors that take no parameters. Your program can easily make instances of those classes and possibly use their methods. Example programs `UseReflectionTools` and `UseDiscoveryLib` (described later in this chapter) demonstrate this technique.

Exploring Enumerations

The .NET Framework includes many enumerations, including some that are very large such as `HatchStyle` with 56 entries and `Color` with 141 entries. Suppose you are building a drawing program and you want to let the user pick from among these values.

Building the lists of `HatchStyles` and `Colors` would be a lot of work. It would also make maintenance more difficult. If a later release of the .NET Framework defined new colors, for example, you would have to figure out which ones were new and add them to your list.

An alternative solution is to use reflection to make the `HatchStyle` and `Color` types list their own values.

Example program `ShowHatchBrushes` (available for download at `www.vb-helper.com/one_on_one.htm`) uses the following code to show samples of the defined `HatchStyle` values:

```
' Display brush samples.
Private Sub Form1_Paint(ByVal sender As Object, _
```

```
 ByVal e As System.Windows.Forms.PaintEventArgs) Handles Me.Paint
    e.Graphics.Clear(Me.BackColor)
    Dim x As Integer = XMIN
    Dim y As Integer = XMIN

    ' Enumerate the HatchBrush styles.
    Dim hatch_style_type As Type = GetType(HatchStyle)

    Dim field_infos() As FieldInfo = hatch_style_type.GetFields()
    For Each field_info As FieldInfo In field_infos
        ' See if this is a static (Shared) property.
        ' We only want the Shared properties such as Horizontal
        ' and not the instance properties such as value__.
        If field_info.IsStatic Then
            ' Get this brush.
            Dim style_obj As Object = field_info.GetValue(Nothing)
            Dim hatch_style As HatchStyle = DirectCast(style_obj, HatchStyle)

            ' Make the brush and draw the sample.
            Using br As New HatchBrush(hatch_style, Color.Black, Color.White)
                DrawSample(e.Graphics, x, y, br, field_info.Name)
            End Using
        End If
    Next field_info
End Sub

' Draw the sample and move (x, y) to a new position.
Private Sub DrawSample(ByVal gr As Graphics, ByRef x As Integer, _
 ByRef y As Integer, ByVal br As Brush, ByVal brush_name As String)
    ' Draw the sample.
    gr.FillRectangle(br, x, y, SAMPLE_WID, SAMPLE_HGT)
    gr.DrawRectangle(Pens.Red, x, y, SAMPLE_WID, SAMPLE_HGT)

    ' Draw the brush's name.
    Dim string_format As New StringFormat()
    string_format.Alignment = StringAlignment.Center
    string_format.LineAlignment = StringAlignment.Near
    gr.DrawString(brush_name, Me.Font, Brushes.Blue, _
        x + SAMPLE_WID \ 2, y + SAMPLE_HGT, string_format)

    ' Update x and y.
    x += SAMPLE_WID + X_MARGIN
    If x + SAMPLE_WID > Me.ClientSize.Width Then
        x = XMIN
        y += SAMPLE_HGT + Y_MARGIN
    End If
End Sub
```

The form's `Paint` event handler gets a `Type` object representing the `HatchStyle` type. It then loops through the `FieldInfo` objects representing the type's fields. It uses each `FieldInfo`'s `IsStatic` method to determine whether a field is a constant, and calls subroutine `DrawSample` to draw a sample of the static fields.

Subroutine `DrawSample` fills a rectangle with the sample brush, draws a rectangle around it, and displays the style's name underneath. It then updates the X and Y coordinates where it will draw the next sample.

Figure 22-2 shows program `ShowHatchBrushes` displaying the hatch styles defined by the `HatchStyle` type.

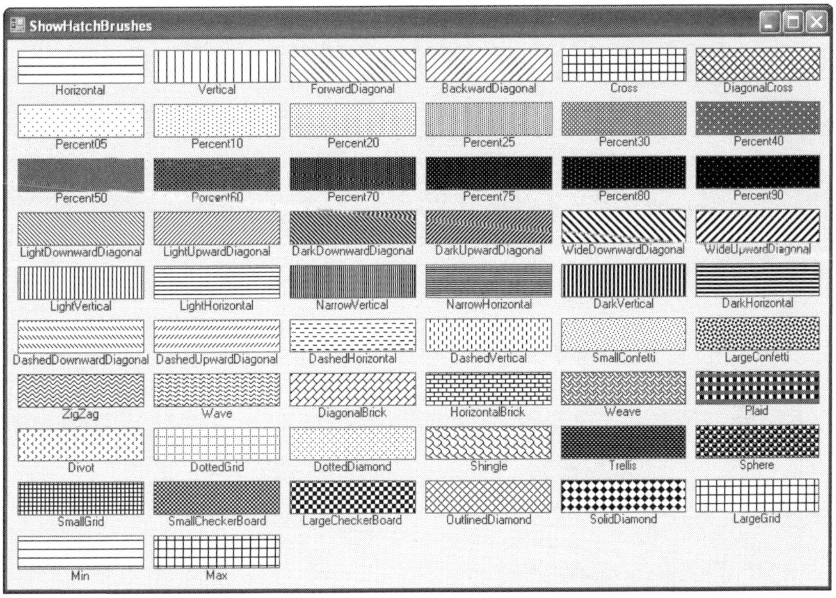

Figure 22-2: Program `ShowHatchBrushes` displays samples of the values defined by the `HatchStyle` type.

Example program `ShowSystemColors` (available for download at `www.vb-helper.com/one_on_one.htm`) uses the following code to fill arrays with the values and names of colors defined by the `SystemColors` type. This code loops through the type's properties rather than its fields, because these values are defined by properties, not fields.

```
Private m_Colors As New List(Of Color)
Private m_ColorNames As New List(Of String)

Private Sub Form1_Load(ByVal sender As System.Object, _
 ByVal e As System.EventArgs) Handles MyBase.Load
    ' Enumerate the SystemColors styles.
    Dim system_colors_type As Type = GetType(SystemColors)
    Dim property_infos() As PropertyInfo = system_colors_type.GetProperties()
    For Each property_info As PropertyInfo In property_infos
        ' Get this color.
        Dim color_obj As Object = property_info.GetValue(Nothing, Nothing)
        Dim system_color As Color = DirectCast(color_obj, Color)

        ' Save the color and name.
```

```
            m_Colors.Add(system_color)
            m_ColorNames.Add(property_info.Name)
        Next property_info

        ' Prepare for Paint events.
        Me.SetStyle( _
            ControlStyles.AllPaintingInWmPaint Or _
            ControlStyles.ResizeRedraw Or _
            ControlStyles.OptimizedDoubleBuffer, _
            True)
        Me.UpdateStyles()

        Me.ClientSize = New Size( _
            2 * XMIN + 6 * SAMPLE_WID + 5 * X_MARGIN, _
            3 * XMIN + 6 * SAMPLE_HGT + 5 * Y_MARGIN)
    End Sub
```

The form's `Paint` event handler draws samples of the colors in the `m_Colors` array. Download the code to see the details.

Figure 22-3 shows program `ShowSystemColors` in action.

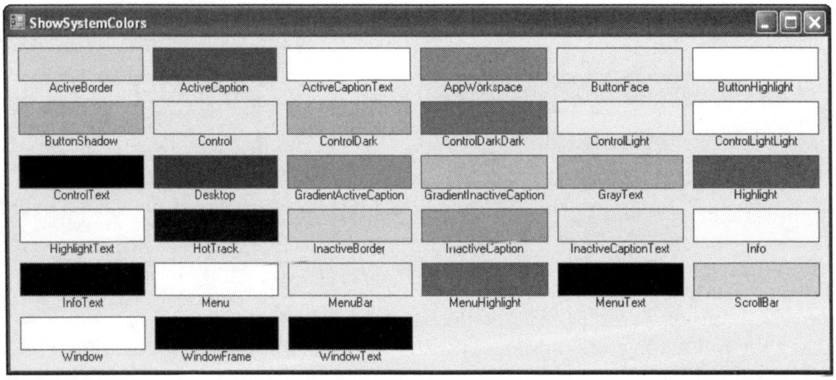

Figure 22-3: Program `ShowSystemColors` draws samples of the values defined by `SystemColors`.

The following table lists this chapter's example programs that display samples of enumerations. All of these are available for download at the book's Web site (`www.vb-helper.com/one_on_one.htm`.)

Program	Enumeration
`ShowDashStyle`	`DashStyle`
`ShowHatchBrushes`	`HatchStyle`
`ShowNamedColors`	`Color`

Program	Enumeration
ShowSystemColors	SystemColors
ShowSystemIcons	SystemIcons
ShowSystemPens	SystemPens

Loading Classes Dynamically

Chapter 9, "Scripting," explains some ways you can add new functionality to an application. In particular it explains how you can make an application compile and execute new Visual Basic code at run-time. Using this technique, you can add new features to a previously compiled application.

Chapter 18, "Deployment," discusses different methods that you can use to deploy an application. If you don't change a method's signature, you may be able to change its behavior to provide new features for an existing application. For example, suppose you build a class library that defines a `Tools` class. This class provides an `InstallTools` method that adds new items to the main program's menus and handles the new items' `Click` events. If you are careful, you can change the way `InstallTools` works and copy a new DLL into the program's directory without breaking the application.

Reflection gives you another option for loading and executing new code. Instead of compiling new code at run-time or relying on the classes in a DLL not changing in significant ways, a program can use reflection to open an assembly, find useful classes in it, and use them.

The `ReflectionTools` example project (available for download at `www.vb-helper.com/one_on_one.htm`) builds a DLL that contains classes that provide tools for another application. The following code shows how the library installs tools:

```
Imports System.Windows.Forms
Imports System.Drawing

' Identifies the tool installer class.
Public Interface IToolInstaller
    Sub InstallTools(ByVal tool_menu As ToolStripMenuItem, _
        ByVal rch As RichTextBox)
End Interface

' Lists the available tool classes.
Public Class ToolInstaller
    Implements IToolInstaller

    ' Install tools for this application.
    Public Sub InstallTools(ByVal tool_menu As ToolStripMenuItem, _
     ByVal rch As System.Windows.Forms.RichTextBox) _
     Implements IToolInstaller.InstallTools
        Dim bold_toggler As New BoldStyleToggler
        bold_toggler.InstallTool(tool_menu, rch)
    End Sub
End Class
```

The `IToolInstaller` interface defines a subroutine named `InstallTools` that takes as parameters a `ToolStripMenuItem` and a rich text box control. The idea is that the menu item is the Tools menu of an application and that the tools will modify the rich text box. In a more complete application, the second parameter would probably be an object that gives the tools access to the main program's object model.

The `ToolInstaller` class implements the `IToolInstaller` interface. In this example, the `InstallTools` routine builds a `BoldStyleToggler` object and calls its `InstallTool` method, passing in the menu item and the rich text box.

The following code shows how the `BoldStyleToggler` class works:

```
Public Interface IRichTool
    ' Return the tool's menu caption.
    Sub InstallTool(ByVal tool_menu As ToolStripMenuItem, _
        ByVal rch As System.Windows.Forms.RichTextBox)
End Interface

' Switches the selected text's Bold font property.
Public Class BoldStyleToggler
    Implements IRichTool

    ' A reference to our menu item.
    Private m_ToolStripMenuItem As ToolStripMenuItem

    ' A reference to our RichTextBox.
    Private m_RichTextBox As RichTextBox

    ' Install the tool.
    Public Sub InstallTool(ByVal tools_menu As ToolStripMenuItem, _
     ByVal rch As System.Windows.Forms.RichTextBox) _
     Implements IRichTool.InstallTool
        ' Create the Tool menu item.
        m_ToolStripMenuItem = New ToolStripMenuItem( _
            "&Bold", Nothing, AddressOf MenuItem_Click)
        m_ToolStripMenuItem.ShortcutKeys = Keys.Control Or Keys.B
        m_ToolStripMenuItem.Visible = True

        ' Add the item to the Tools menu.
        tools_menu.DropDownItems.Add(m_ToolStripMenuItem)

        ' Watch for the Tool menu opening.
        AddHandler tools_menu.DropDownOpening, AddressOf ToolsMenu_DropDownOpening

        ' Save a reference to the RichTextBox.
        m_RichTextBox = rch
    End Sub

    ' The user invoked the tool.
    Private Sub MenuItem_Click(ByVal sender As Object, ByVal e As System.EventArgs)
        Dim tool_item As ToolStripMenuItem = DirectCast(sender, ToolStripMenuItem)

        ' Toggle the style.
        Dim the_style As FontStyle = m_RichTextBox.SelectionFont.Style
        Dim old_bold As Boolean = (the_style And FontStyle.Bold) = FontStyle.Bold
        If old_bold Then
```

```
                ' Make not bold.
                the_style = the_style And Not FontStyle.Bold
            Else
                ' Make bold.
                the_style = the_style Or FontStyle.Bold
            End If
            Dim new_style As FontStyle = the_style

            m_RichTextBox.SelectionFont = _
                New Font(m_RichTextBox.SelectionFont, the_style)
        End Sub

        ' The user opened the Tools menu.
        ' Check or uncheck this menu item.
        Private Sub ToolsMenu_DropDownOpening(ByVal sender As Object, _
         ByVal e As System.EventArgs)
            m_ToolStripMenuItem.Checked = _
                    (m_RichTextBox.SelectionFont.Style And FontStyle.Bold) _
                        = FontStyle.Bold
        End Sub
    End Class
```

The `IRichTool` interface defines an `InstallTool` subroutine that takes a `ToolStripMenuItem` and rich text box as parameters.

The `BoldStyleToggler` class implements the `IRichTool` interface. Its `InstallTool` method saves references to its parameters in local variables. It then makes a new menu item inside the Tools menu item, setting the new item's `Click` event handler to the `MenuItem_Click` subroutine.

`InstallTool` also adds an event handler to the Tools menu's `DropDownOpening` event, so when the user opens the Tools menu, the `ToolsMenu_DropDownOpening` subroutine executes.

When the user clicks the menu item, the `MenuItem_Click` event handler toggles the bold style on the text that is currently selected in the rich text box control.

When the user opens the Tools menu, the `ToolsMenu_DropDownOpening` event handler checks the rich text box control's `SelectionFont.Style` property to see if the selected text is bold. It then checks or unchecks the menu item appropriately.

Example program `UseReflectionTools` (available for download at `www.vb-helper.com/one_on_one.htm`) uses the following code to load the tools in the `ReflectionTools` library:

```
    Try
        ' Find the tools library.
        Dim file_info As New FileInfo(Application.StartupPath & _
            "..\..\..\..\ReflectionTools\bin\Debug\ReflectionTools.dll")

        ' Get the tool library's assembly information.
        Dim tool_assembly As [Assembly] = _
            [Assembly].LoadFrom(file_info.FullName)
        Dim assembly_namespace As String = tool_assembly.GetName().Name

        ' Make arguments for the InstallTools method.
```

```
        Dim args() As Object = {mnuTools, rchDocument}

        ' Loop through available classes looking
        ' for those that implement IToolInstaller.
        For Each class_type As Type In tool_assembly.GetTypes()
            ' See if it implements IToolInstaller.
            If class_type.GetInterface("IToolInstaller") IsNot Nothing Then
                ' Make an instance of the class.
                Dim class_instance As Object = class_type.InvokeMember( _
                    Nothing, BindingFlags.CreateInstance, Nothing, Nothing, Nothing)

                ' Invoke the InstallTools method.
                class_type.InvokeMember( _
                    "InstallTools", BindingFlags.InvokeMethod, _
                    Nothing, class_instance, args)
            End If
        Next class_type
    Catch ex As Exception
        MessageBox.Show( _
            "Error loading tools" & vbCrLf & ex.Message, _
            "Tool Error", MessageBoxButtons.OK, MessageBoxIcon.Exclamation)
    End Try
```

The code starts by making an `Assembly` object representing the library. This example has the location of the library hard-coded in as it appears on my computer. You may need to change it to reflect the location of the compiled library on your own computer.

Next, the code loops through the assembly's types. For any type that implements the `IToolInstaller` interface, the code calls the class type's `InvokeMember` method. The parameters to this method indicate that the program wants to create an instance of the class without passing any parameters to a constructor.

After it has created an installer object, the program uses the type's `InvokeMember` method to call its `InstallTools` subroutine. The parameters to `InvokeMember` indicate that the program wants to call the `InstallTools` method for the newly created object, passing it the Tools menu item, and the `rchDocument` rich text box stored in the `args` array.

Calling `InstallTools` makes the installer install its tools. When the user opens the Tools menu, the tool's event handler checks or unchecks the Bold menu item as appropriate. When the user clicks the Bold menu item, its event handler updates the rich text box.

The `ReflectionTools` project defines a second class named `ItalicStyleToggler`. If you change the library's code so the tool installer also installs this class and then rebuild the library, you can run the same `UseReflectionTools` executable and it will automatically load the new tool.

You could easily extend the `UseReflectionTools` program to look for other tools libraries. For example, you could make it search a tools directory and search every DLL file it found there for classes that implement the `IToolInstaller` interface. Then you could easily add, remove, or modify tools or whole tools libraries.

In this example, the main `UseReflectionTools` program knows very little about the tools library. It looks for classes that implement `IToolInstaller` and calls their `InstallTools` methods, but that's all it knows about the library.

You could make the main program perform more-extensive queries on the library. For example, you could make it search for tools that belong in different menus (other than just the Tools menu), that apply only to particular types of users (for example, clerks, supervisors, or managers), or that belong on different forms in the application. Other methods in the tool classes could give the main program more information. For example, you could give installers an `AppliesTo` method that tells the main program the type of user that should be allowed to use the tool. Once you know how to invoke methods in the library's assembly, you can do just about anything you want.

Invoking Methods Dynamically

The `UseReflectionTools` example described in the previous section looks very specifically for classes that implement the `IToolInstaller` interface. In some cases, you may be able to look for more general classes.

Example program `UseDiscoveryLib` loads an assembly, searches it for types that have default constructors, and lists them. If you select a class, the program searches the class's methods and lists them.

If you select a method, and click the Run button, the program creates an instance of the class. If the method takes no parameters, the program calls it immediately.

If the method requires parameters, the program displays an `InputBox` so that you can enter values separated by commas. When you click the OK button, the code separates the parameters, converts them into appropriate data types, and calls the method passing it the converted parameters.

If the method returns a result, the program converts it into a string and displays it.

Of course, the parameters and return value must make sense as strings. If a method takes a `Form` *object as a parameter, you cannot enter a* `Form` *in the* `InputBox` *function, so the program cannot reasonably convert the string you enter into a* `Form` *and the method call will fail.*

The `DiscoveryLib` project creates a DLL that contains the three classes shown in the following code:

```
Imports System.Math

' This class has no default constructor
' so program UseDiscoveryLib will not use it.
Public Class NoDefaultConstructor
    Public Sub New(ByVal value As Integer)
    End Sub
End Class

' Calculate factorials.
```

```
Public Class FactorialCalculator
    ' Return N!.
    Public Function Factorial(ByVal N As Integer) As Double
        Dim result As Double = 1
        For i As Integer = 2 To N
            result *= i
        Next i
        Return result
    End Function
End Class

' Calculate GCDs and LCMs.
Class LcmCalculator
    ' Return the greatest common divisor of A and B.
    Public Function GCD(ByVal A As Long, ByVal B As Long) As Long
        Dim temp As Long
        Dim remainder As Long

        ' Make sure A >= B.
        A = Abs(A)
        B = Abs(B)
        If A < B Then
            temp = A
            A = B
            B = temp
        End If

        ' Calculate the GCD.
        Do
            remainder = A Mod B
            If remainder = 0 Then Return B
            A = B
            B = remainder
        Loop
    End Function

    ' Return the least common multiple of A and B.
    Public Function LCM(ByVal A As Long, ByVal B As Long) As Long
        Return (A * B) \ GCD(A, B)
    End Function
End Class
```

The `NoDefaultConstructor` class has no default constructor. Because program `UseDiscoveryLib` searches for types that have default constructors, it doesn't list that class.

The `FactorialCalculator` class provides a single function, `Factorial`, which returns the factorial of a number.

The `LcmCalculator` class defines two functions: `GCD` (which returns the greatest common divisor of two numbers) and `LCM` (which returns the least common multiple of two numbers).

The `GCD` of two numbers is the largest integer that evenly divides them both. The `LCM` of two numbers is the smallest integer that is a multiple of them both.

Figure 22-4 shows program `UseDiscoveryLib` in action. Here, the program loaded the `DiscoveryLib` assembly. The user selected the `LcmCalculator` class, picked the `GCD` function, and clicked Run. The program displayed the `InputBox` and the user entered the string "24,92." When the user clicks OK, the program will call the `GCD` function, passing it the values 24 and 92. In this example, `GCD` returns the greatest common divisor of 24 and 92, which is 4, so the program displays the result 4.

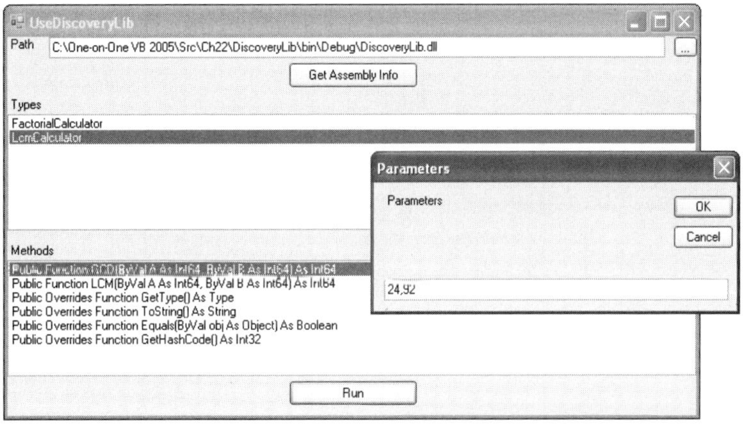

Figure 22-4: Program `UseDiscoveryLib` executes methods of types in assemblies.

Program `UseDiscoveryLib` shows another technique for adding new features to a compiled executable. Before making these methods available to run-of-the-mill end users, you would probably want to restrict the code somewhat. For example, if an application often needs to use numeric calculations, you might want to search the assemblies in a specific directory for functions that take and return numeric parameters. You probably wouldn't want to let users run the `GetHashCode` command (which won't be meaningful) or the `GetType` command (which returns the class's name and isn't very useful).

Discovering Resources

The examples described earlier in this chapter manipulate code, open an assembly, and use its code in different ways. Some list values in enumerations. Others create objects and execute code. Another useful way to manipulate an assembly is to examine and use its resources.

Example project `ResourcesLib` (available for download at `www.vb-helper.com/one_on_one.htm`) is a DLL project that contains several resources. To make the resources easily available to other programs, the resources are embedded in the compiled DLL. To add file resources such as image files and text files to the project, open Solution Explorer and right-click the `Resources` folder. In the context menu, open the Add submenu and select the Existing Item command. Select the file you want to add to the project and click Add.

To embed the file in the project, go to Solution Explorer, open the `Resources` folder, and select the file. Then in the Properties window, set the file's Build Action property to Embedded Resource. Figure 22-5 shows the properties for the file `BigJack.jpg`.

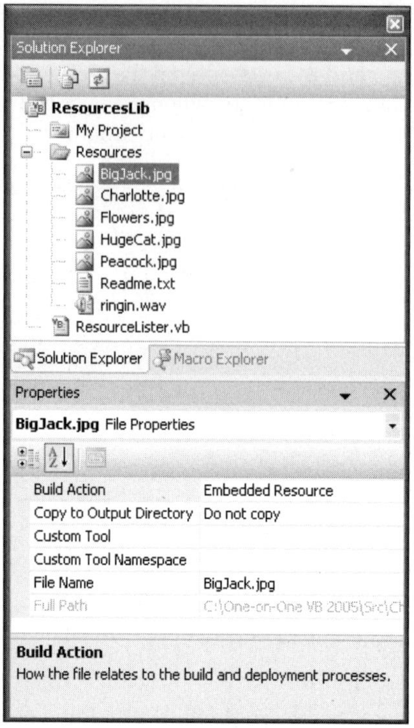

Figure 22-5: Set a resource file's Build Action to Embedded Resource to make it easy to find.

Now, when you compile the DLL, the resources are embedded in the DLL, so they are easy for other programs to find by using reflection.

Example program `GetResources` (available for download at `www.vb-helper.com/one_on_one.htm`) loads resources from the `ResourceLib` DLL at run-time. When you click the Get Resource Info button, the program uses the following code to load the library's assembly and list its resources. It uses the `Assembly` object's `GetManifestResourceNames` method to list the names of the embedded resources and adds those names to its `lstResources` list box.

```
' Get information about the assembly's resources.
Private Sub btnGetResourceInfo_Click(ByVal sender As System.Object, _
 ByVal e As System.EventArgs) Handles btnGetResourceInfo.Click
    ' Get the assembly's information.
    m_Assembly = [Assembly].LoadFrom(txtPath.Text)

    ' Clear results.
    lstResources.Items.Clear()

    ' List the resource names.
    Dim resource_names() As String = m_Assembly.GetManifestResourceNames()
    For Each resource_name As String In resource_names
        ' Skip the resource manifest itself.
```

```
        If Not resource_name.EndsWith(".Resources.resources") Then
            lstResources.Items.Add(resource_name)
        End If
    Next resource_name
End Sub
```

When you click a resource in the list box, the program uses the following code to display your selection:

```
' Display the selected resource.
Private Sub lstResources_SelectedIndexChanged(ByVal sender As System.Object, _
 ByVal e As System.EventArgs) Handles lstResources.SelectedIndexChanged
    panImage.Visible = False
    txtFile.Visible = False

    Dim resource_name As String = lstResources.SelectedItem.ToString
    Dim extension As String = _
        resource_name.Substring(resource_name.LastIndexOf("."))
    Select Case extension
        Case ".bmp", ".gif", ".jpg", ".jpeg"
            Dim bm As New Bitmap( _
                m_Assembly.GetManifestResourceStream(resource_name))
            picImage.Image = bm
            panImage.Visible = True
        Case ".txt"
            Using stream_reader As New _
             StreamReader(m_Assembly.GetManifestResourceStream(resource_name))
                txtFile.Text = stream_reader.ReadToEnd()
                stream_reader.Close()
            End Using
            txtFile.Visible = True
        Case ".wav"
            Using stream_reader As New _
             StreamReader(m_Assembly.GetManifestResourceStream(resource_name))
                My.Computer.Audio.Play(stream_reader.BaseStream, _
                    AudioPlayMode.WaitToComplete)
                stream_reader.Close()
            End Using
        Case Else
            MessageBox.Show("Unknown resource type", _
                "Unknown Resource Type", _
                MessageBoxButtons.OK, _
                MessageBoxIcon.Exclamation)
    End Select
End Sub
```

The code gets the name of the resource and finds its extension. If the extension is `.bmp`, `.gif`, `.jpg`, or `.jpeg`, the program creates a new `Bitmap`, passing its constructor the stream returned by the `Assembly`'s `GetManifestResourceStream` method. It then displays the result in the `picImage` picture box and makes the `panImage` panel that contains it visible.

If the extension is `.txt`, the code makes a `StreamReader`, passing its constructor the stream returned by the `Assembly`'s `GetManifestResourceStream` method. It reads the text file and displays the result in the text box `txtFile`.

If the resource's extension is `.wav`, the code makes a `StreamReader`, passing its constructor the stream returned by `GetManifestResourceStream` and then calls the `My.Computer.Audio.Play` method to play the audio stream.

Figure 22-6 shows program `GetResources` displaying the resource library's `HugeCat.jpg` resource.

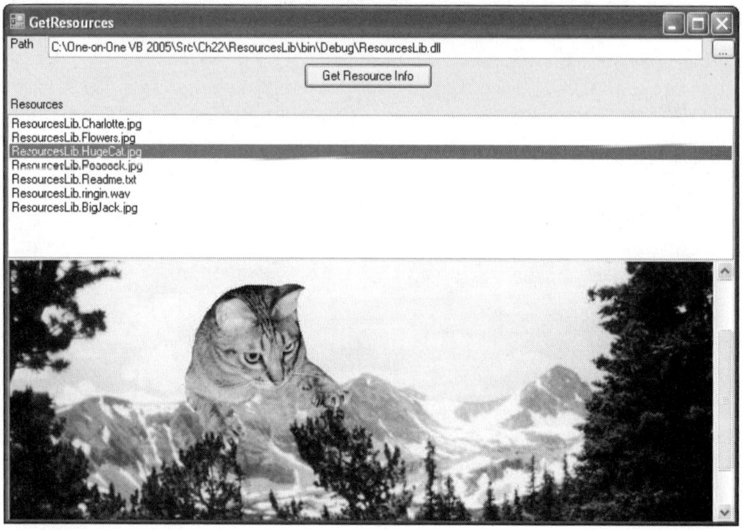

Figure 22-6: Program `GetResource` searches an assembly for embedded resources.

Retrieving Known Resources

In addition to containing embedded resources, an assembly can hold resources that you build in Visual Studio's embedded resource editor. For example, to add a string resource, open Solution Explorer, double-click My Project, and select the Resources tab. In the leftmost drop-down, select Strings. Now, you can add, edit, and remove string resources, as shown in Figure 22-7.

Though the `GetResources` program described in the previous section can see the library's embedded resource files, it cannot see this type of resource string. Even though the program cannot see these resources in the assembly, it can still retrieve them if it knows their names.

> *At least I have yet to find a way. The code that Visual Basic automatically generates for these resources is declared* `Friend`*, so it is inaccessible to code outside of the assembly. The* `GetKnownResources` *program described next uses a* `ResourceManager` *to retrieve these resources, but it doesn't seem to be able to list the resources available. If you figure out how to list these values, email me at* `RodStephens@vb-helper.com` *and I'll add the information to the book's Web site.*

Example program `GetKnownResources` (available for download at `www.vb-helper.com/one_on_one.htm`) uses a `ResourceManager` to fetch this kind of resource. Its list box lists the resources contained in the `ResourceLib` program, including the Greeting string resource.

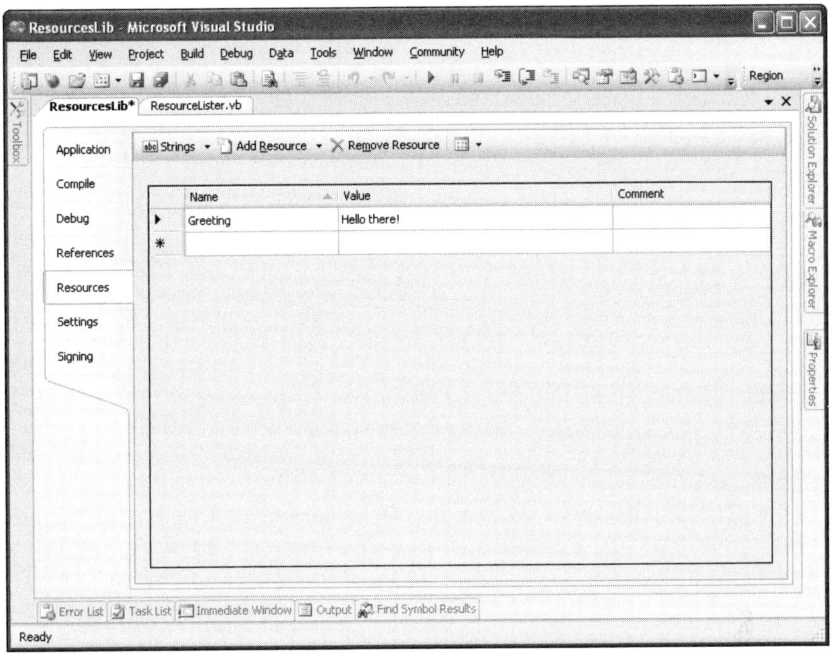

Figure 22-7: Program `GetResources` cannot detect string resources such as Greeting.

When you click the Get Resource Info button, the program loads the resource library's assembly as usual.

When you select an item in the resource list box, the program uses the following code to load the resource:

```
' Display the selected resource.
Private Sub lstResources_SelectedIndexChanged(ByVal sender As System.Object, _
 ByVal e As System.EventArgs) Handles lstResources.SelectedIndexChanged
    If lstResources.SelectedItem Is Nothing Then Exit Sub

    panImage.Visible = False
    txtFile.Visible = False

    ' Make a resource manager.
    Dim resource_manager As ResourceManager = _
        New ResourceManager("ResourcesLib.Resources", m_Assembly)

    ' Get the resource.
    Dim resource_name As String = lstResources.SelectedItem.ToString()
    If resource_name = "ringin" Then
        My.Computer.Audio.Play(resource_manager.GetStream(resource_name), _
            AudioPlayMode.WaitToComplete)
    Else
        Dim obj As Object = resource_manager.GetObject(resource_name)
        If TypeOf obj Is Bitmap Then
```

```
                picImage.Image = DirectCast(obj, Bitmap)
                panImage.Visible = True
            ElseIf TypeOf obj Is String Then
                txtFile.Text = DirectCast(obj, String)
                txtFile.Visible = True
            Else
                MessageBox.Show("Unknown resource type " & TypeName(obj), _
                    "Unknown Resource Type", _
                    MessageBoxButtons.OK, _
                    MessageBoxIcon.Exclamation)
            End If
        End If
    End Sub
```

After checking that an item is selected, and hiding the display picture box and text box, the code creates a `ResourceManager` object, passing its constructor the namespace that contains the library's resources and the library's `Assembly` object.

The program then checks the name of the resource. If the name is `ringin`, the program uses the resource manager's `GetStream` method to get the resource's audio stream and passes it into a call to `My.Computer.Audio.Play`.

If the resource is not `ringin`, the program uses the resource manager's `GetObject` method to fetch an object representing the resource. It then checks the object's type to see if it is a bitmap or string, and displays the object accordingly.

Program `GetKnownResources` is very similar to program `GetResources`, except it can display the `Greeting` string resource in addition to embedded resource files. Unfortunately, it also must have a list of the library's available resource names. That makes the program less flexible because it cannot identify the resources at run-time.

Example program `GetListedResources` (available for download at `www.vb-helper.com/one_on_one.htm`) works around this problem by getting a list of available resources from a class in the resource library.

The following code shows the `ResourceLister` class contained in the `ResourceLib` project. It simply returns an array of the available resource names.

```
Public Class ResourceLister
    Public Shared Function ListResources() As String()
        Return New String() { _
            "Greeting", _
            "BigJack", _
            "Charlotte", _
            "Flowers", _
            "HugeCat", _
            "Peacock", _
            "Readme", _
            "ringin" _
        }
    End Function
End Class
```

The following code shows how program GetListedResources uses the ResourceLister class:

```
' Get information about the assembly's resources.
Private Sub btnGetResourceInfo_Click(ByVal sender As System.Object, _
 ByVal e As System.EventArgs) Handles btnGetResourceInfo.Click
    ' Get the assembly's information.
    m_Assembly = [Assembly].LoadFrom(txtPath.Text)

    ' Get a resource lister type.
    Dim lister_name As String = m_Assembly.GetName.Name & ".ResourceLister"
    Dim lister_type As Type = m_Assembly.GetType(lister_name)

    ' Get the list of resource names.
    Dim resources() As String = _
        DirectCast(lister_type.InvokeMember("ListResources", _
            BindingFlags.InvokeMethod, Nothing, Nothing, Nothing), _
        String())

    ' List the resources.
    lstResources.Items.Clear()
    lstResources.Items.AddRange(resources)
End Sub
```

When you click the Get Resource Info button, the program makes an Assembly object for the library. It then uses the object's GetType method to get a Type object representing the ResourceLister class. It invokes the class's shared ListResources method and adds the returned names to its list box.

When you select a resource from the list box, the program displays it, just as program GetKnown Resources does.

The three resources example programs provide different levels of flexibility and power. Program GetResources can load embedded resource files from any assembly, but it cannot load resource strings.

Program GetKnownResources can load any kind of resource from an assembly but it must know the names of the available resources. So, if you change the resource library, you need to change program GetKnownResources, too.

Program GetListedResources can also load any resource contained in the library. But unlike program GetKnownResources, it gets a list of the available resources from the library's code. That means you can make changes to the library without making changes to the GetListedResources program. You could also make the program load resources from more than one library, as long as each library provides a ResourceLister class.

Summary

Reflection is a remarkably powerful tool that allows a program to examine its own code, or code in other assemblies. That allows it to load classes, execute methods, search enumerations, and load resources from an assembly at run-time.

These techniques are not easy, so they should not be your first choice for implementing most features. If you have defined the tools that you will need to an application, build them into the main program or a library and leave it at that.

However, reflection gives you new opportunities to add flexibility to your programs. The examples in this chapter show how you can use reflection to add, remove, or modify tools and resources for an existing application without recompiling that application.

Reflection tells your application about the code behind an assembly. Another part of the execution infrastructure that lurks behind every application is memory management. Most applications ignore memory management as much as possible, and rely on the .NET Framework and run-time libraries to handle memory issues. While that usually works, there are a few things you can do to make your applications control their memory use more intelligently.

Chapter 23, "Memory Management," describes Visual Basic's memory model and some of the ways you can handle memory efficiently.

23

Memory Management

Normally, developers take memory management for granted, and rightly so. In most cases, the .NET memory-management system handles all the details about creating and destroying objects so that you can concentrate on your application and not bookkeeping details.

However, there are times when it's useful to know a bit about how memory is managed in the application. For certain types of applications, a few changes to the way you handle objects can make a big difference in overall performance.

This chapter explains how memory management works in Visual Basic. It explains some techniques you can use to minimize impact on the memory-management system, and it tells how to make your memory use more efficient.

Before you can learn about specific techniques for managing memory, however, you must understand a little about how the memory system works. In particular, you must know a bit about the garbage collector.

Garbage Collection

Visual Basic .NET uses a garbage-collection memory-management scheme. As a program creates objects, the system takes unused memory from the *managed heap*. When the program no longer has any variables referring to an object, the object is freed and its memory is potentially available for reuse. However, the garbage collector doesn't yet know that the object has been freed.

Over time, the program creates new objects and frees others. Eventually, the managed heap runs out of free memory. At that point, the garbage collector runs.

Actually the garbage collector can execute whenever it thinks it will be profitable to do so. That may be when the managed heap is really empty, or it may be when the garbage collector thinks enough objects have been freed that it would be a good idea to clean things up a bit. Generally, you should assume that the garbage collector might run at any time and not worry about exactly when it runs.

The garbage collector now performs garbage collection to free up memory that was used, but is no longer needed by the program.

The garbage collector manages memory in multiple pieces called *generations*. You can think of these as multiple piles of trash with different distances from the door. The generations closest to the door are easier to recycle than those farthest away.

Initially, the garbage collector sifts through the first pile of trash, called *generation 0* (or *Gen 0* or *gen0*) relatively frequently. When it can no longer find much usable space in generation 0, the garbage collector recycles *generation 1*. When there isn't much unused memory available in generations 0 or 1, it collects *generation 2*.

Again, this is a bit simplified. The garbage collector can recycle any generation whenever it thinks that may be profitable. In general, though, generation 0 collection happens relatively frequently, generation 1 collection happens less often, and generation 2 collection happens rarely.

When it recycles generation 0, the garbage collector finds the objects that are still in use and moves them into a contiguous area in generation 1 so that they are collected less frequently in the future. It then releases the unused memory in generation 0 for future use.

Eventually, if an object lives long enough, the garbage collector promotes it from generation 1 to generation 2. Objects in generation 2 participate in garbage collections only rarely, so these objects will occupy memory for a fairly long time.

Note that the garbage collector need not always use three generations. Currently, Visual Basic .NET uses three garbage generations, but future garbage collectors might use different strategies. If you really need to know, use `GC.MaxGeneration` *to find out how many generations are available. This is described in more detail later in this chapter.*

Ideally, generation 0 contains short-lived objects that are allocated and released fairly quickly, generation 1 contains longer-lived objects that survive generation 0 garbage collection, and generation 2 contains very long-lived objects that the program uses for a long time.

The garbage collector is optimized to make generation 0 collection fast, generation 1 collection slower, and generation 2 collection slowest of all. So, it's important that generation 0 collection occurs most often, generation 1 collection occurs less often, and generation 2 collection occurs only rarely.

For a good article that provides additional detail about how the garbage collector works, see `msdn.microsoft.com/msdnmag/issues/1100/gci`.

Finalization

Some objects refer to other objects that are not controlled by managed .NET code. Because those objects are not referred to by normal references, the garbage collector cannot clean them up automatically as it can other objects.

For example, a `Pen` object uses graphics resources that are not managed by .NET. The garbage collector doesn't understand those resources, so it cannot manage them as it does managed objects.

To free its unmanaged resources, the `Pen` class provides a `Finalize` method. When the program instantiates an object that has a `Finalize` method, the garbage collector adds the object to a *finalization queue*.

Later, when the garbage collector discovers that the object is available for collection, it cannot destroy the object because it has not yet been finalized. Instead, the garbage collector removes the object from the finalization queue and moves it to a list of objects that are ready for finalization. The garbage collector then calls the `Finalize` methods for the objects in the ready list, and removes them from that list.

The next time the garbage collector runs, it will again find that these objects are inaccessible to the program. This time, they are not in the finalization queue, so it can reclaim them. It takes two garbage collections before these objects can be destroyed and their memory made available for reuse.

Example program `FinalizedClass` (available for download at `www.vb-helper.com/one_on_one.htm`) uses the following code to demonstrate finalization:

```
Public Class Form1
    Private Class Big
        Private BigArray(100000) As Integer

        Protected Overrides Sub Finalize()
            Debug.WriteLine("Finalize")
        End Sub
    End Class

    Private m_HasFinalize As Big

    ' Alloctae an object.
    Private Sub btnAllocate_Click(ByVal sender As System.Object, _
     ByVal e As System.EventArgs) Handles btnAllocate.Click
        m_HasFinalize = New Big
        Debug.WriteLine("Allocate: Memory Allocated: " & GC.GetTotalMemory(False))
    End Sub

    ' Release the object.
    Private Sub btnFree_Click(ByVal sender As System.Object, _
     ByVal e As System.EventArgs) Handles btnFree.Click
        Debug.WriteLine("Freeing object")
        m_HasFinalize = Nothing
        Debug.WriteLine("Free: Memory Allocated: " & GC.GetTotalMemory(False))
    End Sub

    ' Force garbage collection.
```

```
        Private Sub btnCollect_Click(ByVal sender As System.Object, _
         ByVal e As System.EventArgs) Handles btnCollect.Click
            GC.Collect()
            Debug.WriteLine("Collect: Memory Allocated: " & GC.GetTotalMemory(False))
        End Sub
    End Class
```

The `Big` class allocates a large chunk of memory and provides a `Finalize` method that displays a message when the object is finalized.

When you click the Allocate button, the program makes a new `Big` object. It then uses the `GC` class's `GetTotalMemory` method to display the estimated amount of memory currently allocated.

When you click the Free button, the program sets its reference to the `Big` object to `Nothing`. At this point the object is a candidate for garbage collection, but garbage collection does not actually occur.

When you click the `Collect` button, the program calls the `GC` class's `Collect` method to force garbage collection in all generations. The first time you click this button, the garbage collector removes the object from the finalization list and calls its `Finalize` method. The second time you click this button, the garbage collector reclaims the object's memory.

The following text shows the output of one test:

```
Allocate: Memory Allocated: 1018164
Freeing object
Free: Memory Allocated: 1059124
Finalize
Collect: Memory Allocated: 936168
Collect: Memory Allocated: 503456
Collect: Memory Allocated: 503444
Collect: Memory Allocated: 503444
```

When I clicked the Allocate button, the program created the new object and reported roughly 1 million allocated bytes of memory.

When I clicked the Free button, the program freed its reference to the object and reported slightly more memory allocated.

Next, I clicked the Collect button. The garbage collector called the object's `Finalize` method and the program reported that about 936,168 bytes were still allocated. Some memory was reclaimed, but the object's memory is still not completely available.

When I clicked the Collect button again, the garbage collector finally freed the object and the program reported much less memory allocated. In fact, the program reports approximately 400,000 fewer bytes allocated and the `Big` object occupies roughly 400,000 bytes (100,000 times 4 bytes per Integer in the array). It is only during this second garbage collection that the object is truly free.

Disposing Resources

An object that has a Finalize method is only completely freed after two garbage-collection passes. The first pass calls the object's Finalize method to release unmanaged resources. The second pass actually releases the object's memory.

Not only does this mean that the garbage collector must run twice to clean up these objects, but it also means the program has little control over when the objects' Finalize methods are eventually called. Your program generally doesn't have much control over when the garbage collector runs, so there's no obvious way for you to know when the Finalize method executes. If you need Finalize to run quickly, that can be a problem. For example, suppose a class writes data into a file and then closes the file in its Finalize method. Because you don't know when that will occur, you cannot rely on the file being closed later.

Because you don't know when a Finalize method will be called, this garbage-collection strategy is called *non-deterministic finalization.*

You can make garbage collection more efficient and more predictable if you dispose of the object's resources without waiting for garbage collection. You know immediately that the object's resources are free and the next garbage collection will reclaim the object completely without requiring a second pass.

You can free a standard .NET Framework object's unmanaged resources by calling its Dispose method. The Dispose method frees the object's unmanaged resources and then calls the GC class's SuppressFinalize routine to tell the garbage collector that it no longer needs to call the object's Finalize method.

Calling Dispose is particularly important for small objects such as Pens and Brushes that an application may create and destroy frequently. For example, a graphics program might create a new Pen and Brush to draw each of the items it is displaying every time it paints its drawing surface. Although these objects are relatively small, they can quickly use up a lot of memory if the program draws a lot of items. They also tie up graphics resources.

The Using keyword makes disposing of these kinds of objects automatic. If you declare the object in a Using statement, Visual Basic automatically calls the object's Dispose method when it exits the Using block.

The following code shows how example program UsingPen (available for download at www.vb-helper.com/one_on_one.htm) draws an ellipse. It defines a Pen object named red_pen in a Using statement. Then it reaches the End Using statement, and the program automatically calls the Pen's Dispose method.

```
Private Sub Form1_Paint(ByVal sender As Object, _
 ByVal e As System.Windows.Forms.PaintEventArgs) Handles Me.Paint
    Using red_pen As New Pen(Color.Red, 5)
        Dim rect As New Rectangle(10, 10, _
            Me.ClientSize.Width - 20, Me.ClientSize.Height - 20)
        e.Graphics.DrawEllipse(red_pen, rect)
    End Using
End Sub
```

A `Using` block always calls the object's `Dispose` method whether the program exits the block by using an `Exit` or `Return` statement, by throwing an exception, or by some other method.

Disposing Custom Classes

If you build a class that uses unmanaged resources, you should make the class implement the `IDisposable` interface so that it can properly handle finalization and the `Dispose` method.

If you start a new class, type **Implements IDisposable**, and press Enter, Visual Basic fills in some of the code you need to build a disposable class for you. Unfortunately, in the version I'm running, at least, the code is incomplete (it doesn't include a `Finalize` method) and misleading (some of the comments are wrong). The following code shows a more complete and correct version:

```
Public Class Big
    Implements IDisposable

    ' Indicates whether we have already been disposed.
    Private m_WasDisposed As Boolean = False

    ' Dispose of resources.
    Protected Overridable Sub Dispose(ByVal disposing As Boolean)
        If Not m_WasDisposed Then
            If disposing Then
                ' Dispose was called explicitly.
                ' Free managed resources.
                ' TODO: Free the managed resources.
            End If

            ' Free unmanaged resources.
            ' TODO: Free the unmanaged resources.
        End If

        m_WasDisposed = True
    End Sub

    ' Dispose of resources explicitly.
    ' Do not change this code. Make changes
    ' to the other version of Dispose.
    Public Sub Dispose() Implements IDisposable.Dispose
        Dispose(True)
        GC.SuppressFinalize(Me)
    End Sub

    ' Finalize the object.
    Protected Overrides Sub Finalize()
        ' Call Dispose passing False to indicate that
        ' we are not running from a program call to Dispose().
        Dispose(False)
    End Sub
End Class
```

The `m_WasDisposed` variable remembers whether the object's resources have already been disposed. The first version of the `Dispose` subroutine uses this value to only dispose of its resources once. If the main program accidentally calls the object's `Dispose` method twice, the code does nothing during the second call.

The first version of `Dispose` takes a parameter named `disposing` that tells it whether the routine is being called explicitly or implicitly by the `Finalize` method. If disposing is `True`, then `Dispose` releases all of the object's managed and unmanaged resources. If disposing is `False`, then `Dispose` releases only its managed resources.

At first, this may seem strange. Why shouldn't the code dispose of managed resources when it is being called from `Finalize`? The reason is that it is not safe to refer to objects that are being finalized. There's no way to determine the order in which objects will be finalized, and the program will throw an exception if it tries to refer to another object that has already been finalized.

How could this happen? Suppose you have a group of several objects that refer to each other. If no other variable in your program refers to any of those objects, the garbage collector will not mark them as in use and will collect them all. It's anybody's guess which objects are collected first, so they must not try to refer to each other during finalization.

In many cases, non-managed resources use handles to operating system objects that are not represented by.NET Framework objects. Often, you can use the `SafeHandle` class and its descendants to manage these resources safely without implementing `IDisposable` yourself.

For example, the `SafeFileHandle` class providers a wrapper for file handles. It provides `IsClosed` and `IsInvalid` methods to indicate whether a handle is open and valid. Its `Close` and `Dispose` methods close the object's file handle.

Before you start writing your own class to deal with an unmanaged handle, check the `SafeHandle` class and its descendants to see if one of them already meets your needs.

Pre-allocating Objects

Normally, your programs should ignore garbage collection and let the garbage collector do its job without interference. Occasionally, you may be able to improve performance if you know something special about how the application works.

For example, suppose you know that your program is about to create several thousand objects, but it will not need them all at the same time. Suppose the program is about to perform 10,000 calculations during each of which it will allocate around 100 objects. If you let the garbage collector handle allocation and deallocation as usual, the program will create and destroy around 1 million objects (10,000 calculations times 100 objects). Depending on the size of the objects, that may lead to several rounds of garbage collection.

Instead of following this "use it and lose it" strategy, suppose the program pre-allocates 100 objects and reuses them as necessary. In that case, the program only creates and destroys 100 objects, so it is unlikely that it will need to perform garbage collection even once.

Example program `Preallocate` (available for download at `www.vb-helper.com/one_on_one.htm`) compares these two strategies. When you click the Run button, the program performs a large number of trials where it builds a linked list of 100 `Cell` objects.

The following code shows the `Cell` class. The `MyForm` variable refers to the program's main form. `Values` is an array of integers that just uses up some memory. `NextCell` is a reference to the next cell in the current list.

```
Public Class Cell
    Public MyForm As Form1

    Public Values(100) As Integer
    Public NextCell As Cell

    Public Sub New(ByVal new_MyForm As Form1)
        MyForm = new_MyForm
    End Sub

    Protected Overrides Sub Finalize()
        If MyForm.GCRunning Then Exit Sub
        Debug.WriteLine("Garbage collecting " & MyForm.NumGCs & "...")
        MyForm.GCRunning = True
        MyForm.NumGCs += 1
    End Sub
End Class
```

The `Cell` class's `Finalize` method checks the form's `GCRunning` variable and exits if the value is `True`. Otherwise, the method prints a message indicating that garbage collection is occurring, sets the form's `GCRunning` variable to `True`, and increments the garbage-collection count.

The following code shows how program `Preallocate` responds when you click the Run button:

```
Public GCRunning As Boolean = False
Public NumGCs As Integer = 0

Private Sub btnRun_Click(ByVal sender As System.Object, _
 ByVal e As System.EventArgs) Handles btnRun.Click
    Dim start_time As Date = Now

    NumGCs = 0
    Dim num_trials As Long = Long.Parse(txtNumTrials.Text)
    For i As Long = 1 To num_trials
        ' Allocate a bunch of objects.
        Dim top As New Cell(Me)
        top.NextCell = Nothing

        For j As Integer = 1 To 99
            Dim new_cell As New Cell(Me)
            new_cell.NextCell = top
            top = new_cell
        Next j

        ' Free the objects.
```

```
            top = Nothing
            GCRunning = False
        Next i

        ' Force a final GC.
        GC.Collect()
        Debug.WriteLine("Done")

        Dim stop_time As Date = Now
        Dim elapsed_time As TimeSpan = stop_time.Subtract(start_time)
        Debug.WriteLine("Elapsed time: " & elapsed_time.TotalSeconds.ToString("0.00"))
    End Sub
```

After recording its start time, the program loops through a number of trials. For each trial, it builds a linked list of 100 `Cell` objects. It then sets the topmost object to `Nothing`, so the program no longer has a reference to the objects and they are candidates for garbage collection.

If garbage collection occurs, any cells that are available for garbage collection execute their `Finalize` methods. The first of those objects displays a message and sets the form's `GCRunning` variable to `True`. After collection is complete, the program resets `GCRunning` to `False` so `Cells` that are finalized later display a new message.

The routine finishes by displaying the elapsed time.

The following code runs when you click the program's Preallocate & Run button:

```
    Private Sub btnPreallocateRun_Click(ByVal sender As System.Object, _
     ByVal e As System.EventArgs) Handles btnPreallocateRun.Click
        Dim start_time As Date = Now

        NumGCs = 0

        ' Preallocate some Cell objects.
        Dim available(100) As Cell
        available(available.Length - 1) = New Cell(Me)
        available(available.Length - 1).NextCell = Nothing
        For i As Integer = available.Length - 2 To 0 Step -1
            available(i) = New Cell(Me)
            available(i).NextCell = available(i + 1)
        Next i
        Dim top_available As Cell = available(0)

        ' Perform the trials.
        Dim num_trials As Long = Long.Parse(txtNumTrials.Text)
        For i As Long = 1 To num_trials
            ' Allocate a bunch of objects.
            Dim top As New Cell(Me)
            top.NextCell = Nothing

            For j As Integer = 1 To 99
                Dim new_cell As Cell = top_available
                top_available = top_available.NextCell

                new_cell.NextCell = top
```

```
            top = new_cell
        Next j

        ' Free the objects.
        Dim last_cell As Cell = top_available
        Do While last_cell.NextCell IsNot Nothing
            last_cell = last_cell.NextCell
        Loop
        last_cell.NextCell = top
        top = Nothing
        GCRunning = False
    Next i

    ' Deallocate the objects.
    top_available = Nothing
    Erase available

    ' Force a final GC.
    GC.Collect()

    Dim stop_time As Date = Now
    Dim elapsed_time As TimeSpan = stop_time.Subtract(start_time)
    Debug.WriteLine("Elapsed time: " & elapsed_time.TotalSeconds.ToString("0.00"))
End Sub
```

This code starts by pre-allocating an array of 101 `Cell` objects. It initializes the objects so that they form a linked list and sets `top_available` to refer to the first object in the array.

The program then performs its trials much as before. This time, however, it doesn't create new `Cell` objects from scratch. Instead, when it needs a new `Cell` object, it takes one from the top of the available list. When it finishes a trial, the program places the `Cells` it has used back in the available array for later reuse.

After it finishes its trials, the program sets `top_available` to `Nothing` and erases the available array so the program has no references to the `Cell` objects. It forces a final garbage collection and displays the elapsed time.

In one test, letting the garbage collector run without interference required eight garbage collections and took 5.28 seconds. Pre-allocating the `Cell` objects required a single garbage collection at the end and took 1.17 seconds.

This example demonstrates a very special case. Usually, the garbage collector does just fine by itself, but if you know that the program must repeatedly allocate and deallocate many objects while keeping only a few alive at one time, then you may be able to improve performance by pre-allocating the objects.

There is a danger to using this method, however. If garbage collection runs while the pre-allocated objects are in use, they will be promoted to generation 1. That will mean they will not be candidates for future garbage collection until the garbage collector performs generation 1 garbage collection, which could be quite awhile later. Of course, it's entirely possible that a lot of the temporary objects would be in use if you leave the garbage collector alone, so it's not certain that pre-allocating objects is worse.

You can call `GC.Collect(1)` *to force a generation 1 garbage collection when the long series of calculations is finished.*

Usually, you should leave the garbage collector alone and only tamper with its behavior if you know the program has a special structure (as in this example) and you know you are having performance problems.

Weak References

If a program uses a lot of very large objects, it can quickly use up a lot of memory. If the program uses too much memory, it may spend a lot of time paging to the system's page file. It may also spend a lot of time performing garbage collection and it may have a lot of objects stuck in generation 1 or 2.

One way to avoid these problems is to not save large objects. Instead of storing large objects for later use, some programs can release the objects and re-create them later when they are needed. Unfortunately, this solution makes the program spend extra time rebuilding the objects when they are needed.

The `WeakReference` class provides a compromise. It lets a program keep a reference to an object for later use. If the program runs low on memory, however, the garbage collector is allowed to reclaim the object. If that happens, the program must re-create the object when it needs it again. The program gets a bit of the advantages of both scenarios: the large object doesn't tie up memory permanently, but sometimes it's still available, so the program doesn't need to re-create it.

To use a weak reference, create a `WeakReference` object and set its `Target` property to the object you want to save. If the program has other "strong" references to the object, then the object is not available for garbage collection. If the `WeakReference` object's `Target` property is the only reference to the object, the garbage collector can reclaim the object if necessary.

Example program `WeakReferences` (available for download at `www.vb-helper.com/one_on_one.htm`) shown in Figure 23-1 stores weak references to large objects. Each time you click the Allocate button, the program creates a new large object and saves a `WeakReference` pointing to it. When memory becomes too full, the garbage collector runs and reclaims some of the weakly referenced objects.

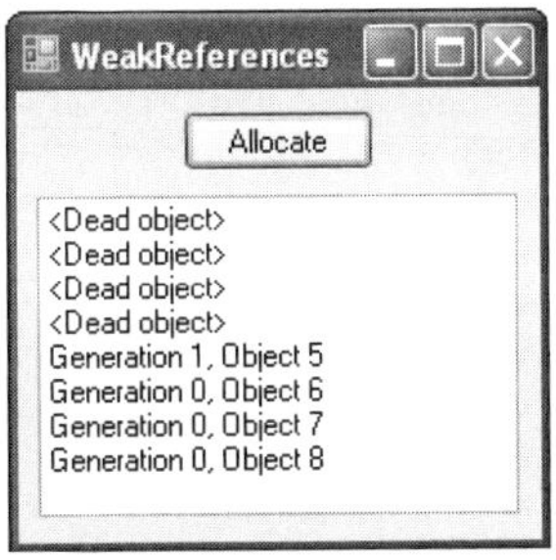

Figure 23-1: Program `WeakReferences` demonstrates weak references to large objects.

In Figure 23-1, I clicked the Allocate button eight times. The first four times, the program created new objects. When I clicked the button the fifth time, the program created another large object. While the code still had a temporary strong reference to the object, the program ran the garbage collector. The collector reclaimed the first four objects and promoted the new object to generation 1. At that point, the button's `Click` event handler exited, so the only reference the program had to the new object was its weak reference.

Next, I clicked the Allocate button three more times and the program created more objects with weak references. If I were to click the button again, the program would repeat the previous round of garbage collection: make a new object, reclaim the previous objects, and promote the new object to generation 1.

The following code shows the `Big` class that program `WeakReferences` uses to allocate approximately 256 KB of memory. Its `Values` variable is an array that occupies 256 KB. The constructor and `Finalize` methods display messages in the `Output` window so that you can see when objects are created and destroyed.

```
' A Big object occupies about 256 KB.
Public Class Big
    Private Const KB256 As Integer = 1024 * 256
    Private Values(KB256) As Byte
    Public Name As Integer

    Public Sub New(ByVal new_Name As Integer)
        Name = new_Name
        Debug.WriteLine("Created " & Name)
    End Sub

    Protected Overrides Sub Finalize()
        Debug.WriteLine("Destroyed " & Name)
    End Sub
End Class
```

The following code shows how program `WeakReferences` uses the `Big` class. The `m_WeakReferences` list holds the `WeakReference` objects that point to the `Big` objects.

```
Private m_WeakReferences As New List(Of WeakReference)

' Allocate a new object.
Private Sub btnAllocate_Click(ByVal sender As System.Object, _
 ByVal e As System.EventArgs) Handles btnAllocate.Click
    ' Make the new Big object.
    Dim new_big As New Big(m_WeakReferences.Count + 1)

    ' Associate it with a WeakReference object.
    Dim weak_reference As New WeakReference(new_big)
    m_WeakReferences.Add(weak_reference)

    ' Display information about the active objects.
    lstObjects.Items.Clear()
    For Each wr As WeakReference In m_WeakReferences
        If wr.IsAlive Then
            Dim the_big As Big = _
                DirectCast(wr.Target, Big)
            lstObjects.Items.Add("Generation " & GC.GetGeneration(the_big) & _
                ", Object " & the_big.Name)
```

```
            Else
                lstObjects.Items.Add("<Dead object>")
            End If
        Next wr

        Debug.WriteLine("Memory Allocated: " & GC.GetTotalMemory(False))
    End Sub
```

When you click the Allocate button, the program creates a new `Big` object. While the variable `new_big` is in scope, the program has a strong reference to this object, so it is not a candidate for garbage collection.

Next the program creates a `WeakReference` object. The object's constructor sets its `Target` property to the new `Big` object.

The program clears its list box and the loops through the `WeakReference` objects in the `m_WeakReferences` list. A `WeakReference` object's `IsAlive` property returns `True` if the `WeakReference`'s `Target` object is still available, and returns `False` if the `Target` object has been reclaimed by the garbage collector. If the object is still alive, the program uses `DirectCast` to convert the `Target` value into a `Big` object and displays the object's `Name` property. If the object is dead, then the program simply says so.

If a `WeakReference` *object's* `IsAlive` *property is* `False`*, its* `Target` *property is* `Nothing`*.*

Unfortunately, there is no way to prioritize weak references. For example, it might be nice to indicate that the garbage collector should reclaim some objects before others, that it should only reclaim an object if it is performing a generation 1 or 2 collection, or that it should reclaim an object if a certain percentage of the available memory is in use. You can make strong or weak references to an object, but that's the only control you have over this.

Improving Garbage Collection

Normally, the garbage collector does fine on its own. But there are a few considerations that you can keep in mind while developing to make the garbage collector a bit more effective.

Most importantly, don't let your program hold on to large numbers of objects for a long time. If the program is holding a lot of objects when a garbage collection occurs, those objects will be promoted to generation 1. That not only takes longer than freeing the objects if they were not in use, but it also means the program will need to spend extra time later freeing those objects again during a generation 1 garbage collection.

If the program will use an object frequently over a long time, keeping a reference to the object makes sense. If the object is used only infrequently, use it and lose it. Pens and brushes are good examples. Suppose an application uses a class to represent items (ellipses, rectangles, text, and so forth) that it draws during its `Paint` event. You could store a pen and brush to draw each item in its class. A better approach is to store information about the pen and brush that an object needs. Then, each object can re-create its pen and brush when it needs to draw. The garbage collector is designed to reclaim many small objects such as pens and brushes frequently, so it's better to do so than to make these objects stick around for a long time.

If an object has a `Dispose` method, use it when you are done with the object. That allows the garbage collector to reclaim the object in a single pass, instead of merely running the object's `Finalize` method in one pass and then reclaiming the object in the next. The `Using` statement makes calling the `Dispose` method automatic, so use it when you can.

Because finalizers take awhile to execute and prevent the garbage collector from reclaiming an object in a single pass, avoid building `Finalize` methods. If an object uses a resource that must be freed when the object is destroyed, by all means, build a finalizer. But if there's another way to structure the program to avoid this, use it. If you do write a `Finalize` routine, also write a `Dispose` method and call it when you are finished with the object.

Release temporary objects before starting a long calculation, particularly if the calculation will use lots of memory. If the calculation causes a garbage collection, then the fewer objects you have loaded the better.

If the code has just finished a very involved calculation, you may have reason to believe that many unused objects are available for reclamation. In particular, if you think a lot of objects are in generation 1 and 2, you may get some benefit from flushing them out by calling `GC.Collect`. A parameter to `GC.Collect` tells the garbage collector what generation to collect. If you omit the parameter, it collects garbage in all generations.

When you call `GC.Collect`, the garbage collector only runs the `Finalize` methods for any objects that are in the finalization queue. To ensure that the finalizers have a chance to run, you can call `GC.WaitForPendingFinalizers`. Then you can reclaim those objects by calling `GC.Collect` again, as shown in the following code:

```
GC.Collect()                        ' Reclaim unused objects and run finalizers.
GC.WaitForPendingFinalizers()       ' Wait for finalizers to finish.
GC.Collect()                        ' Reclaim objects that ran finalizers.
```

You can help the garbage collector by minimizing the program's use of objects. The fewer objects the program uses, the less often it will need to perform garbage collection.

Finally, reduce the program's use of references. When the garbage collector runs, it must follow every object reference to mark the target object as in use. If your data structures have a lot of references, the garbage collector must do a lot of work.

Example program `ManyReferences` (available for download at `www.vb-helper.com/one_on_one.htm`) shown in Figure 23-2 allocates an array of `Cell` objects. Enter the number of objects you want to create and click the `MakeObjects` button. Click the `Collect` button to force garbage collection. The program displays the elapsed number of seconds in the label below the button.

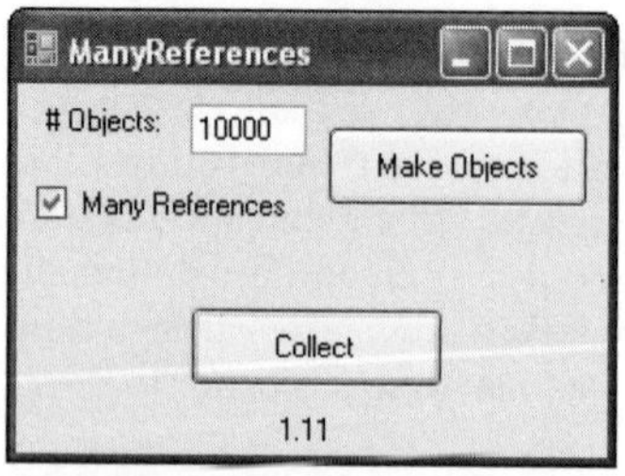

Figure 23-2: Program `ManyReferences` can make the garbage collector follow a huge number of references.

Each `Cell` object has a `Neighbors` property that contains a list of references to other `Cell` objects. If you leave the Many References box unchecked when you create objects, the program gives each `Cell` a single neighbor. If you check the Many References box, the program adds every `Cell` to every other `Cell`'s neighbor list.

In Figure 23-2 the program created 10,000 objects, each having 9,999 neighbors for a total of slightly less than 100 million neighbor references. Performing garbage collection while these objects were allocated took 1.11 seconds. Note that there were no unused objects available for the garbage collector to reclaim. All of these references were contained in active objects, so the garbage collector was forced to follow them all. Just having all of these references around makes garbage collection slower.

When I ran the test without the Many References button checked, the program created only 10,000 neighbor references and took around 0.01 seconds to perform garbage collection.

The program also took almost no time to perform garbage collection as soon as the highly linked objects were destroyed, even though the objects and their references were still around waiting for garbage collection. The garbage collector only needs to follow references that are reachable from the program's variables, so references contained in unused objects don't slow performance.

Summary

Usually, you should ignore the garbage collector and focus on the application's code. The garbage collector is designed to reclaim unused memory fairly efficiently, and meddling with the way it works often degrades its performance.

To make garbage collection as efficient as possible, always call an object's `Dispose` method when you are finished with it. When you build your own classes, avoid using a `Finalize` method if you can. If you must use `Finalize`, also provide a `Dispose` method and use it.

In some applications, you can improve performance by pre-allocating objects before using them, or by forcing garbage collection after a long calculation has promoted many items to generation 1 or 2. These measures can interfere with the garbage collector's normal behavior, however, so only consider them if you have special information about the application that indicates that they will help and you know that there is a performance problem. In most cases, the garbage collector does just fine without extra help.

Finally, use the `WeakReference` class to keep references to large objects that you may need later but that you can re-create if necessary. These allow you to reuse objects sometimes without unduly restricting the garbage collector.

Index

SYMBOLS

A

D

F

M

N

O

P

S

T

U

V